HEILONGJIANG

KIRIN

Mukden

MONGOLIA

Yanan

Pingliang

ISU WEI RIVER YELLO

SHAANXI

Ping-le

RIVER

Chungking

YANGTZE DONGTING L

HUN

GUIZHOU

GUANGXI

Teng

Leizho

Hainan

ANCESTORS

A portrait of Qin Guan, painted during his lifetime

ANCESTORS
900 YEARS IN THE LIFE OF A CHINESE FAMILY

FRANK CHING

William Morrow and Company, Inc.
New York

James J. Y. Liu, *Major Lyricists of the Northern Sung: A.D. 960–1126*. Copyright © 1974 by Princeton University Press. Excerpts reprinted with permission of Princeton University Press.

Library of Congress Cataloging-in-Publication Data

Ching, Frank.
  Ancestors: nine hundred years in the life of a Chinese family.
  Includes index.
  1. Chin family. 2. Ching, Frank—Frank.
3. China—Biography. 4. Chinese Americans—Biography.
5. China—Genealogy. I. Title.
CT1827.5.C47C47 1988   951'.009'92 [B] 87-28289
ISBN 0-688-04461-1

Printed in the United States of America

First Edition

1 2 3 4 5 6 7 8 9 10

BOOK DESIGN BY BRIAN MOLLOY

This book is dedicated to
my mother

A NOTE ON SPELLING

Throughout the book, I have used the *pinyin* system of romanization, which is gaining widespread acceptance. Thus my surname is spelled Qin instead of Ch'in (as in the old system; our family added a final "g" because of the pronunciation of the word in the Shanghai dialect). Exceptions arise when an old form, such as Peking, is so widely recognized that I have opted to retain that rather than to change it to, in this instance, Beijing. There are also instances when the original materials were in English, and there seemed no point in altering the spellings.

ACKNOWLEDGMENTS

This book could not have been written without the assistance and cooperation of countless individuals and institutions over a period of more than six years. Above all, the information supplied by members of my family was vital. I wish to thank my mother and stepfather as well as all my siblings and in-laws for their help and their patience during the years of research and writing. And many other relatives gave their assistance.

In particular, I wish to thank my cousin in Wuxi, Qin Zhihao, who spent numerous hours doing research and transcribing by hand on my behalf; the head of the Qin clan of Wuxi, Qin Zhifen, who was the source of a great deal of information, hand-copied documents and ancestral portraits; my uncle Professor Y. H. Ku of Philadelphia; my aunt in Taiwan, the writer Lin Hai-yin; my niece Linda, as well as relatives in Shanghai: my aunt and uncle Qin Wanhua and Jin Honglin, and my cousin Chen Yanheng and her husband, Zhang Renying.

I am also deeply indebted to the First Historical Archives of China, especially Mr. Qin Guojin and Madame Fu Meiying. I am grateful to Mr. Wang Daorui and Mr. Liu Kui and their colleagues for locating key documents in the archives. The staff of the Peking Library supplied much appreciated services, as did the Peking University.

I am happy to acknowledge the help of Deputy Director Chang Pi-te, Nancy C. H. Wang, librarian, Ms. Hung Ming-chu and their colleagues in the National Palace Museum in Taipei. In addition, I am grateful to Mr. Chang Wejen for information from the archives of the Institute of History and Philology of the Academia Sinica in Taiwan.

The Chinese Academy of Social Sciences provided me with access to its various institutes, such as the History Institute, the Modern History Institute and the Law Institute, and also provided numerous introductions.

The Shanghai Academy of Social Sciences, too, was extremely cooperative. I wish to give special thanks to Mr. Zhou Yi-zheng of its Foreign Affairs Division and Mr. Ni Zhengmou of its Law Institute. The Shanghai Municipal Archives and the Shanghai Library also yielded many nuggets.

In addition, I wish to thank the Zhejiang Academy of Social Sciences, especially its vice-president, Mr. Wei Qiao, and Mr. Wang Baomin.

The University of Hong Kong, especially the Centre of Asian Studies headed by Professor Edward K. Y. Chen, extended research facilities, including the library collections, over the years. In this regard I am particularly grateful to Mrs. Coonoor Kripalani-Thadani.

Columbia University's East Asian Library, in particular Mr. Jack Jacoby, first opened my eyes to the rich resources available in such institutions, both in the United States and in China.

There is a host of individuals without whose help this book would be a much poorer product. Among them are Dr. Peter Bol, Dr. Jerry P. Dennerline, the late Professor Fang Chaoying, Ms. Wendy Locks, Dr. Dian Hechtner Murray, Dr. Charles O. Hucker, Dr. Hilary K. Josephs, Dr. James T. C. Liu, Dr. Elizabeth Sinn, Madame Wang Pao-chen and Dr. Wei Peh T'i.

Mr. Zhu Xiyuan of the Cultural Bureau in Gaoyou and the curator of the Wuxi Museum, Mr. Gu Wenbi, rendered signal assistance.

And, this book could never have been written without the help of Raphael Chan, who spent years translating passages from classical Chinese into English, and my teacher, Mr. Lin Zhengzong.

CONTENTS

Contents

ANCESTORS

Chart 1. Genealogical diagram of the Qin clan beginning with the Song dynasty poet Qin Guan, showing the descent of Qin Yubo, the City God of Shanghai, and Qin Weizheng, progenitor of the Qin family in Wuxi

Chart 2. Genealogical diagram of the Qin clan in Wuxi from Qin Weizheng to Qin Decao, from whom both parents of the author are descended

Chart 3. The descendants of Qin Decao, culminating with Zhaohua, the author's mother, and Liankui, his father

The Search for a 900-Year-Old Grave

My first conscious memory, as a five-year-old in the summer of 1946, is of peeping out of a porthole of a passenger liner as it churned through the South China Sea, taking our family to exile in Hong Kong.

I grew up in postwar Hong Kong, cut off from the land of my ancestors and cast adrift from the network of familial relationships in which Chinese children are raised: grandparents, uncles, aunts, cousins. Because my father had three wives, with different sets of children living in separate households, I didn't even know how many brothers and sisters I had until long after I became an adult.

My father, Qin Liankui, was born in 1888, the fourteenth year of the reign of Emperor Guangxu, five years before the birth of Mao Zedong and one year after that of Chiang Kai-shek. He grew up in a time of political and social ferment, as China's last dynasty tottered and fell, to be replaced by a weak and unstable republic. While in his twenties, my father took a young former courtesan, Cao Yueheng, into his household without going through the formality of an arranged marriage. Together, they brought up six children, three sons and three daughters.

At that time a man was not considered properly married unless the bride was of the same social standing and the marriage was arranged by matchmakers. Bigamy, or even polygamy, was common. So my father was still eligible. After his union with his Suzhou beauty, he acquired a "formal" wife, named Xu Peihua, the younger sister of a former teacher of his. He had never set eyes on her before the wedding. One of his older sisters had visited her on behalf of the family, and described her as "quite attractive." However, after the wedding ceremony, when my father lifted the red veil that covered her head, he saw before him a plain-looking woman with small, slitlike eyes. It was not long before he returned to his first love, leaving his legal wife alone.

By the time my father married my mother, both his earlier wives had died. According to Chinese terminology, my mother was a *tian-fang*, or "replacement wife," that is, one who married a widower. Because my father's earlier children were close to my mother in age, most of them did not live with us. Thus, when I was growing up in Hong Kong, I knew only my mother's other children and the youngest child of my father's first wife.

I attended a Roman Catholic missionary school, which, like other such schools in Hong Kong, tried to turn Chinese boys into little English gentlemen. We waved miniature British flags, marveled at the glory of the British empire and learned to do sums in pounds, shillings and pence. While boys in China were being taught to engage in class struggle to combat the remnants of feudalism and imperialism, I was learning Western ways in a British colony on China's doorstep, one of the last outposts of freewheeling capitalism.

By the time I was twelve, my world had shrunk to three people: a sick, querulous old man whom I called father; my mother, a much younger, strong-willed woman with whom he constantly squabbled; and Priscilla, the sister closest to me in age. I was the youngest, born when my father was in his fifties. Little did I know that this crotchety man had been an architect of China's constitution and had chosen poverty and exile to remain true to his principles. In 1949, on the eve of the partitioning of China, he chose not to endorse either the Kuomintang of Chiang Kai-shek or the Communist party of Mao Zedong, but instead closed his law offices in Shanghai and voluntarily exiled himself to Hong Kong to join his family.

There, my father spent the last ten years of his life, unable to practice British law and becoming increasingly ill and eccentric. We lived in rented rooms in a three-story building in a relatively good area, sharing a kitchen with another family. We had a flush toilet installed, but I still remember the cry of the night-soil carriers, who used to come late each night to empty the contents of our neighbors' lavatories. Our neighbors, like most people in Hong Kong, spoke Cantonese, while we knew only the Shanghai dialect. Although Hong Kong-born, I did not have a sense of belonging. This feeling of alienation was accentuated by our increasing poverty. My school permitted poor children to pay reduced tuition. The fees were collected monthly, and the amount each boy paid was read out by the

14

teacher in front of the whole class. My name was always near the bottom, because I paid less than anyone else.

I longed for comfort and security, for a past I had never known. I did not realize it then, but already I had embarked on what was to be a decades-long search for details of my family history. Much later, I understood that I was acting in the best Chinese tradition, for one of the most scathing comments one Chinese can make of another is that he has *wang ben*, or "forgotten his origins."

When I was nineteen, I left Hong Kong for the United States, but the same sense of alienation haunted me in my new home. The only way to exorcise this ghost, I knew, was to delve into my past. And my past lay in China.

But it was not until the early 1970s and the thaw in U.S.-Chinese relations that I determined to return to China to become acquainted with relatives whose names were strange to me and whose very existences were, in many cases, unknown to me.

I approached the newly established Chinese embassy in Ottawa for a visa, but although I was applying to go in a personal capacity, the fact that I was then on the foreign desk of *The New York Times* caused the embassy to view me with suspicion. I was told I needed the approval of the Foreign Ministry in Peking. Finally, I flew to Hong Kong to plead my case before the China Travel Service, a mainland governmental agency. I argued for the right to visit China as a "compatriot," since I had been born in Hong Kong, which, according to Peking, remains Chinese territory despite the British administration there. Compatriots, unlike foreigners, are not required to have visas to enter China, since theoretically they are merely moving from one part of the country to another. After repeated visits, my request was granted. I was issued an "Introduction for Return to Native Village."

On August 1, 1973, at age thirty-two, I boarded an old diesel train that took China-bound passengers to Lowu, a town on the Hong Kong side of the border. Sedate, well-dressed men and women, foreigners and overseas Chinese, entered the first-class compartments. Since I was a compatriot, China Travel Service had arranged for me to travel third class. There, men and women clawed their way onto the train, passing goods and children through windows and often climbing in after them because the narrow entranceways were jammed. Many people carried shoulder poles from which dangled live chickens, baskets of food and other gifts for relatives in

China. Even standing room was scarce. I squeezed my way aboard, gaining a foothold on the bottom rung of a carriage and hung on to the handrail to prevent myself from falling off. In this fashion, I was slowly borne by the chugging train toward China.

At the border, we walked across a rickety wooden bridge that separated British-ruled Hong Kong from the Communist mainland. The Union Jack fluttered on one side of the bridge, China's red flag with five yellow stars on the other. Once across the bridge, all the passengers were led into a vast shed to be interrogated by immigration and customs officials.

I was interviewed by a man who questioned me at length on my background, my job, my relatives and my friends. He made me empty all my pockets. In one pocket, I was carrying the calling cards of several people I had met in Hong Kong. My interrogator was extremely interested in all of them. He also questioned me about my parents and my brothers and sisters. He wrote down all the answers. Then he asked me the same questions all over again, in different ways. The interrogation stretched into the second hour.

Finally satisfied that I did not present an immediate threat to the security of the Chinese state, he allowed me to go through customs. There, Hong Kong newspapers I had with me were confiscated.

The ride to Canton was a pleasant contrast to my journey from Hong Kong to the border. The train was the only air-conditioned one in China, and it was on the Shenzhen-Canton run for the benefit of foreigners. I sat back in my soft seat and watched the green fields of Guangdong province roll by. The loudspeaker played "The East Is Red," a paean in praise of Chairman Mao Zedong that had virtually become China's national anthem during the Cultural Revolution.

When we finally pulled into the Canton station, the loudspeakers thanked the passengers for helping the crew to complete their mission successfully.

The China Travel Service in Hong Kong had advised me to stay at the Overseas Chinese Hotel in Canton, but the young woman behind the counter there told me the hotel was full and refused to refer me to another hotel. "Hong Kong compatriots usually stay with relatives," she said. "We only serve guests from overseas." I was in a quandary. I had entered China as a compatriot and, because of that, I was refused a hotel room. If I confessed I was really from New York, I feared there might be trouble. But I had no choice. So

16

I produced American identification and explained that, though a Hong Kong compatriot, I lived in New York. The change in the clerk's attitude was remarkable. A selection of rooms was available, she said. The best room, for ten dollars a night, had a bathroom, a telephone and an electric fan. I took it.

The next day, I boarded a plane for Shanghai with a keen sense of anticipation. For in Shanghai I would begin my search for long-lost relatives.

I had the address of my uncle Qin Kaihua, my mother's brother, whom I had never met. He and my mother were never close. He had disapproved of my parents' marriage because my father and mother were related, albeit distantly. But in 1973 this uncle was my one point of contact with my entire family in China. I located the address on a street map and, to avoid attracting attention, decided to walk there. When I arrived at the entrance, I tapped gently on the door, trying not to arouse the suspicions of the neighbors. A skinny, elderly man dressed only in shorts and an undershirt appeared. He turned out to be my uncle. I introduced myself by my Chinese name, Qin Jiacong, the son of Zhaohua, and he waved me in. I walked into a dingy room with a wooden bed, then through a doorway into a small sitting room. It was the height of summer, and the heat was stifling. As we stood facing each other across the room, neither of us could think of anything to say. Finally, my uncle switched on the electric fan and directed it at me full blast while cooling himself with an old-fashioned straw fan. He introduced me to his wife and their sixteen-year-old daughter.

In the presence of these strangers I felt curiously at home. I told them about the various members of the family outside China and what they were doing. And before leaving, I invited them to my hotel for dinner the following evening.

The next day, I received a call from the reception desk telling me I had visitors waiting in the lobby. I went down and found an argument going on between my relatives and the hotel personnel, who were insisting that each of them produce identification. They were told to fill in forms in triplicate, giving their name, address and place of employment, plus their relationship to the person they were visiting. Only after that were they allowed to enter the elevator and go to the dining room. After dinner, when I invited them to my room, the elevator operator refused to take them, saying they had no permission. In the lobby, we were informed that only parents or children of hotel guests were allowed in rooms; all other visitors had to be entertained in the lobby. After much ado, another set of registration forms was filled out and my relatives were allowed up as a special dispensation. Not surprisingly, they never visited me again.

But they made me welcome in their home. I spent almost every evening with my uncle and aunt and learned things about China and about my family that I had never dreamed of.

Before leaving Shanghai, I bought a birthday present for my aunt. I went to the Friendship Store, which was open only to foreigners, and purchased a Chinese-made watch, one of the more expensive brands. I also gave my uncle some knickknacks that I had with me. In return, he gave me a small jade rabbit that had belonged to his grandfather, one of the few things of value that he possessed. Jade to a Chinese is more than another precious stone. The popular belief ascribes to jade the power to protect the wearer from danger and evil. When my uncle offered me the jade rabbit, he was, in a sense, giving me part of himself.

From Shanghai, I went north to Peking. The contrast between the two cities was striking. Shanghai was depressing, a shell of its flamboyant, cosmopolitan past, its Western-style buildings crumbling away after a quarter century of neglect. Peking was magnificent, with the Great Wall winding north of the city, the vast Tiananmen Square in the city center, where Chairman Mao had reviewed millions of Red Guards at the start of the Cultural Revolution, and the Boulevard of Eternal Peace, the main street built in the fifteenth century during the Ming dynasty and wide enough for more than ten lanes of traffic. The whole city conveyed a sense of history, of being the center of an ancient and still vibrant civilization.

Despite its brevity, the trip to China was exhilarating: It marked the culmination of years of longing and dreaming. I had learned more about my homeland than I could have from years of reading. More than ever, I felt compelled to fill in the blanks concerning my family.

The following year, in July 1974, I made a second trip to China. This time, I joined a Hong Kong tour group, which spent a week in Guangdong province, adjoining Hong Kong, visiting Canton, Foshan and the Xichao hot-springs resort frequented by Chinese leaders.

At the end of the week, the rest of the group returned to Hong Kong, but I headed for Shanghai to visit my uncle and his family.

I sent a telegram, telling my uncle I was arriving. But, unused to sending Chinese telegrams, I accidentally overlooked the signature line. When I walked into his house that night, he was clearly surprised.

"Oh, it's you," he said, and I sensed the disappointment in his voice. "I thought it was your mother."

Despite their checkered relationship, my mother's kindnesses to him over the years had mellowed him, and he badly wanted to see her again. So when the unsigned telegram arrived, he had busied himself buying wine, chicken and other hard-to-get items, preparing a feast for their reunion.

After dinner, I proposed a game of Chinese chess, which I knew he enjoyed playing. At the end of the game he sat back, looked at his wife and exclaimed with a hint of sadness: "Never in my wildest dreams did I think that the son of Zhaohua would come and play chess with me."

My uncle's wish to see my mother again was never fulfilled. The next year, my aunt wrote and told me that he had died of a liver ailment. With this link to my Chinese past gone, I became anxious to get news of my half brothers in China. I consulted my half sister Margaret, one of the siblings left behind in China when the rest of us went to Hong Kong. She and her husband, Henry, had now settled in Taiwan. She gave me the address of a Mao Xungou in Shanghai and suggested that I write to ask him about my half brothers. I wrote to Mr. Mao, explaining who I was, and waited months for a reply that never came. It would be over a year before I found out that he was dead. His widow had no information.

In January 1976, Premier Zhou Enlai died after a long bout with cancer. His death plunged the country into grief bordering on despair, culminating with riots in Peking's Tiananmen Square in April 1976. Five months later Chairman Mao died and, within weeks, his widow and his closest political associates of the last decade were in prison, accused of having formed a "gang of four" to seize power.

By this time, I had moved from New York back to Hong Kong. As a reporter now for *The Asian Wall Street Journal*, I made frequent trips into China. Because of my job, I was able to travel both to the mainland and to Taiwan when necessary. In late 1978, I went to Taiwan to say good-bye to Margaret and Henry, who had decided to emigrate to Australia to be closer to their daughter, who was married to a restaurateur there. One evening after supper, Margaret

19

emerged from a back room holding a plastic bag containing a bundle of dusty old books. Thrusting them at me, she said, "Here, I've kept these long enough. It's time they went to a son."

The bag contained books and papers that were among our father's meager possessions when he died in 1959, and which Margaret had salvaged and stored away for two decades. Carefully, I removed the plastic covering and looked at the three books in the bag. Two of them were official publications of the Republican government containing father's name and photograph as a member of the National Assembly.

The third was old, bound in thread, and printed on thin rice paper. On the cover, in old Chinese script, was the title: "Ancestral Genealogy of the Qin Clan of Wuxi."

I was holding in one fragile volume the names of all of my ancestors for the last thirty-three generations, going back in time nine hundred years, to the eleventh century, and to one name: Qin Guan. It was from this prominent poet of the Song dynasty (960–1279) that both my father's and my mother's ancestors were descended. There were thirty-three generations from Qin Guan to myself on my father's side, thirty-four on my mother's side.

When the family records of the Qin clan of Wuxi were first given to me, I did not realize what a rarity such books are today. But I soon found out that even in the past, only prominent, well-established families maintained clan records, or zong pu.

These books served to instill a sense of pride in members of the clan. If an individual rose to a position of power and wealth, his relatives almost inevitably benefited from his good fortune. Similarly, if a man fell in disgrace, his entire clan shared in the blame.

Whole clans have been slaughtered because of the wrongdoings of one member. Most severe of all the punishments that could be meted out was the execution of all members of nine generations of a family—that of the offender, his father, his grandfather, his great-grandfather and his great-great-grandfather, as well as the generations of the offender's children, grandchildren, great-grandchildren and great-great-grandchildren, along with their siblings, spouses and offspring. The elimination of nine generations of an offender meant, in effect, that all those descended from his great-great-grandfather would be executed. The scholar Zhuang Tinglong wrote a history of the Ming dynasty that angered the Manchu rulers of China. The work was not discovered until after his death, but the Manchus reacted to it with a vengeance. Zhuang Tinglong's corpse and that of his father were dug up and burned and the Zhuang family and the families of other scholars implicated were almost wiped out. The printers and purchasers of the book were executed. In all seventy persons were killed and many others exiled.

Most people in China, like those in the West, know only their immediate forebears, and even families with genealogical records are rarely able to trace their ancestry for more than two or three hundred years.

The upkeep of clan histories required much organization. Each family kept a record of births and deaths of its males. Female births were recorded, but since girls could not continue the family line, their records were thin. In our family, the names of daughters were included, as well as the families into which they married, but there are no biographies of the women, as there are for all the men. The only exceptions are accounts of "chaste widows," usually women whose husbands died early—sometimes even before the actual wedding service—and who remained single, devoting the rest of their lives to caring for the deceased's aged parents.

Each family within the clan submitted information regarding births, deaths and marriages. The biographical information given was generally quite brief: formal name, son of so-and-so, his style name (which he picked for himself and usually reflected his ambitions and outlook on life), rank, activities, writings, date of birth, date of death, name of wife, daughter of so-and-so, of which hometown, date of her birth and death, names of sons and daughters, and burial site.

Inclusion of a man's name in the family genealogical records meant that he had been accepted as a member of the clan in good standing. Those who were considered to have disgraced the clan were, in effect, expelled. An interesting example of this is Qin Qi, an early Communist labor organizer and the most important of seven executed in 1927 in Wuxi[1] when Chiang Kai-shek launched his massacre of Communists in Shanghai. His head was cut off and hung from the city wall as a warning to others not to join the Communists. I do not know just how we were related, since his name cannot be found in the last edition of our family records, which were compiled only a year or two after his death. The man who ordered his execution was Qin Yuliu, also a member of the Qin clan, a prominent activist in the Kuomintang who organized anti-Manchu activities with

21

Dr. Sun Yatsen, and who was one of the main compilers of the last edition.

The attention given to family history reflected pride in Chinese civilization and culture as well as in the clan. That pride was dealt a series of devastating blows in the nineteenth century, when China was repeatedly humiliated by Western powers and much of the country was carved into spheres of influence by European countries. Jolted from their complacency by such stark evidence of their nation's backwardness, many reform-minded Chinese turned to Western ideas of science and democracy to cure China's ills, and rejected traditional values. Family histories were regarded as a remnant of China's feudal legacy. The age-old practice of maintaining genealogical records virtually died out after the Communists gained power in 1949.

Many genealogical records still in private hands were lost in the Cultural Revolution. In response to Chairman Mao's call to "sweep away the four olds"—old culture, old habits, old customs and old ideas—youthful Red Guards ransacked homes and carted off or burned everything they considered to be remnants of the former exploiting classes. Many people, fearful of persecution, destroyed precious records handed down by their fathers. The losses suffered are incalculable, both on a personal level and to China as a whole. Fortunately, Western bibliographers in the 1930s and 1940s collected many such volumes so that today major American universities have substantial collections of Chinese genealogies, some of which are no longer found in China itself.

Much of my own family's history was destroyed or lost because of the Cultural Revolution. Fearful clan members burned ancestral portraits and genealogical records before they could be found by fanatical Red Guards. But one relative, risking political persecution, saved several pages detailing the most recent generations. It was from him that I first obtained the clan biographies of my father and my grandfather. My grandmother had written two volumes of essays and poems, of which all her children's families had copies. After the Cultural Revolution, they had vanished, save for a single copy of one volume, which a cousin hid from the Red Guards and, later, generously gave to me.[2]

On December 15, 1978, it was announced that the United States would recognize the government in Peking as the sole legal government of China and would withdraw diplomatic recognition from the Kuomintang government in Taipei.

Together with over a dozen other American reporters, mostly Hong Kong–based, I flew to Peking at the end of December to cover the formal opening of relations between America and China. Five months later, China allowed four American newspapers to establish bureaus in Peking—*The Wall Street Journal*, *The New York Times*, *The Washington Post* and the *Los Angeles Times*. I was chosen by *The Wall Street Journal* as its correspondent in China.

I flew to Peking in June 1979 and established *The Wall Street Journal*'s bureau in a room in the Peking Hotel, a modern, eighteen-story building, the tallest in the Chinese capital. It was a heady time, for China was in the midst of dramatic changes. Pent-up emotions were being let loose in an explosion of unofficial publications and wall posters; the most sacred tenets of Mao were being overturned and billions of dollars' worth of business contracts were being signed. Between my hours as a reporter, documenting one of the most important periods in China in decades, I was burrowing into my personal history—making phone calls, writing letters and meeting people. Each contact was a new excitement. I even made contact with two of my half brothers, both of whom I learned had spent about two decades in prison camps, victims of the Maoist regime. They were released in the fall of 1979, beneficiaries of the more liberal line adopted by Deng Xiaoping.

When I began my research into the past, I did not know what to look for, since I had no idea what materials existed. At a China bibliographer's suggestion, I checked the rare books collection of Columbia University's East Asian Library and discovered a twelve-volume edition of my family genealogy, published in 1873. It contained biographies of important members of the clan, given in generational order. One of the most interesting volumes was a *nien pu*, or year by year account, of the life of Qin Guan, the eleventh-century Song-dynasty poet. The family's genealogical records were updated about every fifty years until 1929, when the last edition appeared. The book I had gotten was part of a seventeen-volume set. It would be seven years before I was able to obtain the other volumes. When I did, it was with some surprise that I read that my father, who had never even lived in Wuxi, had been involved in the compilation, so tenacious was the grip of the ancestral hometown.

23

ANCESTORS

I learned more about my family's past when I was introduced to a cousin who lives in Wuxi. Qin Zhihao proved to be my closest living relative there. We are fourth cousins, that is, we share a common great-great-grandfather. In China, fourth cousins are the dividing point between close and distant relatives: distant relatives do not participate in mourning but those within the "five degrees of kinship," including fourth cousins, are obligated to mourn. Through this cousin, a quiet, unassuming man in his seventies, I discovered that our clan, though greatly weakened, was still nominally functioning even after the People's Republic was proclaimed and, in fact, that the clan's existence was accorded recognition by the Communist government until the Cultural Revolution erupted.

In the old days, almost all clans maintained ancestral halls, buildings where clan records were kept and clan members gathered regularly to honor their ancestors. I wanted to visit the old Qin ancestral hall, built originally in the sixteenth century on Sixth Arrow River. But waterways such as Sixth Arrow River are no more. Cousin Zhihao told me it had been filled in during Republican times and turned into one of the city's main east-west thoroughfares, Cong Ning Road, the very street he lived on. According to him, there was a time when almost every family on the street was named Qin. Our ancestral hall, he said, was the large building adjacent to his home.

I walked around the building where many generations of Qins had gathered to honor their ancestors. It was big, more than twice the size of other nearby buildings. In the old days, upon crossing the threshhold, a visitor was confronted by a large wooden signboard proclaiming this to be the ancestral hall of Qin Guan. A large rock on each side symbolized stability and endurance, a function also performed by two flanking wooden columns. Beyond this was another gate, guarded by stone lions.

Now there is little about the exterior that betrays the structure's original function: The building is home for a dozen families. Inside, however, hidden behind cupboards and other furniture, engraved stone plaques can still be discerned. The words are difficult to make out because the current residents have painted them over. In one corner, set into the wall, is a plaque in honor of someone not of the Qin clan, Wang Yazhou. He was a local official who, some twenty-three generations ago, befriended the first Qin to settle in the vicinity of Wuxi and married one of his three daughters to him. Because

Wang had no sons, the Qin clan had offered him sacrifices and honored him as one of their own ancestors.

None of the original furnishings of the ancestral hall—including the wooden "spirit tablets" that represented the presence of the ancestors, old portraits or the two sedan chairs used by my grandfather—had survived the ravages of time and of the Cultural Revolution. I scrutinized the furniture used by the various households, hoping to uncover some relic. But there was nothing.

Back in the capital, I frequented the Peking Library, the largest in the country. There, I found genealogical records of branches of the Qin clan that had spread to other parts of China. I also found voluminous writings by members of the clan in Wuxi, collected and bound into separate volumes of prose and poetry. I was frequently accompanied to the library by my Chinese teacher, a gentle learned man named Lin Zhengzong, who helped me with materials written in classical Chinese. Because photocopying was not always possible, we spent many hours laboriously hand-copying materials, sitting in the dimly lit reading room. Even my driver, Xiao Yu, volunteered to be a copyist and scoured bookstores looking for anything that might be of interest to me.

From 1984 to 1986, I also spent long periods closeted in the First Historical Archives of China, which has almost ten million documents from China's last two dynasties, the Ming (1368–1664) and the Qing (1664–1912). There, I was able to locate poems dedicated to the emperor by clan members, as well as imperial decrees concerning clan members who were officials, and memorials—documents addressed to the emperor—written by them.

It was my driver, Xiao Yu, who drew my attention to an item in a Shanghai newspaper[3] that reported that a set of genealogical records of descendants belonging to the Sijing branch of the Song dynasty poet Qin Guan had been found in the home of a peasant family outside Shanghai.

Delighted, I asked relatives in Shanghai to approach the peasant family. I could not do it myself because foreigners, especially journalists, were not allowed to go to the Chinese countryside without special permission. By coincidence, an old friend from the United States, a filmmaker named Shirley Sun, had discovered that the city god of Shanghai was Qin Yubo, who was a great-great-great-great-grandson of Qin Guan, and that there was a temple dedicated to him.

25

ANCESTORS

I flew to Shanghai and found that Qin Yubo belonged to the Sijing branch of the family. The Sijing records contained a portrait of him and letters he exchanged with the first emperor of the Ming dynasty in the fourteenth century. After Qin Yubo's death, this emperor appointed him the city god of Shanghai. In subsequent centuries, he was credited with saving Shanghai residents from a massacre and with bringing a number of murderers to justice. I visited his temple in an old section of the city and was saddened to find that the building, reconstructed in 1927, had been converted into a shopping bazaar. The statue of him which used to dominate the interior was gone.

While in Shanghai, I received a tip from my relatives: There was another man on the trail of Qin Guan and his descendants. This man, Zhu Xiyuan, was an official responsible for cultural affairs in Gaoyou, the hometown of Qin Guan. I telephoned Gaoyou and, after considerable difficulty, located Mr. Zhu. He told me he had been crisscrossing the country visiting libraries, reading ancient steles and uncovering gravesites in search of information about Qin Guan and his numerous descendants.

We did not meet until some months later, back in Shanghai. And then it was late at night. At that first meeting, I felt as if he were a member of the family as we sat on his bed and talked about Qin Guan, his descendants, family genealogies and my own place within the clan. Mr. Zhu turned out to be a largely self-educated, intense man who was fiercely proud of Gaoyou's native son, Qin Guan.

The next day, over lunch, Mr. Zhu told me about his research. He had been to Changzhou, where Qin Guan's son had settled, to look for traces of the poet's descendants. There, he had met many peasants named Qin whose ancestors were from Gaoyou. He had also been to Wuxi and had found old graves and inscriptions.

And he was a mine of stories, including one about a wealthy outsider who wanted to be accepted into the prestigious clan. Clan elders set three conditions, two of which he gladly accepted: that he donate fifty *mu* of paddy field, about seven and a half acres, and contribute 200 piculs of rice to the clan. But he balked at the third: that he be considered the most junior clan member and pay respects to all others, even infants.

Mr. Zhu suggested that I formally apply for permission to visit Gaoyou, saying that if I was officially welcomed by the local leadership it would be much easier for him to show me around. I did, and to my delight my request was granted. Mr. Zhu was with me when I registered at the government hostel. When under "Reason for Visit" I put, out of habit, "To gather information," Mr. Zhu immediately changed it to "To visit ancestral home."

I was treated royally that night; almost the entire leadership of Gaoyou turned out for a banquet in my honor. I felt that I was being received as one of their own. I went to bed with a feeling of great warmth, which was not wholly induced by the fiery local liquor.

Next morning, I was confronted with another aspect of reality. I was led into the same dining room where I had been feted the night before, but this time I was to eat my breakfast in solitary splendor. Mr. Zhu showed up while I was eating but declined to join me. From then on, during the rest of my stay in Gaoyou, I ate alone. My pleas to Mr. Zhu and others for companionship were to no avail. I was a foreigner and had to be set apart from the ordinary people.

But Mr. Zhu and the other officials of Gaoyou extended me every courtesy. They showed me the site of the proposed Qin Guan exhibition hall, at a pavilion known as the Terrace of Literature and Leisure. I climbed a series of stone steps to be confronted by an incredible sight: a room with walls covered from top to bottom with engraved calligraphy. They were those of Qin Guan, his brothers, and other Song scholars. I was amazed at the care with which the Gaoyou authorities had preserved these engravings.

They took me by boat along the old Grand Canal and showed me an area, about one block square, still known locally as "the Qin family courtyard," though no one named Qin lives there anymore.

On my last day in Gaoyou, Mr. Zhu gave me a poem that he had written to mark my visit, in which he was very generous in his praise of me for returning to my ancestor's hometown. So China's poetic tradition continues to this day.

My visit to Gaoyou spurred me into making greater efforts to find out more about Qin Guan's descendants. I visited Changzhou, where Qin Guan's son had made his home, and Loyang, a township outside Changzhou, where two thirds of the current population of two thousand are surnamed Qin. I was introduced to many people as fellow clansmen, including a doctor in his eighties and a young peasant. All knew the generation to which they belonged within the clan structure. Some even produced genealogical records which had somehow survived the ravages of the Cultural Revolution. I picked up a copy and read: "Ancestral Genealogy of the Qin Clan of Piling." Piling was the name for Changzhou in Song times.

Asked where their ancestors had come from, almost all of the Qins I met replied: "Qin Village," about halfway between Changzhou and Wuxi. It was from that village that a boy by the name of Qin Wei-zheng had journeyed to Wuxi. He is today revered as the founder of the Wuxi branch of the clan. So the Loyang Qins and the Qins of Wuxi are both descended from the son of the Song poet, who settled in the Changzhou area.

In November 1980, I had visited the old Qin family garden in Wuxi. At the entrance to Ji Chang Garden, I had seen a wooden signboard. Though the wood was cracked, the words were in the simplified Chinese characters developed by the People's Republic. The words began: "This garden was built by Qin Jin in the Zhengde period (1506–1510) of the Ming dynasty, and was named 'Fenggu Xingwo,' ['Phoenix Valley Villa']. In the 27th year of the Emperor Wanli (1599), it was restored by Qin Yao and renamed Ji Chang Garden."

I knew Qin Jin was the man who edited the first edition of our family genealogy. I had never heard of Qin Yao, who turned out to be my great-great-great-great-great-great-great-great-great-great-great-grandfather.

The signboard went on to describe the various scenes within the garden, and to say that an eighteenth-century emperor had a replica of it built in the Summer Palace in Peking.

I had left Wuxi determined to return, and I did—the next year, with my sister Julia and her husband, Will Oxtoby. Both of them teach in the religion and philosophy department of the University of Toronto and had come to China on a honeymoon-cum-sabbatical. It was Julia, a historian as well as a philosopher, who suggested that we look for Qin Guan's grave on Mount Hui in Wuxi. I was skeptical that the grave of a man who had died almost nine hundred years ago would still exist, but I agreed to take part in her project.

We arrived in Wuxi, northwest of Shanghai, on a balmy fall day. We were met by a Mr. Wu, from the local travel service, who was taken aback when we told him we wanted to find a twelfth-century grave. He sought help from the Wuxi Museum, where an old man said he had read that Qin Guan was buried beneath the second peak of Mount Hui. We drove to the western suburbs and stopped at the foot of Mount Hui, then started the long climb up.

Julia stopped a local resident and asked if he knew where Qin Guan's tomb was. "Don't waste your breath," Mr. Wu said. "He doesn't even know who Qin Guan was." Other residents we talked to had vaguely heard of a "big Qin tomb" but did not know its location. After a few hours of climbing steep hillsides, tramping through bamboo groves and leaping across gullies with us, Mr. Wu suddenly gave out a whoop: He had spotted some graves in the distance. We ran down the mountain and drove to a point near the graves, where we began our ascent again. When we got there, however, we were disappointed: All the graves were relatively recent.

Mr. Wu and I continued the climb while Julia and Will fell behind. Gradually, even Mr. Wu's enthusiasm flagged, and I found myself alone as I edged my way up the hill, with gravel and loose rocks making every step hazardous. Then I, too, despaired.

On my descent, I discovered that Julia and Will had run into an elderly man who, though he did not know the site of Qin Guan's tomb, knew of other Qin graves in the area. He led us to a spot where there were several gravestones. Strangely enough, they were all blank. But the old man picked up a rock and started to chip away at one of them. Bits of plaster fell off, revealing an inscription that proclaimed the grave's occupant as a Qing dynasty official. The old man explained that during the Cultural Revolution the Red Guards had dug up the graves of people considered to have been feudal overlords. To prevent that, peasants came up the hills and plastered over the tombstones so the Red Guards could not tell who was buried where.

The old man discovered an unusual gravestone lying flat on the ground. It had many tiny characters carved on it. We rubbed it with wet leaves and spittle to make part of the inscription legible. The grave belonged to a woman whose husband was a member of the Qin clan; we had at long last found the resting place of a family member. But it was getting late; our search had to be abandoned.

A year later, my sister Alice from New York visited China for the first time since she had left it more than three decades before. And she too expressed interest in looking for our ancestor's grave.

So, early one morning, accompanied by Jiaju, our father's oldest son, we boarded a train for Wuxi. When we got to the foot of Mount Hui we decided that we would go straight to the top and work our way down. The path we took led to the first of the three peaks. It was a steep climb, at the very top of which was an old temple that now served as a gift shop, selling such trinkets as the little clay dolls for which Wuxi is famous.

We asked the shopkeeper, a man in his seventies, if he knew the location of Qin Guan's tomb, and explained that we were descendants of the poet. He told us he knew of an old grave in the vicinity, but he could not leave his store untended to take us there. I was so impatient that I wanted to buy his whole stock so he could lock up, but Alice and Jiaju talked further to the man and discovered that his wife would be back soon from doing her laundry at a nearby stream and would be able to act as our guide. But when she came back and was told of our quest, she seemed in no hurry. She took her wet, rolled-up laundry piece by piece from a pail and, at a leisurely pace, hung it on a clothesline. We suspected that she wanted to know how she stood to benefit if she were to help us, so we assured her on that score. And slow as she was to start, when she finally set off she walked briskly despite her seventy years. We marched from the first peak down a valley and up to the second peak, on which a television relay station had been constructed. From there, the old woman veered downhill and, about halfway, she pointed.

We saw a circle of stones that used to be a rock wall, in the middle of which stood a single slab of stone. Cautiously, we inched our way to the front of the white slab, since there was no road and the tall grass was treacherous, snagging socks and trousers and covering up holes and trenches.

The stone slab was indeed a gravestone—eroded by the elements for hundreds of years. On it were carved four characters: QIN LONG TU MU, or GRAVE OF QIN LONG TU. I was afraid we had stumbled onto the tomb of a different Qin. But my brother told me that LONG TU was a title, not a name. So I took out the biography of Qin Guan and, sure enough, he had been appointed "Scholar of the Long Tu Pavilion" in 1130, thirty years after his death. We had actually found the grave of our ancestor.

As we took turns standing behind the tombstone to have our pictures taken, I felt a sense of elation mixed with a hint of sadness. The discovery of the grave marked the culmination of an odyssey that had started when I was a boy in Hong Kong more than thirty years before.

My article about our discovery of the Song dynasty poet's grave appeared on the front page of *The Wall Street Journal*[4] and was promptly translated into Chinese and reprinted in newspapers and journals across China. Interest in it inside and outside China mounted steadily until, in 1984, the Chinese government instructed the local authorities in Wuxi to make preparations for the restoration of the tomb, a task that was completed in 1986.[5] That autumn, scholars all across China congregated in Gaoyou, his hometown, for a seminar on Qin Guan. The wheel had finally come full circle. This traditionalist poet, who died in disgrace only to be posthumously rehabilitated, was being rehabilitated a second time, this time by Communists. The irony would not have been lost on Qin Guan.

CHAPTER ONE

Qin Guan: The Romantic Poet

On a wintry day in 1074, a man in his late thirties went to the Daming Buddhist Monastery in Yangzhou. He was wearing the hat and gown of an official, and was accompanied by a small entourage, as befitted someone in his station in life. He was later to be known as Su Dongbo. (His birth name, Su Shi, was an indication that his father hoped he would become a man of vision: *Shi* was a carriage handrail to be grasped if the passenger wanted a better view. His original courtesy name was Zizhan, "son who is farsighted." But to posterity he is Su Dongbo, "Su of the Eastern Slope.") He had just finished a three-year tour as vice-administrator of Hangzhou, the Chinese empire's second-largest city. At thirty-eight years of age, Su Dongbo had already served as an official for fifteen years, both in the capital of Kaifeng and in the provinces. And he was widely acclaimed as one of the most talented poets in the country.

When he entered the monastery's Pingshan Hall, he caught sight of some writing on the wall. Moving closer, he recognized it as a newly inscribed poem, for the fresh ink still glistened. The poem was written in his own style; even the handwriting resembled his. Who was the mystery poet who could so well imitate his distinctive style? And why had he put this poem on the wall?

Later, Su Dongbo related the incident to his old friend Sun Jue, who listened silently, then handed him several dozen poems saying, "These were written by a friend. Let me know what you think of them."

Su Dongbo was astonished by the volume and quality of the writings. Then he understood. "This must be the same man who inscribed the poem on the wall," he cried.[1]

He was right. Sun Jue explained that the poems had been composed by a relatively unknown scholar named Qin Guan, a fellow townsman from Gaoyou. The young man had long admired Su Dongbo and wanted to meet him. Hearing that Su Dongbo would be passing through Yangzhou, Qin Guan was sure that he would be drawn to the Daming Monastery and visit Pingshan Hall, erected by his late mentor. So, to arouse Su Dongbo's curiosity, Qin Guan had written his poem on the wall. When Su Dongbo heard the story, he was delighted.

This incident occurred in the sixth year of the reign of the Emperor Shenzong, great-grandnephew of Taizu, founder of the Song dynasty. In Europe, the Battle of Hastings had been fought eight years before, and William the Conqueror was on the English throne.

Yangzhou was one of the largest cities in China, the major commercial port of the lower Yangtze valley. It was connected by river to the great interior of China as well as to communities along the eastern coast. The Grand Canal, dug in the Sui dynasty (590–617), linked it with northern China through a series of waterways that reached the Yellow River. Long trains of barges carried salt from the coast and the Yangtze delta to the merchants of Yangzhou. The city was such an important commercial center that as early as the tenth century it had a significant community of foreign traders, including Persians and men from Champa, a country at the southern tip of what is now Vietnam.[2] Two centuries later, a Venetian merchant named Marco Polo would be sent by the Mongol Emperor Kublai Khan to govern Yangzhou for three years. Marco Polo described Yangzhou as "so large and powerful that it has twenty-seven other cities dependent upon it, all of them large, wealthy and thriving with trade."[3]

The first meeting between Su Dongbo and Qin Guan started a friendship that would bind the two men together for the rest of their lives, the older man offering guidance and encouragement, Qin Guan responding with respect and admiration. Qin Guan came to be one of Su's four main disciples, referred to by historians as "The Four Eminent Scholars of the Su School." In later years, his political fortunes were inextricably linked with those of Su Dongbo, just as Su's own political fortunes became entangled in the web of factional infighting that characterized life at the pinnacle of power in the capital.

Qin Guan was born in 1049 into a scholastic family. At the time of his birth, his grandfather, Qin Zhengyi, was journeying along the

33

Yangtze River to take up a post in Nankang, in present-day Jiangxi province. With him were his son and daughter-in-law, who was big with child. The family stopped at Jiujiang ("the city of nine rivers"), nestled on several hills along the Yangtze. There, the baby was born.

Qin Guan lived in Nankang with his grandfather until he was four, when the family returned to Gaoyou. Although he was his father's firstborn, he ranked seventh among his cousins, and so was called "Qin the Seventh." Then, because his father, Qin Yuanhua, admired a fellow student, Wang Guan, at the prestigious National Academy in the capital, he named his son Guan in the hope that he, too, would become a great scholar.[4]

His father was not disappointed. Qin Guan was a child prodigy. He started his studies at home, under his mother's tutelage, learning how to read and write even before he entered school at the age of five.[5] Chinese, like Western languages, evolved from pictographs. But unlike with Western languages, an alphabet was never developed. The result is that Chinese characters have to be learned by rote. At least two thousand to three thousand of a total of about fifty thousand characters have to be memorized before a person is considered literate, making Chinese one of the hardest languages to learn.

Schoolboys at the time of Qin Guan used such texts as the *San Zi Xun*,[6] or *Three Character Primer*, the *Hundred Surnames*, and the *Primer of a Thousand Characters*, in which sentences illustrate the use of a thousand words, none of which is repeated.[7] Each day Qin Guan memorized a few more characters, starting with the most commonly used ones. After learning the pronunciation and meaning of a character, he practiced writing it with a brush tipped with rabbit's hair. He learned how to produce ink by grinding an ink stick made from the heavy residue of oil against a porous ink stone onto which a little water had been poured. He ground and ground until the ink was a rich, thick black. Gradually, he became adept with the brush, wielding it so deftly that the resulting characters seemed to take on a life of their own. Calligraphy was then, as it is now, much more than the equivalent of good penmanship: It was an art form, more highly esteemed than painting.

In Gaoyou, the boy began a course of study that included composition, calligraphy and the recitation and memorization of the classics, histories and poetry. By the time he was nine, Qin Guan knew by heart the *Book of Filial Piety*, *The Analects* of Confucius, *Mencius*, and the *Great Learning*.[8]

From the *Book of Songs*, Qin Guan learned the poems of ancient China, some of which were written two thousand years before he was born. Qin Guan also learned to recite those of the Tang dynasty (618–907), during which Chinese poetry reached its zenith. The *shi* form of poetry, written in lines of five characters, was usually chanted by schoolboys. The seven-syllable line was a later innovation. Even today, scholars say, "After reading 300 Tang poems one knows at least how to hum if not how to compose."

The Tang and Song were the two Chinese dynasties noted for their poetry. In the latter emerged the *ci* form, which was more flexible. The *ci*, or lyrical poetry, had lines of unequal length, and also an irregular meter. While the *shi* was chanted, the *ci* was usually sung and, in fact, was written to tunes. Instead of "composing," poets were said to "fill in" *ci* by making up lyrics for a preexisting tune. Only rarely did a poet create a new tune. The poems were then sung in teahouses and brothels by female entertainers.

Qin Guan practiced his calligraphy and learned how to compose essays and poetry, sprinkling them with classical and historical allusions. Such accomplishments set the scholar apart from everyone else. The scholar was at the apex of an extremely class-conscious society, in which the bulk of the population was illiterate. He was followed in rank by the landowning farmer, the artisan and the merchant. But it was the scholar class from which government officials were drawn. As officials, scholars possessed power and wealth; when out of office, they enjoyed great prestige in their hometowns, where they were usually from landowning families. Though their positions could not be inherited, the scions of scholarly families traditionally were scholars. Such families tended to be wealthy, and only they could afford to let their sons study for long years in preparing for the government-sponsored examinations. The less well-to-do had to send their sons to work in the fields at an early age. Yet many a poor peasant family toiled and saved so that one son could go to school, in the hope that he would pass the highest-level examinations to win an official position for himself and honor for his family.

Merchants had been held in contempt because they were often seen as economic parasites who did not produce wealth but who

35

profited from buying and selling the fruits of other people's labor. But by the Song dynasty, the role of the mercantile class was widely appreciated and scholar-officials themselves occasionally dabbled in business. Successful merchants frequently sought respectability by buying official positions through donations to the government or by linking their families with those of the scholar-gentry through marriage.

People involved in "base" occupations, such as actors and operators of brothels, as well as their children and grandchildren, were not even allowed to take the government-sponsored examinations.

By the time of Qin Guan, the scholar's special position had been confirmed by a tradition of over a thousand years. China's First Emperor, Qin Shi Huang-di, using the state of Qin as his base, had unified the country by vanquishing all rival states. The First Emperor built the Great Wall to keep out northern barbarians, and established the Qin dynasty (221–207 B.C.). The magnificence of his court can be deduced from the vast army of terra-cotta soldiers that have been uncovered guarding his grave in Xi'an, near his ancient capital. But intolerant of critics of his harsh, legalistic rule, he persecuted Confucian scholars, burying hundreds of them alive and burning their books. The dynasty he established, which he thought would last for "ten thousand generations," disintegrated within three years of his death. The brevity of this dynasty has been traditionally attributed to the cruelty of its rulers.

Because Qin is pronounced Chin, the dynasty gave the country the name by which it is known in the West: China. Chinese themselves call their country *Zhongguo*, or Middle Kingdom. Some scholars believe people bearing the surname Qin, like Qin Guan, were descendants of the original inhabitants of the Qin state, in northwest China, or even of its royal household. The First Emperor's own surname was Ying, but after the dynasty collapsed, his family changed their name to Qin to avoid persecution. According to one story, a grandson of the First Emperor eventually settled in Gaoyou, which before then had no residents named Qin. Afterward, the Qins of Gaoyou evolved into a major clan. If credence is to be given to this story, then Qin Guan could have been a direct descendant of the First Emperor himself, a distinction that I would similarly inherit. But this is merely conjecture.

The demise of the Qin dynasty led to a period of internal warfare, from which an uneducated soldier, Liu Bang, emerged victorious as founder of the Han dynasty (206 B.C.–A.D. 220). It was this rough-and-ready peasant emperor who helped restore Confucian scholars to their position of honor. The story is told of how Liu Bang was convinced of the value of Confucian scholars by his chamberlain, Lu Jia, who frequently quoted to him classical annals and odes.

"I conquered the empire on horseback," the exasperated emperor cried one day. "What is the good of these annals and odes?"

Lu Jia replied: "That is true, but it is not on horseback that you will be able to govern it. War and peace are two aspects of an eternal art. If the Qin, having become masters of the empire, had governed it in humanity and righteousness, if they had imitated the ancient sages, you would not have got it."

The emperor turned pale, and said: "Show me then what it was that lost the empire for the Qin, and how it was that I got it, and what it was that won or lost kingdoms of old."

Thereafter, the emperor became a willing pupil of Lu Jia.[9] By the time of his great-grandson, Emperor Wu-di, Confucian scholars were firmly entrenched at court, having eclipsed their Daoist rivals. An examination system was set up to recruit scholars into government service, the first civil-service examinations in the world. Though the examinations were primarily for scholars from aristocratic families and were suspended after the Han dynasty collapsed, they provided the inspiration for the establishment in the sixth century of a much more systematic way of recruiting officials into the bureaucracy.

While the examination system underwent changes over the centuries, it produced scholars who shared the same basic values of Confucianism. All over the country, men were studying the same Confucian classics, which taught them such virtues as righteousness, benevolence, filial piety and harmony.[10] By the Song dynasty, hereditary aristocrats had vanished and the ranks of scholars were filled by those of plebian origins or families of bureaucrats. The examination system remained the major path to an official career up to the twentieth century. My father's early education was in preparation for them before the examinations were abolished in 1905.

It was to prepare himself to take these examinations that the young Qin Guan studied the classics. Like other young men of his time, he dreamed of distinguishing himself.

The death of Qin Guan's father in 1063, the same year Emperor Renzong died, was a severe blow to the family. He had appeared destined for a successful career in the government. Now, only in his thirties, he was dead, and had left behind a widow, three sons and his aging parents. Qin Guan, fourteen, and his two younger brothers had to observe a nominal three years of mourning, as prescribed since the Zhou dynasty (1122–256 B.C.). For the first two days, they fasted, after which they were allowed to eat a watery rice gruel. For three months, the sons refrained from washing their hair as a sign of grief. They wore white, the color of mourning. Their coarse unhemmed garments, if torn, were not mended. The rituals decreed that a son should weep continuously for three days after a parent's death. In the following three months, he should cry frequently and pay respects to the dead; after the first year, he should sob whenever he attended a mourning service. Special music was played to mark the end of the mourning period.[11]

Filial piety demanded that an official, regardless of rank, had to resign his post and go into mourning. Failure to mourn was a punishable offense.

Qin Guan was seventeen when the mourning period ended. The next year his grandfather, as was customary, arranged for him to take a wife.

Because he was descended from a family of scholars and officials, Qin Guan was considered most eligible, and his grandfather succeeded in matching him with the eldest daughter of Xu Chengfu, head of the richest family in Gaoyou.[12] Mr. Xu was a man who valued education and whose youthful ambition had been to become a scholar. His father had refused to let him take the examinations, insisting that he oversee the family properties. Xu Chengfu vowed that, if he had sons, they would become scholars and, if he had daughters, they would marry scholars.

Following the customs of the Song dynasty,[13] a matchmaker was engaged to act as go-between and pay a series of visits to the future bride's family. The matchmaker carried a card to the girl's family, bearing all the relevant data about the prospective bridegroom, including his name and the date and precise hour of his birth. This was compared with the young woman's date and hour of birth, to see if the two people were compatible. Astrologers were consulted. If the two families decided that the young couple were suited, another set of ornate red cards was exchanged. Each card provided information on the family going back three generations, including the ranks of any family members who were officials and the amount of property owned. If this was satisfactory to both sides, the bridegroom's family delivered two big urns of prized wine, decorated with eight red flowers to symbolize prosperity, to the bride's family. These urns were returned filled with water containing several live fish, plus a pair of chopsticks, the fish signifying prosperity and the chopsticks the early arrival of sons.[14]

The day before the wedding, the bride's family sent maids to the bridegroom's house to decorate the bridal chamber. These servants were tipped with money in red packets, called "lucky money."

On the wedding day, the bridegroom's family dispatched a red palanquin, curtained and decorated with red flowers, to the bride's household, together with a band of musicians. The bride, dressed in red, the color of joy, wore a red veil over her head which completely covered her face. She was helped into the palanquin and, to the accompaniment of music, was carried off to her new home. Before she stepped out of the palanquin, a carpet was unrolled so that she would not touch the ground, since it was believed that a bride who set foot on the ground on the way to her husband's home would bring bad luck. Once she had stepped onto the carpet, a man held a mirror in front of her to ward off evil spirits and led her to the bedroom, where she was seated on the bed. The bridegroom, after making obeisances to the family elders, withdrew into the bedroom, emerging shortly with his bride. The couple each received a piece of silk shaped like a heart. Then they went to pay respects to the family ancestors, whose spirit tablets were kept on an altar in the back of the house. After the young couple, accompanied by family and friends, returned to the bridal chamber, they knelt down and bowed to each other, signifying the honor and respect that they would accord each other in life. Guests threw fruit and money on the bed, wishing the couple a fertile and prosperous union.

The institution of marriage was viewed seriously by both sides. Although a man could take one or more concubines, and frequently was expected to do so, they would not have the same status within the family as his wife. A concubine's rank was only a little more elevated than that of a maid, many concubines having been maids who gradually began ministering to their master's needs. Since sex was a taboo subject for respectable women, many wives did not mind relinquishing that part of their duties to a concubine.

Concubines could be acquired or discarded without much ceremony. But divorce was a course to be avoided if at all possible, and entailed the wife being sent back to her own family. Valid grounds for divorce included failure to care for the husband's parents, failure to provide a male descendant, adultery, jealousy, serious illness or an inclination to gossip. A wife could not be divorced if her parents were dead, or if she had fulfilled three years of mourning for one of her husband's parents. Furthermore, if she had shared the hardships of poverty with her husband, he had no right to divorce her later if he became prosperous.

Xu Wenmei, whose name means "cultured and beautiful," was barely into her teens when she married Qin Guan. Her mother had died after giving birth to a second child, a son. Her father's second wife had six children. As the eldest child in the family, Wenmei grew up learning to care for her younger brothers and sisters.

Women of breeding were sequestered in the home, except for special occasions such as visits to the temple. Even then, they traveled in covered sedan chairs. Once married, they were supposed to serve their mothers-in-law and help them run the household. After all, a wife was chosen not by her husband but by his parents. Only concubines were chosen by the husband. The precedence of the parents over the husband is reflected in the common Chinese expression that a family is "taking a daughter-in-law" rather than a husband "taking a bride."

Eight years after Wenmei's marriage, her father, who was only forty-one years old, died. His grieving widow, Wenmei's stepmother, took poison and followed him to the grave two days later. Qin Guan, as the budding scholar, composed "accounts of record," or funerary biographies, in honor of his deceased in-laws.

The ability to compose such obituaries was a skill that scholars had to acquire. Aside from literary abilities, Qin Guan displayed great interest in affairs of state and in military strategy. He was acutely aware of his country's military weakness.

Vast tracts of land, part of Chinese territory in earlier dynasties, were occupied by hostile people considered "barbarians" by the Chinese. The Khitans, a seminomadic people who were the predecessors of the Mongols, had in the tenth century established an empire called the Liao,[15] with seven million Chinese as their subjects. They controlled an area that stretched south of the Great Wall for sixteen prefectures and included Peking. The word Khitan gave rise to the name Cathay. Even today, Kitai is the Russian word for China.

In addition the Tanguts, a people related to the Tibetans, had established a kingdom in northwestern China, naming it the Xixia.

Previously a Chinese vassal, the Xixia kingdom had managed to achieve independence by the late tenth century. Seven years before the birth of Qin Guan, the Song court, to forestall further encroachments on Chinese territory, was forced to increase the annual tribute it paid to both of these warlike neighbors.

So northern China was a region of constant contention among the Song, the Liao and the Xixia. Because of its military weakness, the Song had to send offerings every year to both the Liao and the Xixia to ensure peace, despite Chinese numerical superiority.

The military weakness of the Song dynasty has been traced by some historians to its founding emperor, Zhao Guangyin, a general of the Later Zhou dynasty. Sent on a mission to halt a Khitan invasion in 960 B.C., he was elevated to power in a coup by his officers. The new emperor, cognizant of his own example, reduced the powers of military commanders and put the army under civilian rule. He invited all the commanders who had supported his rise to power to a banquet where, during the feast, he announced: "I do not sleep peacefully at night."

"Why?" asked the generals.

"It is not hard to understand," the emperor replied. "Which of you does not covet my throne?"

The generals, taken aback, declared their loyalty to him. "Why does your majesty speak thus?" they asked. "The mandate of heaven is now established. Who still has treacherous aims?"

But the emperor replied:

"I do not doubt your loyalty. But if one day one of you is roused at dawn and forced to don the [imperial] yellow robe, even if unwilling, how should he avoid being obliged to overthrow the Song just as I against my will was forced to overthrow the Zhou?"

The generals protested that such a course of action was unthinkable and asked how they might prove their loyalty.

The emperor answered: "The life of man is short. Happiness is to have the wealth and means to enjoy life, and then to leave the same prosperity to one's descendants. If you, my officers, will renounce your military authority, retire to the provinces, and choose there the best lands and the most delightful dwelling places, there to pass the rest of your lives in pleasure and peace until you die of old age, would this not be better than to live a life of peril and uncertainty? So that no shadow of suspicion shall remain between prince and ministers, we will ally our families with marriages, and thus, ruler and subject linked in friendship and amity, we will enjoy tranquillity."

The next day, all the army commanders offered their resignations, using imaginary maladies as excuses, and withdrew to the country districts. The emperor, as he had promised, showered gifts and high honors on them.[16]

Fears of another coup caused the Song emperors to prefer military weakness and to seek peace by appeasing their northern neighbors. The Song emperors were remarkably successful: The military coup of Zhao Guangyin was not repeated in the next thousand years of Chinese history. Dynasties fell as a result of internal uprisings or external invasion, but the military remained under civilian control.

Shortly after his marriage, Qin Guan composed a long poem entitled "Man on Horseback Espies the Enemy," about a famous general of the Tang dynasty who put down a major rebellion led by a "barbarian." In that poem, he implied that strategy rather than brute force would be more effective in bringing about the unification of China. "To be good at hitting and stabbing is not the best in generalship; to dare to kill and attack is not the ultimate in using troops," he wrote.[17]

As Qin Guan's political thinking matured, he took one of the most significant steps of his early life: he assumed a new name. Chinese scholars traditionally have had more than one name. The formal name given by one's parents was rarely used, and then only for official purposes. A scholar normally chose a courtesy or style name, by which he would be known to his friends. The style name reflected his ambitions and outlook on life. As he entered a new, significant phase of his life, published a collection of writings, embarked upon a new career, or went into retirement, he might pick still other names that more closely reflected his status and attitudes.

Qin Guan chose the name Tai Xu, or "Great Void."[18] Years later, he explained to a friend why he had chosen it:

"Today the two enemies [Khitans and Tanguts] are in a losing situation. I wish to put into effect perfect strategies to carry out heavenly punishment . . . to let roll a voice which will never be exhausted and to make plans that will last forever, is this not magnificent! And so I took the style name of Great Void to guide my ambition."

It may seem strange that Great Void can indicate high ideals, but in Daoist philosophy, a void is not a vacuum; it is filled with qi, or "vital force." Great Void, therefore, is suffused with energy and purpose for the realization of the young man's goals, and these were ambitious indeed. He wanted to revitalize the country, regain the lost territory and thus restore China to its previous glory.

Meanwhile, the balance of power at court was changing. In 1067, Emperor Yingzong died after a short reign, and was succeeded by his eldest son. Emperor Shenzong, young and reform-minded, invited a remarkable and talented man, an idiosyncratic scholar named Wang Anshi, to court and put him in charge of almost the whole government.

Wang was noted for his eccentric nature. He was reprimanded by superiors for not washing his face and chastised by friends for not changing his clothes. There is a story that he once attended an imperial banquet at which the guests were supposed to catch fish from a pond for dinner, using the fish bait laid out on plates. Wang Anshi, apparently absentmindedly, picked up the fish bait and ate that.[19]

Before his meteoric rise to power, Wang had served for twenty-five years in a variety of provincial posts, distinguishing himself as a scholar and an administrator, yet spurning positions offered at court. Now Wang Anshi accepted Emperor Shenzong's offer to assume virtually full power. Once in office, Wang Anshi proposed wide-ranging reforms. These measures covered the entire gamut of government administration, including reorganization of state revenues, instituting loans for farmers, stabilizing prices and changing the examination system. These reforms were strongly opposed by conservative officials.[20]

One by one, respected officials who opposed Wang either resigned or were forced into the provinces. Even the censorate was no longer inviolate. Since the time of the First Emperor, there had been censors whose job was to keep other officials under surveillance and to report any wrongdoing to the emperor. In the Song dynasty censors could criticize even the emperor himself if, in their view, he was deviating from the path of benevolence and righteousness.[21] They were appointed to twelve-year terms, did not have to disclose their sources of information and were almost never punished for their criticisms and accusations. They had little real power, save that of moral suasion.

The head of the censorate was Lu Gongqu, who had been appointed by Wang Anshi. But when Lu questioned the silencing of all opposition in court, he, too, was dismissed. As Wang Anshi made clear to the emperor, he "preferred the appointment of ordinary officials with no particular distinction to that of talented ones who would obstruct the government's policy."[22]

One of Wang Anshi's most controversial reforms was an agricultural loans measure, called the Green Sprout Law, designed to assist farmers, many of whom turned to moneylenders each spring to tide them over until the autumn harvest. Under the new law, the government assumed the role of moneylender, charging interest at the rate of 24 percent a year, less than private lenders were demanding. The plan, however, was flawed in its implementation. Instead of allowing them to make a voluntary decision, lower-level officials forced all farmers to seek loans and to pay interest on them—whether they needed the loans or not—or face imprisonment. To ensure that the government's risk was minimal, officials made rich farmers act as guarantors for their poorer neighbors. A clamor of protest arose and was readily echoed at court by opponents of Wang Anshi, many of whom represented landowning interests.

Some officials resigned in protest over the law. Others were demoted by Wang for their opposition to it. The outspoken Sun Jue, whose title was keeper of the imperial diary and whose job was to record the emperor's official activities, was told to investigate. Sun Jue did so and reported that the law was being improperly carried out. The finding so infuriated Wang Anshi that he demanded the dismissal of Sun Jue, even though the two men were friends of long standing. Sun Jue was stripped of his titles and sent off to the provinces.[23]

The demotion of Sun Jue offered Qin Guan an opportunity that he seized. Sun Jue was a friend of the family. So, when it became known that he required a secretary to assist him in his post as prefect of Wuxing, Qin Guan sought and obtained the appointment. Working for Sun Jue placed Qin Guan in a good position to learn about the complicated factionalism at court. And it was through Sun Jue that Qin Guan met Su Dongbo, the man who was to influence him for the rest of his life.

Su Dongbo, too, had opposed Wang Anshi, warning the emperor that Wang's policies spread discord. In retaliation, Wang had charges brought against Su, who resigned and asked for a provincial assignment in the first of a series of attempts to escape entanglement in political disputes. His request was granted, and he was assigned to

Hangzhou. When his three-year tour in Hangzhou ended, he was transferred, and it was while he was traveling to his new post that he passed through Yangzhou and spotted the mysterious verse on the wall of Pingshan Hall.

In 1078, Su Dongbo was serving as prefect of Xuzhou, in present-day Jiangsu province. Qin Guan, then thirty years old, was on his way to Kaifeng to take the prefectural examinations, which were given every three years. Candidates were supposed to take them at their local prefectural seat. For some reason Qin Guan took them in the capital instead. Perhaps, like many others, he wanted to benefit from the higher quota of successful candidates assigned to the capital.

Whatever the reason, Qin Guan went to the capital—and on his way stopped at Xuzhou. His enthusiasm for the meeting with Su Dongbo was reflected in a poem he composed, which included these lines:

> I have no wish to lord over 10,000 households,
> Only to see but once Su [prefect of] Xuzhou.

Success in the examinations was crucial to the career of all scholars, many of whom spent years, even decades, preparing for them. Those who passed the prefectural examinations gained the degree of *juren*, or "recommended man," and were eligible to take the metropolitan examinations.[24] Those who failed could keep taking them until they were in their sixties or seventies. One emperor, upon receiving a group of candidates, noticed that among the scholars kneeling before him was a white-haired elderly man.

"You must have many children and grandchildren already," the emperor remarked to him.

"No, Your Majesty," the man replied. "I am seventy-three years old but I have never married. I have been so busy preparing for the examinations that I never had time to find a wife."

The emperor, feeling compassion for him, assigned a palace woman to be his wife.[25]

Qin Guan arrived in Kaifeng in 1078. The examinations took place in a special compound, surrounded by high walls with only one entrance. Like other candidates, he arrived at the examination compound before daybreak, carrying with him a bundle that contained brushes, paper, ink stones, a water pitcher, an earthenware pot, bedding, a curtain for the entrance to his examination cell, and a supply of food. The examination was divided into three sessions, over a period of eight days. No one was allowed to leave the examination compound during a session.

After all the candidates were assembled, they were led through a gate into the examination compound. That gate was then closed and sealed, not to be reopened until the end of the session. Each candidate underwent a thorough search, conducted by soldiers, who went about their task with great zeal. Then each was issued an identification number and assigned to a cell with a dirt floor.[26] The cell had no furniture other than three boards, which could be used as a shelf, a seat and a desk. To obtain a modicum of privacy, Qin Guan, like the other candidates, hung a curtain across his cell. By this time, most of the first day had passed.

Early the next day, before sunrise, the questions were distributed. Officials verified the name, age and physical characteristics of the candidates, as written on folders containing the thick white answer sheets. The physical description of the candidate was required to guard against cases of fraud, lest a substitute be hired to take the examination. All through the day and through much of the night, Qin Guan and the other candidates attempted to answer the questions, which focused on explication of passages from the classics and comments on government policies. There was no literary composition, thanks to one of Wang Anshi's reforms. Like the other candidates, Qin Guan rose occasionally to fetch water from the large jars placed at the entrance of each aisle leading to the individual cells. The water was both for drinking and for making ink. After dark, he lighted a candle and continued with his writing. The next morning he handed in his paper and was allowed to leave the compound. The first session was over.

After resting for a day, Qin Guan returned for the second session, which also lasted a full day and a full night, as did the third. Eight days after he first set foot in the examination compound, Qin Guan's ordeal was over. Now he had to wait for the results to be proclaimed. It took a month.

During that time, clerks were frantically copying all of the examination papers. These were then checked against the originals. The examiners saw only the copies, which bore the candidate's number but no name. This was done in case the examiners might know the names of some of the candidates, or recognize their handwriting.

The two chief examiners were officials sent from the capital. They were assisted by local officials of outstanding scholarship. All the examiners remained in the compound until the publication of the results. Including the time they were locked up before the candidates arrived, many spent almost two months cut off from normal life.

When the results were published, Qin Guan learned that he had failed. But this did not seem to depress him. He joined Su Dongbo and a monk, Can-liao, who was also a major poet, on a tour of scenic places along the east coast. It was not uncommon for Buddhist monks, who spurned worldly honors, to become men of erudition, though they were barred from taking part in the examinations. Su Dongbo was traveling to a new assignment in Huzhou, a growing prefecture of about 150,000 households, and Qin Guan was going to Kuaiqi, where his uncle was an official. This trip provided Qin Guan with the subject matter for a series of compositions. In addition, he was able to meet famous monks and literary figures such as Xianyu Xian, the new prefect of Yangzhou, who became another of his mentors.

Qin Guan, Su Dongbo and Can-liao traveled to Wuxi, by beautiful Lake Tai, and climbed Mount Hui. The three men wrote and dedicated poems to one another in those peaceful, scenic surroundings. But within weeks one of them would be in prison facing a possible death sentence. At Huzhou Su Dongbo left the others to assume his duties as prefect, while Qin Guan and Can-liao continued on their tour. Before they had gone much farther, the two travelers heard that Su Dongbo had been arrested on a charge of slandering the emperor.

It seems that he had written the emperor to thank him for his new post, a customary practice. However, he also showed his contempt for the self-important bureaucrats at court by using a term variously translated as "young upstarts" or "newcomers in their patronage-derived posts."[27] These men, who were pitted against the conservative officials linked with Su Dongbo, chose to interpret this not as a direct slight on themselves but as an indirect insult to the emperor who had appointed them. Given the opportunity they were looking for, they moved swiftly, accusing Su Dongbo of slandering the emperor and of treason. He was arrested by officers of the Censorial Police and escorted to Kaifeng, where he was imprisoned.

The trial of Su Dongbo was used to spearhead an attack on all the leaders of the opposition, many of whom were personal friends of his. The death penalty was invoked for Su and for some of his closest friends, including Sun Jue. Along with the offending letter, over a hundred poems written by Su Dongbo were produced in evidence. He was accused of using historical allusions to criticize high officials and, implicitly, to insult the emperor who had appointed them. (The use of historical allusions to attack contemporary figures was an ancient device among Chinese intellectuals, and continued well into the 1960s, when a play about a Ming dynasty emperor, by the eminent historian Wu Han, was widely seen as an attack on Chairman Mao Zedong. Criticism of the play and persecution of the playwright was one of the first salvos of the Cultural Revolution.)

When Su Dongbo's trial ended, Emperor Shenzong rejected demands for the death penalty but sentenced Su to exile in Huangzhou, near present-day Wuhan. The sanctified principle of guilt by association was applied, and Su's brother, too, was demoted and exiled.

Upon hearing of the arrest, Qin Guan and Can-liao had gone immediately to Wuxing to obtain more information. But they were in no position to oppose the formidable forces that had brought down Su Dongbo. Powerless to help, the two men continued on their journey. Qin Guan went to Lake Tai and visited the temple there dedicated to Yu the Great, a legendary sage-king credited with having made superhuman efforts to save China from disastrous floods by channeling the waters into the ocean. Qin Guan was a guest of the prefect of Yuezhou and stayed in a building called the Penglai Pavilion. Some of his best-known poems were written during this period, including the celebrated "Fickle Youth":

> Mountains rubbed by light clouds
> Sky adhering to the withered grass,
> The painted horn's sound breaks at the watch-tower.
> Let me stop my traveling boat
> And share a farewell cup with you for a while!
> How many past events of Fairyland—
> To look back is futile: only scattered mists remain.
> Beyond the slanting sun:
> A few dots of cold crows,
> A river winds round a solitary village.[28]

Toward the end of 1079, Qin Guan finally returned to Gaoyou. He rose to the defense of Su Dongbo, saying that "though his honor's magnificent talent has been rejected by the world," yet his poetry and calligraphy "have awed the age." He received a letter from Su Dongbo, telling him of his life in exile:

"When I first arrived in Huangzhou, I was very much worried about how I would get along, since my salary had been cut off and my household is a fairly large one. However, by practicing the strictest economy, we manage to spend no more than 150 cash a day. On the first of each month, I get out 4,500 cash and divide it into thirty bundles, which I then hang from the rafters of the ceiling. Every morning I take the picture-hanging rod and fish down one bundle, and then I put the rod away. I also keep a large section of bamboo in which I put anything left over at the end of the day so I will have something to entertain visitors with. I figure I still have enough money left to last us a year or more, and after that we'll think of something else."[29]

Although paper money was used in the Song dynasty, the main unit of currency was still the pierced copper piece, or "cash." For larger transactions, 1,000 cash were strung together and called a "string." Su Dongbo spent four years in exile, and his money eventually did run out. He became a farmer, using land that was on the site of an abandoned military garrison. The land lay on the eastern slope of a mountain. It was then that the poet adopted "Dongbo," or "Eastern Slope," as his name.

Though in exile, Su Dongbo continued to offer advice and encouragement to Qin Guan, and urged him to take the examinations again. In 1081, Qin Guan made a second attempt at the prefectural examinations, this time in Yangzhou. He passed, and early the next year he returned to Kaifeng for the metropolitan examinations. In order to become a *jinshi*, or "presented scholar," he had to take a two-part examination. The first, the departmental examination, was the responsibility of the minister of rites and was held in the Kaibao Temple, where the candidates sat in tiny monks' cells. Successful candidates then submitted a written autobiography to the ministry. There, reexaminers compared the handwriting on the papers with that of the autobiography. If everything was in order, the results were submitted to the throne.

The palace examination system was started in the Song dynasty to enhance the role of the emperor.[30] The examination was held in the palace, and questions were set by the emperor himself or by others in his name. Of course, he did not personally read all the papers. But the examiners sent him the ten best papers, and he was free to change the recommended ranking. Those who were ranked first, second and third were given special honors. As a rule, all those who passed the departmental exams also passed the palace exams.

Qin Guan failed them. This time, his disappointment was great. He returned to Gaoyou to undertake a fundamental reassessment of his goals in life.

Qin Guan secluded himself for forty-nine days. In a letter to Su Dongbo, he explained that he was withdrawing from the world in order to restore his wholeness, to balance himself by giving more attention to his own internal cultivation. To purify himself, he became a vegetarian. During this period, in a departure from traditional scholarly pursuits, Qin Guan wrote a book on sericulture, the raising of silkworms for the production of raw silk. He had observed his wife raising silkworms, watched her combing and spinning the silk. His book was a scientific treatise, with sections on mutants, food, metamorphosis, morphology and the equipment used. Silk was an important product of the Yangtze valley and the export for which China was best known. The Romans dubbed the people who manufactured silk Seres, and their country Serica. Seres was the name that Columbus used for the Chinese. Not until the sixteenth century did the Western world realize that Cathay, China and Serica were the same country.

Qin Guan emerged from his soul-searching a mature man no longer possessed of youth's dreams. Instead of seeking to remake the world, he sought to conquer himself. To reflect this profound change, he decided to adopt another name. He was no longer the ambitious Great Void of his youth.

The name he chose was that of a little-known poet of the Han dynasty, Ma Shaoyou. The literal meaning of "Shaoyou" is "roamed when young." Qin Guan may have decided that the time had come for him to settle down. In explaining the name change, he said to a friend:

"Today my years have come upon me and reflection is easy.
Without waiting until I tread into danger remorse reaches me.
I desire to give back the affairs of the four quarters of the realm
and return to grow old at home like Ma Shaoyou."[31]

Qin Guan was only thirty-five years old. But he had aged prematurely. A portrait of him, painted the year he changed his name, showed a man whose wispy beard and eyebrows had turned gray. His long fingernails proclaimed him a scholar who did not labor with his hands. His eyes had a look of serenity but his back was slightly bent.

His life had reached a turning point. Only persuasion by his mentor, Su Dongbo, convinced him to give the metropolitan examinations another try. In 1085, at the age of thirty-six, Qin Guan finally succeeded. The success that had eluded him when he was consumed with ambition fell into his lap almost as soon as he had decided to renounce the world and seek fulfillment in self-cultivation. Passing the examination opened the doors to officialdom. Then, try as he would, he would not be able to disengage himself from the political forces that were tearing the dynasty apart.

CHAPTER TWO

Qin Guan: The Grieving Exile

Qin Guan's first official post was modest: registrar of Dinghai district, of which Mingzhou city was the prefectural seat. Mingzhou, now called Ningbo, was a bustling port, more important then than it is today. Ships from Japan brought gold, pearls and lumber. From Korea came textiles, lacquer and ginseng, a herb prized for its myriad medicinal, longevity and aphrodisiac qualities. And from the south, from present-day Vietnam, came a variety of spices. The city was ideally suited for trade, since the Grand Canal linked it with Hangzhou and cities inland.

Qin Guan's duties as registrar were to assist the district magistrate, or chief executive, of Dinghai. The magistrate compiled registers and collected taxes, administered justice, provided for disaster relief, made public government orders and in general was responsible for the welfare of the people. The registrar was concerned with the civil aspects of government. The sheriff and military officials preserved order, suppressed uprisings or arrested bandits.

It is not known if Qin Guan's wife joined him in Dinghai. In all likelihood, she remained in Gaoyou. In any event, Qin Guan did not remain long as registrar. He was soon promoted to instructor and transferred to Caizhou prefecture, near the capital, where he was in charge of the Confucian school. But he was soon caught in a series of setbacks and humiliations and tossed about by political storms, for the eleventh century was a period of great intellectual and political ferment. The greatest struggle in Qin Guan's youth had been between the reformer Wang Anshi and those loosely branded as conservatives or traditionalists. Strangely enough, both sides declared their aim to be the return of China to the legendary period when the country was ruled by sage-kings. China was backward-looking, with philosophers and statesmen lamenting the departure of later generations from an idealized past. Even the reformer Wang Anshi had cited the legendary sage-kings Yao and Shun as models to Emperor Shenzong. Qin Guan, as a young idealist, had supported the need for reform, but all his mentors were opponents of Wang Anshi. Inevitably, Qin Guan became identified with them, so that their enemies became his also.

Shortly after Qin Guan's transfer to Caizhou, Emperor Shenzong, the champion of reform, died. Overnight, the political landscape changed. The new emperor was a boy of nine. His grandmother, Empress Dowager Gao, assumed power as regent. As she disapproved of the changes her son had brought about, she recalled to court old officials who had gone into seclusion. Sima Guang, an arch-opponent of Wang Anshi, became prime minister and promptly abolished the entire reform program. Su Dongbo, his brother Su Zhe, and Qin Guan's other mentors, Sun Jue and Xianyu Xian, were all given high office. Wang Anshi's followers were dismissed or exiled, while the disillusioned Wang himself lived in retirement.

The downfall of Wang Anshi's followers did not signal an end to factionalism. The traditionalists divided into several cliques, on the basis of personal loyalties and regional interests. One faction centered on Su Dongbo and his adherents, another consisted of the followers of Cheng Yi, who played a key role in determining the development of neo-Confucianism. While the Su group was flexible in the interpretation of the Confucian classics and was interested in exploring other teachings, such as Buddhism and Daoism, the Cheng school was rigidly orthodox, denouncing Buddha himself as a "barbarian." Cheng Yi criticized Buddha, who had left home to live the life of an itinerant preacher, as being unfilial by "deserting his father and leaving his family" and "severing all human relationships."[1] Cheng Yi, as tutor of the young emperor, frequently warned him against the wiles of wicked women.

Even in Caizhou, Qin Guan felt the effect of these new struggles at court. But compared to his later years in the capital, this period of his official life was idyllic. Several of his best-known poems were written then, some of them inspired by courtesans with whom he had romantic involvements. At the time, it was customary for poets and statesmen to be entertained by courtesans, many of whom were accomplished in literature and music. Because women from respectable families did not appear at public functions, the courtesans provided the only feminine companionship at official banquets, serving

wine, reciting poetry, singing and playing musical instruments. They
were similar to the geishas of Japan in that sexual favors were not
automatically part of their service. But the moralistic Cheng Yi and
his followers did not associate with female entertainers. And, inevitably, Cheng Yi's partisans found fault with the behavior of Su
Dongbo and his associates.[2]

One of Qin Guan's courtesans was called Eastern Jade. Nothing
is known about her except for the poem that he wrote in her honor,
called "Song of the Water Dragon," where he describes a woman
who has just bidden her lover good-bye:

> Double gates beneath the blossoms,
> Sequestered lanes by the willows,
> She cannot bear to think back.
> Remembering their love, all that's the way it was
> Is the bright moon of bygone days
> Facing her as before.[3]

A poem written to another courtesan is titled "Bend in the River":

> Plaintive eyebrows, intoxicated eyes—
> Truly, when you just take a peep at them,
> Your soul is bewildered and lost!
> I remember well that time:
> To the west of the little winding rails,
> With her cloud-like hair loose,
> She walked in her silk stockings;
> Her lilac of a tongue laughingly put forth, with
> endless charm.
> In a low voice she softly murmured,
> "When have I ever been used to this?"
> Before the clouds had produced rain,
> They were blown away by the east wind, all too soon!
> It hurts you so much,
> But heaven doesn't care![4]

This is one of Qin Guan's best-known poems. Given the social
atmosphere of the time, it was daringly erotic. Qin Guan uses a
thinly veiled allusion to the act of making love ("clouds producing

rain"). The woman, on her part, coyly denies that she is accustomed to amorous encounters.

Qin Guan's poems have been likened to those of Keats and the Rosettis. But poetry in China and in the West developed differently and played different roles. Chinese poems were lyrical and closely related to music. The narrative quality found in Western drama and epics was largely missing. Moreover, the rhythmic quality of Chinese verse was not based on stressed and unstressed syllables as in English poetry, but on rhyme schemes and tonal patterns. But perhaps the most important difference was that in China poetry was an integral part of the life of all educated men. Because poetic skills were necessary for passing the civil-service examinations—virtually the only route to advancement—all the intelligentsia were, in a sense, poets. By definition, every official could write poetry, and many did.

Poems were written for friends, lovers, even the emperor. And the emperor, too, composed poems. So pervasive was the desire to compose poems to mark any and every occasion that even peasant households would put couplets outside their doorways during Chinese New Year or other feasts. Those who could not compose their own couplets sought the services of those who could. It was a common practice for friends to exchange poems. A man who received a poem would frequently write one to his friend using the same rhyme-words as the original, or using the same tune if it was a *ci* poem. Even today, scholars of the old school still engage in such poetic games.

The tunes of a *ci* poem bore no relation to the subject matter, and many people wrote to the same tune poems that were of totally different moods. Thus, a tune used by Qin Guan to write:

> The long night is deep, deep like water.
> The wind blows hard; the post-house firmly
>   shut.
>   Dream broken—a mouse peeps at the
>   lamp.
> Frost sends the chill of dawn to invade the
>   coverlet.
>   No sleep!
>   No sleep!
> Outside, horses neigh and people get up.[5]

was used more than eight hundred years later by Mao Zedong to write a poem whose spirit was quite different:

Ninghua, Chingliu, Kueihua—
What narrow paths, deep woods and slippery
   moss!
Whither are we bound today?
Straight to the foot of Wuyi Mountain.
   To the mountain,
   The foot of the mountain,
Red flags stream in the wind in a blaze of glory.[6]

Was Qin Guan a great poet? Contemporary critics debated it. One critic said: "The only one whose feelings match his words is Qin Guan."[7] However, another critic thought his poems too sentimental, and dismissed them as "maiden's poetry."[8]

While Qin Guan was serving in Caizhou, his friends in the capital tried repeatedly to have him promoted. In 1087, Su Dongbo and Xianyu Xian, former head of his home prefecture, recommended him to the court as "wise, good, upright and correct."[9] Recommendations for public office by high officials carried great weight and were not made lightly. If an individual promoted on the strength of a recommendation subsequently committed a crime, his sponsor would be severely punished.

Until the era of Wang Anshi, the designation "wise, good, upright and correct" had been given to only a small handful of people who had passed a special court examination intended to find men qualified for specially difficult work and offer them a means of rising rapidly to positions of responsibility. Wang had abolished these examinations, but in their absence, the court was now assured that Qin Guan was just such a talented man. Such praise, however, exposed him to the attacks of those opposed to Su Dongbo, and the recommendation came to naught.

A year later, in 1088, the special court examinations were revived. Qin Guan, offering himself as a candidate, went to the capital. The examination consisted of two parts. Qin Guan had to write twenty "disquisitions" and thirty "stratagems." The subject matter ranged from the role of the emperor to military strategy—with emphasis on protecting the empire from northern barbarians—to factionalism to finance. Ordinarily, those who passed the first test went on to take the imperial examination, which was conducted by the emperor personally or, if he was too young, by others in his name. But, again because of political maneuverings by the Cheng Yi faction, Qin Guan was barred from the imperial examination on the ground of unspecified immoral conduct.[10]

By coincidence, Qin Guan's uncle, Li Changning, also went to Kaifeng in 1088 to take the examinations. For thirty years, he had failed at each sitting. But in 1088 he not only passed but came first of all the candidates throughout the country. As soon as the results were announced, Li received a number of imperial presents: a green robe, a stiff gauze hat and an ivory tablet, called a *hu*. The gauze hat, painted black with "ears" protruding, proclaimed its wearer an official and the green robe signified his rank. The ivory tablet was to be held in both hands at chest level by an official with his eyes firmly fixed on it when in the emperor's presence. Li Changning received the title of assistant secretary in the literary college and was also appointed to a high military position. Success and honor were finally his. But only months later, he was dead.

In his eulogy, Qin Guan wrote: "He did not succeed in the examinations for thirty years, and served as an official for only a few months. Why was it so difficult to attain, and so easy to lose?" As events were to show, these sentiments could well have been applied to Qin Guan himself.

In 1090, Qin Guan was offered the post of professor of the National Academy where his father had studied, but the offer was withdrawn because of further unspecified allegations of immoral conduct. Most likely, his frequent amorous encounters with courtesans and his erotic poetry made him anathema to the puritanical Cheng Yi partisans. The following month he was appointed rectifier of the imperial library collections, a relatively minor but politically sensitive post.

Qin Guan spent five years in the capital working in an editorial capacity. He enjoyed honor and respect, and associated with some of the highest officers of the land. He lived in an exclusive neighborhood, and his office was in the inner city, not far from the emperor's palace.

Living in Kaifeng was considered a privilege. The capital was a major metropolis with an inner city appointed in imperial splendor and an outer city buzzing with commercial activity. The main roads were lined with shops whose goods ranged from fine silks and expensive jewelry to herbal medicines. Restaurants offered cuisines from every corner of the empire. Wineshops were particularly popular, their presence designated by triangular banners.

The National Academy and imperial temples were in the southern city, where pedestrians, horse carriages, sedan chairs, bull carts and two-wheeled wagons pulled by men competed for road space. The Xiangguo Temple, the most famous in the capital, overlooked the Bian River, its courtyards filled with peddlers hawking feathers, cats, dogs and such household utensils as basins and bedding. Resident Buddhist nuns, too, took part, selling needlework and head ornaments. Books, paintings and perfumes were available in booths at the back.[11]

Kaifeng boasted an incredible night life. The best known combination restaurant and wineshop was the Chang Xing Lou, with a chain of seventy-two establishments scattered across the city. Thick curtains between tables provided privacy for the customers, who were often entertained by girls who sang and offered their services. Toward the southeast, eagles and falcons could be purchased from pet shops, while stables rented out horses, mules and donkeys. Gambling houses started business at midnight and remained open until dawn.

Qin Guan frequented the wineshops, often with other officials. During these excursions, he wrote lyrics that became the equivalent of modern-day pop songs. They were especially popular with courtesans, who entertained their customers with them.[12]

While Kaifeng was a rich city, Qin Guan's remuneration as a literary official did not allow him to live in luxury. In fact, his pay was so low that he wrote a poem about it:

> Three years in the capital, side locks gone gray,
> From old branches again I see new flowers unfold.
> This daily pawning of spring clothes—it's not to buy wine.
> Things are bad—at home we eat mostly gruel.

He sent this verse to the minister of revenue, who responded by sending him two sacks of rice as a present.[13]

Financial problems were not the most serious of Qin Guan's worries; factional squabbles were far worse. His patron, Su Dongbo, anxious to avoid entanglement in political infighting, repeatedly petitioned for a provincial post. In mid-1089, his request was finally granted, and Su was assigned to Hangzhou, where he served as prefect for two years.

With Su Dongbo having eluded his critics, they concentrated their attacks on his associates, especially the Four Scholars—Qin Guan, Huang Tingjian, Chang Lei and Zhao Puzhi—all of whom were working in editorial capacities in the capital.

An incident recorded in the diary of Prime Minister Liu Zhi in 1091 illustrates the atmosphere of political intrigue in the capital.[14] Zhao Junxi, president of the censorate, recommended that Qin Guan be promoted one grade, from rectifier to corrector of characters. Almost immediately, however, Jia Yi—a member of the Cheng Yi faction—submitted a memorial to the throne claiming that Qin Guan was unworthy of the post because of unspecified bad conduct. Zhao, fearful of being accused of favoring Su Dongbo's faction, immediately reversed his position. In a memorial submitted the same day, he announced:

"Previously, I proposed Qin Guan for the post because of his erudition. However, I have discovered that he is guilty of bad conduct. I now wish to withdraw my recommendation. I accept full responsibility for having made an inappropriate recommendation."

Memorials to the throne were supposed to be confidential, but somehow Qin Guan learned of their contents, possibly from allies in the office of the prime minister. The very next day, he called on Zhao and warned him that Jia Yi wanted to replace Zhao with someone from his own faction. "Why not," Qin Guan proposed, "submit another memorial exposing Jia Yi? This would settle the whole matter."

But Zhao refused. He had already decided to appease Jia Yi and sacrifice Qin Guan. Shortly after Qin Guan departed, Zhao received another visitor bringing a message from Su Dongbo. In this Su upbraided Zhao for first recommending Qin Guan and then reneging. It was to be expected that Jia Yi would oppose the nomination, Su said, but why had Zhao been so intimidated? But the following month, Zhao submitted yet another memorial, criticizing his two visitors and accusing them of using Su to put pressure on him.

Qin Guan did not gain the post of corrector of characters until two years later, when he was recommended by the prime minister himself. That same year, he was also appointed compiler in the Bureau of National History to work on the official history of the reformist late Emperor Shenzong.[15] Upon his appointment, Qin

Guan received as imperial gifts the "four treasures of the study," namely fine brushes, paper, ink and ink slabs.

The history of Shenzong's reign was said to have been based on Sima Guang's diary, which was very critical of the regime of Wang Anshi. The compilers of the Veritable Records of the late emperor intended to thoroughly discredit the Wang reformers by giving an unfavorable account of their period in power. For this purpose, the office for preparing the records was filled with supporters of Sima Guang and Su Dongbo. All four of Su's disciples were there.

The tense atmosphere at court drove Qin Guan to inquire more deeply into the mysteries of Daoism. Tired of his libertine past and in search of an inner peace, he decided to renounce the pleasures of the flesh by becoming a celibate. This did not necessarily mean forsaking his wife for, in all probability, she had not left her hometown after their marriage. It did, however, mean relinquishing his beloved twenty-year-old concubine.[16]

Bian Zhaohua was an eighteen-year-old maidservant when she became the concubine of the forty-one-year-old poet. Very little is known of her, aside from Qin Guan's intense love for her, and her passionate devotion to him. She had undoubtedly grown up without the benefits of education and upper-class society that his wife had enjoyed. But the biggest difference between Qin Guan's wife, Xu Wenmei, and Zhaohua was that the former had been selected by Qin Guan's family, while the latter was his own choice.

In celebration of the day when she first became his concubine, Qin Guan wrote these joyous lines:

> Across the fence, the wind tossed the moon into
> my chamber.
> In the silent night, the magpies are quiet.
> On my pillow, I find my weaving girl.
> With great joy, we are transported to heaven.

The three passionate years Qin Guan and Zhaohua spent together in Kaifeng were overshadowed by his increasing political problems. Daoism offered him an alternative to worldly strife. While some Daoists sought physical immortality through the pursuit of an "elixir of life," others, less ambitious, sought immortality of the spirit. To achieve this end, asceticism was prescribed.

When Qin Guan decided to send Zhaohua away, she refused to

go. He offered silver and fine fabrics to her father, to help her acquire a husband. She was inconsolable. The night before she was to leave, she wept until dawn. In an attempt to comfort her, Qin Guan composed a poem just before her departure:

> Misty and gloomy is the moon;
> In sadness the first knock of the morn.
> My heart breaks as she waves farewell.
> No need to weep again before the
>   lamp.
> In life, partings are inevitable.

Qin Guan was not as steadfast as his words, however. Three weeks later, Zhaohua's father came to see him bearing an appeal from his distraught daughter, begging the poet to take her back. Qin Guan relented. And so it was that as his political fortunes began their long, downhill slide, Zhaohua was again at his side.

The year after Zhaohua's return, the empress dowager died, and her grandson, Emperor Zhezong, began to rule in his own right. The young emperor, reform-minded like his father Shenzong, immediately brought back to power the supporters of Wang Anshi's policies. To mark the change he bestowed the name *Shaosheng*— "turning to the sage"—on his reign period. In reverting to the policies of his father, he honored him as a wise man.

The restored followers of Wang Anshi without delay proceeded to persecute those who had served the empress dowager. Su Dongbo, accused of disrespect to the late emperor, was banished to Hainan Island, then one of the most remote corners of the empire. Qin Guan and others were accused of falsifying the facts in the compilation of the late emperor's *Veritable Records*.[17] Wang Anshi's son-in-law, Cai Bian, proposed that the records be revised. This time, they reportedly were based on Wang Anshi's own diary entries. The controversy over the accuracy of the records raged for decades, with history rewritten each time a new faction gained power, until the beginning of the Southern Song dynasty, by which time all of northern China was in alien hands.

Qin Guan, attacked for "knowing that there is a Su Dongbo but not knowing that there is a court," was demoted to vice-prefect of Hangzhou. Although Hangzhou at the time was the second biggest city in the empire, it was hundreds of miles from the capital. Ac-

companied by Zhaohua, he began the long journey there. Banishment from Kaifeng—the center of all learning, civilization and culture,
indeed all that was valuable in life—was a severe punishment indeed.
Bereft of worldly honors, he again thought of seeking spiritual immortality. Near the Huai River, almost in the middle of his journey,
he encountered a Daoist priest with whom he entered into a long
philosophical discussion.[18] As a result, he resolved once more to lead
an ascetic life. A messenger was thus dispatched back to the capital
to ask Zhaohua's father to come and fetch his daughter home. This
time Qin Guan was resolute and his concubine's entreaties were to
no avail. From the moment the heartbroken Zhaohua left his life,
nothing more is known of her. Possibly she became another man's
concubine, or perhaps she insisted on remaining faithful to Qin
Guan's memory. It is even possible that she killed herself.

Before Qin Guan reached Hangzhou, word arrived from the capital that he had been further demoted. With this imperial edict, the
man who once dreamed of driving away the barbarians, reforming
the government and revitalizing the sick land was ordered to the
small town of Chuzhou as the local tea, salt and wine tax collector.

All of Su Dongbo's principal disciples were similarly humiliated.
In the depths of despair, deprived by others of position and respect,
and deprived by himself of Zhaohua's love, Qin Guan had a dream
in Chuzhou that was later interpreted as a premonition of his own
death. In the dream, he composed a poem, which upon awakening
he immediately wrote down:

> By the road in spring, rain has added flowers,
> And the flowers have stirred up a hillful of spring colors.
> I walk to the deep-hidden source of a little stream
> Where are hundreds and thousands of yellow orioles.
> The flying clouds opposite me turn into dragons and
>   snakes
> Soaring and twisting in the azure air.
> Lying drunk under a shady ancient wisteria
> I cannot tell South from North at all.[19]

Qin Guan's lot was further exacerbated by his being ordered to
the even more remote town of Zhenzhou, in the southern part of
what is now Hunan province. As Qin Guan continued wearily on

his way, his depressed state of mind was well reflected in the lines penned on his way there:

> The sad-singing shamaness is on the other side of the
> shrine grove,
> Starving rats pursue one another in the decayed wall.
> The traveler from the north thinks of home and can hardly
> sleep.
> In the bleak mountains the whole night rain is
> blown by the wind.[20]

On the shore of Dongting Lake, Qin Guan offered sacrifices to the lake's god, asking for a smooth voyage. His prayers were answered and at the end of the year he reached Zhenzhou, where he stayed until 1098. Then, victim of another wholesale transfer of banished officials, Qin Guan was sent to Hengzhou, in Guangxi, near the border with Burma, still as tax collector. The next year, he was moved again, this time to Leizhou, across the strait from Hainan Island, where Su Dongbo was living in exile. Hainan was at that time so remote that Su termed his home "the edge of the sky and the corner of the ocean." Because each man was confined to his place of residence, the two friends could not see each other; but they could correspond. During this time, Qin Guan wrote a series of mournful poems in one of which he said: "Days are long, time drags. How can I turn into stone so I won't think of home?"

In the spring of 1100, Emperor Zhezong died childless at age twenty-four and was succeeded by his brother, Emperor Huizong, who was not yet of age. Once more, a conservative older woman took charge. Empress Dowager Xiang, principal consort of Emperor Shenzong, decreed a partial amnesty and gave exiled officials permission to move closer to the capital, though not to Kaifeng itself. Su Dongbo was allowed to go to Lianzhou, on the mainland, while Qin Guan was transferred to Hengzhou, in Hunan. At Su Dongbo's suggestion, the two men met at Xuwen, where they had an emotional reunion.

Then the two lifelong friends separated, realizing that they would probably never meet again. Qin Guan set off for Hengzhou but he never reached there. He became ill in Teng prefecture and was forced to prolong his stay. One day, he went to the Guanghua Pavilion to rest after a bout of drinking to numb his depressed spirits. While lying on a couch, he startled the two servants accompanying him by telling them of the poem he had composed in a dream, which ended with the lines:

> Lying drunk under a shady ancient wisteria,
> I cannot tell South from North at all.

Now the words seemed prophetic. The name Teng means "wisteria," and he was lying intoxicated, unable to distinguish directions.

Thirsty, he asked for water. When one of the servants returned, holding a jade bowl full of fresh spring water, Qin Guan looked up with a smile and died. He was fifty-one years old.[21]

In 1102, two years after his death, his name was one of about a hundred prominent officials of the reign of Empress Dowager Gao to appear on a stone tablet blacklist on the eastern wall of the Palace of Culture and Virtue. Those named and their families were forbidden to enter the capital. The following year all districts and counties across the country were ordered to erect similar stone tablets, and students as well as relatives of those ostracized were barred from Kaifeng. Emperor Huizong ordered the writings of Su Dongbo, Qin Guan and others destroyed.[22] The official portraits of the deceased prime ministers Sima Guang, Liu Zhi and Lu Dafang were burned. The scope of persecution was widened with the drawing up of another list, this time containing 309 names.

In 1106, a comet was sighted in the west, and the stone tablet on the wall of the Palace of Culture and Virtue was sundered by lightning. These occurrences were taken as signs of heavenly displeasure. To avert impending disaster, an immediate halt to the persecution was ordered.

Ten years later, Qin Guan's son, Qin Zhan, became deputy administrator of Changzhou, a prefecture that included Wuxi county.[23] When Xu Wenmei died, Qin Zhan had his father's remains brought to Wuxi and buried with those of his mother on Mount Hui.[24] An auspicious site was selected for the grave, so that the poet's descendants would be numerous and prosperous. That grave, untended for many years, was the one that I discovered nine centuries later.

In 1126, Emperor Huizong, hard-pressed by invaders from the north, abdicated in favor of his son, who became the Emperor Qinzong. But the invaders inflicted a humiliating defeat and took captive both the former and current emperor. The northern half of the country, including the capital of Kaifeng, was seized.

The surviving members of the royal house fled south and installed Huizong's ninth son as Emperor Gaozong. Thus began the period known to historians as the Southern Song dynasty, with its capital in Hangzhou. The shock of losing half the country galvanized Emperor Gaozong into action. He repudiated the policies of his immediate predecessors and posthumously honored Empress Dowager Gao and her trusted advisers.

Three years after Emperor Gaozong ascended the throne, he completed the rehabilitation by bestowing posthumous honors on Su Dongbo and his disciples. Qin Guan and the three other scholars were given the honorary title "Scholars of the Long Tu Pavilion."[25] Qin Guan's tomb in Wuxi was refurbished. A pavilion was built next to the grave and stone tablets with the images of Qin Guan and his two brothers were erected. Visitors to the site reported that from the middle of Qin Guan's grave a wisteria plant had sprouted.[26]

CHAPTER THREE

Qin Kui: The Traitor in Our Midst?

Back in the early 1970s, when I was working at *The New York Times*, I achieved a certain notoriety when a story I wrote on the changing attitudes of the Chinese-American community toward Peking and Taiwan drew the wrath of the Chinatown establishment.[1] A demonstration was held outside the *Times* office, in Times Square in New York, where copies of the newspaper were burned. A Chinatown newspaper declared that "a descendant of Qin Kui is stirring up trouble." To anyone unfamiliar with Chinese history this allusion would mean nothing, but a Chinese would know immediately that I was being declared not only a rogue but a traitor.

According to orthodox Chinese historiography, Qin Kui is the archetype villain, infamous for betraying his country to foreign invaders. Conventional wisdom has it that he, as chief councillor of the embattled Song dynasty in the twelfth century, negotiated a peace agreement with the hated Jurchen, who occupied all of northern China. In the process, he murdered Yue Fei, a heroic general who had attempted to drive the invaders from Chinese territory. Through the centuries, the name Yue Fei has stood for valor and patriotism, while that of Qin Kui has been synonymous with treachery and treason.

Even today in Hangzhou, which was the capital during the Southern Song Dynasty, statues of Qin Kui and his wife, kneeling and caged behind metal grilles, are spat upon by visitors. This happens so frequently that when I visited Hangzhou in mid-1985, I noticed that the authorities had posted a sign asking people to refrain for health reasons from spitting at the statues. The two figures kneel perpetually in front of Yue Fei's tomb. An adjacent temple is dominated by a majestic, larger than life statue of Yue Fei, resplendent in the robes of a general, sitting with his hand resting on the handle of his sword. Inscribed on a gilt signboard hung above his head is his well-known saying: "Give us back our rivers and mountains."

At the time, though stung by the Chinatown newspaper's remark, I felt it was gratuitous mudslinging. I was not yet in possession of our genealogical records, and did not think it was possible to determine one way or another whether I was related to the traitor. Years later, however, scholars both in China and abroad told me about a general belief that the Qin clan of Wuxi is related to Qin Kui.

In the first volume of our genealogical records,[2] I discovered a discussion of the allegation that we are descended from Qin Kui, followed by three arguments that sought to prove it totally unfounded.

The three arguments were as follows:

One: Qin Kui's family was from Nanking and there are still Qins in Nanking. None of our ancestors moved to Wuxi from Nanking. From Qin Guan on down, each generation could be verified.

Two: Qin Guan's tomb is on Mount Hui. His son, Zhan, while living in Changzhou, moved his father's body to Wuxi. During the Kaixi reign period (1205–1207), the magistrate Ying Chunzhi rebuilt the tomb which had fallen into a state of disrepair and admitted the descendants of Qin Guan to the local college.[3] They were paid a monthly stipend to enable them to honor their ancestor. Thus, even at that time the Qins of Wuxi were regarded as the descendants of Qin Guan.

Three: According to historical sources, all the descendants of Qin Kui's only son, who was adopted, were later killed. The great-grandson of Qin Kui, Qin Chu, was the vice-prefect of Chizhou. When that city was attacked by the Jurchens, Qin Chu and the military defender Li Chengzhi fought to save it by leading their troops in street to street battles. When all was lost, Qin Chu went inside his house and set fire to it. An old soldier dragged him out, but Qin Chu cried: "I don't want to live. I would rather die for the country." He then flung himself into the flames and his two sons perished with him. Thus, according to the official history of the Song dynasty, all of Qin Kui's descendants died.

The editor of our clan genealogy traced the origin of the slander that we were descended from the traitor to Emperor Yongzheng, who reigned from 1723 to 1736, the third Manchu to sit on China's Dragon Throne. This emperor had come to power only after a bitter struggle involving several of his brothers, all of whom later paid for their ambition with their lives. The teacher of one of these brothers was a member of our clan named Qin Daoran, who earned Yong-zheng's hatred and spent the entire period of his reign in prison. One day the emperor, while commenting on the descendants of Sunu, a member of the imperial family who had supported a rival claimant to the throne, wrote in an aside: "Now Qin Daoran is actually descended from Qin Kui, and everybody knows this."[4] As was often the case, the emperor's word was taken as the truth. From that time on, stories began to appear linking the Qins of Wuxi with the traitor Qin Kui.

The curator of the Wuxi Museum, Mr. Gu Wenbi, told me that this injustice to the Qin clan could not be rectified by anyone named Qin. "I will reverse this verdict for you," he said, using contemporary Chinese political terminology. "I will write something to clarify the whole situation." And he did. Mr. Gu wrote a long article in which he asserted that there was no truth to the rumor and explained that it stemmed from the Yongzheng emperor.

Whether or not Qin Kui was a member of our clan, the widespread belief that he is associated with it, together with the clan's vigorous denial of this, was, I decided, a persuasive reason for including him in this account of our family history.

Qin Kui was from Jiangning, now called Nanking. He gained the *jinshi* degree by passing the metropolitan examination in 1112, twelve years after the death of the poet Qin Guan, and was appointed instructor in Mizhou, in Shandong province. Later, he was promoted to serve at the National University in the capital, Kaifeng. Subsequently, he became a censor and, by 1126, he held the post of vice censor in chief.

Those were chaotic times. The Song dynasty, which governed a vast area populated by tens of millions of people, had for years been menaced by the Khitan kingdom and consistently bested by a mere 750,000 Khitans. But by the second decade of the twelfth century, the once warlike Khitans had become increasingly Sinicized. With their new civilization had come military weakness.

Now the Khitans found themselves in a perilous state, for from among their formal vassals, the Jurchens, had emerged a leader named A-ku-ta, who forged his people into a formidable fighting force. In 1115, he led a rebellion, declaring himself emperor.

The Song court, gratified to see their Khitan enemies in such a predicament and oblivious to the long-term threat of the much stronger Jurchens, began negotiating a pact with the Jurchens to destroy the Khitan kingdom. In 1121, a Song army of 150,000 marched against the Khitans and suffered a humiliating defeat. A second Song army, launched in 1122, was almost wiped out. Then the Jurchens attacked by themselves and roundly defeated the Khitans. In 1122 the Jurchens proclaimed their own dynasty, the Golden Dynasty, named after a river in their homeland.[5]

By a treaty between the Jurchens and the Song, Peking and its surrounding province of Yan were returned to the Chinese. The Song court, in turn, agreed to compensate the Jurchens for their loss of revenue from the province by transferring their annual tribute to the Khitan to the new Jurchen empire, and by paying in addition 200,000 taels of silver, 300,000 bolts of silk, and a million strings of cash—each containing 1,000 copper coins.[6]

The pact did not last long. The Song emperor, Huizong, persuaded the administrator of Pingzhou prefecture to defect from the Jurchens and then laid claim to Pingzhou, precipitating a Jurchen invasion of the Song heartland.

As the military situation deteriorated, Huizong abdicated in favor of his son. The Jurchen army advanced to the walls of the Song capital and laid siege to Kaifeng itself. The new emperor, Qinzong, sought an accord with the Jurchen commander, who stated his terms for lifting the siege: the cession of three prefectures as well as vast indemnity payments, a harbinger of what China would be confronted with more than seven hundred years later when "barbarians" from the West appeared at her doorstep.

The Song court deliberated upon the demands for three days, with most of the high officials seeing no possible recourse but acceptance. In view of Qin Kui's later reputation as a traitor, it is interesting to note that, at least at this juncture, while serving as vice-minister of rites, he adamantly counseled resistance at all costs. Surrendering three prefectures, he warned, would only whet the Jurchen appetite for even more intolerable exactions. He proposed to gain time by relinquishing only one of the prefectures. As soon as the Jurchen troops withdrew, he said, the Song should strengthen their defenses. In addition, he proposed upholding the dignity of the Song court by refusing the Jurchen emissary entry into the palace, thus keeping the barbarian in his place.

At the end of the three-day period, a Song delegation led by

Prince Kang and a high official, Zhang Bangchang, proceeded to the Jurchen encampment to offer themselves as hostages while terms were negotiated.

As a result of the negotiations, the Song emperor agreed to yield all three prefectures and to pay 5 million taels of gold, 50 million taels of silver, a million bolts of outer garment textiles, a million bolts of silk, ten thousand horses, ten thousand cattle and ten thousand mules, plus a thousand camels.

"The above mentioned items are based on what is available within the town [Kaifeng] and will be taken from the palace precincts and the various offices as well as from the gentry and civilian population, Buddhist and Daoist monasteries, etc.," the Song petitioners told the Jurchen commander. "We have already gone to the very roots and peeled off our skin."[7]

Even more galling, the Song emperor had to debase himself. While the 1123 treaty had been one more or less between equals, the 1126 treaty referred to the Song emperor as "nephew" of his "uncle, the August Emperor of the Great Golden Dynasty." Given the rigid hierarchical structure of Oriental societies, by the agreement the Song emperor symbolically prostrated himself before the conquering Jurchens.

Again, the peace with the Golden Dynasty did not last long. Within months, the Jurchen forces were again camped near the capital. An emergency meeting of the emperor's top advisers was held at the aptly named Prolonging Peace Palace. About seventy officials recommended that the emperor accede to new Jurchen demands. But Qin Kui and thirty-six others disagreed.

Time was running out. The following month, the Jurchens attacked and scored an easy victory against the Song, capturing the capital. To consolidate their position, the Jurchen set up a puppet state, declared that no member of the royal house of Zhao could serve as emperor, and proposed instead Zhang Bangchang, a high Song-dynasty official. Song loyalists including Qin Kui, now prisoners of the Jurchens, objected strongly.

"All my life I have benefited from the state and am ashamed not to be able to repay the state," he wrote to the conquering Jurchens. "Now the Jurchens possess powerful troops, control our lives and even seek to change our emperor. I cannot consent to this. The Zhao family, from the time of the founding emperor, has been in power for a hundred and seventy years. Now, because of treacherous officials and poorly formulated policies, the dynasty is doomed. We have agreed to cede our rivers and our mountains and to act as vassals.

"The Song has been a great and united dynasty. Although it may be fated to fall, the supplanting of the emperor should not be undertaken lightly. When Zhang Bangchang worked for our emperor, he implemented many erroneous policies. He shares the blame for our collapse. our citizens abhor him. If he is enthroned, rebellions will erupt everywhere, and he will not be able to serve the Jurchen well. Even if those in the capital agree to his becoming emperor, the rest of the country will not accept it. Even if the descendants of the Song vanish from the capital, they will not disappear from the rest of the country. My comments are made with the interests of both the Song and the Golden Dynasty in mind."

But Qin Kui's plea was ignored. The puppet state, named Chu, was set up with Zhang Bangchang as emperor, and his Jurchen masters took as captives both the Song emperor, Qinzong, and his father, the former Emperor Huizong, as well as almost the entire court, about three thousand officials. The Jurchens controlled virtually all of China north of the Huai River, leaving the Song loyalists in southern China.

Adherents of the Song dynasty selected a new emperor to rally around. Their choice was the Prince of Kang, the captured Huizong's ninth son and the only one still at liberty. He was enthroned as the Emperor Gaozong in 1127 and began the period known to historians as the Southern Song dynasty.

Gradually, the Song dynasty was able to consolidate its control of southern China, with a capital in Hangzhou. That city, named Lin'an, or "Temporary Peace," served as the Song capital for the remaining 150 years of the dynasty.

Meanwhile, in Peking, the Jurchens sought the services of Qin Kui, whom they respected. He was placed under Ta-lan, a son of the Jurchen emperor. Before long he and his whole family managed to make their way southward to Hangzhou. Whether he escaped or was released by the Jurchens on an understanding that he would work for them has never been ascertained.

Because of Qin Kui's patent ability and his reputation for loyalty, he was immediately appointed minister of rites at the Song court. He urged peace between the Southern Song and the Golden Dynasty, and proclaimed that the Song should administer the south and the Jurchens the north.

Within two years, Qin Kui had become chief councillor, one of the two most powerful officials at court. Chief Minister Lu Yihao was responsible for military affairs while Qin Kui took care of all other matters. However, in 1132, Qin Kui was removed from office in temporary disgrace for supporting what was considered to be a shameful peace with the Jurchens. He did not regain his position until five years later.

At the time, there were two contending groups at the Song court. One consisted of military revanchists, who wanted to roll back the Jurchen army, release the imprisoned imperial hostages and recover the lost territory. It had among its leading members General Yue Fei.

Little is known about the details of Yue Fei's life, partly because he died in ignominy and so no official biography of him was prepared. But there are a multitude of legends. It is said that his father, a farmer, was killed in a flood when Yue Fei was only a month old. His mother brought him up and inculcated in him a strong sense of patriotism, tattooing on his back the characters "Boundless loyalty to the nation." As a young man, he was endowed with unusual physical strength. Discipline, loyalty and patriotism were his hallmarks. When he was nineteen years old, he joined in an abortive attempt by the Song to capture Peking.

He was twenty-three years old when the Northern Song collapsed. A call was issued for soldiers to come to the assistance of the dynasty. Thousands of peasants espoused the cause, and Yue Fei was one of them. The resistance could not withstand Jurchen military superiority, and the volunteers fell back to the Yangtze River. In the regrouping, Yue Fei assembled his own army. It eventually became the third largest army in the diminished Song empire, mainly because it absorbed members of peasant uprisings that Yue Fei quelled.

Yue Fei quickly gained a reputation for enforcing strict discipline. He ordered his own son's execution when the young man's horse stumbled and fell while he was in full armor; only when all his officers knelt down to plead for mercy did he relent, and even then he insisted on his son being flogged. Asked when the empire would have peace, Yue Fei replied: "When the civilian officials do not love money and when the military officials are not afraid to die."

The tension between the war and peace factions was symbolized by the antagonism between General Yue Fei and Qin Kui. In the background, of course, was the emperor himself, Gaozong. From the standpoint of self-interest, he had little to gain in the unlikely event that his forces triumphed over the Jurchens and released the legitimate emperor, his brother, for that would result in an end to his reign.

One school of thought has it that Gaozong himself masterminded the weakening of the war faction, and that Qin Kui was merely carrying out his bidding. More recent historians impute to Gaozong a less selfish motive. In this view, the emperor was realistic enough to know that it was militarily impossible to vanquish the Jurchens, and that an agreement to preserve the peace was the best he could hope for.

Still another theory casts the emperor as the pawn of the evil prime minister who plotted to murder the country's savior in order to make peace with the enemy. It is this version of Qin Kui that has been predominant in China.

In 1138, Qin Kui was again in political difficulties for accepting another humiliating peace treaty. When that was violated by the Jurchens in 1140, Qin Kui undertook to negotiate a new peace agreement.

While the diplomats negotiated, the generals continued the fighting. During this campaign, Yue Fei scored major successes against both the puppet Chi forces and the Jurchen army. His men advanced towards the Northern Song capital, Kaifeng. So badly routed were the Jurchens that it seemed they might withdraw north of the Yellow River.

Song civilian officials, however, feared this military success might jeopardize their chances of reaching a new peace agreement. So all Song forces were ordered to fall back. It is said that Yue Fei received twelve urgent dispatches from the emperor before he finally consented to do so.

Then the emperor stripped all of his military commanders, including Yue Fei, of their commands and gave them titles with no real power. The military grew restive. Charges were brought against one of Yue Fei's sons and a chief subordinate. The two were accused of plotting a revolt. Yue Fei himself was charged with complicity and imprisoned.

The new peace agreement with the Jurchens, reached in 1141,

made the Huai River the border between the two states and called for the emperor of the Golden Dynasty to bestow on the Song emperor the legitimacy to rule.[8]

The Song dynasty was to be a vassal. The agreement refers to the Golden Dynasty as "your superior state," while calling the Song "our inferior state."

After the conclusion of the agreement, in mid-1142, the Golden Dynasty sent an official, Liu Gua, to invest Gaozong as the Song emperor. The certificate of appointment was very offensive. It referred to the Song emperor by his personal name as though he were a commoner, and it voiced the hope that the Song would remain "for generations an obedient subject" of the Jurchens.

Together with this insulting message of investiture, Liu brought with him the bodies of the members of the imperial family who had died in captivity, and Gaozong's mother, who was still living.

During that same period, Yue Fei was murdered in prison, apparently under orders from Qin Kui. It was a hasty killing, not a formal execution, possibly because the general still commanded a significant following.

Qin Kui himself died in 1155. At first he was honored with the name *Zhong Xian*, or "Loyal and Wise." The peace accord he had negotiated held for almost two decades. It was violated in 1160 when a Jurchen ruler made unprovoked attacks on the Song.

But in the years following his death, the reputation of Qin Kui steadily worsened.[9] The Emperor Gaozong claimed that all the wrongdoings under the peace policy had been his minister's fault. He said that Qin Kui controlled many people in the palace, including the imperial physician, so that the emperor himself had not dared oppose him.

Just as Qin Kui's reputation grew worse, so that of Yue Fei rose. After the battles of 1160 his remains were exhumed and given a glorious reburial at the present site of his tomb in Hangzhou. During the Ming dynasty—the last native Chinese dynasty, which came after that of the Mongols and before that of the Manchus—Yue Fei's loyalty was lauded in novels and plays, and numerous temples were built in his honor.

He was revered as one of China's greatest heroes for eight hundred years until the Cultural Revolution in 1966. Then his grave was desecrated and he was denounced as a feudal warlord. In 1979, in the aftermath of the death of Mao and the overthrow of the Gang of Four, Yue Fei's tomb was again repaired and opened to the public.

Nowadays, objective historians evaluate Qin Kui and Yue Fei quite differently. One eminent Song historian calls Qin Kui the "scapegoat" of the Gaozong emperor.[10] According to him, both Yue Fei and Qin Kui were loyal, each in his own way. Yue Fei was loyal to what he saw as an ideal, while Qin Kui gave his personal loyalty to the emperor, carrying out his will. As to who should be blamed for Yue Fei's death, he says:

"Most historians took the orthodox line of condemning Qin Kui, the chief councillor, while criticizing the emperor only mildly." However, he adds, "It must be emphasized that the old histories generally refrained from attacking any emperor, except the most abusive and the stereotyped bad last emperors."

The reason is simple: Historians were not only afraid of retribution from the emperor's successors, but also were afraid of being accused of pretending to criticize past rulers while actually attacking the present one.

In the popular Chinese mind there is no doubt that one was the superhero and the other an archvillain. Such was Qin Kui's reputation after his death that nearly all people surnamed Qin felt tainted. By the Ming dynasty, popular stories told of how Qin Kui was being incarcerated in the deepest recesses of hell, in the company of other notorious traitors in Chinese history. In the Qing dynasty, one official named Qin Dashi, who had placed first in the palace examinations of 1752 but was from Qin Kui's hometown, went to Hangzhou and knelt before the tomb of Yue Fei and reflected the common hatred for Qin Kui in a couplet:

> Ever since the Song no one has been named Kui,
> Now before this grave I am ashamed to be a Qin.

CHAPTER FOUR

Qin Yubo: The City God of Shanghai

"China's feudal rulers created two sets of officials to control the masses," the Shanghai Museum curator explained. "There was one set of officials for this world and another for the next. That way, the common people believed that there was no hope of escape from their rulers, even after death. That is why each city had its own city god."[1]

When I went to the museum in the fall of 1982 in search of information about Qin Yubo, the city god of Shanghai and my distant forebear, I learned that city gods did not begin life as spiritual entities but had, at one time, been ordinary human beings.

The city god I was pursuing was a seventh-generation descendant of Qin Guan.[2] By the time Qin Guan was posthumously accorded the title Scholar of the Long Tu Pavilion in 1130, half the country was already in alien hands. And little more than a century later, the whole of China was, for the first time, under the rule of foreign invaders, the Mongols. Led by Genghis Khan, these fierce warriors swept out of the arid northern steppes, bent on conquest.

Ultimately, the Mongols became rulers of the greatest land empire known to history, which extended from the east coast of Asia to the Black Sea and from the Siberian steppes to the frontiers of India.

In 1279, the remnants of the Song forces were defeated in a naval battle off Hong Kong. The Mongols established a Chinese-style dynasty, which they called Yuan, or "First Beginning," indicating their belief that they alone would go down in history as the founders of the first truly great empire.[3] Vastly outnumbered by their subjects, they sought to govern with the help of foreigners. Thus it is not surprising that Kublai Khan, grandson of Genghis Khan and the first Mongol emperor of China, accepted a Venetian, Marco Polo, into his service.[4]

76

While distrusting all Chinese in general, the Mongols were especially suspicious of southerners. Northern Chinese, who had lived under alien rule for over a century, were considered less hostile. History was to prove the Mongols right, for the rebellions that finally brought about their overthrow were led by southerners.

The Mongols, hoping to strengthen their hold, made the study of their language mandatory. Shortly after Marco Polo ended his long sojourn in China in 1292, the Yuan court ordered the setting up of schools in each county for the teaching of Mongolian. The Mongols realized they had to prevent themselves from being absorbed by the more numerous and culturally superior Chinese.

The five sons of Qin Tianyou, great-great-grandson of Qin Guan, had fled south across the Yangtze River before the onslaught of the Mongol forces. The eldest, Qin Zhirou,[5] had taken up residence in Shanghai, at the time a coastal township.

Qin Zhirou had two sons, Liangxian and Lianghao,[6] who grew up under Mongol rule. Lianghao traveled to Daming, a major center of learning in northern China, to study under a well-known Mongol scholar. Soon he became the foremost Mongol scholar in the land. He translated over three hundred important passages from ancient documents and compiled them into a volume entitled *A Compendium of Knowledge*. So distinguished was he that Temur Khan, who succeeded his grandfather, Kublai Khan, as emperor in 1295, granted him the title professor of the imperial college.

Lianghao's first son, Yubo, was born in Daming in the summer of 1295 and went to school there with his brother, Hengbo. He attained the highest degree, that of *jinshi*, in 1344, at the age of forty-nine. In 1350 he was appointed to serve as a magistrate in Shandong province. His three years there won him great popularity because he carried out many projects, including reviewing the taxation system, reconstructing the temple of Confucius (who was a native of Shandong), setting up forty-two schools, repairing the city wall, and establishing a welfare system. He devised a system for storing grain when the harvest was plentiful and distributing it during lean years.

After Shandong, Yubo was promoted departmental director of the provincial government of Fujian and won a reputation as a just and able administrator. But he submitted his resignation after only a year because, as a Confucian scholar, he felt that the Mongols had lost what the great philosopher Mencius called the mandate of heaven, or the moral right to rule.

The Chinese called their emperor the Son of Heaven, and believed that he constituted a living link between heaven and the people. When the emperor was just and virtuous, all lived in harmony. Earthquakes, droughts and other natural disasters were interpreted as signs of celestial displeasure with the emperor. When these occurred, he was expected to reform and offer sacrifices to appease heaven. Social upheavals, too, were seen as an indication of imbalance within society. If uprisings were quelled, then heaven had indicated the ruling dynasty should continue in power. If a rebellion was successful, it was proof positive that the mandate to rule had been transferred to the new dynasty.

Qin Yubo saw that the situation in the country was deteriorating. In Peking, then known to the Mongols as Dadu, or the Great Capital, Mongol princes were involved in power struggles with one another while, in southern China, revolts were multiplying.[7] The area controlled by the central government was steadily shrinking. So in 1354, at the age of fifty-eight, Qin Yubo returned to Shanghai to live in retirement with his aged mother. But the political situation in China was such that he was not allowed to do so in peace.

At the time, southern China was ruled, in effect, by warlords, each of whom was trying to enlarge his territory. The two most important of these were Zhang Shicheng and Zhu Yuanzhang.

Zhang Shicheng[8] and his brothers were boatmen who, when confronted with exorbitant government duties and exploitative merchants, went into open rebellion, leading a small band of followers in 1353. The Yuan court tried to entice Zhang to end his revolt by offering him high posts, but he detained or killed the emissaries. His area of influence continued to increase and, in 1354, Zhang revealed his ambitions by conferring on himself the title of Prince Cheng. Two years later, he crossed the Yangtze and seized most of the country east of Lake Tai, in China's richest agricultural area. He made present-day Suzhou his capital, setting up his headquarters in a former Buddhist monastery. Soldiers from other rebel armies rallied to him, and he had little trouble recruiting scholars to serve in the bureaucracy that he was establishing.

Suzhou is only twenty-five miles from Shanghai. When Zhang learned that Qin Yubo was living in retirement there, he solicited his support, knowing of Qin Yubo's prestige and reputation as a scholar.[9] Twice he approached him, and twice he was rejected.

The Mongols, too, tried to court Qin Yubo by offering him the post of traveling censor[10] and later the position of minister of agriculture and water resources of Fujian province, but neither of these overtures was successful.

Qin Yubo's refusal to join Zhang Shicheng was judicious. Within a year, Zhang lost four cities to the forces of his rival, Zhu Yuanzhang. He offered to surrender to the Mongols in return for a princedom, but eventually settled for the less prestigious rank of grand commandant. Though nominally loyal to the Yuan dynasty, Zhang continued to rule the area under his control and, in fact, was able to expand his empire. For eight years, Zhang and Zhu maneuvered for advantage. Then, in 1366, Zhu won a decisive victory and most of Zhang's cities capitulated. His capital, Suzhou, fell after a ten-month siege and Zhang himself was taken to Nanking, Zhu's headquarters, where he was put to death.[11] Many of his officials and advisers were also killed—as Qin Yubo would have been if he had succumbed to Zhang's blandishments.

Zhu Yuanzhang came from a poor family. His parents and his elder brother died in a famine. Zhu himself survived by begging for food. At the age of twenty, he joined a Buddhist monastery and became a monk. After four years, however, he returned to secular life. The country was in chaos, and Zhu was ambitious to shape the new order. He joined a rebel band and, by marrying the commander's daughter, eventually was acknowledged as the group's leader. Perhaps because of his Buddhist background, he enforced strong discipline over his men, prohibiting wanton killing and plunder. Keenly aware of his own lack of education, Zhu recruited scholars to act as his mentors.

As soon as he had defeated Zhang Shicheng, Zhu assumed the title Prince of Wu. With his new status, his need for talented advisers became more urgent. So, within days of his assumption of the title of prince, Zhu personally wrote a letter to Qin Yubo, appealing for his assistance:[12]

> . . . This year, I have conquered half of Guangdong and Guangxi, Fujian has been pacified and Shandong, too, is under my control. My troops have taken Kaifeng as well as territories

along the Yellow River. My intention was not to crown myself emperor. However, I saw that there were no genuine leaders among those spurious heroes who arose at the coast and who, not knowing what they were doing, brought suffering to the people. I have analyzed the situation and it is clear that the Yuan dynasty has lost the mandate of heaven and will be overthrown. Since I am a Chinese, I have the right to start a new era.

My intention is to lead the Chinese people to eradicate the northern barbarians and excise the country's ills. Though I have enough troops and supplies, I need assistance. People tell me that Yubo is a man of consistent rectitude, and that is why I have traced your whereabouts. Now that I know where you reside, I am sending my envoy to bring this invitation to you. I hope you will come voluntarily and without any reservations and assist me in ruling the country according to correct principles. However, if you choose not to, you should move your place of residence for your own safety. The people who live along the coast are of a bellicose nature, and it is extremely dangerous for you to live there.

Yubo, please consider my request carefully. I lay my heart bare in writing this letter. I do not know how to embellish because I am uneducated, and I am writing this letter without any help from scholars.

Qin Yubo, after much reflection, decided against linking his fortunes to the rising ones of Zhu Yuanzhang. In his reply, addressed to Zhu Yuanzhang's minister, he tried to explain why:

I was a sojourner in Daming. When I was young, I followed my father to the Yuan capital. Though undeserving, I was fortunate enough to be accepted into the government academy, from which I graduated. Our family has been granted honors and emoluments by the Yuan dynasty. We resided in Yangzhou. In 1354 I sought refuge in Songjiang prefecture. My mother was eighty years old at the time. Mr. Zhang of Pingjiang [Zhang Shicheng] twice asked for my assistance, but I refused. The Yuan government offered me an official post in Zhejiang, but I declined. On the eighteenth day of the tenth month [1365], my aged mother passed away. I buried her in Changren Village of Shanghai County and followed the traditional regulations in mourning for one's parents. Now I have received this invitation, delivered with all propriety, to serve as an official. I regret that, for reasons of ritual, I have to decline.

For over twenty years, I have been the recipient of emoluments from the Yuan dynasty. If I turn my back on the past and join in opposing the Yuan, I will be acting disloyally. Moreover, if I do not complete the observance of mourning for my mother, I will be unfilial.[13]

I have observed that the court [of Zhu Yuanzhang], acting on behalf of heaven and the people, has put down disturbances and restored order, and is now governing with benevolence and justice, selecting officials on the basis of loyalty and filial piety. Now men of talent are approached to take part in running the government. I can foresee peace everywhere, and I am sure I will benefit from such good government.

I am a person of little talent and in poor health. If I can be allowed to lead a quiet, leisurely life on a farm, to live out my years as a simple commoner, teaching the younger generation, and enjoying peace, I shall be exceedingly grateful.

If I turn against my benefactor and ignore my duty to my mother and shamelessly seek power and wealth by accepting an official position, I will be held in contempt and the wise and far-sighted Prince of Wu will surely condemn me and punish me as a warning to other new officials.

I beg you to show me clemency and convey my sincere wishes to the Prince of Wu. If my petition is granted, I shall be appreciative of my extreme good fortune. If punishments are to be meted out to me, I shall endure them willingly. I ask you to forgive my poor composition and writing, as I am in a state of perplexity and anxiety.

But Zhu Yuanzhang was not a man to brook refusal. A second letter was dispatched to Qin Yubo, this time couched in much less courteous terms. It read:

In the old days, loyalty between the sovereign and the minister was based on mutual understanding and a respect created by generations of ministers and sovereigns, with the sovereign heeding the counsel of his ministers. However, when a dynasty began to weaken, the advice of talented ministers was disregarded and men of strength lacked opportunities to demonstrate their courage. When the sovereign died, the ministers perished with him, and that was considered loyalty. However, there were also sagacious men of unsurpassed virtue and ability who could recognize the signs portending the end of a dynasty: an ineffective sovereign and power-hungry ministers who lacked understanding of each other, with the sovereign ignoring their recommendations. Such men of discernment and ability would select another great leader to follow, and their distinguished service usually resulted in the beginning of a new era, with their names being recorded for posterity. Every generation has its share of such farsighted men.

I have never heard of a minister being acclaimed for his loyalty who, when the country was in danger, preferred to hide in the wilderness rather than work. With this I cannot agree. Although I am uneducated, I have heard of Wei Qing [of the Tang dynasty] who, citing Confucius, asked what official would not come to the aid of his sovereign in his hour of need, or not help him if he were failing? Can such a man be considered a loyal minister? Now I have seen your letter. I know that you previously worked for the Yuan dynasty, and that you refused the bandit Zhang Shicheng, who tried to usurp power. Even if you had wanted to serve me, you did not have the opportunity. This I regret. The northern barbarians were, indeed, your master. There is a difference between the northern barbarians and me. A righteous man should know which path to take. Since you do not intend to serve me, I should enable you to serve your former master again. What if I send officials to escort you to Yanjing [Peking]?

When Qin Yubo received this second summons, he knew that there was no avenue of escape for him. The Yuan dynasty was fast sinking.

Seriously troubled, Qin Yubo carefully composed his answer, which began:

I, Qin Yubo, was educated by the Yuan dynasty and received their emoluments for more than thirty years. Now it is heaven's will that I should become a commoner, living as a simple fisherman or farmer. The summons from his highness shows his benevolence and wisdom: benevolence in sparing my life and wisdom in gathering around him men of talent. However, I dare not accept his invitation because of my observation of the mourning period in honor of my mother, and my own ill health. Moreover, I am also restrained by a sense of shame. A scholar without shame uses his lord as a mere fishtrap. A woman without shame values her husband as a hairpin. If a nation loses its sense of shame, the nation is finished.

I humbly beg you to entreat his highness to have pity on me. Let me be free, like the deer in the mountains and the fish in the ocean.

Qin Yubo was already in his seventies and may well have been in poor health. But Zhu Yuanzhang was in no mood to accept his excuses. He dispatched yet a third summons in which he said bluntly:

On the twenty-fourth day of the fourth month, I led my troops to Longjiang. There I met two Confucian scholars named Pan and Qin who came to my boat for a discussion. Mr. Pan showed me a poem of yours, in your own handwriting. It was a very fine one. I think that when the sky turns bright, a true man should be willing to cooperate with his lord, and advise him how to govern the country. But I see from your poem that you admire the character of hermits. I know this noble sentiment of yours will inspire future generations. But I am so discouraged by you that I will not discuss my plans for ruling the country with you again.

You are still bound by the mourning ceremonies. I will not interfere with the respect that you show to the dead. When the mourning period for your mother ends, however, I shall give you an escort so that you and your whole family can return with dignity to the northern barbarians where you can demonstrate your allegiance to them. If their dynasty collapses and their emperor dies, and you have no benefactor and still refuse to join me, I shall grant you gifts and honors in order to show the world my magnanimity. Do you not find that laudable?

Now you still have your dynasty and your emperor. If I made you stay within my jurisdiction, I would be forcing you to be disloyal. That is why I must let you go. But if you have my permission to leave and still choose to remain, then you will have to stop talking about your high ideals of fealty. You will become a laughingstock. I am sure you agree. After you have read this

83

letter, you should carefully reflect on your situation. In less than ten months your mourning period will be over. Then I will proceed as planned.

The old poem says, "Barbarian horses sigh at the northern breeze and migrating birds build their nests on the southern branches of trees."[14] Even birds and animals know where they belong, what about man?

Yubo, you cannot deny that you are born of Chinese parents. It is unfortunate that you worked for the barbarians and refuse to join me, a fellow Chinese. I am not a man of letters, but I have heard that when the Shang dynasty was about to fall, one minister offered the new rulers the instruments for playing ritual music, while another stayed to teach the new Zhou dynasty the correct principles of government.

Your poem has stimulated my interest in studying history. I have found that every emperor made use of officials from the previous dynasty to help him rule benevolently. From this I see that all your protestations of reverence for loyalty and principles must be lies!

While Qin Yubo was exchanging letters with Zhu Yuanzhang, the Yuan dynasty collapsed in 1368. Zhu Yuanzhang proclaimed a new, Chinese, dynasty. His choice of Ming, or "enlightened," as its name reflected the founding emperor's Buddhist background. Installed on the throne by his military commanders, Zhu heaped rewards on them.

Although Zhu recognized that the Confucian bureaucracy was indispensable for the administration of the empire, he did not invest it with much real authority. Instead, he concentrated power in his own hands, abolished the office of prime minister and ordered the heads of ministries to report directly to him. He declared that, even after his death, anyone advocating the restoration of the office of prime minister should be executed. He set up a new institution, the Grand Secretariat, but it was theoretically powerless, performing only liaison and drafting functions. During the entire 276 years of the Ming dynasty, the post of prime minister was never restored. But there were several instances when a grand secretary, by sheer force of personality, was able to dominate the government.[15]

Zhu tried to impose his will on posterity in other ways too. Mindful of the interference of eunuchs and palace women in state affairs in previous dynasties, he limited their number to less than a hundred. This was flouted by the fifteen emperors who succeeded him, most of whom lacked his vision and his dynamism. Toward the end of the dynasty, the Ming palace swarmed with up to nine thousand palace women, and the number of eunuchs in the capital had soared to seventy thousand. Emperors engaged in the pursuit of pleasure and neglected state affairs, thus permitting eunuchs to seize power, usually with disastrous consequences.

The founding emperor not only distrusted his officials but also had little confidence in his children and grandchildren. To forestall intrigue on the part of the princes, he allowed only the heir apparent to reside in the capital. His other sons were sent to garrison the northern and western borders, or to provincial estates where they lived royally, with generous allocations of servingmen, land and stipends. He made provisions for all of his progeny but could not foresee that by the end of the dynasty his direct male descendants would number 100,000, resulting in an intolerable financial burden on the state.[16]

After Qin Yubo received Zhu Yuanzhang's third letter, he had no choice but to acquiesce. Reluctantly, he entered the emperor's service at the new "southern capital," Nanking. Yubo was appointed reader-in-waiting to the prestigious Hanlin Academy, which provided literary and scholarly assistance to the emperor.

In 1370, at the age of seventy-four, Yubo was named one of the chief examination officials in the capital, a position to which only the most erudite could aspire. Later, apparently because of a disagreement with the emperor, he was demoted to prefect of Longzhou, in the south, where he died at the age of seventy-eight. He was buried, together with his wife, west of Longevity Temple in Shanghai, to the south of his father's tomb. As the couple was childless, a son of Yubo's brother, Hengbo, was adopted by Yubo to continue his family line. But this son died in childhood and so Yubo had no direct descendants.

But the story of Qin Yubo does not end with his death. In fact, his death merely marked the beginning of a new phase. For legend has it that when Emperor Zhu heard of Qin Yubo's death, he declared: "Yubo was reluctant to serve me in life. Now let his spirit serve me after death." With that, he appointed Qin Yubo the city god of Shanghai.[17]

Though this appeared to be a way of punishing Qin Yubo, the

people of Shanghai considered it an honor. Over the centuries, stories were told of how the city god came to the aid of the citizens of Shanghai.

One such extraordinary occurrence was the rescue of Shanghai residents from an impending massacre shortly after the fall of the Ming dynasty and the founding of the Qing. In 1653, about 250 years after Qin Yubo's death, General Wang Jing led troops against pirates in the Shanghai area. The operation failed because of General Wang's cowardice and ineptitude. Governor Zhou was ordered to investigate. General Wang, fearful that his lack of courage and bad judgment would be exposed, reported to the governor that the pirates had escaped because they had many accomplices among the people of Shanghai. He recommended that all the adult male inhabitants along a certain stretch of the coast should be executed. The newly established Qing dynasty was particularly sensitive to the activities of pirates because some were assisting Ming loyalists determined to overthrow the dynasty. So when General Wang proposed the mass executions, Governor Zhou consented.

The night before the executions were to take place, a delegation of prominent Shanghai residents came and knelt before the governor, appealing to him for mercy, declaring that those condemned were innocent. The governor, however, refused to rescind the order and stated the executions would proceed at sunrise.

That night, an apparition manifested itself before the governor. It was Qin Yubo, the city god of Shanghai, in his official robes, covered with a red cloak, and holding an ivory tablet in both hands. Without uttering a word, he slowly shook his head. Then he vanished. Governor Zhou dismissed the vision as the product of his overwrought mind and returned to his responsibilities. Again, Qin Yubo appeared, shaking his head in disagreement. Four times the governor remained obdurate and four times he received a visitation from the city god. By morning, Governor Zhou, convinced, ordered a stay of execution.

When word got around that those under sentence of death had been saved by the intervention of the city god, the relieved Shanghai residents streamed to Qin Yubo's temple to give thanks. Large sums of money were donated for the renovation of the temple, which had been under the charge of Daoist priests since the early days of the Ming dynasty, and a terrace was built to mark the miraculous event.

Another Qin Yubo miracle was recorded as late as 1826. A fisherman, Wang Abao, was murdered. His brother, Wang Ruizeng, reported that the two men had been involved in a fight with another group of fishermen led by Gu Chinguan. In the brawling, Wang Ruizeng said, both he and his brother were seriously injured, and when he visited his brother the next day, he found him dead.

The magistrate of Shanghai, responsible for the investigation, went to the victim's boat and found the corpse on the cabin floor, turned toward the wall. The face was covered with blood, but there were no bloodstains on the floor. There were two head wounds, both on the left side, and two chest wounds. The latter were so deep that bones and muscle had been exposed. From the depth of the wounds it appeared that the deceased had been attacked with a metal instrument other than a knife.

The magistrate issued a warrant and arrested Gu Chinguan and his six friends. Gu admitted there had been an altercation, but in his account the quarrel over fishing territories took place in a restaurant. Gu said he had thrown a bowl at Wang Ruizeng and injured his forehead. Then, before the dispute grew more serious, mutual friends had separated the two parties. Gu's account also contained the firm assertion that the murder victim Wang Abao had not even been present.

The magistrate began to suspect that the murderer was perhaps the brother, Wang Ruizeng, but he lacked evidence and so decided to solicit the help of Qin Yubo.

The magistrate, accompanied by his retinue, brought Wang Ruizeng one evening to the temple of the city god and prayed to Qin Yubo to help him solve the case. Then he waited. Just after midnight, Wang Ruizeng fell into a trance in which he confessed that he had killed his old and weak brother, Abao, and blamed the murder on Gu. He said that Gu fished the upper reaches of the river, while he and Abao had to be satisified with the lower. He had quarreled with Gu over this in the restaurant, but Gu and his friends were stronger. When he returned home that night, he found Abao asleep. Wang Ruizeng hit upon a plan to get rid of both his antagonist Gu and his useless brother. He killed his brother in his sleep and accused Gu of the deed.

The murder weapons, a blood-stained ax and a pair of scissors, were found in a creek behind Ruizeng's house. Thanks to the aid of the city god, the real murderer was convicted and executed.

87

Miracles attributed to Qin Yubo mounted. Belief in his supernatural powers was such that people used to take the ashes of joss sticks from the temple to mix with medicine.

While most stories illustrate how Qin Yubo brought succor to the citizens of Shanghai, in one the city god himself is in distress. In 1748, during the reign of Emperor Qianlong, Wang Ting, district magistrate of Shanghai, had a dream in which Qin Yubo appeared and appealed for help. Magistrate Wang awoke convinced something was seriously wrong; he rushed to the city god's temple and found it ablaze. Without regard for his own safety, he dashed into the flames and managed to salvage the statue of Qin Yubo, its stern red face signifying justice and righteousness, before the fire devoured it and the whole building. The magistrate then had the temple rebuilt.

In the nineteenth century, the Qing dynasty became progressively weaker. As in the declining years of the Yuan dynasty, the central government was beset by revolts. But this time, the situation was aggravated by the encroachment of Western powers, each of which tried to carve out its own sphere of influence in China. The most notorious event was the Opium War of 1839–1842, when Britain sent gunboats to safeguard its export of opium to China.

In 1842, British troops forced the surrender of Shanghai. Led by Sir Henry Pottinger, they marched into Shanghai on May 11. For want of a better location, they were billeted in the temple of the city god. Luckily, they remained there only five days and caused little damage.

Thirteen years later, in 1853, the temple was again seized. Local insurgents, called the Small Sword Society, took control of most of the city, establishing their headquarters in Qin Yubo's temple. The central government was unable to quell the rebellion and fighting continued intermittently for eighteen months. Eventually, in 1855, imperial government forces, supported by French troops, captured the city and the rebel leader was killed. Unfortunately, the long occupation of the temple and the desperate fighting had damaged the temple extensively.

In 1860, a joint Franco-British force entered Shanghai at the request of the Chinese government to protect it from the Taiping rebels, who were rapidly gaining strength. Once more, the temple was transformed into a barracks, this time for French and British soldiers. An artificial hill in the temple grounds was leveled and a pond filled in for the construction of temporary billets. By the time the Taiping threat waned and the foreign forces were withdrawn, the area around the temple had been so transformed it was almost unrecognizable.

In the late 1860s, there was a large-scale renovation of the temple. By the late nineteenth century, the temple was attracting pleasure-seekers from around Shanghai, and its grounds were a focus of entertainment in the city. On holidays and festivals, flower shows and celebrations took place there. Inevitably, in the wake of celebrants came merchants, and the commerce further detracted from the temple's former solemnity.

A series of fires in the early 1920s seriously damaged the temple, but a group of philanthropists donated large sums of money and, in 1927, a totally new steel and cement structure rose on the site. Inside was housed a statue of the red-faced city god, dressed like a Ming dynasty official, seated behind his desk. Its arms were movable, to facilitate the changing of its official robes with the changing of the seasons. Several times a year, on religious festivals, the god was placed in a sedan chair and paraded through the tortuous maze of narrow streets that made up the old city. As the god was responsible for the maintenance of order in Shanghai, regular tours were essential. A 1935 report in the English-language *North China Herald* described one procession:

"First came 24 horsemen, clad in red and purple, and bearing spears and bows and arrows executed in the classical style; they were closely followed by a large body of men, dressed in flowing robes of red and white, with an occasional variation of purple and red, and wearing black paper top hats, or so they appeared to western eyes.

"The clashing of gongs grew louder, and the smell of incense, from burners borne by coolies in sedan chairs, or carried by acolytes, stronger. Black and white gowns, worn by men carrying silver chains, were followed by blue robes, the wearers of which wore beautiful fan-shaped peacock plumes at the back of their heads."

The procession extended for two to three miles and lasted for many hours. From time to time, the city god was borne to a temporary temple set up in his honor, where, the newspaper account said, the god "rested awhile, receiving the worship and adoration of hundreds of his subjects, before proceeding through another fourteen or fifteen streets on his return trip to the City Temple. The festivities did not end until 11 o'clock at night."[18]

89

Despite the increasing commercialization of the city god, believers continued to worship at the temple, even after the Communists took power in 1949. But by April 1966, on the eve of the Cultural Revolution, all churches and temples in Shanghai were closed.[19] Daoist priests removed the statue of the city god and placed it and other religious objects in a compound for safekeeping. On the night of August 23, virtually all temples in Shanghai came under attack. The youthful Red Guards forced their way into the Daoist compound and destroyed or carted away all religious artifacts, including the statue of Qin Yubo.

After that, the temple was converted into a shopping bazaar. In mid-1986, I was told by a spokesman for the Daoist Association of China that plans were being drawn up to reopen the temple. I hope a new statue of Qin Yubo will soon grace the interior. Shanghai today is China's most prosperous city, bustling with industry and commerce. I like to think that Qin Yubo, the city god, is still concerned with its welfare.

CHAPTER FIVE

Qin Weizheng: The Clan's "Firm Roots"

In the Room for Singing Merits, the main chamber of our clan's ancestral hall in Wuxi, hung a portrait of Qin Guan. To the left was one of his son, Qin Zhan. Both men were wearing their splendid official robes. To the right was the portrait of a man wearing the simple hat and gown of a commoner. The unimposing subject was Qin Weizheng, progenitor of the Wuxi branch of our clan and an eleventh-generation descendant of Qin Guan.[1]

The rise and fall of Qin Guan's fortunes after death affected his children and grandchildren. By the second decade of the twelfth century, Qin Guan's posthumous rehabilitation made it possible for his son, Qin Zhan, to become deputy administrator of Changzhou prefecture.

The Chinese have traditionally viewed each individual as but a link in a chain, connected with both his ancestors before him and his descendants. Thus, emperors frequently posthumously honored the parents, grandparents and even great-grandparents of an official who had rendered signal service. Similarly, a family often benefited for generations because of the meritorious actions of one man.

But for succeeding generations of Qin Guan's family members, the positions served were progressively lower. While Qin Zhan was deputy head of a prefecture, his grandson achieved only the much lower rank of instructor, and his great-grandson held the post of county registrar, one of the lowest rungs on the bureaucratic ladder. Toward the end of the Song dynasty, even such low-level bureaucratic posts eluded the family.

Nonetheless, the scholarly tradition was preserved, and each generation had its share of hermit poets, people who either had no zest for politics, preferring the rustic life, or who had failed to overcome the examination hurdles that lay in the path of an official career.[2]

91

Such a hermit was Qin Huai, a ninth-generation descendant of Qin Guan. He and his sons lived as recluses, content with simple bucolic pleasures. Inevitably, the family's economic standing declined as its land holdings were divided and subdivided among the children of each generation. Qin Huai's younger son, Qin Mo, was reduced to a state of genteel poverty. Qin Mo's first wife gave him no sons, but his second, whom he married late in life, bore him three. When Qin Mo died at the age of seventy-five, his second son, Weizheng, was but a child.[3] His third and last son, Ruiba, was an infant.

Before long, Weizheng's mother also died, and he and his brothers had to fend for themselves at an early age.[4] The family fortunes were at their lowest. The young Weizheng decided to strike out on his own. He must have been in straitened circumstances indeed, for he took a drastic step. He forsook Qin Village, named after his ancestors, where his family had lived for ten generations. And he abrogated his responsibility to tend his parents' graves and honor those of his ancestors.

Weizheng, his meager belongings in a bundle on his back, headed east, in the direction of Wuxi, then a medium-sized town and the seat of Wuxi District. By nightfall, he had walked almost eighteen miles and was approaching Hudai, a township that was part of Wuxi District. Exhausted, he lay down to rest on the Zhuangyuan Bridge, planning to continue on his journey in the morning. The name of the bridge was symbolic, for *zhuangyuan* was the title given to the candidate who came first in the triennial nationwide examinations for the highest degree in the capital.

There lived in Hudai a man named Wang Yazhou, who held the post of registrar. He and his wife had three children, all daughters, and longed for a son. Since both he and his wife were no longer young, they were concerned that there would be no male heir to tend their graves or offer sacrifices to ancestors.

That night, Registrar Wang had a strange dream. In it he saw a beautiful white crane, an auspicious symbol, standing proudly on Zhuangyuan Bridge. Underneath the bridge thousands of fledglings flapped their wings. He awoke so intrigued that he and his wife left their house early the next morning and went to Zhuangyuan Bridge seeking a clue to the meaning of the dream.[5]

There they saw a young man, not much more than a boy, fast asleep on the bridge. Though dusty from his journey, the stranger had more the appearance of a student than someone from peasant stock. The Wangs woke up Weizheng and questioned him. After hearing his story, Wang decided that the crane in his dream represented the unusual young man, the fledglings his numerous progeny.

The Wangs took the surprised youth home and treated him as their son. Weizheng proved himself a bright student. He took the local examinations, and became a licentiate, or *xiucai*, "flowering talent." This meant that he had been admitted into the ranks of scholars, and enjoyed certain privileges, such as exemption from labor service and corporal punishment.

When Weizheng reached marriageable age, his benefactor made him a proposition. He offered one of his three daughters to him in marriage, on the understanding that the couple's first son would be surnamed Wang, to continue the father-in-law's family line.[6] This would guarantee that the Wang family's ancestral altars would be looked after and that prayers would be offered annually to their spirits.

The practice of "adopting a son-in-law," though uncommon, was not unheard of. As in this case, the offer was usually made by a family without a male heir to an impoverished prospective bridegroom. Instead of the wife joining the husband's family, he joined hers. Few men were willing to consider this, believing it degrading.

Perhaps Weizheng also found it shameful, but agreed out of a feeling of obligation to the Wang family for their charity. He had three sons by the Wang daughter. Because Weizheng, like his grandfather, was something of a recluse and loved nature, he named his sons Songyin "Pine Hermit," Zhuyin "Bamboo Hermit" and Meiyin "Plum Hermit".

Unfortunately, fate intervened to prevent Wang from realizing his wish. Songyin, Weizheng's firstborn, who was to continue the Wang family line, died in childhood. Then the descendants of the two other sons took it upon themselves to honor Weizheng's benefactor. That is why, later on, members of the Qin clan every year honored Wang[7] at the same time that they offered sacrifices to their own ancestors, especially to Qin Guan and Weizheng.

Qin Weizheng was a scholar and an artist. Only a single poem, originally written on one of his paintings, is extant. The painting is that of a pine tree. On it, he wrote:

My life is at an impasse, I curse my fate,
The tired earth is tossed about in storms,
My hometown looks unfamiliar,
Rootless, my adopted home is Hudai.
The tall spreading pine delights,
The fragrant grass greens,
No more reunions with my brethren
A toast to being master in a strange land.[8]

Because Weizheng never became an official, he is not mentioned in the official literature. We can assume that, since he had earned the degree of licentiate, he enjoyed a certain amount of prestige locally, especially in a small community like Hudai. But in all likelihood his life was relatively undistinguished.

The only contemporary account we have of his life that survives to this day was written by his brother-in-law, Yin Bangzhan, who had married another of the Wang sisters. Perhaps by far the most important information in this brief account was the following statement: "His eleventh-generation ancestor was Qin Shaoyou, who was famous for his poetry and his deeds."[9] From this it is clear that, even during the lifetime of Weizheng in the late Song dynasty, his descent from Qin Guan was accepted as fact.

Weizheng was buried on Guishan, ("Homecoming Knoll"). Later, his father-in-law, Wang Yazhou, was buried beside him. Wang's widow constructed a temple near the two graves, and placed inside it a huge statue of Guanyin, the Goddess of Mercy. This had been the dying wish of her late husband, who was a devout believer in Buddhism. When the building was finished, it was named Zifu ("Obtaining Happiness") Temple. The spirit tablets of Wang and Weizheng were placed inside. A plot of farmland was set aside, to be worked by monks. The proceeds were used to maintain the monks and to defray the costs of incense and sacrificial paper money.

In 1777 Liu Yong, one of the era's most outstanding scholar-officials, composed an epitaph giving credit to Weizheng for the Wuxi Qin clan's prominence: "For a tree to be tall the roots must be firm, for a river to flow far, its source must be inexhaustible. The same can be said of man. From time immemorial, venerable clans and revered families traced their origins to gifted individuals."[10]

Liu Yong was a student of a member of the Qin clan. He composed this epitaph at a time when a new plaque was being erected at the ancestral tomb. The Chinese believed that the site of a man's tomb could influence the fortunes of his descendants. Liu Yong wrote in the epitaph that Weizheng's tomb "clawed onto Dragon Mountain on one side and leaned on Phoenix Hill on the other; no wonder the Qin family produced such a multitude of talented scholars." In China, the dragon symbolizes the emperor and the phoenix represents the empress.

And another scholar said of the founder of the Qin clan of Wuxi: "Although his biography was not included in the Annals of the Song Dynasty, his descendants, including famous officials and filial sons, reflect the reward that heaven bestowed on him for his virtues."[11]

Wuxi today is one of the most developed medium-sized cities on the lower Yangtze valley, linked to Shanghai and Nanking by road and rail. It is in the heart of China's most prosperous region, known to the Chinese as "a land of rice and fish." At the time Weizheng moved in with the Wang family, Wuxi already had a population of almost half a million people. It was an ancient community, whose origins stemmed from the early years of recorded history, long before the overthrow of the Shang dynasty (1766–1122 B.C.) by King Wu, who established the successor Zhou dynasty. Tradition has it that King Wu's great-grandfather had three sons. The eldest, Tai Po, realizing that his father wanted to pass the throne to his younger brother, moved south of the Yangtze River to live among the barbarians, on the pretext of gathering medicinal herbs. He was accompanied by thousands of his followers and their families. There they founded their own state, which they named Wu and which was centered in the vicinity of present-day Wuxi.

About the fifth century B.C., during the time of Confucius, around the time of the fall of Babylon to the Persians, the Chinese empire had fragmented into half a dozen states, each of which paid lip service to the impotent Zhou emperor. In southern China, the big struggle for dominance was between Wu and its neighbor, Yue.

In 496 B.C., King He-lu of Wu attacked Yue, but was mortally wounded by the Yue king, Gou-jian. As He-lu lay dying, he made his son, Fu-cha, swear to avenge his death.

Three years later, Gou-jian heard that King Fu-cha was training troops to avenge himself. He decided to strike first, ignoring the counsel of his minister Fan Li.

95

But in the ensuing battle, his forces were routed and he was besieged by the king of Wu.

A remorseful Gou-jian told Fan Li: "This comes of not following your advice. What shall I do now?"

Fan Li replied, "One who overcomes self-satisfaction gains the help of heaven, one who can turn a disastrous situation into a secure one gains the help of men, and one who practices frugality gains the help of the earth. Try to placate him with humble words and rich gifts. And if that fails, offer yourself as a hostage."

So King Gou-jian sent his minister Wen Zhong to sue for peace. Approaching on his knees, Wen Zhong said to the king of Wu, "Your worthless subject Gou-jian sends his slave with the request that he may be your subject and his wife your serving maid."

The king's adviser said, "Heaven has delivered Yue into our hands. Don't accept." He added: "If you do not destroy Yue now, you will live to regret it. Gou-jian is an able ruler and Wen Zhong and Fan Li are good ministers. If you let them return to Yue they will make trouble." But the king, ignoring his advice, decided not to destroy Yue.

Gou-jian spent the next few years as the slave of the king of Wu, cleaning his stables. He humbled himself in the king's presence until Fu-cha was convinced of his loyalty and released him.

Free, Gou-jian and his ministers plotted revenge. He kept gall by his sleeping mat, looking at it while seated or lying down and tasting it while eating, to remind himself of his previous humiliation. He tilled the fields himself, made his wife spin cloth, went without meat and wore no colored silks. He became an ideal ruler, treating men of talent respectfully and his protégés handsomely, helping the poor, mourning the dead and sharing his people's toil. He did this for twenty years, and his people were devoted to him. Like him, they wanted vengeance.

Meanwhile, his minister Fan Li, knowing King Fu-cha's weakness for women, scoured the kingdom looking for beauties. One day he discovered, on the bank of a river, a lovely maiden named Xishi, the daughter of humble parents. She was so beautiful that her father, a woodcutter, charged one gold coin of anyone who wanted to look at his daughter. Fan Li recruited her and trained her in the arts of pleasing men. Then, even though he himself had fallen in love with her, Fan Li sent her to King Fu-cha. Just as he hoped, the king became so infatuated with her that he lost all interest in affairs of state, and the power of Wu gradually declined.

When Fan Li judged that the time was ripe, King Gou-jian mobilized his forces to attack Wu. They scored a great victory, killing the crown prince, but Gou-jian was unable to destroy Wu. Four years later Gou-jian attacked again, this time routing the Wu forces and besieging their capital. King Fu-cha sent an envoy to Gou-jian, who advanced upon his knees with bared back and begged the king of Yue for peace.

"Your subject Fu-cha presumes to lay bare his heart to you," the envoy said. "In days gone by he wronged you at Kuaiqi, but complied with your request for peace. Now that you have advanced in majesty to mete out punishment, he must obey your commands. Will you pardon his offence, as he pardoned yours at Kuaiqi?"

Gou-jian was moved but Fan Li countered, "At Kuaiqi, heaven delivered us into their hands, but they did not seize their chance. Now heaven has delivered them into our hands: Is Yue to oppose the will of heaven? Twenty-two years you have been planning this: How can you throw away your victory now? One who spurns what heaven offers will suffer for it."

When Fu-cha heard this, he decided to commit suicide. As he dealt himself the death blow, he covered his face with his long hair saying, "How can I face Wu Zixu?" Wu Zixu was the minister who had warned him against trusting Gou-jian, and whom King Fu-cha had subsequently condemned to death. Before the minister died, he had said: "Pluck out my eyes and hang them over the East Gate to see when the Yue invaders break through and destroy our state."

Shortly after his triumph, Fan Li resigned. Then, in a note to his long-time associate, Wen Zhong, he warned:

"When all the birds are killed the good bow is put away. When the cunning hares are dead the hounds are made into stew. The king of Yue with his long neck and predatory mouth is a good companion in time of trouble but not in time of peace. You had better leave."

The loyal Wen Zhong chose to stay and, just as Fan Li foresaw, was eventually put to death by King Gou-jian.[12]

According to legend, Fan Li and the beautiful Xishi slipped away by boat one night, after which he shunned politics, made a fortune as a merchant, and settled down by the shore of lovely Lake Tai, one of China's five major lakes. Even today in Wuxi, on the north shore of Lake Tai, there is a garden, Li Yuan, which is named after Fan Li and stands on the site of his former home. People say that Xishi's beauty was such that when she walked along a river, the fish would swim to the bottom, ashamed to compete with her. Even today, the Chinese have a saying, "From a lover's eyes a Xishi springs."

The name Wuxi means "No Tin." During the Zhou dynasty, it is said, there was a tin mine on a peak east of Huishan, or Mount Hui. In the Han dynasty two thousand years ago, the tin was exhausted, and so the town's name was changed from "Have Tin" to "No Tin." In the Han dynasty a stone plaque was dug up from the mountain with the following engraved on it:

> When there is tin, weapons, wars;
> When no tin, peace prevails;
> When there is tin, chaos emerges,
> When no tin, harmony presides.

From then on, the mountain was called Tin Mountain, which has become synonymous with Wuxi itself. The highest point in the area, it dominated the city.

Like almost all towns of the time, Wuxi was surrounded by a city wall. There was a major canal that ran the length of the city from north to south, while rivers ran parallel to each other from west to east. On a map, Wuxi had the appearance of a bow drawn taut, with the east-west rivers resembling arrows. These came to be named "First Arrow River," "Second Arrow River," down to "Ninth Arrow River." In the center of town was the "Sixth Arrow River."

Wuxi boasted a government college, to the south of the city, where ceremonies were held twice a year in honor of Confucius and his disciples. During these, people offered sacrifices of vegetables, silk and wine. In addition, a pig, a cow and a sheep were slaughtered.

Besides the official college, there was a private one, called the Donglin ("Eastern Groves") Academy, located in the eastern part of Wuxi, where there was a grove of willow trees. It was started in the Song dynasty by a lone scholar and gradually developed into an academy. Such privately established academies flourished in the Song dynasty, supplementing the efforts of government schools in preparing young men for the civil-service examinations. In the Ming dynasty, the Donglin Academy reached its zenith and became a major political force. Members of the academy were highly regarded by intellectuals across the country for their integrity and uncompromising stance against eunuchs who were abusing power at court.

Because of its historical origins and scenic surroundings, the literature on Wuxi is vast. Many of the poems sing the praises of Huishan, considered to be the most beautiful mountain in east China. Other writers have praised the clear waters of beautiful Lake Tai, and the "Second Spring Under Heaven," at the foot of the mountain. The spring in Wuxi was valued for its tea-brewing qualities. The ranking was done by Lu Yu, a connoisseur of the Tang dynasty, who traveled around the country testing the quality of the water of a score of springs.[13]

Spring water was superior to well water, and well water to river water. The sweetness of Wuxi's spring water has been attributed to the presence of tin. A Song-dynasty tea enthusiast conducted an experiment by putting tin into a well whose water was bitter. Years later the water turned sweet, and he concluded that tin can change the taste of food or water. To the best of my knowledge, this has never been scientifically proven.

Ever since Lu Yu praised the Second Spring Under Heaven, it has been famous. In the Qing dynasty, two emperors, Kangxi and his grandson Qianlong, both loved the water from this spring. When Kangxi toured the south, he brought his family with him to taste the water. Kangxi granted the Qin family a plaque with the words "Noble Spring" carved on it. This they placed inside their family garden, the Ji Chang Garden, which is adjacent to the spring. Today, the spring is almost dry but its romantic past lives on.

The garden, a small one set in the foothills of Mount Hui, was landscaped in such a way that it provides a feeling of spaciousness as though Mount Hui itself were within the garden's confines. The twisting paths heighten the sense of beauty and romance, hiding each scene from view until the mind has fully absorbed the last one. The artificial lake was cleverly shaped so that it appeared to stretch well beyond its actual limits.

There are many stories related to the garden, some of which may be apocryphal. In one corner, for example, is a sign that reads "Board of Shame." Legend has it that the Qianlong Emperor played chess there once with a monk. The emperor, who was traveling incognito, was not accustomed to losing. The monk, noticing the nervousness of the people around Qianlong, realized that he was no ordinary man. The monk thereupon used his skill to let the emperor win. But that night the emperor, thinking about the game, realized that the monk had lost on purpose and was overcome by a sense of shame.

One part of the garden is named "Know Fish Pond," after a story concerning two philosophers. One of them, looking at the fish swimming in the pond, remarked: "How happy and peaceful the fish are!" His friend countered by saying, "How do you know the fish are happy, since you are not a fish?" But the first man said in rejoinder: "How do you know that I don't know, since you are not me?"

The garden is no longer the property of the Qin family, having been turned over to the state after the Communist victory in 1949, but it is being well taken care of and is considered a cultural treasure, preserved and maintained at the expense of the government.

But in Weizheng's time, the garden did not yet exist. His sons continued to live quietly in Hudai. Then a grandson, Qin Ranhe, moved into Wuxi city and lived along Sixth Arrow River. In time the Qins multiplied until almost every family who lived along the bank of Sixth Arrow River bore that name.

The family records for the three generations from Weizheng to his grandsons are incomplete. But from the time of his great-grand-sons, the records are much more detailed. Beginning from the time of Ranhe's son, Jisheng, the year, month and date of birth of each person is available. Jisheng himself was born on the seventh day of the third month of 1382, during the reign of the first emperor of the Ming dynasty.

Jisheng's son, Qin Xu, is the best known of this long line of rustic poets and recluses.

CHAPTER SIX

Qin Xu: The Blue Mountain
and the Bamboo Stove Story

In 1407, Qin Jisheng, the twenty-six-year-old great-grandson of Weizheng, was traveling by boat on Lake Tai one stormy day on his way to Maji Mountain when he saw an old monk struggling for his life in the waters. Jisheng stripped off his outer garments and dived in to rescue him.

In gratitude the monk knelt in front of his benefactor and said, "Though I cannot repay you for what you have done for me in this life, I will do so in my next incarnation."

Three years later, Jisheng's wife was with child. The family rejoiced and prayed for a boy. When his wife was in labor, Jisheng paced restlessly in the adjacent room. Suddenly he saw the spirit of the monk whose life he had saved enter his wife's chamber. Soon, a lusty cry was heard and a midwife emerged holding Jisheng's first-born son.[1]

The story illustrates the Chinese maxim that "good will be rewarded with good, evil with evil." It also shows that the circumstances of the baby's birth were a portent of the future.

Jisheng named his son Xu, which means "Dawn."[2] Qin Xu was the great-great-grandson of the founder of the Wuxi branch of the family and my direct ancestor eighteen generations ago. Qin Xu continued the family tradition and became a hermit poet, a life that was consistent with the legend that he was the reincarnation of the Buddhist monk.

He was born during the twenty-two-year reign of the Ming emperor Zhu Di, who adopted the reign name Yong-le or "Eternal Contentment." Under his vigorous guidance, the Ming dynasty extended its frontiers, rebuffing Mongol attempts to resume control of China, sending expeditions into the northeast to subdue the

Jurchens, and even annexing Annam (now Vietnam), though the Annamese did not remain long under Chinese control.

The Yong-le Emperor also shifted the capital to Peking while maintaining Nanking as a secondary capital, with all the trappings of a central government, including its own set of ministers who reported directly to the emperor.

During Qin Xu's early years, the empire was in strong, capable hands. The splendor of the Ming capital was known far and wide. In 1419, when Qin Xu was nine years old, the Persian emperor Shahrukh, son of the renowned Timur, sent an embassy to Peking, and its members recorded in some detail the magnificence of the Chinese court. The Persian court historian wrote of the Chinese New Year celebrations thus:

"While it was yet midnight the officer-in-charge came and awakened them [the Persian guests] and having mounted them on horseback conducted them to the palace. It was a magnificent building which had only now been finished after 19 years. That night in that huge city every person had so illuminated his house and shop with torches, candles and lamps that you would have thought the sun had risen already. So much so that if a needle fell it would be visible.

"That night the cold was much abated. Everybody was admitted into the New Palace. There were to be found in that palace 100,000 people who had come from all parts of Cathay, China, Machin, Qalmaq, Tibet, Qamul, Qara-Khoja, Churche, and the sea coasts as well as other countries the names of which are not known. The Emperor gave an entertainment to his officers of state. He had caused the envoys to be seated just outside his throne-room. Thus a concourse of 200,000 men stood with swords, maces, halberds, lances, staves, javelins, battle-axes and other weapons of war in their hands. About one to two thousand men held in their hands the Chinese fans of variegated colors and designs, each being about the size of a shield and slung up across their shoulders. The acrobats and boys danced in ever new fashions, and they wore such dresses with robes and coronets that it is not possible to give an adequate description thereof."[3]

But Qin Xu grew up unaware of palace luxury. He tasted sorrow early for his mother died when he was only five years old. His father remarried and from this union another son was born many years later.

As a teen-ager, Qin Xu astonished all the village elders by his retentive memory, his industriousness and his brilliance. They urged Jisheng to encourage him to take the civil-service examinations. But Qin Xu's father objected, having himself shunned officialdom. He told the village elders: "I have heard that one should serve one's parents with one's heart, but not serve them by gaining fame and fortune." Besides, he wanted to keep his only son by his side. Qin Xu, being a filial child, obeyed his father.

Jisheng obtained the services of a private tutor for his son, a local scholar. His teacher considered Qin Xu an outstanding student.

Qin Xu worked for a while as a village official responsible for food storage. But his real interest lay in literary pursuits. He selected for himself the courtesy name Xiujing, which means, appropriately, "Cultivation and Respect." He may have taken seriously the story of his being the reincarnation of a monk, for he served his father well and when his father was on his deathbed, Qin Xu kowtowed at night to the North Star, which was supposed to govern the dead, and prayed that he could die in his father's place. It is said that upon his father's demise, his grief was such that his hair turned white. He then devoted himself to caring for his stepmother, his young half brother and two half sisters.

His biographers describe him as a taciturn man who seldom laughed. Solemnity was considered a virtue in China. A strict disciplinarian, he expected his sons to live up to his high standards. But he was said to have been generous and charitable.

Once, he loaned a hundred pieces of silver to a merchant named Wu. Unfortunately, all Wu's merchandise was lost in a shipwreck. Desperate and despondent, the man wanted to commit suicide. Qin Xu consoled him by pointing out, "You are very fortunate not to be inside the belly of some big fish. Why worry about money?" With that, he tore up the promissory note that Wu had given him.[4]

Qin Xu enjoyed the typical, idealized life of a Chinese hermit-poet, pursuing the leisure, tranquillity and domestic peace sought after by so many scholars.

During his eighty-five years, he witnessed great growth in the clan's fortunes. From the time of Weizheng, scholars within the family had never proceeded beyond the first examination hurdle, which conferred on them the title of licentiate, in some ways comparable to that of holders of a bachelor's degree today.

In 1459, the Qin clan made a breakthrough when two of its members, Qin Xu's son Kuai and his nephew Fu, journeyed to Nanking and succeeded in passing the provincial examinations. They became the first *juren* produced by the clan in Wuxi. Successful candidates were entitled to official posts, and Qin Fu became a local official in Yunnan province. But Kuai went on to Peking the following spring as a candidate in the metropolitan examinations, the third and final hurdle. These, too, were held once in three years, and were even harder to pass than the provincial examinations. But Kuai proved himself equal to the challenge. He thus became the first member of the clan to gain the highest degree of *jinshi*, often likened to the modern-day doctorate, at the age of twenty-six.

Those were politically complex times. Ten years before Qin Kuai took his provincial examinations, the Yingzong Emperor had been captured by the Mongols while personally leading an expedition against them. While he was held captive, his brother ascended the throne. A year later, when the Mongols released the original emperor, the brother refused to yield the throne and put the Yingzong Emperor under house arrest for the next six and a half years. The former emperor was restored to the throne in 1457, as the result of a coup.

Qin Kuai became secretary of the Bureau of Provisions of the Nanking Ministry of War, one of four bureaus within the ministry. One can imagine Qin Xu's pride as he saw his son resplendent in the official blue pongee robe with a square on his chest showing an egret standing on one foot with wings extended. The bird motif signified civil officials, while the costumes of military men displayed such animals as lions, leopards, bears and tigers.[5] In the next few years, Qin Kuai moved up the ladder of the Ministry of War, rising to become director of the Bureau of Provisions. With the rise in rank, he swapped the egret on his chest for a silver pheasant. He gained local experience in his next two postings as a prefect, a rank that entitled him to don the red robes of the highest-level officials, with a wild goose in flight on the square on his chest.

While a prefect in Wuchang, a major commercial center in southern China, Qin Kuai instituted a policy of balanced taxation. His standing was further enhanced by two rescues he performed. While walking along the bank of a river after worshiping at the temple, he chanced upon a frightening sight: a woman, bound tightly with ropes, half buried in the sand. After releasing her, he listened to her story. She and her husband, a merchant, were traveling by boat from Hangzhou when they encountered pirates, who killed her husband and tried to rape her. She fought them off so fiercely that they tied her up and left her half buried in the sand to die. After taking her home, Qin Kuai pursued the pirates, seizing them that same night. On another occasion, a pretty young lady from a wealthy local family was kidnapped by a brothel owner who intended to sell her into prostitution. The girl's cousin, in the provincial capital to take the examination, told Kuai about this. He caught the kidnapper and freed the girl. So high was his prestige that he was praised as the first official in Hunan who had governed well.

While Kuai was serving as prefect in Jianchang four years later, his mother died and he returned home to observe a mourning period of twenty-seven months. After his return to office, his reputation for integrity and sagacity rose by the way he handled two other cases. In one, a commoner, surnamed He, was planning to lodge a complaint against the deputy magistrate of Guangchang. The official found out about this and got someone to make a false accusation against He, who was subsequently sentenced to death. Sensing a frame-up, Kuai reopened the case and the accuser, under interrogation, confessed.

The second involved a dispute between two clans, the Pengs and the Wus, each of whom brought accusations against the other. Hundreds of people were implicated. To minimize the possibility of collusion, Qin Kuai wished to question each person individually. Because so many people were involved, the prefectural office was not large enough, so Kuai used an open field as his interrogation chamber. He had hundreds of wooden posts planted in the ground ten feet apart from each other and tied each person to a post. Then he interrogated each person individually. Ten days later he had resolved the matter.

In 1485 he became administration commissioner of Jiangxi province. As such, Qin Kuai had reached almost the top of the civil service, just below the highest rank of minister. Instead of being bedecked with clusters of mixed flowers, his red robe of office now boasted a solitary floral design three inches in diameter, while the square on his chest revealed a golden pheasant.

Now in his fifties and in poor health, he retired from office and returned to his hometown, where he spent his last decade in the company of his father and brothers, living a life of tranquillity.

The success of his son's career raised Qin Xu's status in Wuxi, both financially and socially. Honorary titles were showered on him, but he retained an innocence that was reflected in his poems.

At the age of seventy-one, Qin Xu organized the Blue Mountain Poetry Society. Though it had only ten members, all were intellectuals who, like Qin Xu, had little interest in political involvement. None held government office. All, however, had standing in the community.

Since a career in politics was precarious, many of the gentry preferred to live their lives in peace. Such an attitude was widely admired, indicating a man of lofty ideals, unsullied by the scramble for wealth and power that preoccupied lesser men.

Qin Xu set forth the objectives of his poetry society thus:

"We do not have the responsibilities of government officials, nor the heavy work load of farmers, laborers and merchants. Our sole responsibility is, of course, to praise the peace and prosperity of our country. However, we should not behave like parasites as it has been warned that scholars should use their minds. Henceforth, we should persuade one another with discipline, rectitude and kindness so that we will not disgrace our ancestors and can set good examples for our descendants. Otherwise, even if our poems are artistic and beautiful, we may later be criticized."

The ten men built a "cottage" at the foot of Mount Hui in which to meet once a month. It included a huge meeting hall, the "Hall of the Ten Elders," a study, a dining room, a kitchen and a garden through which creeks ran and in which pines and bamboos flourished. The society attracted the attention of many scholars and poets, and banquets were held whenever guests arrived from other provinces.

Qin Xu, at seventy-three, was one of the oldest members of the group. The nine others ranged in age from forty-nine to seventy-four. In those days, a man in his late forties was considered old since, in all likelihood, he was already a grandfather, but Chinese society venerated the elderly.

Every month, those present would divide into groups; some sang, some painted, while others discussed philosophy. A painting by Shen Zhou, one of the four great painters of the Ming dynasty, showed Qin Xu, seated, practicing his calligraphy while another elderly man looked on. One was holding his writing brushes, while two others admired his calligraphy. Another was sketching. Still another was carving his poems onto bamboo segments. The others were looking at the cranes in the garden.

Whenever the monthly meeting was canceled for some reason, Qin Xu would go to the mountains with two young servants to visit some old monks. Occasionally, at their request, he would compose a poem.

When Qin Kuai retired as administration commissioner of Jiangxi province and returned to Wuxi, he became one of the most active members of the Blue Mountain Poetry Society. Though some of his fellow townsmen thought it a pity that Kuai should retire at such a relatively young age, Qin Xu was ecstatic, as shown in the poem he wrote at the news:

> The sky will be complete after your return,
> I hope the news of your coming is true,
> You can share my madness at the Society,
> And watch others fight for a place at court,
> We will dance, drink and enjoy the scenery,
> The blue waters and green hills will accompany us,
> If I have my son with me in my old age,
> I will never complain about the years that have passed.

Qin Xu lived not only to see his son retire but also, in his eighties, to see his grandnephew, Qin Jin, embark on his career. Qin Jin was the highest official produced by our family, serving as head of three ministries in Nanking and two in Peking.

Qin Xu enjoyed good health most of his life. The day before he died at age eighty-five, he got up, dressed, sat on his bed and chatted with his sons. They asked him if he had any final words, and he replied, "Life has been good to me, what more can I say?"

At the time of his death, he had three sons, four grandsons, ten granddaughters and three great-grandchildren. He was buried next to his wife on Dragon Hill.

The death of Qin Xu was widely mourned by his close friends in Wuxi and by people who knew him by reputation. The custom at the time was for the emperor to accord high officials posthumously with a name that captured the essence of the person. Since Qin Xu was never an official, he could not receive such a name from the court. So his close friends decided to bestow one on him. They chose Chen-jing, or "Upright and Peaceful."

NOTES

The death of Qin Xu, followed by the death of his son Kuai[6] the following year, left the Blue Mountain Poetry Society without a leader. The other members, all old men, died one by one and by the early 1520s, only one of them survived. The original society was no more.

Very much a part of the history of the Blue Mountain Poetry Society is the story of the bamboo stove, though the stove itself is even older.[7]

The original bamboo stove was made in the late fourteenth century, during the reign of the founding emperor of the Ming dynasty. At that time, two famous painters, Wang Zhongbi and Pan Kecheng, resided in the Ting Song Temple in Wuxi. One day Zhen Gong, a bamboo artisan from Huzhou, passed through Wuxi and the temple keeper, a monk named Xing-hai, asked him to make a stove on which he could boil water for tea. Zhen Gong made it according to the monk's specifications, which included the surprising use of bamboo to form the frame of the stove. The sides were cemented with clay. The inside wall of the stove and the ring on the top were reinforced with molten iron. The stove was about a foot tall, the top was cylindrical and the bottom was square, reminiscent of the Qian Kun ("Heaven-Earth") Pot of Chinese mythology. After the bamboo stove was finished, the two painters made pictures to illustrate its marvels, and poems were written praising it. The paintings and the poems were mounted on a scroll, known as "The Bamboo Stove Painting Scroll."

Some years later the monk Xing-hai moved to Hangzhou. He left the bamboo stove and the scroll with Pan Kecheng, one of the two painters, as a gift. The stove was kept in Pan's house for almost sixty years; Pan's grandson then gave the stove to a wealthy man named Yang Mengxian.

It was three years after Yang's death when Qin Xu's son Qin Kuai retired from his government post and returned to Wuxi to become a regular member of the Blue Mountain Poetry Society. He stayed in the Ting Song Temple. The temple keeper then was the grandson of Xing-hai. One day he showed Kuai the Bamboo Stove Painting Scroll. Kuai so loved the poems about the stove that he started a search for the stove itself—and found it with Yang Mengxian's brother, Yang Mengjing. Kuai persuaded him to return it to the temple.

Qin Xu and the other members of the society were delighted to have the stove about which they had heard so much. They held a special meeting and a banquet in celebration. It was attended by famous poets from throughout the country, each of whom wrote a poem about the remarkable event, and the poems were copied onto the scroll, making it longer than ever. Qin Xu, as head of the society, wrote:

"The bamboo stove of Ting Song Temple was the handiwork of Zhen Gong. It had been lost for more than fifty years. The grandson of the temple keeper, with the help of my son Kuai, fortunately recovered this treasure. Surprisingly, the stove is almost like new even after so many generations. This roll of poems will be kept in the temple forever as an encouragement to people of future generations to try to recover treasured old artifacts."

But neither the stove nor the scroll was destined to remain in the temple forever. Toward the end of the Ming dynasty, in the first half of the seventeenth century, the stove vanished again. By this time, age had taken its toll and the clay was falling off, though the frame was still intact. Because the whole country was in turmoil, its absence was not immediately noticed, and when it was, no one actively attempted to recover it. Later, the Ting Song Temple was destroyed in a fire and, in the confusion, even the scroll of paintings and poems was lost.

It is generally believed that the scroll resurfaced during the reign of the Kangxi Emperor (1662–1722) when a famous Manchu poet and official, Singde, eldest son of Grand Secretary Mingju, bought it from an unknown person at the capital. He showed it to his best friend, a poet from Wuxi named Gu Zhenguan, who was head of the imperial library. Gu borrowed the scroll and fashioned two bamboo stoves, using the drawings as a guide. Because the scroll was so long, he split it up into four rolls. At the time, there were four paintings, thirteen essays and ninety-two poems on the four rolls. Gu took the two new stoves and the four rolls to Mount Hui, where a new Ting Song Temple was built to store these treasures. In the ensuing celebrations, more people put brush to paper to express their appreciation.

Ironically, at about the same time that Gu had duplicates of the stove fashioned, the original surfaced again. A monk, Song-chuan, stumbled across it in a farmer's house. The farmer told him that the stove had been brought to his house some generations earlier by one of his relatives who had once served as a monk in a temple on Mount Hui. When the monk had become disillusioned with Buddhism, he had returned to his family farm, bringing with him the bamboo stove and a tea set. Over the years the tea set was broken, but the bamboo stove was still largely intact.

Song-chuan retrieved the stove from the farmer to return it to Wuxi. He took it to an official of the Ministry of Rites and asked him to compose an account of the stove that could be engraved permanently on stone. The official wrote the account, then decided that since the stove was first discovered by the Qin family and since Qin Xu was the leader of the poets who wrote about its first recovery, the artifact was "not only the legacy of Wuxi but also that of the Qin family." Accordingly, he sent Song-chuan to the head of the Qin clan, Qin Daoran, and suggested that he contribute a poem to mark the second recovery. He did and ended it by enjoining the monks of the temple to care for the bamboo stove as they would their robes and begging bowls, which are passed on from generation to generation.

In 1751, a few years after the stove was returned to the temple, the Qianlong Emperor made an inspection tour of his southern dominions and stopped at the temple, because the fame of the bamboo stove had long since reached the capital. Later, he wrote of it:

"Much has been written about the stove. It was lost and a replica was made. Later the original reappeared and a picture of it was painted. All the essays and poems were mounted on four rolls. During my reign, the magistrate of Wuxi endorsed the rolls and sent them to the temple for storage. Since then the bamboo stove and the Second Spring Under Heaven have kept each other company. When I passed through Wuxi, I remembered that my grandfather had visited this famous spring. So I came to see how good the bamboo stove really was for making tea."

The original purpose for making the bamboo stove was probably decorative rather than utilitarian. Bamboo symbolizes purity and lofty ideals, like clear tea itself. But it is unclear why the stove was later said to possess special tea-making qualities.

The emperor wrote four poems about the stove, praising its beauty and referring to its long history. The tea made from Second Spring water boiled on the stove also pleased him.

Six years later, the Qianlong Emperor paid his second visit to Wuxi. Again, he went to the Ting Song Temple and drank tea made with spring water boiled on the bamboo stove. On this occasion, he composed two poems, "Tea-Making at Ting Song Temple" and "Using Spring Water From Mount Hui Boiled on the Bamboo

Stove." He also bestowed the name "The Bamboo Stove Mountain Chamber" on the room in the temple where the stove was kept. And, after his return to Peking, he ordered a duplicate of the stove made and constructed another Bamboo Stove Mountain Chamber in the Western Hills, part of a vast area of imperial pleasure grounds outside the capital.

In the next decade the Qianlong Emperor made two more southern tours and each time visited Wuxi, wrote poems about the bamboo stove and tasted its tea.

In 1768 the emperor, a prolific poet, felt dissatisfied with his writings and had all his old poems sent back to the capital so he could polish them. Among the poems the emperor reworked were those about the bamboo stove. When he returned the four rolls to Wuxi, the magistrate took them to his official residence to be mounted anew. Unfortunately, a fire broke out and the four historic rolls of paintings and poems were reduced to ashes. The emperor, furious, fined the government officials involved 200 taels of silver—a considerable sum—to be given to the monks of Ting Song Temple as compensation for their loss. The emperor determined to have the four rolls reproduced. He personally took on the task of re-creating the first roll—presumably working with copies that were then extant—and ordered one of his sons to do the second roll. Two senior officials were given the jobs of re-creating the third and fourth rolls. These copies were then deposited in Ting Song Temple. And in the years that followed, the emperor paid repeated visits to the temple and added more poems to the new rolls.

The emperor also took from the imperial collection a painting by Wang Zhongbi, one of the two Ming artists who had made the first painting of the bamboo stove four hundred years earlier, and donated it to the temple as additional compensation. The painting was titled "Hermit Fisherman."

Soon, the painting by Wang Zhongbi became as famous as the bamboo stove itself. Every visitor to Ting Song Temple asked to see the "Hermit Fisherman."

In 1860, tragedy struck again. Wuxi was occupied by forces of the Taiping Rebellion and in the fighting Ting Song Temple was destroyed. The rolls of poems, as well as Wang Zhongbi's painting, vanished.

Four years later, Qin Xiangye, one of our clan's outstanding scholars in the Qing dynasty, discovered the rolls in Shanghai. He took

111

them back to Wuxi only to find Ting Song Temple in ruins, with just the foundation intact. During the chaotic postwar period, it was not possible for the temple to be rebuilt. In 1865, a memorial in honor of soldiers killed in the long bloody war with the Taiping rebels was built on the site of the temple. Qin Xiangye gave up hope that the "Bamboo Stove Mountain Room" would be reconstructed and donated the paintings to the monks in charge of another temple.

So the four rolls were again deposited with monks at a temple in Wuxi. But the "Hermit Fisherman" painting was still missing. In the mid-1860s, a cousin of Qin Xiangye located the painting in the city of Dongting. He paid a high price for it, brought it back to Wuxi, and donated it to the temple that had the rolls.

Qin Xiangye's account of the four-centuries-long saga of the bamboo stove ended thus:

"Alas, the poems and paintings changed hands so many times, it was like smoke and mist clouding one's eyes. Our ancestors had their own way of wielding the brush, and I fear their style cannot be duplicated. These rolls of paintings are unique, outstripping paintings by the Tang dynasty's Wu Chen. They were lost, and now they have been recovered. This is an event worth celebrating. As to Ting Song Temple, it began in the Tang dynasty [618–907] and lasted until the present era. It was built, destroyed, rebuilt and again destroyed over a thousand-year period. Maybe that was its intended fate."

CHAPTER SEVEN

Filial Sons of the Qin Family

China has changed greatly since the Communists came to power in 1949. Instead of filial piety, loyalty to the Communist party and to the state is placed first. But as recently as my parents' generation, filial piety was the virtue most extolled in China. Our clan produced a number of "filial sons" and there are many stories about them, and many poems written in their honor. The clan naturally kept no record of unfilial sons. If they existed, their deeds were considered shameful and hence not to be recorded, and they themselves would have been expunged from our genealogical records.

I remember as a child being moved by traditional stories of filial piety. Such stories were told to almost all Chinese children to foster in them the proper attitudes toward their elders. One I especially liked was about an eight-year-old boy, Wu Meng, who belonged to a family too poor to buy mosquito netting. The boy used to expose himself to droves of mosquitoes every night, hoping that after feasting on his blood, the mosquitoes would spare his parents and let them have a good night's rest.[1] Such stories made me feel unworthy since I knew I could never be so selfless.

The *Xiao Jing*, or *Book of Filial Piety*, an important Chinese classic, cites Confucius as saying that "filial piety is the root of all virtue, and that from which all teaching comes. Our bodies, in every hair and bit of skin, are received by us from our parents, and we must not venture to injure or scar them. This is the beginning of filial piety. When we have established ourselves in the practice of the Way (Tao), so as to make our name famous in future ages and thereby glorify our parents, this is the goal of filial piety. It commences with the service of parents; it proceeds to the service of the ruler; it is completed by the establishment of one's own personality."[2] In sum, filial piety is the one virtue from which all other virtues flow. For

113

love of one's parents, one should not do anything that might bring them shame. Also for love of one's parents, one should strive for success in life to bring them honor.[3]

Officials, known as censors, crisscrossed the country, meting out punishment for dereliction of duty and proposing rewards for the virtuous, especially filial sons and chaste women. The Ministry of Rites conducted rigorous investigations before granting official recognition of filial deeds. Few people received the coveted honor of being officially designated as a "filial son." It was even more unusual for two brothers—or cousins—to win that distinction. The Qin family, however, distinguished itself by producing several pairs of filial sons from the fifteenth to the nineteenth century.

Yongfu and Chongfu, Qin Xu's younger sons, made up the first pair. They remained at home to take care of their parents while their older brother, Kuai, won honors as a high government official. When Kuai began his official career, he said to his two younger brothers: "I studied in order to win honor for our parents. I may not be able to serve them properly so you two must care for them."

The two brothers were junior members of the Blue Mountain Poetry Society. Yongfu was quiet and serious and a painter of note. Shy by nature, he is said to have blushed whenever the young men he was with talked about sex. He was devoted to his father and, if Qin Xu was angry, Yongfu would get down on his knees and remain kneeling until his father's mood had dissipated.[4] It is from Yongfu that both my parents are descended.

The youngest son, Chongfu, was a man of many talents, though his poems were considered inferior to those of Yongfu. After Kuai began his official career in Nanking, Qin Xu sent Chongfu to him to study. However, it is said, he pined for his father and told Kuai he preferred to return home. When Qin Xu started to suffer the afflictions of age, Chongfu took up the study of medicine. After a few years, he became quite knowledgeable.

When Qin Xu was fifty-three years old, he developed a heart disease that troubled him every ten days or so. Medicine did not seem to have any effect, and the two brothers could do nothing but pray. Their father recovered but had a more serious relapse the next year. His sons repeatedly struck themselves on the chest so that they could share his pain. Then Chongfu found out from ancient medical texts that rabbit's blood could be used to treat the ailment. He decided that human blood would be better. Perhaps he was

114

influenced by the traditional Chinese belief that a serious sickness can be cured if the patient eats the flesh of someone who loves him deeply. (Even in New York, I came across a woman who had tried, unsuccessfully, to save her cancer-stricken husband in this way.)

The two brothers dug their long, sharp fingernails into their chests until the blood ran. They collected the blood in a vessel, mixed it with medicinal wine and gave the potion to their father. Qin Xu recovered and did not have another attack for many years.

On another occasion their mother, the Lady Yan, fell while walking upstairs and injured her knee. She bled profusely and her sons called in the best physicians. In the summer heat, the injury became infected and oozed pus, causing such a stench no one was willing to go near her. The two brothers washed their mother's wound and changed the dressing regularly. At night, they sat beside her bed and fanned her, to relieve her from the heat and to chase away mosquitoes and flies. But the pus continued and the wound refused to heal. The two brothers then took turns licking the wound until all the pus was gone. When winter came, the knee finally healed.[5]

The filial nature of the two brothers was praised by the villagers and eventually news of them reached Changzhou, the prefectural seat. Long Jin, the prefect, conducted an investigation and submitted a detailed report to the Ministry of Rites in Peking in 1473. He concluded:

"Their filial acts are so outstanding that I beg that a testimonial of merit be conferred upon them so that such behavior can be publicized and encouraged."[6]

In 1476, after a thorough investigation, the Ministry of Rites in a memorial to the emperor made an official response to Prefect Long Jin:

"Their filial acts have been substantiated and deserve praise and encouragement. The local county is ordered to set aside 30 taels of silver for the family to build an arch in honor of the filial pair."

The emperor acquiesced. This was a great honor indeed, for it was extremely unusual for two brothers to be so honored at the same time.[7]

When the two brothers were officially proclaimed a "filial pair," Yongfu was forty and Chongfu was thirty-six. Both their parents were still living, so they could share in the honor. A plaque with the words "Double Filial Piety" engraved on it was hung in front of their house.

The Lady Yan, Qin Xu's wife, died in 1478. He survived her by about seventeen years. Now the two brothers had an even greater responsibility to their father, for he no longer had a wife to serve him. Every day, the brothers would neither eat nor bathe until after their father had done so.

Both brothers enjoyed long lives, Chongfu dying at the age of seventy-eight and Yongfu at eighty-eight. Chongfu was in good health until the very end. He died the day after the Chongyang Festival, when Chinese traditionally ascend the heights to escape a legendary devastation of the lowlands. Chongfu was fit enough to attend those festivities and write the following poem:

> In sickness I awaited the festival,
> I climbed the hill, aided by my stick.
> Chrysanthemums teased me for being thin,
> But I still sipped from my cup.
> The sparrows were rushing home,
> Sounds of autumn murmured.
> I can't bear to look in the mirror,
> And won't put a flower in my hair.

In 1521 when Yongfu was eighty-five, the Jiajing Emperor ascended the throne. The new emperor's devotion to his parents was to cause a confrontation between him and virtually his entire bureaucracy, for he heaped honor after honor upon his deceased father and his mother, who was still living. The year after his enthronement, he bestowed on Yongfu imperial gifts of grain and cloth to reward him for his filial acts. It was a fitting culmination to a life dedicated to filial piety, and could not have been bestowed by a more appropriate occupant of the Dragon Throne.

In 1746, more than two hundred years after their deaths, the Qianlong Emperor approved the construction of the Temple of the Filial Pair and awarded the Qin family a plaque. The plaque, engraved with words written in the emperor's own handwriting, read "Family of Filial Piety and Brotherly Love." It was mounted on an arch erected outside the West Gate, that is, outside the city wall, facing Mount Hui. The family was also granted a stone, on which were carved the words "Filial Piety and Brotherly Love." The temple which, like the arch, was next to the Ji Chang Garden, was destroyed during the Second World War by a bomb dropped from a Japanese plane, and the site is now occupied by a public toilet.

The exceptional filial piety of the two brothers continued in Yongfu's son, Tang, and Chongfu's son, Xun. We do not know much about the actual deeds of Xun, except that he was paired with his cousin, but there is considerable information on Tang, my sixteenth-generation ancestor, who took care of his parents until he himself was almost seventy years old.

Tang grew up observing how his father, Yongfu, treated his grandfather until Qin Xu's death in 1494. By then, Yongfu was sixty and Tang was twenty-eight. Gradually, Tang assumed the role of filial son. Two years after Qin Xu's death, Yongfu developed a persistent pain in his leg and was unable to straighten it. Tang prayed for months for his father, repeatedly banging his head on the ground, kowtowing to heaven. He did this so frequently that his forehead bled. Finally, his father recovered.

Tang's early academic life augured a brilliant career. He was at the top of his class through the first few hurdles: a qualifying test to compete in the district examinations, the district examinations themselves, and a qualifying test to enable him to take the provincial examinations. But then things went wrong for him: He did not pass the provincial examinations.

At about this time he married, taking as wife a woman from the Kong family. Tang's wife helped him greatly. When he repeatedly failed the provincial examinations, she comforted him by saying: "Precious things never come easily. If you study hard now you will reap future benefits."

Unfortunately, she died at the age of thirty, leaving three young sons.

Later, he remarried, but this marriage, too, turned out tragically for Tang. Within a year of the wedding, his new bride contracted a heart ailment and became bedridden, dying fifteen years later.

Tang finally succeeded in the provincial examinations, on the seventh attempt in 1504 when he was thirty-eight years old. Next came the final hurdle: the metropolitan examinations. Again he failed repeatedly. In the meantime, the Confucian college he was attending recommended him to go to Peking as a "tribute student," to be examined by officials of the Hanlin Academy. He passed and was enrolled in the National University. Later he was assigned as a novice to the Grand Court of Revision and then to the Ministry of Personnel.

Even after his training period was over, Tang did not get a posting. Most likely he was unable to accept one because of his mother's poor health. She had suffered a stroke in 1507, when she was sixty-nine, and became an invalid. Tang devoted himself to taking care of her.

Tang's mother's health deteriorated to such an extent that she lost the power of speech, and the lower half of her body became paralyzed. In 1517, Tang wanted to forgo the metropolitan examinations, but because his mother's condition was stable, his father almost forced Tang to travel to Peking. Again he failed. At the time, both his parents were in their eighties.

According to Wen Zhengming, a prominent painter, calligrapher and scholar, who composed Tang's epitaph,[8] Tang said after failing the exams: "I left home to travel several thousand miles to obtain an official post. My purpose was to honor my parents. Now I may not get a post and my parents are getting old. I should not try anymore." He stuck to his word. So in 1520, when another opportunity arose to take the examinations, Tang decided against it. In 1523, when the examinations were next given, he passed up the opportunity again. That year, his father died. The next time the examinations were offered, he was in mourning for his mother. He had served her for nineteen years, and would mourn her for three more.

In 1528, the emperor called on his officials to notify him of people who had performed outstanding deeds exemplifying such virtues as filial piety or chastity. The assistant instructor in the Confucian school in Wuxi, together with several scholars, submitted a recommendation to the Changzhou prefecture that Tang be honored as a filial son.

The prefect of Changzhou, Zhang Dalun, held an investigation, going to Wuxi personally to conduct interviews. In his report to the Ministry of Rites in Peking, he enumerated all of Tang's deeds, pointing out that because his mother had lost the power of speech, Tang had had to anticipate her wishes. His devotion to her was such that he even accompanied her to the toilet. Prefect Zhang concluded: "I, as a shepherd, put great emphasis on old customs and virtues. His Majesty's order to report filial characters to be honored made me feel the importance of making this application to honor Qin Tang. If I don't report this and let Qin Tang's filial piety go unnoticed, how can I encourage filial acts in the locality? I would be irresponsible otherwise. I hope His Majesty will accede to my proposal and grant Qin Tang the honor."[9]

This request went to Chen Xiang, grand coordinator and concurrent censor-in-chief, who validated the information and found the recommendation justified. However, the Ministry of Rites turned it down because Qin Tang was still listed as an expectant official and so could still be appointed to a post; if he did get one, it would no longer be true that he had forfeited his career for his parents.[10]

In 1540, when Tang was seventy-four years old, Magistrate Wan Yukai of Wuxi recommended him as a candidate in the following year's metropolitan examination, thirty-six years after he first qualified. Tang rejected the proposal, saying: "In the past, I did what I did for my parents. Now that my parents are gone, why should I do it again?" He added: "Now that I am old and cannot serve the emperor properly, I do not want to compete with my descendants."[11] At the time, six of Tang's sons and grandsons were at various stages of education preparing themselves for official careers.

The following year, Tang's oldest son, Huai, submitted a memorial asking for his father to be honored. In it, Huai explained that his father had been faced with the choice of becoming an official and serving the emperor or remaining at home to serve his parents. "He thought he would have much time to serve Your Majesty but little time to take care of his parents," Huai said, explaining his father's decision. "Since the two mourning ceremonies, my father has become weak and ill, and even though he wanted to serve Your Majesty, he was unable to do so."

Huai argued that if his father could not be honored as a filial son, then he should be given a title. And he asked that his aged and infirm father be exempted from having to travel to the capital for it.[12]

The Ministry of Personnel looked into the precedents cited and decided Huai had a valid case. Qin Tang was granted the title assistant secretary of the Chief Surveillance Office in Nanking.[13] It was an honorary title; Tang never reported for duty. He remained in Wuxi, helping to educate the younger generation.[14]

About that time, another application to win official recognition of Tang's filial nature was filed by two of his neighbors. When Tang heard about it, he requested that the application be withdrawn because he was undeserving of special praise. After all, he argued, he had not served the emperor as an official, and had done only what any son should for his parents, so why should he receive special honors?[15]

When Qin Tang was seventy-two, both his youngest son and a grandson passed the provincial examinations and were assigned government jobs. Their success was said to have been heaven's reward for Tang's filial piety. He died in 1544 at the age of seventy-eight. "My father was a filial son and my sister a chaste woman," he said shortly before his death. "I have nothing to be ashamed of."

In the 1620s, eighty years after his death, a group of scholars made a request to have Tang honored in the local Temple of Worthies. The proposal worked its way to Education Intendant and Censor Sun Zhiyi, who gave it the final approval.[16]

Tang's oldest son, Huai (my fifteenth-generation ancestor), also displayed the qualities of a filial son. He went through the stages that all young men from scholarly families go: one examination after another, until he reached the final step. Then, history repeated itself. His father urged him to go to the capital to take the highest examinations. But Qin Huai, aware that his father was too old and weak to be left alone, and knowing that his father had given up his chance in similar circumstances, refused. He pretended to pack, then used every excuse he could think of to delay the journey. He procrastinated for years, taking care of his father together with his brothers.

Huai's mother died young and he was good to his sickly stepmother, Tang's second wife. After this lady's death, she is said to have appeared to Huai in a dream and said to him: "I have nothing with which to repay you. But I shall pray for you to have a good son and for the family to expand." Huai eventually had four sons. One of them, Qin He, was later successful in attaining the highest-level degree. From him were descended some of the most prominent officials of Wuxi. A few years after Qin Huai's death, his name was added to those honored in the Temple of Worthies in Wuxi.

More than two centuries later, a third filial pair emerged in the Qin family.[17] They were two brothers, Qin Kaijie and Qin Fengxiang. Their father, Qin Yunquan, was a scholar who went to the capital in 1811 to take the examinations, leaving behind in Wuxi his wife and their two sons, aged five years and four months. He failed and instead of returning home, he joined the staff of a prominent

Mongol official, Sung-yun, who was then in Peking as minister of personnel.[18]

Two years later, Sung-yun was named military governor of Xinjiang, in China's far west, an area also known as Chinese Turkestan. When Sung-yun went to Xinjiang, Qin Yunquan accompanied him. Xinjiang—the name means "new frontier region"—was not under Chinese control in the Ming dynasty, and even today is very different from the rest of China. Accounting for roughly one sixth of China's land area, it is sparsely populated, with much of the territory being covered by the Taklamakan ("Go in and you won't come out") Desert.

Today it is possible to fly from Peking to Urumqi, the regional capital, but in the nineteenth century, travel was mostly by camel caravan, following the age-old Silk Road, a journey of several months along a route infested by marauding bandits. Xinjiang was—and is—as far from the heart of Chinese civilization as one can get and still remain within the Chinese empire. The streets are teeming with people whose features are distinctly un-Chinese. The mosques and minarets reflect the influence of Islam. Its predominantly Muslim population includes about six million Uigurs, as well as sizable minorities of Kazakhs, Tajiks, Kirgiz, European-looking Uzbeks, and Xibos, whose women are noted archers. They share the same languages, religion and customs as their cousins on the Soviet side of the border.

In Urumqi, the streets have the aroma of an Arab bazaar, with fierce-looking, mustachioed barbers plying their trade on the sidewalks beside street vendors selling cooked mutton on skewers and dealers in old, handwoven carpets. While in other parts of China there are special restaurants for Muslims, in Xinjiang there are special restaurants for non-Muslim Chinese, so small is their number.

For some unknown reason, Qin Yunquan remained in Xinjiang for the next three decades, although Sung-yun's tour as military governor there lasted only two years. Under Sung-yun's direction, a group of scholars had begun to compile a history of Xinjiang, and it is possible that Qin Yunquan was connected with this project. Or perhaps the reason is that Sung-yun was in disgrace for several years immediately after his stint as military governor: He had incurred the wrath of the emperor by urging him not to visit the ancestral tombs in Manchuria. Since he left Xinjiang under a cloud, perhaps he was unable to take with him his personal entourage.

In any event, Qin Yunquan's sons in Wuxi had become adults, and their mother had aged, in a fatherless family. The mother had succeeded in bringing up the two boys only by practicing the strictest frugality. The two brothers grew up with a desperate desire to find Qin Yunquan. They asked each visitor to Wuxi if he had any information about their father.

One day the younger brother, Fengxiang, dreamed that he was in a foreign land where the houses and the people were very different from those of Wuxi. He also saw an old man who, he thought, bore a resemblance to his father. After he woke up, he related this dream to one of the village elders, who had known his father many, many years ago. This man told Fengxiang that, from his description, the place he had seen in his dream had to be "the land beyond the pass," referring to the pass in the westernmost point of the Great Wall, beyond which were vast territories inhabited by many "barbarian" peoples. From then on, the two brothers paid special attention to travelers who had been to the northwestern territories.[19]

In 1844, Fengxiang met a merchant who had just returned from a business trip to Xinjiang. Fengxiang chatted with him and asked about the geography of the area. He also asked if there were any men from Wuxi living there. "Just one," the merchant said, "and he has been there for so long that his hair is all white." When Fengxiang asked for his name, the merchant replied, "Qin Yunquan."

Fengxiang was so happy that he danced and cried, but when he told Kaijie the news, the two brothers had one of their rare disagreements.

"Let me go and look for our father," Kaijie begged.

"No, brother," Fengxiang replied. "Mother is old now and she needs someone to take care of her. I am not able to support her. That is your responsibility as the older son. Mine is to find our father."

"But you are too young to travel," Kaijie argued, "and the road to the northwestern territories is long and dangerous."

"The territories beyond the pass are still part of the empire," Fengxiang responded. "If a merchant can go there and come back, so can I. There should be no sons in the world without fathers."

And so the argument was settled. The brothers borrowed 50 taels of silver from relatives and friends and prepared large quantities of dried food. Kaijie and their mother traveled with Fengxiang as far as Jiayuguan, or the Jiayu Pass, which today is still regarded as marking the cultural frontier of China.

At Jiayuguan, the two brothers parted. Kaijie escorted their mother back to Wuxi, while Fengxiang pressed on alone, vowing not to return before finding their father. It took five more months of arduous travel before he finally reached Urumqi. By that time, he had spent all his money and consumed all the dried food he had brought with him.

He discovered that his father lived in a place called the Red Temple. He went there and found an old man. He knelt in front of him and wept. The old man, taken aback by the stranger's behavior, demanded, "Who are you?"

"I am your son," Fengxiang replied.

Yunquan was suspicious and refused to believe him. So Fengxiang spent the next two hours telling his father everything concerning their hometown, their friends, their neighbors, and Fengxiang's mother—Yunquan's wife. Finally, Yunquan was convinced. Now it was his turn to cry. Holding his son and clasping his hands, he said tearfully, "You are indeed my son. But what are you doing here?"

Fengxiang then told his father about the search he and his brother had conducted over many years. And he urged his father to return to Wuxi with him.

"I have been away from home for the last thirty-six years," sighed Yunquan. "I thought I would die in this foreign land. Now that you have come, of course I will return home with you. But how are we going to raise the money for such a long trip?"

Fortunately, friends and neighbors were sympathetic. News spread of Fengxiang's feat—how he had traveled thousands of miles to look for a father he had not seen since he was an infant.

Many people put up whatever money they had to help pay for the expenses.

By the time Fengxiang reached his hometown with his father, it had been two and a half years since he first left on his perilous quest. His father was already seventy years old. As soon as the old man saw his wife, he clasped his hands in front of him and bowed to her four times, thanking her for having raised their two sons alone. Then all the villagers joined in rejoicing over the family reunion.

Four years later, Yunquan became seriously ill, and no treatment appeared effective. Out of desperation, Fengxiang said to his brother,

ANCESTORS

"I have heard that, in the old days, illnesses could be cured by giving the patient human flesh. I will cut some flesh from my thigh for father and see if he recovers."

So the two brothers again argued over who should sacrifice himself for the sake of their father. This time, the older brother prevailed.

Before Fengxiang could stop him, Kaijie took out a knife and sliced a piece of flesh from his left thigh. When they mixed this with medicine and gave it to their father without his knowledge, the old man's condition improved.

Unfortunately for Kaijie and Fengxiang, their father's recovery did not last. He had a relapse a few months later and died. Several years afterward, their mother also passed away.

Kaijie, the older brother, was killed in battle in 1860, at the age of fifty-five, during the Taiping Rebellion, when he attempted to rally the villagers to defend their hometown. He left no descendants. After Kaijie's death Fengxiang, wishing to continue his brother's family line, gave his own son, Yongcan, to his brother. But Yongcan, too, was killed in the fighting, which lasted many months, devastated Wuxi and decimated its population. When the war ended, ten of the twenty-four subbranches of our family no longer existed.

Fengxiang reported his brother's death while defending Wuxi to the imperial court, and Kaijie was posthumously honored for his loyalty to the throne. Meanwhile, a movement gathered momentum in Wuxi, urging special honors for the two brothers, whose filial deeds had moved the people.

The process was long and complicated. It went from one level of government to the next, until it reached the Ministry of Rites in Peking. The ministry ordered its own investigation, which concurred with the earlier findings. The ministry then sought confirmation from yet other sources, including the head of the Qin clan and officials at the provincial, prefectural and district levels.

All these reports went to the governor-general of Jiangnan, who called for another investigation by the local authorities. When these investigations, too, confirmed the facts as reported, the file was sent to an expositor-in-waiting of the Hanlin Academy, who gave his approval to honor the two brothers as filial sons.

After this, another detailed report was requested by the Ministry of Rites, which then submitted a summary of the case to the imperial court. The court asked for still another report from the people of Wuxi about the two brothers, a report to be signed by representatives

124

of four groups of people: those related to the Qins by marriage, who presumably would be well informed about the facts; fellow townsmen; neighbors; and representatives of the clan itself.

With this report, the court gave final approval to the request for the two brothers to be honored as filial sons. That final approval was granted in 1896, twenty-one years after the first report. By then even Fengxiang, the younger brother, had been dead eight years.

Four hundred years earlier, the first filial brothers were honored when their parents were still alive. The procedure then was relatively simple, and swiftly carried out. By the nineteenth century, the process had become so complicated that, by the time it was completed, all the principals involved were dead.

CHAPTER EIGHT

Qin Jin: The Scholar-Strategist

Even in April the North China plains are brown and dreary, with few patches of green visible beyond the Great Wall. But the Yangtze River Delta, where Wuxi is situated, is lush with vegetation. On April 5, 1983, I was tramping through the hills outside Wuxi with several companions in search of ancient graves, mostly from the Ming dynasty. By coincidence, it was *Qing Ming*, the "Clear and Bright" Festival when Chinese traditionally honor departed family members by sweeping graves, burning incense and offering sacrifices. Even though the Cultural Revolution, during which such "feudal practices" had been denounced, was over, only a few people ventured forth that day to pay their respects to the dead.

I was most interested in locating *Shangshu Mu*, "The Minister's Grave," the grave of Qin Jin,[1] who, in the sixteenth century, served as minister of revenue, minister of works, minister of rites and minister of war.

Because of his exalted official status, his tomb occupied a vast area. I had seen a sketch of it in a book[2] in the Peking Library and had been struck by the similarity between his grave and the celebrated Ming Tombs northwest of Peking where thirteen of the emperors who ruled China from 1368 to 1644 lie buried. The "Sacred Way" along which the bodies of the deceased emperors were carried is lined with stone animal and human figures. The long path leading to the tomb of Qin Jin was flanked by stone lions, tigers and sheep as well as larger than life statues of civil and military officials.

Now, more than four hundred years later, the long Sacred Way over which his body was carried is overgrown with grass, and the stone figures no longer stand proudly on guard. In 1958, during the Great Leap Forward, a campaign to achieve rapid industrialization, peasants were told to make steel in backyard furnaces, and most of these

Ming dynasty limestone figures were destroyed in that frenzied effort. The few that remain were broken and hidden amid the weeds.

The land on which Qin Jin is buried is now owned by the Homecoming Hill Production Brigade of Hudai Commune and the grave itself is just a yawning hole. I was told that, in 1967, during the Cultural Revolution, the brigade decided to excavate the tomb. "Was it because you needed the land for cultivation?" I asked a brigade member. "No," he responded. "We wanted to see what was inside such a huge grave. We had heard that it was a man who had been decapitated and buried with a golden head. We just wanted to see the golden head. It took us a whole week to open up the grave. The coffin was made of stone, and was covered by heavy stone slabs. We had to drill holes in them before we could lift them up."

But their labor was for nothing. The peasants had been preceded by grave robbers, who probably struck centuries before. All they had to show for their week's effort was the stone slabs they had uncovered. Two were bound together tightly with metal wire. When they were untied, it was discovered that one had the name and title of the occupant of the tomb written in ancient, fancy script. The other contained a detailed account of the life of Qin Jin. The illiterate peasants did not know that this was a *muzhiming*, or "grave record," a biography inscribed on a stone tablet buried with the dead. The inscriptions were of little value to them, but they could use the stone slabs. Ever since, those stone tablets had functioned as washing boards by a pond, on which the peasants laundered their clothes. Years of rubbing has worn the stones smooth, so that now only a few characters can be made out. Fortunately, a local schoolteacher who recognized the historical value of the find had taken the trouble to copy down every word from the four-hundred-year-old blocks before releasing them to the peasants.

Looting of graves in China was a frequent occurrence, despite the caretakers hired to live with their families on the burial grounds. Tombs of dignitaries were sturdily constructed, with stone on all four sides. The top of the burial chamber, too, was covered with heavy stone slabs, so that it was almost impossible for thieves to penetrate. But the Chinese believed that the body had to be in contact with the earth, and so the bottom of the coffin was not lined with stone. Grave robbers could therefore bypass the stone walls by tunneling into the burial chamber from below. The more imposing a tomb, the more likely it would be a target for grave robbers over the centuries.

ANCESTORS

All day, I literally tripped over historical relics, mainly pieces of *muzhiming*. In an area short of wood and stone, they were holding up pigsties, serving as crude stepping-stones in streams and, in one case, propping up the bed in a peasant's house. The heavy stone slabs were also used for flattening the earth. So all the care taken to protect the resting places of the mighty ended in naught, not from malice but from a combination of ignorance and utilitarianism.

The account of Qin Jin's life, copied down by the schoolteacher, says that he was born on the eleventh day of the ninth month of the third year of the reign of the Chenghua emperor of the Ming dynasty, which corresponds to the year 1467. Joan of Arc had been burned at the stake as a heretic sixteen years previously, and Martin Luther would not be born for another sixteen years.

Qin Jin's father, Qin Lin, was the eldest of three sons, an impoverished scholar whose family had made a living by teaching village children for four generations.

The father adopted the courtesy name Beimu, or "Humble Shepherd," a reflection both of his modesty and his role as a teacher. He wrote of his circumstances in the following poem:

> Lacking the treasure to acquire land,
> I built a tiny hut to lodge myself.
> Swallows fly in and out through the holes;
> The low beams knock against my hat.
> With my elbow as a pillow I ponder the future;
> Resting on my haunches, I weigh my
>   ambitions.
> Don't look down on my modest abode;
> In it are ten thousand springs.

Legend has it that Qin Jin was a very unusual youth. It is said that one night his household god appeared to him in a dream and revealed that he would become a great and powerful official. Because even gods had to rise when a great man passed by, the divinity asked that his altar be moved from the main hall to a more remote part of the house so that he would not have to pay obeisance to Qin Jin every time he walked by. The next day, it is said, Qin Jin arranged for the shrine to be moved, because he himself believed in the message imparted in his dream.[3]

As a boy, he used to wander into the homes of relatives when he was tired of studying. Eventually, it was noticed that whenever he entered a household with a sick person, the patient recovered. Friends and relatives concluded that the devils responsible for the illness recognized and feared Qin Jin as someone who was destined to wield great power.

Whatever the truth of such stories, it is clear that, at quite a young age, Qin Jin was regarded as someone marked out by fate.

His self-confidence is reflected in another story about his childhood. When Qin Lin went to tutor the children of the wealthy, his son would accompany him. Often, the teacher would be asked to dinner but the invitation would not be extended to his son. One day, Qin Lin composed the first line of a couplet on that subject and asked Qin Jin to compose a second line, a common teaching device. The father wrote:

The banquet is given but the child is not invited.

Qin Jin immediately paired it with the line:

But the Imperial rolls in Peking will bear his name.

The boy then told him: "Your son's ambition is not to attend dinners. In future, Father, please do not worry about such things for my sake."

As Qin Jin grew older, his father arranged for learned men to instruct him in the art of government as well as the classics. At the age of fourteen, Qin Jin suffered the death of his mother, to whom he was very attached. By then, his education had progressed to the extent that he himself was able to compose a commemorative essay in her honor. He spent the next three years in official mourning. By the end of the mourning period, he was ready to tackle the examination system.

The examination system faced by Qin Jin in the Ming dynasty was significantly different from that with which Qin Guan had to contend four hundred years earlier. It was even more rigorous. There were years of preliminary examinations at the district level and the prefectural level before a candidate could even compete in the real civil-service examinations, which began at the provincial level.

Qin Jin had first to pass a qualifying test to entitle him to compete in the district examinations held in Wuxi, then another to compete in the prefectural examinations. Qin Jin came first in the district examinations, the prefectural examinations and the qualifying examination for the provincial degree of *juren*.

In 1486, when he was only nineteen, he went on to the provincial examinations.

At the time, Wuxi, his hometown, was under Nanking, the southern capital, and so Qin Jin journeyed there to take the hotly contested examination, knowing that of the thousands of candidates competing, less than 1 percent would pass. But he did and was therefore entitled to compete in the capital in the highest-level examination, held once every three years.

Qin Jin's father would not let him attend the metropolitan examinations the following year. Perhaps he was worried about his only son's journeying to far-off Peking at such a tender age. Or perhaps family matters took precedence. For it was about this time his father remarried and also made arrangements for his son's wedding. Qin Jin took as bride a well-brought-up, educated young lady from the Niu family, who was three years his senior. We know little about her background, but we can assume that she came from a relatively well-to-do family because only such a family could afford to educate girls. We may also deduce that she was not a great beauty because it was unusual for a family to have a daughter still unmarried after the age of twenty.

An exemplary wife, she quickly took over the running of the household and got along well both with her father-in-law and with Qin Jin's stepmother. In 1492, when Qin Jin was twenty-five, his wife presented him with a son, Pan. The following year Qin Jin resumed his interrupted academic career and journeyed to Peking for the metropolitan examinations.

Successful candidates were divided into three grades. In the first grade were only three men: the highest graduate, *zhuangyuan*, the second, *bangyan*, and the third, *tanhua*. These names originated with ancient customs. *Tanhua*, for example, literally meant "to look for flowers," and stemmed from a Tang-dynasty custom that two of the youngest and most handsome of the graduates would walk through all of the capital's famous parks to pick the most beautiful peony they could find. These top three graduates received special honors, and were expected to go far in their careers. The number of graduates in the second and third grades varied from year to year.

Qin Jin was in the second grade, placing thirty-second among the 90 graduates, while 205 men graduated in the third grade. The successful candidates were invited to a banquet at the Ministry of Rites, which was responsible for administering the examinations.

The senior grand secretary and chief examiner recommended that Qin Jin join the prestigious Hanlin Academy, which provided literary and scholarly assistance to the emperor and to the court. However, Qin Jin declined, explaining that he had to return to Wuxi to be with his ailing father. The grand secretary was very impressed by a young man who was willing to put his father's welfare ahead of his career.

After spending a year with his father, Qin Jin in 1495 accepted his first official posting with the Ministry of Revenue in Peking, with special responsibility for grain supplies. He eagerly threw himself into his work, inspecting warehouses, granaries and customhouses in prefectures within his jurisdiction, which included part of the Northern Metropolitan Area. The capital depended on grain carried by barge from the south up the Grand Canal. In a period when transportation was by maddeningly slow barges and when it was difficult to predict the weather, a well-run storage system reduced the risk of famine in times of drought. In addition to seeing that supplies in the granaries were properly maintained, Qin Jin weeded out the ineffective and the corrupt in his department.

The following year he was sent by the ministry to Linqing,[4] a town along the Grand Canal, where he ran a customhouse, collecting tolls from vessels using the canal.

During the Ming dynasty a major evaluation of all officials was held every three years. Each official was given a rating by his immediate superior as to whether he was "superior," "adequate" or "inadequate."

Qin Jin received an extremely complimentary commendation from his superior, the minister of revenue. Not only was he promoted to vice-director of the Henan Bureau, but his parents and his wife, too, received imperial honors. Later, Qin Jin was promoted to director of the Shanxi Bureau, whose duties included supplying army posts in the north, along the troubled border with the Mongols. Military colonies were perenially understrength, and keeping them adequately provisioned was one of the most vexing tasks of the Ministry of Revenue.

In 1503, Qin Jin's father died, leaving behind little more than a collection of his poems and a compilation he had made of the legends of Hunan. Qin Jin's career was suspended while he went into mourning. He is said to have grieved so deeply that, for three years, he did not set foot outside his house.

The end of Qin Jin's mourning period coincided with the coronation of a new monarch as the Hongzhi Emperor was laid to rest with his ancestors. He was succeeded by his eldest son, who assumed the dynastic name Zhengde ("Uprightness and Virtue"). Unfortunately, this emperor did not live up to the name. He showed little inclination for affairs of state. He preferred adventure to the often boring role of administrator of the empire. Finding court life stifling, the young emperor spent much time hunting, and he often scandalized his officials by wandering among the local populace dressed as a commoner. His life later degenerated into one of debauchery. With no one running the country, a group of palace eunuchs, known as the Eight Tigers, moved into the power vacuum and dominated the court.

The eunuchs were the only male attendants permitted to live in the imperial palace. Their job was to look after the palace women and to take care of the emperor's personal needs. Normally, they came from poor families who chose to raise their social status by castrating one of their sons to make him acceptable for service in the palace. Eunuchs were commonly looked down upon, and could advance only by winning imperial favor. As a result, they were usually anxious to cater to the emperor's every desire, such as by procuring young ladies for his pleasure. There are many examples in Chinese history of eunuchs who were so successful in winning the emperor's confidence that they became tyrants and actually seized the reins of government themselves.

By the sixteenth century there were twenty-four eunuch offices in the court, with responsibility for such aspects of palace maintenance as the care of utensils, ceremonial equipment, apparel, stables and seals; the provision of fuel, foodstuffs, music, paper and baths; the handling of documents; the upkeep of buildings and grounds; and the manufacture of textiles, art objects and other craft goods. Eunuchs also supervised the palace treasury. The head of the Directorate of Ceremonial, the chief of the palace staff, had under him many thousands of eunuchs.

Qin Jin returned to the Ministry of Revenue as director of the Sichuan Bureau. For his ability, he was awarded the prestige title of

132

Fengzheng Great Officer. His deceased parents were honored, as was his wife. His father received the same titles he had been given. His deceased mother and his wife were both made ladies of the first rank.

But Qin Jin soon got a taste of palace intrigue. While he had been in mourning for his father, a coalition of eunuchs and the emperor's in-laws, eager to line their own pockets, had asked for and received permission to buy and sell salt manufactured above state quotas, thus breaking the state's salt monopoly. Once he was back with the Ministry of Revenue, Qin Jin asked for this permission to be rescinded, arguing that the practice was weakening the country's defenses, since salt was bartered for grain that was earmarked for frontier army posts. The new emperor, however, was in no mood to reverse his father's decision. When the minister of revenue, decrying the vast sums being expended by the imperial family, pleaded with the new emperor to forbid his relatives to trade in surplus salt and called for the dismissal of a number of eunuchs, the minister lost his job. But Qin Jin was able to salvage his.

In 1508, after over a decade of working in the capital, he was assigned to Henan province, where he eventually became education intendant and surveillance vice-commissioner, his first senior posting. The surveillance offices were part of the vast machinery of the censorate, which for two thousand years was responsible for monitoring the performance of the bureaucracy.

Education intendants were censors who approved the admission of students to government schools, examined students and awarded the first of the civil-service degrees—the licentiate, or *xiucai*. As an intendant Qin Jin set himself up as a model for the province's aspiring scholars. He devised a syllabus of very high standards and emphasized the teaching of ethics. At the time, the best-known education intendant was the reformer Shao Bao, Qin Jin's fellow townsman from Wuxi, who was known to his students simply as "The Teacher."

In those days, fortune-tellers exercised great influence by giving advice on auspicious and inauspicious burial dates and sites, so that many students left their parents unburied, sometimes for years, while the coffins were kept at home or in temples. Funerals were also expensive affairs, and many families spent years raising funds to defray such expenses as the buying of land and the engraving of inscriptions. My father did not acquire land for his father's burial until more than twenty years after the latter's death.

Shao Bao was determined to end this practice. He decreed that any scholar who had an unburied parent could not take part in the examinations; a rash of burials occurred as a result. As Qin Jin's reputation grew, his name was often linked with Shao Bao's. The two men became close friends and were known for the large numbers of students they helped to groom, many of whom eventually served in high posts.

In 1510, Qin Jin left the censorate, though he remained in Henan province, and was promoted to administration vice-commissioner.

At that time, the Ming dynasty was being periodically wracked by peasant rebellions. One of the biggest of them began in late 1510, led by two brothers known as Liu the Sixth and Liu the Seventh. The brothers had been forced into banditry after they were unjustly accused of being rebels and their property was confiscated. They rapidly gained a huge following. Their uprising threatened the Peking Metropolitan Area and Shandong, then moved south to overrun the province of Henan. City after city fell before them, with the bandits often slaughtering all the government officials. The terror-stricken local officials sometimes fled, sometimes surrendered with the populace. The commander of Xinyang, in southern Henan, made a stand and was killed in battle. The ancient city of Kaifeng, capital of the Northern Song dynasty, where Qin Guan had worked as a court historian, was then threatened.

At this juncture, Deng Xiang, the governor of Henan, assigned Qin Jin the unenviable task of governing and defending Kaifeng with his local militia. At the same time, the court in Peking ordered Commander Song Chen to lead his troops south to fight the bandits led by Liu the Sixth.

In mid-1511, Qin Jin was on an inspection tour about thirty miles outside Kaifeng when he received information that Liu the Sixth and another bandit leader, Tiger Yang, were moving westward toward Kaifeng. He immediately reported the matter to Governor Deng and started military preparations. Then word arrived that bandit troops led by Tiger Yang were less than thirty miles from Fengqiu, a northern district of Kaifeng.

Just then, Commander Song's forces arrived heading toward Kaifeng. Qin Jin urged him to stay and help defend Fengqiu, but the commander refused. "My orders are to fight Liu the Sixth, not to fight Tiger Yang," he declared before leading his troops on to Kaifeng to report to the governor.

Qin Jin knew that without Commander Song's troops, he stood

little chance of resisting the bandit onslaught. Yet, Fengqiu was so close to Kaifeng that its loss would seriously jeopardize the security of that ancient city. He mounted his horse to ride to Fengqiu, about fifty miles to the northwest. When he arrived, the local officials came out to welcome him, and then, kneeling by the roadside, said:

"The bandits are powerful and confident. You had best leave Fengqiu tonight."

Qin Jin refused. Everyone, he said, must stay to help with the town's defense. "If I leave Fengqiu now," he said, "it will certainly be captured by the bandits. You should not urge me to deviate from the path of righteousness." He then ordered what local forces there were to prepare immediately for battle.[5] Fortunately for Qin Jin, Governor Deng ordered Commander Song Chen's forces to defend Fengqiu.

Soon, the bandit forces were reported at a village less than four miles away. Qin Jin ordered Commander Song to attack. As the commander mounted his horse, Qin Jin raised his hand and pledged: "You will receive our logistical support. But you are the main force and should lead the attack." Qin Jin personally led the local militia in support of the regular troops. Commander Song and his fast-moving troops attacked the bandits' main body and routed them, killing or capturing many. That night, the bandits withdrew their remaining forces to a neighboring village.

The next morning, the bandits surrounded Chen Bridge Township, which was being defended by government troops. With surprise on their side, the bandits easily routed the government troops, who suffered a severe setback. Many soldiers were captured and many civilians killed. When Commander Song's relief forces arrived, the bandits retreated. Song's men went in hot pursuit till they finally caught up with them and defeated them in a fierce battle.

When the soldiers returned to Fengqiu, it was already the hour of the second drum, close to midnight. Intelligence reports placed the bandits in Huanglinggang, where they were planning a counterattack. Qin Jin ordered Commander Song to force the bandits to Changheng.

Meanwhile, Commander Li Qin, who had been pursuing the bandits from Shandong, decided to join forces with Qin Jin. With his thousand soldiers, they chased the bandits to Huaxian, where another battle was fought, but because of a heavy downpour some of the bandits managed to escape.

As Commander Li's troops returned to Fengqiu, the local people were petrified, mistaking them for bandits. Their weeping filled the air. Qin Jin ascended the city wall and, when he discerned the flags of the government soldiers, he laughed and told the people not to be afraid, but to open the city gates and welcome the soldiers.

Governor Deng ordered a convoy to welcome Qin Jin back in triumph to Kaifeng. Qin Jin responded to the praise showered on him by saying: "The victory belongs to the soldiers. I have nothing to do with their success."

But the people of Fengqiu thought differently. "If it were not for Master Qin," they said, "we would have ended up as fish and meat on the bandits' table." So, in an extraordinary gesture, they built a temple west of the local college in honor of a man who was still living. Each year, on his birthday, they made offerings of meat and wine.[6]

The rebellion of Liu the Sixth eventually collapsed in the autumn of 1512. The failure of these Ming dynasty rebels—and of the other large-scale uprisings that have occurred periodically since the First Emperor proclaimed the Qin dynasty more than two thousand years ago—is usually attributed to the absence of a cohesive ideology and adequate organization. A few rebel leaders succeeded in overthrowing a regime and setting up a new one but most attempts have ended in failure. There is a popular Chinese saying, "He who succeeds is emperor; he who fails is a bandit." To the Communists all these rebellions were justified. Mao said the class struggles of the peasant wars "constituted the real motive force of historical development in Chinese feudal society."[7] He is also reported to have referred to himself as the leader of China's last peasant revolution.

As a result of his success at Fengqiu, Qin Jin was promoted to administration commissioner of Shandong,[8] where the rebellion had started. That placed him near the top of the civil-service ladder.

Qin Jin found Shandong, the main battleground in the fighting between government troops and the rebels, devastated by the war. A severe shortage of goods sent prices spiraling, and a small handful of speculators made big fortunes while ordinary people suffered. Qin Jin set about the task of binding up the wounds of war. He immediately banned all black-market activities and instituted price controls.

In 1514, after three years in Shandong, Qin Jin was named Xunfu

("Touring Pacifier"), or governor, of Huguang Province, and also vice censor-in-chief.[9]

He set off, accompanied by two retainers, and used the long overland journey as a chance to "inspect and pacify," taking note of problems in various areas. As a result, he made a series of suggestions to the court, including increasing the number of officials responsible for the crucial task of grain storage, clarifying policies relating to such storage, enlarging the staff of customs inspectors, setting up corps of boundary troops with specified powers, increasing the number of military posts and adopting special policies to look after the Miao, a warlike tribal people who lived in the mountains. But perhaps the most sensitive of his proposals called for removing useless officials and decreasing the powers of eunuchs outside Peking.

When Qin Jin arrived in Huguang, he found the province in virtual chaos. Traditionally, the aboriginal population had been allowed to select its own leaders, whose positions were then confirmed by the conferring of official seals. Qin Jin discovered that, almost a century before, members of tribes from other areas had moved in and taken over these posts. In the resulting confusion, the government canceled the titles. Qin Jin succeeded in identifying the rightful claimants and restored the establishment of aboriginal Pacification Offices.[10] Though these carried purely nominal rank, they conferred prestige and influence on the aboriginal chiefs.

In the summer of 1517, Qin Jin submitted a memorial to the throne regarding an imperial order that Huguang supply over a thousand catties of sturgeon fingerling to the court. He pointed out that the province was poor, often afflicted by roaming bandits and by famines, and could ill afford to meet such a demand. He said the fish could not easily be raised in ponds and catching them was difficult, and added that, because of the long distance to Peking, they might well all be dead by the time they arrived. He asked for the order to be rescinded. The court refused.[11]

Later that year when floods struck some of the principal cities in the province, Qin Jin requested urgent relief from the court. An emergency meeting was called by the Ministry of Revenue in Peking and it was decided to issue grain held in warehouses for the disaster areas. In addition, taxes due from the most devastated areas were waived while those from other less afflicted ones were reduced.

In two batches of proposals, Qin Jin called for a number of military and civil reforms, which were adopted. As a result of his experiences

137

in Huguang, Qin Jin wrote two books, *The Principles of Governing* and *Pacifying Huguang*.

While serving in Huguang, Qin Jin obtained permission to build a temple in honor of his great hero Yue Fei, the Southern Song general who dreamed of ousting the northern barbarians but died in prison as a result of official treachery. Although the Mongols were no longer a threat to the state, they constantly harassed the borders.

And Huguang was notorious for its bandits, who were allied to Miao and Yao tribesmen. Numbering in the tens of thousands and well entrenched in mountainous areas, they moved back and forth across the borders of several provinces, giving support to each other as they eluded the various provincial armies. The problem had reached such magnitude by 1517 that the court ordered a coordinated attempt to crush them. Suppression of this uprising was one of the major achievements in Qin Jin's long career.[12]

Qin Jin led his troops against the bandits in Chengui, an area in southeastern Huguang bordering on Jiangxi, Guangdong and Guangxi. The bandit chieftain, Kong Fuquan, a well-built man with a monstrous appearance, had crowned himself Prince of Yanchi. Five trusted commanders led his formidable troops.

Qin Jin divided his troops into four armies, plus a reserve force. He began his campaign on the second day of the eleventh month and two days later ordered an all-out attack. After a week of fighting, the four armies had captured seven enemy strongpoints and killed hundreds of bandits, taking numerous prisoners. One of the bandit chieftains was executed, along with 134 of his followers.

The bandit troops sought to retreat to their mountain stronghold. Qin Jin deployed his forces to cut off all escape routes while continuing to put pressure on strategic sites.

The vanguard force attacked in two waves a fortnight apart, which resulted in the capture of sixteen enemy strongpoints and the taking of hundreds of prisoners, including two chieftains. Government casualties were minimal, reported by an unofficial chronicler of the war as only four killed and seven wounded.

The other armies did similarly well. The right flank, with the help of informers, pinpointed the exact location of one of the bandit leaders. A battle that raged along the edge of a cliff lasted from morning till dusk, after which the rebel forces were routed. Both the bandit leader and his son were caught. In a series of battles fought over five weeks, this army seized twenty-seven enemy strongpoints, killed three bandit leaders, captured hundreds of enemy soldiers, and put several hundred houses to the torch. Government casualties were listed at nine killed and twenty-five wounded.

The left flank marched to Tiger Hill East, where a group of bandit soldiers was holding out. After three days of fierce fighting, the rebels fled.

Then the army began another series of battles, in which it succeeded in capturing twenty enemy strongpoints and two more bandit leaders. Again, government casualties were surprisingly light, four killed and thirty-one wounded.

The rearguard, too, had its moment of glory. In three engagements over an eight-week period, it seized twenty-two enemy strongpoints and two bandit leaders, while suffering losses of five killed and twenty-two wounded.

There is little doubt that the bandits in Chengui were almost eradicated, as the area was quiet for decades afterward. But the extremely small number of government casualties reported is far from certain. The casualties may have been deliberately cited as low for tactical reasons. It is even possible that some government casualties were counted as bandits, since rewards were offered for each enemy killed and, once a head was severed from the body, there was little to differentiate soldier from bandit.

Despite his armies' victories, Qin Jin was dissatisfied, for the bandit chieftain Kong Fuquan was still at large. Qin Jin issued a warrant offering a reward of five hundred gold pieces for anyone who captured him alive—or two hundred gold pieces for the person who brought in his head. A New Year's Eve battle saw the capture not only of Kong but also of his wife, cousin and daughter. After decades in which the bandits had managed to rally their forces after each government assault, the rebels in the Chengui region were finally exterminated.

Many centuries later, another Chinese leader, Generalissimo Chiang Kai-shek, was confronted with a similar problem. He led five campaigns involving over a million soldiers to "encircle and annihilate" the "Communist bandits" led by Mao Zedong. Each time the Kuomintang government thought it would finish off the Communists, they managed to stage a comeback. Finally, the Communists were forced to flee their mountain stronghold and embark on what became known as the epic Long March of 1935–1936. For over a year they crossed swamps, deserts, torrential rivers and snowy mountains and dealt with hostile tribesmen, all the while dodging the pursuing Nationalist troops, until they finally emerged in arid northwestern China and made their headquarters in the caves of Yanan. Many years later they emerged to sweep Chiang Kai-shek's troops off the mainland onto Taiwan.

After the Chengui battles, Qin Jin rewarded all his commanders and soldiers and gave families of the dead and wounded compensation. In turn, Qin Jin and three of his senior commanders were all promoted a full rank. Qin Jin was given the prestige title Tongyi Dafu, or "Facilitator of Righteousness Great Officer," as were his deceased father and grandfather, while his great-grandfather was given the title Guanglu Great Officer. And his elder son, Pan, was admitted to study in the prestigious Directorate of the Imperial Academy without having to take the usual examination.

Qin Jin refurbished the graves of his ancestors and erected new tombstones inscribed with the new titles. As was customary, he also had portraits of the dead drawn showing them wearing the costumes that their new rank entitled them to.

At about this time, an investigating censor, Zhang Yuli, on a routine tour, arrived in Qin Jin's hometown of Wuxi. It was his responsibility to be the emperor's eyes and ears, to be on the lookout for local officials who were derelict and should be impeached, and for those who deserved commendation. Censor Zhang was approached by Qin Rui, the son of Qin Kuai, for permission to build an ancestral temple in honor of the clan's founder, Qin Guan, on the site of an old temple along Sixth Arrow River that was being torn down. When the censor gave his approval, Qin Rui wrote to his fifth cousin Qin Jin,[13] who offered money and the services of his two sons, Pan and Bian, because he himself could not return to Wuxi.

The ancestral hall was completed in the spring of 1519, the same year that Pan received his degree from the provincial examinations. The building had one main hall, in which hung a portrait of the clan's founder, Qin Guan. There were four back rooms, dedicated to Qin Jin's father and grandfather, representing the "Qins who lived near the western gate," as well as the father and grandfather of Qin Rui, who belonged to the "Qins who lived by the river." Known as the "Temple of the Five Gentlemen," it became the ancestral hall of the entire Qin clan in Wuxi.

CHAPTER NINE

Qin Jin: The "Proper and Agile" Minister

In 1520, the year after the erection of the temple, Qin Jin was appointed at age fifty-three to his first ministerial-level post, as right vice-minister of revenue in Peking. Each ministry had two vice-ministers, left and right, the former being the more senior, though both held the same rank.

Soon thereafter the Zhengde Emperor died at the age of thirty, leaving no heir. During his sixteen-year reign the emperor's depravity and his neglect of his imperial duties had resulted in eunuchs and other court favorites arrogating to themselves his prerogatives. Officials who remonstrated with him about his excesses were flogged, imprisoned and pilloried. For a short time he had even forbidden the raising of hogs because the word for pig had the same pronunciation as the imperial surname.

Upon his death, a thirteen-year-old cousin was chosen to be the eleventh emperor of the Ming dynasty, supposedly as the deathbed wish of the Zhengde Emperor. Traditionally a childless emperor was succeeded by a nephew or someone else of the next generation. The choice of someone of the same generation was to pose severe problems because he could not be adopted as the deceased emperor's son.

The problems surfaced almost as soon as the new emperor was named. They started with the young man's insistence, upon his arrival in Peking from the south, that he be immediately received as emperor, rather than as heir apparent. The court officials gave in, and, the same day that he entered the capital, he was enthroned.

Six days after he ascended the throne, the new emperor directed officials responsible for protocol to decide on an appropriate designation for his own father, the Prince of Xian, who had died two years before. The appropriate honor, he felt, was for his father to

141

be posthumously declared an emperor too. But the majority of his high officials declared that his primary obligation was not to his own parents but to his predecessors on the Ming throne, whom he should honor as his own ancestors. Minister of Rites Mao Cheng proposed that, according to precedents set in earlier dynasties, the new emperor should refer to the Hongzhi Emperor as "imperial father," that is, to regard himself as the younger brother of the previous emperor and the Zhengde Emperor's father as his adopted father, thus providing continuity for the imperial family. His own father, Mao Cheng said, should be honored as "imperial uncle." And his own mother, who was still living, as "imperial aunt." When addressing his mother, he should refer to himself not as her son but as her "imperial nephew."

The emperor refused and called for further consideration of the matter. Seventeen days later, Mao Cheng submitted a memorial reiterating his original proposals. Again, the emperor balked. Then the minister of rites went into great detail to cite precedents from the Song dynasty and the Three Kingdoms period to justify his proposals. The young emperor adamantly maintained his objections.

At this point the ranks of the bureaucracy were split. Some officials, led by Bureau Secretary Zhang Cong, now argued that the emperor should address his deceased father as emperor. The emperor quickly adopted this suggestion, overruled the highest officials in the court and promoted Zhang Cong.

The next step was to welcome the emperor's mother into the capital. Mao Cheng proposed that she be welcomed as a princess, since the late emperor's wife was empress dowager, and enter the Forbidden City through a side gate. But this was vetoed by the emperor, who insisted that his mother and the widow of the previous emperor be given equal treatment. Finally, it was decided that she would enter through the main gate and be accorded all the prerogatives of an empress dowager.

After the enthronement of the new emperor, who adopted the reign name Jiajing, or "Splendid Tranquillity," Qin Jin was made the senior vice-minister of personnel, considered the most important of the six ministries, since it was in charge of the promotions and demotions of officials in all the other ministries, but he did not remain long in that post. Critics accused him of disrupting the workings of the ministry by changing long-established criteria for promotions. Censors accused him and other high officials of being "black sheep" who were unworthy of senior posts. As a result, several officials were ordered to retire. And Qin Jin was transferred back to the Ministry of Revenue, where he again served as the junior vice-minister. Perhaps in protest, he submitted his resignation, which was turned down. A few days later, he applied for sick leave. Again his request was denied. Possibly to placate him, he was raised from right vice-minister of revenue to left. Since the minister was ill, Qin Jin ran the ministry, overseeing the bureaus that dealt with all thirteen provinces and the two metropolitan areas, looking after the salt monopoly, the inland customhouses, the granaries and the imperial stables and pastures.

One of the first memorials he submitted to the new emperor concerned the problem posed by imperial relatives who sought to make use of their positions to enlarge their domains. Qin Jin filed a request with the censorate, citing precedents and asking for the perpetrators to be sent into exile, even though the emperor's own uncle, Shao Xi, was attempting to take over lands around the capital that had always been considered public. In his memorial, he stated:

> Recently an imperial edict was issued saying that all government officials could build and own "imperial housing" and that these officials would have full control over these houses. We, the courtiers, were extremely astonished at this. Traditionally it was thought unreasonable for the higher classes, including the imperial family, to fight with the common people for lands and benefits. Such actions would not occur in an empire at peace. A long time ago, the first Emperor of the Han dynasty ordered that the common people could share the Jing Imperial Garden, and his descendant Emperor Zhao opened up a palace and gave it to the common people. Further, Emperor Yuan gave the public all the farmlands and palaces that were not occupied. During the Song dynasty, the Emperor also let the citizens who lived around the capital farm the grasslands from which they were normally barred. It is obvious that all the good Emperors of the previous dynasties were sympathetic to the common people.
>
> Our first Emperor had considered the area around Nanking the most important place in the empire, yet he allowed the people who lived there to farm the land and to be exempt from taxation. His successors continued this practice. However, since the Zhengde

reign period [1506–1522] cunning groups took advantage of the Emperor's trust and took over farmland around the capital. They offered the land to [eunuch] officials close to Your Majesty, and they suggested to Your Majesty that these lands should be developed for "imperial housing." This suggestion means that the Emperor will take over by force what should belong to the common people.

Another major flaw of this suggestion is that those who are in charge of rents and taxes for such housing will definitely reap personal benefits, and the imperial court will be blamed. The reputation of Your Majesty's newly inaugurated reign will be tarnished. We beg Your Majesty to send officials to examine the case and we suggest that those lands that were taken away from the common people after the Zhengde reign period be returned to the original owners. The common people grieve over the present unjust situation. We beg Your Majesty to right these injustices, which will be beneficial to both the upper and lower classes.[1]

In response, the emperor acknowledged that "important areas around the capital had always been granted by our ancestors to the common people. Recently some people have abused this practice. I know this even though I stay within the palace. Now that I have read your memorial, I have even stronger feelings against those people. Your suggestions are well taken. Let us put them into practice." However, the emperor added that Shao Xi, being his uncle, would be pardoned.

Under Qin Jin's guardianship, the state's revenues gradually increased. At this time, he received a belated award for his extermination of the bandits in Huguang: One of his sons was granted the hereditary title of company commander of the Embroidered-Uniform Guard, a unit that was the emperor's personal bodyguard. Qin Jin declined this honor for his son and his decision was respected, though the reason he gave is not known. Perhaps it was because the Embroidered-Uniform Guard had a sinister side: It cooperated with the eunuchs in secret-service activities; its officers exercised almost unlimited police and judicial authority, and its prison was a feared torture chamber.

The enthronement of the new emperor had been welcomed by old officials like Qin Jin, who had been appalled by the behavior of the previous emperor and who hoped the new ruler, being young, would learn to be conscientious. At first, their wishes seemed to come true. The new ruler got rid of large numbers of palace dependents, curbed the activities of the eunuchs and imposed restraints on the growth of aristocratic estates. But there were no real institutional reforms, and eventually the new emperor began to resemble his predecessor in the neglect of his imperial duties.

The year 1523 was a busy one for Qin Jin. His younger son, Bian, was admitted as a student into the imperial college by special favor, again in recognition of Qin Jin's suppression of the Huguang bandits. (His older son, Pan, had already obtained his *juren* degree.) And Qin Jin was appointed minister of rites in Nanking, his first full ministerial post.

Shortly afterward, the country was afflicted by a drought in the north and floods in the south. These natural phenomena were taken as portents of heaven's displeasure. A virtuous emperor would ensure an abundant harvest and a harmonious society; droughts and famine were brought about by the conduct of a delinquent emperor.

A group of officials, headed by Qin Jin, used the floods in Henan as occasion to remonstrate with the emperor, a step that could easily have led to banishment or death. Qin Jin submitted a memorial to the throne, entitled "An Honest Presentation of Why the Country Is Suffering From Calamities." Beginning with some flowery compliments, Qin Jin went on:

> When Your Majesty first ascended the throne, you made many promises, and people looked forward to their fulfillment, but now they see that these promises have not been kept. So Your Majesty's words are not as credible as before.
>
> When Your Majesty first ascended the throne, idle courtiers were demoted and the diligent rewarded. But now Your Majesty is moved by flattery and fills government positions with those who are incompetent. So your Majesty is not exercising the judgment you used to in seeking virtuous men.
>
> When Your Majesty first ascended the throne, you were open to criticism and complaint at any time of the day or night. But now even when the Nine Chief Ministers memorialize about matters that involve your imperial relatives or the eunuchs, you merely reply: "The matter has already been dealt with." So Your Majesty is not as open to suggestion as before.

145

When Your Majesty first ascended the throne, promotions and transfers were made strictly on the basis of recognized procedure and bribery was not tolerated. Now there is excessive favoritism and appointments are made casually. So Your Majesty is not as careful in the selection of officials as before.

When Your Majesty first ascended the throne, all evildoers were handed over to the three judicial offices, but now the law is loosely applied, showing that respect for the law is not what it was before.

When Your Majesty first ascended the throne, you ordered that the Ministry of Revenue cut the requisition of fodder for horses in half and that Supervising Secretaries and Investigating Censors strictly examine the number of horses required. But now because of such people as the eunuch Xian Hong, you have rescinded your order, so your sympathy for the distress of the people is not what it was before.

When Your Majesty first ascended the throne, you cast aside Buddhism and banished Buddhist monks and nuns. But now altars for offering sacrifices have been set up. In this respect your veneration for the orthodox path is not what it was before.

When Your Majesty first ascended the throne, your physical condition was splendid. Now, your sacred body is in poor health, your countenance has not its original radiance. So your spirits are not what they were before.

In the early days, Your Majesty's rule was enlightened in that decisions of government were made openly in the outer court and no interference was tolerated from a coterie around you. But now the lines of government are confused, since a coterie is making decisions without the knowledge of the outer court. Governance cannot be taken from the hands of the court for a single day; power cannot be delivered into the hands of a coterie. A barrier between the Emperor and his court will result in prejudices, listening to the advice of women and eunuchs will result in disaster. Upholding this general principle, Your Majesty will be able to wield the implements of government as if you had a firm grasp on the handle of the mighty Tai-ah Sword.[2]

The memorial reflected the feelings of many of the officials at court, and the minister of rites in Peking, Wang Chun, persuaded

146

the emperor to accept its wise counsel. Qin Jin not only went un-punished, but was promoted to Nanking minister of war, the highest of the six ministers in the southern capital.

But Qin Jin served as minister of war for only two months. Then he was summoned to Peking to serve as minister of revenue, his first cabinet post. The six ministers in Peking, together with the censor-in-chief, were the seven highest officials in the empire and advised the emperor on the most serious issues. (More important delibera-tions were expanded to include two other men, the heads of the Office of Transmission and the Grand Court of Revision. All to-gether they were referred to as the Nine Chief Ministers.)

When Qin Jin arrived in Peking, he found himself drawn into a political storm, with the emperor on one side and most of the court on the other. In the preceding months, the emperor had continued to heap posthumous honors on his father and to raise the status of his mother. Officials who voiced their opposition were thrown into prison. Hitherto, the emperor had referred to his parents as "my own progenitors." His father, for instance, was "my own progenitor the Emperor Xian." But the emperor disliked the qualifying phrase and, in the summer of 1523, decided to drop it. Almost the entire court was opposed. Qin Jin and the rest of the Nine Chief Ministers all submitted memorials objecting to the change. The emperor shelved the memorials and took no action.

Then, led by the Nine Chief Ministers, hundreds of officials knelt outside a palace gate and, wailing and weeping, staged a protest. When they refused to disperse, the emperor had eight of them thrown into prison. The other officials remained on their knees, loudly lamenting the behavior of the emperor. The emperor then ordered some two hundred officials flogged and thrown into the Embroidered-Uniform Guard jail. More than a dozen did not sur-vive the ordeal. Some of those who did were sent into exile. Two months later, the emperor confirmed that his own father was to be addressed as "imperial father," while the Hongzhi Emperor was to be called "imperial uncle." His mother was to be empress dowager, without the phrase "my own progenitor." The emperor also ordered that a book be written on the Great Rites Controversy.

Because of Qin Jin's rank, his name frequently headed the list of people who were opposed to the Emperor's excessive desire to honor his deceased father. But in the fall of 1524, the actual leader of the

147

protest, He Mengcun, submitted a memorial to the throne, entitled "Acknowledgment of Guilt," in which he called himself the ringleader and absolved Qin Jin and other higher-ranking officials.[3]

Being minister of revenue for a capricious emperor was not easy, especially since the emperor would turn affairs of state over to his eunuchs and other palace servants. Then, too, the Ming emperors were known for abusing their ministers. One of Qin Jin's predecessors was chained to his desk by an emperor who regarded his work as slovenly.

Fortunately for Qin Jin, the Jiajing Emperor viewed him favorably, despite his stance on the Great Rites Controversy. Nevertheless, Qin Jin was involved in several disputes involving the royal family. There were many precedents of imperial relatives seeking advantage from their status. Frequently, these were relatives of the empress, commoners raised to high position because a female member of their family had found imperial favor.

Another of Qin Jin's headaches was the salt monopoly. For many years, there was a tug of war between the emperor, who allowed his favorites to deal privately in surplus salt, and the ministry, which wanted greater control of this sensitive commodity.

It was inevitable that, sooner or later, Qin Jin would have to do battle with the palace eunuchs. In the fall of 1525, a number of censors and other officials protested that the eunuchs were expanding their powers by hiring several thousand additional workers. Since the funds came from the Ministry of Revenue, Qin Jin prepared a memorial to the emperor, in which he declared:

"Money and food are the blood vessels and the life of the country. Now all these workers are getting salaries, which they do not deserve, and they are depleting our treasury and constricting the vessels. This year, due to natural calamities, our coffers are quite empty. We cannot afford the additional expense. We hope Your Majesty will agree and prevent the country from sinking into poverty."[4]

The emperor consented, though the eunuchs continued to enjoy his confidence.

A few months later, a eunuch official, Liang Dong, reported that the palace required additional supplies of gold, pearls and precious stones, and requested the Ministry of Revenue to provide the necessary funds. In his response to the emperor, Qin Jin argued that there were established avenues for the provision of such items. If the need for additional jewelry was urgent, the Ministry of Revenue would see what steps could be taken. But now, the Treasury was almost empty. The provinces could be asked to increase their production but they were already heavily burdened, with Guangdong and Yunnan suffering from natural disasters. The minister added that the palace already had a considerable collection and that, if the emperor were to live frugally, no additional purchases would be necessary.[5] The emperor sided with the eunuch and ordered the minister of revenue to procure additional jewelry.

During the Ming dynasty, it was customary for officials in the capital to undergo merit evaluations every six years. In 1527, the time arrived for such an examination. After it, Qin Jin and another official, Chao Huang, were given "permission" to retire. It is unclear what happened, but the two men apparently had offended some powerful people, possibly as a result of their constant confrontations with the eunuchs.[6] A group of officials petitioned the emperor, urging the retention of the two men, citing the many problems faced by the dynasty, such as strengthening the borders and reviving the economy. The emperor rejected this plea. The two men, however, did not retire in disgrace. They were granted a lifetime salary and travel expenses back to their hometowns.[7] Ordinarily, courtiers had to pay for their own journeys, even while on official business.

His official career apparently over, the sixty-year-old Qin Jin devoted himself to more personal business in Wuxi. the compilation of his family genealogy, a task begun by his great-grandfather. This would be the first time the Qin clan had compiled its own genealogy since its move to Wuxi. In the preface Qin Jin wrote:

"When thousands of people look at an individual, there may be a lot of different opinions, but when an individual looks at the thousands, there should be no differences. It is due to feelings of closeness that we differentiate relatives by degree of kinship and not by wealth.

"I just would like to let the future readers of this book sense the filial relationship and the brotherly feelings toward their fellow countrymen by not regarding them as strangers or outsiders. The book says over and over: 'Remember, respect, receive and develop.' Don't regard them as mere words."

During this period of relative idleness, Qin Jin bought a plot of land near Mount Hui Temple, which was used by the monks as their residence. There he built a beautiful garden, with a villa inside, which he named Phoenix Valley Villa since his courtesy name was

Phoenix Mountain. The fate of the garden was to be associated with the rise and fall of the Qin family's fortunes for the next four hundred years. To mark the completion of its construction, he wrote the following lines:

> Retired, I reside on a famous mountain,
> My lodging is a small villa
> The creek curls around the rocks
> Tall pines dwarf the bushes
> Birds flit around the mountain
> Hill paths are remote and deserted
> Sounds of spring surround me
> Tinkling like a jade musical instrument.

In 1531, after he had spent four years in the political wilderness, Qin Jin was recalled to office. His supporters at court had argued that he was too capable and too young to be retired. However, he was in effect demoted, for his new appointment was as minister of revenue in Nanking. Nevertheless, Qin Jin took up the post in earnest, immediately submitting memorials with suggestions for reforms. His were proposals on pasturelands, transporting hay, building dams of brick to prevent floods, appointing an official responsible for purchasing silk at state-set prices, and regulating the prices of cotton cloth. All were approved.

Just as eleven years previously, a censor had called Qin Jin a "black sheep" unfit to serve the emperor, so now another censor submitted a memorial in which he praised Qin Jin to the skies, and advised that he should be given an appropriate position at court.[8]

Despite this memorial, Qin Jin was kept in Nanking. The following month, apparently disillusioned, he submitted a request to retire, which was denied. At the beginning of 1533, Qin Jin was finally brought back to Peking, this time as minister of works. He was again at the center of power. His chief responsibility was to oversee the building of palaces and the restoration of those damaged by fire or the ravages of time, and to see to the upkeep and repair of canals.

Qin Jin joined with a number of other high officials in requesting an imperial favor: the gift of certain books, including the *Minglun Dadian*, compiled at the behest of the Jiajing Emperor himself. It was an account of the Great Rites Controversy, in which the emperor emerged triumphant from his conflict with officials over the extravagant honors he insisted on giving his parents. By asking for the book, Qin Jin and the other officials who had opposed him were symbolically signaling their capitulation. The emperor happily acceded to the request.

One of Qin Jin's most important tasks as minister of works was the expansion of the imperial ancestral temple, built in 1420, from its original nine chambers to nine separate temples. Toward the end of 1534, he submitted designs of the new temple complex for the emperor's approval. It was to be flanked by two smaller structures, one to honor the imperial family's female members, the other the males. Garments of deceased emperors and empresses were to be housed in the temple, which also featured plaques honoring meritorious officials. The emperor approved the designs after making minor alterations.

But Qin Jin did not remain in office long enough to see the project completed in 1536. And five years after the completion, the new temples were destroyed in a fire caused by a thunderstorm. The superstitious emperor suffered much anguish and decided to rebuild on a more modest scale, reverting to the original design of nine chambers within one temple.

In his last years in office, honors began to be heaped on Qin Jin. In 1534, at age sixty-seven, he became junior guardian of the heir apparent and the following year, grand guardian of the heir apparent, a post that carried with it the highest rank in the civil service. He also received additional tasks to perform, such as acting as examiner in the palace examination. He was granted 20 taels of silver as well as two silk suits for his work in supervising canal construction.

His age began to affect him. He was even unable to attend a ritual at the imperial temple. Yet in 1536, he was transferred to Nanking to act as minister of war and grand adjutant, a post he had held thirteen years earlier.

And despite his age, he showed that his reputation as a military strategist was well founded. He submitted a series of major proposals for the reorganization of the military forces: He called for the collective training of soldiers, setting up a system for keeping watch at night, rebuilding the city walls—the longest of any city in China—setting up individual files on each soldier, reforming the payroll system and increasing the number of administrative personnel.

But within a few months of taking over the post, Qin Jin requested permission to retire. The emperor realized that Qin Jin was becoming increasingly weak but, out of deference to the minister and in order to give him face, turned down his request. But when the seventy-year-old official renewed his request a few months later, approval was granted. Qin Jin was provided with transportation back to his hometown, given a pension of four piculs of rice a month and assigned four personal servants for life.[9] He was given another honorific title, Guanglu Great Officer, and, for a third time, his ancestors for three generations were posthumously honored. All were given the title grand guardian of the heir apparent and Nanking minister of war, and their wives promoted to ladies of the first rank.

Back in Wuxi, Qin Jin again dedicated himself to genealogical research and a study of the Confucian classics. He rebuilt the graves of his ancestors to reflect their new status. Presumably, he also had artists draw portraits of them and their wives in their official finery.

Qin Jin became the typical grandfather, playing with his six grandsons and giving them instructions in the classics. Every day he read the classics himself. When his eyesight finally failed him, he asked two of his servants to read aloud to him daily from the classics and historical works.

He informally revived the Blue Mountain Poetry Society. He and a group of friends met frequently, sometimes at his villa, sometimes at theirs, where they relaxed, enjoyed a few cups of wine and composed verses.

Unlike his ancestor, the Song dynasty poet Qin Guan, he never took a concubine, nor was he ever accused of immoral conduct. Qin Jin was a man of rectitude, a scholar who, when necessary, led troops into battle. But he was not interested only in official glory. He was a family man who took pride in his ancestry and who earned his clan's eternal gratitude by compiling its genealogy and constructing its ancestral hall.

In 1544 Qin Jin died at the age of seventy-six and was buried on Homecoming Mountain, near his father. When the emperor was told of his death, he declared a day of mourning and did not hold court. A record of Qin Jin's official life was compiled and evaluated by the Ministry of Rites. And he was granted, with the emperor's consent, a canonical name, meant to reflect his qualities. The two-character names came from a list of ninety-two words, each of which bore a special significance. Qin Jin was given the name Duan Min, "Proper and Agile," presumably alluding to qualities he had displayed in his long years of service.[10] When the name was conferred,

Qin Jin was said to have "committed no irregularities, grasped righteousness and fulfilled his duties with merit."

The day after his death, his body was given a thorough cleaning, which included the trimming of his beard and the cutting of his fingernails. The nail parings and hair were put in a small bag, to be buried with him. The corpse was dressed, and sacrificial food and wine were offered. The next day, the body was formally dressed before being placed in the coffin. The coffin was stuffed so that the corpse would not roll around when it was carried. Then the feet, head and left and right sides were covered with cloths.[11]

Seven days after Qin Jin's death, the vice-prefect of Changzhou arrived to pay respects at the behest of the emperor. By imperial order, nine mourning altars were set up, and a eulogy composed by the court was read. On the forty-ninth day after the death (a day known to the Chinese as "seven sevens," marking the end of the seven-week mourning period) another nine altars were set up, this time by the prefect of Changzhou.

The burial ground was carefully selected. The main criteria were that the soil had to be bright, the trees and grass luxuriant; furthermore, the site should not be encroached upon by the construction of roads or buildings, nor should it be needed for farmland.

Before the actual burial, there was an elaborate ceremony: the calling back of the soul. Three men shouted out the dead man's name at the tops of their voices while holding his official garments in their hands. These garments were not put in the coffin, but nineteen other sets of clothes were, including a ceremonial court dress and a stiff circular belt signifying rank. The number of garments to be buried with the deceased depended on his rank. Daily utensils, including a sink, a wash basin, towels and a comb for his use in the spirit world were added. The combs were stored in boxes and the robes were stored in bags. The ivory tablet, called a *hu*, held respectfully by a courtier while in the imperial presence, was placed in the hands of the dead man. His mouth was stuffed with cooked rice and jade so that he would not want for food or luxury.

Also buried with him was a flag on which was emblazoned his name for the enlightenment of the gods. The official rank and titles were also recorded. Protocol even dictated the length of the flag, with that of the highest-ranking officials reaching nine feet.

Ming dynasty regulations permitted the burial of up to fifty articles with the dead, such as drums, flags, dusters, saddles, bows, arrows, stoves, water tanks, armor, helmets, spoons, bottles, barrels, spittoons, incense burners, scented boxes, joss sticks, teapots and cups, bowls and dishes, chairs, footrests, wooden horses, spears and swords, tables and beds. Whatever a person was accustomed to in life was not denied him in death.

On the coffin itself was a piece of cloth on which were embroidered clouds and fire, signifying a government official.

The burial of Qin Jin did not take place until the year following his death. That ceremony was presided over by another imperial envoy. And Qin Jin was laid to rest on one side of a double grave. Six years later, when his wife died, she was buried beside him, in solemn ceremonies supervised by the prefect of Changzhou, acting under imperial instructions.

Qin Jin's wife was a woman of character. When her husband was battling bandits in Huguang, there was a report that he had been kidnapped. She reacted to it by saying, "If my lord is dead, I will have no regrets if death claims me too." When thieves and robbers were running rampant in Wuxi, she refused to hire personal bodyguards, saying: "If I hire guards, they will risk their lives to protect me because I pay them. I do not want anyone to risk their lives for money."

A winding path, lined on both sides by trees and stone figures, led to the joint grave of Qin Jin and his wife. Imperial regulations prescribed that for someone of Qin Jin's rank, there should be two stone lions, two stone tigers and two stone sheep, as well as two seven-foot-high stone civilian officials and two military guards. These were the stone figures whose scattered remains I found in 1983.

The hierarchical structure of Chinese society was reflected even in the gravestone used. Qin Jin was entitled to a stone pillar resting on a stone turtle, a symbol of longevity. A lower-ranking official would not merit the stone turtle. The height and width of the stone depended on the rank of the deceased, as did whether the top was flat or rounded.

While there were gravestones and other markers above ground to identify the occupant of the grave, the Chinese made doubly sure that even if the aboveground steles and gravestones should vanish in the course of time, anyone stumbling across the grave would immediately know the identity of the occupant. They did this by burying with each official two vast stone slabs on which were engraved his name and his life story. These two slabs, with

154

the inscriptions facing each other, were tightly bound together with metal cord before being buried either inside the grave or in front of it.

Qin Jin, being of the first rank, was entitled to a burial area of ninety square paces. Officials of the second rank were entitled to eighty square paces, down to the seventh rank, which was allowed only twenty square paces.

An epitaph was composed by his old friend Yan Song, who, that year, was named grand secretary. The epitaph was engraved on a stone pillar known as a *shendaobei*, or "inscription on the sacred way." But Yan Song later earned a reputation as one of the most treacherous officials of the Ming dynasty. So though Yan Song's writings contain poems dedicated to Qin Jin, Qin Jin's collected writings of prose and poetry contain no mention of Yan Song. Someone, for reasons of prudence, obviously winnowed through Qin Jin's writings and removed all evidence of such an unfortunate association, but the epitaph, engraved on stone, could not be conveniently removed.

There is an interesting legend about Qin Jin's burial. It is said that some of the laborers working on the tomb were unhappy with the way they were treated, so one of them cursed the occupant of the tomb, saying, "This family will not become prosperous again unless the stone tortoise in front of the tomb turns over." Since the stone tortoise was held in place by a massive stone plaque, it seemed an unlikely eventuality. Yet in 1600, fifty-six years after Qin Jin's death, a storm toppled the plaque and turned the tortoise over.[12]

CHAPTER TEN

Qin Liang: A Prophecy Come True

The same day that I discovered that Qin Jin's tomb had been dug up in the Cultural Revolution, I was lucky enough to find one that was virtually intact. Hidden behind a bamboo grove, it was on a hillside covered with trees, vines and bushes. In the vicinity, lying amid pink peach blossoms, were remnants of an engraved stone horse and a stone tortoise, as well as four stone pillars, now being used as makeshift bridges over dry gullies.

Gu Wenbi, the Wuxi Museum curator who was accompanying me, became very excited. Reconstructing the tomb with flourishes of his arms, he exclaimed: "This was a typical Ming-dynasty grave, called *san-jian si-chu* ['three chambers with four pillars']." The grave itself was marked by a circular mound of earth, Chinese-style. The tumulus was surrounded by a low wall of lapis lazuli. Even though the grave was four hundred years old, the engraved picture of an old man with a flowing beard was still clearly discernible on the stone wall. To the left of the old man was a deer, while on the other side was a crane, with pine branches arching overhead. Mr. Gu explained that the engravings symbolized longevity and their presence meant the grave had been constructed while its occupant was still alive. Chinese were very concerned about history and their place in it, and this concern extended to where they would be buried. People of prominence often selected their own burial sites while they were still in relatively good health. The Chinese statesman Li Hongzhang, who died in 1901, traveled through Europe in 1896 with a coffin.

The surface gravestone of the tomb in Wuxi was gone but about a hundred yards down the hill was a structure called a *xiang-tang*, or "hall of sacrifice," where the body of the deceased was first laid out more than four hundred years ago. The hall is now used as a recreation room for a leprosy hospital, but several stone engravings embedded in the walls are still legible. Using a wet rag to wipe off the coat of whitewash, Mr. Gu was able to make out without much difficulty an account written by a former grand secretary, in which he explains how this particular grave site was selected in 1564 by Qin Han two years before he died. His son, Liang, chose to be buried at that site when he died in 1578.

From the position of the two graves, it was clear that Liang had buried his father at the more auspicious spot, directly facing Lake Tai, while satisfying himself with a plot on the side as an act of filial piety.

Liang's father, Qin Han, was the great-grandson of Qin Xu, founder of the Blue Mountain Poetry Society, and the son of Tang, the man who had given up an official career by dedicating nineteen years of his life to caring for his sick mother. Qin Han was born in 1493, the sixth year of the reign of the Hongzhi Emperor and the year after Christopher Columbus set sail from Spain in search of India.

By the time he was twenty, Liang's father had become a licentiate and had taken a bride. Two years after his marriage, Liang was born. In *Tales of Wuxi*, a book of anecdotes, it is said that when Liang's mother was pregnant, a neighbor had a dream that the Qin family would produce a child who would become administration commissioner, the second-highest official in a province.[1] Fifty-one years later the prophecy came true.

According to contemporary accounts, Liang was an unusual child. He did not much care for children's games but he loved to fly kites. He had a kite that was ten feet long and ten feet wide, so heavy that several strong men were required to get it into the air.[2]

In 1531 when Liang was sixteen, his father's aunt became a widow. Since both her sons had died before reaching adulthood, she wished to continue her late husband's family line by adopting one of her nephews. Her choice was Liang's father. So Qin Han at age thirty-eight suddenly found himself with a new family name, Wu, and new parentage.[3] Technically he was without a father, and his aunt was transformed into his mother. He took this new role seriously for, three years later, he petitioned the imperial court to honor his adopted mother for her devotion to her late husband. The request was granted.

Eventually Qin Han resumed his original name, though it is not clear why or how. Apparently he found another candidate to replace him as the continuer of the Wu family line.

Liang was a diligent student. At twenty he entered the local government academy where Qin Jin had also studied, to prepare for the series of examinations he must face.[4] Two years later, in 1537, he earned the first degree and became a *xiucai*. But it took him until 1543 to pass the provincial examinations. In 1544 Liang made his first attempt at the metropolitan examinations, but failed and had to wait another three years before he could try again. In the meantime, he became a teacher. He tried to instill into the minds of his students the idea that "as a scholar, one should be true to oneself and not fawn on the rich and powerful." In 1547, at the age of thirty-two, he passed the metropolitan examinations and became a *jinshi*. He was dispatched to Jiangxi province to serve as prefectural judge in Nanchang.

When he arrived in Nanchang, he learned that there was a gang led by a notorious bandit known as Ping the Twelfth, which was raising havoc. The bandit leader was able to elude capture because he was well connected with one of the local police officials. Qin Liang confronted the errant official, who fell on his knees begging for mercy. Liang promised to spare his life if he helped to capture the bandit chief. So the man pretended to continue his cooperation with the bandits while keeping Liang informed of their activities. With the help of a spy in the ranks, Liang was able to enter the bandit lair one night. Ping the Twelfth was captured without a fight and was beheaded in the marketplace as a warning to others.

But Qin Liang did not pronounce the death sentence easily. Before he went to Nanchang, his father had advised him, "Do not be whimsical and treat other people's lives lightly." Liang took these words to heart and scrupulously sifted through the evidence in cases that could result in capital punishment. Once, while Liang was working on a case late into the night, his son knelt down in front of him and begged him to rest. Liang chided him by saying: "You are too young to realize the importance of this work. One mistake on my part may result in the death of an innocent man."

This attitude saved the life of a prisoner who had offended a local provincial intendant. The official had had him arrested and beaten so badly that he was near death. When Liang heard about this, he investigated and ordered the prisoner released.

In 1551, after having served in Nanchang for three years, Liang was transferred to the capital. He was promoted to supervising secretary of the Office of Scrutiny for Personnel. The Offices of Scrutiny were set up to monitor the rest of the bureaucracy.

As the Jiajing Emperor grew older, he became obsessed with the mystical aspects of Daoism, and its search for a formula that would bestow immortality. In pursuit of this, he had special structures erected for Daoist worship and ordered special incense as well as precious metals and gems. He devoted himself to cult practices, including alchemy, and he spent little time on the actual affairs of state.

The year that Liang was transferred to the capital, he incurred the wrath of the emperor. As supervising secretary, part of his job was to criticize wrongdoing, even on the part of the emperor, and to propose policies. Liang offended the emperor by refusing to take part in his mystical ceremonies, and may well have admonished the emperor himself to refrain from such practices. There are few details available. The only extant account of the incident says merely that Liang "refused to offer incense" and so was flogged. Such flogging was administered by blows of a bastinado, a heavy wooden rod capable of inflicting terrible injury. He was beaten so badly that he was fortunate to escape with his life.

When Qin Han heard about the beating meted out to his son, he wrote to him: "Since you have committed your body and soul to serving the emperor, even if you die you should have no regrets, as long as you are dying for something worthwhile." His father also comforted him by saying, "Since it is your official function to offer criticism, you would be derelict in your duty if you did not speak out when necessary. Then, you would really be to blame."[5]

But Qin Liang told his family, "If I cannot change His Majesty's mind I will not die with my eyes closed," meaning that his soul would not be at peace. If Liang hoped to persuade the emperor to abandon Daoism, it was a futile endeavor. The Jiajing Emperor became so fanatical that even high officials like Grand Secretary Yan Song had to cater to his desires by becoming experts at composing Daoist prayers on special paper.

In the first half of the sixteenth century, the Mongols had staged a series of raids south of the Great Wall, edging closer and closer to Peking. In 1550, the Mongols were actually encamped in the capital's suburbs. It became clear that a wall to protect the outer city, where most of the people lived, was urgently needed. Two years later, Qin Liang was one of two supervisors assigned to the project. (The walls around the inner city had been completed 130 years earlier.) He took his work so seriously that he actually slept at the construction site, a section of the wall near the Temple of Heaven, where the emperor went to offer sacrifices on special occasions. Discovering that construction was being delayed because a high official was dipping into the funds for his own purposes, Liang reported this to the emperor and the official was dismissed. In the process, Liang undoubtedly made political enemies.

The wall around the outer city, when completed, was somewhat lower than that protecting the inner city. It measured thirty feet in height, with a width of twenty-five feet at the base and fifteen feet at the top. The outer faces of the walls were strengthened by square buttresses built at intervals of sixty yards, and on the summits of these were the guardhouses for the troops on duty. Each of the sixteen gates of the city was protected by a semicircular enceinte, and was surmounted by a high tower provided with countless loopholes.

Because the construction of the Peking city walls progressed smoothly, Liang received a promotion to the politically sensitive Office of Transmission, which processed all communications among the various agencies of the capital and between them and various provincial authorities, serving first as right assistant administration commissioner, and two years later as left assistant administration commissioner.[6]

During this period, he worked closely with the vice-minister of works, Yan Shifan, son of Grand Secretary Yan Song, who had accumulated so much personal power that he in effect functioned as prime minister, though that post did not exist.

Some historical sources attribute Liang's rapid rise to his close relationship with both the Yan father and son, but others say that Liang offended Yan Shifan because he refused to condone the general practice of paying for promotions. There may be some truth to both versions. On balance, it seems likely that Liang did benefit from the patronage of Yan Song, who was also a close friend of his father, but that later Liang attempted to distance himself from the Yans.

The southern assignment Liang received in 1558 was as vice chief minister of the Nanking Court of the Imperial Stud, which was indirectly under the supervision of the Ministry of War. The Court of the Imperial Stud directed a number of horse pasturages throughout the empire. Liang's office was situated in Chuzhou near Nanking.

In Chuzhou, Liang was able to enjoy the mountains and waters of the south and to be near his father.

While Liang was in Peking, Han composed a poem that showed the profound love he had for his son:

> Suddenly the year is over,
> My mind is a thousand miles away.
> My days are full of sound and motion,
> My nights are filled with loneliness.
> It's too early for the ground to be covered with snow,
> When will the bird fly across the river with news of you?
> Tomorrow marks one full year of separation
> I scratch my head and sleep will not come.

Han decided in 1554 to revive the Blue Mountain Poetry Society, which had been inactive for sixty years. The building had become dilapidated in the decades since the death of his great-grandfather, but with the help of other prominent local scholars, Han had the premises repaired and the main hall, formerly called the Hall of Ten Elders, was renamed Hall for Continuing Cultivation.[7]

Another project that kept Han occupied was the garden built by his uncle Qin Jin on the outskirts of the city, at the foot of Mount Hui. Qin Liang had bought the garden for his own pleasure and that of his father.

In an essay describing the garden, Qin Han said:

"The hill is high, the garden measures several acres. It includes a pond and a thousand bamboos. Trees and flowers of all kinds are there. It is not too big, but large enough for one to relax in. Inside are halls, bridges, buildings and pavilions, as well as rivers, books, wine, songs, musical instruments and a retired old man! I spend my time here as a gardener, a fisherman and a companion of nature, to view the flowers, to keep company with the birds and animals and to enjoy myself. Sometimes I drink a few glasses of wine, sometimes I write a few poems. That is my life. How peaceful."

While Qin Han was enjoying his leisure years, Liang had been promoted to chief minister of the Nanking Court of State Ceremonial, and then within a year named head of the Office of Transmission. Some commentators have pointed to this rare double promotion as evidence that Liang was being backed by Yan Song and his son, who were then at the height of their power.

It is said that after this double promotion Yan Shifan sent an emissary to Liang to say: "You have been promoted twice in a year.

161

Do you know how this came about?" The emissary demanded a substantial payment to Yan Shifan. But by all accounts Liang rebuffed the emissary.[8]

In any event, the power of Yan Song and his son was broken when, after they had dominated the court for almost two decades, they were disgraced. Yan Song was subsequently listed in the official "History of the Ming Dynasty" under the category "Treacherous Officials," accused of having usurped imperial powers, persecuted his critics and condoned his son's corrupt and tyrannical behavior. He lost favor when a young colleague, Grand Secretary Xu Jie, gradually supplanted him in the emperor's eyes. His downfall was precipitated in part by his wife's death in 1561, for his son was required to resign and go into ritual mourning. Bereft of his son's assistance, the eighty-one-year-old Yan Song was unable to continue to please the emperor.

The turning point came when the emperor's palace burned down. Yan Song argued that the palace should not be rebuilt, as it would be too costly, but his rival Xu Jie devised a plan in which it could be rebuilt at reasonable expense. Taking advantage of the opportunity, Yan Song's political opponents moved in and exploited the emperor's displeasure and superstitions. By the following year, Yan Song had been dismissed and his son banished.

As the disgrace of a powerful leader inevitably affected his allies and supporters, so the downfall of the Yans provided a chance for their political opponents to surface and denounce all those who had been associated with them.

In 1563, those newly installed in power used another device to sweep aside those who did not belong to their camp. This was the periodic assessment of metropolitan officials, held every six years, during which each official was expected to examine his own performance in office, find himself unworthy and ask to be relieved of his post, while hoping, of course, that his request would be denied.

It was to be expected that Qin Liang, because of his links to the Yans, would be demoted, and he was. He was assigned to serve as assistant administration commissioner of Zhejiang province, a position that was one grade lower than his previous job of transmission commissioner. Liang's father tried to comfort him with the words Liang had taught his own students years before: "To be demoted for refusing to flatter the rich and powerful is no disgrace."

But though Liang's political career had suffered a setback, it was by no means over, for he was not without friends in the post–Yan Song era. Grand Secretary Xu Jie, who had engineered Yan Song's downfall, was his father's friend. And Li Chunfang, a friend with whom Liang had studied for the *jinshi* examinations, was rising rapidly within the government. So Liang was able to work his way up again.

In the spring of 1564, Liang, then forty-nine years old, was appointed surveillance vice-commissioner responsible for education in Zhejiang. He worked as an examiner for five months, traveling through eleven prefectures and awarding the licentiate degree to fifty-six students. All of them went on to take the provincial examinations and all were successful. Only one successful candidate within his jurisdiction was not spotted by Liang, proof of his excellent judgment in selecting students.

In 1565, Liang's friend and classmate Li Chunfang became a grand secretary. That year, Liang was appointed Huguang surveillance commissioner, which returned him to the rank he had held before his demotion. The following year, he was promoted to administration commissioner of Jiangxi province, thus fulfilling the prophecy of his neighbor's dream before his birth. But he never served in that post.

For in 1565 his father suffered a stroke. Concerned about Han's condition, Liang asked for permission to return home. In Wuxi, he found his father failing rapidly, despite daily ministrations of herbal medicine. Two months later, in 1566, Qin Han died.

Even on his deathbed, Qin Han offered a final word of advice to Liang: "My son," he said, "you should pay attention to this: Fate is not unalterable. Success never comes easily, only from hard work."

Liang suspended his career and went into mourning. But in actuality, he went into permanent retirement, and there is reason to believe that it was not totally voluntary. He was in his early fifties and could look forward to another decade of active political life. Apparently there was still a strong aversion to him on the part of the anti–Yan Song forces. Even though his powerful friend Li Chunfang gave him support and composed an epitaph for Liang's father, the opposition was too great.

Liang spent his twelve remaining years in Wuxi, where he devoted himself to writing. He edited the memorials of Qin Kuai and published a new edition of Qin Jin's book, *Pacification of Huguang*, adding a preface.

Although retired, Liang maintained an active interest in politics. His former students who had become officials wrote to him to seek his opinion. He also became a friend of the local magistrate and persuaded him to simplify the tax system by replacing a multiplicity of taxes with just one tax, a reform known as the single-whip tax system.

In 1574, Magistrate Zhou Bangjie asked him to compile a revised version of the local history and geography, known as the *Wuxi Gazetteer*. Eighty years previously, his great-granduncle Kuai had been involved in editing an earlier edition. Liang agreed and in his preface wrote:

> Countries keep histories and districts have records. The district record is used to provide accurate information for future generations and should be as complete as possible.
>
> Our district has been famous since its exploration by Tai Po. It was known for the beauty of its scenery and the prosperity of its people. However, because such a long time has elapsed and writings have been lost, the earliest records we have are those of Wang Wenyu. During the Jingtai reign period [1450–1456] of this dynasty, Feng Zexian re-edited the manuscript. Early in the Hongzhi period, Wu Fengxiang and Li Xunming also updated this information. From then till now eighty years have elapsed, and much has occurred—births and deaths, changes in district laws, customs, etc. If these are not recorded, we will not be able to trace them in future.
>
> An office was set up in the county magistrate's yamen. Scholars such as Hua Pan, Li Shifang, Yu Yong, Sheng Pan and my cousin Qin Ping helped. We read through the old records, researched the origin of each event, re-edited the complicated and deleted the unnecessary. The period covered is from the third year of the Hongzhi emperor [1524] to the first year of the Wanli reign period [1573]. It has ten categories, in twenty-four chapters. The ten categories are geography (enfeoffments), palaces (and their regulations), food and storage (relating to taxation), military defense (precautions taken), personalities worthy of honoring, including scholars and sage philosophers, officials and how they governed, examinations, literature, unofficial historical accounts (to compensate for lost official histories) and miscellany.[9]

Liang continued by explaining that he had corrected his draft again and again. He finally expressed his fears thus: "The record compiled by Wang was too restricted, that by Feng too complicated. Those of Wu and Li too ungraceful. Restricted, complicated and ungraceful writings should be avoided. Yet I do not know whether this new record will be criticized in future as we criticize the old records now. However, the magistrate's order has been fulfilled and as I write this preface I await the judgment of the future."

Even while Qin Liang was alive, some of his colleagues were unhappy with the way he had edited the *Wuxi Gazetteer*. One of his main collaborators, Hua Pan, privately expressed great dissatisfaction with his work in a letter in which he told a friend that Liang had turned down suggestions for including information on some prominent men just because their descendants were no longer wealthy and powerful. He added: "He is stubborn and refuses to accept the principles of fairness and impartiality. He prints [major historical events in Wuxi] in small characters, but he put the Story of the Bamboo Stove in big characters. Even events of less importance than the Bamboo Stove he would include, as long as they were about Qin family members."

The fact that his great-granduncle had been asked to compose a preface to the 1494 edition, and that Liang himself had edited the latest version, showed that by this time the Qin family was considered an influential part of Wuxi society. From then on, until the last local history of Wuxi was published in 1881, almost every edition was compiled by members of the Qin family.

Like his father, Liang enjoyed visiting his garden on Mount Hui, which he further enlarged while keeping its old name of Phoenix Valley Villa. In a poem written one summer, Liang said:

> This morning I was bothered by the hot weather;
> I went to the Phoenix Valley to search for quietude.
> The red flower's gone—I feel sorrow for the aged;
> The paths and pavilions are being invaded by grass.
> The cicadas hide and sing amid leaves of tall trees;
> The forest-residing cranes dance leisurely;
> I drink alone with the breeze lapping the pines.

That garden was to remain within the same clan for some 450 years.

Qin Liang's best-known piece of writing was a long political essay titled "The Minds of All People Under Heaven" on how a government can best institute policy changes.[10] In it he argued:

"For a country to institute well-thought-out policy changes, three elements are required. First, the change has to be put into effect gradually. Second, it must be done with skill. And third, it must be implemented consistently. In the absence of these three factors, policy changes will turn out to be short-lived, and will yield no benefits."

Like most scholar-officials, Qin Liang wrote a large number of epitaphs for friends and relatives. One of the most interesting was composed for an aunt who had been betrothed to one of Qin Liang's uncles at the age of fifteen. The bridegroom-to-be was only sixteen, but he died before the wedding. Since by convention the two could not meet before the wedding day, she had never laid eyes on him. Yet so seriously were betrothals taken in those days that she attempted to hang herself at his death but was rescued in time by her family.

When she recovered, she vowed never to wed another man. She cut short her hair and severed one of her ears as a sign of her determination to remain chaste. And she demanded that at her death she be buried beside her betrothed. When she reached the age of fifty, news of her extreme devotion to her betrothed reached the court, which bestowed honors on her.

The death of his father had left Liang head of the family, which included his mother and two younger brothers, one of whom was only a child. It was also, of course, his responsibility to arrange suitable marriages for his own children. Since marriages were arranged in those days according to the maxim that "bamboo doors face bamboo doors" and "wooden doors face wooden doors," a good idea of a family's social standing can be obtained by looking at its in-laws. All three sons born to Qin Liang's wife were matched with daughters of prominent families. The son of his concubine was matched with a less prominent family, though that bridegroom was a student in the Imperial Academy. Liang's three daughters all married into families of high officials. His grandchildren, too, were matched with the offspring of families of similar background.

In the autumn of 1577, when Liang was sixty-two years old, he fell ill. In the winter, he caught a lingering cold. But the following spring, on his mother's birthday, he insisted on getting up from his sickbed to pay her ceremonial respects, so she would not worry about his health. He also took part in the extensive celebrations for her.

But in the autumn of 1578, he became mortally ill. His last words, addressed to his children, were these:

"Our family has always worked for the cause of righteousness. I have never done anything to shame my ancestors. I have discharged my responsibilities to the best of my ability and I have never disgraced the family name. My only regret is that I will not be able to fulfill the duties of a son in making arrangements for my mother's funeral. You must take care of your grandmother."[11]

CHAPTER ELEVEN

Qin Yao: Hero and Savior

In the spring of 1985, I found in the mail a letter from my fourth cousin, Zhihao, in Wuxi. It contained five pages of what turned out to be a 381-year-old legal document, neatly copied on thin, red-lined paper: the property settlement of Qin Yao, nephew of Qin Liang, and my ancestor thirteen generations ago.

Such a document—similar to a will in that it appeared to have been prepared before his death, but signed by four witnesses a few weeks after his death in 1604—is extremely rare. And it is of special interest because it was the will of a former high official who possessed incredible wealth, and who had children by both his wife and his concubines.

Qin Yao was born in 1544, during the twenty-third year of the reign of the Jiajing Emperor, a decade after King Henry VIII of England severed ties with the Papacy and established the Church of England. Yao was the younger son of Qin He, who passed the metropolitan examinations and was appointed district magistrate of Wukang, in western Zhejiang province, in 1553. At the time, the power of the pirates was at its height.[1] Numerous towns in the coastal provinces of Zhejiang, Jiangsu and Fujian were captured or besieged by them. Unwalled market towns, such as Wukang, were particularly vulnerable.

The deputy administrator of Zhejiang ordered Qin He to build a city wall to protect Wukang from the pirates, but Qin He refused. He felt that construction of a city wall would be a heavy burden on the citizens. Moreover, he felt that the act of building the wall would enlarge the residents' fears of a pirate attack and weaken the town's ability to withstand one. Instead, Qin He personally trained a local militia of able-bodied young men and charged them with guarding the town.

Qin He himself was the leader of the guards, and his followers confidently awaited the arrival of the pirates. They attacked Wukang several times, but each time they were repulsed. Then they changed their tactics. They sent men dressed as monks into the town in an attempt to gain information on its defenses and to seek opportunities to create disturbances. But Qin He was suspicious. And so he pretended to welcome the "monks," invited them to a banquet and then seized all of them. The next day they were beheaded, and the pirates knew that they stood little chance of being able to sack Wukang.

After finishing his term in Wukang, Qin He was promoted to secretary and then director of the Nanking Ministry of Revenue before being transferred back to Zhejiang in 1562 to serve as prefect of Jinhua.[2] Then, because his cousin Liang received an appointment in the same province, he was reassigned to Yunnan, where he served as prefect of Yongchang until his death in 1566 at the relatively young age of forty-nine. (The practice of preventing the conflicts of interest that might arise if relatives worked in the same province was known as the Law of Avoidance.)

Qin He had been a very generous man, always willing to extend financial help to friends and relatives. After his death, his two sons, Bing, twenty-six, and Yao, twenty-two, wanted to demand repayment. But their mother argued, "If you do not succeed in life, it will not be for want of money. You want to demand repayment for these debts. Do you think your father would approve of your acting in this way?" The two brothers relented and tore up the promissory notes.

Yao went into twenty-seven months of mourning, during which time he took care of his grandfather until he, too, died in 1568. Then, in April 1571, the fifth year of the reign of the Longqing Emperor, Yao took and passed the metropolitan examinations, earning the *jinshi* degree. His chief examiner was Grand Secretary Zhang Juzheng, who was well on his way to becoming the unchallenged head of the government. Zhang took great care to draw up questions appropriate to the times, questions that demonstrated his belief in such concepts as the proper relationship between a ruler and his ministers, the appropriateness of different laws for different periods and the Confucian precept that names must reflect reality: A man can properly be called emperor only if he actually carries out the functions of an emperor.

Zhang was very impressed by Qin Yao, and recommended him

for the prestigious Hanlin Academy,[3] which provided literary and scholarly assistance of all kinds to the emperor and the court.

After three years with the Hanlin Academy, Yao was appointed supervising secretary of the Office of Scrutiny for Punishments, which had the right of special veto over documents, including imperial decrees that were to be promulgated. Documents from provincial officials addressed to the ministries first went to the supervising secretaries, who could rephrase them or, in some cases, even return them for reconsideration if the memorials or decrees were in their view inappropriate or inconsistent with recognized governmental principles.

In addition, the supervising secretaries had the ear of the emperor, and were able to take part in imperial audiences and policy deliberations. They could even remonstrate with the emperor when they felt he was acting unwisely and often were sent by the emperor to the provinces on investigative missions.

By this time Qin Yao was a favorite of the powerful Zhang Juzheng, who had been senior grand secretary since 1572. When the nine-year-old Wanli ascended the throne the following year, Zhang took over the reins of government while also acting as the tutor to the emperor. Zhang, like Yan Song, was one of a handful of Ming grand secretaries who wielded such political power that they were de facto prime ministers.

Each grand secretary worked in one of six designated buildings in the imperial palace. Rarely were all six posts filled; the number of functioning grand secretaries usually fluctuated between three and four. Because they were inside the palace, they were considered part of the "inner court," as distinct from the rest of officialdom in the "outer court." The grand secretaries theoretically held posts without power, but from the fifteenth century on they were given high honorific ranks in the administrative hierarchy. And though they were originally meant to be only secretaries, gradually their role widened so that they drafted responses to memorials for the emperor to approve, approval that became a formality for some of the weaker rulers. Although he was posthumously disgraced, Zhang went down in Chinese history as a good and loyal minister, one of the most capable senior ministers of the Ming dynasty, unlike the notorious Yan Song.

Like other men who possessed power, Zhang was not averse to using it to remove his political enemies and to promote his own protégés, like Yao. For the time being, his political enemies were in no position to retaliate, but their time would come, and when it came after his death, his protégés would suffer.

With the backing of Zhang, Yao's rise was nothing short of meteoric. His promotions did not come at three-year or six-year intervals, as was customary. Instead, he was promoted to right supervising secretary of the Office of Scrutiny for War in 1575 and, a month later, promoted to left supervising secretary of the Office of Scrutiny for Rites.

The following year, the fourteen-year-old Wanli Emperor sent Yao as his personal representative to preside over the investiture of the wife of Hou Ping, the Prince of Qidong, the emperor's grand-uncle. That same year, Yao's mother died and he had to go into mourning, as convention dictated. While he was still in mourning, the father of Grand Secretary Zhang also died, precipitating a crisis at court. The timing was unfortunate, for Zhang had just launched a program of reforms, and he had been put in charge of the young emperor's forthcoming wedding. In the end, Zhang neither attended his father's funeral nor observed the set mourning period, a serious violation of Confucian orthodoxy. Censors and other officials who were bold enough to point to this were severely dealt with for their effrontery.

When Qin Yao returned to Peking, he was named left supervising secretary of the Office of Scrutiny for Punishments and, six months later, was promoted to chief supervising secretary of the Office of Scrutiny for Personnel. While in the latter office, he criticized the minister of personnel for not exercising sufficient care in the choice of candidates for promotion, which resulted in the minister's trying to get him transferred. But Yao was protected by his mentor Zhang.[4]

The grand secretary cautioned Yao on the need to avoid open clashes with political opponents. But Yao insisted on speaking his mind, and so kept up a flow of memorials to the throne, presenting his ideas and criticisms. These covered such subjects as how to make use of men of talent, how to punish the lazy, how to select eunuchs, how to prevent corruption, how to deploy troops and how to maximize the good and minimize the bad effects of any policy.

When he was thirty-seven, he was appointed examiner of the imperial college, a position of potential influence since many of his students later became important officials.

Two years later, in 1582, he went on to become vice-minister of the Court of Imperial Sacrifices, which was in general charge of sacrificial rites and music. Under it was a College of Translators, which dealt with communications to and from tributary states, and a Music and Dance Office.

In 1584, Qin Yao took charge of the College of Translators, an agency whose literal name was the "Office of the Four Kinds of Barbarians," since China considered itself the center of world civilization, surrounded by barbarians to the north, east, south and west. At the time, the main "barbarians" China had to deal with were the various Mongol tribes to the north, who had been masters of China in the previous dynasty, as well as Koreans and Japanese to the east, Uigurs and Tibetans to the west and various aboriginal tribes in the south and southwest. A tiny cloud looming on the horizon was the Manchus under their chief Nurhaci, who were beginning to build a coalition whose forces would sixty years later cross the Great Wall and put all of China once again under alien yoke. But few in China at the time took note of such a threat.

Barbarians from the West, such as the Portuguese and the Italians, were seen as even less of a threat, hardly making an impact on the Chinese consciousness, although by the mid-sixteenth century the Portuguese were engaging in illicit trading with China on a small scale. When Qin Yao became head of the Office of the Four Kinds of Barbarians, the Portuguese were already entrenched in the tiny enclave of Macao. At the time, Matteo Ricci, the Italian missionary, had just launched the Jesuit penetration of China.

In 1582, Grand Secretary Zhang died and he was given posthumous honors, including the title superior pillar of the state. But with his death, his enemies began to emerge. They accused Zhang of everything from corruption to treason. His home was ransacked and his sons tortured to extract confessions from them. His posthumous titles were withdrawn. And men he had put in power were themselves under attack.

Qin Yao was one of them. The vice-administrator of Peking prefecture submitted a memorial in which he accused Yao of having acted as a "bloodhound" for Zhang when Yao was with the Office of Scrutiny for Personnel, criticizing whomever Zhang wanted. He called for Yao's dismissal from his post of vice-minister of the Court of Imperial Sacrifices. Other voices, too, were raised.

And although Yao was not dismissed, his ascent was halted. In the next four years, he made only lateral shifts, being transferred to the Court of the Imperial Stud, then to the Court of Imperial Entertainments, which was indirectly under the Ministry of Rites and was responsible for providing the drinks and delicacies required for sacrifices and ceremonial banquets.

In 1586, he became governor—literally "Inspector and Pacifier" —of Nankan, a rugged region far from any provincial capital. He was given the additional title of assistant censor-in-chief. As governor, Qin Yao was not considered a member of any particular governmental agency but rather a surrogate of the emperor, accountable only to him. The Nankan area had been troubled by bandits, mostly Yao tribesmen, for decades, and during the first decade of the Wanli era, they grew active again.

One large group was led by Li Pei, grandson of the leader against whom Wang Yangming had fought at the time of Qin Jin. A second group was led by Li Yuanlang, a monk who was a member of the White Lotus Sect, a mystical religious cult that formed the basis of rebel movements up to the twentieth century, and who had a large following among the superstitious local people, especially young men.

That year, a drought struck Longnan, in Jiangxi; no crops could be grown and many people, faced with famine, rose in rebellion. Li Yuanlang proclaimed himself king and declared that he had been sent by heaven to take over the empire. Making use of charms and spells, he ordered the various armies to dress in black and to synchronize their attacks. He raised his own flag, a banner sporting the symbol of a mountain, and went to Longnan, a place of strategic importance, with several hundred followers, and selected a date on which to perform a special ceremony to inaugurate his uprising. After chanting prayers, he and his followers launched attacks on travelers, seizing large numbers of horses.

Three days after Qin Yao's arrival in Nankan, he ordered an attack on the bandit lair of Shengang. Li Pei was caught in a surprise swoop and his army was eliminated.

However, Li Yuanlang's forces were still intact. When they attacked the town of Nanxiong, the local defenders requested reinforcements and Qin Yao, with the help of several generals, moved his armies to cut off the supply lines of the bandits. A decisive battle took place at Nanshao, and Li Yuanlang, instead of fighting, resorted to spells and incantations. Many of the rebels were slain and Li

Yuanlang and twenty of his key followers were taken alive. Eventually, Li Yuanlang and fifteen of his men were executed at Longnan, while others were jailed.[5]

After the battles, Qin Yao and three of his colleagues filed a joint memorial reporting their success in clearing the bandits from the area, and proposing measures to help the people of the war-torn region.

As a result of his triumph in the Shengang battle, Qin Yao was promoted a full rank and awarded 20 taels of silver. The emperor wrote in his own hand four characters, "Qin-hou You-gong," that is, "Meritorious in Bandit-Catching," on a plaque that stayed in the family for generations.

It is interesting to note that, in 1587, the year the Shengang fighting began, Qin Yao was required to submit a memorial evaluating his own performance in government. Such evaluations, as we have seen, were often used by grand secretaries and the minister of personnel to get rid of their political opponents and promote their allies.

The form of the self-examination memorial was stylized and the language stilted, filled with terms of the most abject humility.

In his self-examination, Qin Yao summarized his career, listing all his appointments, then added:

"I realize that I am stupid and without talent, and that only because of good fortune have I been able to draw a salary from the court for seventeen years. My work has been superficial and unimportant. I am deeply ashamed of occupying a post of which I am unworthy, and I fear I am not capable of performing my duties well.

"The area where I am based is at the boundary of four provinces [Jiangxi, Guangdong, Guangxi and Fujian] and the official in charge holds the key to the area. I am far too foolish and irresponsible to hold such a position. I beg Your Majesty to order the Ministry of Personnel to have me demoted and replaced by someone more talented, so that Your Majesty's mind may rest at ease, and so that I myself will feel less anxious. I beg your forgiveness and I await your instructions."

Naturally, no such action was taken, not after Qin Yao's triumphs over the Shengang rebels. Instead, in late 1589 he was made governor of Huguang province and promoted to vice censor-in-chief. History was repeating itself. Qin Yao, born the year of Qin Jin's death, now held the same post that Qin Jin had occupied seventy-three years earlier, and at the same age.

When Yao arrived in Huguang, the province was plagued with drought. He memorialized the court, requesting help for the affected areas and asking for local taxes to be spent on famine relief. He graphically described the devastation he had seen while traveling to his new post. He wrote:

I went to Huangmei from Jiujiang and traveled slowly through the province. What I saw was tragic and shocking. Between Hanyang, Jiangshan and Yingcheng, the roads were full of corpses. I felt so shaken that I feared that most of the nearby regions were in a similar state. I sent notices out to all those in charge of prefectures, subprefectures and counties to use government funds to hire laborers to bury all the exposed corpses. When I finished with these errands and returned to the city, I saw that the hungry had streamed in from the countryside. They no longer resembled human beings, with their long hair and naked bodies. They thronged in, crying and screaming. Although the government warehouses were thrown open and food provided, many died. Again, I ordered all the local government leaders to bury the dead without delay.

I mention these sights because I witnessed them. Regarding what I did not observe, I have no idea how many thousands are involved. I asked the local elders, and they told me, "Calamities have occurred many times, but nothing like this has ever happened before. Last spring the soil was so bad that the rice seedlings could not be transplanted. In autumn locusts came. Last winter, people ate grass and ferns; this year, even these are gone. We can survive another fortnight, but our food will be depleted by winter. The old and the weak are awaiting death. Even the strong are hungry and, once they fall, they cannot rise. The richer families are trying to sell their farms at low prices but can find no buyers. The poor try to give away their children but can find none willing to adopt them."

After I heard these words, I could not sleep and I lost my appetite. I am trying to find a way to save these people. When I first assumed this job, I ordered all those in charge of the financial affairs of prefectures and counties for a full account of what they could provide. All of them have reported that their areas were flooded in the fourteenth and fifteenth years [1586 and 1587] and struck by drought in the sixteenth [1588]. They have no money or food left to help other areas. Furthermore, bandits appeared from Qihuang, Changsha and elsewhere and they preyed on the merchants. I, with the help of local officials, have taken action to suppress their activities. Now the bandit problem has somewhat subsided, but such manifestations are an indication of chaos. It has been said, "When people are poor, bandits arise; when bandits arise, people get poorer." The southern people are cunning and violent. The future fills me with apprehension.

I understand that Your Majesty took pity on the population of Zhejiang and the Southern Metropolitan Region after they suffered calamities by waiving their requirement to deliver tribute grain to the north and allowing them to use these funds to pay for local military expenditures. This policy was welcomed by both soldiers and civilians. Now, of the 123 counties within the 15 prefectures in my jurisdiction, I have discovered that 117 of them have been struck by natural calamities, and only 6 have not been affected. The extent of damage is greater than that of Zhejiang and the Southern Metropolitan Region. Your Majesty's family originated in the southern provinces and you must have a special affection for the people in this region. I hope Your Majesty will have pity on them.

The people have always been the foundation of a country. No ruler has ever been at peace without the support of his people. Now all the people in the south are dying. It is appropriate to save them using the policy Your Majesty approved for Zhejiang and the Southern Metropolitan Region. However, Huguang is 2,000 li [about 700 miles] from Peking, and money from the central treasury may take a long time to arrive. I dare not request you to send us funds. But, on behalf of the people, I would like to beg that fines levied on Huguang that remain unpaid and 30 percent of the tribute rice due, together with silver from customs duty levied at Jingzhou, be waived so that the money can be spent locally. I realize that this request has no precedent. The money is due to be sent to Peking soon. But we wish to retain these funds to help the people or else we have no way to survive. I dare to present this memorial to Your Majesty because, just as I cannot cook without rice, so I cannot withhold information from Your Majesty. The order to remit the fines and taxes has arrived, and I am bold enough to request that Your Majesty reverse the order because of the merit that Your Majesty would gain from such an act.

The people of Huguang are weak and dying. This is the worst calamity they have ever suffered. If we do not do something for them, then when further misfortune occurs, it will be too late.[6]

Qin Yao's request was approved, and he was subsequently credited with saving the lives of several hundred thousand people. By the time Yao left Huguang a year later, the price of grain had fallen and refugees who had fled the devastated province had returned.

In the spring of 1590, Qin Yao was called upon to put down a bandit uprising in the south near Guangdong province. In a three-week campaign, he captured the bandit leader and wiped out several hundred of the bandit troops.

Qin Yao, forty-five, was in the prime of life and appeared to have at least two more decades to advance his career. But fate determined otherwise.

With the posthumous disgrace of Grand Secretary Zhang, Qin Yao had become vulnerable. Although the first attempts to get rid of him were unsuccessful, another attempt was made seven years later. This time it succeeded.

The exact sequence of events is unclear, but it seems the attack against him was launched toward the end of 1590. A censor fired the first broadside, submitting a memorial in which he accused Yao of factionalism. This was followed by one from another censor accusing Yao of sycophantic behavior toward those in power. The minister of personnel also called for his dismissal. As a result of these and other criticisms, Yao was suspended from his post, but the imperial order made it clear that he was to await a new assignment.

About this time, another charge was leveled against Yao. Evidently, Yao had attempted to win himself the support of influential officials by making them substantial gifts of money, a common enough practice at the time. The charge, however, was that Yao had used government funds in order to buy influence. The issue, therefore, was not one of mere bribery but the more serious one of embezzlement of government funds. Apparently, Yao's defense was that the money did not come from the government treasury but had come from fines, and that use of such funds for entertainment and other official purposes was long sanctioned by practice.

Qin Yao went to Peking to answer the charges brought against him. He found temporary lodgings in a temple. In those days, temples, like inns, offered accommodations for travelers, and the facilities were often of a high quality, though the food served was all vegetarian, with the charges for room and board paid in the form of donations. When he went to court to defend himself, he submitted a memorial in his own defense, and expected that at most he would be given a mild punishment. But Li Zhen, his successor as governor of Huguang, criticized him very strongly.

At the time, there was a rumor that an extremely favorable report on Yao's bandit-suppression activities was about to come in from Guangdong. The belief spread that the emperor would reinstate him. But just then, one of Yao's subordinates, Shen Fu, in charge of the subprefecture of Hengzhou, submitted an extremely detailed list of accusations against Yao, specifying dates when his personal servants visited each prefecture and county, the names of the servants, and the amounts exacted from each local government. Shen Fu accused Yao of having embezzled well over 100,000 taels of silver from local authorities in Huguang province.

This tipped the balance against Yao. An investigation into the charges was ordered. The Office of Scrutiny for Personnel eventually presented a long and detailed case against Qin Yao.

"We have found that one or two governors were extremely greedy, often using government funds for private business. They pocketed fines and, when they left their posts, bribed their superiors with thousands of taels of silver. If the official turned down the bribe, they put the money in their own pockets. These courtiers bring shame upon the government. They were assigned to administer large areas. With such examples, how will local officials behave?

"Now the subprefect of Hengzhou, Shen Fu, has filed charges against Qin Yao, who has been forced to step down. Qin Yao dipped his hands into the treasuries of fifteen prefectures and stole over 100,000 taels of silver.

"In the eleventh month of the eighteenth year of Wanli [1590], Censor Guo Shi accused Qin Yao and he was suspended. The light sentence was a result of Qin Yao being protected by the powerful. Yao despaired over being reinstated. On the second and nineteenth day of that month, however, he ordered his servants Liu Yingwang and Liu Sheng to deliver a note to Shengzhou and Yongzhou prefectures to obtain 800 taels of silver. With this money, he sent 200 taels each to Grand Secretary Shen, Grand Secretary Xu and Grand

Secretary Wang; he obtained 300 taels from Guiyang, Shenzhou and Taozhou and used the money to bribe Guangxi Commander Li and Joint Military Commander of Guangdong and Guangxi Liu, giving 40 taels to the former and 60 taels to the latter. He obtained 80 taels from each of the following places: Laiyang, Hengyang, Chiyang, Lingling, and 60 taels each from Anyan, Yinwu, Changning, Hengshan, Lanshan, Ningyuan, Jianghua and Yungou and sent the money to Military Commander of Guangdong and Guangxi Liu, Guangxi Pacifier Cai and Guangxi Commander Zhang. The note also stipulated that the money should be given to the servant and no record was to be kept."

This damning account of Yao's nefarious activities was followed by a recitation of previous wrongdoings, some of which were petty. Once, the Office of Scrutiny said, Yao sent his servants to buy cloth, presumably as presents for influential officials, and the servants shortchanged local officials by 9 taels of silver. On another occasion, officials in one locality had to turn over a hundred bolts of cloth to Yao's servants without payment. "So we can see that the local officials had to bear a heavy burden to satisfy Yao," the report concluded.

As a result of the investigation, Yao was found guilty as charged. He was told to repay the embezzled amount, totaling perhaps 100,000 taels of silver. Worse, he was ordered into exile.

Qin Yao paid the fine, which reportedly amounted to one-tenth of his estate, but, for some reason, he did not go into exile. That portion of his sentence was commuted, so it is said, through the influence of a princess to whom Yao paid the astronomical bribe of 100,000 taels of silver. Though the identity of this lady was never disclosed, she was presumably an older member of the imperial family, who exercised some influence over the emperor. Nevertheless, as far as the official record is concerned, there was no such commutation.

There are several unverifiable stories relating to how Qin Yao amassed his vast fortune. One story is that when he was ordered to fight bandit forces, he would announce ahead of time when his troops would storm their mountain strongholds. Forewarned, the bandits would flee, but without their booty. When Yao's troops arrived, they were spared a battle and Yao confiscated all the gold and silver.

That particular story generated a serious debate long after his death—a debate that once again illustrates the Chinese perception of life, which sees the actions of a person affecting his descendants, whether for good or ill. If a person accumulates merits during his lifetime, the reasoning goes, his descendants for many generations will benefit. And vice versa.

Many of Yao's descendants in later years became prosperous and successful, and some people attributed this to Yao's having accumulated much merit during his lifetime. These merits, it was said, were earned because Yao had saved lives by giving the bandits time to escape instead of engaging them in battle.

Others disagreed. According to a book that contains fascinating accounts of Wuxi and its personalities, "If the bandits were not harmful to the people, they should have been pacified but not attacked. But if they were harmful, they should have been attacked. When these bandits heard about an attack they fled, so they obviously were not very fierce. Even if an official received an order from the court to wipe out these groups, the general in charge ought to give them the chance to surrender. In this way, we can say that the merit gained is indeed great. But no merit can be earned by anyone who allowed the bandits to flee and then seized their property."[7]

The dismissal of Qin Yao in the winter of 1590–1591 occurred when the Wanli Emperor was twenty-seven years old, while he still took some interest in governance. Soon thereafter, his interest began to wane, so that eventually he neglected virtually all his imperial duties. Traditionally, the emperor held daily audiences with his ministers to discuss affairs of state. The Wanli Emperor, however, even when young, held court irregularly and reluctantly. In 1589 he stopped attending general audiences at court. In 1591, he stopped participating in public ceremonial activities. For the next thirty years of his reign, power lay in the hands of others.[8]

The emperor's interest in affairs of state extended only to taxes levied to satisfy his whims. He instituted new taxes and authorized eunuchs to travel around the country to collect them. He refused even to meet with his grand secretaries, dealing with them only through his eunuchs. From 1603 to 1614 he held only one meeting with his grand secretaries. He held another audience in 1615, and another just before his death in 1620.

Such negligence meant that much of the machinery of government was paralyzed. Memorials lay unanswered. The refusal of the emperor to respond to them, even to those requesting permission to retire, resulted in aging, ill or just disillusioned officials leaving their posts and retiring without permission. At one time, a single minister simultaneously headed three of the six ministries. The others were headed only by vice-ministers. In the provinces, half the local positions were unfilled.

Yet no one could assume responsibility for the government because such an act would amount to usurpation. By default, the eunuchs rose to power, since they alone had access to the emperor. Factions multiplied. The Wanli Emperor's legacy was government paralysis, deep-seated factionalism and a weakened bureaucratic as well as military structure that was to lead to the eventual downfall of the dynasty. His inept heirs hastened the decline so that, within twenty-four years of the death of the Wanli Emperor, Peking fell first to the rebel leader Li Zicheng, then to the Manchus, who went on to conquer all of China.

There is no parallel for this in Chinese history. The only other period in peacetime when the Chinese government was unable to function normally, though for very different reasons, was during the Cultural Revolution decade of 1966–1976, when again many government positions were left unfilled as their incumbents were denounced as "capitalist roaders" and purged, or sent down to the countryside for "reeducation" in an orgy of political fanaticism. For years, the country did not have a head of state. Ministers and heads of bureaus and departments vanished, to be replaced by untitled "responsible persons." Mao, the modern-day emperor, was inaccessible to all but a small clique whose members conveyed messages to and from him to those who theoretically had the responsibility for running the country.

Qin Yao spent the last thirteen years of his life living like a hermit in Wuxi. The famous garden built by Qin Jin and taken over by Qin Liang was bought by Qin Yao, who renamed it Ji Chang Yuan, or "The Garden of Leisure." He had it landscaped once more. When the work was finished, the garden had twenty sites, each of which depicted special scenery. Qin Yao wrote twenty poems, one for each of the scenes, and had them published as a book. In the preface, he said:

"The collective name of my garden is Leisure. It is ideal for ascending the heights or for composing poems while listening to the music of the streams."[9]

Qin Yao also built a shrine to Guan Di, the god of war, revered not only for his bravery but also for his rectitude and loyalty. By

181

honoring Guan Di, Yao was saying that he, too, was not only a man of courage but also of personal integrity.

But the disgrace of Qin Yao was considered such a stain on the family honor that, eight generations later, one of his descendants, Qin Ying, wrote a defense of his ancestor called "Refuting a Frame-up."[10] In this, he declared that Yao had been victimized, and pointed to the fate of his accusers as evidence. None of them came to a good end, he said. Shen Fu, his main accuser, was later executed for corruption and his father was forced to commit suicide. Qin Ying wrote: "Right after my ancestor's death, misfortune befell Shen Fu and his father, probably because my ancestor's spirit had lodged a complaint in the netherworld and won the case."

Qin Yao died in 1604. The month after his death, Yao's enormous estate was divided among his heirs. The property-settlement document, properly drawn up, was witnessed by four persons: Yao's brother, his brother-in-law, his son-in-law and his nephew.

The heirs were listed in hierarchical order, with the wife before the concubines, the sons before the daughters, and the sons of the wife before the sons of the concubine. However, the sons' inheritance was much greater than that of their mothers. The daughters obtained the least. One adopted daughter, in fact, did not receive anything directly, but she was expected to inherit her adopted mother's share after the older woman's demise.

Yao's income came from two primary sources: rent from farmlands and moneylending. So vast were Yao's holdings that, even after they had been divided and subdivided, his children, grandchildren and great-grandchildren were considered among the wealthiest people in Wuxi.

Although Yao died in 1604, he was not buried until six years later, presumably because his children wanted to be sure of an auspicious burial date. The burial site itself was chosen by Yao himself while he was still alive. As was the practice at the time, a plot of land near the grave was given in perpetuity to a peasant family named Zhou, whose responsibility it was to look after the grave from generation to generation.

Incredibly enough, in mid-1985, when I made another research trip to Wuxi, I uncovered this grave, and met the descendants of the Zhou family. I was sure the grave had been destroyed because the *muzhiming* had been dug up and damaged to such an extent that rubbings made of them were largely illegible. If the underground burial stones had been dug up, I assumed, the grave itself must be empty.

I couldn't have been more wrong. Following a crude map of the gravesite, I went with my cousin Zhihao, the museum curator Gu Wenbi, my sister Priscilla and her two sons in search of the grave. Gu Wenbi located a peasant named Shao, who led us to the site, only a short distance up a hill from the road. On the other side of the road were vegetable patches and the rump of what used to be a stone sheep, as well as part of another stone animal that had stood guard along the path to the grave.

Shao took us to see a young woman named Zhou Jinfu, a descendant of the family that had been entrusted with caring for the grave in 1610. She told us that they had discharged their obligations right up to the time of the Cultural Revolution. But then, she said, they were unable to continue to do so because of the political turmoil. It turned out that the Red Guards did attempt to dig up the grave, but it was so solidly built they were not able to make much of a dent. The Red Guards managed to dig up the burial tablets, which they shattered.

I could not help being amazed by the continuity of Chinese society. Here was a peasant family that had faithfully tended my ancestor's grave for over a dozen generations. They had continued to discharge their obligations despite changes in dynasty, revolutions, wars and natural disasters. It made me more aware of the great cohesion underlying Chinese society, a cohesion that remains despite all the changes.

CHAPTER TWELVE

Qin Yong: Ming Loyalist and Philosopher

In the northeastern section of Wuxi stands a cluster of undistinguished buildings of the type that abounds in China today: unimaginative, utilitarian, no-nonsense structures of brick and concrete. These house the Donglin Elementary School, where pupils, many of whom wear around their necks the red scarf that marks them as members of the Young Pioneers, scamper around the basketball court when class is out. In the midst of this sea of children stands a magnificent three-tiered stone arch about thirty feet high supported by four columns. Each tier is marked by latticed masonry that culminates on both ends with upturned eaves topped by curlicues resembling rearing sea lions. In the center of the arch is a plaque with four words written in the old manner, from right to left. They say "Old Traces of Donglin."

Behind the arch is a large, walled compound of relatively recent vintage but built in the old style, with sloping tiled roofs. This is the Donglin Museum, built in the 1980s to commemorate events that occurred more than three hundred years ago. The museum stands on the site of the old Donglin Academy, which for several decades during the seventeenth century was a major political force.

The Donglin Academy was the nub of a nationwide intellectual ferment to restore Confucian political and philosophical values to the debilitated Ming court. As we have seen, by the seventeenth century, the caliber of the Ming emperors had so degenerated that most lacked any interest in governance, permitting their eunuchs, wet nurses and in-laws to abuse the imperial authority.

The Donglin Academy attempted to restore moral values to the court. Its adherents spanned the empire, though most of its strength was concentrated in cities along the Yangtze River valley. In its heyday, it dominated the upper echelons of the government. But

184

its success was short-lived, and in the mid-1620s, members of the banned "Donglin Party" were subjected to horrifying persecution by the most notorious eunuch dictator in Chinese history, Wei Zhongxian.

Members of the academy were dismissed from government posts, imprisoned, exiled, tortured and killed. The academy's leader, Gao Panlong, committed suicide by drowning himself in a pond, dressed in his robes of office, when news that members of the eunuch-controlled Embroidered-Uniform Guard were in Wuxi to arrest him. After Gao's death, Chief Eunuch Wei ordered the complete physical destruction of the academy: Not a stone was left upon a stone. The struggle was between the leaders of a moral crusade and the forces represented by Eunuch Wei, who had usurped the powers of the emperor and was using them for his own glorification. The emperor, having no interest in affairs of state, devoted himself to his favorite hobby, carpentry.

What struck me when I visited the Donglin Museum was that the Ming dynasty academy still remains a symbol of righteousness and that there are people in China today who see themselves as the heirs of this moral tradition.

Among them is Liao Mosha, a well-known intellectual, who lays claim to being the contemporary heir to the Donglin spirit.

Liao Mosha was a member of a coterie of prominent intellectuals known as the Three Family Village, which included the historian Wu Han and an outstanding writer and editor named Deng Tuo, who served as vice-mayor of Peking. All three men were viciously persecuted in the Cultural Revolution, and Liao Mosha spent eight years in prison. But at least he survived the ordeal. His two colleagues did not.[1]

One of the first broadsides that signaled the launching of the Cultural Revolution was a criticism of a play written by Wu Han about an upright Ming dynasty official who was dismissed after having criticized the emperor. Wu Han was accused of ostensibly criticizing the Ming emperor for the dismissal while actually attacking Chairman Mao for having dismissed the popular defense minister who had dared to speak out against the Great Leap Forward, Mao's disastrous attempt to achieve China's rapid industrialization.[2]

These members of the Three Family Village were persecuted as a direct result of their views of the Donglin Academy. Deng Tuo was an admirer of the founder of the academy, Gu Xiancheng, and in a newspaper article had singled out a couplet written by Gu Xiancheng in which the Ming dynasty philosopher called on people in general to take an interest in affairs of state. Deng Tuo's critics pointed out that the Donglin Academy was in effect an opposition party to the Ming court and that by praising it Deng Tuo was advocating opposition to rule by the Communist party.

But in 1982, six years after China emerged from the Cultural Revolution, the authorities of Wuxi decided to open the Donglin Museum. To mark the opening, the only survivor of Three Family Village was invited to provide a sample of his calligraphy that could be displayed in the main hall. Liao Mosha agreed and submitted two lines, which turned out to be the couplet written by the founder of the academy and praised by Deng Tuo. And those words are now on two wooden pillars in the main hall.

The political significance of Liao Mosha's calligraphy in the Donglin Museum would not be lost on the Chinese. Most people in China, for instance, know that the masthead of the official newspaper, the *People's Daily*, was inscribed by Mao, as was the name of the Peking Railway Station. It is considered a great honor for an institution to have its name inscribed by a well-known political or cultural figure.

A particularly telling example is that of the *Chungking Daily*, the main paper in Sichuan, Deng Xiaoping's home province. The paper had requested Deng, a native son, to provide a specimen of his calligraphy to use on its masthead, and Deng had complied. Then, when Deng was purged in the Cultural Revolution as the "No. 2 person in authority in the party taking the capitalist road," his calligraphy was taken down by the paper's politically canny editors. In 1975, when Deng was temporarily rehabilitated to assist the cancer-stricken Premier Zhou Enlai in running the country, the *Chungking Daily* resurrected his masthead. But the following year, when Deng fell from power a second time immediately after the death of Premier Zhou, down came the masthead again. After the death of Mao and the return to power of Deng, the *Chungking Daily* once more proudly displayed on its masthead the calligraphy of China's top leader.

The Donglin Academy was started by Gu Xiancheng, a major philosopher and politician, in 1604—the year Qin Yao died—after he was forced into retirement by factional infighting at court. The founders included Gu's brother, Gu Yuncheng, Gao Panlong, An Xifan and several other leading philosophers from Wuxi and its environs. Gu and his associates not only expounded on Confucian precepts, they also criticized the policies of the imperial court. So influential did their academy become that similar institutes sprang up in neighboring cities, the members of which also became identified as Donglin partisans.

Though far from the capital, the Donglin Academy was able to exert considerable influence, thwarting the appointment of people it deemed unsuitable for high office. The death of the Wanli Emperor in 1620 marked a turning point. He was succeeded by his son Taichang, who died the following month. So Wanli's fifteen-year-old grandson ascended the throne as the Tianqi Emperor. Because the chief eunuch, Wang An, was sympathetic to the Donglin partisans, many of them were recalled to court, some after having spent the last twenty or twenty-five years in retirement. By that time, Gu Xiancheng had died and Gao Panlong had taken over as head of the academy. He and other Donglin men were given high posts. The Donglin party was no longer the opposition. It was at the height of its power.

Though the rise of the Donglin partisans was rapid, their fall was even more precipitous, for their ally, Chief Eunuch Wang An, was framed and murdered by his rival, Eunuch Wei Zhongxian, in that same year of 1620. The Tianqi Emperor left the government in the hands of his trusted Eunuch Wei, and his former wet-nurse, the Lady Ke. These two forged a formidable alliance and dominated the inner court.

Events came to a head when a protégé of the senior grand secretary ordered the flogging of a eunuch. Wei's eunuch army surrounded the house of the senior grand secretary, humiliating the old man into submitting his resignation. A political bloodbath followed, as Donglin men, including Gao Panlong, were either disgraced or forced into retirement. Lists were drawn up of Donglin partisans, and hundreds of men were marked for persecution. Chief Eunuch Wei was not satisfied with ousting them from office. He had them struck off the rolls of officials and reduced to the status of commoners or sent to remote frontier regions to serve as foot soldiers. More than a dozen leading Donglin figures were arrested and tortured to death in the palace prison.[3]

In April 1626, a detachment of imperial guardsmen arrived in Wuxi to arrest Gao Panlong, who, as we know, committed suicide. The eunuch Wei charged Gao's elder son with failure to prevent his father's death and sent him to the frontier to serve as a common soldier.

The Donglin Academy had set up rules and regulations, encapsulating them into easy-to-remember formulas known as the "Nine Advantages" and the "Nine Harms."

The teachings of Gao Panlong and the other founders of the Donglin Academy had a great impact on their disciples. Gao was a staunch upholder of traditional Confucianism. He always started with introspection, saying, "Only he who knows how to reflect and examine himself is truly able to investigate things," adding, "If, upon examining ourselves, we find ourselves sincere, all things of the world without exception are within us."[4]

Philosophy was for Gao the practical task of self-perfection, which he pursued with great earnestness. He exercised strict self-control and subjected himself to a rigorous daily routine to achieve quiescence of mind. For Gao this was a restful return of the mind to itself, a passive awareness of its nature.

To achieve this end, Gao advocated meditation or, literally, "sitting quietly" without thinking. He wrote: "To sit quietly, clear the mind and be intimately aware of the heavenly norm, means that at the time of sitting quietly our mind, being cleared from all affairs, is identical with the so-called heavenly norm, and all one has to do at this time is to be silently aware of this inner self."

The concept of sudden enlightenment, which is found in Zen Buddhism, has a place in Gao's thinking. Indeed, he spoke of his own: "Thereupon," he said, "as if cut off, all the entanglements of my worries were gone, and suddenly something like a burden of a hundred pounds fell with a crash to the ground. It furthermore penetrated my body and my soul like a flash of lightning, and thereupon I became fused with the Great Change. There was no longer a separation of heaven and man, interior and exterior; now I saw that the six points [east, south, west, north, zenith, nadir] are all mind, that the breast is its realm, and the square-inch [heart] is its proper seat. If one understands it deeply one cannot speak of a location at all."[5]

As a result of this enlightenment, he gained the insight that all external happenings are only relative, that "fundamentally there is no life and no death," which made him view death as "a return" and enabled him to meet it with composure.

One of Gao Panlong's favorite disciples in the Donglin Academy was Qin Ercai, grandson of Qin Liang.

As a student at the Donglin Academy, Qin Ercai used to go to Gao's cottage by the river to seek his instruction and to meditate, or "sit quietly."

On one occasion, Ercai asked Gao about self-cultivation. Gao told him, "When a person becomes confused, it is occasioned by the near and not the far. Take your clan for example. It is very big. There are those who are cold and hungry. They are right before your eyes but you don't see them. Your heart is withering. How can you talk about cultivation?"

Ercai was delighted by these remarks, and he explained, "I have been thinking of the poor for a long time. I have always wanted to honor the filial sons and to use 300 mou of southern farmland to help the poor, but I have not done it."[6]

A year after enrolling in the academy as a student, Ercai became an associate lecturer. However, he died two years later, leaving behind his widow and three sons. When he died Gao was at his side. Ercai commanded his oldest son, ten-year-old Yong, to kneel before Gao and ask to be accepted as his student. Gao composed Ercai's epitaph, which read in part:

"He was a naturally good person. To turn a good person toward the good is as easy as channeling water down the valley or lighting firewood. However, to turn him toward evil ways is like taking fire out from a pond or extracting water from the flames. To lead him toward the good is like listening to exquisite music or eating delicacies. To lead him toward evil is like sticking a thorn in the eye or inhaling foul odors."

Gao tutored Yong for fourteen years until he became one of the primary exponents of Gao's philosophy.

In 1621, when the Donglin partisans were in the ascendancy, Gao was summoned to Peking to be vice minister of the Grand Court of Revision. Two years later, having offended powerful interests by his insistence on the application of strict moral codes, he retired to Wuxi and resumed the running of the academy. At this time, Yong finally became a licentiate at the age of twenty-six.

The following year, Gao was called out of retirement; he accepted the post of vice-minister of justice, and later, that of censor-in-chief. But his tenure in office was brief. Gao accused a regional inspector of venality; that official sought the protection of Eunuch Wei, pledging to be his adopted son. In the subsequent test of strength, the Donglin partisans were roundly defeated and Gao was back in Wuxi by the end of the year.

Over the next few years, the persecution continued: Donglin men were being arrested and tortured, the Donglin Academy was declared subversive and ordered destroyed and Gao himself committed suicide. But by the time Yong passed the provincial examinations in 1630, the Donglin controversy was largely over.

On the death of the Tianqi Emperor, Eunuch Wei and his supporters fell from power. The eunuch was ordered to commit suicide by strangling himself, and when Yong gained the highest degree in 1637, the academy had resumed functioning. In fact, that year saw a large number of Donglin adherents win the highest degree.

Gao Shitai, nephew of Gao Panlong and a fellow student and friend of Yong's, took over the running of the Donglin Academy for the remaining thirty years of his life, well into the beginning of the Qing dynasty.

Qin Yong's official career began in 1637, as the Ming dynasty was drawing to a close. The signs were clear. In the northwest, a bandit leader, styled the "Dashing General," put himself at the head of a vast rebel army. In the north, Manchu forces were being consolidated under a leader who moved his capital progressively closer to the Chinese border. Still, the Ming court remained oblivious. The imperial coffers were almost empty, their contents having been frittered away by the Wanli Emperor and his descendants. Infighting by eunuchs and outer-court officials had further weakened the government. The most capable officials had become casualties and many were disgraced, exiled or executed.

In this atmosphere Yong took up his first post as magistrate of Qingjiang district, in Jiangxi. To familiarize himself with the history and geography of the place, Yong asked for a copy of the latest edition of the local gazetteer. When he learned that there had not been a written record for over three hundred years, he spent all his free time reconstructing the history of the district. When he came across the names of deceased village elders, he tried to find out about their lives from their descendants; when he traveled in the countryside, he spoke to the illiterate farmers; and when he came across old plaques erected by the roadside, he would copy down whatever inscriptions were still legible. The residents cooperated by occasionally sending him essays on local events and customs. He also held discussions with older members of the community, seeking their counsel. Finally, in 1641, he started writing.

He traced the history of Qingjiang all the way back to the founding of the Ming dynasty in the fourteenth century. In explaining his own action, Yong said: "Although Qingjiang is a small place, it is an important part of Jiangxi. The source of its mountains and rivers, the details of its farming and taxation, the rise and fall of individuals, more than half of this information was missing since the era of Hongwu and Yong-le. If I say I don't have time to do it now and leave it to someone else, after several decades or several hundred years a lot more information will be missing. Now, even though the book contains gaps and some of the information is erratic, it may still be of some use to future scholars. I felt that as long as one thousandth of the information could be retained, it was worthwhile. I regard Qingjiang as my family and the people there as my fathers, my sons and my brothers. When I leave, I will think of them and they will think of me. Whenever I pick up a copy of this book to read, I will feel that I am once more walking on this soil and seeing the people."[7]

As an official, Yong put into practice the teachings of the Donglin Academy. At the time, the area was struck by famine and banditry was rife. The wealthy had themselves categorized as families responsible for keeping horses that could be requisitioned in case of war, thus winning tax exemptions. The tax burden on others was oppressively heavy. To give some relief to the poor, Yong ordered those who had joined the lower levels of government service to pay taxes.[8]

At the time, bandits were active in the vicinity of Tianchang. Yong set a trap for them by dressing his soldiers like farmers and sending them to Tianchang. The bandit leader, lured by the seemingly defenseless farmers, tried to rob them and was caught, together with his whole gang.

Another bandit leader had successfully evaded capture until Yong devised a strategy to deal with him. He pretended to lead his troops on a mission that took them past the bandit's home. Seeing that Yong was headed elsewhere, the bandit relaxed his vigilance. Once Yong's troops passed his house, however, they turned back and caught him off guard.

Yong wrote a series of songs to be sung by the farmers while working. Known as the "Songs of the Four Prohibitions" and the

191

"Songs of Five Persuasions," they each had their own moral message, exhorting people to live as good members of society.

The Four Prohibitions told people not to steal or rob, not to go against established social customs, not to be too quick to lodge accusations with the government against other people, and not to take life too lightly and commit suicide.

The Five Persuasions recommended paying taxes promptly, working on communal water-conservancy projects, working industriously at one's assigned task, fulfilling neighborhood security obligations and building storehouses for grain.

Judging by the songs, what upset Yong the most appears to have been a growing custom for young men to join the families of their brides, presumably because the bride's family had no sons. Yong saw this as a perversion of nature, which intended girls to leave their homes and join the households of their husbands. His song condemning this practice went to fifty-four lines, more than three times the length of the others. Part of it went like this:

> It's unreal, like a puppet show.
> Flesh and blood are reversed.
> Oh, sorrowful are the parents
> To see their son depart.
> Money is as heavy as the mountains
> While bone and flesh are light as feathers.
> Adoption of the son-in-law
> Is turning the whole world mad.
> What is needed is a return
> To the good customs of yore.[9]

Yong served in Qingjiang for five years. When he left, the townspeople were reluctant to see him go. They accompanied him for over a day, and escorted him almost a hundred miles beyond the city walls. They brought food with them, as well as wine and fruit, and served him a meal every few hours.

From Qingjiang, Yong went to the capital. In the summer of 1643, Yong and twenty-six colleagues went to the Ministry of Personnel for reassignment. At that time, the northeastern areas had been hit by fighting, and officials were required to replace those who had either died or vacated their posts. Yong was named magistrate of

Fenglai district in Shandong, which had been the scene of three major battles. He spent six months there.

In 1644, Yong was due to be reassigned again, but first he went home to Wuxi for a vacation. It was while Yong was on holiday that the dynasty came to an end. A huge rebel force led by "Dashing General" Li Zicheng laid siege to Peking. The nearest Ming army was encamped at the Great Wall to keep the Manchus at bay. Bereft of aid, Emperor Chongzhen, fifteenth successor of Founding Emperor Zhu Yuanzhang, hanged himself from a tree on Coal Hill.[10] The Ming dynasty had finally lost the mandate of heaven.

The day the emperor committed suicide, not a single official came to the mourning audience. Li Zicheng marched into Peking at the head of his troops, unaware that the emperor was dead, and encountered no resistance. The Ming cause had no champions left in the capital.

Among those who had abandoned the dynasty was Qin Xian, Yong's nephew. Xian and some other officials, all Wuxi men, decided to throw in their lot with the rebels.[11] Xian knelt by the roadside to welcome Li. He shouted, "Qin Xian, bureau secretary of the Ministry of War, bids Your Majesty welcome." But he could not be heard above the clatter of horses' hooves. He yelled again, even louder, but still was not heard amid the general hubbub. Some of Li's followers, however, noticed him.[12]

Several days later, Chao Yushen, uncle of Xian, and Wang Sunhui, a close friend and fellow townsman from Wuxi, hurried off to register themselves as applicants for positions with the new dynasty, even before the official enthronement. On their way they met Xian, and all three agreed to offer their services to Li Zicheng.[13]

After they registered their names with the new authorities, all of them were assigned new homes and forbidden to return to their old ones. This was to enable Li's forces to loot the homes of former Ming officials, many of whom had buried their money and valuables when the rebel army marched in.

The newly enlisted officials were told to report to General Liu Congmin, one of Li's most trusted henchmen. In violation of instructions, Xian secretly returned to his house to recover his valuables. When he did not report to General Liu at the designated time, soldiers were dispatched to arrest him. At that moment he arrived at the general's compound. Apologizing profusely, he got down on his hands and knees and repeatedly kowtowed to the general, but the officer was not appeased. General Liu, who had had his men devise torture instruments designed to crush human bones in order to extract the last ingot of silver from former Ming officials, now had Xian tortured. Xian screamed: "His most intelligent majesty wants to capture the south of the Yangtze and he needs people. If you spare my life, I will do my utmost." His friend Wang also spoke on behalf of Xian and Xian was finally released, on condition that he pay a fine of 500 taels of silver.[14]

And Xian's wish to join the new dynasty was indeed granted—but since Li did not trust defectors from the Ming cause, he appointed him only to the lowly job of a county official in distant Sichuan province, an area that may not even have been under the control of his forces.

Then, even more unfortunately for Xian, Li did not succeed in establishing a new dynasty. His troops were roundly defeated by a combined force led by a Ming general, Wu Sangui, and the Manchus. (General Wu had decided to throw in his lot with the Manchus after he learned that his favorite concubine had been ravished by Li.) After this defeat, Li rushed back to Peking, melted down all the gold and silver imperial treasures, proclaimed himself emperor and fled the next day after having set fire to the palace. He held Peking for thirty-nine days, and was emperor for only one.

Qin Xian was twenty-eight years old when he offered his services to Li. He lived to regret it for the next fifty years. The Manchus made an effort to win over former Ming officials, but they regarded those who had joined Li's rebellion as renegades. With the defeat of Li, Xian returned to Wuxi. There he lived for the rest of his life in the deserted premises of the Blue Mountain Poetry Society until he died at the age of eighty-two.

The Manchus proclaimed the Qing ("Pure") dynasty, and said they had come to China to avenge the last Ming emperor, who had been unseated by Li. They gave Chongzhen an emperor's burial, and declared that he had been ill served by his ministers.

Although the Manchus were firmly entrenched in Peking, Ming loyalists did not give up the fight. They rallied around a cousin of the late emperor, the Prince of Fu, who was proclaimed emperor in Nanking. Playing the Manchus' game, the new emperor sent a delegation to Peking to thank them for driving out Li and promised them cession of all territory north of the Great Wall as well as an annual tribute if they would now withdraw. The Manchus made a counteroffer: If the Nanking court gave up all claims to be the legitimate government of the whole empire and accepted the status of a dependent kingdom, the Manchus would tolerate its existence. This compromise was rejected.

News of the death of the Chongzhen Emperor reached Yong two weeks after his return to Wuxi. Yong was appointed investigating censor of Henan province by the newly enthroned Southern Ming emperor.

At that time, a powerful official sent an emissary to Yong with a message: "Come and see me. I can get you a promotion." Yong refused to go. Later, they met in court. The official respectfully joined his hands together and raised them in a gesture of honor to Yong, saying to all the assembled officials: "Censor Qin refused to accept a reward privately. He is a fine disciple of the emperor."

Unfortunately, the Southern Ming court, like its predecessor in Peking, was riven with factional disputes. Yong's memorials fell on deaf ears, and he soon realized that there was nothing he could do to prevent the fall of the dynasty. He tried to hang himself, but was saved by members of his family. Then he asked for and received permission to retire.

Instead of uniting in the face of the Manchus, the Southern court became embroiled in a mini–civil war. This so weakened its forces that the Manchus were able to capture Nanking. The Southern Ming emperor was taken prisoner to Peking, where he died. And Yong went into hiding in a monastery in the east of Wuxi.

Yet the Ming cause was still not without champions. Another member of the Ming royal house, the Prince of Tang, based in Fuzhou, proclaimed himself administrator of the realm and emperor. Then another prince in Shaoxing titled himself administrator of the realm and denied allegiance to the emperor in Fuzhou. This prince was forced to flee in the summer of 1646, when a Qing army reached Shaoxing. By October, the Fuzhou-based emperor had been captured and killed.

One of his brothers escaped to Canton, where he established a court and was declared emperor in late 1646. A few days later, another grandson of the Wanli Emperor, the Prince of Gui, declared himself emperor.

The Qing drive southward was inexorable. The emperor in

195

Canton was beset by internal dissent and had to crush one of his challengers on the battlefield. Then the Manchus easily defeated his exhausted army. When Canton fell, he committed suicide rather than be taken prisoner.

Now, only the Prince of Gui was left. Pursued by Manchu forces, he fled first to Wuzhou, then to Ping-le in Guangxi. When the Manchus took Ping-le, he retreated to Chuanzhou; when they laid siege to Guilin in April 1647, he moved to Wukang, in Hunan. He was pursued until there was no refuge anywhere, and he finally held court on boats.

The prince's household—though not the prince—had been converted to Catholicism through the good offices of a eunuch who had been baptized in Peking by a Jesuit missionary. The prince's mother had taken the Christian name Anna, while his father's principal wife—who became empress dowager when the prince ascended the throne—was baptized Helena.

In November 1650, with the situation grimmer by the month, Empress Dowager Helena sent a personal appeal to Rome, asking Pope Innocent X and the Jesuit General to intercede with prayers and to send more missionaries to China. The letters did not reach Venice until the end of 1652, by which time Innocent X was dead. The newly elected pontiff, Alexander VII, penned a reply but the courier did not reach China until 1659. By then, the Empress Dowager Helena had already been dead for more than seven years.

The Prince of Gui found temporary refuge in remote Yunnan Province in the 1650s. Then, when even Yunnan was no longer safe, he sought asylum in Burma, where he was treated virtually as a prisoner for the next two years. Early in 1662, a Qing army arrived at the Burmese border and demanded he be handed over. The Burmese complied and the last of the Southern Ming emperors was strangled to death with a bowstring.

Yong had left the Wuxi monastery and settled north of it in an old house he named the "Hall of a Thousand Rests." For the next seventeen years, he rarely ventured out, except to sacrifice in the ancestral temple during festivals. He had no concubines and no interest in material possessions. His passion was collecting books. To avoid persecution, he did not discuss politics and refused to see even old friends who were serving as officials. He would discuss philosophy only on rare occasions with one or two of his closest friends.

Among them was Gao Panlong's nephew, Gao Shitai, who had taken charge of the Donglin Academy.

During his retirement, Yong spent much of his time writing and reading, especially the *Book of Changes*, becoming an expert in it. He also compiled a new edition of the family genealogy, which was published in 1660. When Qin Jin first published a genealogy in 1528, he proposed that it be updated every thirty years. In the intervening 132 years, there had been only one updating, by a grandson of one of the filial sons. The two earlier editions had consisted largely of charts that showed the lines of descent of various branches of the family. Yong fleshed out the genealogy by providing biographies of each individual about whom he could obtain information. He spent a decade on this project and revised his draft three times.

In his edition, Yong discussed the question of major and minor branches of the family, concluding that the senior branch—the descendants of the eldest son of the eldest son down through the years—was not necessarily the most important. He cited the filial brothers and Qin Jin as examples of members of branches that had become even more numerous. The prosperity and success of these branches, he said, was due to the fact that they had produced descendants who were virtuous and wise. He summed it up this way: "If one practices kindness, the major branch will remain major and the minor branches will grow." He urged that all members of the clan "unite and not forget their ancestors." This way, he said, "sons will respect their fathers, younger brothers will respect their elder brothers, and from generation to generation, all will honor their ancestors."

Yong also fixed up the ancestral tombs and revived the practice of setting aside land from which income would be used for honoring the ancestors.

Until 1661, the year he died, he enjoyed discussing philosophy with his grandnephew Songdai, a lecturer at the Donglin Academy. The day before he died at age sixty-four, Yong called his brother to his bedside and told him to write down his last words:

"The end of righteousness is benevolence. This is the business of holy sages. I have not achieved that stage. And I sigh at the past. In the Hall of a Thousand Rests, I thought of that day and night for seventeen years. I am quite satisfied. I am prepared to die tonight."

His brother wanted Yong's last moments to be spent in comfort and suggested moving him into his own house. Yong opened his eyes and said, "Have you forgotten my will?" So his brother kept silent. The next morning, he woke up, washed, bathed and went to bed again. His brother and his nephews surrounded him. When evening came, his limbs turned cold. Suddenly he raised his right hand to wipe his forehead and scratch his arms. Then he leaned on a servant. His face did not show any fear, he did not cry out in pain. He died peacefully. It was September 11, 1661, seven months after the death of Shunzhi, the first Manchu emperor of China.

When the people in Qingjiang heard about Yong's death, they showed their respect for him by placing his spirit tablet in the Temple of Famous Officials. His tablet was also lodged in the Daonan Temple, built for those closely associated with the Donglin Academy. Later, his tablet was placed in a temple specially erected for him, on the site of his old home.

A critique by a contemporary, Zhang Youyu,[15] said of Yong:

"His hard work, his belief and his knowledge allowed him to be the greatest philosopher to emerge after those of the Song dynasty."

CHAPTER THIRTEEN

Qin Dezao: My Parents' Common Ancestor

My parents shared a common ancestor who lived in the seventeenth century, but I was to find that tracing their lineage was more complicated than running a finger along genealogical charts.

For a while, I thought that their closest common ancestor was Qin Zhongxi, the second of three brothers born to Governor Qin Yao's oldest son, Jun, an extremely wealthy man who enjoyed high standing in his hometown as a member of the gentry. But it turned out that the closest of their ancestors was from the next generation.

Zhongxi was a student at the National University, but he never became an official, evidently because he was in poor health most of his life. He spent much of his wealth collecting calligraphy and paintings. He was described as gifted, with special insight into the writings of ancient scholars.

He died when only in his forties, leaving three sons: Decheng, Dezao and Dezhan. I can claim descent from all three brothers. Decheng, the eldest, had a weak constitution and died at the age of twenty-three in 1638, leaving a young daughter and a widow who honored his memory by never remarrying.

Our genealogical records show that my father was descended from one of Decheng's brothers and my mother from the other. But because Decheng left no sons, each of those two younger brothers later gave one of their sons to be adopted by him posthumously, one of whom was my mother's ancestor. That is why I can say that I am descended from all three brothers.

The first son given to Decheng posthumously was Songdai, son of Dezhan. Ordinarily, one male adoption was thought sufficient to continue the family line. But because Dezao's infant son, Songling, was born near the time of Decheng's death, he was regarded in a sense as Decheng's reincarnation and so also became his posthumous adopted son, by a custom known as "paired adoption."

There may have been more practical reasons for this double adoption. Since the family was wealthy, it may have seemed fairer to divide the oldest brother's estate between his younger brothers. The primary purpose of such adoptions was to ensure that no family line should die out. The infants would grow up with two mothers, the natural mother and the adopted one, who in all likelihood would be part of the same household.

In our family tree the lines of descent show not the blood relationship but the adopted one, and so my mother is shown as descended from Songdai. But Songdai had no sons. When he died heirless, one of his "brother" Songling's sons was assigned to continue his family line in still a second case of posthumous adoption. So my mother was actually descended from Songling, the first son of Dezao.

My father in turn was descended from Dezao's second son, Songqi. This made my father and my mother eighth cousins once removed, a relationship so distant as not to be a legal impediment to marriage either in China or in the West, though because our clan was particularly closely knit, and the two branches had maintained contact throughout, their union precipitated a scandal.

That closest common ancestor, Dezao, was born in 1617. His early life took a predictable path: He prepared himself for the civil-service examinations and showed promise as a youth, having passed the licentiate examination while still in his early teens. Then, in 1634, when he was seventeen, he took and passed an examination for licentiates, which entitled him to an annual stipend to study in the government school while preparing himself for the provincial examinations.

But Dezao never went beyond the licentiate stage. As a result, he did not have an official career but followed in the footsteps of Qin Xu and Qin Han, enjoying a life of leisure while his sons, especially the oldest, Songling, joined the court and for a while was a favorite of the emperor. Dezao became prominent in the clan not so much for his deeds but for his longevity and his numerous descendants, many of whom achieved prominence. When he died at the age of eighty-five, he was survived by well over a hundred descendants. He enjoyed the rare distinction of realizing the traditional Chinese ideal of having five generations of a family living under one roof.

Partly because of sheer strength of numbers, his descendants dominated the clan. His grandsons formed twenty-four sub-branches, and from them sprang scholars, hermits, poets and officials as well as simple farmers. Dezao witnessed the growth of the clan into a prosperous and powerful institution whose status would be widely recognized for the next two centuries. On my father's side I am a member of the eleventh sub-branch, descended from Dezao's grandson Xianran, the second son of Songqi. On my mother's side I am a member of the sixth sub-branch, descended from Dezao's grandson Shiran, second son of Songling.

As our clan was consolidating its position in Wuxi, another very different one was rising in the north, beyond the Great Wall. Just as Genghis Khan forged the Mongols into an invincible fighting force in the thirteenth century, so four centuries later the various Manchu tribes were rallying around a charismatic leader, Nurhaci.

In 1590, when Zhongxi was an infant in Wuxi, Nurhaci led a band of Manchu chieftains to pay tribute to the Ming court. Five years later the Wanli Emperor bestowed on him the title "Dragon-Tiger General" for offering to lead his troops to assist Korea in resisting a Japanese invasion. But Nurhaci, while accepting the Ming honors, was nursing long-range ambitions for the total conquest of China.

He bided his time for three decades, carefully forging alliances through dynastic marriages among the various tribes or bludgeoning the more recalcitrant ones into obedience. Gradually he subjugated one Manchu tribe after another, forming them into units distinguished by the color of the banners they carried. Eventually, eight separate banners were established, two each of yellow, white, blue and red, but four of them with borders around the banners. As Mongols and Chinese flocked to his side, sixteen more banners were set up, eight for the Mongols and eight for the Chinese. Banner members included warriors as well as women and children.

As part of the preparation for their invasion of the Chinese heartland, the Manchus studied how each one of their predecessors, including the Khitans, the Jurchens and the Mongols, had fared. Chinese books discussing those historic events were translated into Manchu, so that lessons could be learned and mistakes avoided.

Just as Genghis Khan never lived to see the Mongol conquest of China, so Nurhaci, too, died before the Manchu takeover of the Celestial Empire. But by the time of his death in 1625, plans for the invasion of China were well developed. A capital had been established the year before in Shenyang, in northeastern China.

Nurhaci's eighth son, the thirty-three-year-old military hero Abahai, assumed leadership and responsibility for the realization of his father's dream. He subdued Korea in the east and turned it into a vassal state while, to the north, he extended Manchu control to the region around the Amur River, which today marks the northern border between China and the Soviet Union. From 1629 on, his troops successfully breached the Great Wall almost every other year, raiding Chinese cities and camping in the environs of Peking. He brought the Manchu plans for conquest almost to fruition, but he, too, never sat on the Dragon Throne. In 1643, the year before the fall of Peking, he died.

The death of Abahai precipitated a power struggle between his oldest son, the thirty-four-year-old Haoge, who had already proven himself a capable general, and Haoge's brother Dorgon who also had considerable support. In the end, a compromise was reached under which Abahai's youngest son, a boy of five, was named his heir but Dorgon was appointed regent, which put him in effective control. When the Manchu troops rode into Peking, establishing the Qing dynasty, Dorgon was at their head. He and Haoge remained enemies and, in 1648, Dorgon had him imprisoned on trumped-up charges. Within weeks, Haoge was dead. Dorgon then took Haoge's wife into his own household and continued as regent until his death in 1650, when the boy monarch, who was reigning as the Shunzhi Emperor, was thirteen years old.

Shunzhi, the first Manchu to sit on China's Dragon Throne, was a remarkably mature child. He realized that his knowledge of the Chinese language was not adequate for him to conduct affairs of state, since he was unable even to read the memorials submitted, and thereupon applied himself diligently to studying the language. He became so proficient in a few years that he was able not only to read and write it but also to grade the papers of the candidates taking part in the palace examinations.

He was thoughtful, precocious, and had an especially pious nature. He became friendly with the German Jesuit Adam Schall, who had served the Ming court first as an astronomer and then as an expert in the casting of cannons, and was retained by the country's new rulers as director of the Astronomical Board. The young emperor used to visit Father Schall and engage the learned man in conversation about a host of subjects, displaying an inquiring mind that was open to new ideas. After each of Shunzhi's visits, the Jesuit had to set aside the chair in which his visitor had sat, for no one could sit in a chair that had held the imperial person.[1]

It was the Jesuits' desire to convert the Qing royal family to Catholicism, just as they had successfully converted the family of the last Southern Ming emperor. They did not succeed, but the favors showered on them by the court certainly facilitated their attempts to proselytize both in the capital and in the provinces.

While interested in Christianity, the young emperor, who had been brought up as a Buddhist, never gave up his original faith. His devotion to Buddhism became stronger, especially after the visit to Peking by the Dalai Lama, Tibet's spiritual and temporal ruler. It is not known whether the Shunzhi Emperor really died in 1661 at the age of twenty-three or whether he abdicated in favor of his seven-year-old son, in order to spend the rest of his life as an obscure monk.[2] Legends of the Shunzhi Emperor's secret life as a monk abound, and include stories that his son Hsuan-yeh, the Kangxi Emperor, used to visit him in his monk's cell in a temple on the sacred Wutai Mountain.

In any event, after taking Peking, the Manchu forces swept south, led by Dodo, another brother of Dorgon's. There was scattered resistance by loyalists to the Ming, such as in Yangzhou and in Jiading, which were taken by force and their populaces massacred.

Elsewhere, there was a general, if sullen, acceptance of the new order. There was, however, widespread resentment against a decree that all men must shave the front of their heads in the Manchu style, while letting the hair grow long at the back to braid into a queue. This was perceived as a humiliating symbol of submission to the alien conquerors, and many men, preferring to lose their lives and keep their hair, committed suicide before the arrival of the Qing forces.[3] In many places, in the interim between the flight of the Ming officials and the arrival of the new Qing representatives, there was a period bordering on anarchy, with servants rising against masters, looting and much senseless violence.

The twenty-eight-year-old Qin Dezao, upon the request of his widowed mother, escorted her and his wife to the safety of the countryside. He then returned to the city to take care of his grandparents, who were too weak to make the journey. By the fall of 1645, the Qing had virtually crushed all resistance in the province surrounding Wuxi.

The following year, though not all southern China had been pacified, the Manchus demonstrated their ability to administer the land and their acceptance of Chinese institutions by holding the metropolitan examinations as usual in Peking. Because of continuing disturbances in the south, 95 percent of the successful candidates came from four northern provinces. Three years later, in the 1649 examination, Qin Huazhong, second cousin of Dezao's father, was one of a handful of southern scholars to gain the highest degree. He was appointed magistrate of Fuquan county of Ping-le prefecture in Guangxi province, serving there for three years.

When the Manchu court started a coordinated attack against the Ming loyalists, Huazhong was ordered to join it. In the ensuing battles, towns and cities changed hands many times. In 1653, Huazhong was taken prisoner in Ping-le by the Ming general Li Dingguo. Told by the common people that Huazhong was a good man, General Li tried to win him over to the Southern Ming cause, offering him a choice between death and high honor. Huazhong tried to hang himself, but was thwarted when the cries of his sons alerted the guards. Soon, General Li was driven out of Ping-le by returning Manchu troops and, during the retreat, Huazhong, still a prisoner, jumped into a river and drowned himself. Because of his courage and loyalty, he was posthumously promoted by the Qing court in Peking.

The martyrdom of Huazhong could only have raised the family's status in the eyes of the Manchus, who were skeptical of the loyalty of their southern subjects. By taking part in the state-sponsored examination system and by accepting official postings, southern scholars implicitly acknowledged the legitimacy of the Qing dynasty. Under the Manchus the Qin clan prospered as its members surpassed their ancestors in gaining power and prominence.

Qin Dezao appears never to have taken part in the Qing civil-service examinations, but this does not necessarily mean that he was opposed to the new regime. It can easily be accounted for by the turmoil of the times and his family problems. Dezao's academic career had been interrupted by the death of his father. Hardly before the mourning period was over, his older brother died, leaving him, at the age of twenty-one, the head of the household, having to care for his brother's widow and daughter as well as his own family, which included his mother and his grandparents. As a filial son, he tried so hard to please his mother that, though not a Buddhist, he observed Buddhist rites for her.

His firstborn, Songling, passed the provincial examination in 1654 and the following year, at the age of nineteen, was successful in the metropolitan examinations. That winter, two other members of the clan were also successful—Qin Shi and Qin Lu. Qin Lu was assigned as prefectural judge in Wenzhou prefecture in Zhejiang province. Qin Shi distinguished himself by coming in first in the metropolitan examinations, and was ranked third in the palace exams, the position known as *tanhua*. The emperor was so pleased that he bestowed on Qin Shi a cloak, ordinarily given only to the first-ranking candidate, as a sign of imperial favor. Qin Shi was then appointed compiler of the Hanlin Academy.

Songling was also assigned to work in the Hanlin Academy.

Dezao fathered five other sons, three born of his wife, the Lady Hou, and two born of his concubine, who was surnamed Zhang. His youngest son, Weihang, was a devout Buddhist from youth. After he grew up, he decided to become a monk and so did not have any descendants. A monk in Chinese is *chu-jia-ren,* or "someone who has left his family," because such an act implies repudiation of his relatives. For that reason, Weihang's name is omitted from some of our family records. Just as he rejected his family, so they responded likewise.

Because Songling was adopted posthumously by his uncle, Dezao's second son, Songqi, my father's ancestor, was considered head of the senior branch of Dezao's descendants. Songqi was a licentiate and was assigned various posts but elected to remain in Wuxi to serve his father. In 1714, he updated the family genealogy and published its fourth edition.

Songqiao also began life as a scholar but never assumed any government office. He lived to the age of eighty-one. He was kind and unworldly, and children called him "The No. 3 Old Buddha," since he was the third son.

The fourth son, Songru, served as a district magistrate in the southern province of Guangdong. There was great unrest in that region, since General Wu Sangui and two other Ming commanders, who had initially thrown in their lot with the Qing court, rose in rebellion. Songru suggested that the tax burden on the peasants should be lightened, but since the court in Peking was anxious to raise funds to defray the costs of the war, he was dismissed. However, two years later, the court reversed its own taxation policy and Songru was rehabilitated. Appreciative inhabitants of Guangdong built a temple in his honor.

Dezao's fifth son, Songqiu, born of a concubine, was a student of the National Academy and died at the relatively young age of thirty-three.

One by one, Dezao's elders, peers and even some members of the younger generation died before him. As patriarch, he ministered to the needs of his large family. When his deceased brother's daughter married a poor man from the Hua family, he gave her some land as a dowry, sufficient for her and her husband to live on.

In 1660, when Dezao was forty-four, his wife died after twenty-six years of marriage. Dezao took the unusual step of honoring her by writing a long account of her life. He said:

> My wife's ancestors were rich and famous. Her father was bureau secretary of the Ministry of Revenue while her great-grandfather was minister of the Court of the Imperial Stud.
>
> Before her marriage, my wife was taught by her grandmother, a widow who raised her sons and grandsons to pass the highest level of the metropolitan examinations. She loved my wife and said my wife resembled her. After my wife married me, my father died and I was in deep sorrow. She assumed all household responsibilities and tried to ease my pain. In 1641, our house caught fire, and my father's coffin, which was in the main hall, was in danger of being burnt. My mother screamed and wanted to jump into the flames. My wife organized the servants and saved the body just in time. During that incident, I was at my grandfather's tomb.
>
> My mother has always been physically weak. My wife took good care of her. When the dynasty changed, she accompanied my mother to live in the countryside while I lived with my grandparents in the city. Whenever I went to visit my mother, my wife would say, "I shall take care of mother and you should take care of the grandparents." She lived with my mother for almost thirty years and never gave any cause for complaint. When she died, my mother wept and cried out her name every night.
>
> My wife respected me. She took care of the whole family and she always asked for my opinion and decisions. She loved the

children, but she also disciplined them. I remember one winter evening we were sitting around the fire. Songling complained about the cold. My wife scolded him and said that a lot of people were dying in the snow without food and clothing, and that Songling should not grumble about the cold while wearing furs and sitting beside a fire. When Songling became a *jinshi*, she wrote and told him not to become arrogant, but to earn the respect of others. She also told him not to worry about her but to work hard for the emperor. She was in charge of household affairs for over twenty years. She never wore beautiful clothes and was always willing to help the poor. She had an aversion to monks and nuns. She said she only had sympathy for the poor, and did not count monks and nuns among them.

The year after his wife's death, Dezao's mother died at the age of seventy-one. She had spent her last twenty-seven years as a widow. On her seventieth birthday, Qin Yong composed an essay in her honor.

According to Yong, the Lady Yu had little to do when she first married except to dress in her finery every day, look charming and please her mother-in-law. However, when her husband became ill she nursed him until his death, and then raised their sons. After the death of her son Dezhan, she developed a heart condition and had to be constantly on medication. At the age of fifty, she became a vegetarian and devoted herself to Buddhist prayer and meditation.

In 1684, the Kangxi Emperor took the first of six elaborate trips to view his southern domains. His reasons for traveling to the south were, officially, to inspect the construction of dams along the Yellow River and to see at first hand the life of the common people. A third, unmentioned, reason—undoubtedly the most important one—was for the emperor to win the support and respect of the large numbers of influential families in southern China, many of whom were not yet reconciled to the idea of Manchu rule.[4]

The first of his southern tours lasted two months. He showed his awareness of the sensitivies of his Chinese subjects by skirting Yangzhou and Jiading, where resistance to Manchu rule had been the strongest in the 1640s and where brutal massacres had therefore taken place.

During these journeys south, the Kangxi Emperor emphasized

his respect for Chinese culture and traditions. While in Shandong, the home province of Confucius, he visited the temple in honor of the sage. In Nanking, the original Ming capital, he officiated at sacrificial ceremonies at the tomb of Zhu Yuanzhang, the Ming founding emperor, and sought to show the legitimacy of the Manchus as the successors of the Ming rulers. To win the support of southern gentry families, he increased the quota of students from the two southern provinces of Jiangnan and Zhejiang who could qualify for admission to local colleges.

The imperial procession reached Wuxi by way of the Grand Canal.[5] On the first journey, the imperial barge docked at a jetty on the western outskirts of the city, near the foot of Mount Hui, where officials awaited its arrival. Scholars gathered at a temple to the north. From the jetty, it was only a short distance to the Ji Chang Garden. As the emperor approached the garden, he was welcomed by the clan's patriarch, Qin Dezao, and four of his sons, all of whom were kneeling by the side of the road.

When the emperor met Dezao,[6] he asked the patriarch his age and, according to eyewitness accounts, gave the old man a penetrating look. Then he turned to Songqi, the oldest son present, and asked him if he was related to Qin Songling. "He is my brother," Songqi responded.[7]

Dezao was sixty-seven years old then. Aside from his six sons, he already had sixteen grandsons and two great-grandsons, not counting female descendants.

In the next twenty-three years, the emperor paid more visits to Wuxi, and each time he returned to the garden. He loved the garden so much that he made it his "traveling palace" and lived there while visiting Wuxi.

In January 1689, the emperor made a second trip south and ordered a group of noted artists under the direction of the most famous painter of the time, Wang Hui, to prepare for posterity scrolls depicting his travels. Starting with the emperor departing the capital, the pictures capture key points of the imperial journey and show the scenery, life-style and traditions in great detail. For example, in the Nanking section, the emperor, dressed in a long orange robe under a turquoise silk cloak and wearing a red hat and white shoes, is shown walking toward the temple, flanked by four guards, one of whom shields him from the sun with an umbrella with a big yellow canopy. Another holds a sword in his hand while two others are armed with bows and arrows. Behind them are twenty-four other armed guards, while civilian officials bring up the rear.

From figures visible on the various scrolls, it appears that there were some three thousand officials and soldiers in the emperor's entourage. When the emperor emerged from the Forbidden City through the Yongdingmen, or Gate of Eternal Pacification, soldiers lined both sides of the road. More soldiers followed in the train of the royal party. Marching south, the procession passed the old imperial hunting grounds at Nanyuan and proceeded through the Great Red Gate. The leading group, divided into lines along each side of the road, held twenty pairs of big-canopied umbrellas of different colors. The sides of the umbrellas were decorated with dragons and special grass that was considered auspicious, while the tops were embroidered with flowers. Behind them came two officers holding staffs.

A second group of twenty people lined the sides of the road, each holding a fan as a shield against wind and dust. On one side the fans were square, on the other, round. They were of red and yellow, decorated with one or two dragons.

The third group was a double file of people, twenty-three in each line, all of whom carried poles from which fluttered banners, pennants, tasseled feathered streamers or red yak tails adorned with white feathers. The fourth group held aloft 109 kinds of flags. These were followed by two pairs of staff carriers, who preceded the fifth group—pairs of foot soldiers armed with various types of weapons, including golden curved axes, star-shaped and melon-shaped axes, gold-tipped wooden staffs and swords.

Behind them came the musicians carrying various instruments, including forty-eight drummers beating waist-high drums, four large drums for bands of drummers, clapping boards, twelve bamboo flutes mounted with carved dragon heads, four brass cymbals, twenty-four painted horns, four golden gongs, eight small trumpets and eight large trumpets. Among the musicians marched six lantern bearers, two abreast, each carrying a red gauze lantern shaped by wire in the middle of which was a candle holder.

Directly behind the musicians were the conveyances used by the most important personages accompanying the emperor. Both a grand carriage and a jade carriage were drawn by a pair of elephants, followed by a grand coach, drawn by a team of eight horses, and a smaller, two-wheeled horse-drawn coach. A huge palanquin was carried on long poles by twenty-eight men. They were followed by five elephants, each laden with a large barrel to quench the thirst of the travelers. Four other elephants were used to clear away any obstruction that the imperial party might encounter.

Then came the emperor on horseback, shielded from the sun by a mounted soldier carrying a large umbrella. The emperor was preceded by twenty cavalry, all on white horses, and protected from behind by his imperial bodyguard, who carried halberds, lances bearing leopard's tails, bows and arrows and scimitars. The imperial pennant, a red-bordered triangular yellow banner emblazoned with a dragon, came next.

Bringing up the rear were large numbers of attendants, marching two abreast, carrying such items as a gold incense burner, boxes of incense, basins and pitchers made of gold, as well as headrests. Also in the procession were princes, imperial relatives, including members of the emperor's own clan, officials of the inner court, such as grand secretaries and eunuchs, as well as representatives from all the ministries. All the officials who remained behind in the capital came to see the emperor off, kneeling by the roadside.

On this trip, Kangxi again stopped in Wuxi, to the delight of the local inhabitants. Parades and singing welcomed the imperial visitor, who spent the night in the city. The next day, His Majesty visited the Second Spring Under Heaven. As was customary, all the commoners knelt in his presence. Suddenly it rained, turning the earth into mud. The emperor immediately told them that they did not have to kneel in the mud. The crowds rose and shouted, *"Wan sui! wan sui! wan wan sui!"* "May Your Majesty live for ten thousand times ten thousand years."

In Wuxi, the royal barge docked at the Sparing Life Pond, a section of a river set apart for the purpose of liberating fish and other aquatic creatures. This was a Buddhist practice that is still observed today. After visiting the Second Spring Under Heaven, the emperor proceeded to the Ji Chang Garden. This time, Songling was there with the rest of the Qin family to welcome the imperial visitor. In the five years since the emperor's first visit, Dezao's family had increased by three more grandsons and three more great-grandsons. It was probably during this visit that Dezao obtained imperial approval for his great-grandfather Yao to be honored by having his statue placed in the Temple of Sages in Wuxi.

Ten years later, in 1699 the Kangxi Emperor initiated a third southern tour. This was the last time that Dezao met him. The venerable patriarch was then eighty-two years old. In the intervening decade, his family had grown with the addition of five more grand-sons and twelve more great-grandsons. The old man again welcomed the emperor to the family garden, and this time, the emperor and his mother spent the night as guests of the Qin family. Kangxi granted two samples of his handwriting to Dezao. Such was his fondness for the garden that he gave imperial sanction for its name, Ji Chang Garden.

In 1701, Dezao died at the age of eighty-five. Though he never became an official and hence, from one point of view, did not achieve anything of import, he was revered and respected during his life-time. He was seen as a model of filial piety, of brotherly love and of scholarly integrity.

After his death, one of his contemporaries, Yan Shengsun, eval-uated Dezao's life by saying: "I admire the men of old, hermits such as Qin Xu. They loved ancient traditions, enjoyed reading, and lived long. Their poems were peaceful and reflected the customs of that period. Two hundred years later, Qin Dezao appeared and was very similar to his ancestors. He was a descendant of Qin Xu of the ninth generation. Just as Xu was filial, with filial sons, so Dezao was filial, with filial sons. Xu lived a long life and was without arrogance, Dezao also lived a long life and never quarreled with anyone.

"Since the olden days, good fortune has been defined as longevity, wealth, a peaceful life, accumulation of merits and a good death. Dezao was blessed with all of these."[8]

CHAPTER FOURTEEN

Qin Songling: Hanlin Academy's Youngest Member

In the fall of 1983, I was invited to attend a genealogical conference in Taiwan. One of the participants was a scholar named Chang Pi-te, who was in charge of the Qing dynasty archives at the Palace Museum in Taipei. With his help, I looked up all the Qins in the museum files and found much biographical information on Qin Songling, the eldest son of Dezao and my maternal great-great-great-great-great-great-great-great-grandfather.

There was not one biography of Songling but six different drafts. The alterations were usually refinements of fact. The first draft, for example, started off as is customary by giving his name and his hometown, saying that he was from "Wuxi, of Jiangnan." Jiangnan was a province only from the 1640s to the 1660s, so in the second draft, this was corrected to read "Wuxi, of Jiangsu." In addition, there were also a few more details, such as the exact year an event occurred, or the length of time Songling served in a particular office. Affixed to the top, there were also notes written on slips of paper, pointing out errors or asking for certain facts to be verified. The third draft was a cleaner copy, written in neat characters, giving the name of the person who had acted as proofreader. The fourth draft had again been checked carefully for accuracy, and more details, such as Songling's courtesy name, were added. Slips of paper with marginal notations were pasted on so that further checks could be made. By the fifth draft, the biography was almost in final form. All the literary conventions were followed, such as elevating any references to the emperor by three spaces. The sixth, and final, version ran to five and a half pages. All the characters were beautifully written and there was only one correction, of a word that had been wrongly written.

It was the job of court historians to prepare biographies of officials, leading literary figures and other people of merit after their deaths. On the whole, the biographies were brief, and dealt only with the highlights of an official career.

Songling was born in 1637. He began his studies early and all information extant indicates he was exceptionally talented. At the age of six, he studied the Confucian classic *Doctrine of the Mean* and impressed his teacher by his understanding of the concept "nature." He was clearly precocious because he earned the first degree, that of licentiate, at the age of eleven. By the time he was seventeen he had become a *juren*. The following year, in 1655, he went to Peking and successfully competed in the metropolitan examinations, earning the *jinshi* degree at the age of eighteen, before he was even married, an almost unheard-of occurrence.[1] After that he was appointed bachelor of the Hanlin Academy, the youngest man ever to serve in the Hanlin. Then his father arranged for him to marry a young woman from the Wu family.

At that time, the Shunzhi Emperor ordered a poetry-writing competition, with "crane" being the topic. Songling submitted the following lines:

> He often sings loudly to the moon,
> A dancer who doesn't welcome people.

Emperor Shunzhi loved the lines and ranked Songling's poem above the rest, telling his courtiers that here was a man of fine character.

One of Songling's responsibilities at the Hanlin Academy was, in effect, to be the emperor's ghost-writer. In this capacity, he was well placed to observe what went on at court, and he helped give voice to the emperor's sentiments. One day, for example, he was asked to draft an essay in honor of an obscure secondary consort of the late Prince Haoge, brother of the Shunzhi Emperor. The essay, though brief, reflected not only the affection Shunzhi felt for his dead brother but also his hatred for his uncle Dorgon, who as regent before Shunzhi was old enough to rule had imprisoned Prince Haoge and caused his death. By the time Shunzhi became of age, Dorgon was already dead, but the emperor still issued a decree denouncing him for having usurped power.

In 1657, when Songling was twenty years old, he was appointed corrector of the State Historiographer's Office, among the youngest to serve in this important post. He seemed destined to rise to great heights, for he had impressed the emperor favorably with his talents. But suddenly disaster struck.

The seeds of the storm had been sown years ago. In the first dozen years of the Qing dynasty, when the Manchus were in firm control of only the northern provinces, they were constantly engaged in battles to subdue the south. These military engagements drained the Treasury in Peking. So the Manchus canceled most of the tax exemptions granted in the Ming dynasty to families of officials and scholars. This resulted in widespread tax evasion. Beginning in 1657, the new regime began to exert greater pressure on local authorities to gather taxes from wealthy southern families to meet the central government's budgetary needs. In 1658, the Shunzhi Emperor issued a decree to the Ministry of Revenue in which he castigated the southern gentry for evading taxes and singled out Wuxi for special attention:

"Wuxi in Jiangnan and other districts owe much in tax arrears, over several hundred thousand taels. The local officials have done nothing about this. Obviously, the problem lies with them. The high officials do not conduct inspections seriously and the lower-level officials pocket the taxes. Some officials have accepted bribes from powerful local dignitaries and are afraid of pressing them to pay taxes. The ministry should investigate cases similar to those in Wuxi and report to me."[2]

As an imperial ghost-writer, Songling undoubtedly knew of the increasing pressure to collect taxes from the wealthy southeastern provinces, and he made sure that he scrupulously paid taxes on the eight acres of farmland that he owned. But he could not have foreseen that events beyond his control were about to engulf him.

In 1660, Songling's mother died and he returned home for the mourning ceremonies. While he was absent, he was suspended from his post on charges of nonpayment of taxes. It turned out that a widowed aunt of his, in order to evade taxes, had registered property in Songling's name without his knowledge. Songling's father advised him not to contest the charge so as to spare the aunt from public humiliation, and worse.[3] Songling consented, although undoubtedly with great reluctance. As a result, he was found guilty, stripped of his degrees and dismissed from his post. Without his degrees, he was no longer eligible for any government posts. All he could look forward to was a lifetime of obscurity.

In 1661, while Songling was still in mourning for his mother, the sudden death of the Shunzhi Emperor was reported. The mystery of his death was compounded by the publication of a will, generally believed to have been forged, in which the young emperor castigated himself for a number of sins, including his preference for Chinese officials over Manchus and his lack of filial piety toward his mother. The will is thought to have been forged by his mother and four Manchu leaders, who were named regents during the minority of Shunzhi's son, the Kangxi Emperor. These four regents, especially Oboi, who later became a virtual dictator, were Manchu conservatives who treated their Chinese subjects as conquered people and made little attempt to accept or even understand their culture and history. They were responsible for the wave of tax-persecution cases in Jiangnan.[4]

Because resistance to the Manchus had been strongest in the two southeastern provinces of Jiangnan and Zhejiang, Manchu suppression there had also been the strongest. For most of the first two decades of their rule, the Manchus decided that men from four of these provinces' prefectures—Suzhou, Changzhou, Zhenjiang and Songjiang—should be prohibited from holding high metropolitan posts. Wuxi was part of Changzhou prefecture and even top-level graduates from Wuxi were barred from the highest honors in the capital. And since these provinces were the wealthiest in the country, the tax rates imposed there were particularly high.

The 1661 Jiangnan taxation case illustrates the tensions between Manchus and Chinese. The wrath of the Manchus against the people of Wuxi and the rest of Jiangnan and Zhejiang was fueled by the sympathy that the populace had felt for the rebel Koxinga. In 1659, Koxinga had been able to penetrate deep into Jiangnan, all the way to Nanking, before he suffered a crushing defeat. So the Manchus made serious efforts to collect all taxes, even trifling amounts, and subjected those found delinquent to harsh penalties.

Tax records were deliberately not kept, or perhaps were subsequently destroyed so there would be no evidence of this instance of Manchu persecution of the Chinese. There were, however, unofficial accounts. According to one, the tax rate in Jiangnan, especially in the prefectures of Suzhou and Songjiang, was a hundred times higher than elsewhere. "Often, people have not yet finished one tax before another is due," this account said. "So hundreds of thousands of taels of silver were unpaid." During that 1661 taxation crackdown,

"Governor Zhu Guozhi listed 13,000 people as tax delinquents. All of them were removed from office, and some were even flogged."[5]

Ultimately, 13,567 people in Jiangnan were deprived of their degrees as a result of tax cases. When some of those affected protested against their treatment by local officials, their protests were treated as evidence of disloyalty to the new regime, which resulted in arrests and floggings, and triggered off more demonstrations. It all culminated in a mass execution in Nanking in August 1661 when eighteen people were beheaded, not on charges of tax evasion but on charges of plotting rebellion. About three thousand people were jailed.

Though Songling officially accepted responsibility on the tax-evasion charge, he did not want his former mentor, Hu Shaolong, who had played a critical role in starting him off on his career, to think ill of him. Songling therefore wrote to him, explaining what had happened:

> I was a poor student and was fortunate to be chosen by you. His Majesty employed me as his servant and granted me many favors. I regarded the emperor as the sky and you as my father. The sky will never fall and who would not love his father. I studied hard to maintain my position and tried to be worthy of your choice.
>
> When I went home for [my mother's] mourning ceremony, the taxation case broke out. The tax record of my hometown showed that I owed no taxes. However, my widowed aunt, who lives in the next city and who had not been in touch with my family for some time, put my name on her list. I do not know where she learned such a trick and I only knew about it when the imperial order suspending me was handed down. The department concerned called for a hearing and asked me to defend myself against the accusations. I realize that I should have done so. I also know, however, that my poor aunt has no descendants and I was afraid that if she was found guilty, it would cost her her life. So I did not put up any defense.
>
> This year I have been sick several times and I found myself physically deteriorating though I am not even thirty. Though I will not challenge the charges, I remember the favors shown by His Majesty and how you were my benefactor. By accepting guilt

as a tax evader, I have brought shame on you. There is nothing I can do to compensate for this but discipline myself by studying harder. After I have improved myself and people know me, they will say that this is the former history official of the emperor and the former disciple of Mr. Hu, and that this man was once guilty of an offense but finally turned out to be a law-abiding person. This is the only way I know how to repay you.

After his removal from office, Songling spent thirteen years in Wuxi. Being from a wealthy family, he enjoyed a life of leisure, savoring domestic joys. His wife, the Lady Wu, had given him a daughter, whose name has not been preserved, and a son, Daoran. The daughter turned out to be extremely bright, but the son was dull. Many a time, Songling lamented the fact that his daughter had not been born a male.

His wife died when the children were still infants. Songling remarried, taking as *tianfang,* or replacement wife, a woman from the Hua family, whose father served in the Hanlin Academy. The higher status of his second wife's family reflected the rise in Songling's own station. Though dismissed from office, he was still addressed by his former titles and accorded great respect. He also took a concubine, surnamed Fei. The Lady Hua presented him with a second son, Shiran, my mother's ancestor, and concubine Fei produced four more sons.

In 1666, he went to visit his cousin, Qin Shi, known as "Elder Qin," who was the judicial commissioner in Jiangxi province. Unlike Songling, Elder Qin was quite poor and so, very frugal. Many years later, when Elder Qin died, Songling wrote his epitaph and said that his cousin slept on a wooden bed for three years and could barely afford daily necessities, but he was so loved by the people that they supplied him with food and wine. While in Jiangxi, he could not even afford a secretary and so had to cope with the voluminous paperwork himself.

The wealthy Songling was, however, able to occupy himself by studying philosophy and the classics. Two stories from this period of his life illustrate the pastimes of the wealthy gentry in those days.

The first has to do with a tenacious form of Chinese folk religion, in which it is said that the spirit of a person long dead can be summoned to dwell temporarily in a living being. Thus, it would be

217

possible theoretically for someone with no understanding of English to summon the spirit of William Shakespeare and suddenly recite lines from *Hamlet*.

According to the tale, Qin Songling had in his home a special room with an altar set up for the purpose of invoking spirits. He also had a resident medium. One day, Songling returned home accompanied by the magistrate of Wuxi, Wu Xingzu. Wu, who was a close friend of the family, did not believe in mediums and spirits, but when he heard that the medium in Songling's household was going to invoke the spirit of the great eighth-century Tang poet Li Bo, he decided to see what would happen.

After they stepped into the room, the medium wrote with a stick in a tray of sand in front of him: "Wu Xingzu, why aren't you kneeling?"

To which the magistrate replied, "Please compose a poem for me. If it is good, I will certainly kneel before you."

Li Bo, through the medium, asked: "What theme?" The magistrate, who happened to see a cat curled up in the corner, answered: "Cats!"

"What rhyme words do you require?" the spirit asked, evidently very confident of his abilities. The magistrate then picked three words that rhymed in Chinese: "nine," "leeks," and "wine," to be used at the end of the first, second and fourth lines of the poem.

The medium immediately smoothed out the sand in the tray in front of him and wrote out the following lines:

> Of ten parts of a tiger the cat has nine;
> He eats fish and prawns but not leeks.
> He became wild when chasing a rat,
> Spilling what was atop the bed—wine.

Convinced, the magistrate fell on his knees, paying homage to Li Bo's spirit.[6]

Another story of life in Songling's household was related by a guest who was invited to an open-air soiree held at the family garden in 1670, almost a decade after Songling was dismissed.

The narrator was Yu Huai, a famous poet and music lover from Fujian province, known for his writings about the singing girls of Nanking in the seventeenth century. Yu Huai had a good friend named Xu Sheng, one of the best singers of the period.

According to Yu Huai, Xu Sheng's voice was such that when he sang the birds became silent and the fish stopped swimming to listen in rapt attention. One day Xu Sheng said to him: "I am old and I am afraid my voice won't last. I taught my techniques to six or seven students who are now with the father of the court historian, Qin Songling, in Wuxi. If you travel to the region of the Nine Mountains and the Second Spring Under Heaven, do not forget to go and listen to the music."

In 1670, Yu Huai attended a party hosted by Songling. According to Yu Huai's account, Songling, in the company of six or seven singers, arrived at the foot of Mount Hui in a gaily decorated boat, which docked near the Ji Chang Garden. All the singers carried musical instruments.

"At that time," Yu Huai recalled, "it was between autumn and winter. The leaves had already fallen. We stayed in the Long Corridor [in the garden], watching the mountain scenery and listening to the sound of the spring water. The singers wore green garments and silk shoes, and looked like scholars. They went to the rocks, and some played the flutes while others plucked string instruments. After a while a song was sung and the sound was so beautiful that it reminded one of perfectly shaped pearls. At that moment the clouds seemed motionless and all other sounds were stilled. I cried out, 'Xu Sheng! Xu Sheng! You did not exaggerate!' "[7]

In 1674, more than ten years after the tax incident, Songling, then aged thirty-seven, was partially rehabilitated. He was given an unofficial posting, one attained through recommendation by a sponsor and not part of the regular bureaucracy. He was appointed lecturer to troops fighting in Huguang. In this way, he participated in one of the major events of the Kangxi emperor's reign: the suppression of the Revolt of the Three Feudatories.

General Wu Sangui, who had helped the Manchus gain power in 1644 by switching his allegiance from the Ming dynasty, had been rewarded with a fiefdom in the southwest. In 1674, however, he led an uprising against the Qing, and was soon joined by two other former Ming generals who had been given feudatories in the south.

Governor-General Cai Yurong of Huguang was ordered to quell the insurgency. Despite his efforts, all of Hunan was seized by Wu Sangui, who declared himself emperor of a new dynasty, thus posing a real threat to the Manchus.

219

Songling lectured to the troops on the teachings of Song dynasty philosophers, as well as on loyalty and filial piety, to keep the soldiers loyal to their Manchu rulers.

He remained with General Cai's forces for four years, until the death of the rebel general Wu Sangui in 1678. By then, it was clear that the victory of the Qing dynasty was assured. To celebrate the triumphant culmination of this long military campaign, Songling composed a poem, which included these lines:

> The emperor ruled against a slaughter;
> The rewards were tremendous.
> The farmlands are plowed again
> And the soldiers have gone home.
> Music is again heard in the palace
> And wineglasses are in use again.

The revolt of Wu Sangui underlined the precarious hold of the Manchus on southern China. Emperor Kangxi was anxious to win over Chinese who were unreconciled to Manchu rule. He decided to follow his father's example and increasingly Sinicized his administration. Chinese institutions were adopted, Chinese learning was emphasized, with the emperor setting a personal example. To win the support of outstanding scholars, the emperor devised a special examination, the *boxue hongru,* or "great scholars of extensive learning," to entice such people into his service.[8]

In the spring of 1678, the emperor issued a decree to the Ministry of Personnel that stated:

"From ancient times, whenever a dynasty arose, of necessity there were profound scholars of vast learning who fostered the literary development, expounded the Classics and Histories, and enriched the literary style, thus preparing themselves for selection as advisers and writers. I, in my spare time after enacting the 10,000 affairs, gladden my heart with literature, and it is my wish to obtain scholars of vast learning who could be used as aides in the classical studies. Since the foundation of our dynasty, the scholars have been held in esteem, the Way [Dao] has been emphasized and talents have been cultivated. . . . I herewith order, within the capital those officials whose ranks are above the third grade and those who are in the censorate, and outside the capital the viceroys and governors, the provincial administration commissioners and the provincial judicial commissioners, all to recommend three of whom they know, so that I might personally submit them to an examination for appointment."[9]

Governor-General Cai Yurong, whom Songling had served for four years, recommended him as a candidate. The examination was held in the spring of 1679. All together, 202 scholars of high repute were recommended. Some of those, diehard Ming loyalists, refused to take the examination, pleading illness.

In the end, 152 persons took the examinations. The emperor himself acted as chief examiner, assisted by his highest literary officials. Fifty of the candidates were successful. Of these, the top twenty were placed in the first rank. Songling passed in the first rank.[10]

The fifty successful candidates were assigned to the Hanlin Academy. Songling was reinstated with all his former degrees and titles. He became one of only a few people in the Qing dynasty to be admitted twice into this prestigious institution.[11] Once more, he was corrector of the State Historiographer's Office, the post he had held twenty-two years earlier. At the age of forty-two, he was given a fresh beginning to his official career. Like other successful candidates, he was assigned to work on compiling a history of the Ming dynasty. This, too, was a strategic move by the wily Kangxi emperor. By engaging to record its history people whose loyalties might still lie with the vanquished Ming dynasty, he was able to obtain their services and, at the same time, their recognition of the legitimacy of Manchu rule.

In China, each dynasty traditionally prepared an official history of its predecessor. So it was that, in the Qing dynasty, court historians were assigned to edit an official history of the Ming, just as Ming historians had prepared a history of the Yuan dynasty of the Mongols. Today, the People's Republic of China, much to the chagrin of the authorities on Taiwan, is engaged in a compilation of the history of the Republic of China, even though the government on Taiwan still calls itself by that name.

Compilation of the Ming dynastic history was a vast project, requiring large numbers of scholars. It was also politically sensitive. In fact, an unauthorized version had been compiled in earlier years by scholars loyal to the previous dynasty. Because that history used Southern Ming reign titles rather than the new Qing dynastic titles, its compilers were considered traitors. The families of those most intimately involved in the compilation of the book were wiped out.

All males over the age of fifteen were executed and all women and children were made slaves. Even officials who were not involved with the project but who knew about it and had not reported its existence were executed. The corpse of the main compiler, who had died before the work was finished, was exhumed and burned. Songling stayed with the Ming history project for only two years.

In 1681, when he was forty-four, Qin Songling was appointed chief examiner of that year's triennial examinations in Jiangxi province. Being examiner was an honor, since only the most learned men were appointed, but it was also a perilous task because, during the Kangxi period, there were a number of examination scandals in which corruption was alleged. In 1657, for example, there had been a scandal in the examinations held in Peking of such proportions that several hundred people were punished.[12] The case involved bribery, blackmail, mistaken identity, anonymous letters and other abuses. Fortunately for Songling, the 1681 Jiangxi provincial examinations proceeded smoothly.

Later that year, Songling was appointed keeper of the imperial diary, one of a handful of officials whose job it was to record the emperor's official daily activities. As such, he was in constant contact with the emperor. An examination of the records kept by Songling of the emperor's day-to-day activities is extremely revealing.

Kangxi's day typically began with an early morning meeting with his courtiers, who gathered in the compound outside his palace before dawn. Much of the discussion had to do with personnel matters, such as the filling of vacant posts or whether to grant requests for retirements. The emperor clearly knew in advance the issues that were to be broached.

And daily, if possible, the emperor went to Five Dragon Pavilion to pay his respects to his grandmother, the grand empress dowager. It was she who had provided parental guidance to him when he was growing up, since both his parents died early.

Because the corps of imperial diarists did the job in rotation, Songling's name does not appear at the end of every entry. But on the twenty-seventh day of the seventh month of the twenty-first year of the reign of the Kangxi Emperor, that is, August 23, 1682, Songling recorded the following:

"His Majesty arrived at the Yingtai Pavilion and listened to reports from all the departments. After these had been presented, the Grand Secretary [Mingju] requested permission for the Ministry of Personnel to propose that the post of assistant reader of the grand secretariat be filled, and recommended Investigating Censor Wang Guochang as the main candidate and Investigating Censor Wu Xingzu as a second choice.

"His Majesty asked: 'How learned is Wang Guochang?'

"Replied Grand Secretary Mingju: 'Wang Guochang is an excellent scholar. He is the brother of the previous Reader Wang Guo'an and is a good replacement.'

"His Majesty asked: 'How is Wu Xingzu's learning?'

"Mingju replied: 'Among the investigating censors, except for Wang Guochang, Wu Xingzu's learning is second to none. He was recommended as an alternate candidate previously to replace Jin Ruxiang.' "

"His Majesty said: 'Since Wu Xingzu was an alternate choice previously, have him fill the vacancy this time.' "

Having disposed of this matter, the emperor went on to other issues. Songling recorded:

"The governor of the Metropolitan Region, Ko-erh-ku-te, had reported that the coastal areas of the region consisted of sandy soil and no farmland could be developed.

"His Majesty said: 'There is a lot of farmland along the coast near Tianjin and other places. If these farmlands are worked by commoners they will have to pay tax and there will be no arguments. But if the lands are taken over by bannermen, they will not pay tax and thus decrease governmental income. Have the local officials carry out a detailed investigation and report.' "

A request arrived from the governor of Guizhou for tax exemption because Guizhou was hit by famine.

"His Majesty said: 'Guizhou is a large area, the government troops haven't been there for very long. Regulations for tax exemption have been clearly drawn up. This request is obviously designed to please the local inhabitants. Not granted.' "[13]

On the eighteenth day of the ninth month, the Kangxi Emperor held court at the Gate of Celestial Purity, in front of which stood two gilded bronze lions. A throne was placed at the gate for the emperor from which to hear reports from high officials and issue his decisions. Behind the throne was a screen, which shielded the imperial apartments from the gaze of his officials, and before it was a yellow-topped desk. In front of the desk and to the left was placed a cushion on which the official making a report knelt.

Early in the morning, guards arrived and stood along the sides of the throne. These imperial bodyguards used the leopard's tail as their emblem. Those holding lances stood to the right of the throne, while those wielding broadswords stood to the left.

Representatives of the various ministries, who constituted the outer court, had come before dawn to await the emperor's arrival. They stood in a row, facing west. Across from them stood other officials, those from the inner court, such as members of the Hanlin Academy. When the emperor arrived, borne on a sedan chair, and took his seat, the keeper of the imperial diary moved over to a platform on the side, ready to take notes. A minister brought out a box containing the memorials, knelt and placed the box on the emperor's desk. Then he rose, walking backward to his original place, before kneeling to report.

On this occasion, Songling recorded:

"His Majesty arrived at at the Gate of Celestial Purity to listen to the reports from officials of all departments.

"The Grand Secretary [Mingju] requested permission for the Ministry of Personnel to offer Huang Jiuchou of Guizhou, [a former rebel who turned himself in] the position of assistant secretary.

"His Majesty said, 'Huang Jiuchou is the loyal follower of Wang Fuchen [a deceased rebel general]. He is cunning and is a cheat. Never offer him any position. This kind of bandit should never be appointed even if he surrenders.'

"[One memorial was from] Minister Huang Ji, who requested permission to retire, citing old age as the reason.

"His Majesty said, 'Huang Ji is a careful man. He does not have too many friends, and can still work well despite his age. Have him remain in his position.'

"His Majesty also told the grand secretaries and others: 'During the battles, the common people bore the burden of paying for supplies. I said previously that when peace came I would exempt them from tax. This year reports of famine and calamities are at a minimum. You can check the taxation accounts with the Ministry of Revenue, paying special attention to the province of Shaanxi since it has been worst hit and its tax should be exempted.'

"Mingju responded: 'Your Majesty is great. Now the world is at peace and we should give the people some respite.' "[14]

On the twentieth day of the twelfth month, in his last report before the Chinese New Year, Songling recorded:

"His Majesty arrived at the Palace of Celestial Purity.

"The issue of reconstructing the Palace of Tranquillity and Longevity was brought up; the Ministry of Works had spent too much, causing the impeachment of Vice Ministers Subai and Jin Ding.

"His Majesty said, 'The success of construction work depends on finances, and the budget has to be realistic and properly managed. Now I see that neither the schedule nor the budget is being followed. They [the two officials] have been taking advantage of the financial situation. I ordered them to reform but they did not listen. Such an attitude should be severely punished. I see, however, that the construction work itself is proceeding well and there are no irresponsible acts, so Subai and Jin Ding may remain at their posts but are demoted by two ranks. The same demotion will apply to the official Bai Erlai. They will continue to work on the construction of the palace. No action is to be taken by the Ministry of Punishments.' "[15]

After the Lunar New Year, on the first day of the second month, Songling made an entry directly related to his work and showed the politically sensitive nature of his job, which the Kangxi Emperor clearly thought was open to abuse. Because the emperor himself did not have access to the imperial diary, he was apprehensive that his actions could be distorted and he himself depicted in a bad light. Songling reported:

"At the hour of the dragon [7 to 9 A.M.] His Majesty arrived at the Gate of Celestial Purity.

"The Hanlin Academy reported that the records of the keeper of the imperial diary for the twenty-first year of the Kangxi era were ready to be filed away after inspection by members of the Grand Secretariat.

"His Majesty said, 'Records of the keepers of the imperial diary are very important, since they contain history. There may be cases where something was never reported to me directly but which only reached the notice of the Office of the Keepers of the Imperial Diary. Some diarists may write their own reports and send them on to the office. There are only two officers on duty every day. They may have friends who want them to include only the words of praise while not recording negative matters. So the keepers of the imperial diary have to be trustworthy. But are they? I do not intend to review the records. What I have done will be remembered by the people even if no records were kept. Ask the Nine Chief Ministers to set up a review board and go over the records carefully. Punish those responsible for falsifying the records.' "[16]

Songling's next entry was on the seventh day of the fourth month of the twenty-second year of the Kangxi era, that is, May 3, 1683:

"Hour of the dragon [7 to 9 A.M.]. His Majesty arrived at the Gate of Celestial Purity. The grand secretaries and the Subchancellors asked the Ministry of Personnel to propose candidates for the post of administration commissioner of Gansu province. The first choice was Secretary Shih-te-ku and the second choice was Pa-hsi.

"His Majesty said, 'Shih-te-ku is too old. Pa-hsi seems worth considering. What do you think?'

"Grand Secretary Mingju said, 'Indeed, there is nothing outstanding about Shih-te-ku, while Pa-hsi has been secretary of the Ministry of Personnel for quite a long time.'

"Grand Secretary Le-te-hung said, 'Pa-hsi is experienced and careful.'

"His Majesty said, 'Pa-hsi's learning may only be average, but he is still useful. Since he is experienced and careful, let him be the administration commissioner.' "[17]

On the twenty-seventh day of the fifth month, Songling reported that the emperor had discharged a ritual duty as the Son of Heaven, the intermediary between heaven and all his subjects, by praying for a bountiful harvest:

"Morning. His Majesty went to the Altar of Land to offer sacrifices because of the summer solstice.

[It was customary for the emperor to spend one or more days in the Palace of Abstinence before a ritual sacrifice. When he left the palace to perform sacrificial rites, bells in the pavilions would be sounded, and when he went to the Taimiao, or Imperial Ancestral Temple, to offer sacrifices, drums were beaten.]

"At the hour of the snake [9 to 11 A.M.], His Majesty went to pay his respects to the grand empress dowager [his grandmother] and the empress dowager, [his stepmother]."[18]

On the twenty-third day of the eighth month, there was an entry recorded by one of Songling's colleagues. It is unclear if that was purely due to rotation of the various diarists or because of the subject matter, for on that day the emperor discussed the promotion of Songling. The issue was the selection of an official to serve as secretary of the Supervisorate of Imperial Instruction, which was charged with the direction of the studies of the heir apparent. Emperor

Kangxi had picked his second son, the eight-year-old Yin-jeng, whose mother, the empress, had died in childbirth, as heir apparent, and a large bureaucracy was entrusted with the important task of seeing to his education.

The imperial diarist recorded:

"Grand Secretary Mingju reported, 'I have asked Chancellors Niu Niu and Zhang Yushu, and they both said that among the Hanlin academicians, the present Keeper of the Imperial Diary Qin Songling is excellent both in character and in learning, and has served for quite a long period. My officers also say that Qin Songling is excellent and fit for promotion.'

"His Majesty said, 'I know that Qin Songling is excellent scholastically and is of good character. Let us promote him to fill the vacancy.' "[19]

So Songling was promoted to secretary of the Supervisorate of Imperial Instruction while continuing to work as an imperial diarist. It is ironic that Songling took part in the education of Heir Apparent Yin-jeng, for Songling's son Daoran was later appointed tutor to the Kangxi Emperor's ninth son, Prince Yin-tang. The two princely half brothers would become bitter enemies, and Yin-tang would be implicated in a conspiracy to assassinate the crown prince.

To Songling, 1683 must have seemed a very good year. At the age of forty-six, he had successfully resumed his official career and had been promoted twice in a short time. The Kangxi Emperor was well disposed toward him, and he could look forward to making up for the long years spent in enforced idleness. Until, that is, the following year.

CHAPTER FIFTEEN

Qin Songling: Keeper of the Imperial Diary

During Songling's second year as an imperial diarist, the decades-long Qing campaign against the Ming loyalists holding out in Taiwan finally culminated in success. On September 4, 1683, Koxinga's remaining men, by this time led by his grandson, surrendered to Qing naval troops.

The Qing court had tried to weaken Taiwan by denying it food and other supplies. It went so far as to forcibly evacuate the entire coastal population facing Taiwan. But the Manchus were not able to impose their rule on Taiwan until they had built up a fleet strong enough to dislodge the Ming loyalists.

The strategist behind the Qing campaign was Yao Qisheng, governor-general of Fujian province, across the strait from Taiwan. The governor-general assembled a powerful fleet with a well-trained landing force, but entrusted the execution of the campaign to Admiral Shi Lang. The admiral's report of his victory, in which he evidently did not dwell on Yao's role, was sent directly by sea and reached Peking twenty days before the governor-general's report, which went by land. This resulted in the Kangxi Emperor's thinking that Yao Qisheng was trying to claim credit for Shi Lang's achievement.[1]

The emperor's bias against Yao Qisheng was evident in the court proceedings of October 28, 1683, when, as Songling reported, the emperor dealt with a memorial by Yao Qisheng recommending the economic development of coastal regions:

"His Majesty said,'Yao Qisheng's proposal is without substance. When Shi Lang attacked, Yao Qisheng could not even provide the military supplies on time. The warships constructed under his supervision were mostly useless. He even reported raising funds of 170,000 to 180,000 taels of silver. I think he lied. Yao Qisheng is undeserving, yet he dares to claim that he joined in planning the attack on Taiwan. Now that Taiwan is free of all the pirates, the coastal areas will be developed gradually. Yao Qisheng filed the memorial mainly to show that he cares for the people. His proposal is denied.'

"Mingju responded, 'Yao Qisheng is without honor, as Your Majesty said.'

"His Majesty said, 'Beware of him.' "[2]

It was the custom during the Qing dynasty for the emperor to review personally once a year all criminal cases for which capital punishment had been ordered. The emperor would decide if the execution should go ahead—and, if so, what form of execution should be employed—or whether it should be deferred pending further investigation, or whether it should be commuted. The annual review was conducted in the fall, in a session known as the Autumn Assizes.

Often, the main criterion of the gravity of the crime was not the nature of the act itself but the relationship between the perpetrator and the victim. Thus, a son who killed his father would be guilty of a much more serious offense than a father who killed his son, since the son owed filial piety to the father, and the father had no such obligation to the son. Similarly, a servant striking, or simply vilifying, his master was guilty of a heinous offense, while masters who struck or even killed their servants would be treated leniently.

The theory sustaining such practices was the hierarchical nature of society, with the emperor at the top. By logical extension, sanctioning of a man who raised his hand against his master or his father would lead to the condoning of regicide. The position of servitude was especially pronounced in Manchu households, where bondservants, who had a status comparable to slaves, were common.

The ceremonies at the Autumn Assizes were impressive.[3] Usually, the sessions were held at dawn, in the presence of all the emperor's chief officials, including members of the Grand Council, the chancellors and the subchancellors, the Nine Chief Ministers, censors and court officials, and the imperial guard. In deference to the solemnity of the occasion, the emperor wore plain white silk, a sign of light mourning.

After the emperor was seated on his throne, a chancellor handed him documents, which had been placed on a table before the throne. After reading these, the emperor issued rescripts indicating which criminals were to be executed. The names of those thus condemned were marked with a red hook. This practice continues in China today.

After this the documents were translated into Manchu and shown to the emperor, who verified the accuracy of the translation. The documents were then given to a censor, to be copied at the Censorate before being transferred to the Ministry of Justice. The ministry sent the imperial rescripts to the provinces concerned for the orders to be carried out.

One such session was recorded by Songling on December 1, 1683. An unusual feature about this session was that it was not held at dawn, but rather in the late morning, after routine matters had been handled, and after the emperor had paid his usual respects to the grand empress dowager and the empress dowager. Songling recorded:

"At the hour of the horse [11 A.M. to 1 P.M.], the emperor arrived at the Hall of Earnest Diligence [in the Forbidden City] and summoned the grand secretaries and chancellors to deliberate and come to a decision on the major criminal cases before the Autumn Assizes in the capital.

"His Majesty asked the grand secretaries, chancellors and others to be seated.

"His Majesty personally reviewed all the cases in detail. For those whose guilt was not in doubt and who could not be pardoned, His Majesty confirmed the verdicts reached."

Then the emperor moved on to other cases, where he felt there was an element of doubt, or where there were extenuating circumstances. In all of them, he spared the accused. They included:

• A murder case in which a man, Ku Na, had been convicted of killing his master and sentenced to death by slicing:

"His Majesty said, 'Although Ku Na was convicted, he never admitted his guilt. This is suspicious. That is why he has not been executed for so many years. Keep him in prison. We will make a decision when there is more evidence.'" (Confession of guilt, though not essential, was considered desirable. When prisoners refused to confess even under torture, then a serious question was raised as to whether they were really guilty.)

• An adulterer who had killed his lover's husband:

"His Majesty said, 'Liang Changshou and Yan Zigui's wife had an affair and [Liang] killed Zigui. He is utterly detestable. But his brother was killed in battle. So I will spare him.'"

• A forgery case:

"His Majesty said, 'Ko-erh-pa secretly made a counterfeit seal and cheated the Treasury of more than 2,000 taels of silver. Although both crimes [making the seal and cheating] call for capital punishment, he was forced into such acts because of his poverty.' "

• A case of black magic:

"His Majesty said, 'Heizi wrote out a spell and put it inside his master's clothes and believed the magic would harm him. Though it is unforgivable, it was the act of an ignorant person. Spells never do anyone harm.' "

• A gang fight in which several people were mortally wounded:

"His Majesty said, 'Although Li Da and the rest fought with Wang Qiang and other people, killing Kai Ji and two others, one of those involved, Yu Wu, has already been executed. There are too many people involved and we cannot behead all of them.' "

• A conspiracy to commit murder:

"His Majesty said, 'Ko-ba-ku was poor and could not pay back the money he owed Yan Tu, so he plotted with Shi Se to kill him. Shi Se is not the person who initiated the crime and so should be spared.' "

• Death due to a misunderstanding:

"His Majesty said, 'Because Sun Liansheng saw Liu Da enter his house naked, he mistook Liu Da for a thief and killed him. The two men did not know each other, so he can be pardoned.' "

• Self-defense:

"His Majesty said, 'Wan Jian, a watchman, was on duty in the garden. Pan Guofu struck him first. Wan Jian defended himself and fought. He was under the influence of alcohol. It was not as if he started the fight or wanted to kill his attacker.' "

• Swindling:

"His Majesty said, 'Li Song deceived a member of his family and sold that person for 5 taels of silver. This is not a serious crime and the amount involved was small.' "

Summing up the results of the day's work, in which he had overruled all the death sentences where there were extenuating circumstances, the emperor said: "Life is of the utmost importance. That is why I wished all of you to come to the inner court to discuss these matters. If there are any extenuating circumstances, we must spare a person's life. The work today has been tiring. Now you can go and eat."[4]

At one court session, the Kangxi Emperor asked how the editing of the History of the Ming Dynasty was progressing. And then, according to Songling, he added:

"History books are for future generations. They are of great importance. They have to be accurate and substantiated. We see that nowadays people do not like to have their essays corrected by others. This attitude is wrong. Any essay may have mistakes and therefore should be corrected. One should be modest and open to criticism. Never be stubborn and regard oneself as infallible."

Songling continued:

"Then His Majesty told Chancellor Niu Niu and the others, 'Even my writings should be corrected when appropriate.'

"Li Wei reported, 'Your Majesty's order is right. The essays written of course are not perfect and can be edited.'

"His Majesty said, 'Yes, look at the Hanlin Academy; the funeral odes and inscriptions that they prepare are not without flaws, yet they dislike their being corrected. Make sure the history editors know this.' "[5]

The emperor's word was law. The only constraints on him were moral. He attempted always to project an image of paternal concern for the people. Thus, on April 24, 1684, when there was a fire in a residential area outside Zhengyang Gate, the Kangxi Emperor went personally to the scene and supervised the fire-fighting operation. To prevent the fire from spreading, he ordered the destruction of neighboring houses. Members of the inner court were drafted to assist. Eventually, with the help of waterguns, the blaze was put under control.[6]

The last entry in the imperial diary registered by Songling was dated May 6, 1684. On that day, the Kangxi Emperor asked the Hanlin Academy to translate an essay composed by him on the contribution of Buddhist and Confucian philosophy.

That year, Songling was promoted from secretary to admonisher in the Supervisorate of Imperial Instruction with responsibility for giving moral and social guidance to the ten-year-old heir apparent, from which position he moved on in the same year to become senior adviser to the Supervisorate. Simultaneously, he worked as an editor of the Hanlin Academy. At the age of forty-seven, he seemed well launched on his career for a second time.

But then Songling was appointed chief examiner of Shuntian prefecture,[7] the area that included Peking, responsible for overseeing the examinations that year, a task that normally took several months.

The examiner bore a heavy responsibility: Because of the small number of successful candidates allowed, he was bound to fail the vast majority, thus blocking their only avenue to an official career. And he had to be careful about the candidates he passed, because all papers graded by the examiners went to officials of the Ministry of Rites for a process known as "thorough checking" in which minute details of phraseology and syntax were studied to see if any prohibitions had been violated.

If mistakes were found, the candidates might not only lose their degree but also be barred from participating in future examinations. The examiners could be disciplined by registration of demerits, by being made to forfeit their salaries for a fixed period of time, or worse. If bribery or nepotism was involved, the officials could be exiled or even executed.

The official records indicate that during the thorough-checking process that year, three of the successful candidates were found to have made mistakes in formats, while two others were found to have employed "ridiculous reasoning" in their papers. There were no charges of cheating or bribery, but all of the examiners from Songling on down were dismissed from their posts,[8] the most serious punishment meted out for examination offenses in the more than two decades since Kangxi ascended the throne. And curiously, despite the severity of the punishment, very little information exists regarding what really happened.

Historians today believe that there was a deliberate cover-up of those events. The eminent Qing historian Meng Sen attributes Songling's downfall to a desire for revenge by Gao Shiqi, at that time a favorite of the Kangxi Emperor. Songling had earned Gao's displeasure when he rejected a request of Gao's to compose a preface to a collection of Gao's writings. Songling despised Gao for his constant fawning on the emperor.

What gave Gao the excuse was that all the successful southern graduates of that 1684 examination were from the culturally advanced provinces of Jiangnan and Zhejiang, with none from the more backward provinces of Huguang, Jiangxi and Fujian. This was seized upon as suspicious and so the papers of the successful candidates were ordered subjected to especially strict scrutiny. Moreover, two of the successful candidates were from the family of the outstanding scholar Xu Qianxue—his son and his nephew. As a result of the thorough checking, the son's degree was revoked.[9]

These facts are consistent with our family's own account of what had happened. Qin Ying, Songling's great-great-grandson, said that the story handed down within the family was also that Gao Shiqi had used the examination incident as a pretext to get rid of Songling. Ying could well have heard the story from members of his father's generation, who were old enough to have known the facts. As one historian said, "Songling's son Daoran, Daoran's younger brother Jingran, Daoran's son Huitian, and Huitian's son Taijun were all members of the Hanlin Academy and served as government officials. The story handed down through the generations should be viewed as reliable."[10]

It is not known what were the "ridiculous reasonings" uncovered in two of the papers. If there was ambiguous wording that could have been interpreted as insulting to the ruling Manchus, the consequences would have been grave, since the Manchus were aware of their unpopularity with much of the educated Chinese elite. After all, the uprising by General Wu Sangui and his allies, which lasted for eight years, had been put down only three years before.

A famous example of the literary inquisition that marked the rule of the Manchus had to do with an examination in which a phrase used by Confucius, "where the people rest," was made the subject of an essay. It happened that the first and last words of the phrase resembled the two-character reign name of the emperor, minus the top few strokes. Charges were brought that the examiner who had chosen the subject of the essay cherished a desire to decapitate the emperor. He was thrown into prison and, after his death there, his body was dismembered. His two brothers were also imprisoned and his wife exiled.

There may have been further factors as well that led to the draconian punishment meted out to Songling and the other examiners. He is known to have made several powerful enemies. He had, for instance, antagonized Songgotu, uncle of the empress, by snubbing him on several occasions when Songgotu invited Songling to banquets. Antagonizing members of the Manchu royal family was certainly not calculated to enhance Songling's position at court.

For the second time in his life, Songling found his official life cut short. At the age of forty-seven, he was forced to leave office. But he was even now considered a person of renown, at least in the scholarly world. His official career was over, but he was not disgraced.

He lived out the rest of his life in Wuxi, and was the recipient of imperial favors to the end.

Five years after Songling's dismissal, the Kangxi Emperor paid a visit to Wuxi. He arrived on the evening of February 21, 1689. Hundreds of lanterns were lit to welcome him. The next day, the Kangxi Emperor and his entourage visited the Qin family garden, where the plum flowers were in bloom. Songling was there to welcome him, his presence confirming that he was not in disgrace. In the garden, Kangxi noticed a camphor tree whose trunk measured sixty spans. Turning to Songling, he asked: "How old is this tree that is in your family garden?"

Songling replied: "We have had this garden for two hundred years, and the tree was here even before the garden. We don't know how old it is."[11]

Then the emperor went to see the Second Spring Under Heaven nearby.

After admiring it, the emperor asked for ink, writing brush and paper and wrote out two characters, *pin quan*, or "Noble Spring." He bestowed this on Songling and asked him to keep the written characters himself while having them engraved on stone for posterity. That autumn, a solemn ceremony was held to mark the unveiling of the engraving of the imperial calligraphy.[12]

During this second period of enforced official idleness, Songling completed the work begun years before on the *Wuxi Gazetteer*. He conceded that so many people of note had appeared that it was difficult to decide whom to include and whom to omit. "When changes are great, records are difficult to write," he said. "When too many people are worthy, it is difficult to record them all. If some details are left out, the record may be biased. If all details are noted, they may confuse. In recording history, the writer initially wants to put everything down. When the record is finished, one may find it to be either too detailed or too brief."

Songling's lasting contribution to Chinese literature was his annotation of the classic *The Book of Poetry*. His short official career may well have been a blessing in disguise, for it afforded him additional time for literary efforts. As one Qing dynasty scholar wrote, while the Qin family in Wuxi was known for Confucian scholarship and for the large numbers of officials it produced during the Ming dynasty, it was not until the time of Songling that they were known for their writings. In fact, his biography in the official history of the Qing dynasty appears in the section on literary figures, not government officials.

After he had finished his work on the *Wuxi Gazetteer*, Songling and his brother Songqi began updating the family genealogy. Though he did not live to see this third edition of the Wuxi clan's history appear in print, he did contribute a preface. In it, Songling described the duty of clan members to help each other, a practice that began in the Zhou dynasty (1122–255 B.C.): "People with the same surname supported each other during sickness and hard times. They shared the expenses of burying the dead. They cared for the old, the weak and the handicapped. They reminded one another to offer sacrifices and helped one another at weddings, funerals or in times of famine. If anyone refused to help another, he would be expelled." Songling lamented that these good traditions had disappeared and added that if anyone acted like that now, he would be mocked.

In 1703, when Songling was sixty-six years old, the emperor paid another visit to Wuxi. It was during this trip that the emperor restored to Songling his original titles and ranks, thus formally ending any lingering doubt that, nineteen years after his dismissal as a result of the Shuntian examination affair, he was once more in the emperor's good graces.

On this journey, Kangxi gave the clearest indication yet that he did not suspect Songling of harboring treasonous thoughts. For he asked Songling and Songqi which member of their household would be most appropriate as a tutor for one of his sons. Songqi recommended Qin Daoran, Songling's forty-five-year-old firstborn. When the emperor went north to Peking, he took Daoran with him as tutor of his ninth son, Yin-tang.

In 1713, when Songling was seventy-seven, he journeyed to the capital to celebrate the Kangxi Emperor's sixtieth birthday. For many days the imperial birthday was celebrated in lavish style and splendor.

Father Matteo Ripa, a Catholic missionary employed by the Kangxi Emperor, describes the birthday celebrations in his memoirs:

> On the fourth day of April, the chief mandarins from all parts of the empire arrived at Peking to assist at the celebration, and take part in the splendid rejoicings which were made upon this occasion. Every one offered to the sovereign gifts of the rarest description, according to his rank and power.
>
> On this occasion the whole city of Peking wore an appearance of festivity. All were habited in gala dresses, banquets were given without end, fireworks discharged, and every kind of rejoicing carried on as at the new year. But that which above all things

struck me with astonishment, was the spectacle exhibited upon the royal road from Chang Chun Yuan (the Park of Everlasting Spring) to Peking, which is about three miles in length. This road was adorned on both sides with an artificial wall composed of mats, and entirely covered with silks of the most beautiful workmanship, while at certain distances were erected fanciful houses, temples, altars, triumphal arches and theatres, in which musical dramas were represented.

So great was the abundance of silk, that we Europeans all agreed in thinking that no kingdom in Europe possessed so much. Public prayers were also delivered by the mandarins in the numerous temples of the capital, for the safety of the Emperor and the continuation of his line; and at the same time various prostrations and sacrifices were made before a picture representing the monarch.

On the eleventh of the same month the Emperor went in state from Chang Chun Yuan (the Park of Everlasting Spring) to his palace in Peking, allowing every one to see him. On ordinary occasions His Majesty is always preceded by a great number of horsemen, who clear the streets entirely, causing all the houses and shops to be shut, and a canvas to be drawn before every opening, so that no one might see him. Upon this celebration of the sixtieth anniversary of the Emperor's birth, the openings were not stopped nor the doors shut, nor were the people driven away. The streets and roads were now crowded with countless multitudes desirous of beholding their sovereign. He rode on horseback, wearing a robe covered with dragons, magnificently embroidered in gold, and having five claws, the five-clawed dragon being exclusively worn by the imperial family. He was preceded by about two thousand horse-soldiers, in splendid array, and immediately followed by the princes of the blood, who were succeeded by a great number of mandarins.

A vast number of aged but healthy men had been sent to Peking from all the provinces. They were in companies, bearing the banner of their respective provinces. They afterwards assembled together in a place where the Emperor went to see them; and it was found that this venerable company amounted to four thousand in number. His Majesty was highly gratified with this spectacle; he inquired the age of many, and treated them all with the greatest affability and condescension. He even invited

237

them all to a banquet, at which he made them sit in his presence, and commanded his sons and grandsons to serve them with drink. After this, with his own hand, he presented every one of them with something; to one who was the most aged of the whole assembly, being nearly a hundred and eleven years old, he gave a mandarin's suit complete, together with a staff, an inkstand, and other things.[13]

The celebration of longevity is a constant theme in Chinese history, and association with the elderly is itself considered auspicious.

The celebrations were on such a scale that preparations for them had gone on for almost a year. As a retired official, Songling presented his felicitations at a ceremony at the Palace of Supreme Harmony in a group in which senior officials performed acts of obeisance to honor the emperor, and were followed by foreign envoys, chiefs of tribal groups and retired officials. To mark the imperial birthday, all offered gifts to the emperor, from the highest princes to the lowest commoner who had come to Peking. The presents ranged from ancient books, religious statues, snuff bottles, brocades and ivory carvings to horses and fresh fish.

At the same time, there was an outpouring of poems written by officials in praise of the emperor. Songling wrote ten poems in all, preceding them with a preface that alluded to Emperor Kangxi's southern trips:

"When His Majesty inspected river construction in the east, the country was at peace. All the people in the south danced with joy to welcome him. Now we celebrate His Majesty's birthday, and we offer our wishes for his longevity. I have served two emperors, and my transgressions have been forgiven. Now my teeth are loose and I still am the recipient of imperial favors. His Majesty's merits are boundless and cannot be expressed in words. I have written ten poems, but they are but a drop of water in a lake of praise for His Majesty."

One of the poems of praise for Kangxi went as follows:

> He works day and night without complaint;
> He holds the world in his hands.
> The wind blows at his beard at night;
> The moon is reflected in his teacup.
> He holds court in three palaces;

He picks the best men for office.
I remember a tortoise served him
At the dawn of his career long ago.

The tortoise, of course, was Songling's modest way of describing himself.

Songling was among those invited to a grand banquet for over two thousand elderly people from Jiangnan and nearby provinces, held in the Park of Everlasting Spring. The feast included eight main courses, including six types of grain, and concluded by serving one hundred kinds of fruits. Guests were ranked in order of seniority. Since Songling was seventy-seven years old, and had won his *jinshi* degree fifty-eight years previously, he was given a seat of honor.

After the banquet, an imperial decree extolling the virtue of filial piety was read out to the guests. The emperor invited all those over the age of eighty to move to the front, and he personally toasted them. Presents were distributed to the guests. Each person's present depended on his rank. Songling was granted a warm hat, two robes decorated with coiled dragons and an inkstand made of turquoise.[14]

While in Peking, Songling met Prince Yin-tang, the student of his son Daoran. After the birthday celebrations, Songling was escorted back to Wuxi by Daoran.

The following year, 1714, Songling died at the age of seventy-eight. The day he died, he took a bath, put his hand on his head, smiled, got dressed and lay down in bed, where he expired peacefully.

Songling died a contented man. His family had survived the change in dynasties well. Even though he had twice suffered the ignominy of dismissal, he had been restored to a position of honor. His son was the tutor of the emperor's son and a member of the distinguished Hanlin Academy. His nephew Jingran was also a Hanlin academician. His grandson Zhitian was already carving out his official career. His family was favored by the emperor, respected by the citizens of Wuxi and remained one of the wealthiest south of the Yangtze River. Yet, within a decade of his death, the family was in disgrace politically and reduced to impoverishment.

CHAPTER SIXTEEN

Qin Daoran: Tutor of the Ninth Prince

I first heard of Qin Daoran, the oldest son of Songling, my mother's great-great-great-great-great-great-great-grandfather, in April 1983, when I returned to Wuxi and had the opportunity to meet local historians and distant relatives. Then I set out to learn much more about this ancestor who spent thirteen years in prison as the victim of a spiteful emperor.[1]

When he was a child, Daoran was considered slow-witted. His teacher, in fact, advised Songling to withdraw him from school. But Daoran determined to compensate for his handicap by studying harder than anyone else in his class. Rote memory was and is an important part of Chinese education. Daoran forced himself to commit essays to memory, even if he had to read them over two or three hundred times.[2] With practice, this became easier. Finally, he could memorize an essay after reading it only a few times. He felt he had removed a mental block, and he told friends that his former stupidity was due to a shadow on his heart. With the shadow gone, he developed a remarkable memory and applied himself to the study of the classics, history and philosophy.

At age fifteen, he passed the entrance examination at the local academy, after having first become a licentiate. He not only memorized other people's work but also learned to compose fine essays of his own. By the time he was sixteen, he and three cousins were known as "the four scholars of the Qin family."[3] He also gained a reputation as an outstanding calligrapher.[4] Yet, in spite of all his efforts, he failed repeatedly in the provincial examinations. It took him ten attempts before he finally passed. Since the exams were given only once every three years, he spent nearly thirty years trying to obtain the *juren* degree.

During those three decades, Daoran started a literary society with two other local scholars. Named the Discussing Virtue Society, it was located at the foot of Tin Mountain and was established along the lines of the former Donglin Academy. Meetings were held regularly at which scholars discussed political philosophy.[5]

Daoran's tranquil life as a local scholar and aspiring official came to an end in 1703, with the Kangxi Emperor's fourth southern tour. At this time, largely unknown to all but a small handful of people at court, the emperor was experiencing severe problems with his heir apparent—his second son and the only one born of his late empress. Kangxi had received reports that Prince Yin-jeng had been associating with men of evil character and indulging in immoral practices. His plan was to groom his other sons so that one of them could be named his heir instead. So, the year before, he had enlisted an outstanding scholar from Suzhou, He Chao, to be the tutor of his eighth son.[6] And then, while visiting the Qin family garden, the emperor had met Daoran and had taken him back to the capital as his ninth son's tutor.

In Peking, Daoran worked in the Imperial Study, an institution also known as the South Library, which was set up by Kangxi. It consisted of high literary officials appointed at the emperor's pleasure and had been established in part to counter the bureaucracy of literary officials who had control over the examination system. During the Kangxi years, there were a number of scandals that showed that merit was frequently not the only determinant of success in examinations. Personal animosities and friendships played a large part, despite all attempts to keep the identity of the candidates from the examiners. He Chao, the scholar who became the eighth prince's tutor, had repeatedly failed the provincial examinations because he had antagonized the chief examiner. In 1700 the emperor denounced the officials responsible for the metropolitan examinations and pointed out that most of the successful candidates were children of high officials. As a result, new rules were drawn up under which children of such officials were tested separately and could account for no more than one tenth of all graduates. Although the idea was to give less privileged students a better chance, the result was that relatives of officials were allocated a quota totally disproportionate to their numbers.

To show his regard for He Chao, the emperor conferred on him and two other South Library scholars the *juren* degree, so that they would be eligible to take the metropolitan examinations. With a bold

241

disregard for imperial partiality, the examiners failed all three protégés, whereupon the emperor again demonstrated his omnipotence by conferring on the candidates, by special fiat, the highest degree of the land.

Therefore it was perhaps not surprising that, though Daoran had repeatedly failed the provincial exams, he was still chosen by the emperor to serve in the South Library.

Prince Yin-tang, whom Daoran was brought to Peking to tutor, was then already twenty years old. His mother was the imperial concubine I-fei, who had also given birth to the emperor's fifth son. After the death of the empress, I-fei was one of the emperor's favorite concubines, along with Te-fei, mother of the fourth son and of the fourteenth son. The mother of the eighth son, Yin-ssu, was a lowly palace maid, daughter of an imperial bond servant. Her humble origins proved a major disadvantage to her son's claim to the right of succession.

The education of princes was viewed as a matter of great consequence. Lessons started early in the morning, sometimes before dawn, and included reading and composition. The syllabus was similar to that of scholars preparing for the civil-service examinations. A tutor could, when necessary, discipline his royal charge. When they were young, relatives of the same age were allowed to study with a prince to keep him company.[7]

Apart from studying the Chinese classics, history and philosophy, princes of the Qing dynasty were required to learn their own language, Manchu. So as not to lose their cultural heritage, they also took lessons in horsemanship and the martial arts, archery in particular.

Every day, the Kangxi Emperor personally saw to the education of his sons. According to one contemporary account, he would expound on the classics to his children before holding morning audience with his ministers.[8]

Daoran was soon to be aware of the political intrigues of the various princes. He arrived in Peking on April 30, 1703, and it was only two months later when the emperor ordered the imprisonment of Songgotu, an elder statesman who, as grand-uncle of the heir apparent, exercised considerable influence over him. Songgotu's disgrace alerted all of Kangxi's sons to the fact that the heir apparent was in disfavor and precipitated a scramble for power among them. The major aspirants were the emperor's firstborn, Yin-shih, and the eighth son, Yin-ssu, the latter supported by the ninth son, Yin-tang, as well as by the thirteenth son, Yin-hsiang. The emperor's brother, Prince Yu, was a strong advocate of the eighth son. On his deathbed in 1703, he disclosed to the emperor that the heir apparent had engaged in illicit activities and he praised Yin-ssu as a man of talent and moral integrity who should be named heir apparent.[9] Thus began a savage succession struggle lasting two decades, one of the longest in China's history. But while there was much concealed chicanery, there was little overt action since Yin-jeng was still officially the heir apparent.

Two years after his arrival in Peking, Daoran obtained his *juren* degree. By then, he was forty-seven years old and his oldest son, Zhitian, had caught up with him. Both father and son passed the examinations the same year. Three years later, in the autumn of 1708, the Kangxi Emperor finally stripped Yin-jeng of the title of heir apparent. In a dramatic confrontation, he had his son brought before him in chains at his hunting lodge. There, in the presence of high Manchu and Chinese officials, the emperor denounced his son for unfilial conduct, sexual debauchery and other iniquitous behavior. Most heinous was the accusation that the crown prince had crept into the emperor's tent late at night in an attempt to assassinate his father and secure the throne for himself. The prince was placed under arrest, and almost immediately cliques emerged supporting the various brothers contending for the vacant title.[10]

The day Yin-jeng was imprisoned, his elder brother, the firstborn Yin-shih, approached the emperor in support of the eighth son's cause. He went so far as to suggest that the former heir apparent could be eliminated, apparently through assassination. Greatly alarmed, the emperor immediately took steps to protect Yin-jeng. He also ordered the arrest of his eighth son. When Kangxi learned that Yin-shih had paid Daoist priests to cast spells on the former heir apparent and had effigies used for black magic in his own house, the emperor issued a decree to incarcerate his firstborn in solitary confinement for life, holding him responsible for the deviant behavior of the former crown prince.

Kangxi was bitterly disappointed by his sons. At one point, he voiced the fear that "at my deathbed, some of you will fight each other for the throne, swinging your swords over my corpse!"[11] Grief and stress undermined his health. His cheeks were sunken and his eyes were deeply lined while his goatee of a beard became predominantly gray. Toward the end of 1708, the emperor was so gravely ill that he sought the advice of his ministers on the choice of a new heir apparent. With the exception of Yin-shih, he was prepared to accept any son they recommended, he said. To his chagrin and surprise, the ministers almost unanimously nominated his eighth son, Yin-ssu. The lone dissenter was Kangxi's close adviser Li Guangdi, who adopted a neutral position.[12]

Despite his pledge to respect his ministers' decision, Kangxi vetoed their choice, citing the fact that Yin-ssu had just been imprisoned for his involvement in an assassination plot and that his mother was of low birth. But the support for Yin-ssu continued so strong that the emperor was fearful he would be forced to abdicate in favor of his eighth son.

At this stage, Kangxi began to lean toward the reinstatement of Yin-jeng as heir apparent, since he was convinced that his son had been the victim of black magic, and that his earlier behavior was the work of ghosts that had possessed him. And the following spring, with the "ghosts" exorcised, Kangxi formally reinstated Yin-jeng as heir apparent, dashing the hopes of Yin-ssu and his supporter Yin-tang.

Yin-tang was given the title Prince of the Fourth Rank, along with Yin-ti, the emperor's fourteenth son. But the emperor's older sons were given higher honors. With the firstborn out of contention for having employed black magic, the third son, Yin-chih, was made a Prince of the First Rank, as was the fourth son, Yin-chen. Yin-tang apparently was piqued that his status had not been as elevated as his older brothers'. That year, Daoran became a *jinshi* by passing the metropolitan examinations.

In 1712, Daoran was appointed compiler of the Hanlin Academy while continuing to teach Prince Yin-tang and acting as his confidant. As a member of the academy, Daoran had access to information about the emperor's moods and partialities, information that could serve Yin-tang's interests. He Chao, tutor of Yin-ssu, was also a member of the Hanlin Academy and worked similarly for his prince.

During that year, Kangxi, despairing of his second son, who was again exhibiting strange behavior, and fearing that he would be forced to abdicate, once again stripped Yin-jeng of the title of heir apparent, placed him under permanent confinement, and decreed that Yin-jeng and those of his brothers who supported him should receive corporal punishment. The Jesuit priest Matteo Ripa witnessed the scene and described it in these words:

"When we arrived at Chang-Choon-Yuan [the Park of Everlasting Spring], the imperial residence near Peking, to our great terror we saw in the garden of that great palace eight or ten mandarins and two eunuchs upon their knees, bareheaded, and with their hands tied behind them. At a small distance from them the sons of the Emperor were standing in a row, also with their heads bare, and their hands bound upon their breasts. Shortly after, the Emperor came out of his apartments in an open sedan, and proceeded to the place where the princes were undergoing punishment. On reaching the spot he broke out with the fury of a tiger, loading the Heir Apparent with reproaches, and confined him to his own palace, together with his family and court."[13]

From then on until his death a decade later, the emperor rejected numerous appeals to designate another heir apparent, and severely punished those officials who urged him to do so or who promoted the candidacy of one prince over another.

In 1714, Daoran's father died and Daoran returned to Wuxi for the customary mourning rites.

When he returned to Peking, he was appointed keeper of the imperial diary, recording the emperor's official activities as his father had done more than three decades earlier. Always a sensitive position, it was made even more so by the power struggle for the throne.

In 1715, He Chao was arrested and his house searched, on suspicion that he was involved in promoting the ambitions of the eighth prince. As the battle among the princes became more acute, each contender strove to plant his own men in the emperor's inner sanctum so as to be kept informed of imperial preferences, opinions and changes in mood.

It was for this reason that the emperor decided in 1717 that his diarists should no longer record all his decisions. He instructed that orders given orally should not be recorded. He also tried to limit access to the records. That same year, Daoran was named deputy examiner at the provincial examinations in Jiangxi, an indication of the esteem in which he was held.

At this time, the empress dowager became seriously ill. Her stepson, the emperor, was himself in his sixties and in poor health, suffering from dizzy spells and painful, bloated feet that made movement difficult. Believing himself to be on the verge of death, Kangxi at the end of 1717 issued a valedictory to all his sons and the highest officials of the land. In it, he revealed his innermost thoughts on life and death:

"I have enjoyed the veneration of my country and the riches of the world; there is no object I do not have, nothing I have not experienced. But now that I have reached old age I cannot rest easy for a moment. Therefore, I regard the whole country as a worn-out sandal, and all riches as mud and sand. If I can die without there being an outbreak of trouble, my desires will be fulfilled."[14]

The illness of the empress dowager sparked rumors that, as a sign of filial piety, Emperor Kangxi would finally name an heir apparent so that his stepmother would be able to see the new crown prince before her death. Such rumors inevitably heightened tensions among the emperor's sons.

Early in 1718, toward the end of the fifty-sixth year of the reign of the Kangxi Emperor, Daoran recorded:

"The empress dowager's condition is gradually worsening. His Majesty, moved by grief and worry, fell ill. He is becoming thin and has severe pains in his feet so that he can walk only with difficulty. He was concerned that he would not be able to perform the rituals expected of him if the empress dowager should meet with misfortune.

"His ministers said: 'Your Majesty's filial devotions toward the grand empress dowager and the empress dowager have exceeded those of all your predecessors. Your Majesty served them day and night. Though Your Majesty's grandmother, the grand empress dowager, passed away thirty years ago, yet Your Majesty still weeps whenever her name is mentioned. Your Majesty is the most filial emperor since the period of the legendary sage kings. Now the empress dowager is sick and Your Majesty is worried that you may not be able to perform all the rituals. According to the *Book of Rites*, a mourner over the age of fifty need not be broken down, a mourner over the age of sixty need not grieve excessively, a mourner over the age of seventy may drink wine and eat meat and remain indoors instead of spending the mourning period beside the grave. That is the rule for an ordinary person who is in good health. Now Your Majesty is close to seventy years of age and you are in poor health. Your Majesty should follow historical precedents. In addition, the empress dowager has been the recipient of your filial devotions for more than sixty years and is in her eighth decade. That, too, is extremely rare. If anything should happen to her, all the appropriate arrangements will be made by the princes and courtiers. We hope Your Majesty will be mindful of your ancestors and of the welfare of the nation. It is the desire of all your ministers and your people that Your Majesty should restore your strength by not exerting yourself too much. Taking care of your own health is part of your filial obligations.' "[15]

In spite of the inflammation and painful swelling of his feet, the emperor was determined to continue to pay regular visits to the empress dowager at the Palace of Tranquillity and Longevity, which was at the northeastern end of the Forbidden City, a considerable distance from his own residence, the Palace of Celestial Purity. This regimen was strongly opposed by his highest ministers. Thus, three days later, Daoran recorded:

"At the hour of the dragon [7 to 9 A.M.], Prince Cheng [the third son], Prince Yong [the fourth son] and Sixteenth Master presented an imperial edict, which read:

" 'The condition of the empress dowager is deteriorating. We, mother and son, have been together happily for years. Now this misfortune has come upon us. Though my body is sick, my mind cannot rest. How can I not visit her? However, my own ailment makes it difficult for me to travel. I will see how my physical condition is. If at all possible, I will continue to make the visits. If I cannot withstand the journey, I will refrain.'

"Prince Cheng and Prince Yong transmitted another imperial edict, which said: 'As to the matter of the various princes, let all the ministers, the grand secretaries, the high Manchu and Chinese officials in the Ministry of Rites and the Nine Chief Ministers meet and discuss whether the princes should cut off their queues [as a sign of mourning if the Empress Dowager dies] and then memorialize.' "[16]

In response to the emperor's bidding, the court's highest officials assembled to determine the proper mourning rites for his stepmother. For this purpose, they examined imperial precedents, particularly the mourning for Kangxi's own mother when he was a mere boy. That afternoon, the officials were ready with their report. Daoran recorded:

"At the hour of the monkey [3 to 5 P.M.], Minister of Rites Tunju and other officials memorialized: 'We have had a meeting to discuss imperial precedents. In the past, emperors normally wore mourning garments of spun silk. For the mourning of the Compassionate and Harmonious Empress Dowager [Kangxi's mother], Your Majesty wore silk. Now, in the case of the empress dowager, we should according to tradition prepare white mourning costumes of spun silk for Your Majesty and the imperial family.

" 'We have also ascertained that when the Compassionate and Harmonious Empress Dowager passed away, Your Majesty did not cut off your queue. So Your Majesty must not do so when mourning the empress dowager.' "

That is to say, Kangxi must not go into deeper mourning for his stepmother than he had for his mother. According to Manchu tradition, the queue was cut off only while mourning one's father or grandfather. The emperor had violated this rule three decades earlier when his beloved grandmother, the grand empress dowager, died.

After reading the memorial from the Ministry of Rites, Kangxi penned a reply on it, written in red ink, as was the emperor's prerogative. With a few flourishes of his vermilion brush, the stubborn emperor declared:

"Mourning clothes should be made of cotton cloth. There is no regulation that says elderly mourners may not cut off their queues. If the empress dowager dies, I shall certainly cut off mine."

That same day, he issued another edict, which was transmitted to his officials through Prince Cheng, calling on them to do additional research into traditional practices.

Officials of the Nine Chief Ministries met and reported after their meeting: "According to Manchu tradition, a sick and elderly person should shun mourning clothes. Now Your Majesty is close to seventy and is physically weak. Your intention to wear mourning garments is already an extreme expression of your filial feelings. During the mourning for the Compassionate and Harmonious Empress Dowager, Your Majesty did not cut off your queue. On this occasion, Your Majesty must act likewise."

To which His Majesty replied: "My order is clear. You should obey my order."

Daoran observed:

"Today, His Majesty's feet were so swollen that he could not move. Because of the seriousness of his condition, His Majesty, when he went to the Palace of Tranquillity and Longevity, was borne on a sedan chair and his feet were wrapped in handkerchiefs. He held the hand of the empress dowager and asked how she was. He stayed until he felt so unwell that he could not endure it any longer."[17]

That night, Kangxi did not return to his palace. Instead, he slept in a tent that he pitched outdoors, by the Changchen Gate, in another gesture of his profound devotion to the empress dowager. Thirty years previously, when his grandmother had died, the emperor had behaved similarly, sleeping in a shabby tent outside his palace.

The next day, the emperor issued another edict in which he described in moving terms his visit with the empress dowager:

"The empress dowager's condition is deteriorating. If I remain in my residence, I become anxious. Now I am sick and my feet are painful. I cannot sleep. Yesterday I went by a sedan chair to see the empress dowager. That made me feel worse. I held the empress dowager's hand and said, 'Mother, I am here.' She opened her eyes, but was sensitive to the light. She held my hands. I wanted to stay, but the people attending me saw that I could not bear it any longer and persuaded me to leave. After all the exertion I felt great discomfort and grew dizzy. The Fifth Prince urged me to go saying that he would do all that was necessary for his grandmother. But I replied since I was present, why should he do it for me? Since the second month of this year I have been feeling unwell with palpitations of the heart and dizzy spells. Though I am still ill I am better now than when I was in Rehe [the country residence in Inner Mongolia where the Emperor spent his summers]."[18]

The following day, the emperor's officials continued to press him to think of his own health and not tax himself physically while showing his filial devotion to the empress dowager. Daoran recorded:

"The hour of the dragon [7 to 9 A.M.].

"The courtiers memorialized: 'The empress dowager has received your services for over sixty years, which is her good fortune. No one in history can compare with the filial piety of Your Majesty. Your Majesty should be less demanding on yourself. We courtiers know how to make the mourning preparations. We have found that the Confucian scholar Zheng Kangcheng said in the Tang dynasty that a mourner over the age of sixty can remain seated while his descendants perform the sacrificial ceremony. We beg Your Majesty to follow this precedent and think of the welfare of the empire.'

"His Majesty responded: 'If the empress dowager passes away, I shall perform all the requisite ceremonies, despite my sickness. Since you all have parents, you can understand my feelings. Do not try to persuade me otherwise, for it will only add to my sorrow.' "

Later that day, the emperor issued the following edict: "If misfortune befalls the empress dowager, I shall perform the sacrificial ceremonies every two or three days up until the time the casket is moved. When the casket is moved, I shall follow it to the gate of the Palace of Tranquillity and Longevity, or even to the Flowery Eastern Gate if I have the strength." It was the custom in those days not to keep the deceased in the palace long but to transfer the corpse to a funeral house, because of the Manchu belief that the presence of a dead person in the palace would shorten the life of the emperor.

That evening, the event that had been the preoccupation of the emperor and the whole court for such a long time finally occurred. Daoran recorded:

"At the hour of the fowl [5 to 7 P.M.], the empress dowager passed away at the Palace of Tranquillity and Longevity.

"His Majesty immediately cut off his queue, changed to mourning clothes made of cloth and cried and wailed incessantly. Neither the princes nor the servants could bear to look at him. They knelt down and pleaded: 'Your Majesty is old. Please consider your own health and the welfare of the empire and do not feel too sad. Please return to the palace.'

"They begged several times, but His Majesty refused. He saw to the arrangement of the casket, poured the libation, and only after repeated begging by the princes did His Majesty leave and return to his tent at the Changchen Gate."[19]

The pouring of the libation was an integral part of the mourning ceremonies, and was performed on many occasions. Usually, a vessel of wine was first presented to the emperor by the minister of rites. The emperor then poured it into a large golden bowl. When the master of ceremonies gave a signal, all officials present prostrated themselves.

For the next eleven days, the emperor continued to camp outside his palace. On the eleventh day, the casket of the empress dowager was transferred to an outside funeral house. Daoran recorded:

"His Majesty went to the Palace of Tranquillity and Longevity and offered the ritual sacrifice. He wept and called out 'Mother!' All his retinue cried. When the casket was moved through the Eastern Flowery Gate to be deposited at the funeral house outside the Chaoyang

Gate, all the princes helped His Majesty to the West Terrace. As the coffin was borne forward, His Majesty cried again. After repeated entreaties, His Majesty returned to his tent at the Changchen Gate."[20]

With ceremonial troops leading the way, the solemn procession passed by the Xiehe Gate, the eastern gate leading from the vast courtyard facing the Hall of Supreme Harmony, and wound its way to Dengshikou Street and Red Temple Avenue until it arrived at the funeral house outside the Chaoyang Gate. At each spot were gathered, according to rank, princes and high officials who knelt and wept as the casket was borne past. At the funeral house, princesses, consorts and wives of high officials were assembled. The casket was carried into the middle of a field surrounded by two layers of fences. The women mourners were allowed through the first entrance, where they knelt. Inside, the princes performed the libation ceremony. When the wine was poured onto the ground, all the princesses and consorts kowtowed, knocking their heads on the ground.

On the eighteenth, Daoran made one last brief entry:

"In the morning, princes and ministers, Manchus and Chinese, civil and military officials, the Nine Chief Ministers and other officials all came to the emperor's tent at Changchen Gate and petitioned: 'The ceremony to transfer the body of the empress dowager to the funeral house is over. It is now extremely cold and we hope that Your Majesty will have some concern for yourself, consider the welfare of the country, and return to the Palace of Supreme Harmony.' "[21]

But the mourning for the empress dowager continued, marked by the Clear and Bright Festival in the spring, when the dead are honored. It concluded with the burial of the empress dowager in a mausoleum on the outskirts of Peking. Although Kangxi wanted to accompany the body there himself, in the end he bowed to the wishes of his ministers and announced that, considering his state of health, he would forgo the journey. On the fourteenth day of the third month of the fifty-seventh year of his reign [April 14, 1718], a hundred days after the death of the empress dowager, the Kangxi Emperor finally consented to return to his normal routine by moving to the Park of Everlasting Spring in the outskirts of Peking.

Daoran's career as an imperial diarist ended later that year when Kangxi abolished the Office of the Keepers of the Imperial Diary.[22] Daoran was appointed professor of the Department of Study, where

Hanlin bachelors studied for examinations, and then named supervising secretary of the Office of Scrutiny for Rites, which made him an official critic of the Ministry of Rites. Six months before he was appointed to this post, Prince Yin-tang had made him his household and financial manager, a position that only a Manchu bond servant was supposed to hold.[23]

After he became supervising secretary, Daoran asked Yin-tang to relieve him of his duties as family treasurer, since he felt it was incompatible with his new role. The prince was adamant. During this period, Daoran several times requested permission to retire from government service, but it was never granted. Afterward, people said it was as if he had had a premonition that his life was in danger.

In the last few years of the Kangxi Emperor, Prince Yin-tang was one of the main contenders for the throne. He strengthened his position by amassing great wealth and using money to win support for himself and members of his faction.

Yin-tang had influential allies, but he never found favor with his father. Once it became apparent that his chances were slight, the leading contenders became Prince Yin-chen, the fourth son, and Prince Yin-ti, the fourteenth son. Born of the same mother and thus full brothers, they were, however, deadly rivals. The out-of-favor Yin-tang used his vast wealth to help Yin-ti. And in his last years, the emperor appeared to be leaning more and more toward Yin-ti. In 1718, he appointed Yin-ti commander in chief of troops at Xining in the northwest, his mission to hurl back the Western Mongols, who had invaded Tibet, a Chinese vassal state. The thirty-two-year-old generalissimo was seen off with much pomp and ceremony, and the feeling grew that this was the emperor's favorite son. Because of the emperor's frail condition, Yin-tang made arrangements for a messenger to ride from Peking to Yin-ti's encampment to keep the prince informed of any developments. Though Daoran was not a party to these events, he was aware of them. Before Yin-ti left for the front, Daoran, under instructions from Yin-tang, paid him a courtesy call. Yin-ti was too busy to see him, but presented him, via a servant, with a hat.

Yin-ti was summoned back to the capital for consultations after two years, and remained in Peking for six months. Before he left again for the front at the end of May 1722, Daoran called on him at Yin-tang's suggestion. This time, the two men did talk.

Seven months later, the Kangxi Emperor died suddenly at the age of sixty-eight, having sat on the Dragon Throne for sixty-one years, the longest-serving emperor in several millennia of Chinese history. His reign had seen the Manchus transformed from alien conquerors into Sinicized rulers of China. He had sought, with a large measure of success, to unify and strengthen the empire. But on a personal level he had had the sorrow of the enmity among his sons.

The death of the emperor did not precipitate an armed conflict among the brothers, because Fourth Prince Yin-chen acted promptly and accomplished his takeover with almost military precision. The ambitions of Yin-tang, Yin-ssu and Yin-ti, as well as those of their supporters, such as Qin Daoran, were thwarted. For them, the enthronement of the new emperor was to be an unmitigated disaster.

CHAPTER SEVENTEEN

Qin Daoran: Political Prisoner

News of the death of Emperor Kangxi reached Yin-ti in Xining. Though the thirty-four-year-old prince had troops under his command, he was unable to promote his own cause, for by the time he was informed, his brother, Fourth Prince Yin-chen, had been proclaimed the new emperor. And Yin-chen, who took the reign name Yongzheng, immediately removed the threat posed by his brother. The day after Kangxi's death, Emperor Yongzheng recalled Yin-ti to Peking and stripped him of his command.

Though Yin-tang was in Peking when Kangxi died, he and Yin-ssu were also rendered powerless by the speed of events. The commander of the Peking gendarmerie had thrown in his lot with Yin-chen and been instrumental in overseeing a smooth takeover by the Fourth Prince. Furthermore, the new emperor sent Yin-tang out of Peking, where he had powerful supporters, to remote Xining, even before their father's funeral.

And Yongzheng lost no time in beginning to gather evidence against his sibling rivals. One of the first things he did was question Yin-tang about the role played by Qin Daoran. Why, he asked, did Yin-tang ask Daoran, a Chinese, to manage his family affairs? Yin-tang pretended that Daoran had not actually been in charge of these, but only concerned with educational matters.

It may never be known if Yin-chen was really his father's choice. Some historians argue that Yin-ti was the intended heir, and that Kangxi's will was altered from "fourteenth son" to "fourth son."[1] Such stories circulated almost immediately after Kangxi's death. Some accounts go so far as to claim the Fourth Prince murdered his father to ensure his own succession.

What is certain is that contemporary records were tampered with on the orders of the new emperor. The Veritable Records of the

Kangxi Emperor's reign were edited so that unfavorable references to the fourth son—and favorable references to the others—were expunged. For these services, Emperor Yongzheng gave the editor of the records the highest possible honors.[2]

About ten days after Yongzheng's enthronement, Daoran received an emissary with a secret message from Yin-tang. It was: "The emperor has asked about you. He says that you are a Chinese, so why were you in charge of family affairs, and why did Prince Yin-tang show you such favor? I am afraid you may be summoned for questioning. You have to be prepared to answer these questions."[3]

The messenger told Daoran what Yin-tang had answered and urged him to corroborate that account. Most probably, Daoran was taken in for questioning soon after and detained. The first mention of Daoran in the Veritable Records of the Yongzheng period occurs on March 16, 1723, the tenth day of the second month of the first year of his reign. On that day, Yongzheng issued an edict against Lesiheng, a staunch supporter of Yin-tang. In it, Yongzheng disclosed that Lesiheng's crime was violating his injunction not to maintain records of the punishment of persons close to his brothers.

Emperor Yongzheng outwardly took the position that his brothers were the victims of evil men in their households who would be punished. But the new emperor said in his edict, "I told Lesiheng: 'The penalties are a matter of family discipline for punishing servants, so no official record is necessary.' However, Lesiheng disobeyed my orders. Now, Lesiheng is removed from his position and ordered exiled to Xining to serve Yin-tang."

And while on the subject of Yin-tang, the emperor asked rhetorically, "He could have appointed anyone as his family manager; why did he pick a Chinese, Supervising Secretary Qin Daoran?" The emperor answered his own question by saying that Yin-tang wanted to win the support of Chinese officials through Daoran. In spite of all that Yin-tang had done, Yongzheng said, "I did not take away his title. I did not reduce his income, and I did not take away his family servants. I have only sentenced one or two of the wicked men and the eunuch."[4]

Unfortunately, Daoran was one of the "wicked men" punished along with the eunuch He Yuzhu.

On November 8, 1723, the Yongzheng Emperor commented on a recommendation by the Ministry of Punishments that Daoran be immediately executed. The emperor responded: "Qin Daoran has performed many wicked acts while relying on powerful supporters. He has cheated people of a large sum of money. We shall postpone his execution but jail him in Jiangnan. Have him pay back the money first, then report to me again."[5]

Though the Yongzheng Emperor did not immediately openly persecute his brothers, much less delicate treatment was meted out to his other political opponents. Father Ripa, in his memoirs, describes the death of one high official condemned by Yongzheng:

"He [Mo-lao] was informed that the Emperor condemned him to die by his own hands, and the executioner, after freeing him from his chains, gave him a cup of poison, a halter, and a dagger, that he might choose for himself whichever death he preferred, but he left him no food. The next day the executioner returned, expecting to find him dead; but seeing that he was still alive, he urged the necessity of instant execution; Mo-lao then taking off a coat of mail adorned with gold, gave it to the man to get more time allowed. The executioner accepted the gift, and went to the mandarins to report that he had not yet killed himself; but on the following day, finding him once more alive, he stifled him beneath a sack of sand. After this his body was burnt, and, to complete the tragedy, his ashes were scattered to the winds."[6]

For three years, Yongzheng consolidated his position while gradually whittling down the authority of his potential opponents. By the beginning of 1726, the fourth year of his reign, he was ready for further measures. A letter was intercepted from Yin-tang to his son. It was written not in Chinese characters but in the Cyrillic alphabet, which the Ninth Prince had learned from the Portuguese missionary Jean Mourao. Yin-tang was accused of conspiracy and his brother Yin-ssu of clandestine contact with Yin-tang. Both were expelled from the imperial clan, making them liable to punishment as commoners. To add to their humiliation, Yin-ssu was forced to take the name Acina, which means "cur," and Yin-tang, Seshe, or "pig."

The web that Yongzheng wove around his brothers was finely spun. He first gathered evidence against those who were in a position to incriminate the princes. The testimony of Daoran was crucial. To attempt to obtain his cooperation, Yongzheng first built a case against him, using testimony by Shao Yuanlong,[7] his former colleague who had been spurned by Yin-tang, and by Yao Zixiao, a retainer in Yin-

A branch of the Grand Canal in Gaoyou, Qin Guan's hometown

The mountains of China are covered with engravings of calligraphy left behind by visiting scholars.

Statues of the traitor Qin Kui and his wife kneel behind metal bars. Sign on wall warns visitors not to spit on the statues "for hygienic reasons."

Larger-than-life statue of China's famous patriot, General Yue Fei, dominates temple in his honor in Hangzhou.

The temple of the City God of Shanghai has been converted into a shopping mall.

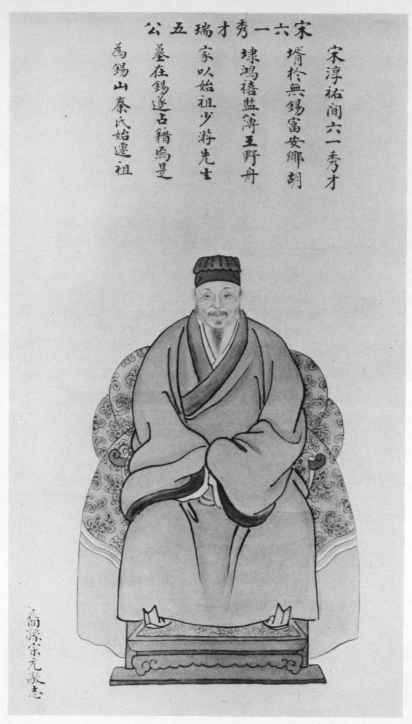

宋淳祐間六一秀才
宋壻於無錫富安鄉胡
一六隸鴻禧監簿王野舟
才秀家以始祖少游先生
瑞才墓在錫遂占籍為是
五公墓在錫遂占籍為是
公為錫山秦氏始遷祖

Ancestral portrait of Qin Weizheng, progenitor of the Qin family of
Wuxi, wearing the clothing of a commoner. Portrait was part of a series
commissioned in the early nineteenth century.

寄 畅 园

明王朝弘治年间（公元1506至1510年）秦金修造，称"凤谷行窝"。
万历二十七年（公元1599年），秦耀改造，易名"寄畅园"。
园内水陆面积各半，水曲"锦汇漪"是全园中心。池东有
"郁盘廊"、"知鱼槛"、"涵碧亭"等临水建筑，"七星桥"横贯池
上，别饶风趣。登池西北高坡，可眺望全园景物。坡下有幽
曲小溪"八音涧"，深入流水，迴响其间，池边小径叫"锦步滩"。
寄畅园座落锡山、惠山之间，夏阴敞日，古木参天。东
看锡山古塔，雄峙栋前，西望九龙惠山，蜿蜒屏后，疏林
茂草，宛如一幅"云林山水"借景特色，素为古今造园家推
崇，是江南著名古园。北京颐和园内的"谐趣园"，就是清
帝南巡按照京份"寄畅园"造的。
历代变乱，名园荒芜，解放后送经整修，池沼假山、迴廊
曲槛，顿萌生机，使我园古代造园艺术珍品，重放光彩。

Cracked signboard outside the Ji Chang Garden, or "Garden of Leisure," in Wuxi says it was begun by Qin Jin in the early sixteenth century. It remained in the hands of the Qin family for over four centuries.

A scene of the Ji Chang Garden, a favorite of two emperors of the Qing Dynasty. A replica can be found in the Summer Palace in Peking.

明水樂武昌府知府

明南京兵部主事晉中

武昌府憲大夫封承德郎惠

府知山碧山吟社十老之

修敬公首江南通志郡志邑

志有傳

Portrait of the recluse-scholar Qin Xu, whose oldest son won honors in officialdom and whose two other sons were honored as "filial sons." He is shown here in the robes of an official. Though he never served in an actual post, he was given the official ranking in recognition of his oldest son's achievements.

A stone horse lies amid the grass along the "Sacred Way" leading to the tomb of Qin Jin, a high-ranking official who died in 1544. His grave was dug up during the Cultural Revolution.

The grave of Qin Liang (1514–1578) probably was not desecrated by Red Guards because it was behind a leprosy hospital. The engraving of an old man on the wall signifies that the grave was constructed while its occupant was still living.

Mr. Gu Wenbi speaking with a woman named Zhou, whose family cared for the tomb of Governor Qin Yao (1544–1604) for over three centuries.

An arch commemorates the site of the Donglin Academy, whose members were persecuted by the Eunuch Wei Zhongxian toward the end of the Ming Dynasty.

The career of the seventeenth-century scholar Qin Songling, the youngest man ever to win admittance to the Hanlin Academy, was cut short because of Manchu persecution of the Chinese.

Minister of Punishments Qin Huitian, who came third in the nationwide examinations, was favored by the Qianlong Emperor.

An endorsement by the emperor, written in vermilion ink, stipulates the forfeiture of three months' salary by Qin Huitian for an error in judgment.

Provincial Judge and Vice-Minister of Punishments Qin Ying in his later years

"Distinguished Failure" Qin Xiangye was known as a poet and historian. He officiated at the wedding of author's grandparents in Hangzhou.

The author's grandmother standing in a garden holding a musical instrument. The picture is from a posthumously published collection of her essays and poems.

Qin Liankui, the author's father, taken in his mid-forties, when he was in his prime

Zhaohua, the author's mother, at age seventeen, when she was married

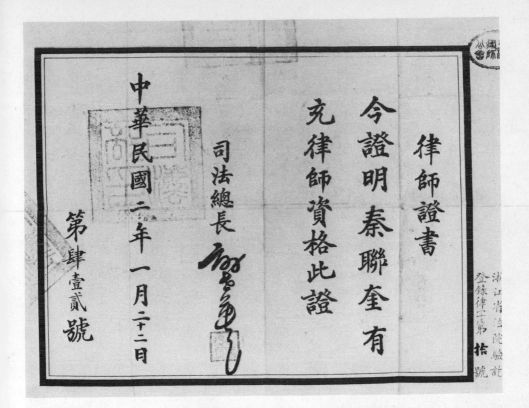

The certificate issued by the Ministry of Justice in 1913 authorizing Qin Liankui to practice law.

The certificate issued by the Kuomintang government after its successful Northern Expedition to overthrow the warlord government in Peking in 1927, when Qin Liankui was a moving force behind the Shanghai Bar Association, of which he was a founder

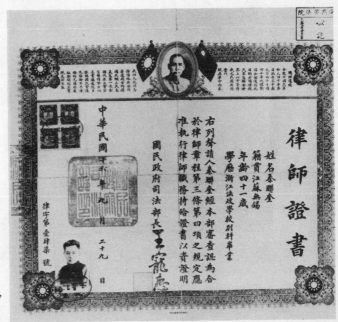

The defendants and their lawyers in the "Seven Gentlemen" case of 1936–1937. Qin Liankui is in the second row, extreme right.

The 1938 graduating class of the Zhengshi Middle School in Shanghai, which was owned by the notorious Du Yuesheng. The Communist martyr is seated in the front row, extreme left. His elder brother, Jiaju, is third from the right.

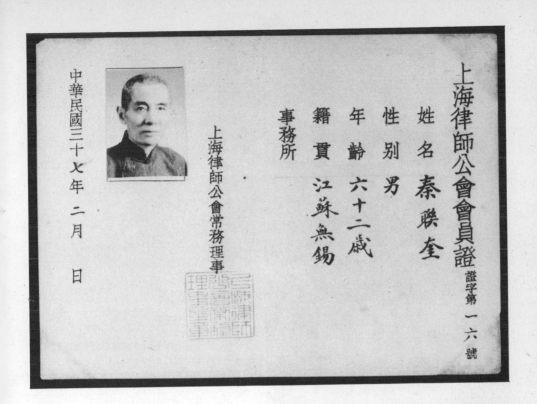

Qin Liankui's Shanghai Bar
Association membership card, issued
in 1948. His membership number
was 16.

Family portrait of the author's family, showing the aged father and young mother with their four children. The author is the youngest shown.

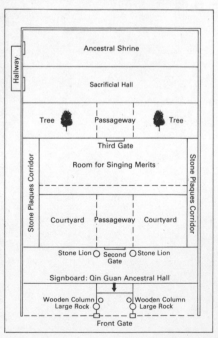

Floor Plan of the Qin Guan Ancestral Hall

North

Floor plan of the Qin Guan Ancestral Hall in Wuxi, built during the Ming Dynasty (1368–1644)

tang's household who had acted as a messenger to keep Yin-ti at the front informed of his father's moods and state of health.

On March 10, 1726, the Yongzheng Emperor issued an edict instructing Vice Minister of Punishments Huang Bing and Cha-pi-na, governor general of Zhejiang and Jiangnan, to conduct an interrogation of Daoran, who was then in prison in Nanking. The edict said:

"You must investigate Qin Daoran and question him in detail. Bring with you the case of Shao Yuanlong and Yao Zixiao. Qin Daoran is a Chinese and so is different from the others. Why did he help Yin-tang in his wicked activities to oppress people? His actions are iniquitous. He even declared that Yin-tang had the countenance of an emperor. This kind of plot merits death. Tell him if he confesses everything concerning Yin-tang, Yin-ssu and Yin-ti I will spare him. After he has told the truth, report to me. Then remain there until further orders."[8]

Daoran's testimony was extracted without resorting to physical torture, although great psychological pressure was brought to bear. He was constantly made to understand that his life would be spared only on the condition that he "spoke the truth."

A transcript of the cross-examination has been preserved.[9] Written in the form of a series of questions and answers, this document is a prime source of information on Emperor Yongzheng's case against his brothers—the Eighth, Ninth and Fourteenth Princes. However, the document raises almost as many questions as it answers. For one thing, it reveals that there had been earlier interrogations and other proceedings, for which records are no longer extant. In all likelihood, they were either not kept or destroyed on the order of the Yongzheng Emperor.

It is clear, in any event, that by the time of this interrogation, Daoran had been in prison for four years, the first three of which were spent in the Ministry of Punishments prison in Peking. We do not know exactly when he was sent to the south. The record remains blank in many areas.

Reading between the lines of the questions and answers, it also becomes evident that, at some point, Daoran was fined the astronomical sum of 100,000 taels of silver, and given six months in which to raise the money. By the time of the interrogation, he had raised only one tenth of that amount. The fine was euphemistically described as "raising funds for the military."

The first charge leveled against Daoran was that, being a Chinese, he should not have become involved in the family affairs of the Manchu royal family, that is, the power struggle among the various princes.

Daoran's response was an abject admission of guilt, tempered by an assertion that he had tried to quit Yin-tang's service. He then turned informant and betrayed his former patron, reciting a long listing of Yin-tang's "crimes," together with his own role in them.

Daoran repeatedly asserted that he was guilty of heinous crimes deserving of the death penalty many times over. He recounted numerous occasions when Yin-tang had engaged in extortion. Such acts included a demand for payment of the sum of 80,000 taels of silver to "adopt" someone as his daughter, since it was considered a great honor to be related to the emperor's family. Imperial relatives, governors and governors general, as well as lower-level officials, made large gifts of money to Yin-tang when he put pressure on them.

The biggest corruption case concerned Yin-tang's own son-in-law, grandson of the wealthy Grand Secretary Mingju, who paid 300,000 taels. It cannot be ascertained what power Yin-tang had over the people from whom he extracted vast sums, what threats or promises he made. As a result of his role in these activities, Daoran had received a small share of the proceeds—a total of just over 3,000 taels of silver. The Ninth Prince had also promoted his financial position through dealing in contraband ginseng, which he had smuggled in from Manchuria to sell in the south, ginseng being highly valued for its life-prolonging qualities. Because ginseng was an important source of revenue, its cultivation, gathering, transportation and sale were carefully regulated.

Yin-tang was by far the wealthiest of the princes. He more than doubled his assets by marrying into the family of Grand Secretary Mingju. Yet he had not hoarded wealth. He had gathered it in order to further his political ambitions and those of his two brothers. In effect, through the years, he built up an impressive war chest to pay for the expected succession struggle.

Daoran had played a key part in Yin-tang's plans, representing the southern scholars. Just as the Kangxi Emperor had to Sinicize his administration to win over the Chinese, so the various princes needed supporters to strengthen their positions. Daoran had provided access for Yin-tang to the Chinese intelligentsia. The relationship between Yin-tang and Daoran can be gauged from the fact that Daoran frequently went to Yin-tang's house late in the evening, remaining there until early morning. In all likelihood, Daoran was a key strategist in the three brothers' attempt to gain power.

Daoran must have been realistic enough to know that Yin-tang's chances to be the next emperor were slim, given the Kangxi Emperor's known dislike for this son, as well as for the eighth son, Yin-ssu. Nevertheless, Daoran also knew that should his student become emperor one day, his own position would be exalted. And so Daoran on occasion had told people that Yin-tang's countenance "manifests an imperial air."

He said in his deposition, "I told people that Yin-tang was kind and generous in order to make people think he was good. This was because I harbored improper desires, and for this I deserve to die ten thousand times."

In his testimony, Daoran also provided information on other unlawful or unseemly behavior by Yin-tang. Slavery was an accepted practice at the time, so the buying and selling of girls was not in itself illegal, except with the use of force or deception. But it made a great difference whether the girls came from respectable or low-class theatrical families. Yin-tang had obtained girls through his eunuch, He Yuzhu. Ironically, the eunuch had pretended to be the son of a wealthy salt merchant, and had "married" girls from respectable families. His victims were then transported to Peking and into Yin-tang's bedchamber.

Daoran's evidence concerning his former pupil and confidant was crucial in forming the basis of serious charges against Yin-tang. For example, Daoran said that Yin-tang was unhappy with having been named a Prince of the Fourth Rank when some of his siblings had been named Prince of the First Rank. One day, Daoran said, Yin-tang pulled the ceremonial feather indicating rank from his head to show to everyone and said that it did not look very grand. This was taken to indicate that he harbored resentment against his imperial father.

On another occasion, Yin-tang feigned illness and encouraged his eighth brother to do likewise because they were lazy and did not want to perform tasks assigned by their father, thus deceiving the emperor. When Kangxi stripped the heir apparent of his title and put him in chains, Yin-tang felt the punishment for his brother was not severe enough. Such a sentiment was interpreted as an expression of disloyalty and lack of filial piety.

As the questioning went on, Daoran furnished information that ensnared not only Yin-tang but also Yin-ssu and Yin-ti.

Daoran described Yin-ssu as an impostor and a hypocrite, someone who pretended to be virtuous in order to acquire a good reputation. Yin-ssu had used his Chinese tutor, He Chao, to further his political ends, Daoran said, but the evidence Daoran was able to give was rather insubstantial. Yin-ssu, he said, used to ask his tutor's brother to buy books for him in the south so as to impress southern scholars and gain their support.

Yin-ssu was such a poor scholar and his handwriting was so bad that the Kangxi Emperor had ordered him to practice his calligraphy daily. Instead, he hired someone to do his homework, thus deceiving the emperor.

Moreover, Daoran said, Yin-ssu disobeyed his father's order to abstain from alcohol. He drank intemperately and when intoxicated became violent. Yin-ssu was also guilty of the serious crime of being henpecked. His wife, Daoran said, gave orders within the household. Since this was intolerable even in the home of a commoner, how could it have been permitted in the palace?

As to Yin-ti, Daoran said that he used illness as an excuse to avoid accompanying the emperor on a trip. Kangxi punished him by taking away his servants and making them do the most menial jobs. Yin-ti then apologized to his servants, saying that he was the cause of their suffering. This act, Daoran said, showed disloyalty and lack of filial piety, for if everyone felt grateful to Yin-ti, what did they think of the emperor?

All three brothers, Yin-tang, Yin-ssu and Yin-ti, had frequently voiced their resentment of the heir apparent. Daoran condemned this as improper and disloyal conduct.

Daoran's testimony shed new light on an intriguing incident that highlights the brothers' intense behind-the-scenes power struggle. This was the case of the physiognomist Chang Ming-te, whom Yin-ssu had consulted to find out what the future held. Chang told him what he wanted to hear: that he would be emperor one day. Chang also proposed that the former heir apparent, who had been stripped of his title by Kangxi, be assassinated. Though the brothers ignored this recommendation, when news of it came to light in 1708, Chang was executed by the cruelest form of capital punishment: death by slicing. Yin-ssu, Yin-tang and Yin-ti were forced to watch the execution.

And because of this incident, Yin-ssu was imprisoned. The brothers Yin-tang and Yin-ti appealed to their father on his behalf. This only succeeded in angering the emperor more. "Are you two placing your hope on Yin-ssu's becoming the heir apparent so that once he is enthroned you may be made Prince of the First Rank?" he asked. "You want to show that you are men of unswerving loyalty and faithfulness to each other and you are real heroes; but I think you are like the bandits of the Water Margin at Liang Mountain."

The hot-tempered Yin-ti swore an oath, which so infuriated the Kangxi Emperor that he drew his dagger and said, "If you want to die, you can die right now." Those present begged the emperor to spare his son. Kangxi then sheathed his dagger but struck Yin-ti with a rod. Yin-tang knelt down and grasped the rod before it could be used again. Kangxi slapped him twice on the face so hard that it was swollen for days. He then ordered that Yin-ti be flogged.

Much of the questioning of Daoran centered on the relationship between Yin-tang and Yin-ti. Daoran revealed the secret arrangement between the Ninth and Fourteenth Princes under which Yin-tang sent messengers to Yin-ti in Xining to keep him informed of the state of affairs in the capital, and most particularly of the Kangxi Emperor's health.

According to Daoran's testimony, Yin-tang wanted his brother to score a resounding triumph on the battlefield so that he would be nominated heir apparent. Yin-tang had told Daoran: "In the event that the Fourteenth Prince becomes heir apparent, he will certainly seek my advice." After assuming his command in Xining, Yin-ti not only drove the invaders from Tibet but pursued them into their own territory. But he was thousands of miles away when Kangxi died and so in no position to have any influence on the question of the succession.

Throughout the interrogation, Daoran suggested that his had been an insignificant role in the princes' conspiracy.

Toward the end of the interrogation, the vice-minister made a comment that was pure conjecture. "There is still much that you have not disclosed," he said. "I will give you time to think. Then confess item by item. If you try to conceal anything from us, we will torture you severely. You are a scholar. You know what is important.

You are guilty of having deceived heaven and your emperor. But now is the time for you to repent."

The pressure on Daoran was great. He had to convince his questioners of his sincerity and eagerness to cooperate. "I deserve ten thousand deaths," he repeated. "Now the imperial court has ordered an investigation. If I tell the truth, I shall live; if I lie, I shall die. This is most magnanimous. Though I am only an animal, I can think and I am grateful to His Majesty for not executing me. How would I dare conceal anything? In the last few days, I have told you everything concerning the disloyalty and the unfilial behavior of Yin-tang, Yin-ssu and Yin-ti, their clandestine activities, their using money to win over people, their extortion of wealth. I even told the truth about my own crimes, which deserve death. I have concealed nothing. His Majesty's intelligence is so penetrating, he will know my honesty. I dare not deceive him."

As a result of the interrogation, the vice-minister and the governor general informed the Yongzheng emperor:

"We found that Qin Daoran is very cunning and wicked. Since the late emperor appointed him tutor of Yin-tang, he not only did not oppose all the wicked activities of Yin-tang but even encouraged them. There were numerous illegal acts, such as taking care of Yin-tang's family matters, extorting money from Man-pi and others, and praising Yin-tang in public. He has admitted all the charges by Shao Yuanlong. Qin Daoran is a thief but Yin-tang treated him as his confidant and kept no secrets from him. Qin Daoran then used such information to cheat and blackmail. Such a wicked person should receive the most severe punishment to set an example to others who violate the law. Governor General Cha-pi-na will press his family members to make good the fine of 100,000 taels for military expenses, together with the 2,320 taels he extorted that he has been ordered to return. The money will be remitted to the court as it is collected."

Since Daoran had been able to raise only one tenth of the fine of 100,000 taels, great pressure would be put on his family to provide the rest.

The vice-minister and the governor general then enumerated the crimes of the three princes, based on Daoran's evidence:

"Concerning Yin-tang, Yin-ssu and Yin-ti, their wicked acts are beyond numbering.

"Yin-tang:

"First count of grave disrespect: criticizing the late emperor for only naming him a Prince of the Fourth Rank.

"Second count of grave disrespect: feigning illness and telling Yin-ssu to pretend to be sick also.

"Third count of grave disrespect: complaining to Qin Daoran that the Kangxi Emperor was too lenient in the treatment of his First Brother.

"Fourth count of grave disrespect: warning Qin Daoran that he was about to be interrogated after Your Majesty had been enthroned with the intention of deceiving Your Majesty.

"First count of harboring evil designs: meeting with Yin-ti almost every other day, and talking in secret until midnight, before Yin-ti left to lead his troops.

"Second count of harboring evil designs: sending Yao Zixiao as a messenger back and forth.

"Third count of harboring evil designs: giving money and goods to others with the intention of buying their support.

"Yin-ssu:

"First count of harboring evil designs: being deceitful, crafty, pretending to be pleasant and agreeable, seeking praise and a good reputation, buying loyalty.

"Second count of harboring evil designs: repeatedly forming a faction with Yin-tang and Yin-ti.

"Third count of harboring evil designs: having transactions with practitioners of black magic before the heir apparent was dismissed.

"First count of grave disrespect: deceiving the late emperor by hiring someone else to practice his calligraphy.

"Second count of grave disrespect: beating the official and lying to the late emperor.

"Third count of grave disrespect: violating the late emperor's ban on imbibing liquor and beating servants when drunk."

In addition, the officials reported to the emperor, further investigation would be carried out concerning other aspects of the case. As to the charges against the Fourteenth Prince:

"Yin-ti:

"First count of grave disrespect: holding a grudge against the late emperor over taking his servants with him on the Rehe trip, seeing them off personally, and giving them the word 'peace.'

"Second count of grave disrespect: telling Yin-tang that the late emperor was getting old and asking him to prepare to send 'the message' [whenever the emperor died]. Even a courtier would not make such an unfeeling request."

The report added that all the charges against Yin-tang, Yin-ti and Yin-ssu were substantiated by Qin Daoran's statement. Qin Daoran had told the truth without torture. It recommended that the punishment of Yin-tang, Yin-ssu and Yin-ti should be meted out in accordance with the law, and that the money they had obtained illegally should be traced and forfeited.

In conclusion, the report, signed by both Vice-Minister Huang and Governor General Cha-pi-na, said:

"The statement by Qin Daoran is credible and reasonable. We await your Majesty's decision and judgment."

Evidently, the Yongzheng Emperor ordered Vice-Minister Huang to transport Daoran back to Peking from Nanking for, six weeks later, he was again interrogated, this time in the capital. While en route to Peking, he was cooped up in a caged cart and was practically starved. This humiliation stripped him of his self-respect, and he was reduced to saying almost anything his accusers wanted to hear, while continuing to beg for his life.

This interrogation took place in mid-1726, when all three princely targets of the new emperor were in prison. Other figures involved were similarly brought to Peking and questioned. These included the Catholic missionary, Father Jean Mourao, the eunuch Chang the Blind, and Yin-tang's literary friend He Tu.

A partial transcript of the interrogation[10] has been preserved, probably an edited, authorized version. It contains only two questions, followed by Daoran's answers, as well as many instances when the text says "further testimony" without the questions being reproduced.

Again, torture apparently was not used, though clearly there were threats. As Daoran said, "If I do not tell everything about my crimes and the crimes of Yin-ssu, Yin-tang and Yin-ti, I not only risk my own life but also the lives of my wife and children.

"Now I will recall carefully and tell more," Daoran said in this confession. "Yin-tang is stupid and ignorant. The Kangxi Emperor knew that, so he never said anything good about Yin-tang and never gave him special tasks to perform. Though he always said he himself stood little chance of being chosen [as heir apparent] he always harbored hopes. I know."

The interrogators then asked: "Since you knew that Yin-tang was stupid and ignorant, why did you help him in his wicked deeds? How do you know that Yin-tang harbored hopes in his heart even though he knew that he did not stand a chance?"

Daoran's answer: "Yin-tang once told me: 'When my mother was pregnant, she felt sick. She dreamed that a bodhisattva gave her a red biscuit which looked like the sun. She ate the biscuit and recovered from the sickness. She also said that I had a tumor behind my ear when I was a child. I was in convulsions. Suddenly I heard a loud noise and when I opened my eyes, I saw a lot of gods wearing golden armor around me, and I recovered. These incidents showed that I was born with good fortune.' He always remembered these things, and I saw how he acted. That's why I know he harbored wild dreams and I am the only one who knows this. Otherwise there is no way to account for his relating stories about dreams and unnatural phenomena, such as the sun descending into his mother's abdomen when she was pregnant with him. As to why I stayed with him even though I knew he was stupid, that is why I say I deserve to die."

In further testimony, Daoran provided additional information to be used against his former patrons. "Before the Second Prince's title was taken away from him," Daoran disclosed, "Yin-tang always told me bad things about him and how badly the Second Prince had treated him, Yin-ssu and Yin-ti. So they conspired to bring about the downfall of the heir apparent through treacherous means. They made every effort to please old Prince Yu and asked him to recommend Yin-ssu to the emperor. Therefore, even while seriously ill, Prince Yu strongly commended Yin-ssu to the emperor for his talent and virtue."

In addition, Daoran said, when the Kangxi Emperor asked his ministers to propose a new heir apparent in 1708, the princely brothers and their co-conspirators reached secret agreements with other officials to jointly support the candidacy of Eighth Prince Yin-ssu. "Everyone wrote the character 'eight' on his palm [to show support for the Eighth Prince]," Daoran disclosed. "They recommended Yin-ssu to the emperor and thought they would succeed. But they did not know this was against the desire of the Kangxi Emperor. Yin-ssu, Yin-tang and Yin-ti were surprised and disappointed. These incidents were known not only to me but to everybody."

Daoran then disclosed that Yin-tang interpreted the recall of Yin-ti for consultations in the middle of his military campaign as a sign that Kangxi wanted to prevent this son from scoring a military triumph.

Daoran said: "He told me, 'Our imperial father is obviously unwilling to let Yin-ti succeed in the expedition, lest he should become too difficult to handle in the future.'

"Yin-tang wanted to know everything that occurred in the inner court," Daoran continued. "So he lavishly bribed two eunuchs named Chen Fu and Li Kun to observe and report on the emperor's daily moods and movements and asked them to keep him informed of all such matters constantly. We can see what he was planning."

The remainder of the testimony consisted of bits and pieces of information. The impression is of someone dredging his memory for anything that might satisfy his interrogators.

"Yin-ssu also realized how stupid Yin-tang was," Daoran said. "The reason why Yin-ssu was close to Yin-tang was because he wanted money from Yin-tang to buy people's loyalty. Yin-ssu found a lot of magicians and hid them in secret rooms at his home. Whenever he needed to pay these people, he asked Yin-tang for money, sometimes 100 taels, sometimes 200 taels. I saw many such people. I often heard from messengers that money was dispatched to Yin-ssu's house. That is why I know. But to whom this money was given, I truly don't know."

Along with Qin Daoran, all other involved parties were closely questioned, such as Jean Mourao, He Tu, Chang the Blind, messengers and eunuchs. As a result of the testimony, the Yongzheng Emperor issued an edict on July 1, 1726, listing twenty-eight "crimes" of Yin-tang and forty "crimes" of Yin-ssu. The two brothers were never allowed to speak in their defense. Within three months of the charges being published, both brothers had died in prison from severe maltreatment.

But even after their deaths, Yongzheng was not content. After Yin-tang's death, the emperor asked to be informed if anyone came to view the body and wept. Ten days after his death, Yongzheng was told that no one had come, but the emperor was not satisfied and called for continued vigilance in case anyone wept over the death. Yin-tang's widow wasn't allowed to claim the body until the prince had been dead three months.[11]

Because of Daoran's willingness to cooperate, his life was spared. The Yongzheng Emperor magnanimously permitted him to be imprisoned in Wuxi, his hometown. The following year, because of inquiries conducted by the Court of the Imperial Clan, he was brought back to Peking for additional questioning. Shortly after this, the emperor showed his personal attitude toward Daoran by commenting that evil officials were fated to have their names vilified by later generations. He said: "Now, Qin Daoran is actually descended from Qin Kui [the Song dynasty traitor], and everybody knows this. He denies his ancestry and you can see that such a bad person comes to no good end."[12]

Daoran's plight affected the entire family. Pressure was brought to bear on family members to discharge their debt. When Daoran's brother Shiran vowed to share Daoran's misfortune and offered to exchange places with him, the local magistrate pointed out that since Shiran had been adopted by his uncle, they were legally no longer brothers and so he had no obligation to Daoran. But Shiran, with tears in his eyes, replied:

"I became the heir of another branch and separated from my brother, but we were born from the same body. I wasn't implicated in the sentence, which was the generosity of the court. But my character cannot change because it was given to me by nature. If my brother lives, I live. If he dies, so do I."[13] He sold all his property to help pay part of Daoran's fine, but the result was negligible.

Throughout the rest of the reign of the Yongzheng Emperor, the fortunes of the Qin family were not reversed. Daoran's inability to pay the fine meant that family properties, including the famed Ji Chang Garden, were confiscated. The whole family was impoverished and penalized. Those who succeeded in gaining the highest degree never rose to positions of prominence. It appeared that the Qins of Wuxi were destined to fade into oblivion.

CHAPTER EIGHTEEN

Qin Huitian: "The Man Who Looked for Flowers"

In October 1735, the Yongzheng Emperor, the third Manchu to sit on China's Dragon Throne, died at the age of fifty-six after a reign of thirteen years. Mystery surrounded his death, just as it had cast a shadow over his ascension to the throne. Despite the official announcement that he had died peacefully in the Park of Everlasting Peace, rumors spread that he had been murdered by the daughter of a man whom he had executed.

Mindful of the vicious succession struggle from which he had emerged victorious, Yongzheng had avoided publicly naming an heir apparent. Instead, he had announced that he had put the name of his choice on paper. This he deposited in a sealed box, which was kept behind a wooden tablet hung in the Palace of Celestial Purity. The box yielded its secret after his death, and the fourth of Yongzheng's ten sons, born of an imperial concubine of the second rank, became the new emperor; he assumed the reign name Qianlong.

The Manchu emperors paid great attention to the education of their sons and selected as heir the one most capable of maintaining Manchu rule in China, whether he be born of the empress or an imperial concubine.

During his six decades in power, the Qianlong Emperor saw the Chinese empire expand to its zenith of power and influence. At its height, he held sway over territory that extended an astounding five and a quarter million square miles—one and a half times the size of the United States. But by the end of his reign signs of dynastic decline were already discernible. Secure in the superiority of his empire over all its neighbors, the Qianlong Emperor was woefully ignorant of developments across the seas, where Europeans were rapidly outstripping Chinese technology, especially in military areas. Toward the end of his reign, Emperor Qianlong scornfully told

European envoys that the Celestial Empire was totally self-sufficient, having no need for their manufactures.

It was a confident young man of twenty-five, with clear eyes, long nose and slightly protruding ears, who ascended the throne in 1735. He had been well educated in the martial arts that characterized his Manchu heritage as well as in the Chinese classics, painting and calligraphy. Qianlong, in fact, prided himself on his literary accomplishments and, by the end of his reign, was credited with authorship of over 43,000 poems.[1]

Qianlong gradually started to undo the work of his father and near the end of his reign ordered the posthumous reinstatement of his uncles Yin-tang and Yin-ssu to the Imperial Clan, exonerating them of treason.

One of the first acts of the new emperor was to declare a general amnesty, but it did not extend to those under sentence of death and to other special cases, like Qin Daoran's.

In April 1736, scholars from around the nation gathered in the capital to compete in the triennial metropolitan examinations, the first held under the Qianlong reign. Among the contenders was thirty-three-year-old Qin Huitian, Daoran's youngest son, born of a concubine surnamed Pu. He had done what he could to alleviate the sufferings of his father. When Daoran had been transported from one city to another in a wooden cage, Huitian had mingled with the guards, bribing them to ease his father's lot as best he could.[2] After Daoran had been sentenced and virtually all family property sold to help pay the enormous fine, Huitian imposed strict discipline on himself, forcing himself to study and promising himself that one day he would buy back all the lands and houses that had to be sold.

Huitian was instrumental in easing the conditions of his father's imprisonment in his hometown. The local magistrate, Wang Qiaolin, was impressed by Huitian and accepted him as his protégé. He then gave Daoran special privileges, including his own room, and allowed him to give lectures as well as to receive unlimited visits from his relatives, who daily brought him home-cooked dishes. Life was made as pleasant as possible, although Daoran had to remain in prison. This was consistent with the instructions of the Yongzheng Emperor, who had stipulated that Daoran "need not be too harshly treated."

Magistrate Wang also helped Huitian advance his career, recommending him to posts first in Nanking and later in Canton while the young man prepared himself for the examinations. Huitian knew that official recognition was the only channel through which he could clear the family name and possibly gain his father's release.

Huitian was among 352 candidates out of about twenty times that number from around the country who were successful and were thus guaranteed an official career. But before they returned home, they had to take the palace examinations, which were conducted by the emperor himself. The first three candidates would be immediately catapulted to nationwide prominence.

The questions were set by court officials of outstanding literary ability, who also read the papers but did not grade them. The candidates were seated in the grand and imposing Palace of Preserved Harmony, the last of the three great outer palaces that led to the imperial living quarters. They had to address themselves to various comments made by the emperor about governance, such as "Sincerity must be applied in all situations," "Policies emanate from the top and customs grow from the bottom" and "Politeness and righteousness arise only when people have enough food and clothing; education can begin only when the nation is wealthy and the harvest is good."[3] In a long discourse, Huitian wrote, "The rule of an emperor depends on the Way, and the Way is rooted in the mind. The mind is the basis of peace and the modification of nature. The structure has to be justice, such that merit will emerge and all will be in harmony. The most important element is sincerity. According to the Doctrine of the Mean, there is only one principle—sincerity and moderation."[4]

The examiners presented to the emperor their choice of the top ten of the several hundred papers, but he was free to change this order in any way. On the morning of May 14, 1736, Emperor Qianlong reviewed the ten best papers at his western apartment, the Palace of Mental Cultivation.

The Qianlong Emperor discharged his duties conscientiously, and read through the papers himself. He then summoned the members of the Commission of Imperial Revisors, high officials whose task it was to evaluate the papers. "In the paper that you ranked first," he told the officials, "there appears a phrase referring to the emperor setting an example for farmers by personally plowing the earth. I have not yet conducted such a demonstration. The phrase is inappropriate. The paper can only be ranked second." He was alluding to the fact that he had not yet performed the traditional spring ceremony in which the emperor personally drove the plow, importuning heaven for a bountiful harvest. His choice for first place was a paper originally ranked sixth.

After he had made each choice, the emperor ordered the seal over the candidate's name removed. When the seal was lifted from the name of the third-ranking candidate (originally the second), it was Qin Huitian.[5]

The next day, an elaborate ceremony was held in the Palace of Supreme Harmony, the most impressive building in the vast compound of palaces, to announce the results. The candidates were assembled in the rear, behind the high officials resplendent in their court robes. The emperor's entrance was heralded by the ringing of bells and the beating of drums. After Qianlong mounted his throne, the master of ceremonies cracked his whip three times, music started and the candidates were led to the front, where an imperial decree was read bestowing on them the *jinshi* degree. Then began a procedure known as the calling of names. The name of the top-ranking graduate, Jin Deying, was called out three times. He was brought to the front of the group and knelt down before the emperor. Next was the turn of Huang Sunmou, who knelt down beside Jin. Finally Qin Huitian's name was called, and he joined the other two, behind Jin.[6]

Eight days later, the emperor issued decrees appointing these three men compilers of the Hanlin Academy,[7] where Huitian's father and his grandfather had served. Other specially promising graduates were also nominated to the academy, either as compilers or as lower-ranking bachelors. The remaining graduates were given provincial posts. On May 30, the three top men were accorded the further honor of being assigned to work in the Imperial Study, the emperor's personal literary advisorate, in which Huitian's father had also worked.[8]

That month, Huitian's mother died and Huitian returned to Wuxi for her mourning ceremonies. He did not have to remain in mourning for three years because, though she was his natural mother, she was not his legal mother: His grandfather Songling had decided years earlier that Huitian was to continue the family line of Daoran's brother Yiran, who had died without heirs.[9]

Because both his adoptive parents had died early, Huitian had actually known only his real parents. When he mentioned his deceased adoptive ones, he referred to them as "father" and "mother," but when he spoke of his natural parents, he called them "my mother-by-birth" and "my father-by-birth."

Soon after his mother's mourning ceremonies ended, Huitian staked his career, for which he had worked so long and so hard, on an appeal to the new emperor. Very carefully, he composed a memorial to Emperor Qianlong, pleading for his father's release,[10] though never suggesting that there had been any injustice on the part of Qianlong's father, Emperor Yongzheng, who had ordered his imprisonment. The long memorial said in part:

"My father-by-birth Qin Daoran committed a serious offense but was graciously spared. Because he could not pay the fine, he was imprisoned. Now, my father is eighty and extremely frail. In the fifth and sixth months of this year, he suffered from the hot and humid weather and had fevers and chills, which almost killed him. Since I am his own flesh and blood, I could not help grieving. At the end of the seventh month he recovered slightly. Now I have an official position in the palace, and work in close proximity to Your Majesty. But I cannot help thinking of my father, and the fact that he is eighty, infirm and imprisoned, with no prospect of being released. This so distresses me that I cannot concentrate on my work. If I pretend to work and continue to accept a salary, my sense of shame will increase and I will become an embarrassment to the literary world. I beg Your Majesty to be magnanimous. My father-by-birth Qin Daoran is eighty and nearing the end of his life. If he can be so fortunate as to be able to enjoy the remaining years of his life as a free man, I am willing to have my ranks and titles removed while devoting myself entirely to Your Majesty's service."[11]

Huitian was praised by his contemporaries as one of the two filial sons of the era.[12] But the risk he had taken was considerable. Given the capriciousness of imperial behavior, he could well have been dismissed or even charged with a serious offense, such as disrespect to the late emperor. It is not for nothing that there was a saying among court officials that "keeping company with the emperor is akin to keeping company with a tiger."

Fortunately for Huitian, the Qianlong Emperor responded by issuing the following order: "Qin Daoran is permitted to be released, and the unpaid fine waived. The governor-general and the governor must inform local officials that he is to be watched closely and not allowed to leave the area to stir up trouble."[13]

Daoran was allowed to live at home, where family members could take care of him, but he could not travel freely outside Wuxi. Evidently, Qianlong felt that he could not be completely trusted. Daoran wrote a book on his reflections during his thirteen-year ordeal, but unfortunately it has not been preserved.

By the reprieve Emperor Qianlong gained in Huitian a loyal official who would serve him literally to his dying day. Though Huitian was already in his mid-thirties when he began his career, he would serve the emperor for the next three decades. So devoted to his work was he that he apparently spent little time with his family. By the time Huitian began his official career, his wife, surnamed Hou, had given him three sons, one of whom died in infancy, and a daughter. Later, a concubine would present him with another son and daughter.

Evidently, the new emperor favored his new courtier, whose grandfather had served both Qianlong's grandfather, the great Kangxi Emperor, and his great-grandfather, the first Manchu to sit on the Dragon Throne. At the end of the second year of his reign, just before the Chinese New Year, Qianlong personally granted Huitian the word *fu*, or "fortune," in his own handwriting. It was customary to paste the word on the portal during the New Year celebrations, in order to bring good fortune in the coming year.[14] The display of imperial calligraphy on one's door was regarded as a signal honor. On New Year's Eve, the emperor bestowed other gifts on Huitian: A box of ink and a set of brushes, appropriate gifts for a scholar, as well as two sable skins, small purses, a silk handkerchief, two Western cloth handkerchiefs and two deer tails, which, like powdered deer antlers, were considered to have medicinal and aphrodisiac properties, a deer, a goat, four fish and four pheasants.[15]

Throughout Huitian's three decades of service to the emperor, such gifts were forthcoming five or six times a year. Each occasion was carefully recorded by Huitian in his diaries, two volumes of which have survived.

Soon after Huitian joined the Hanlin Academy, he was ordered to participate in a monumental project, the compilation of the *Comprehensive Geography of the Empire*, which had been begun sixty years earlier during the Kangxi era. The project was finally completed in 1744. Consisting of 356 chapters, it is a definitive description of the empire at the time, including not only details of the geography but also of the administrative system, both in the capital and in the provinces.

In the spring of 1738, Qin Huitian accompanied the Qianlong Emperor as he performed the ritual of imperial plowing. China being an agricultural society, it was essential to ensure a good harvest every year, and to this end heaven had to be won over. At dawn on April 11, the emperor, after having cleansed himself spiritually and physically by fasting and bathing, emerged from his palace, dressed in full imperial regalia, complete with a handsome headgear weighed down with pearls and a cloak emblazoned with the imperial dragon. Together with civil and military officials, he headed a grand procession that wended its way to the Altar of the Creator of Agriculture in the southwest of Peking, where he offered sacrifices to the legendary sage-king Shen Nong, credited with teaching agriculture to the Chinese people thousands of years before. There, the emperor prayed for an abundant harvest.

Having offered the sacrifice as the Son of Heaven, the intermediary between heaven and all his subjects, Qianlong then divested himself of his ceremonial robes and donned garments more appropriate for his next task: that of farmer. The emperor and his entourage proceeded to the Fengzeyuan, northwest of the Ying Pavilion, where a plot of about an acre was set aside for use on such occasions. This plot was carefully tended and its grain used in imperial sacrificial ceremonies. The emperor, witnessed not only by his highest officials but by a hundred old peasants selected from those who lived near the capital, grasped the plow to which an ox was hitched and made several furrows in the field. After that his officials, in order of precedence, followed suit. The rest of the plowing was completed by the specially chosen farmers.

This ancient ceremony exhorted peasants to work harder by following the imperial example. On the other hand, by humbling himself in this manner, it was thought, the emperor was more likely to understand the bitter life of the peasantry and win favor from heaven. At the end of the ceremony, Emperor Qianlong walked along the field and chatted with the farmers before departing to the strains of music.[16]

That year, Huitian submitted his first self-examination, the routine expected of metropolitan officials every three years. The emperor was apparently pleased with him, for he granted him an audience and raised him by one rank. Four months later, Huitian was appointed associate examiner for the provincial examinations in Peking. Later, he was also made assistant examiner of the provincial military examinations, which emphasized such skills as archery and horsemanship over literary accomplishments.

In 1739, the fourth year of the Qianlong era, the palace examinations were held again. That year, the third-ranking candidate was Qin Yongjun, Huitian's cousin.[17] This feat—two cousins among the top three places in the palace examinations—was duplicated by only four other families in the 260 years spanning the Qing dynasty.[18]

In 1742, Huitian was appointed to the Palace School for Princes, established under Emperor Yongzheng.[19] He became tutor to Emperor Qianlong's sons, just as his father had taught Kangxi's son Yin-tang.

Qianlong did not announce which of his sons was heir apparent. Like his father, he wrote down the name of his successor and deposited it in a sealed box hidden behind a wooden placard that hung in the Palace of Celestial Purity. In fact, because of the fierce power struggle among the princes that had characterized the last decades of the Kangxi era, the custom of appointing an heir apparent was permanently abandoned.

Huitian's rise in the government was rapid. In September 1742, he was named commissioner of the Office of Transmissions, which handled documents passing between the emperor and his officials. In this, the ninth year of his reign, Qianlong made the unusual decision to go on a pilgrimage and honor his distant ancestors who were buried near Mukden, in the Manchurian heartland.

Preparations for the journey precipitated dozens of memorials, which must have fully occupied Huitian in the Office of Transmissions. The principal ones were from the Ministry of Rites, and concerned protocol: how the emperor, the empress dowager and other members of the party should approach the various tombs and make sacrifices. The tombs in question were: that of Abahai, father of the first Manchu emperor, Shunzhi; that of Abahai's father, the great Nurhaci; and a tomb known as Yongling, or Eternal Tomb, constructed by Nurhaci to house the remains of four of his ancestors. It was the considered view of the Ministry of Rites that the Yongling Tomb was to be given the most elaborate treatment, since it contained the remains of the earliest ancestors of the Manchu emperors.

On November 1, 1743, the imperial party arrived at the Yongling Tomb. There, the emperor, his mother, the empress dowager, and his wife performed the prescribed ceremonies. The Qianlong Emperor, dressed in the plain costume befitting such an occasion, was escorted by an official of the Ministry of Rites into the mausoleum, which occupied a large walled compound, with several structures housing the remains of the deceased and their consorts. The emperor entered through the left entrance of the outer door, known as the Chiyun Gate. Then he walked down a narrow passageway along the side of the Chiyun Hall to a series of steps that led to the main tomb. There, on the steps, he knelt on a cushion and, bending over, knocked his head against the ground. Then he straightened himself and, very reverentially, performed the kowtowing ritual two more times. After that he arose, only to kneel down again to perform the three prostrations three times. The emperor thus offered his ancestors the same homage that his living subjects offered him every day at imperial audiences, a ritual known as the three kneelings and nine prostrations.

This done, he proceeded into the tomb. Inside, he performed the most solemn ceremony of all: He knelt four times, knocking his head against the ground thrice each time. With each prostration, he offered in sacrifice a libation of wine, which he splashed onto the ground. He then stood up, faced west, and cried out in lamentation. Meanwhile, princes and high officials stood on both sides of the Chiyun Hall performing similar ceremonies outside.

The empress dowager, the empress and other imperial womenfolk were ushered in by the wives of the keepers of the mausoleum. They stepped in through the right entrance, walked along the opposite side of the Chiyun Hall and performed a ritual known as the "six bowings and three prostrations," with the empress dowager standing directly in front of the empress. The empress dowager then went into the tomb, followed by the empress. Inside, they performed the same ceremonies as the emperor, then rose facing east, mourning aloud. At the conclusion, the emperor and the women parted, leaving by different exits.

The following day, the royal entourage returned for yet more rituals. After having entered the Chiyun Gate, the emperor knelt and burned incense. Again, he proceeded to the cushion, where he performed the three kneelings and the nine prostrations. After pouring libations of wine, he read out a funeral ode, which was then burned. Then, after bowing three times, he performed a second and a third sacrificial ceremony, concluding with three kneelings and nine bowings. Finally, he again faced west and raised his voice in lamentation.

Similar rites, on a slightly reduced scale, were later held at the tombs of Nurhaci and Abahai. High officials accompanying the emperor stood on the side while the offerings were made.[20]

Huitian was commissioner of transmissions for only three months before he was named vice-minister of rites.[21] While in that position, he submitted his earliest substantive memorials that still survive. In one, Huitian pointed out that in many districts, local officials were confronted with wealthy gentry who could influence official decisions to their own advantage. He urged that the demarcation between officials and civilians be clearly drawn, and that power should reside only in the hands of the former.[22] He thus drew attention to one of the most serious administrative problems of the time. His solution was to implement the Confucian precepts of governance, under which ritual was all-important since it set out the proper order of the universe, with the emperor, or Son of Heaven, acting as both the ruler of the people and their intermediary with heaven. As long as everyone had a proper sense of hierarchical order, the job of emperor would be easy.

In another memorial, he proposed that the system of taxation be modified so that money as well as grain could be acceptable as payment, depending on the circumstances. He pointed out that, for practical reasons, grain could not be stored over a long period of time whereas money was easily stored and transported. Besides, he added, it did not make sense to collect a locality's taxes in grain, only to have the province import grain later for its own consumption.[23]

In 1745, while Huitian was serving in Peking as vice-minister of rites, the Qin clan in Wuxi decided to update its genealogical records. The last edition had been prepared thirty-one years previously, and the only man still alive who had participated in that fourth edition was Daoran, but he was now too old to take an active part in such work.

With his father's ninetieth birthday approaching, Huitian asked for, and obtained, permission to return to Wuxi to take part in the celebrations.

This birthday was an intensely emotional experience for Daoran. He had spent his eightieth in prison and now he was surrounded by relatives and friends. The celebrations went on for a year. While he had been the cause for the clan's decline a quarter of a century earlier, he was now revered as its grand old man because his son's success had reversed the clan's plummeting fortunes.

While Huitian was in Wuxi, he helped work on the new genealogical records, compiling information from the various branches. In all likelihood, this was also when he began to buy back, piece by piece, all the property that the family had lost.

Several years earlier, the government had finally returned Ji Chang Garden to the Qin family. It was overgrown and dilapidated, not having been tended for well over a decade. Daoran helped draw up plans for its restoration. The Qianlong Emperor offered to contribute a thousand taels of silver, but the clan declined to accept the money.

By then the garden had been in the hands of the clan for quite a few generations. It, too, had had its ups and downs. After the death of Qin Yao it was divided among his four sons, and was not reunified until the time of Dezao. To prevent any future division, the clan, led by Daoran, decided to build an ancestral hall within the garden, specially for honoring the Ming-dynasty filial sons. This would serve the dual purpose of encouraging filial piety and of ensuring that the garden would never be divided or sold. Forty *mu* of farmlands were set aside, the income of which would be for the upkeep of the temple and the annual spring and autumn sacrifices. The proposal made by Daoran was prepared by Huitian.

After the birthday celebrations, Huitian kept postponing his return to the capital because he was reluctant to leave his father. But Daoran told his son: "His Majesty has been so generous to us. You must do your utmost to serve him. Hurry back to your post. Though I am old, I am strong both in body and mind. Do not worry about me." With that, Huitian took his leave.

The proposal to build an ancestral temple required official approval, and so Huitian submitted it to the Ministry of Rites. Permission was duly granted and the Temple of the Filial Pair was constructed to the left of the garden. Qianlong also gave permission for Qin Yao, Huitian's great-great-great-great-grandfather, to be honored as well. A hall was also constructed to store the plaques inscribed by the Kangxi Emperor on his various visits.

In 1747, the twelfth year of the Qianlong era, Huitian filed another prescribed self-examination. Couching it in extremely self-derogatory terms, he described himself as unworthy of his post and begged to be dismissed. Huitian went so far as to propose a specific replacement for himself. He said:

"I am a stupid person and have been appointed to such high

positions and granted great honors by His Majesty. I know I have performed poorly and I beg for demotion or dismissal.... The governor of Shuntian Prefecture, Sun Hao, is capable and knowledgeable. I recommend that he be appointed in my place." Four days later, Emperor Qianlong brushed this aside by ordering: "Qin Huitian is to stay and serve in the same post."

That year, Huitian's father died in the fifth month. He returned to Wuxi and was in mourning until the following year. During that time, he studied the important work on mourning rites compiled by a scholar colleague of his grandfather Songling. He also devoted himself to his own monumental work, *Wu-li Tung-kao,* or *Comprehensive Study of the Five Rites,* a study he had begun as a young man of twenty-one, when he met regularly with other scholars to discuss the classics. It would take him thirty-eight years to complete.

Soon after Huitian came out of mourning, news arrived from the southwest of a military victory over the Jin-chuan, a minority people in remote western Sichuan. These hardy rebels had built thousands of formidable stone fortress-towers that had proved virtually impregnable. Two military commanders had been executed for failing in their mission to subdue these people. Now finally, the Manchu commander Fu-heng, the emperor's brother-in-law, had managed to quell them. The Qianlong Emperor later regarded this as the first of ten great military campaigns in his sixty-year reign, but he paid a high price for his military expeditions: It was estimated that the battles against the Jin-chuans alone cost 20 million taels of silver, more than a quarter of the government's annual revenues.

The pacification of the Sichuan area prompted the Qianlong Emperor to plan a major tour of his southern domains, as his grandfather, the Kangxi Emperor, had done so many times. Qianlong had an inordinate regard for his grandfather and measured himself against him. When he first mounted the throne, he prayed that he would be given almost as long a reign as that of Kangxi, who had ruled for sixty-one years. Considering that his grandfather was only seven when he became emperor and Qianlong was twenty-five, this appeared unlikely. But heaven granted Qianlong his wish.

The reason given for the long and costly southern journey was fully in accordance with Confucian values: filial piety. The trip, though planned in 1749, was scheduled for two years later, to coincide with celebrations of Qianlong's mother's sixtieth birthday.

When Huitian first learned of the emperor's plans to travel southward, he proposed that Qianlong make a stop at the Qin family garden, which the Kangxi Emperor had loved. An imperial visit would have been a great honor for the family, and would have been a sign to the whole world of imperial favor. In response, Qianlong declared that he would visit the Ji Chang Garden to pay respect to his grandfather, who had left samples of his writing there. However, he said, he did not want to create trouble for people who lived in the vicinity. Moreover, Huitian would not be traveling with the imperial party, because the emperor feared Huitian might cause his fellow townsmen and clansmen to go to great lengths to accommodate the emperor in order to win favor.

Apparently, Qianlong feared that Huitian might use his proximity to the emperor to further his own ends in Wuxi. Qianlong said that since the garden housed the writings of the Kangxi Emperor, the expenses should be borne not by the Qin family but by the local authorities and merchants.[24] Despite the emperor's injunctions, the clan naturally spared no expense to get the garden in readiness for the imperial visit. It went so far as to place antiques in the garden for the emperor's amusement. The restoration of the garden took two years and cost 5,000 taels of silver.

The authorities in Wuxi, like those in communities everywhere along the route, went to great lengths to ensure the imperial visit's success. Although the entire trip lasted three and a half months, each stop was only for a day or two. To prepare for the visit, officials in Wuxi rebuilt a section of the city wall that had collapsed. But since the imperial barge traveling along the Grand Canal would be exposed to only one view of the wall, only its exterior was repaired. From the canal, the wall appeared sturdy but actually it was hollow in parts. Still, as long as it stood up for the duration of the imperial visit, all would be fine. A bridge under which the emperor's barge would pass was found to be too low because of recent floods; it was torn down and rebuilt. Streets that the imperial party was likely to travel on were repaved and the city gates were repainted. To please the imperial eye, lanterns and silk decorations were hung everywhere, and bamboo was planted over a five-mile stretch.

For the accommodation of the imperial party, two areas, one south of the city and one to the north, totaling ninety acres, were designated as encampment sites. Since the imperial party would be arriving by boat via the Grand Canal, old piers were dismantled and new ones constructed, each with a gold-plated dragon's head, signifying the imperial presence. The piers were decorated with silks of five colors. Red carpets led from all the piers. The cost was astronomical. And, throughout the length of the southern tour, similar preparations were made.

Mount Hui, or Huishan, was the main attraction in Wuxi. Parts of Mount Hui Temple, which housed the historic bamboo stove and its associated scrolls, were rebuilt. The construction took a year and was finished only days before the emperor's arrival. Moreover, to ensure that the Second Spring Under Heaven would be unimpaired, the officials barred anyone from carrying water from the spring for a year before Qianlong's arrival.[25]

Thus, all was in readiness when the imperial entourage arrived in Wuxi on March 16, 1751, thirty-six days after leaving Peking. The emperor's vessel dropped anchor near the aptly named Welcome Dragon Bridge—since the dragon was the symbol of the emperor—on the northwestern edge of the city, across from the northern encampment site. The empress dowager and her party were a few miles behind. The procession of imperial vessels stretched as far as the eye could see. That night, while soldiers and some other members of the entourage slept on land, the emperor and his family spent the night on their barges.

The following morning, Qianlong began his sightseeing in Wuxi. The day began with breakfast with his mother in the Qin family garden.[26]

Members of the Qin family awaited their imperial guest at the entrance to the garden. The welcoming party consisted of twenty-four adult males from the Qin family, headed by nine men above the age of sixty, all of whom were kneeling by the roadside. They made an impressive sight. Their bowed heads were covered with white hair, and their eyebrows and beards were also white. The Qianlong Emperor asked their leader his age. He was Xiaoran, Songling's nephew, ninety. Next was Songling's son, the eighty-seven-year-old Shiran, who had helped welcome Emperor Kangxi to the garden more than four decades ago. Also present was the sixty-six-year-old Shouran, another son of Songling's. The other senior members of the family were their cousins, Jingran, eighty-five, Yongran, seventy, the wealthy Ruixi, sixty-one, as well as their nephews, Daoran's oldest son Zhitian, seventy-six, and Xintian, sixty. The eighty-five-year-old Jingran's son, Dongtian, was himself sixty-two. Together, they made up what later became known as the Nine Old Men of the Qin family.

The Qianlong Emperor asked each person his name, age and title. He then bestowed on the two eldest members of the family two characters ("venerable eminence") in his own handwriting which they were authorized to have engraved on a plaque to put over the entrance of the street where they lived. Ordinarily, such an honor was reserved for those over ninety, but because there were so many old men in the Qin family, the emperor decided to make an exception.[27]

Longevity was regarded as a reward for a virtuous life. So the sight of so many old men, all from one family, was not only unusual but considered extremely auspicious. The emperor ordered that a record be made of this occasion when he was greeted by Nine Old Men whose total ages added up to well over six hundred. After the elaborate greetings from the Nine Old Men, Emperor Qianlong and his entourage proceeded to tour the Qin family garden, leaving their hosts on their knees outside.

The garden's artificial lakes and mountains, its zigzag bridges, pavilions and green willows enchanted the Qianlong Emperor on this, his first visit. While touring it, he entered a special pavilion where the engraved poems composed by his grandfather, Kangxi, were kept. The garden, his grandfather's writings and the encounter with the Nine Old Men moved Qianlong to compose a poem. After writing it out, he ordered a grand councillor to take it out and read it to the Qin family members, still assembled on their knees by the entrance.[28]

From the Qin family garden, the emperor went to Mount Hui Temple, where he sipped tea made with water from the Second Spring and boiled over the bamboo stove. Afterward, the emperor recalled: "I remembered that the famous Huishan spring had been visited by my beloved grandfather, so I tried the tea made with the bamboo stove. I also wrote two poems on the rolls and gave them to the monks for safekeeping."

After the tea, the emperor and his party proceeded to the Hall of Ripples, where they viewed the Second Spring Under Heaven. That sight, too, stirred the emperor's imagination, and he composed a poem, as he also did when he visited the site nearby of the old Blue Mountain Poetry Society. Then Qianlong and his entourage moved on to Tin Mountain, from which Wuxi ("No Tin") derived its name. From the Viewing Lake Pagoda, the emperor commanded a spectacular view of Lake Tai. However, because it started to rain, he returned to the imperial barge.

One of the emperor's stops was the Filial Son Temple of the Hua family. When Qianlong arrived, he found an old man on his knees. Asked who he was, the old man replied that his name was Hua Xiyan. A graduate of the provincial examinations, he was awaiting an official assignment. By that time, graduates outnumbered the official posts available. Those who did not have the highest degree often waited years before obtaining a position. "How old are you?" the emperor enquired. "Eighty," was the response. "You need wait no longer," Qianlong promised him. He was given the rank and perquisites of a district magistrate, but with no district to run. The grateful Hua followed the emperor back to the southern encampment, and was rewarded with gifts of silk and a sable skin.

Before the imperial party continued on its southward journey, Qianlong ordered twenty-eight rolls of silk to be bestowed on members of the Qin family who had welcomed him to the Ji Chang Garden. And on his return journey to Peking, the emperor stopped again in Wuxi. The entire Qin clan gathered at Xin'an to thank the emperor for his beneficence and welcomed him once more to their garden. All nine submitted poems that they had written, following the same rhyme patterns as that of the poem written by the emperor. These were graciously accepted. After touring the garden, the emperor gave Xiaoran, the oldest member, a special poem entitled "A Second Tribute to the Ji Chang Garden." And when he returned to Peking, he ordered a replica of the Ji Chang Garden to be landscaped within the Summer Palace.

He explained: "Of all the gardens in South China, the Garden of the Qins at Huishan has the longest history. My royal grandfather favored it with the name Ji Chang. In 1751, I went on an inspection tour of the south. Because I liked its charm and seclusion so much, I came back with a design of it and ordered a similar garden to be built on the earthen slope of the Hill of Longevity and named it 'Huishan Garden.' Every pavilion and path in it was constructed to match the original."[29]

The garden in the Summer Palace is still enjoyed by visitors today, but its name has been changed to Garden of Harmonious Interest.

CHAPTER NINETEEN

Qin Huitian: Minister of Punishments

Huitian became the most distinguished member of our family in the Qing dynasty, just as Qin Jin had been the most outstanding in the Ming.

In 1752, the year after Qianlong's return from the south, Huitian was appointed vice-minister of punishments, a job in which it was almost impossible to avoid offending or making enemies of influential people. Those who worked in the Ministry of Punishments were liable to punishment themselves if the emperor should disagree with their judgments. The Chinese concept of justice included a precisely appropriate punishment for each offense. And if an official punished an innocent person, he was liable for punishment himself. Moreover, even if a person was found guilty, an official could be penalized if the punishment was deemed incommensurate with the crime, either too lenient or too severe. Moreover, often an official had to deal with cases in which different Confucian principles were in direct conflict.

Each ministry in the Qing dynasty had two heads, one Manchu and one Chinese, with the Manchu automatically outranking the Chinese. There were four vice-ministers, equally divided between the two ethnic groups.

As vice-minister of punishments, Huitian was responsible for dealing with some of the most difficult cases in the empire. One case he handled involved a man who caught his wife in the act of adultery. Enraged, he picked up a chopper and attacked the couple, killing his wife and wounding the other man. He was arrested not for killing his wife but for wounding the other man, who happened to be his uncle. According to Confucian principles, to raise one's hand against one's elders was a most grievous offense. Even though the uncle was ordered to be executed for adultery, the husband was also condemned to death for having struck his uncle.

Huitian expressed his views on this legal and moral dilemma to the emperor in this fashion:

"According to the law, when a husband catches his wife and her lover in bed and kills them, the husband is not guilty of murder. So, if the husband injures a senior relative in an incident of adultery, no sentence should be suggested. According to the law, any relatives of a couple can be allowed to seize an adulterer, but if a man kills someone who is his elder, he will face a charge of murder. However the law only mentions 'killing,' not 'injuring.' So the husband who, in the course of seizing an adulterer, injures his elder, should not be found guilty.

"When an elder commits adultery with a junior member of the family, according to law he should be sentenced to capital punishment. The law allows the husband to seize the adulterer and it is difficult to prevent injury in such cases. We have thoroughly researched the issue and could find no precedent for executing a husband who injured a senior relative who was committing adultery."[1] Qianlong apparently found the argument persuasive. The husband was pardoned.

But Huitian was not always successful in obtaining the emperor's approval. The emperor was unhappy with the ministry's handling of a case concerning several individuals convicted of murder and robbery in the provinces, who were due to be transported to the capital for sentencing. They had pleaded illness, and the ministry had agreed to a three-month delay. The emperor found this too lenient and called on a special panel, headed by his brother-in-law, to decide how to penalize the top officials of the Ministry of Punishments.

The twenty-eight-man panel, which included the Manchu and Chinese ministers of personnel and war as well as the deputy heads of several ministries, recommended that the top five officials of the ministry involved all forfeit a year's salary. The emperor concurred.[2] But the punishment, though severe, may not have been as draconian as it sounded. The Qing dynasty operated under a system of merits and demerits, which could be used to cancel out each other. Thus, forfeitures of salary could be balanced against advancements in grade or recordings of merit. Often, both penalties and awards were only on paper. Of course, if an official had no merits with which to offset his demerits, he could actually end up losing his salary. In this case, Huitian actually forfeited a year's salary.

However, an official's salary was actually the smallest part of his income. An official also received a subsidy in grain that was almost equivalent to his salary, as well as an allowance "to nurture incorruptness," which was many times greater. Moreover, officials were expected to supplement their income from outside sources, such as contributions and gifts, and so long as these were not excessive, such officials were not deemed to be corrupt.

An indication of the real income of an official is the annual assessments that some clans made of their members. Thus, one clan expected an annual contribution of 80,000 taels of silver from a second-ranking official, such as Huitian was at this time, though his salary was only 150 taels a year. In general, officials in the provinces, even those of lower rank, enjoyed a considerably higher level of outside income than those in Peking, because in the capital there were so many more high-ranking officials to share the contributions. The wealth that almost always accompanied the holding of office is reflected in the Chinese saying "May you be promoted in office and become rich."[3]

In 1754, Huitian was given the additional job of assistant superintendent of the Astronomical College.

Huitian's appointment to the Astronomical College was a reflection of the wide range of his academic achievements. He was known not only for his literary attainments but also for his knowledge of the classics, of rites, of the law and of music. In a real sense, he was a Renaissance man.

That year his oldest son, Taijun, passed the palace examinations and was named a compiler of the Hanlin Academy, following in the footsteps of his father, grandfather and great-grandfather. In the Qing dynasty, only one family in the whole country exceeded this achievement of having four successive generations serve in the prestigious Hanlin Academy—that of Zhang Ying, whose family produced Hanlin scholars for six generations in a row.[4]

The following year, Huitian was named lecturer of the Classics Colloquium, that is, he became a teacher of the emperor,[5] an extremely prestigious position he held simultaneously with his other posts. Lectures to the emperor were ordinarily delivered twice a year, during the spring and autumn. We have two accounts of Huitian's performance of that task. One occasion was the mid-spring festival, at which a sacrificial ceremony was presided over by the emperor himself. After the sacrifice, Emperor Qianlong, accompanied by officials of the Nine Chief Ministries and the grand secretaries, arrived at the Wenhuadian, or Hall of Literary Glory, where the emperor attended lectures. Four learned men were scheduled to lecture that day, each on his particular specialty. Huitian lectured on one section of the *I Ching*, or *Book of Changes*, considered the most obscure—and most profound—of all Chinese classics.[6]

Ordinarily, on formal occasions, officials had to perform the ceremony known as the three kneelings and nine prostrations before the emperor. On this occasion, however, because they were acting as his teachers, the ritual was reduced to two kneelings and six prostrations.

Though the topic was obscure, Huitian made his lecture relevant to the administration of the empire. An emperor, he said, is faced with myriad decisions, and it is not easy to make the right ones. Besides, even if the emperor makes the proper decisions, officials charged with their implementation may err. For example, Huitian said, the correct policy is to buy and store grains in years when the harvest is plentiful. However, if this good policy is badly carried out, there will be insufficient grain during the lean years, and prices may be high even in the good years.

Huitian urged that care should be taken that government purchases not disrupt the market by driving prices up. Such purchases, he said, should be made cautiously so that wealthy men will not be able to drive the price up through hoarding.

Another problem was taxation. Huitian said that officials press landowners to pay taxes. But frequently these landowners have to depend on their tenant farmers to pay them rent before they are able to pay taxes. If the farmers do not pay rent, then the landowners, especially small landowners, are unable to pay taxes. Officials, he said, put pressure on the landowners but not on the farmers. As a result, the landowners are forced to sell their land at a low price, often in small lots. Even then, no one dares to buy except powerful farmers. Some of the land is in remote areas where local officials are in league with powerful farmers. When tax collectors arrive, they are greeted by insults.

These problems, Huitian said, can be traced to defects in the system. Officials in the capital, he said, transmit orders to those in the provinces, who directly govern. But often those in the capital do not understand the situation in the provinces, and those in the

287

provinces do not understand the situation in the capital. The solution, Huitian said, is for them to rotate. In the past, he said, there was such a practice, but it has fallen into disuse. The ministers in Peking evaluate the performance of provincial governors, he said, but some of them are too old and others are incompetent. The problem was serious, Huitian said, but could still be remedied.[7]

After the lectures the emperor presented his own views. Then he hosted a banquet for the lecturers and other high officials.[8]

On another occasion, also after a mid-spring ceremony, the Qianlong Emperor and his ministers again adjourned to the Hall of Literary Glory to listen to Huitian and another scholar expound on an obscure saying by the sage Mencius: "Shun understood what was real, proceeding from benevolence; he investigated human nature, but did not act from benevolence." Shun was the second of China's three legendary sage-kings. He was known as a keen student of nature and understood the intricacies of human relationships. He taught that whether an act was benevolent or righteous depended not on the nature of the act but on the motivation behind it.

In his lecture, Huitian said that both Shun and Yu, another legendary sage-king, possessed two important qualities, honesty and strength. Since the empire is too large for one man to run alone, the emperor has to appoint officials to assist him. In conformity with Confucian values, Huitian said the most important thing was to appoint good officials and get rid of the evil ones. To judge whether an official is good or bad, he said, one has to see through to the heart of the person; to do that, it is necessary to analyze his actions to see if they benefit the public at large or the individual himself. Good officials, he said, do not care for position or money; they do not shun difficult tasks, or fear criticisms. They treat their superiors with respect, not flattery. Bad officials, on the other hand, put their own interests first. They hide their true feelings and, to avoid making mistakes, always keep silent on controversial issues. Those of high rank do not take the initiative, merely attempting to please the emperor, while those of low rank will bribe their superiors to safeguard their jobs and possessions.

A lax emperor, Huitian warned, will be taken in by the flattery and reward such officials. In time, the situation will degenerate, officials will lose their diligence and rules and regulations will no longer be enforced. And, of course, the evil officials will remain.

An honest emperor, Huitian said, will listen with an open mind to his courtiers, be willing to delegate authority, pardon minor transgressions and not be fearful that power will slip from his own hand. He will not hesitate to make use of virtuous officials, nor will he hesitate to dismiss wicked ones. If the emperor is honest and strong, officials will naturally follow his example.[9]

In 1757, Emperor Qianlong decided once more to personally inspect his southern domains. This time, Huitian was part of his entourage—on a journey that began with a new high point in Huitian's career. The imperial party set off on February 28 and, the very next day, Huitian was promoted to minister of works. The ministry was responsible for such projects as dam construction.

In Wuxi, Huitian was able to play host to Qianlong at the Ji Chang Garden, where the emperor stayed the night. Among the members of the Qin family who greeted the emperor were four of the original Nine Old Men, the rest having died. All were granted new honors.[10]

While in Wuxi, Huitian was asked for advice on how to resolve some long-standing clan problems. Cousin Dongtian told him that, since the clan was rapidly expanding, it was no longer able to care for all its indigent members. In the past, he said, there were many wealthy people within the clan, each of whom took care of his own immediate family members. But now, with the expansion of the clan, there were families that could no longer make ends meet. Huitian considered the matter urgent. He recommended that the clan acquire sufficient farmlands, to be administered by the clan, to care for indigent members. Huitian set the target at a thousand *mu*, or about 150 acres. But, aside from offering this advice, Huitian was not in a position to do anything further at that time. As a high official, he enjoyed a good income. But the income of officials in the capital did not compare with that of those who served in lower-level posts in the provinces.

On this visit, Qianlong was as prolific as he had been six years previously. To celebrate his trip, he composed a poem titled "A Visit to the Ji Chang Garden."

In response, Huitian penned the following lines, based on the same rhyme pattern:

> Rain celebrates the imperial visit;
> The river's flow is smooth.
> Footpaths on which the emperor's feet
> Trod will glow for a hundred years.

> The fish in the pond and the birds
> In the air also know they are happy.

Then the emperor, spotting a pointed rock called Beauty Stone, decided that it was inappropriately named. Believing the stone looked masculine, he peremptorily changed its name to Jie-ru-feng, or Peak of Purity, and wrote a poem about it.

Again, Huitian composed a poem in response, using the same rhyme patterns and length of lines. He praised the emperor's poem for having added to the beauty of the rock and other scenery. Nature herself, he wrote, gazed upon the emperor and said in admiration: "He is outstanding and towers above all."

After his return to Peking, Huitian discovered a serious flaw in his ministry's procedures, and he submitted a memorial proposing some changes. "The Ministry of Works collectively manages all construction works," he said. "The degree of difficulty varies from project to project, and officials shun the difficult ones. Now I propose that the Ministry of Works follow the example of the Ministry of Punishments. That is, assignments should be decided by the drawing of lots. We should categorize all the construction projects according to their degree of difficulty. For those involving over 100 taels of silver, the lots will be drawn by the director or vice-director of a bureau. For those involving less than 30 taels, the lots will be drawn by clerks. The head of the ministry will inspect the work and decide on rewards and punishments." Qianlong accepted Huitian's suggestion.[11]

But Huitian soon again experienced the risks that went with the holding of high office. He was a member of the Nine Chief Ministers of State—the heads of the six ministries plus the Censorate, the Office of Transmissions and the Grand Court of Revision. Collectively, they were responsible for advising the emperor on how matters of great consequence should be handled. If the emperor disagreed with them, they had to suffer the consequences.

Now it happened that before Huitian became a minister, the administration commissioner of Hunan province had been arrested for having accepted more than 3,000 taels of silver in bribes. Because the money had been returned, the governor of Hunan, Jiang Bing, proposed a sentence of "suspended execution," whereby a convicted criminal was under sentence of death but the sentence was not carried out for the time being, and often was later commuted. That case appeared on the docket of the Autumn Assizes in 1757, and the Nine Chief Ministers had to deal with it before it went to the emperor. All, including Huitian, concurred with Governor Jiang Bing's proposal. Emperor Qianlong, however, declared angrily: "This kind of greedy official should be immediately decapitated. If a high-ranking official can escape punishment by repaying the money, even higher officials will consider bribery as unimportant."

Not only did the emperor order the man's immediate execution, but he also ordered that Governor Jiang Bing be penalized for having suggested such an inappropriate sentence, along with the officials of the Nine Chief Ministries for "misusing their power to protect their colleague." As a result, Governor Jiang Bing's properties were confiscated and he was demoted to the rank of vice-director of a bureau. Punishment of the even higher-ranking officials was meted out in accordance with the extent of their responsibility. Six ministers or vice-ministers were nominally discharged though retained at their posts—a common penalty in which an offender could regain his original title if he survived four years with an unblemished record—and three had demerits recorded in their files. Huitian fell into the latter category.[12]

Despite this case, Emperor Qianlong's confidence in Huitian's ability to administer justice evidently remained undiminished, for only a few months later, he was named minister of punishments.[13] His successor as minister of works was Ji Huang, whose son, it so happened, was married to Huitian's daughter.

One of Huitian's first memorials in his new position was on counterfeiting, a problem as serious then as it is today. Copper coins were the main form of currency at the time, and forgers often made coins of baser metals, such as lead, or they chipped the edges off the real coins, melted the scrap down and recast them as genuine copper coins. In his memorial, Huitian pointed out that one should differentiate between the various types of crimes involved, such as manufacturing fake money and destroying real money. "The punishment for those who privately make coins is delayed capital punishment," he wrote, "while that for those who privately destroy money is immediate capital punishment." However, Huitian said, such sentences were being carried out without regard for other factors, such as the number of coins created or damaged. He suggested that a scale of punishments be drawn up that would be uniformly applied in all provinces. What he proposed was immediate execution of those guilty of forging more than ten thousand copper coins, while those whose crime was on a smaller scale should be sent into exile. Those who repeated the offence, even on a small scale, would be executed. Thus, he eliminated the sentence of delayed capital punishment under which a case would be reheard during the Autumn Assizes every year until a final decision was made, an extremely time-consuming process requiring the attention of both the emperor and his highest officials.[14]

During that year's Autumn Assizes, Qianlong disagreed with the sentences proposed by the Ministry of Punishments in three cases. For their poor judgment, Huitian, his Manchu colleague, as well as two vice-ministers were each punished by foregoing six months' salary in each case.

The year after Huitian became minister of punishments, Qianlong decided to review criminal records of the previous five years to trace those responsible for the delays in processing cases. Fifty-five officials—present and former—were punished. Only one man, who was already retired and living on a pension, was spared.

Huitian was soon appointed to serve concurrently as grand minister of the Board of State Music, proof of his multifaceted talents.

But now in his mid-fifties, Huitian began to experience physical problems. His eyesight deteriorated, a fact which put him in serious trouble on a number of occasions, for Qianlong, almost a decade younger, penalized his officials each time he spotted a mistake on a document, even if the meaning was clear. Thus, in July 1759, Huitian and his colleagues in the Ministry of Punishments were penalized with a loss of one month's salary because a copyist had accidentally repeated one line of a document, which was forwarded to the emperor without their noticing it.[15] The following month, Huitian applied for sick leave, citing his eye problems. He was given two days off which evidently did not improve his condition.

He was then given the additional responsibility of being chancellor of the Hanlin Academy. Though a great honor, it only added to his already heavy burden as minister of punishments, lecturer of the Classics Colloquium and grand minister of the Board of State Music. In addition, he was often given extra assignments, such as selecting personnel to serve in provincial posts, or presiding over the civil-service examinations.

As minister of punishments, Huitian tackled a social phenomenon that had defied solution for many years: the problem of people who, for one reason or another, had been uprooted from their native villages and who had become vagrants, often forming unruly bands that caused trouble to local authorities.

He suggested that all the homeless and beggars in each province be rounded up and sent back to their native villages, where there was a system of mutual responsibility known as the *bao-jia* system, under which a hundred households formed a *jia* and ten *jia* formed a *bao*. Each person was part of a household, and each household had to register the names of its adult males and report their movements to the *jia*. Moreover, within a *bao*, members of each *jia* were responsible for each other's security and acted as each other's guarantor. Because responsibility was shared collectively, households kept an eye on each other and the head of each household saw to it that those for whom he was responsible acted within the law. Once reintegrated into this network of mutual security, Huitian argued, these rootless wanderers would lose their potential for making trouble.

The Qianlong Emperor agreed in principle with the suggestion, but he modified it somewhat. In his edict he stated: "What Qin Huitian proposed was right, and his suggestion is the best method of clearing up prison and court cases, but these people move around quite often. They ought to be caught and investigated, then sent back to their home province and watched under the *bao-jia* system, but this is quite tedious. Let them be put under surveillance in whichever province they happen to be without sending them back to their original one. All local officials should instruct those responsible for the *bao-jia* system to watch these people and control them in order to prevent them from causing trouble."[16]

It was about this time that Huitian became involved in a long and complicated affair having to do with the examination system, which was central to the administration of the country. Normally, papers of the successful candidates in the provincial examinations were sent to the capital, where they were reviewed by officials of the Ministry of Rites for thorough checking on phraseology and syntax, to see if any prohibitions had been violated. Since 99 percent of candidates failed, the papers of the small handful who passed were expected to be flawless in every way. As we saw earlier, if papers of successful candidates were found to contain mistakes, the candidates could be stripped of their degree and barred from future participation in examinations. Officials who had passed them would be punished, in the most severe cases by dismissal or exile.

In 1759, the triennial provincial examinations were held throughout the country. The papers of the graduates were reviewed by the Ministry of Rites. However, to ensure that the reviewers themselves had not erred, another group of four officials, headed by Huitian, was set up to check them. In an edict, Qianlong said that many candidates were poor in poetry and essay writing, and that while a weakness in the former could be understood, there was no excuse for poorly written essays, since this was the main subject. The reviewers were instructed to detect candidates who, despite their poorly written essays, had been passed. "If any such essays are missed in the review and eventually discovered by me," he warned, "the reviewers will be held responsible."

By early 1760, the group had finished its work. However, on March 16, the supervising secretary of the Ministry of Rites, Zhu Pilie, submitted a memorial that in effect accused Huitian and the other members of the panel of serious dereliction of duty. According to Zhu, who was in the first group of reviewers, he personally reviewed forty-one papers and found twenty-five of them so seriously flawed that both their authors and the examiners who passed them should be punished. The candidates, he said, should be disqualified and barred from participation in future examinations from one to three times, depending on the severity of their mistakes, the chief examiner involved should be demoted and transferred, while the readers of the papers should be demoted or their salaries forfeited. All these suggestions, he said, were in line with regulations laid down by the Ministry of Rites. However, he complained, the panel headed by Huitian had followed his proposed penalties in only fifteen of the cases. Zhu implied that by lightening the penalties in ten of the cases, Huitian and his associates were guilty of favoring certain examiners who were their friends or distant relatives.

In his memorial, Zhu said he had written his comments on slips that were then pasted onto the examination papers. He said that some of his comments might have been deliberately altered, adding that he had kept copies of all of them. He concluded with a string of innuendoes: that the Jiangxi chief examiner was not only from the same prefecture as Huitian but also a good friend of another panel member, Qian Rucheng; that the Fujian chief examiner was a student of Huitian's and came from his hometown; and that the Guangxi chief examiner was a distant relative of Qian's. "Therefore," he said, "I cannot help but suspect that their lenient treatment of the candidates is due to personal relationships." Zhu then requested that the emperor personally review all twenty-five papers.

Qianlong took immediate action. Two days later, he issued the following decree:

> The accusation regarding the review of examination papers by Qin Huitian and others by Zhu Pilie has been investigated by me. I have interrogated the reviewers and the papers have been reexamined by me in conjunction with officials of the Grand Council. We found that Qin Huitian and the other reviewers have indeed overlooked things they should not have missed and they cannot be excused for such negligence. We are still investigating the charge that the reviewers have shielded people with whom they have personal relationships. . . . We also found that there has been no modification, addition or deletion of comments [made by Zhu]. I have also called upon [Zhu] for a meeting and found that the accusation is not substantiated. So the reviewers were definitely not unjust. The main purpose of the thorough checking of papers is to warn and persuade students to learn the proper form of writing and to maintain the examiners' vigilance in selecting candidates. If examiners select their own relatives or students and if the reviewers protect the examiners, of course I will not let them escape punishment. Now Qin Huitian and the other reviewers have not committed such an offense. Though they have overlooked a few faulty papers, I do not consider the mistakes as unforgivable. The suspicions of Zhu Pilie and his accusations are unsubstantiated and false and I cannot agree with him. Moreover, so many papers were reviewed at once and it is obvious that Qin Huitian together with three or four other reviewers could not detect all mistakes. If I ask other officials to review once more the papers read by Zhu Pilie himself, who claims to be extremely careful and who only reviewed a few tens of papers, can he guarantee that no new mistakes would be spotted?
>
> At the end of the Ming dynasty, courtiers formed cliques to attack their opponents, and continuous feuding took place. The emperor was unable to prevent this, so finally factional fighting resulted in the fall of the empire. I do not want this review case to lead to the formation of factions and future feuds.
>
> In conclusion, punishment for negligence by Qin Huitian,

> Guan-bao and Qian Rucheng should be discussed by the departments concerned, and the punishment of Zhu Pilie for making false and unsubstantiated accusations should also be discussed.[17]

As a result of this episode, the Ministry of Personnel decided that two demerits be recorded against Huitian. He immediately submitted a memorial thanking the emperor for his generosity, acknowledging his negligence and attributing this to his lack of learning and poor eyesight. Huitian also proposed a method to standardize the way in which reviewers commented on papers.[18] On November 6, Qianlong issued an edict again emphasizing the need for care in selecting those examination papers that would be passed and the importance of the review process. He added that one or two minor errors could be overlooked.

The following year Huitian was named chief examiner of the metropolitan examinations. Knowing the emperor's personal interest in the selection process, Huitian, instead of submitting the traditional top ten papers to the emperor for his final decision, asked for and was granted permission to submit twelve, a reflection of his caution and modesty.[19] That same year his son, Qin Taijun, was named deputy examiner for the provincial examinations in Zhejiang. In recognition of the honor that the Qianlong Emperor was bestowing on his son, Huitian composed a memorial thanking him.

Huitian's deteriorating eyesight caused him further trouble two years later, when he was penalized on three occasions: once for not noticing that the name of a convict had been copied wrongly on a Ministry of Punishments document, once for not noticing a misprint on an examination paper, and once because a scribe had mistakenly substituted one word for another with the same sound. It may appear strange that the head of a ministry should be held responsible for what are basically minor copyists' errors, but it was considered disrespectful to present to the Son of Heaven any document that was not perfect.

In 1761, after thirty-eight years of labor, Huitian finished his magnum opus, the *Wu-li Tung-kao*, or *Comprehensive Study of the Five Rites*, in 120 volumes. The five categories of rites he studied were those employed in sacrifice, those for festive occasions, rites proper to host and guest, rites for military circles and rites for death and misfortune. Under these were seventy-five subdivisions. Huitian added music for all the ceremonies. Though largely of a historical and philosophical nature, it was considered a handbook on practical statecraft, a complete guide to social and administrative practices. The work was hand-copied into the mammoth *Siku Quanshu*, or *Complete Library in Four Branches of Literature*, a massive literary project undertaken in the 1770s and 1780s to collect, compile and preserve rare and precious books.

Toward the end of 1761, the emperor granted requests to his courtiers to have their ancestors posthumously honored. Huitian asked for, and obtained, honors for his adopted father and his natural father,[20] as well as for Songling, his grandfather, and Songling's adopted father and natural father. In addition, Huitian's four mothers were all honored—his natural mother and his adopted mother, as well as his father's first two wives.

On April 23, 1762, Huitian and his Manchu fellow minister of punishments were reprimanded by the emperor for their handling of a case. The perpetrator of the crime had cheated his mother, a widow, of money and food. There was no dispute over his guilt. The debate was over his sentence. The Ministry of Punishments decided on exile, and the emperor considered the place of exile inappropriate and changed it. "I did not concentrate on reviewing this case because I was on my southern tour," the emperor explained. "Fortunately, I have reviewed this case in detail or else the decision would have been wrong." He ordered that both the Chinese and Manchu ministers of punishments be disciplined.[21]

The following year, a case occurred that was potentially disastrous for Huitian, since it involved his nephew, Qin Rong, a provincial official.

It happened that Gao Cheng, the provincial judge of Guizhou, accused Qin Rong, a prefect in his province, of having tortured a prisoner to death while investigating a robbery that involved two prisoners with similar names. There were suspicions that Rong had communicated privately with his uncle in order to protect himself. The ramifications of the case were so great that the emperor gave it his personal attention.

On June 28, 1763, Qianlong declared in an edict that it was the Ministry of Punishments that first detected the mistake made by provincial officials who had confused the identities of the two men. "The report from Gao Cheng showed that he tried to cover up the mistakes and to lay the blame on Qin Rong, the original prefect, accusing Qin Rong of having killed a robber named Ma Xiang through torture," the emperor said. "Actually, an official can use torture to extract a confession in an important case, and the official should not be found guilty if the prisoner expires as a result."

The emperor went on: "Qin Rong became the target of accusation because the Ministry of Punishments discovered mistakes in the handling of the case. Qin Rong is the nephew of Minister Qin Huitian, so Qin Rong was suspected of having communicated through a private channel about this case. This is unfounded. If Qin Rong had misjudged the case and secretly reported through private channels, he would be guilty, and so would Qin Huitian.

"Now, the case revealed that the officials concerned had released those guilty of robbery and condemned the innocent. All officials of that province, including the governor-general, governor, administration commissioner and provincial judge acted in collusion. Qin Rong was right to report directly to the ministry."

A series of investigations was ordered by the emperor, and as the truth was gradually disclosed, more and more high provincial officials became implicated. As a result, the governor-general, the governor and the provincial judge were all dismissed, as well as many lower-level officials. The governor-general, in addition to being dismissed, was sent into exile.

The emperor decided to promote Qin Rong from acting prefect to prefect. "This case was first reviewed by Qin Rong, who collected evidence by going to the scene of the crime," he said. "This official is diligent and capable and should be rewarded. When he comes back from mourning, have him appointed as prefect."

To assure impartiality in the treatment of this case, Huitian was not involved in its investigation. The emperor sent two of his deputies instead. "When robbers incriminate the innocent," Qianlong said, "government officials are supposed to vindicate the victims. Now, the governor and provincial judge were involved in the frame-up, so who could determine the truth?"[22]

In 1763, Huitian was again chief examiner of the metropolitan examinations, and late that year was granted the exalted title grand guardian of the heir apparent, a title that had continued to be granted as an honor though the practice of naming an heir apparent had been long discontinued.

Though exonerated in the case involving his nephew, Huitian had been penalized on so many other occasions, several times through nominal dismissals, that when he put his name to a document, he had to sign himself "Lecturer of the Classics, Grand Guardian of the Heir Apparent, Minister of Punishments, Concurrently Grand Minister of the State Board of Music, Dismissed and Retained at the Post, Pardoned and Retained at the Post and Again Pardoned and Retained at the Post."

In May 1764, he became so ill that he requested permission to resign. Though Emperor Qianlong acted to lighten Huitian's workload, he refused to let him go. "It is not necessary for Qin Huitian to retire," the emperor said in an edict. "All memorials will be looked at through the normal procedures. He does not need to countersign, so he can have more time to rest." Relieving Huitian of the responsibility of countersigning all ministry documents meant that he would no longer be held responsible for any mistakes discovered.

Despite his decreased workload, the sixty-two-year-old Huitian's health continued to worsen. In September, he again asked for permission to resign so he could return home to recuperate. On September 11, Emperor Qianlong ordered the Manchu minister of punishments, Shu-ho-te, to report on Huitian's condition.[23] Evidently, he reported that Huitian was indeed seriously ill, for on September 14, 1764, the emperor finally relented and decreed: "Minister Qin Huitian, who has still not recovered from his illness, requested permission to retire so he could go home to receive medical attention. Let him take leave to go south for medical treatment. The environment of his hometown is also more congenial to him and will help speed his recovery. But he does not need to resign. Let Liu Lun be in charge of the affairs of the ministry for the time being."[24]

On September 23, Huitian filed a memorial informing the emperor that he was boarding a boat to begin his homeward journey. That was the last communication between the minister and the emperor he had served for almost three decades. The imperial rescript consisted of one word: "Noted."

Huitian never reached his hometown. On the morning of October 4, 1764, he died on a boat on the Grand Canal that linked Peking with Wuxi. Eight days later, when word of Huitian's death reached the court, the emperor issued an edict: "Minister Qin Huitian served in the Ministry of Punishments and was extremely hardworking. He requested leave and was given permission to return home for medical care. I hoped that he would recover. Now I hear that he died on the way home. I am profoundly grieved. I have ordered a report as to what honors should be granted to him according to precedents. In addition, I add a thousand taels of silver as extra funds for his mourning ceremony to show my especially deep concern."[25] Huitian was given the posthumous title of Wen-Gong, or "Cultured and Respectful."

With the death of Huitian, his son Taijun also chose to go into retirement. However, other generations of Qins would continue to serve the Qianlong Emperor.

CHAPTER TWENTY

Qin Zhenjun: An Hour of Glory

When Emperor Qianlong visited Wuxi in 1757, accompanied by Minister Qin Huitian, one of the youngest members of the family to meet him was the shy, withdrawing twenty-two-year-old Qin Zhenjun. Already an accomplished calligrapher, he had compiled in one volume all the poems on the Ji Chang Garden composed by Qianlong during his first visit, as well as writings by scholars and officials in earlier times. This he presented to the emperor, who graciously accepted it and, in return, gave Zhenjun presents of books and silk.[1] The next time they met was not in the beautiful setting of a garden, but in the bloody suppression of an uprising that sought to overthrow the Qing dynasty. And the hero of the hour was Zhenjun.

Zhenjun was the great-grandson of Songling, the grandson of Shiran (Daoran's brother) and the son of Chuntian, Huitian's cousin who had been one of the Nine Old Men to welcome the emperor to the Qin family garden. He was born in 1735, at the beginning of the Qianlong reign, the fourth of six sons. His older brothers were the children of his father's wife, the Lady Lu. Zhenjun and his younger brothers were born of a concubine, the Lady Huang. While young, he studied at home under his eldest brother, Hongjun, a disillusioned scholar who repeatedly failed the civil-service examinations and who, from the age of thirty-six on, gave up all thought of an official career of his own and instead concentrated on educating his sons as well as his younger brothers.

In instructing his charges, Zhenjun's brother said: "Our family has been known for its scholarship since the Ming dynasty, and quite a few members have been important government officials. Even now we have the most scholars of any family south of the Yangtze river. Today, young people are lazy and refuse to study. In the old days, it was said that whenever people saw well-disciplined youngsters on the streets, they knew they were from the Qin family. Now that tradition seems to have been lost."[2] Zhenjun's brother suggested that a clan school be set up to ensure that family members would have a chance to study. It was an idea that Zhenjun and his oldest nephew, Qin Ying, would later try to bring to fruition.

Instead of studying in Wuxi, Zhenjun became a student at the National Academy in Peking at the age of twenty-one, after having purchased the title of *jiansheng*, by now a common practice, which entitled him to take the provincial examinations. Thus began a frustrating period of study and examinations, during which he repeatedly failed to gain the provincial-level degree of *juren*. He finally abandoned these attempts and decided that, if he could not further his career through success at the examinations, he would do so by purchasing an office. The practice of purchasing a post was one long sanctioned as another means of gaining entry into officialdom. However, since he possessed only the lowest degree, and that through purchase, his prospects of rising to high office were slight. Zhenjun purchased the position of assistant magistrate, a post near the bottom of the bureaucratic hierarchy.

In 1770, Zhenjun was assigned to the Donga district of Tai'an prefecture east of the Grand Canal. He performed his duties satisfactorily and, the following year, was posted as assistant subprefect to Linqing, one of the most important cities in north China, about 60 miles from Donga and 290 miles due south of Peking. Linqing, a commercial and trading center, was strategically situated on the Grand Canal along whose waters moved barges laden with southern grain for the tables of Peking.

According to an old Chinese saying, some heroes create situations in which they perform heroic deeds, while some situations create heroes. Linqing was to create a hero.

For some years a man named Wang Lun, a native of Shouzhang, not far from Donga, had been gathering disciples around him, preaching to them the doctrines of the White Lotus sect.[3] As a religious sect, the White Lotus probably came into existence in the fifth century as an offshoot of Amidist Buddhism, one that emphasized asceticism. Early in the fourteenth century, it became overtly political as a result of widespread governmental abuses by the Yuan dynasty. Zhu Yuanzhang mobilized the support of White Lotus sect members to help him establish the Ming dynasty. Then, as soon as he was safely enthroned, the first Ming emperor denounced the sect for its heterodox views and attempted ruthlessly to crush it. The sect went underground and continued to attract adherents by emphasizing personal salvation, the curing of diseases and the martial arts. For hundreds of years, despite repeated persecutions during both the Ming and Qing dynasties, the sect continued to maintain a grip on a small part of the populace, often people who were unable to identify with the Confucianism of the scholars and officials. In contrast to orthodox Buddhist sects, the supreme deity of White Lotus believers was a goddess called the Supreme and Venerable Mother.

The family of White Lotus leader Wang Lun had lived in Tangjia village in Shouzhang district for over two hundred years. Wang Lun himself was probably born in the 1740s into a peasant family. While still a teenager, he began practicing the martial arts, learning to fight with his hands and feet as well as with a staff or sword. Eventually he became an acknowledged master, despite the fact that he was small, less than five feet tall.

For a while he worked as a runner in the government office of neighboring Yangku district, becoming acquainted with policemen, runners and other low-level government employees in Yangku and other districts, some of whom later became his followers. He taught them not only the arts of fighting but also yoga, meditation, breathing exercises and fasting. His sect was given the appellation "Pure Water Sect" because of Wang Lun's ability to go without food for long periods after drinking "purified water." He taught that this would be necessary to survive the catastrophe that would inevitably accompany the arrival on earth of the Buddha Maitreya, an event that would signal the passing of the world into the next great stage of history.

Wang Lun was also a self-taught physician, and won much goodwill, in addition to income, through his healing powers. Eventually his followers, male and female, included not only peasants and low-level government employees but also those who lived on the margins of society, such as itinerant actors and actresses, monks—at least one of whom claimed the ability to enter the netherworld and return—and sorceresses. The White Lotus disciples shared the traditional Chinese belief that the universe was governed by the two opposing yet complementary forces of *yin* and *yang*, *yin* identified with the female and *yang* with the male. The former was considered dark, wet and negative, the latter bright, active and positive.

Although the number of his immediate disciples was small, perhaps a few dozen, some of whom he adopted as his sons, they recruited others, passing on his teachings. By the 1770s, after two decades of disseminating his message, the followers of Wang Lun and their followers numbered in the hundreds, possibly thousands, in Shouzhang and the surrounding districts. There were even adherents in Henan province, adjoining Shandong.

In the early 1770s—about the time when Zhenjun was first posted to Linqing—Wang Lun began to speak in vague terms of pending cataclysmic changes. At first in veiled form, then more explicitly, he disclosed to his followers that he himself was the incarnation of the Buddha Maitreya. He reinforced this claim by speaking of dreams and other revelations. In his mind the new phase into which the world was about to enter was inextricably linked with the overthrow of the existing dynasty. Wang Lun made it clear that he was destined to become emperor. Gradually, he prepared his followers for action. Knowing that they and their knives, sticks and pitchforks were no match for the well-armed Qing forces, Wang Lun taught them protective chants that, he said, would make them invulnerable to bullets and arrows.

By the summer of 1774, his plans had almost matured. As more and more people became involved, rumors spread that a rebellion was imminent. The magistrate of Shouzhang, Shen Qiyi, was told by an informer that some people in Yangku were connected to the rebellion. He sent a message asking his counterpart there to arrest sect members. But one of his subordinates, a constable named Liu Huan, was a follower of Wang Lun and alerted his leader. Wang Lun decided on immediate action. The uprising would begin at midnight on the twenty-eighth day of the eighth month, that is, October 3, 1774.

The first target was Shouzhang City,[4] seat of the district in which Wang Lun lived. Wang Lun's followers from several districts were ordered to arm themselves that night and converge on Shouzhang. Since Magistrate Shen and the military authorities had been warned of the impending rebellion, the troops in Shouzhang were on guard and reconnaissance patrols scoured the countryside, but they reported nothing untoward. Inside the walled city, some forty soldiers were assigned to each of the four gates, but that night Constable Liu Huan and other sect members managed to open one gate. The rebel force, led by some of Wang Lun's most trusted disciples, entered Shouzhang. Quickly, they subdued the guards and silently made their way to the offices of the city's military and civilian officials. The chief military officer, Major Kan-fu, effected his escape and headed for Yangku. But Magistrate Shen was less fortunate. Upon refusing to join the sect members, he was stabbed to death.

With the city in their hands, the rebels looted the treasury, confiscated the contents of the granary and released prisoners held in the local jail, whom they invited to join their ranks.

That same evening, one of Wang Lun's principal disciples, Wang Jinglong, staged an uprising in his home village, Chang-ssu-ku, north of Shouzhang. Acting in concert with the rebels in Shouzhang, he and his followers took control of the village with relative ease, killing over a dozen people and setting fire to half the houses. But they did not attempt to hold it, for the next day, they set out to join their fellows in Shouzhang.

On that day, October 4, Wang Lun and his household arrived in Shouzhang. He was greeted in style, with each rebel soldier kowtowing to him eight times. Nine kowtows were performed for the Eternal Venerable Mother herself. The rebels remained in Shouzhang for several days, during which time their ranks were swollen by some of the populace of the city and its environs as well as people from Tangjia, Wang Lun's home village. The success of the rebels in seizing and holding Shouzhang, the seat of the district, gained additional recruits for their cause.

It was at this time that Zhenjun[5] first heard reports of the trouble. The subprefect of Linching was away, and so the thirty-nine-year-old Zhenjun was temporarily in charge. As his diary of the events relates, villagers fleeing from Chang-ssu-ku arrived in Linqing, bringing news of the uprising. Zhenjun was still unaware of the capture of Shouzhang. As acting subprefect, he did not hesitate to take prompt countermeasures. Together with the local military commander, Colonel Ye Xin, who had fewer than three hundred soldiers under his command, Zhenjun went to Chang-ssu-ku arriving there on the morning of October 5. He found the village devastated. Most of the rebels had withdrawn, but his troops did succeed in seizing nineteen men and two women, including the wife of Wang Jinglong. It was while in Chang-ssu-ku that Zhenjun learned of the fall of Shouzhang and, fearing the worst, hurried back to prepare the defense of Linqing. The prisoners were sent to Tangyi, the district seat, to be put in the custody of the acting magistrate there.

305

Back in Linqing, Zhenjun ordered a curfew and submitted a detailed report to the governor of Shandong, Xu Ji, on both the uprising in Chang-ssu-ku and the successful assault on Shouzhang by "white-turbaned bandits."

Zhenjun's report reached the governor's office in Ji'nan, the provincial capital, at noon of October 6. Governor Xu, in turn, submitted a report to Emperor Qianlong, who was in Rehe, the imperial summer retreat north of Peking. This memorial reached the emperor on October 9, by which time the rebels had abandoned Shouzhang. Since the emperor could not know this, he ordered Governor Xu to surround Shouzhang with his troops and prevent the rebels from escaping. Qianlong also ordered that those taken prisoner by Zhenjun in Chang-ssu-ku should be sent immediately to Ji'nan, the provincial capital, to prevent their being rescued.[6] This showed insight, but it was too late.

For on October 6 the rebels had already started their trek northward, their ultimate destination being Peking itself. On October 7 the rebels, now numbering over a thousand, attacked Yangku. That city was defenseless for, in what would have been a comedy of errors had the consequences not been so tragic, all the soldiers in Yangku were marching to relieve Shouzhang at the request of Major Kan-fu, the chief military officer who had managed to flee that city. Somehow, in the dark, the soldiers and the rebel forces had passed each other undetected. So when the rebels arrived in Yangku, they found that the highest remaining official was the jail warden. Both he and the few others who opposed the rebels were easily dispatched. As in Shouzhang, the rebels emptied the prisons and welcomed those willing to join them into their ranks. They also helped themselves to the contents of the city treasury.

Having encountered little resistance entering the city, they were, however, forced to engage in battle upon their departure. Troops under Brigade General Wei-i and Major Kan-fu, rushing back to Yangku, entered the city through the east gate just as the rebels were leaving via the south gate. In the ensuing skirmish, both sides suffered casualties. Major Kan-fu was killed. The rebel cavalcade then continued its march northward.

That day, October 7, Governor Xu Ji, acting on information that had already been overtaken by events, ordered Colonel Ye Xin to dispatch two hundred soldiers from Linqing to help relieve Shouzhang, thus leaving Linqing defenseless. The governor did not realize that Shouzhang was no longer in rebel hands, nor that Colonel Ye's troops would be hopelessly outnumbered by the rebel forces, now in the thousands.

Having successfully achieved all their objectives thus far, the rebels continued northward. There were two possible goals, Dongchang, on the east of the Grand Canal, and Tangyi. They decided that Tangyi would offer the least resistance and so headed there, thirty-two miles away. The city wall around Tangyi had collapsed in several places and the defense was weak. When the rebels arrived, they met with little opposition. The official in charge, Acting Magistrate Chen Mei, attempted to escape on a horse his servant brought him, but Chen, grossly obese, was unable to mount it. Thus he was captured while attempting to flee on foot. One of the rebel leaders, a salt smuggler who had been caught before and sentenced by Chen, now exacted vengeance. He had Chen first flogged, then castrated, his genitals stuffed into his mouth before he was dismembered. When the prison doors were opened, the rebels captured by Zhenjun at Chang-ssu-ku and sent to the Tangyi authorities were released, as Qianlong had feared earlier.

The rebels did not try to hold Tangyi. After emptying its treasury, they continued northward to the village of Liulin. By now the Victorious Force, as they called themselves, had taken every city and village they attacked, defeated what Qing armies stood in their path, and were less than fifteen miles from the rich city of Linqing.

When news of these events reached Linqing, the people were petrified. Linqing consisted of a large Old City, crowded with shops, where most of the inhabitants lived, and a smaller New City. The perimeter of the Old City roughly followed the Grand Canal as it wound its way to join the Wei River. The wall surrounding the Old City was about fifteen miles long, encompassing the waterway. But much of it had long since crumbled and so afforded little protection. The walls of the New City, tucked in the northeastern corner of Linqing, were high and sturdy. While the headquarters of the local military forces were in the Old City, the office of the subprefect as well as the granary and the treasury were situated in the New City.

With Colonel Ye and most of the troops elsewhere, the fears of the citizens were exacerbated. As Linqing verged on panic, Zhenjun went into the Old City to calm the civilians. He advised the elderly and sick to move into the New City, and urged that valuables be carefully hidden. The terror was such that all but one of Zhenjun's personal assistants fled. But the one who remained, a man named Deng, helped him immensely in the coming days in formulating a strategy to counter the White Lotus rebels.

Since the wall surrounding the Old City provided no defense, the Grand Canal was the main barrier between the rebels and the New City. The obvious place for the rebels to cross the canal was at a wooden sluice in the south of the Old City. Zhenjun ordered the dismantling of the movable bridge there. To prevent the rebels from crossing by boat, he ordered all boats in the area removed. He also sent an urgent request to Governor Xu for reinforcements. Before the arrival of regular troops, he organized the militia, consisting of about eight hundred men.

Meanwhile, Wang Lun and his rebel force were still encamped at Liulin. Governor Xu, learning of this, personally led an army of several hundred troops against them, moving in from the south, and ordered Brigade General Wei-i and his troops to close in simultaneously from the north. This news heartened Zhenjun and the Linqing inhabitants, for it appeared as if the uprising would be quelled before it engulfed Linqing. But instead, the governor's troops were surprised north of Liulin. The governor found himself surrounded and in peril. Only the arrival of Brigade General Wei-i enabled him to extricate himself and lead his soldiers to the safety of Dongchang. Governor Xu was so impressed by the display of rebel skill and valor that he reported to the Qianlong Emperor: "I saw that one of the leaders held knives in both hands and moved his arms and legs so swiftly that he flew about like a monkey. The others were just as unafraid of death and made no attempt to evade our firearms."[7] Little wonder that word spread that the White Lotus rebels were immune to firearms due to their ability to invoke magical powers.

Governor Xu's memorial on this October 7 encounter did not reach the emperor until October 16. But Qianlong, aware that his provincial forces might be unable to quell the uprising, had already taken action five days previously. He had appointed Grand Secretary Shu-ho-te[8] special commissioner to deal with the disturbances and ordered him to go to Tianjin with secret instructions for the brigade general there to have one or two thousand Green Standard soldiers in readiness. In addition, several hundred Manchu soldiers stationed at Cangzhou and Qingzhou were to be put on alert, ready for action. "If the situation is not under control by the time you reach Dezhou," the emperor said, "then take several hundred Manchu soldiers from there and go to the spot. Transfer in as many others as you think necessary."[9]

If Wang Lun had been aware of the forces that were being deployed against him by the emperor, he might have acted differently. But, oblivious of decisions being made hundreds of miles away and fresh from dealing a resounding blow to the governor, Wang Lun's forces now began to close in on Linqing.

Fortunately for Linqing, Colonel Ye and his troops had returned to the city. As soon as they were within sight, Zhenjun rode out alone to welcome them. Another force of a hundred and forty soldiers arrived from Dezhou on the morning of October 11, raising the number of soldiers in the New City to slightly under four hundred. These troops were deployed in the southwestern section of the New City. The reinforcements arrived none too soon for, within hours, the vanguard of the rebel forces appeared.

The White Lotus fighters headed straight for the wooden sluice and, finding the bridge destroyed, immediately set to work building a new one. The Grand Canal was several hundred feet wide at that point. The rebels tore wooden planks from houses, lashed them together into rafts, and tied the rafts together into a floating bridge. By noon, more than a hundred rebels had poured across the bridge, establishing a beachhead inside Linqing.

This first wave of rebels attempted to storm the west and south gates of the New City but they were repulsed by volleys of musket fire and showers of arrows from defenders atop the wall. Nevertheless, by late afternoon, the bulk of the rebel force, several thousand strong, was on the north side of the canal. They marched up the main avenue, setting fire to Colonel Ye's office as they passed it, the blaze lighting up the evening sky.

Zhenjun, from the vantage point of the city wall, saw a weird sight as the rebel force advanced now on the south gate. In their forefront was a group of women waving white fans and muttering chants. Accompanying them were several monks, each with a sword in one hand and a banner in the other, directing the attack.

The sight of the turbaned rebels, led by sorceresses and monks, struck fear into the hearts of the defenders. Bullets and arrows failed to find their marks and the soldiers became disheartened. The defenders sought to break the spell of the rebels, who were chanting "guns will not fire," by deploying *yin* magic to neutralize *yang* magic.

Prostitutes were summoned up to the city wall, where they loosed their hair and removed their garments, so that their genitals were exposed. Then, according to Zhenjun's account, dogs were slaughtered and their blood sprayed on the wall, apparently to simulate menstrual flow to counter the "black magic" of the White Lotus sect.

The rebel spell was broken, the cannons on the city wall roared and a hail of bricks and stones was hurled down on the sect members. The rebels, finding their incantations ineffective, became demoralized and withdrew. The first attack had been successfully repulsed.[10]

After dark, the rebels moved forward again, using another tactic. Dashing through the hail of gunfire, they piled straw outside the city gate, hoping to set it on fire. At the same time, other rebels crept up to the city wall in an attempt to tunnel beneath it. Zhenjun rallied his men and called for volunteers, declaring, "Anyone willing to go down to fight the bandits will be richly rewarded." Several civilians, evidently members of the militia, came forward and were lowered down the wall under cover of darkness. Hiding in a ditch by the gate, they slashed out at the legs of the rebels with sickles when they ran in with bundles of straw. Meanwhile, other soldiers on the wall kept up a steady stream of fire with muskets and arrows, some with dynamite wrapped around them. Zhenjun estimated that in this encounter more than two hundred rebel soldiers were killed. About midnight, the rebels disengaged.

Although the rebels controlled the Old City and were in a position to attack the west and south gates, Zhenjun maintained contact with the governor by dispatching messengers through the north and east gates of the New City, which led to open countryside not under rebel control. His report was transmitted by Governor Xu to the Qianlong Emperor, who issued a decree commending the defenders of Linqing and ordering that all the officials involved be rewarded, including the soldiers who were lowered down the city wall to engage in hand-to-hand combat with the rebels. All of them, he said, should be promoted to sergeant. Other soldiers were granted an additional month's rations and pay. The emperor instructed Governor Xu to record Zhenjun's merits and, after the uprising was over, to arrange for Zhenjun to be presented to the emperor at an audience.[11]

The next morning the assault on the New City resumed. The rebels hitched oxen to a cart and loaded it with cannons, which they had apparently located in the Old City. Then they drove the cart to the west gate, planning to batter down the gate, but the Dezhou troops on the wall, armed with muskets, cut down the leader and the other rebels scattered. With the oxcart stalled, soldiers were lowered to the ground by ropes. They slew the oxen and carried the cannons and ammunition into the city. That day, two rebel soldiers were seized outside the south gate.

On October 13, the third day of the siege, the attack on the west gate resumed in the late afternoon. The rebels hid in the old Yuan Di Temple near the gate, which shielded them from the marksmen and archers on the wall. Then, at intermittent intervals, bands of them rushed out, each person carrying a bundle of dried millet stalks. These they piled up by the city gate and set them on fire. The gate started to burn and a loud crack signaled that the wood was splitting. Again, Zhenjun called for volunteers, who descended the wall and doused the blaze. But holes had appeared in the city wall. Amid the din of battle, men and women took bricks from temples inside the New City and, mixing them with earth, repaired the wall. And thanks to both soldiers and citizens, another crisis was overcome. During this engagement, Zhenjun calculated, more than a hundred rebels were killed.

The next day, Zhenjun and the other leaders of the city decided to reward the civilians who had played such an important role in defending the city by giving each of them a picul of grain. The wealthier citizens of Linqing donated the grain, which was distributed to the soldiers. That morning, instructions from the governor arrived. He ordered that one of the captured bandits be executed by slicing. The other captive rebel was already dead, but his corpse was to be decapitated.

The defenders had successfully repelled every onslaught, but the rebels were learning to stay beyond the range of bullets and arrows. Meantime, they brought into play weapons they had seized in the Old City. No longer were they limited by their knives and other crude weapons. As Zhenjun wrote, "Flying shells entered the city, sounding like a flock of wild geese." The defenders returned fire, and shooting by both sides continued late into the night. But as long as the rebels were sheltered by the Yuan Di Temple, the soldiers' guns were largely ineffective. And ammunition supplies were running dangerously low. So that night, the defenders took the initiative.

Volunteers were again sent down the city wall by ropes. Quietly, they crept up to the temple and set it on fire, destroying it and thereby depriving the rebels of their sanctuary.

This was the first foray into enemy territory by the defenders of Linqing. To celebrate it, cattle and pigs were slaughtered and a big feast was held in honor of the soldiers.

The following day there was a lull in the fighting, though the rebels tried to draw the defenders' fire to force them to waste their ammunition. Since October 11, four days after the first attack on Linqing, Wang Lun and his followers had abandoned their camps outside the Old City and moved into the houses there, to show their determination to stay in Linqing until the New City had fallen. The capture of such an important metropolis would, they knew, give their movement much-needed momentum.

The rebels moved into the main buildings in the Old City, including the Monastery of Great Tranquillity, or Big Temple. As a sign of their control, they flew banners from the temple that were visible at great distances and, at night, hung huge lamps. Shops were ransacked and the residents were made prisoners. The men were forced to work while many of the women were raped. Only a corner of the Old City that was inhabited by Muslims remained intact, because the Muslims put up a strong resistance.

There were few shops inside the New City and after several days of siege most of the supplies were used up or dwindling. Oil was burned in place of candles, pieces of cloth were tied together for use as ropes and tin objects were melted down and forged into bullets. Zhenjun wrote to the governor impressing on him the urgency of the situation and sent appeals to neighboring towns and cities for emergency supplies.

On October 15, a hundred soldiers arrived to help in the defense of the city and, on the sixteenth, Brigade General Wei-i and Commander Ke-tu-ken appeared with five hundred men. General Wei-i set up camp to the northeast of the city, away from the rebel forces to the south and west. That afternoon their camp was attacked by several hundred White Lotus rebels. Zhenjun and the city's defenders watched the fighting from the city wall but were unable to help for fear of hitting Wei-i's soldiers. The well-armed Qing soldiers, struck by panic, broke ranks and fled. The White Lotus fighters pursued them for several miles before returning to Linqing.

Having regrouped, the sect members renewed their assault on the

New City, bombarding the south gate. A cannonball flew into the subprefect's office, smashing a stone plaque, but fortunately Zhenjun was unhurt. The battle raged until dawn when the rebels withdrew.

For the next six days, there were no major rebel assaults. Within the embattled walls of the New City, Zhenjun worked to maintain the morale of the troops. As the top official in Linqing, it was his responsibility to inspire confidence despite the gravity of the situation. He distributed money and clothes to the soldiers to reward them for their efforts. He also distributed grain, buns, cakes and gruel to the civilians to raise their spirits. And he sent another urgent message to the governor.

The next day, Zhenjun received gratifying news. The emperor had instructed three of his highest officials—a grand secretary, his own seventh son-in-law, and the president of the Censorate—to lead armies to crush the White Lotus rebels. Troops in the neighboring provinces of Zhili and Henan were being mobilized to cut off escape routes. Meanwhile, gunpowder, fuses and ammunition arrived.

While the lull in the fighting persisted, there was sporadic shooting by both sides, and supplies were running low. Crude spears, made by melting down hoes and other metal objects, were distributed to the soldiers. Food was almost exhausted for both man and beast. Volunteers had to leave the safety of the wall to gather fodder for the horses. Trees were felled for firewood and when there were no more, houses were taken apart so the wood could be used for fuel.

On October 20, while Zhenjun was inspecting the city's defenses, he noticed an arrow that had been shot by the rebels. It was embedded horizontally. He knew that if it had been fired from the ground, it would have slanted in landing. So Zhenjun decided that the rebels must have established themselves in a building as high as the city wall. The only such structure was a pawnshop to the southwest, a building tall enough for the White Lotus rebels to peer over the city wall and spy on the defenders. Zhenjun ordered another foray. The dozen men who volunteered for it were lowered down the city wall at night, each with a load of straw strapped to his back. They succeeded in reaching the pawnshop undetected. Peeping through the window, they saw that all inside were asleep, except for two men who were drinking. Quietly, they lit their fires and soon the building was ablaze. The White Lotus rebels poured out of the pawnshop as the soldiers ran back toward the New City, with three women in black, wielding daggers, pursuing them almost to the city gate. The

313

guards on the wall opened fire. The women, said to be adopted daughters of Wang Lun, waved defiantly at them but fell back.

Meanwhile, unknown to Zhenjun, the Qianlong Emperor, pleased with the way the defenders were holding out, issued an edict promoting Zhenjun to subprefect of Linqing, effective immediately. His handling of the White Lotus uprising had, within a matter of weeks, raised him to a position of prominence that might otherwise have taken him decades to attain.[12]

On October 23, the rebels mounted another major attack on the New City. Their strategy was devised by a new adherent of the sect, Wu Zhaolong, who had received military training. Hitherto, the rebels had been unable to approach the city gates safely because of the bullets and arrows that rained down on them. Wu drew up a plan that provided cover for the rebels as they advanced with a load of explosives. Long planks were placed across three carts, protruding like wings from the sides. Under cover of night each cart, borne on the backs of seven or eight men, inched forward toward the south gate.

Because of the darkness, the carts were not discovered by the defenders until one of them was already perilously close to the gate. Realizing the dire situation, Zhenjun ordered his soldiers to throw down bricks and stones to obstruct the front cart. Before long, debris a foot high blocked the entrance.

Bricks and stones were hurled also at the other two carts. They became so heavy that the men beneath the planks could no longer sustain the weight and fled, abandoning their loads. Zhenjun then ordered the carts set on fire, but there were no flaming arrows left. So he had gunpowder wrapped in cloth tied around an arrow and a lit incense stick stuck in it as a fuse. In this way, the two abandoned carts were blown up, but the front cart was too close to the gate for that, so Zhenjun ordered soldiers lowered down the wall. They quickly dispatched the six rebels hiding beneath the planks, then poured water on the explosives to render them harmless. And the last major assault on the New City by the White Lotus sect members was repulsed.

Soon afterward, the rebels were forced to turn their attention from attacking the New City to defending their position in the Old City. On October 24, the first contingents of Qing reinforcements arrived on the northern outskirts of the city and set up camp. Wang Lun, wishing to retain the initiative, marshaled his forces and staged a surprise attack on them, but this time the Qing soldiers stood their ground and eventually the rebels had to withdraw. It was their first defeat since they began the assault on Shouzhang twenty-two days previously.

The next day, Zhenjun left the New City, the first time he had done so since the beginning of the siege. Taking a circuitous route, he traveled southward until he came to the camp of Governor Xu and his troops. Zhenjun brought with him a scout familiar with the terrain to assist the governor in the coordinated assault on the Old City planned for the following day. Then Zhenjun returned to his New City bastion.

The arrival of the governor's troops on the morning of October 27 was heralded by loud cannon fire from the south. Before long troops from the north also joined the action. By noon, Imperial Commissioner Shu-ho-te and his banner troops were at the scene. The rebels, hemmed in on all sides, were forced to retreat, suffering heavy losses. Many sought shelter inside houses, which the Qing troops simply put to the torch.

Though the rebel cause was now clearly hopeless, the White Lotus sect members continued to fight. The Qing troops pressed forward, but the presence of civilians made their progress slow as each street and each house had to be taken over and searched. The fighting continued for several days.

Even overwhelmingly outnumbered, the White Lotus sect members proved themselves formidable opponents, willing to confront guns with knives and spears. One woman, described by Zhenjun as a "sorceress," proved particularly difficult to subdue. Wu San-niang, or "Third Daughter of the Wu Family," was a beautiful woman of about twenty, who was both Wang Lun's pupil and his concubine. An itinerant performer, she was an expert in the martial arts and seemed to possess magical powers. Even though all her own followers were killed, she remained defiant. Dressed in imperial yellow and brandishing a short sword in each hand, she was elusive even when surrounded. She fought fiercely and, though shot at from all directions, was unscathed. Eyewitnesses described how she leaped from her horse onto a building, and from there onto a taller building. The Qing soldiers fired guns and shot arrows, but she, seemingly invulnerable, merely waved her sleeves. The struggle against her went on for hours until the Qing troops feared she would escape when it became dark. Then an old soldier decided to counter her

315

yin force with *yang* powers. He cut the genitals from the body of a dead rebel, placed them on a cannon, and fired. San-niang fell to the ground, and her body was immediately chopped to pieces.

The street-to-street fighting inevitably took its toll of innocent civilians. On October 28, a thick fog covered the city. Several thousand refugees from the fighting, residents of the Old City, came to the walls of the New City clamoring for sanctuary. None of the officials, military or civilian, dared let them in for fear of infiltrators. But Zhenjun said, "These are our own people; how can we leave them out to die? If anything untoward occurs, I will assume responsibility." But to minimize the danger of infiltration, Zhenjun ordered that only women, children and the elderly were to be given refuge. They were taken to the various temples and fed.

That day, a public execution was held before all the troops. On the orders of the emperor, Brigade General Wei-i and Commander Ke-tu-ken were condemned to death for having lost the battle of October 16, when their well-equipped troops were routed by an untrained and poorly armed White Lotus force. The execution was timed to coincide with the final assault on the rebels to make sure that the Qing soldiers would do their utmost.

Although the back of the rebellion had been broken, resistance in the Old City continued. Moreover, Wang Lun himself was still at large. The rebel leader was almost captured on October 30. On that day, Sublieutenant Xian Heling was told that Wang Lun might be hiding on Horse-Market Street, in a large house built by a former high official. Xian Heling and an imperial bodyguard, Yin-chi-tu, took about twenty men with them, climbed over the wall of the compound and found Wang Lun. The sublieutenant grabbed his queue while Yin-chi-tu held him by his body and wrestled him to the ground in an attempt to take him alive. Wang Lun's bodyguards immediately came to his rescue. One struck the sublieutenant on the neck with a sword, seriously wounding him. Yin-chi-tu, too, sustained many injuries, but tenaciously clung to Wang Lun. Then a spear pierced Yin-chi-tu's throat and he released his grip on the rebel leader, who was carried indoors by his followers.

Qing soldiers now cordoned off Wang Lun's hideout to ensure that no one would escape. At midnight on October 31, rebels tried to break through the encirclement, but all were either killed or captured or driven back by the heavy gunfire. Wang Lun's brother was among those killed.

Wang Lun was entrenched in a tower within the compound. Several of the captured rebels, trying to win time for their leader, claimed to be Wang Lun. In the confusion, no attempt was made to storm the tower in which he was still hiding. But Wang Lun knew that there was no escape. On November 1, to avoid being taken alive, he set fire to the tower in which he and a handful of his followers remained. Some, unable to withstand the heat and smoke, jumped out the window. Wang Lun stayed. His sword and his bracelets later formed the basis of the identification of his charred body.

The rebellion, which had taken so many lives, had lasted exactly twenty-nine days. Over a thousand prisoners were executed, while their leaders were taken to Peking under armed escort for questioning before execution.

The Wang Lun uprising turned out to be but the first of a series of major rebellions against Qing authority. Later attempts to topple the Manchus were on a much larger scale and proved considerably harder to put down. The White Lotus rebellion of 1774, though quelled in less than a month, was the harbinger of a period of decline for the dynasty that lasted for more than a century, until it finally fell in 1911.

With Wang Lun dead and his uprising at an end, Imperial Commissioner Shu-ho-te set about preparing for the postwar rehabilitation of Linqing. He did not think Zhenjun, who had performed so admirably under enemy fire, suitable for the task of running Linqing in peacetime. Possibly he was unimpressed with Zhenjun's unassuming personality. In any event, a memorial to Qianlong, jointly signed by Shu-ho-te, the imperial son-in-law, the president of the Censorate and Governor Xu Ji asserted that they feared that Zhenjun might not be able to handle the complex and pressing matters confronting postwar Linqing. They recommended that Li Tao, district magistrate of Feicheng, be appointed instead. They also proposed that Zhenjun take over Li's old position, thus in effect demoting him, though allowing him to retain the rank of subprefect. The emperor acquiesced and praised the imperial commissioner for having the courage to propose the reversal of an imperial decision.[13]

On June 20, 1775, Qianlong received both Zhenjun and the new subprefect, Li Tao, in Peking and questioned them closely about the situation in Linqing. Evidently, Zhenjun did not impress the emperor. In any event, after the audience, the emperor said that Li

317

Tao showed a good understanding of the situation and that Zhenjun was a person of honesty and sincerity. And the emperor said that since Zhenjun had defended the city night and day with all his energy, and since his merits were obvious, he should be appointed to a subprefecture whenever a suitable opening arose.[14]

In the meantime, Zhenjun continued as district magistrate of Feicheng, which was part of Tai'an prefecture. Subprefectures were categorized by the degree of complexity of their administration. While Linqing was classified as a strategic post that was "difficult" and "busy," Feicheng was listed as a "simple" post. "Difficult" meant an insecure locale, while "busy" signified a post where much official business was conducted. A "simple" post was one in which the population size, the level of public revenue and the extent of the legal caseload were considered to be not too challenging.

The following spring the emperor, on an inspection of his eastern domains, passed through Shandong. When he arrived at Linqing, he wrote two poems commemorating the suppression of Wang Lun's rebellion. And he issued an edict in which he recalled that although Zhenjun had been given the rank of subprefect, he still lacked such a post. Qianlong ordered that he be given a subprefecture as soon as possible. In the meantime, he bestowed on him two bolts of silk.[15]

Not long after that, forty-one-year-old Zhenjun was finally given a chance to demonstrate that he could run a subprefecture. He was named head of Pingdu, also in Shandong, which was categorized as "difficult." Zhenjun set about proving himself a capable administrator. He concentrated his efforts on education, renovating the local college. Twice every month, he lectured to the students on the importance of moral behavior as well as on literature and writing.

Zhenjun also went to great lengths to care for the poor and for sojourners. Each winter, he ordered warm clothes distributed to the poor. Travelers who were stranded in Pingdu were offered shelter until the spring.[16]

Although the judicial commissioner was ultimately responsible for court cases, much of the investigation of crimes and the arrest and trial of suspects was done by district magistrates and other provincial officials. One of the murder cases that Zhenjun had to deal with was particularly gruesome. A corpse covered with multiple wounds was discovered in Pingdu. The murderer, apparently in an attempt to make it difficult for the authorities to identify the body, had removed the facial skin of the victim. But Zhenjun learned that the clothing on the corpse had belonged to a man named Zhu. And further investigation showed that Zhu and a man named Cao had been feuding. Zhenjun then conducted a secret search of Cao's house. Bloodstains were found, Cao was questioned and he confessed.[17]

Zhenjun's performance at Pingdu was considered to have been so good that after a three-year tour, he was promoted to prefect and assigned to Xining, in northwestern Gansu province. He turned down the promotion because of his elderly parents. If he stayed in Shandong province, his parents could live in relative comfort in Ji'nan, the provincial capital, but Gansu was much more backward and remote. So he elected to remain in Pingdu. In 1783, at the end of his second tour there, he was again offered a promotion to prefect, this time of Caozhou, one of Shandong's eleven prefectures. Zhenjun accepted, but before he could assume his new duties his father died. He accompanied his father's coffin back to Wuxi and began to observe the official mourning period, which was prolonged because, during it, his mother also died.

In 1786, having completed mourning for both his parents, Zhenjun returned to work. Again, he was assigned to Gansu, this time as prefect of Pingliang. He accepted. Pingliang was important as a transportation center but its soil was poor. Zhenjun did his best for the economy by improving transportation facilities and upgrading agriculture.

But his most important achievement in Pingliang was his decision to rebuild the local academy, which had not functioned in decades. With money collected from fines, he asked local officials to hire workers and obtain construction materials. After it was completed, Zhenjun decided to enlarge its scope, providing for more and bigger buildings. He had the heads of all the districts in the prefecture raise additional funds, and with that money hills were leveled, ponds dug and soon the academy's buildings rose from the ground. Thirty of the smartest students were accepted and teachers were recruited to instruct them. All these efforts were vindicated when, the year after the academy's reopening, one of its students brought honor on the entire prefecture by passing the provincial examinations. This was followed by two brothers, who were also successful examination candidates.[18] The reopening of the academy won Zhenjun the gratitude of the local residents, since it allowed them access to officialdom.

In 1793, Zhenjun was again promoted, this time to grain commissioner in Shaanxi with his base in the ancient city of Xi'an, the provincial capital. The people of Pingliang were sorry to see him go, and the following year, as his sixtieth birthday neared, a delegation went to the office of Magistrate Kong Jinghan and expressed the desire to visit Zhenjun in Xi'an and celebrate his birthday "by presenting him with a glass of wine." Magistrate Kong advised them against the long journey, saying it was too arduous for the elderly and the children. "I shall tell him of your good intentions," he said, "and that all of you have practiced filial piety and brotherly love as he had taught you. I am sure he will be happy to hear that. So it is not necessary to go in person to offer him a glass of wine." Instead, poems in honor of Zhenjun were composed, and Magistrate Kong compiled them into a book for which he wrote a preface.[19]

In mid-1794 Zhenjun was promoted again, this time to salt controller of Zhejiang. This was a lucrative post, since the incumbent was often plied with gifts from wealthy salt merchants. He stayed there for a year and then, apparently because of a difference of opinion with a superior, he pleaded ill health and was allowed to retire to Wuxi at the age of sixty-one.

While in retirement, Zhenjun devoted himself to the welfare of the clan. He and another clan member, Qin Yunjin, searched for and ultimately found all the graves of the ancestors from the Song poet Qin Guan down to Weizheng. Their success meant that the clan had located the graves of all twenty-five generations from Qin Guan down to their own time. Plaques were set up to honor the ancestors, and annual sacrificial rites were set up. Portraits of fourteen ancestors were painted.

Zhenjun also substantially enlarged the clan's common land holdings, known as charitable land, since it was for the welfare of clan members who were less well off financially. Zhenjun's uncle, Huitian, had set as the goal a thousand *mu* of land, or slightly more than a hundred and fifty acres. This was considered a large estate, and few clans had such holdings. In 1774, Zhenjun made a contribution of a hundred *mu*, while others, such as Huitian's son Taijun, added an additional three hundred and sixty *mu* to the original holdings of slightly more than fifty *mu*. But they were still far short of their target. In 1795, after his retirement, Zhenjun made an additional contribution of four hundred and ninety *mu*, finally reaching the clan target of a thousand *mu*. In effect, he converted almost his entire personal fortune into clan properties, doing much more for the clan than had others who were better scholars or had served in higher positions.

Qin Jin had put together the first genealogy, Qin Rui had built the ancestral hall, Qin Daoran had spearheaded the planning of the temple to honor filial sons, Qin Huitian had drawn up rules and regulations to be observed by clan members, and now Qin Zhenjun had fulfilled the long-held desire to put the clan on a firm foundation by seeing to it that its poorer members would have a regular source of income. What was still missing, however, was a clan school.

Zhenjun next devoted himself to this effort. He set aside an additional fifteen acres of farmland for the eventual setting up of a clan school, an idea that his brother and tutor had instilled in him when he was young. At the same time his nephew Ying donated fifteen acres. Income from the land was to be used to hire good scholars to teach. "I hope our family descendants who enter this school will learn to serve the country and follow the example set by our ancestors," Zhenjun wrote. "I hope they will be filial and brotherly."

Zhenjun's own descendants swelled the ranks of the clan. He had four sons and a daughter. By the time of his death, he also had three grandsons, seven granddaughters and three great-grandsons.

For an unexplained reason, in 1803, when he was sixty-eight years old, Zhenjun came out of retirement. Perhaps the official who had caused him to go into retirement was no longer in office. In any event, he was appointed circuit intendant in Shandong province, in charge of the prefectures of Ji'nan, the provincial capital, and Dongchang, Tai'an, Wuting and Linqing. These prefectures constituted by far the most important of the three circuits into which the province was divided.

At that time there was a serious flood in neighboring Henan province, which affected Shandong. Zhenjun was the first official to ask the court for disaster relief. He also ordered that dams be built to control floodwaters and arranged for two hundred vessels to transport food to help the flood victims. In the winter of 1806 he became the province's acting judicial commissioner, although some of his subordinates possessed higher degrees than he.

In the autumn of 1807, while traveling from Dongchang to Jining, he fell ill and, a few weeks later, he died in his office at the age of seventy-two. Although Zhenjun worked as an official for decades and rose to a third-ranking position, a rare achievement for someone who did not hold either a metropolitan or provincial degree, he is remembered best for his three-week defense of the city of Linqing.

CHAPTER TWENTY-ONE

Qin Ying: Pirate-Fighter and Provincial Judge

"In previous generations our family produced many members who were prominent scholars, but your great-grandfather and grand-father were both unfortunate, like myself," Hongjun told his oldest son, Ying. "Now, all my hopes are placed in you."

When Ying's granduncle Huitian accompanied Emperor Qian-long to Wuxi on his southern tour, Ying was only twelve years old but already recognized as a precocious literary talent in the area. He became a licentiate at the age of fifteen. But it took him an additional nineteen years to pass the provincial examinations and, despite six attempts over the next fifteen years, he never did pass the metropolitan examinations. In fact, Qin Ying, my mother's great-great-great-grandfather, was one of a handful of people to rise to high office without having attained the degree ordinarily needed for such posts, that of *jinshi*.

Ying, the eldest of five sons and three daughters, was born to Hongjun, the brother of Zhenjun, on February 22, 1743. His mother was descended from a famous scholar and official, Xu Qianxue, friend and colleague of Songling. Actually, the Xu and Qin families were intermarried several times over. The grandson of Xu married Songling's granddaughter, a union that produced a daughter, who returned to the Qin family by marrying her first cousin Hongjun.

Though his granduncle was a high official, Ying's family was not well off. In fact, after he married at the age of eighteen a daughter of the Zhu family, he lived with them for the first year, while his father worked as lecturer in an academy in a different town in order to support his large family.

Some years after becoming a licentiate, Ying went to the capital to study in the Imperial Academy while his granduncle Huitian was minister of punishments. He became Huitian's assistant and learned about the work of the ministry from the inside. The experience would stand him in good stead later in life.

In 1774, Ying finally passed the provincial examinations and became a *juren* at the age of thirty-one. That year, his favorite uncle Zhenjun gained honor for defending the besieged city of Linqing. Two years later the emperor journeyed through Shandong province and while in Tai'an held an examination in search of local talent. Qin Ying took part in that examination, graduating in the first rank. The emperor immediately appointed the thirty-three-year-old Qin Ying a secretary in the Manchu-dominated Central Drafting Office of the Grand Secretariat.[1]

Before assuming his post, he returned to Wuxi to see his parents. It was to be his last meeting with his mother. The year after Ying moved to Peking, his wife and two sons joined him in the capital. Ying did not return to Wuxi for seven years, but his thoughts were with his family, and he secured honorary titles for his parents.

In 1781, Ying was named to serve concurrently as a secretary in the Grand Council, which had replaced the Grand Secretariat as the locus of power. It was a much-sought-after post. That year, he was assigned to assist in the compilation of the *Siku Quanshu,* or *Complete Library in Four Branches of Literature.* This was the most ambitious bibliographical project in the Qing dynasty, entailing the copying by hand of about 3,450 rare books and manuscripts, including those on the classics, history, philosophy and belles-lettres.

Ying worked on the project for four years, under Director-General Ho-shen, a young Manchu who was the favorite of the Qianlong Emperor. Rumors spread that the aging emperor was having a homosexual love affair with the handsome former imperial bodyguard. Other stories held that the emperor saw in the young man the reincarnation of a woman he had loved in his youth. Ho-shen placed his men in key positions and crushed those who opposed him. He was a far more powerful person than any of the emperor's sons, so it was not surprising that, after the death of the Qianlong Emperor, his son and successor, Emperor Jiaqing, ordered Ho-shen to commit suicide. History has condemned Ho-shen as extremely corrupt, incompetent and power hungry.

Ying was part of a small army of literary workers responsible for checking the work of copyists and editors. The manuscripts he worked on were then rechecked by other officials. If they caught any mistakes that Ying had missed, he was penalized by having demerits recorded

323

against him. During his four years on the project, Ying received a total of thirty-six demerits. In 1782, however, no demerits were recorded against him. In fact, that year, he was rewarded by the emperor with gifts that included a rubbing, a scepter and satin, as well as ink, brush and ink slab.[2]

Early in 1783, Ying had a dream that appeared to be portentous. In the dream, an ancient pine tree that grew outside his home in Wuxi had toppled over. When he heard a few weeks later about the death of his grandfather, he was relieved, thinking that his dream had come to pass and that at least his parents were safe.

That autumn, the Qianlong Emperor, then seventy-two years old, made a trip to the Manchurian capital of Mukden, and Ying was part of his entourage. He received a letter from his father telling him that his sixty-two-year-old mother had a chest disease, but Ying was unable to take time off to go to see her.

When he returned to the capital, he heard that his mother had died. Seven months later, his father followed her to the grave. News of his father's death was said to have been such a shock to Ying's younger brother, Lian, that he coughed blood and died within weeks.[3] In a matter of months, Ying had lost three of the people closest to him. The death of his parents caused a temporary retirement while he went into official mourning.

In 1787, Ying and his family returned to the capital, and he resumed his position in the Grand Council. As soon as he returned, he was immersed in the latest crisis, a serious uprising in Taiwan, which was not quelled until the following year. This was followed in 1789 by Qianlong's military intervention in a civil war in Annam—now known as Vietnam. He ultimately brought the territory under Chinese suzerainty in what he considered one of the ten great campaigns of his reign, but the Annamese civil war would have severe repercussions in later years that would affect Ying.

In 1789, the triennial evaluation of all metropolitan officials was held, and Ying came in the first category. As a result he was promoted to assistant reader of the Grand Secretariat, a department dominated by Manchus. Chinese could hold only two of the sixteen posts.

Ying was moving upward. Though not allied with Ho-shen, he was clearly not an opponent of his former superior. Ying himself acknowledged that he and Ho-shen were on friendly terms, but biographers friendly to Ying attempted to portray Ho-shen as an antagonist who was forced to recommend Ying's promotion only because the Qianlong Emperor thought highly of him.

In 1792, Ying was appointed secretary of the Jiangxi Bureau of the Ministry of Revenue. His job was to look after financial matters relating to Jiangxi from his office in Peking. Though his work kept him busy, Ying spent what time he could spare on the education of his two sons, Xiangwu and Xiangwen. His older son was in his early twenties and his younger was a teen-ager. He wrote poems to them exhorting them to study hard.[4] To Xiangwu he said:

> Your essays do not lack force
> But they require more depth.
> Your gold is mixed with sand
> And your jade with stones.

To Xiangwen:

> You are already fifteen years old
> But know no history or literature.
> I am poor and own only a few old books
> Study now or regret in old age.

In 1793, Ying was appointed circuit intendant in Zhejiang province. So it was that he missed the historic visit to Peking that summer of Lord Macartney, envoy of King George III of England. The envoy's mission was to persuade Qianlong to permit the stationing of an English ambassador in Peking and to widen trade, but much of his time and energies were spent resisting Chinese efforts to make him perform the kowtow in the presence of the emperor. Macartney felt the ceremony too degrading, and agreed only to accord the Chinese emperor the same respect that he accorded to his sovereign.

The Chinese empire was then at its height, and Qianlong was in no mood to acknowledge the English sovereign as his equal. In a rebuff to George III, Qianlong issued a decree that said in part:

"As to what you have requested in your message, O King, namely to be allowed to send one of your subjects to reside in the Celestial Empire to look after your country's trade, this does not conform to the Celestial Empire's ceremonial system, and definitely cannot be done. . . .

"The Celestial Empire, ruling all within the four seas, simply concentrates on carrying out the affairs of government properly, and

325

does not value rare and precious things. . . . In fact, the virtue and power of the Celestial Dynasty has penetrated afar to the myriad kingdoms, which have come to render homage, and so all kinds of precious things from 'over mountain and sea' have been collected here, things which your chief envoy and others have seen for themselves. Nevertheless we have never valued ingenious articles, nor do we have the slightest need of your country's manufactures."5

This insular Chinese attitude bore the seeds of the dynasty's downfall, and within decades of Qianlong's death, the mighty empire was humbled as foreign troops and cannon easily defeated Chinese armies, marking the beginning of a century of humiliation.

When Ying was sent to Zhejiang as circuit intendant in 1793, he was already fifty years old. He was responsible for the two prefectures of Wenzhou and Chuzhou, one of four circuits into which the province was divided.

Ying's lasting contribution to the governance of his circuit stemmed from his discovery that it was the practice of local officials to appoint village heads who were then held responsible for the collection of taxes and liable for any unpaid taxes. Members of wealthy families were chosen for this task, since they were the ones who could afford to pay. They were also liable to perform forced labor on government projects.

Many families, to avoid such an onerous burden, bribed the local officials to spare them this obligation. But even if they were spared one year, they would be appointed the next. The result, as Ying discovered after his arrival, was that after several decades of such a practice, there were no wealthy families left in Wenzhou.

The officials would not change the system because they knew that if these village heads were absolved of the burden of making up for delinquent taxes, then the responsibility for collecting taxes due would fall on their own shoulders. So complaints to local officials went unheeded, while complaints to higher officials were simply passed back down to the local officials who were benefiting from the system.

But in 1794, the year after his arrival, Ying called for the abandonment of the system, telling the prefect of Wenzhou: "Seeing to it that taxes are paid is the responsibility of the officials. Why should this responsibility be shifted onto village heads? Why should the common people be burdened with the duties of government officials?"

So Ying asked the governor to approve the dismantling of the system and the practice was abandoned throughout the province. To ensure that there would be no abuse, Ying had his orders engraved on stone. The grateful villagers said to him: "Your Honor has released us from slavery, and we will make sure that we pay our taxes promptly so as not to embarrass you." They erected a plaque in his honor next to the Temple of the God of Agriculture.[6]

While in Wenzhou, Ying was named Zhejiang's acting judicial commissioner, or provincial judge. That made him the third most senior civil official in the province, ranking next to the governor and the administration commissioner, who was responsible for financial matters. As provincial judge, he was directly involved with antipirate activities and observed the weakness of government troops, who were unable to eradicate piracy along the coast.

In the late eighteenth and early nineteenth centuries, piracy was at its height. The provinces most seriously affected were Zhejiang, Fujian and Guangdong. In addition to indigenous pirates, there were those from Annam preying on coastal shipping. In a sense, this was the legacy of Qianlong's intervention in the Annamese civil war for, although the new Nguyen dynasty accepted tributary status, its ruler permitted the Annamese navy to raid the Chinese coast and gave shelter to Chinese pirates.

So, when Ying became acting provincial judge, the pirates were his biggest problem. They outnumbered and outgunned government vessels, and were usually able to carry out their raids unimpeded. Chinese military commanders often shunned encounters with the pirates, staying out of sight as the pirates went about their plundering, then moving in when the pirates were gone and arresting the victims as pirates.

It was Ying's wife who brought to his attention the hazards of judging pirate cases. Once, when he was working in the evening with her at his side, she said: "I hear that most of the suspected pirates are from Fujian and we don't even know their dialect. When there is no material evidence, shouldn't there be some doubt as to the truth of the matter?" Ying reviewed the cases and found that many men charged with being pirates were actually refugees who had been falsely accused.[7]

In the spring of 1795, Ying was formally moved to Hangzhou, as circuit intendant of the most important area of Zhejiang, in charge of the three prefectures of Hangzhou, Jiaxing and Huzhou. He

327

continued to serve concurrently as the acting provincial judge. Within months, his wife died, at the relatively young age of fifty-four. In a eulogy, Ying praised her as an ideal wife and helpmeet, lamenting, "We used to argue on occasion but she was usually right. Now that she is gone, who is there to advise me?"

Ying's grief did not prevent him from taking a fifteen-year-old concubine the following year, when he was fifty-three. The young woman, who was from a poor Wuxi family named Dai, was ten years younger than her oldest stepson, who four years later would make her a grandmother.

The year of Ying's remarriage, Emperor Qianlong formally abdicated at the age of eighty-five, after having ruled for sixty years. He had prayed for a reign almost as long as that of his grandfather, Emperor Kangxi, and out of filial feelings did not want to be seen exceeding the sixty-one-year-reign of that great man. But in the remaining two and a half years of his life, he continued to run the country, though his son formally reigned as the Jiaqing Emperor.

Ying bought a piece of land on Gushan, a peninsula that juts into West Lake, and built a temple there in honor of his ancestor, the Song dynasty poet Qin Guan, who had served briefly as deputy prefect of Hangzhou. He also constructed another temple in honor of Qin Guan's mentor, Su Dongbo, who had been prefect of Hangzhou. His forebears were constantly in Ying's mind, especially Songling, who was widely regarded as an outstanding man of letters. Ying gathered together the writings of his great-great-grandfather and had them published.

Because Songling had assumed the courtesy name Cangxian, or "Green Hill," Ying deferentially adopted as his own courtesy name Xiaoxian, or "Little Hill." During his years in Zhejiang, Ying gathered around him a coterie of local scholars whom he entertained at wine parties where poems were exchanged. He even helped publish the collected prose writings of a well-known Zhejiang scholar, Ji Shaonan. Together with his friend of many years, Ruan Yuan, the director of education, he edited a six-chapter volume on the works of Jiangsu and Zhejiang poets.

As circuit intendant resident in Hangzhou, Ying was responsible for coastal defense in the three prefectures under his jurisdiction. And, as Zhejiang's judicial commissioner, he presided over the province's highest court. Thus, he was involved in antipirate activities on two levels. While inland waterways were the responsibility of civil officials, security on the high seas was the responsibility of the military. The military units combating the pirates were commanded by a brigade general, who was responsible to the provincial commander in chief.

Pirate vessels were normally indistinguishable from others, and could thus mask their intentions until they were almost alongside their intended victims. In addition to plundering cargo, the pirates often expanded their fleets by taking over merchant ships and kidnapping the crews and passengers, the former to work for them and the latter to be held for ransom. It was not unusual for some of the kidnap victims to be subjected to homosexual rape before being forced to join the pirates' ranks.

At the time, local officials were expected to make an arrest within several months of a crime or be punished themselves. Often, Qin Ying recommended that the same officials be punished time and again for failing to make arrests. This system acted as an incentive for some officials to arrest innocent men and accuse them of piracy, so that they themselves would escape punishment.

In 1797 alone, Ying recommended on more than ten occasions the punishment of officials who had failed to apprehend pirates. Some of the cases were two or three years old. Those punished were military officials from the brigade general on down, including company commanders and assistant commanders.

In one case, a merchant named Wang, who had bought a ship to ferry cargo, encountered pirates, who seized his load of sugar and tobacco and kidnapped three of his workers. On the return journey two months later, the unfortunate merchant ran into pirates again. This time, no one was kidnapped but he lost his entire cargo of tobacco. When after a year, there were still no arrests, Ying recommended that a brigade general and three acting company commanders be punished. The Jiaqing Emperor concurred and ordered the Ministries of War and Punishments to consider the appropriate penalties.[8]

Ying himself also suffered from the system of justice. On one occasion, he had convicted a woman prisoner and sentenced her to death, but before the sentence could be carried out, she hanged herself in prison. And Ying was held responsible for her death! It seems that since suicide deprived the state of the right to mete out the punishment due to her, Ying, as the provincial judge, was negligent, and the Ministry of Personnel proposed that he be demoted

329

and transferred. However, Emperor Jiaqing decided to keep him at his post.

Aside from pirate raids on the open sea, there were also cases that occurred along rivers or in harbors, the responsibility of civil officials. In 1800, Ying investigated the plundering of a cargo ship carrying a load of sugar. The incident itself had occurred two years previously and no one had been brought to justice. A gang of pirates was subsequently arrested in neighboring Fujian province. These pirates confessed to having robbed the sugar merchant in Zhejiang. Ying, in submitting his list of civil officials to be punished, included a circuit intendant, a subprefectural magistrate, a vice-magistrate and an assistant magistrate. He said that although the robbers were apprehended, they had been arrested in another province for a different offense, and thus the officials in Zhejiang were still guilty of negligence.

Though pirate cases accounted for much of his time, Ying was also responsible for other cases. Thus, in late 1799, he dealt with a case involving people who were smuggling salt, the transportation and sale of which was a state monopoly. Ying's report stated:

"On the evening of July 21, three local officers were on duty looking for salt smugglers. The officers hired a boat steered by Wu Kexiang. When they encountered a boatload of salt smugglers, they ordered the boatman to give chase. Wu rowed their boat until it caught up with the smugglers, and he held onto the other boat with his hand. One of the smugglers struck Wu Kexiang's hand with a pointed bamboo, and he fell into the water and was drowned. The smugglers escaped. An order for their arrest has been filed. Since the incident, six months have gone by and no one has been apprehended."

Ying found the three officers guilty of negligence in the death of the boatman.

Another case involved the eighteenth-century equivalent of a bank robbery. On February 26, 1799, two men, owners of a financial establishment, hired a vessel to carry over 4,000 taels of silver to another city, to be exchanged for Spanish silver dollars. However, as night fell, two other boats closed in. The robbers overpowered the captain and crew, tied up the bankers and fled with the money. Over the next four months, five of the criminals were caught, but seven others, including the gang's leader, remained at large. Ying recommended that four officials be punished.

In another case, a fire started in the house of a neighbor of a merchant named Ding. The merchant, fearful that the fire might spread, moved all his money and valuables onto two boats, satisfied that the fire would not reach them. However, six or seven sampans closed in on his boats and more than ten robbers clambered aboard. Ding's loss amounted to 619 taels of silver. Again, the case was unsolved for many months and civil officials were disciplined.

Ying established a reputation for being a shrewd judge of character. Once, a serving girl, acting with an accomplice, murdered her husband, then accused her master of the act. The master, under torture, confessed to a crime he did not commit. When the case went to Ying, he conducted a new investigation and established the identities of the true murderers. The man at first denied his guilt, but Ying said: "I saw seven of you in court. Five were clearly worried and nervous, but only you and the woman appeared calm and pleased. It is obvious that you are the murderers." The man confessed, though it is not recorded whether torture was used to extract his confession.

At the end of 1799, Ying's friend Ruan Yuan was named acting governor. Ruan thus became his immediate superior and the two men developed a good working relationship.

Shortly after Ruan Yuan's assumption of office, Ying drew upon his many years of antipirate experience and put his thoughts in writing for the benefit of the new governor:

> The plundering of rice ships is due to the oceans' not being pacified, and the oceans are not pacified because of our neglect of military preparations. In Zhejiang, military commands have been set up at Huangyan, Dinghai and Wenzhou, and the military units there are quite adequately manned. Aside from warships, there are also newly constructed vessels for intercepting pirates. This force should be sufficient. If the men are properly trained and the soldiers are courageous and show initiative, then patrolling vessels will go to the rescue of any rice ship that encounters pirates.
>
> Now, soldiers are never at hand when a crime is committed. Instead, they go into hiding. Rice ships are usually robbed in the inner harbor, and the pirates remain there with impunity for days after the crime, robbing incoming vessels. The ships on patrol never seem to be aware of these events, staying out to sea. The military commanders, too, do not immediately order the

ships back to the harbor to fight the pirates. Instead, the military vessels hide among the islands while the commanders are unable to maintain discipline.

For example, in the case of Ningbo, the circuit intendant and prefects had raised money for the construction of twenty-six ships for intercepting pirates. But all the ships were taken out to sea by the soldiers; none remained in the harbor to help. All the people who live in the three strategic points in eastern Zhejiang are frightened and furious. Although there is a military command at Dinghai, that lonely island has only eight warships, which is far from adequate. If the pirates land, how can they be repulsed? Fortunately, I hear that you have ordered that forty patrol ships be sent from Huangyan as reinforcements, and that the military officers Li Hong and Chan Tian, both capable men, have been ordered to Dinghai to seize the pirates operating there. This news has helped to calm the people.

Ying turned to a more immediate problem:

Pirate ships have been lurking in the vicinity of Changtushan near Dinghai for days, and there is no sign of any of our warships. In my opinion, these pirates are only untrained riffraff, and the hardened criminals number no more than a dozen or so. The rest are common people from Changchuan who, because of famine, were forced into banditry. The weapons they use are also quite poor, and some of the pirates don't even know how to use them. Now if we can take them by surprise while they are moored, it may be possible to clean them up in one swoop. While caution is important in military affairs, swift action is also necessary and surprise is a major factor in ensuring success. The pirates have been here for some days and their guard is down. If we attack quickly, we will surely win. If we miss this chance and let them sail away, it will be extremely difficult to find them at sea as it is so vast and the weather is so unpredictable.

If we do not act and let the pirates leave, they will return to cause trouble when our troops are away. This is our opportunity, now that they are all gathered at Changtu. I am pained by the procrastination. Our squadron commanders have very bad habits that they cannot get rid of. They confuse cowardice with caution. You worry every day, while they delay and observe at a distance, so no robbers have been captured. If we want to win, we have to demonstrate our power, and to demonstrate our power, we have to make clear our ability to bestow rewards and inflict punishment. You must reward those who obey orders and punish those who do not. Once discipline is maintained, the strength of our forces will be made manifest and it will be an easy matter to vanquish the pirates and bring joy to the people."[9]

In December 1799, Acting Governor Ruan Yuan had the satisfaction of reporting on two successful antipirate operations and the judgments delivered by Acting Provincial Judge Qin Ying.[10]

In the first case, government soldiers captured a pirate ship off Ninghai. In the fighting, six pirates were killed and four captured. In the hold were found seven of their captives.

The second group of pirates was captured off Xiangshan district. One pirate ship was seized and two pirates were killed, five captured and nine kidnap victims released.

All the prisoners were sent to Hangzhou for questioning. After the hearings, sentences were proposed by Provincial Judge Qin Ying and approved by Governor Ruan Yuan, who then forwarded the proposals in a memorial to the emperor for final approval. One of the captured pirates in the first case was named Ding Dong, a native of Fujian. Ding was originally a fisherman. On May 18, 1799, while he was fishing, he was robbed and made a prisoner by the pirate leader Fei Xing. Ding then joined the gang, which included eighteen other members. One of the eighteen, Zhu Jin, had also started off his pirate career as a kidnap victim, and joined the gang after he was raped by Fei Xing.

According to Ding, the gang engaged in four robberies in five months, their targets either fishing boats, cargo ships or salt carriers. One ship was ransomed for 1,500 silver dollars. The raids netted them twelve prisoners, three of whom were released after payment of ransom, which took the form of money, fish and rice. Two of the captives agreed to join the gang, and the rest were incarcerated in the hold. On November 16, the ship commanded by Fei Xing was sailing with four other pirate ships when they encountered the government warships. In the ensuing fight, Fei Xing and some of the other pirates were killed. The kidnap victims were released.

In his judgment, approved by the governor, Provincial Judge Qin Ying sentenced Ding to death by beheading, along with another pirate. Their heads were then put on display as a warning to others. Zhu Jin was sentenced to be flogged and then exiled for three years.

In the second case, it was discovered that one of the pirates, Mao Amao, was also a fisherman who had joined the pirate gang after he was kidnapped. In the ensuing five months, he took part in several raids on merchant ships with cargoes of rice, sugar and fish and seized a fishing boat. Mao assisted the pirates by gathering together the booty and by helping to steer the ship. During this period, the gang also increased its numbers through kidnappings. One kidnap victim, Li Yingxiao, joined the gang, while others were assigned to such duties as cooking. Li was among the five pirates seized alive.

Another captured pirate, Weng Youwen, also turned out to have been originally a kidnap victim. After taking part in a couple of raids, he asked to be released so he could visit his mother. Later, he joined another pirate gang, this time voluntarily. Thus, three of the five arrested pirates turned out to have been pirate victims originally.

Although Mao and Li started off as victims of pirates, they were condemned to death because they had taken part in pirate activities. Weng's sentence was more lenient. Because he was involved not in the robberies but only in the collection of the plunder, he was to be exiled.

The decisions reached in the two cases were according to regulations and precedents. The practice was that pirates should be immediately executed and their heads put on display. Executions were conducted publicly in the marketplace and presided over by the judicial commissioner. Those who aided pirates without actually taking part in the violence were sent into exile, with the place of exile depending on their degree of guilt. So kidnap victims were faced with a hard choice: oppose the pirates and accept the consequences or cooperate with them and risk death or exile.

In 1800, Ying wrote a second letter to Governor Ruan Yuan about the pirate menace. This time, he was less concerned about the pirates than about the behavior of soldiers who, instead of fighting them, framed innocent men:

> In the last three months, you personally supervised the arrest of pirates, but they have not yet been totally eliminated. All officials and civilians hate the pirates and will not be content even if they are skinned and cooked. The failure to eliminate the pirates is due to the incompetence of the commanders, who

leave the real pirates alone but who falsely accuse innocent people on merchant ships as pirates. The damage they do is worse than that of the pirates. There are two possible explanations why merchant ships are taken for pirate vessels:

1. After pirates rob a merchant ship, they sail away before the arrival of government soldiers, who mistakenly arrest the victims and report them as pirates.

2. The government warships do not dare get close to pirate vessels. When they encounter merchant ships, they ask for bribes. When the demands are refused, they arrest the merchants and accuse them of being pirates.

With regard to the first explanation, to misidentify merchant ships as pirate ships is no explanation at all. The second explanation is even more incredible. What can one say?

Ying then went on to discuss a case at hand, involving twelve people who, he felt, were falsely accused but had already been found guilty and sentenced:

Recently, twelve persons were arrested in Dinghai and charged as pirates. I have made a thorough investigation and have discovered that they are only ordinary people, not pirates. They are fish merchants from Fujian. Their ships had been licensed in Fujian. The grain on their ships was purchased from Tayushan and not obtained through robbery. They had encountered pirates on the seas but they managed to escape and went to Dinghai. When their ships anchored in the harbor, officials went and asked for money and they refused to pay. As a result they were charged with being pirates. Yesterday they were transferred from Dinghai to Ningbo. Actually, eight hundred to nine hundred of their fellow villagers, who were transporting grain to Fujian, cried and pleaded for them, proclaiming their innocence. I am sure they are all victimized civilians. The officials let the pirates go while preying on the common people and they frame the innocent as robbers. Such behavior is outrageous.

I am now sending these twelve people to you for further interrogation. I am sure your honor, being so intelligent, will have no difficulty discerning the truth immediately. I am writing this letter because I am afraid that your honor might first let your subordinates conduct the interrogation and those officials may use torture to obtain statements in order to strengthen the false accusations. A lot of lives are at stake. These poor people met their first misfortune at the hands of the pirates, then they encountered corrupt officials, and then the judicial staff. How unfortunate they are. They are poor civilians and are like our own sons. If real pirates are released, it is unlawful. If common people are falsely accused and sentenced, it is a violation of the principle of benevolence. You are benevolent and the common people treat you as their father. I am sure these twelve persons will be set free by your honor.[11]

Governor Ruan Yuan agreed with Ying and released the men who had been falsely accused.

Ruan Yuan's tenure as governor proved beneficial to Ying. He gave Ying the greater responsibility of acting administration commissioner for a few months, the second-highest post in the province and one that was primarily concerned with finance, taxation and personnel affairs. Thus, when a subprefect was dismissed on grounds of insanity for having forged imperial orders, Ying was instrumental in recommending a replacement. It was difficult to find suitable people to fill vacancies, as candidates serving in other provinces might not be familiar with local conditions, and officials were barred from serving in their home province under a long-standing rule known as the Law of Avoidance. So, most of the time, a replacement had to be found from within the pool of officials, or expectant officials, within Zhejiang.

As acting administration commissioner Qin Ying was still involved with antipirate work. One problem was that, often, the cannons were so old that they blew up when being fired. Moreover, the ammunition frequently did not match the bore of the weapons used by the soldiers. So Ying recommended that old cannons and guns should be melted down and recast. Ying provided estimates of the cost involved in such an operation, including the amount of coal needed.

In 1800, three prefectures in eastern Zhejiang suffered from serious floods, which were followed by famine. But the local officials, fearful of being blamed if they requested funds over their budget to cope with the famine, were reluctant to report the situation to the capital. Ying wrote to Ruan Yuan saying: "Budget reports are only an estimate and they may not always reflect the real situation. The flood was unexpected and we should report the truth to His

Majesty. How can we watch the commoners die?" The situation was reported to the capital and supplies were requested. The extent of the devastation is reflected in a poem Ying wrote:

> The black wind swept the hill, the dragon reared,
> The thunder roared and the lightning was swift.
> The mountain collapsed, struck by the god's head
> As his foot kicked up waves a hundred steps
>   high.
> Stones and tiles fled before the clouds;
> Not a door or window remained in any village.
>
> In this world no chickens or dogs existed;
> Only the owls and eagles could be heard.
> Everywhere was covered by the horror.
> Corpses littered the roads,
> Skeletons hung from trees like monkeys.
> The dead were gone, but pity the living.
>
> Widows cried for their husbands,
> Sons for their fathers.
> Hungry and naked they lay in ditches.
> The balance of nature was disrupted.
> We are officials without conscience;
> How can the common people live?

In December 1800, Ying was finally confirmed in his post as judicial commissioner, a job he had carried out in an acting capacity for six years.[12] But after having waited so long for the post, Ying found himself transferred the next year to Hunan province as judicial commissioner.[13]

When Ying arrived in Hunan, one of its prefectures, Hengzhou, was afflicted by famine. The harvest had been poor the previous year, and this led to the emergence of robber bands who struck not only at the outlying counties but also at major cities, such as Changsha and Hengyang. Information about these bands had been suppressed by the local authorities. Ying informed the governor of the situation, and Hengzhou received assistance from other localities in the province.[14] The bandit ringleaders were brought to justice by Ying.

In 1802, Qin Ying, now fifty-nine years old, became ill with an ailment that affected his arm. Because of it, he was given sick leave for two years. After his recovery in mid-1804, he was named judicial commissioner of Guangdong province. The Jiaqing Emperor issued an edict to him that said: "The lives of civilians are most important. It is essential to find out the truth. Although the official work is complicated, you should never relax your vigilance. Never release those who deserve execution, but for those who are innocent, you should not lay one blow on their bodies. You should adhere to this principle in your work."[15]

The pirate menace in Guangdong was, if anything, worse than in Zhejiang, since the province was close to Vietnam. Pirates were running rampant. Government forces simply ignored the raids, and the people were left to their own devices.

Ying set about the task of countering the pirates and was moderately successful. Under his supervision, two of their leaders were captured.

And he gained the reputation of being a fair-minded man who was more interested in establishing the facts than in convictions. One case he handled toward the end of his tour in the province is illustrative: A merchant, Lin Wu, was framed by pirates, and Ying was convinced of his innocence. But just at that time, he was promoted to be administration commissioner of Zhejiang and so left Guangdong. After his departure, the man was condemned and executed. Just before his execution, the prisoner screamed: "If Judicial Commissioner Qin were here, I would not have to die."[16]

CHAPTER TWENTY-TWO

Qin Ying: Peking Minister

Qin Ying is "a man of limited knowledge and ability," Na-yen-cheng, governor-general of Guangdong and Guangxi, wrote to the emperor. "The delay in quite a number of cases was due to his tardiness. When I first arrived, I instructed him to uncover the connections between bandits and pirates. However, he disagreed with me and never followed my instructions."[1]

The comments were made just after Ying's tour of duty in Guangdong had ended. That tour had been much less pleasant for Ying than his years in Zhejiang, primarily because he had to work with Governor-General Na-yen-cheng, a Manchu who had been appointed in 1804 because of his good record as a military commander.[2]

Emperor Jiaqing was seriously concerned about the pirate menace and wanted it cleared up. He allotted more than 40,000 taels of silver for the repair of antipirate war vessels, and said that the salt tax of 140,000 taels was also available for use by the new governor-general. "Na-yen-cheng is young and strong," the emperor declared. "He should be able to clean up the robbers and pirates." But it was easier said than done.

Ying's early months in Guangdong were busy ones, as he supervised the capture of several pirate leaders, including one Liang Xiuping. The capture of Liang was preceded by that of six confederates in May 1804, at the border between two districts, Xinhui and Houshan. It was known that Liang's band wanted vengeance and was planning to stage an attack. Ying ordered special measures for the defense of the area. A curfew was imposed. A system of gong signals was devised to inform forces in each area about the movements of the pirates. The system was rigidly enforced and any lapses were subject to punitive actions. When Pirate Liang and his followers arrived,

339

they ran into this defense network. Twenty-eight pirates, including Liang, were seized in Houshan District.[3]

After the new governor-general arrived, he took personal charge of the antipirate campaign as the emperor desired. However, the government soldiers under Na-yen-cheng were no match for the predatory sea bandits of Guangdong. Harsh measures were adopted against the pirates, and torture was liberally used whenever any were captured. In one case, when eighteen pirate suspects were arrested, Governor-General Na-yen-cheng reported that eleven had "died of illness" after being interrogated. Those sent into exile had the word "bandit" tattooed on their faces.

Contrary to established procedure, which provided for the provincial judge to hear all pirate cases, Governor-General Na-yen-cheng, without the knowledge of the emperor, set up a special unit, called a Military Work Office, to deal with pirates.

On the whole the battle against the pirates was a losing one: For each one caught, many more got away. And the pirates were constantly making new recruits from their prisoners. Thus, Ying again found himself recommending penalties for officials who failed to arrest the perpetrators of crimes.

The Annamese connection of some of the pirates was clear. One such case involved the pirate leader Fu Laohong, who escaped to Annam in 1801, after ninety-nine members of his gang were captured. There, he was named commander of an Annamese military vessel, and began his career of plunder anew. Fu preyed on foreign shipping as well as junks transporting salt, and extorted protection money from government grain vessels. He was sentenced to death by slicing after interrogation not only by the administration commissioner, the provincial judge, and the prefect of Canton, but by the salt controller as well. After his execution in the marketplace in Canton, his head was sent back to Haikang, his hometown, to be displayed as a warning.

To prevent arms from falling into the wrong hands, the private manufacture of munitions was forbidden. This led to a paradoxical situation. Merchant ships, wanting to defend themselves against piracy, turned to illegal manufacturers. One resourceful group learned in 1800 of the demand for cannons, and immediately went into the cannon-making business. The group collected waste metal and, by December 1800, had constructed five cannons. By May 1801, they had made three more. The privately made cannons were getting heavier and, of course, more expensive. The following September, the illegal arms merchants were manufacturing cannons that weighed 364 pounds each; by year end they were producing 455-pounders. Altogether, they constructed forty-three cannons, which cost them 427 silver dollars, but which they sold for 2,284 dollars. Before long, another group heard of the lucrative cannon-manufacturing business and set up shop for itself, constructing twenty cannons in all before it was stopped. The arms manufacturers were caught in 1805 and charged with the illegal private construction of cannons and of smuggling explosives. Eleven men were condemned to death.[4]

One of the government's rare successes in its campaign against piracy occurred in mid-1805 when a major pirate, Zheng Yalu, virtually stumbled into the arms of a naval squadron. He and his gang had been high on the list of wanted pirates, and Zheng had escaped narrowly the year before after one of his relatives secretly promised government officials to lead him into a trap. Zheng had uncovered the plot and lured the unfortunate relative aboard his ship, where he was killed and his body dismembered before it was dumped into the sea.

Zheng's downfall came in the wake of a successful raid on a merchant ship, when his men were then set upon by a rival pirate, Zhu Fen. In fleeing Zhu Fen, Zheng ran right into the arms of some soldiers who just happened to be in the vicinity. He and forty of his supporters were caught. The initial interrogation was conducted by the local magistrate, who reported that five of the prisoners had "died of illness" after making a full confession. The prisoners were then interrogated by the prefect of Canton before they were again interrogated by Na-yen-cheng himself, together with Ying and some other officials. Zheng was sentenced to death by slicing, his brother to death by beheading, and four of the corpses were also decapitated. The other prisoners were ordered flogged or exiled or both. Only two were freed, one because of his youth and the other because he was a kidnap victim.[5]

In the summer of 1805, Jiaqing promoted Ying to be administration commissioner of Zhejiang province. So he was preparing to leave Guangdong when his adversary, Na-yen-cheng, was secretly attacked.

That fall, the governor of Guangdong filed a secret memorial accusing his superior, Governor-General Na-yen-cheng, of neglecting his duties while indulging in wine and other pleasures, such as

attending theatrical performances. Emperor Jiaqing, like his predecessors, encouraged the submission of secret reports as one way of
gathering information. The emperor sent an emissary, Mou Yuan-
ming, to investigate the charge, but Mou reported that there was no
substance to it. The Jiaqing Emperor, suspicious, ordered Governor-
General Wu Xiongguang of Huguang to interrogate Mou, who broke
down and confessed that he had filed a favorable report after he
had been feted by Na-yen-cheng. Emperor Jiaqing asked Na-yen-
cheng to account for his stewardship of Guangdong.

In justification of his conduct, Na-yen-cheng filed a memorial in
which he said his plan was to deal first with robbers on land before
tackling the bandits at sea since, he reasoned, once the land robbers
were eradicated, the pirates would lose their source of food and
other supplies. Otherwise, he said, even if thousands of pirates were
killed, thousands more would replace them. To achieve his goal, he
said, he needed the cooperation of other officials, such as the administration commissioner and the provincial judge. In addition,
Na-yen-cheng said, he wanted interrogation of suspects to be handled swiftly and efficiently, with special emphasis on ascertaining
the links between land robbers and sea bandits.

The governor-general insisted that his plan had worked well, with
over three thousand pirates turning themselves in within a few months.
However, he said, while Administration Commissioner Kuang-hou
understood his sense of urgency, "the former Judicial Commissioner
Qin Ying" would not cooperate with him. This may well have been
the case, since Ying's experience in Zhejiang had taught him to move
cautiously lest innocent men be tortured into making confessions.

Moreover, Na-yen-cheng said, when there was a "joint
interrogation"—presumably at a session of the Military Work
Office—at the court, the judicial commissioner was supposed to be
in charge, but Qin Ying used to fall asleep in court and "I once had
to order a constable to wake him up. He was physically weak and
stupid." Na-yen-cheng added that he had been planning to submit
a secret memorial to the emperor about Ying, but that it was too
late since the emperor had already announced his promotion. Na-
yen-cheng's protestations failed to set to rest the emperor's doubts
about him. Ying may not have known about the governor-general's
criticism of him, but he soon would have a chance to present his
side of the story during an imperial audience.

One of the last cases reported on by Na-yen-cheng before Ying's departure from Guangdong had to do with an important pirate, Li Chongyu, whom the emperor had expressly ordered Na-yen-cheng to arrest when he was first assigned to Guangdong. The governor-general did not bring about Li's arrest, but did hold several hearings to determine the culpability of the officers who had failed to capture him. Na-yen-cheng personally presided over the interrogations, once with Governor Bai-ling, and once with Administration Commissioner Kuang-hou and Judicial Commissioner Qin Ying.

It turned out that early in the spring, information as to the whereabouts of Pirate Li fell into official hands, and a plan was made to take him by surprise. To prevent his escape by sea, ships blockaded the harbor while on land a strong force, including five cannons, sixty soldiers armed with guns and over a hundred foot soldiers converged on Li's hideout. Such was the fear of Li and his rebel army that, when the government troops were closing in, they ignored the original order to take him by stealth, and sought to bolster their courage by firing their weapons. In the ensuing battle, twenty-five of Li's cohorts were captured, but Li himself escaped. After the interrogations, all the officers were exonerated of any suspicion of collusion with the pirate, but the commander who gave the order to fire confessed to cowardice. The officers received varying degrees of punishment, including exile, dismissal and flogging. The interrogations also established that by the time the soldiers started to move in, Pirate Li had long since left the scene.[6]

Pirate Li was never caught. Later in the year, he accepted an offer by Na-yen-cheng to "surrender" in return for which he was made a lieutenant and allowed to keep a substantial number of his own men under him. In addition, Li was given several thousand taels of silver and the honor of wearing the insignia of a fourth-rank military official. The surrender of Li was part of Na-yen-cheng's policy of winning the pirates over, since he could not defeat them in battle. The governor-general paid 10 taels of silver to each pirate who turned himself in. Altogether, five thousand pirates took advantage of this offer. Thus, funds earmarked for antipirate activities were being used to pay the pirates. The governor of Guangdong disagreed with this policy, which was also being implemented in other provinces, and warned the emperor against the risks of recruiting pirates as soldiers.

As was customary, Ying had to return to Peking for an imperial audience, to be formally appointed before taking up his new position

343

in Zhejiang. The meeting took place on December 1. On that occasion, Ying was given an opportunity to report to the emperor on the situation in Guangdong. Emperor Jiaqing asked about Na-yen-cheng's performance of his duties and the antipirate campaign.

After the meeting, the emperor issued an angry edict:

> Today Qin Ying, having arrived in the capital, had an audience with me. I asked him about Na-yen-cheng's situation in Guangdong. He said it was true that Na-yen-cheng had set up a Military Work Office. The office consists of seven members, the administration commissioner, the judicial commissioner, the salt controller, intendants and prefects and the regimental commander. All the pirate and bandit cases are dealt with by the Military Work Office before going to the judicial commissioner for reexamination. The members used torture during the interrogation, and this was reported to the governor.
>
> Although there are a lot of cases in Guangdong, the procedure of interrogation should follow the traditional way and be carried out by the judicial commissioner. If the judicial commissioner is too busy and cannot do the job, he should be criticized. The Military Work Office is a ridiculous setup. The administration commissioner and salt controller have their own offices and their work is clearly prescribed; besides, the regimental commander should not be involved in the hearing of criminal cases. How dare Na-yen-cheng change traditional procedures! Na-yen-cheng had worked for the Grand Council and should know better, but he has now set up such a terrible system. I hereby order him to abandon this practice.
>
> Concerning the memorial filed by [Governor of Guangdong] Bai-ling criticizing Na-yen-cheng for drinking and going to the theater, Qin Ying has told me that Na-yen-cheng's office holds banquets and theatrical performances three or four times each month. Na-yen-cheng also invited [Administration Commissioner] Kuang-hou to go to Yan Feng's home to watch performances several times a month. So, each month, Na-yen-cheng attends theatrical performances many times; how can he do his work properly?[7]

An investigation into Na-yen-cheng's conduct was launched, and the governor-general was eventually dismissed. The emperor ordered him exiled to Xinjiang, where he remained for two years before again being entrusted with a position of power.

During the imperial audience, Ying requested that he be allowed to work in the capital, instead of taking the position in Zhejiang. The emperor agreed, in view of Ying's advancing age, and he was made minister of the Court of Imperial Entertainments. Shortly afterward, he was appointed minister of the Court of Imperial Sacrifices.[8] While in the latter position, he prepared his most important memorial in which he analyzed the pirate situation in Guangdong and set forth his ideas on how to counter this menace.[9]

The major pirate gangs, he said, were getting bigger and bigger, while smaller groups of pirates were proliferating.

He said that government forces were ineffective because they did not have sufficient funds and weaponry and lacked capable leaders. The military commanders, he said, always looked for excuses for not going out to intercept pirates, citing the condition of their vessels, or the weather. And when they did go out, "they hid behind uninhabited islands, purposely missing the chance of encountering the pirates. And when they did meet the pirates, the cunning pirates would sail away, leaving behind one or two plundered merchant ships for the government troops to arrest. The government troops would arrest the merchants, then report to their superiors that they had caught the pirates. The soldiers then stopped pursuing the real pirates but just sent the innocent victims to the provincial capital, where they would be sentenced and executed. Executions were carried out almost every day, but the pirates continued to multiply."

The military commanders were irresponsible, he said, and pointed out despairingly that "when Sun Quanmou was demoted, his replacement, Wei Dabin, was another Sun Quanmou. How can we know that Wei Dabin's replacement won't be another Wei Dabin?"

He then went on to make several proposals, the main points of which were:

> • Strengthen the Military. Squadrons are understrength and inadequately equipped for lack of funds. Foreign merchants and salt traders are willing to make financial contributions, but officials handling these transactions may seek to enrich themselves. Besides, the military commanders are still haughty and indolent. It is necessary to set up strict regulations to prevent abuses so that our forces are strong in fact and not just on paper.

345

• Raise the Prestige of the Military. The pirates have numerous spies. Unless we first instill fear in their hearts they will view our troops with disdain. Before troops are dispatched, it would be appropriate for the governor-general to meet with them and drink to their success. Those who return with merits should be publicly rewarded; those who disobeyed orders should be executed without mercy.

• Guard Against False Appearances. It is essential that only real pirates are arrested. In seeking rewards, soldiers will disregard the truth in favor of arresting the innocent. On rare occasions some of the victims are released by the judges, but even then the matter is not further investigated. From now on it is hoped that only real pirates will be arrested, without indulgence and without prejudice. Where defense is concerned it is also necessary to replace false strength with true strength. Artillery emplacements are used to protect our coast but the coastline is long and military posts are few, so sea bandits finding a place weakly defended sail right in. The patrol craft are insufficient to cope with the pirates and end up as their property. As to the *bao-jia* system [of mutual defense], it is superficial and has become a means for low-level functionaries to exact extortions. If it is desired to set up a *bao-jia* or militia system, it is necessary first to win the trust of the people. It is my belief that to provide proper defenses we must first reform the system of administration, and to reform the administration it is necessary to look after the interests of the people.

• Speed Up Court Cases. People of Guangdong are prone to level accusations against each other so an imperial edict should be issued sternly ordering that legal cases should be disposed of swiftly, regardless of whether the matter in dispute is big or small. Delay in hearing of cases is dangerous as local bullies and pettifoggers take advantage of the situation to use undue influence and confuse the issues until finally the particulars of the evidence are frequently conflicting and it is impossible to find out the truth. The only solution is to order the officials at district and prefectural level to clear up each case as it arises and eliminate the opportunities for abuse.

• Reduce What Is Excessive. Recently Haizhou District set up a fund to defray the expenses of seizing and transporting prisoners. It is important to economize so that the financial burden is not too heavy. When a magistrate arrives at a new post, he is immediately given recommendations for private secretaries and servants; with so many people to feed, it is impossible for him to maintain his integrity. Holders of minor posts and military officials only look for benefits; once vested with power, they will intimidate civil officials. A proliferation of minor posts will also result in enormous expenditures.

• Punish Rapacious Underlings. Officials have to use functionaries who know local conditions well, but if they become too close to them, it will be disastrous for the people. In Guangdong, many of them actually accept bribes from pirates. Such activities must be severely punished.

If these proposals are carried out, the administration will be cleansed; once the administration is cleansed, the confidence of the people will be won over; once the confidence of the people is won over, it will be possible to set up *bao-jia* or militia systems. As a result, the province will be well defended.

After the emperor read Ying's memorial, he told the Grand Council to order the new governor-general in Guangdong to act on Ying's advice. Copies of the memorial were made and distributed to coastal officials for implementation.

Before long, Ying was named governor of Shuntian prefecture, which surrounds the capital, an important post both actually and symbolically. When the emperor was not disposed to discharge his ceremonial duties, the governor stepped in as his representative. The importance of this post was also reflected in the trappings of office: While the seals of other such offices were made of bronze, that of the governor of Shuntian was made of silver.

As soon as he assumed the office, Qin Ying found himself in the middle of an unresolved case. The plaintiff accused the defendant of assault and of forcibly occupying his land and harvesting his crop. The former governor, Mo Zhanmou, had first ordered the defendant released and, upon encountering objections, had taken him to his own home where the governor said he would privately investigate the matter. The Ministry of Punishments had learned about this and accused the governor of not following proper procedure. After Ying's arrival, he was ordered to investigate the actions of his predecessor, who had not yet departed. In his report, he said that the proper procedure was for all cases to be dealt with by his office, then submitted to the Ministry of Punishments. Private interrogation, he said, was not permitted. Ying also pointed out that the case came up before he had assumed office.

The Jiaqing Emperor, in an edict, asserted that bribery must have been involved. Otherwise, he said, why was the accused first released and then questioned in private? Former Governor Mo, he ordered, should be dismissed immediately, arrested and sentenced. Furthermore, the district magistrate of Daxing county, which is part of Shuntian Prefecture, should be investigated to see if he was involved. Ying, too, was punished on the ground that he had not reported the improper actions of his predecessor.[10]

Early in 1807, Ying was appointed vice-minister of punishments. That June, he was subjected to disciplinary action because he and other officials had celebrated the traditional Mid-Autumn Festival. The Jiaqing Emperor had declared that because of a drought in the Peking area, there should be no celebration unless it rained. Yet on the day of the festival, princes and officials went to the Yuan Ming Yuan Imperial Park to extend festive greetings to the emperor and to celebrate. "We should not be celebrating," the emperor said in an edict. "The princes and officials, on their way here, should have seen how the common people live. If we hold a feast before any rainfall, the commoners will think that I do not care about their difficulties but only know how to enjoy and celebrate. Why can't the princes and courtiers understand my feelings?" He then decreed that all those who had gone to the Yuan Ming Yuan Park, including princes, imperial relatives, grand secretaries, ministers and vice-ministers (of which Qin Ying was one) would be deprived of their salaries for three months.[11]

At the Ministry of Punishments, Ying again had to deal with cases that stemmed from earlier years. One of the most embarrassing cases for the ministry was the fact that its own treasury had been broken into in 1804 and about 19,000 taels of silver taken. For several years, an investigation had dragged on, but the culprits were not apprehended and no money was recovered, despite the arrest and torture of scores of people. The investigators were punished for failing in their job and officials in charge of the ministry were ordered to make restitution.

In September 1807, when the annual Autumn Assizes were being prepared, the cases from Hunan were found to be behind schedule. Because he had been provincial judge there, Ying was held responsible. The Ministry of Personnel suggested that he be demoted by two grades and transferred. However, the Jiaqing Emperor decided to keep him at his post.

One of Ying's duties as vice-minister of punishments was to preside over the execution of people guilty of heinous crimes. One such case occurred in December 1807, that of a man named Zhong Kuan, accused of practicing black magic. Zhong had been tried and condemned to death earlier, sentenced to the most lenient form of execution, death by strangulation. It was considered lenient because it left the body intact. A more severe form of punishment was decapitation, after which the head was often put on display as a warning to the public. The most severe form of capital punishment, of course, was *lingchi*, or death by slicing, under which the victim was tied to a cross and then cut up bit by bit, with the final cut severing the head from the body.

In the Zhong case, the convicted man invoked a time-honored custom of delaying his execution by loudly proclaiming his innocence, an act that automatically stayed the executioner's hand until another investigation was completed. As a result, Emperor Jiaqing assigned Grand Secretary Qing-gui to interrogate Zhong and hold a new investigation. But the grand secretary confirmed the guilty verdict, and recommended raising the punishment to death by decapitation. The Jiaqing Emperor approved this, and ordered that Zhong be punished with forty blows of the bamboo before the execution "as a warning to future criminals."

Ying and a colleague were ordered to preside and announce that the more severe punishment was due to Zhong's having falsely proclaimed his innocence. "From now on," Emperor Jiaqing concluded, "if a review conducted as a result of a criminal declaring his innocence confirms that fact, the officials in charge will be punished. But if he is found guilty, a more serious punishment will be meted out."[12]

Executions, though common, could not be ordered or carried out on just any day. Just as certain days were considered auspicious or inauspicious for events such as weddings, there were days that were considered inappropriate for ordering capital punishment. Thus, in mid-1808, the emperor ordered that on days when banquets were to be held in the palace, cases involving sentences of immediate execution should not be submitted. Also, during the period celebrating the birthdays of the emperor and his consort, no criminal cases were to be submitted. However, he turned down a suggestion that criminal cases not be submitted on the birthdays of princes and other members of the imperial family.[13]

As vice-minister of punishments, Ying was involved also in cases that were sensitive from a political or security viewpoint. In 1808, for instance, his ministry handled a case involving a colonel of the elite Guards Division who stabbed someone to death in a military camp. The victim had tried to intervene in an argument between the colonel and another person, and had been stabbed for his pains. Because the camp was close to the Forbidden City, the colonel was sentenced to be flogged in front of his troops before his execution, which was presided over by Ying and the captain-general responsible for that military section.[14]

Since China was very much a hierarchical society, with the Chinese under the Manchus, the common people under the officials, sons under their fathers, and everyone under the emperor, the greatest crime possible was the upsetting of the social order. For if a servant were to go unpunished for raising his hand against his master or a son against his father, it would be tantamount to sanctioning regicide. So the severest penalties were meted out to slaves or servants who attacked or, worse yet, killed their masters. One such case, handled by Ying, had to do with men who plotted against their master, Li Yuchang. One of the men involved had, through forgery, obtained 23,000 taels of silver that were sent to Shandong province to relieve the famine there. Li Yuchang found out about it but, before he could take action, the forger had Li poisoned. And when the death was investigated, the official in charge was paid a 2,000-tael bribe. Eventually, the case reached the Ministry of Punishments, and, through the ministry, the emperor. Jiaqing ordered the chief culprit taken to the tomb of his master, tortured and beheaded, after which his heart was to be torn out and offered in sacrifice to the spirit of the deceased. Qin Ying was ordered to escort the two accomplices to the marketplace, where he presided over their execution. As for the corrupt official, he was sentenced to death by strangulation.[15]

The following year, Ying found himself in a quandary. An imperial relative, Min-xue, was involved in a murder case. The case was handled jointly by the Ministry of Punishments and the Imperial Clan Court, which had jurisdiction over judicial and disciplinary affairs involving members of the imperial family. Officials of both organizations, aware of the sensitive nature of the case, sought excuses for releasing Min-xue. However, because the report was full of conflicts, it was reviewed by other ministers, who recommended that officials involved in the original investigation be dismissed. Qin Ying was demoted by three grades and transferred. The Jiaqing Emperor, in an edict, said Ying had not paid sufficient attention to the case, adding that he was "old and useless."[16]

So, in February 1809, he found himself once again in the position of minister of the Court of Imperial Entertainments. However, over the next twelve months, Ying gradually regained the emperor's confidence by serving in six different posts.

In April, Ying was made vice-president of the Censorate,[17] and though he had never obtained the *jinshi* degree, he was honored by being designated supervisor of that year's metropolitan examinations. When three candidates who had concealed essays on their persons were caught, the delighted emperor rewarded all the examination officials involved.[18]

In June 1809, Ying was appointed superintendent of government granaries.[19] Again, as soon as he arrived at his post, he found himself in the midst of a scandal. The warehouses his department was responsible for had not been well looked after. Grain from the Old Taichang Warehouse had turned black and was so rotten that it was inedible. This was the second time within a three-month period that the problem had occurred, and a detailed investigation was ordered. As usual, the men in charge were held responsible. Ying's two predecessors were demoted and told to work for four years without a salary. Other officials were also punished for negligence and two grain inspectors were fired. It turned out that the grain had gone bad from the humidity: The inspectors had neglected to dry the grain periodically. Each spring, when the climate turned muggy, the grain from the south had to be inspected and dried if necessary. Although the emperor absolved Qin Ying of any responsibility,[20] he decided that the post of superintendent of granaries was so exacting that it should be filled by a younger man. So Ying was officially in the post for only a matter of days before he was again named vice-president of the Censorate.

In July, a serious shortfall was discovered in the grain held at a warehouse in Tongzhou, outside Peking. A special panel of four men, including Vice-President of the Censorate Qin Ying, was set up to investigate and told to report to the emperor every five days. Their job was to determine if theft was involved and, if so, whether it occurred before the grain was stored in the warehouse or afterward.[21]

The result of the investigation was devastating. The panel found that hundreds of thousands of piculs of rice had been stolen and false records were kept. One report said that the thieves had soaked the rice in a solution that caused it to expand, and so the bins looked fuller than they actually were. However, Ying conducted an experiment with the solution, and found that it did not work. He reported his finding to the emperor, who disclosed that he himself had performed the same experiment and had obtained the same result. That act won him the emperor's trust, since Ying was not content to accept what was said to him, but insistent on uncovering the truth for himself. Because of his experiment, Ying was able to prove the innocence of a number of people who had been accused of selling, storing or buying the solution.[22]

Later in July, Qin Ying was promoted to subchancellor of the Grand Secretariat and concurrently vice-minister of rites. He was then named vice-minister of war before being named, in August, acting senior vice-minister of punishments. That winter, he became senior vice-minister of war. And in February 1810, he was confirmed in the position of vice-minister of punishments. Almost exactly a year after his demotion over the case of the imperial relative who was accused of murder, Ying had regained his former title.[23]

That September, Ying served concurrently as vice-minister of works in charge of the Coinage Office, thus having been vice-minister of five of the six ministries.

Late in 1810, Qin Ying, age sixty-eight, asked for permission to retire. His eyesight was bothering him and, as his granduncle Huitian had shown, this could be dangerous for someone in his position. In his memorial, Ying said that he had suffered from a bad cold in the fall, which caused his eyes to become red, swollen and inflamed. Even though he had recovered from his cold, his eyesight was deteriorating. "When I went to court I found it difficult to see my way," he wrote, "and when I read documents, my eyes became blurred. Also my ears echoed and I could not hear too well." Ying asked for permission to leave the following spring, after Emperor Jiaqing departed on his annual journey to the northeast.

In his response, the emperor granted Ying's request and summed up his career as follows: "Qin Ying has served the court for years and has been extremely careful. When he worked in the provinces his reputation was also good. Now because of a bad cold he has an eye ailment and is unable to recover in a short time. I now allow him to retire and rest. He can leave for home after seeing me off next spring. His eye problem is due to a bad cold and should be easy to cure. When he recovers, he can return to the capital and wait for another appointment."

In his farewell memorial to the emperor, Ying replied: "I am without any special talent, yet Your Majesty still wants me to serve the court after my recovery from sickness. If I am so fortunate as to recover from my eyesight and hearing problems, I shall come back and serve the court. I dare not stay away and lead an easy life."

Early in 1811, Ying returned home to Wuxi. There, he devoted his remaining years to literary efforts. He not only helped to update another edition of the family genealogy, he also did very thorough research into the life of his ancestor, the Song poet Qin Guan, and annotated the year-by-year biography of the poet first prepared by the Ming scholar Qin Yong. He was also the chief compiler of another edition of the *Wuxi Gazetteer*, which came out in 1813.

That his health was good was attested by the fact that, in 1813, at the age of seventy, Ying fathered another son, born of a concubine, whom he named Xiangye. This son of his twilight years would continue the family's scholarly tradition far more successfully than his older and better-born brothers.

In 1818, at the age of seventy-five, Ying celebrated the sixtieth anniversary of his earning his first degree. It was rare for people to live long enough to be able to celebrate the sixtieth anniversary. The anniversary was important because the Chinese measured time in sixty-year cycles. What added to the joy on that occasion was that, that year, one of Ying's grandsons entered the local academy after obtaining the same degree.

On July 21, 1821, Qin Ying wrote to an old friend Chen Yong-guang asking him to prepare his obituary. "My sickness is getting serious and I am afraid I shall die soon," Ying wrote. "You know me, and you know classical literature well. I make bold to request you to prepare my tombstone. My personal character and my life were not clearly understood by my sons and my students." He died on August 7, 1821, just as China was celebrating the reign of a new emperor, Daoguang.

CHAPTER TWENTY-THREE

Qin Xiangye: The "Distinguished Failure"

"Have you forgotten what your father taught you?" Qin Ying's widow tearfully asked her son, Xiangye, as she exhorted him to greater efforts.[1]

Because of the wide age gap between Xiangye and his father's earlier children—his oldest brother, Xiangwu,[2] was forty-two years his senior—he did not grow up with them. But he did grow up under the tutelage of his mother. When he returned home after school, she made him repeat all he had learned that day. She was delighted if he performed well, but forced him to study late into the night if he failed. Whenever her son appeared to be flagging, she would resort to the carefully preserved slips of paper on which her late husband had written the boy's lessons.

Xiangye's early scholastic record was good. By the time he was in his late teens, he had compiled a small collection of poetry of which he was quite proud. Wishing to have his poems published, he sent them to his father's good friend Ruan Yuan, asking for the favor of a preface, but his presumption was apparently ignored by that august personage, who had risen to become a grand secretary.

Xiangye's mother arranged his marriage to his second cousin, a Wang three years his senior, when he was in his late teens. His bride's maternal grandfather was a Qin. The marriage of cousins was quite common and acceptable provided the surnames were different. Such a marriage was described as "adding closeness to an already close relationship." This one linked the wealthy Wangs with the prestigious Qins, producing a strong alliance.

Xiangye successfully followed the normal pattern of an aspiring scholar until he gained his licentiate degree. In 1835, at the age of twenty-two, he went to Peking as a student in the National Academy to prepare for the provincial-level examinations, like his father be-

354

fore him. But though he spent almost two decades in the capital, the second degree of *juren* eluded him.

During this period, the weakness of the Chinese state was becoming increasingly apparent. In 1839, the Daoguang Emperor was convinced that it was essential to move against British traders who were importing opium into China in ever-increasing amounts to pay for purchases of tea, silk and porcelain. Not only was this resulting in a significant drain on national finances, but also it was sapping the moral fiber of the empire.

In March 1839, Imperial Commissioner Lin Zexu arrived in Canton, the seat of commerce between Chinese and foreigners, empowered to stamp out the evils of opium smoking. The opium came from British India and the British traders were the most active in this lucrative business. The commissioner confiscated and destroyed more than twenty thousand chests of opium from British traders. The Chinese still had an unrealistic sense of their power; the emperor threatened to ban exports of tea, thinking that the British could not survive without it.

But while the captains of fifty-five ships of various nations had agreed to sign a guarantee not to deal in opium, only one British ship signed and thirty-two refused. The British traders persuaded Lord Palmerston, the prime minister, to assemble an expeditionary force against China, precipitating the Opium War of 1839–1842.

The Chinese expected the expedition, which consisted of about twenty warships carrying four thousand British and Indian soldiers, to attack Canton. They were taken by surprise when the ships sailed northward. On July 5, Dinghai in Zhejiang province, almost defenseless, fell to the British after a sustained bombardment by the warships.

The following month, the British fleet reached Tianjin, posing a direct threat to Peking itself. The British presented a letter from Lord Palmerston to the emperor containing a series of demands, including compensation for the confiscated opium and the expenses of the British expedition.

The Chinese court agreed to negotiate on condition that the British forces withdraw to the south. The negotiations dragged on and the British, impatient, demonstrated the might of their cannons by attacking and capturing the forts of Chuanbi, guarding Canton, in January 1841 and annihilating most of the Chinese fleet. This show of force worked: Within two weeks, the Chinese in Canton agreed to demands that included the ceding of Hong Kong island to Britain, the paying of an indemnity of six million dollars and the reopening of Canton to trade.

Before the agreement was ratified by either side, British troops occupied Hong Kong. As a result, the agreement was repudiated by Peking, and the Chinese court poured troops into the Canton area with the aim of exterminating the British. The following month, the British attacked again, easily occupying the forts and foreign factories. Making use of the network of waterways, British warships gained control of the countryside, while local officials, fearing the wrath of the emperor, hid the true state of affairs from the court in their reports.

The British, realizing that officials in Canton could not make good on the promises made to them, decided on a second military expedition to the north. They easily took city after city along the coast, seizing the city of Shanghai in June 1842. The British then sailed up the Yangtze River, subduing Zhenjiang and threatening Nanking. With British military superiority clearly established, the emperor finally yielded and negotiations were conducted in Nanking.

The result was the Treaty of Nanking, signed in 1842. Under this treaty, China agreed to cede Hong Kong island, pay an indemnity of twenty-one million dollars, open five ports—Canton, Amoy, Fuzhou, Ningbo and Shanghai—to foreign trade and recognize diplomatic equality between Chinese and British officials. Six million dollars of the indemnity was earmarked as compensation for the seized opium. Thus, even though opium was not specifically mentioned in the treaty, trade in the drug was tacitly recognized.

While the Opium War, as it came to be called, is now viewed as a watershed in China's history, its full significance was not apparent to many in the capital, who were merely relieved when the foreign forces withdrew, convinced that Western "barbarians" could never alter the centuries-old ways of the Celestial Empire.

Xiangye was undoubtedly drawn into discussions about these developments with scholars in the capital. Unfortunately, almost all his writings from this period have been lost as a result of later military conflicts.

In 1846, Xiangye made another attempt to gain the degree of *juren* and failed. This time, however, he came so close to passing that he was listed in a separate group of forty who received honorary mention as "Distinguished Failures." Buoyed by this achievement, he tried and failed several more times. Distinguished Failure would be his highest academic achievement. It also characterized much of his life. Despite his ambitious plans for the salvation of his beleaguered country, he would never gain a post high enough to put them into effect. But, while he failed to realize all his ambitions, he did succeed in earning a reputation in later years as a scholar and historian.

Before he reached the age of forty, he had five sons and a daughter. Though he had been left a modest inheritance and his wife was from a wealthy family, he was increasingly faced with the need to earn a living. So primarily for financial reasons, Xiangye began to work as a private secretary, one of the few available outlets for scholars who failed to achieve official posts. He worked for the director of education, first in Shandong province and later in Anhui. Already approaching middle age, he entered the government bureaucracy as a lowly copyist and, from that position, he was promoted to salt examiner.

Though as a licentiate he was technically qualified to serve in the official bureaucracy, by now the number of aspiring officials was so great and the number of posts so small that getting one often entailed years of waiting. The government had developed a system by which candidates had to pay to have their names placed on waiting lists for various provincial postings. Xiangye made a substantial financial investment to become a first-class subprefect, one of the higher positions in local government. In 1856, he was sent to Zhejiang province by the Xianfeng Emperor, to wait until a subprefectural post became available.

While Xiangye waited, he drew no salary, but he was given temporary assignments, lasting weeks or months, for which he was paid. One such task was to travel between Suzhou and Changzhou, raising supplies for the military. As a result, he was promoted to the rank of prefect but still lacked a prefecture to run.

In the 1850s, southern China was torn by an uprising, the Taiping Rebellion, led by a man named Hong Xiuquan—like Xiangye, a licentiate who had repeatedly failed the provincial-level examinations. This uprising, which convulsed the country for fourteen years—roughly coinciding with the American Civil War—and in which thirty million people died, appeared to portend the end of the reigning dynasty.

Hong Xiuquan had witnessed the superiority of western arms in

the Opium War. Attracted by Christianity, which was being prop-
agated by missionaries who came in the wake of the gunboats, Hong
read the religious tracts and one day fell into a trance, after which
he proclaimed himself the younger brother of Jesus and, like him,
Son of God. He and his supporters proclaimed a new kingdom, the
Taiping Heavenly Kingdom. Their mission was not just to overthrow
the Manchus and restore China to Chinese rule, but to spread their
own brand of Christianity. Because of the link to Christianity, initially
Westerners were sympathetic to the movement. But eventually, they
felt that their political and mercantile interests were best served by
the Qing, so they joined forces with the Chinese armies to crush the
rebels.

The rebel soldiers at first encountered little resistance as they
advanced, capturing one city after another, including in 1853 the
key city of Nanking, the early Ming capital. Nanking thus became
the capital of the Taiping Heavenly Kingdom.

When news of the fall of Nanking reached Wuxi, the citizens
panicked. In April 1853, during the annual Qing Ming Festival,
when deceased relatives are honored, it was rumored that rebel
forces were approaching. In the resulting pandemonium, twenty-
seven people died, either by falling from the city wall or by being
trampled to death. A beggar threw away his begging bowl and attempted suicide.

As a peddler passed two loyal regiments guarding the city to the
north, he hawked his wares, as was customary, by slapping together
two sticks of bamboo to announce his presence. However, the sight
of him in the distance and the clacking noise caused the nervous
soldiers to open fire. Thinking that they were under attack, some
other soldiers attempted to flee and became entangled with each
other. In the ensuing melee, more than ten soldiers died. The hawker,
however, escaped unscathed.

The expected attack was years in coming. During this period, the
city's jangled nerves were stretched taut and both civilians and soldiers remained tense.

With most of the two richest provinces, Jiangsu and Zhejiang, in
rebel hands, the central government's revenues shrank, and soldiers'
rations were cut. In March 1860, fifty thousand soldiers guarding
Wuxi deserted. A militia was formed to defend the city, and in May,
reinforcements arrived. Five days later, the long-awaited attack came.
The commanding officer went out to meet a frontal assault, taking

all his troops with him. With the city now bereft of defenders, another rebel force easily moved in from the west and captured the city.

On entering the city, the Taiping rebels posted notices saying that they would not harm anyone. However, the very next day, the rebel soldiers, with red kerchiefs tied around their heads, went on a rampage, killing the men and kidnapping and raping the womenfolk.[3]

The Taipings tried to recruit local people to work for them, but pockets of resistance remained outside the city, including one at Tangkou township led by Xiangye's friend Hua Yilun, whose daughter had married Xiangye's eldest son. Hua's forces tied white kerchiefs around their heads to distinguish themselves from the rebels.

The central government in Peking was in no position to render aid to the provinces. It had been under constant pressure from Western powers to open up the interior of China for travel and trade, to tolerate the activities of missionaries, and, most important, to allow the stationing of ambassadors in Peking on a basis of diplomatic equality. Failing to achieve their objectives by negotiations, the Western powers resorted to force. In 1858, Canton was occupied by British and French troops, and, that same year, the Treaty of Tianjin was signed with Britain, France, the United States and Russia, as an Anglo-French force threatened to march on the capital.

When the British and French returned to Tianjin the next year with a large naval force to exchange the ratified treaties, they were repulsed by the Chinese. As a result, allied troops marched on Peking in 1860, causing the Xianfeng Emperor to flee the capital under the pretext that he was going hunting in his northern domains. The occupation of Peking and the burning of the imperial Yuan Ming Yuan pleasure grounds finally awoke China to its vulnerability in the face of Western military technology. The Convention of Peking signed under such pressure guaranteed the right of foreign envoys to reside in the capital, opened Tianjin as an additional treaty port and increased the indemnities China was to pay. The Russians, taking advantage of Chinese weakness, exacted a treaty under which China ceded all territory east of the Ussuri River. The series of crises confronting him caused the emperor's health to deteriorate rapidly and brought about his early death in 1861, at the age of thirty. His five-year-old son succeeded him, but the power behind the throne for the next half century would be a woman known to history as the notorious Empress Dowager Cixi.

Back in Wuxi, the Taiping Rebellion proved the most serious calamity to strike in a thousand years. The Heavenly Kingdom retained control of Wuxi for four years. In the first month, more than 190,000 men, women and children were killed. During the four-year period, many committed suicide by hanging or throwing themselves into wells and rivers. The locality became a wasteland as fields lay untended. Even sparrows were not to be found. Toward the end, before the area was pacified, the survivors were forced into cannibalism. People from one community would raid a neighboring community for the purpose of obtaining corpses for consumption.

Xiangye was living in Hangzhou when Wuxi was about to be lost to the rebels, but his mother was in Wuxi. Xiangye's oldest son, Guangjian, carried his grandmother to safety in the countryside. Xiangye managed to flee Hangzhou before the arrival of the rebel forces there. He hid in the wilderness for over a month before he found a boat that took him back to Wuxi. He stayed at Tangkou township, which was held by the militia commanded by his friend Hua Yilun.

With virtually all of Zhejiang province in rebel hands, Xiangye was unable to hold office. So, in the spring of 1862, he went to Shanghai with Hua. There, they met General Li Hongzhang, who had just been named acting governor of Jiangsu, and became his private secretaries and advisers.

Xiangye was joined in Shanghai by his mother and the rest of his family in the autumn. Though safe from the Taiping rebels, the interlude in Shanghai was not a happy time for Xiangye. His fourth son had died in infancy and now his second son, Guanghan, succumbed to the rigors of wartime living conditions. Moreover, Guangjian's two children, a girl and a boy, both contracted smallpox, and the disease killed the boy. Xiangye took it upon himself to teach poetry to his beloved granddaughter. He lamented the fact that the house was so small there was no room for his children and grandchildren to study properly.

In late 1863, Li Hongzhang and his forces succeeded in driving the Taiping rebels from Wuxi and Suzhou. But by the time Wuxi was recovered, 90 percent of the city had been destroyed, including many houses along Sixth Arrow River, where members of the Qin family were concentrated. The rebels had taken care to preserve the best houses for their own use, but when the government troops arrived, street-to-street fighting caused widespread destruction and, after the government soldiers won, they went on a spree of violence and destruction that far exceeded anything perpetrated by the Heavenly Kingdom's troops.

After the recapture of Wuxi, Xiangye wrote to the newly appointed district magistrate there, and indicated that he would like to return to official life but lacked the funds needed to purchase an office. "I am poor and my family responsibilities are heavy," he wrote. "Though I have many wealthy friends, it is not easy for me to raise sufficient money."[4]

Somehow, Xiangye must have succeeded eventually in raising the required sum, for in 1864 he left the employ of Governor Li and moved the family to Suzhou. The following year he reentered officialdom.

In 1866, he served as acting salt controller of Zhejiang. Xiangye conducted an experiment in which salt would not have to be physically transported from one area to another, and sometimes back again. Instead, he issued coupons, or promissory notes, that pledged payment of a certain amount of salt. However, he was never in a position to put his ideas into effect because he did not have the governor's support.

That year, after an extremely hot summer and an exceedingly cold winter, both his mother and his son Guangzu fell sick and died within three days of each other. He took them back to Wuxi to be buried. In an obituary on his mother, Xiangye lamented that just when his income started to improve, his eighty-five-year-old mother had died and he did not have a chance to repay her properly for having nurtured him.[5]

Xiangye's remaining years in Zhejiang were spent in a number of capacities, increasingly in the literary recordings of major political events. He was ordered by the governor of Zhejiang to compile a record of how the province was wrested back from the Taiping rebels by General Zuo Zongtang. The result was *A Record of the Pacification of Zhejiang*, which took two years to complete.

In this officially sponsored book, Xiangye drew entirely from government sources, such as imperial decrees and reports made by officials. Naturally, he made no attempt to record events from the point of view of the Taiping rebels, but by focusing on the situation in Zhejiang, he was able to show what had happened in the country as a whole.

Many parts of Zhejiang were lost and recovered several times as the tides of war washed over the province. During those long years of struggle, uncounted people lost their lives. The provincial capital, Hangzhou, had a population of 810,000 before the war began, including those who lived outside the city walls. When fighting ended, it was reduced by more than 90 percent.

When Hangzhou was under siege in 1860, he recounted, the price of rice soared as the capital's grain reserves ran out. Eventually, there was no grain to be purchased. Lotus leaves, banana skins, the roots of grass and the bark of trees were consumed. The troops had their own supplies but even those ran out. Then horses and donkeys were slaughtered. The commanding officers were reduced to eating candles. With the soldiers weakened by hunger and their ranks thinned by deaths, the city finally fell. None of the capital's officials, numbering between five hundred to six hundred, escaped. The rebels went on a rampage, robbing and killing. The streets flowed with blood and the rivers were clogged with bodies of women who had drowned themselves.

In remote areas, he said, there was less destruction as the people went into hiding. But even in these areas, he added, only little more than half the population survived.

The pacification of Zhejiang and the province's gradual economic revival meant that taxes could again be raised from this normally wealthy area. However, Xiangye and two other provincial officials jointly submitted a request for tax commutation. They explained that after so many years of warfare, it would take time for the people to recover. They argued that the government should not press for the payment of back taxes for 1862, when Zhejiang was still under rebel control. "Taxes should be collected only for the period after 1862, to allow the people to recuperate," they said.

Xiangye was intimately connected with the tax-reform efforts in the wake of the Taiping Rebellion. In a preface he wrote to a book on the subject, published in 1868, he explained how the tax rates were reduced. He compared the high grain-tribute tax rates in Zhejiang with those in Jiangsu, where the taxation was among the heaviest and had been the cause of many uprisings. "Actually," Xiangye said, "there were no grain storage houses in Jiangsu's subprefectures and counties. People paid their grain taxes and then had to buy the grain back. In years of poor harvest the farmers would have to exchange two piculs of their grain for one picul from the government."

But in 1864, a taxation office was set up under Expectant Prefect

Tai Yunlin. "Mr. Tai was a knowledgeable official," Xiangye wrote. "After thorough research he proposed to reduce the tax rate by eight-thirtieths, which amounted to 260,670 piculs of grain. People were so relieved it was as if a sickness had left their bodies or as if they had been saved from fire or drowning. This was the biggest event within the last several hundred years."

With the province once again able to pay grain tribute to the imperial court, the question of transportation of the grain arose. An issue that had confronted Zhejiang for most of the previous half century was whether sea transportation routes should be developed to replace the Grand Canal, which had become increasingly impassable because of alternate silting and flooding. It was essential to keep open some route for the transport of southern rice to feed the court in Peking as well as the provinces of northern China.

As early as 1803, when the Yellow River flooded and its silt blocked the Grand Canal, proposals for developing a sea route had been put forward, recalling the use of such routes in earlier dynasties. However, the problem was put aside with the end of the floods. Interest was revived seriously in the 1820s, when a section of the Grand Canal was destroyed, thus crippling the grain-distribution network. Therefore, in 1826, a flotilla of 1,562 junks was used to deliver rice from Shanghai to Tianjin. Even then, however, the emperor declared that this was a temporary measure and, the following year, the inland route was used again after repairs to the canal.

In the 1840s, the problem had become increasingly serious and resulted in food shortages in the capital. In 1849, the Grand Canal became impassable and a sea route was employed. The Taiping Rebellion, which disrupted inland transportation, had ended all talk of reviving the Grand Canal.

The history of how Zhejiang province developed a sea route to the north was enshrined in a book published in the name of Governor Ma Xinyi. Xiangye contributed a preface to the volume, which appeared under the governor's name.

Sea transport, Xiangye concluded, was less costly, required less labor and took less time than transport via the Grand Canal. However, he did see problems, especially as the province continued to recover from the ravages of war and production increased. Then, he said, there might not be enough vessels to carry all the tax grain to the north. "Recently," Xiangye said, "merchants have started using foreign ships, and Chinese-made ships have been virtually given up."

In 1871, he again served as acting salt controller. He discovered that many posts within the salt administration were actually unfilled and administrators used the salaries to line their own pockets. Xiangye then made an example of an official who was one of the worst abusers of the system, checking his accounts page by page and exposing his corrupt practices. After that, other officials involved in the salt administration no longer dared pad their accounts and posts were properly filled.

Another problem Xiangye tackled had to do with violations of the state salt monopoly. The government had quotas on the manufacture of salt, and the price was set at a high level to bolster state revenues. However, many people were manufacturing and selling salt privately. The city of Daishan was the biggest offender. Since the city was on the coast, salt could be produced by evaporation of seawater, entailing little capital or labor. The resultant salt was sold at a fraction of what the government charged. Xiangye proposed that, instead of banning such production, the government should tax the producers. This idea was adopted and Daishan salt was openly sold and taxes were paid on it. However, despite his urging, this system was not extended to other parts of the province and the production, distribution and sale of salt remained a major problem for decades. Xiangye repeatedly lamented that the salt controller lacked power to put policies into effect.

Like his father, Ying, Xiangye had many friends who were prominent writers and poets. In 1867, he and some other poets set up a literary society. They met twice a month and intended to publish a compilation of their poems. However, the society disbanded because some of the members were assigned to posts elsewhere and some of the older men had died. A few years later, in 1873, Xiangye was approached by another poet, Bai Shaxi, who showed him not only his own poems but writings by seven or eight other scholars, most of whom were expectant officials awaiting posts. That coterie of poets, too, had broken up; the members had either died or moved away. Bai asked Xiangye to select the poems that he considered the best and publish them as a collection, and he gladly complied.

About this time he was asked to be the chief editor of a new edition of the family genealogy. His father had been the chief editor of the previous one, which appeared in 1819. Many of his nephews and grandnephews had gained higher degrees than Xiangye, and they also participated in this clan-wide project. But Xiangye was not only one of the most senior persons in the clan in terms of generational rank, he was also the most distinguished scholar.

In his preface, Xiangye ascribed the delay in such a new version to the turmoil of the Taiping Rebellion—as a result, many people were killed or had fled from Wuxi and much of the information was missing. Comparing the past with the present, he said that the clan had been highly successful during both the Ming dynasty and the Qianlong and Jiaqing reigns of the Qing dynasty, sometimes with "tens of people serving simultaneously either in the capital or in the provinces," many of whom were high officials. The Qin family, he said, produced numerous successful examination candidates who became famous courtiers, good officials, prominent scholars or filial sons.

But now, he said, "there are hardly any scholars or students left; there are fewer people now who seek the licentiate degree than there used to be taking the provincial examinations." Clearly in his mind the Qin clan, like the dynasty itself, had entered a period of decline.

The clan's rise and fall can be reflected statistically. In the fifteenth century, the clan produced two *jinshi*. In the sixteenth century it produced three. In the seventeenth century, the figure jumped to nine, and this soared to sixteen in the eighteenth century. But in the nineteenth century, it plummeted to two. The number of *juren*, too, rose from ten in the sixteenth century to fourteen in the seventeenth, jumped to thirty-one in the eighteenth and dropped back to sixteen in the nineteenth century. Clearly, the clan's fortunes had peaked in the eighteenth century, especially during the Qianlong era. Xiangye bemoaned his own inability to reverse the tide. "As I write this preface," he concluded, "how ashamed I am and how bad I feel."

It is interesting that over a century later, the curator of the Wuxi Museum drew a parallel between the decline of the Qin family and that of the dynasty.

"The fall of the Qin family of Wuxi actually reflects a historical trend that marked the twilight of feudalistic society in China," he wrote. "Feudal officials and landlords had contracted an incurable terminal disease, and could not halt their decline."

In 1875, a curious thing happened. Xiangye's grandnephew Baoji, a well-known scholar in his own right, was in Shanxi province and in a store came across the booklet of poems written by Xiangye as a young man and sent to Ruan Yuan almost half a century ago. That official, of course, had long since died. Baoji bought the book of poems and presented them to his granduncle. The old Xiangye considered them not worth publishing.

By this time Xiangye himself was in demand as a contributor of prefaces to collections of works by younger writers.

Tragedy struck in 1878, with the death of Xiangye's wife of over forty years. In his obituary of her, Xiangye wrote that throughout their marriage, "we were mired in poverty or plagued by sorrow." When she knew she was dying, Xiangye said, "she took out her hairpins and bracelets and gave them to her granddaughters and her maid. Then she gave me all her savings and asked me to prepare a coffin for her. She knew that I was poor and did not want to burden me with the expense of her funeral services."

The following year, upon the recommendation of Li Hongzhang, now a grand secretary, Xiangye was named acting intendant in charge of the prefectures of Jinhua, Chuzhou and Yanzhou. At the time, there were bands of bandits in the mountains who were so organized that they operated like a government unto themselves, with their own seals and banners. Xiangye seized their leaders and sent them to the provincial capital for trial, but to his disappointment, they were released. However, while there were disturbances in other circuits, his prefectures remained calm.

Though no longer an adviser to Li Hongzhang, Xiangye retained a keen interest in national and international affairs. He showed this by writing to Li and offering his views on major developments.

At that time, the Chinese were involved in a territorial dispute with the Russians, who had occupied the far-western territory of Ili in 1871 under the pretext of administering it on China's behalf until the Chinese were able to take it over. But when the Chinese informed the Russians in 1878 that their services as administrators were no longer required, Moscow was reluctant to return the territory. Negotiations were held and, in 1879, the Chinese envoy agreed that Russia could keep two thirds of the territory and, in addition, would receive a large indemnity from China. It was at this point that Xiangye wrote to Grand Secretary Li, by then arguably the most powerful official in the country.

Xiangye excoriated the Russians for being greedy for Chinese territory and expressed indignation at them for sending gunboats into Chinese waters to increase their bargaining leverage. He said that if the Russians were lured ashore they could be defeated since their warships and cannons would no longer be effective and "our heroic troops will surely defeat them."

On the whole, however, he cautioned moderation. Xiangye felt that the coastal provinces were poorly defended. "In Zhejang," he wrote, "the six cities of Wenzhou, Ningzhou, Taizhou, Shaoxing, Hangzhou and Jiaxing are all on the coast. If one city is careless [and is taken], all the others will be shaken."

Part of China's internal weakness, Xiangye said, was due to mal-administration. "This year, after the famine, officials tried to raise the harvest figures to show their superiors that there was a surplus, which resulted in increasing the taxes," he wrote. "That is why there has been a series of rebellions in the three prefectures of Hangzhou, Jiaxing and Huzhou. These have led to a loss of confidence on the part of the people." If rebels and smugglers should stir up trouble internally when the country was confronting a Russian threat externally, "the situation could be disastrous."

To sum up, Xiangye said, "It is not right to bargain for peace; but if we consider our southeast situation, we should not go to war."

In his next letter, Xiangye drew the grand secretary's attention to what he felt were important differences between the Russians and the Japanese on the one hand and the British on the other.

The main reason the Russians had not made a military move, Xiangye declared, was because of internal political problems. In a recitation of Russian misdeeds of the past, he said that they had assisted Japan when that country coveted Taiwan, then had wanted to take over strategic locations in Mongolia. "They acted like bullies and everyone was furious and wanted to go to war with them," Xiangye said. But, he added, China still was not prepared for war. "Although Zhejiang is starting to buy cannons and is trying to strengthen its coastal defenses, I am afraid the preparation may not be good enough. This is also true of Fujian and Guangdong.

"Russia and Japan are different from Britain," Xiangye went on. "The British only want trade, and the peace between Britain and us will last. The Russians and the Japanese want more land, so a peace treaty is unreliable. In a few years, they will stir up trouble and attack us while we are unprepared."

Looking into the future, Xiangye suggested that even if China opted for peace, "we should strengthen our frontier troops and lower taxes in order to win the support of the people.

367

"In the future, if battles break out, we should fight on land while guarding the harbors. That way, I am sure we will win," Xiangye said, echoing a commonly held Chinese belief that foreigners could fight well only from the safety of their gunboats and that, once on land, they could be annihilated. "To recollect historical facts, the Russians attacked us twice during the Kangxi reign period, and we repulsed them twice. This shows that we can fight them on land." As for the Japanese, Xiangye said that they were "equipped with warships and cannons, and so we can only guard our harbor but cannot fight them at sea."

Zhejiang province had set up an official publishing house. In 1880, Xiangye, in view of his literary attainments, was named its general manager and oversaw the publication of works of historical value not only to Zhejiang but to scholars across the country. One of the biggest projects was a supplement to the twelfth-century study of the Northern Song period by the historian Li Tao titled *Chronological Continuation of a Comprehensive Mirror to Aid in Government*.

Under the editorship of Xiangye, the Zhejiang Publishing House restored sections of the Li Tao work that had become lost over the years, including records for the periods of Emperors Huizong and Qinzong, the two Northern Song emperors who were taken prisoner by the Jurchens.

According to a preface written by Xiangye, "This book exhausted the physical and mental strength of eight to nine people, who had to check a large number of references, and it took two years to complete. We can say that much care has been taken."

In September 1881, a new governor, Chen Shijie, assumed office and asked local officials to advise him on the running of the province. Xiangye, who had spent almost a quarter of a century as an official in the province, advised Governor Chen that the main problems were financial.

Xiangye began with the problems of the state salt monopoly. As he had ten years earlier, he urged that private salt production be legalized and the manufacturers taxed. However, the salt administration was not revamped until the second decade of the twentieth century, when it came under foreign management.

As for tribute grain, Xiangye said that since the reduction in rates that came into effect after the Taiping Rebellion, the people were happy. However, he pointed out, problems remained. He said that, while the tax was paid to local officials in kind, it had to be delivered to the Ministry of Revenue in Peking in cash. So officials had to sell the grain they received, often back to the peasants who had paid it in, at a state-set price of 3,600 *wen* per picul, regardless of the harvest or the market price. While other taxes could be reduced or remitted in years of poor harvest, the tribute grain was set at a definite amount each year. Since the harvest varied from year to year the market price of grain, in effect the peasants' tax burden, varied from year to year. The obligation was less burdensome when the harvest was good, but when it was poor, it became onerous.

In the past, he said, officials vied to be responsible for collecting tribute grain because it was lucrative, but lately they considered it a burden since they had to make up any deficits if the peasants were unable to meet their obligations. Xiangye said the situation was so absurd that he had heard of people praying for famine so that the price of grain would rise. Presumably, this would have raised market prices higher than the state-set rate of 3,600 *wen* per picul, and the peasants would have benefited from such purchases. "The only suggestion I can make," Xiangye said, "is to vary the price of grain instead of fixing it at 3,600 *wen* per picul. Perhaps the problem can be solved if we keep it at 20 to 30 percent above the market price, depending on the harvest."

Xiangye then turned his attention to the *likin* tax, a local tax on commodities in transit. He pointed out that this did not exist before the Taiping Rebellion but was introduced at that time specifically to raise revenue for military expenditures. Still, after the end of the uprising, the tax was not abolished. "The people did not complain when the government needed the funds to end the state of chaos," Xiangye said. "But now the country has been at peace for over a decade. The money now goes to the construction of ponds, coastal defense and other projects." Xiangye said that, to administer this tax, a large bureaucracy had been built up and so costs were high and corrupt practices had emerged.

"When I was working for the provincial office," he said, "I discussed with the administration commissioner the setting up of new regulations and the laying off of excess staff. Whom to dismiss would depend on the performance of individual officials. This would encourage people to work harder and increase revenues. If the same number of officials was hired irrespective of the workload, the situation would invite corruption." His advice was apparently not accepted at the time.

In conclusion, Xiangye said that he was getting old and had decided to retire. However, he said, it did not really matter if he remained in the government as long as his advice was heeded. "I believe that if a high official will not listen to an individual, he will not make use of him; but if his words are accepted, it is the same as if he had been given a post. I cannot be the judge of my own words, so I will let your honor be the judge."

One of his last official acts was to petition for official recognition of the virtue of a young woman, the widow of his great-grandnephew. Within weeks of her marriage her husband died. She vowed that she would not remarry, refused to eat and, a little over a month later, died of hunger at the age of twenty-four. He felt that such a noble gesture should not go unnoticed. So he and some other prominent Wuxi personalities submitted a report on her behalf, asking that she should be honored and held up as a model for other women. The request was approved.

Back in Wuxi, he was asked to update the local gazetteer, the last edition of which had been edited by his father forty years previously in 1813, the year of Xiangye's birth. So Xiangye worked on local historical records, as so many of his forebears had done before him. He had to record the devastation of Wuxi during the Taiping Rebellion, the worst catastrophe to visit his hometown in a thousand years. In the back of the gazetteer, he listed some of the more prominent victims of the rebellion. Over a hundred were from the Qin clan. That 1881 edition has never been updated and remains to this day the definitive record of the history and geography of Wuxi.

Xiangye included in the *Wuxi Gazetteer* his own essay on the inequities of the grain-tribute tax, which was collected in money rather than in kind. While commoners paid according to a fixed rate, he said, "for the gentry households, the rate differed with the degree of strength [of gentry members] and the size of their landholdings." He said he had heard of large gentry landowners who had computed their own tax rate "and forced the officials to accept it.

"The small owners have only a few to several ten *mu* of land," he continued. "After a year's hard labor, the proceeds are not sufficient to support a family of eight mouths. They do not have cash to pay for the grain tribute. They have therefore been forced to sell rice for their daily meals at a low price."[6]

Although Xiangye himself was automatically considered a member of the upper gentry by virtue of his degrees and official positions, he was never a large landowner and his sympathies clearly lay with the poor. The writing of this article was an act of courage, since he was challenging the entrenched interests of the gentry in Wuxi. He offered two possible solutions to the problem posed by the use of different rates of conversion from grain to money. One was to build granaries so that tax could be collected in kind, thus bypassing the problem of conversion rates. The other was to continue to collect the tax in money, but to use prevailing market prices for grain as the conversion rate, with a small surtax to pay for the expenses of tax collection. Like so many of his proposals, this one fell on deaf ears.

Throughout his life, he had been frustrated by not being able to attain high office, so he had sought to do the next best thing, which was to present his ideas to high officials in the hope that he could influence them. His essay on Vietnam was written in 1882 when the French were invading Tonkin and when China and France appeared headed for a conflict over Vietnam.

He pointed out Vietnam's historical and geographical ties with China, claiming, "It is a historical fact that Vietnam belongs to China." While France was across the ocean, Vietnam bordered on the provinces of Yunnan and Guangxi. But Vietnam was so weak that it would easily be swallowed up by the French, Xiangye said. Then Vietnam's fate would be that of the Ryukyu Islands, which had been lost to Japan.

At the time, a former Taiping leader, Liu Yongfu, who had sought refuge in Vietnam, took up arms against the French. He and his "Black Flag" troops won several battles. Xiangye argued that China should pardon Liu and support his efforts. "How can the poor Vietnamese sustain their resistance?" he asked rhetorically. "How can our country just sit by and not send troops to help them?"

However, he recognized that China's own military resources were limited. Although General Li Hongzhang and his troops "have won almost all the battles they engaged in," he said, "if they are dispatched to Vietnam, the rebels in central China may cause trouble. I am afraid that before the foreign troops can be defeated, our country will already be in trouble. Moreover, Vietnam is a long distance away, and our troops will be exhausted before they arrive. Also, they are unused to the climate. So it is not advisable to send our soldiers there."

The solution advocated by Xiangye was to dispatch small forces to the Sino-Vietnamese border to bolster the morale of both the Vietnamese and the forces of Liu Yongfu. In addition, he proposed

371

that Liu Yongfu be pardoned and formally granted a military office of the second or third rank, so that he and his soldiers would constitute an official Chinese force. If the French troops crossed into Chinese territory, he said, they would be caught between Liu's forces and those sent to the Sino-Vietnamese border.

If the French should send a naval force against China, Xiangye said, the Chinese should not oppose them on the open sea but strengthen their defenses on land. The Chinese, he said, should "tempt the French to move inland and then eliminate them. After the French have lost several battles, they will sue for peace." As to other Western nations, Xiangye did not think they would intervene. "The British and the Americans are only interested in trade," he said. "If there is war, the sea-lanes will be blocked and their trade will stop, so they won't agree with the French to fight such battles and the French will lose their support." Isolated, France could not possibly win, he concluded.

But the Chinese authorities denied Liu official recognition and support and sent forces into Vietnam from the south. Liu's troops, denied support, were unable to withstand the French, and regular Chinese soldiers were forced to do battle. These were defeated by the French and a humiliating agreement was signed in which China recognized French interests in Tongking and agreed to open up Yunnan and Guangxi to French trade.

Xiangye's best-known essay was on coastal defense. In it, Xiangye expressed the somewhat unorthodox view that foreigners by and large were not predators. Foreigners, he said, seek only profits in trade and do not relish war. Sometimes, he said, "one or two countries have cunning ambitions," but these were usually curbed by other foreign countries who did not wish to see their interests affected.

"However," he warned, "the Japanese are an exception. They have secret goals and their trade is small." These words were to prove prophetic.

The Japanese had become experts in the manufacture of steel ships, he said, and it was necessary for China to learn to make these too. Warships were expensive, Xiangye pointed out, and China could not afford to buy many of them. Besides, foreigners sold China obsolete products. "Once we learn how to produce something, the foreigners change their techniques. If we only imitate we will never catch up.

"The foreigners are good at sea but they are not good on land," he added, repeating the commonly accepted belief. So China should devote its resources to training a modern army. In addition, he advocated that taxes be remitted so coastal cities would be able to form militias. "The foreigners are more afraid of the civilians than of soldiers," he said, "and they won't dare to move inland. The ships provide them with sanctuary and so they will not leave their vessels. Foreigners live on their ships; they are a long distance from their own countries and find it difficult to get logistical support. But we have no such problems. If the people along the coast can stop the traitors who supply the foreigners, and if we can hire more fishing boats and recruit more pirates, we can stop the foreigners from infesting our harbor and we can easily get rid of those on land. This is what I call 'to use our advantage against their weakness.' "

Besides, he said, a professional army would not only serve to keep the foreigners at bay, but would also be able to quell internal uprisings. Guns, cannons and small ships should also be manufactured to counter any rebels.

At the same time, he urged, the best people should be selected as officials and the people should be educated and living standards improved. "When the people have confidence, the country will be strong and peace will last, and the Westerners and Japanese will no longer dare to have designs upon us," he concluded.

While in retirement, Xiangye lived the life of a poor scholar. All his life he had been in financial straits, except for the brief periods when he served as salt controller. Although he was now almost seventy years old, he was invited to return to Hangzhou to lecture at the Eastern City Academy. Xiangye decided to accept the offer, but had to sell two rolls of paintings to raise funds for traveling. Then, before he could embark on his journey, he fell sick.

His illness began in the fall of 1883 and, fifty days later, he remained bedridden. On November 11, 1883, he died at the age of seventy.

In an epitaph, his friend Sun Yiyan said: "I feel very sad for Xiangye. Though a scholar possessed of great intelligence, he was never appointed to an important position. He worked hard and, if he had been given the same opportunities as his father, he could have done much that would have been beneficial to the country. Unfortunately, his highest position was salt controller and he became a poor retired gentleman. Ah, well, a scholar should not be evaluated by his worldly achievements!"[7]

CHAPTER TWENTY-FOUR

Grandfather: District Magistrate Qin Guojun

In the edition of the family genealogy that Xiangye edited is the following entry concerning my grandfather: "Guojun: Great-great-grandson of Wenjin . . . Styled Leping. Student of the National Academy. Expectant for rank 9b. Born on the seventh day of the twelth month of the second year of the Xianfeng reign era [1852]. Betrothed to Miss Qiu, daughter of Zhejiang Expectant Subprefect Yundong, born on the eighth day of the second month of the first year of Xianfeng [1851]."

So Grandfather was already betrothed, although not yet married, at the time the genealogy was written, and his future wife was more than a year older than he. Also, when this entry was prepared, he had already received, through purchase, the title *jiansheng*, or student of the National Academy. This was the equivalent of a licentiate degree and entitled him to participate in the provincial examinations. In addition, he was an expectant candidate for an office of the ninth rank, the lowest in the government hierarchy, higher only than clerks, runners, secretaries and others who were not considered part of the regular bureaucracy.

His father, Bingbiao, had also purchased a degree and become an assistant magistrate in Zhejiang, but my great-grandfather had died while only in his thirties, leaving his widow and his six-year-old son, Guojun, three earlier sons having died in childhood.

My great-grandmother took her young son to Xi'an, where they were cared for by her brother, but within a few years, she also died. The closest surviving paternal relative was Guojun's father's brother, Bingsu, who was also a local official in Zhejiang. But before long Bingsu and his wife died, childless. This left Guojun, a teen-ager, the sole heir to both his father and his uncle, with the responsibility of continuing both their family lines.

374

While a teen-ager, Guojun joined the army of General Zuo Zong-tang, who as governor-general of Shaanxi and Gansu provinces had to put down a serious Muslim uprising. There are few details of this early phase of Guojun's life, but oral tradition within the family has it that Grandfather served under two of General Zuo's best officers. He supposedly was involved in logistics, ensuring that adequate grain supplies reached the troops.

In February 1871, the rebel leader was defeated and killed. With the expedition to the northwest over, Grandfather began to pursue the career of an official by purchasing the degree of *jiansheng*. The title was relatively inexpensive, costing him roughly a hundred taels of silver, which he paid in two installments, the last one in 1889.[1] While being a *jiansheng* qualified him for office, he had to pay far more substantial amounts before his name could be put on a list of expectant officials, starting at the lowest rung. It was common for an expectant official to wait for years before his name moved up the waiting list and a substantive post became vacant. By the late nineteenth century, the vast majority of men on the lower rungs of officialdom obtained their positions through purchase rather than as a result of taking the examinations, a practice that generated considerable revenue for the government.

Now a member of the scholar-official class, Grandfather went to Zhejiang province to claim his bride. Her father, Qiu Yundong, was a scholar who had served as deputy administrator of Hangzhou, the provincial capital. The story goes that before the wedding, the better-off Qiu family sent servants to Grandfather's home to make prep-arations. They were told to put their hands into the bundled up quilts in the bridal chamber and feel the inside. Smooth quilts meant they were silk; rough signified ordinary cotton cloth. When the ser-vants returned, they reported to the Qiu household that the quilt covers were smooth. The wedding ceremony was presided over by Qin Xiangye, the senior member of the clan, who was then serving his second tour as acting salt controller.

In 1872, the couple produced their first child, a daughter. Ulti-mately, that union produced five daughters and two sons. The elder son, Lianyuan, was assigned to continue his uncle's family line while the younger, Liankui, continued his father's family line. Liankui was my father.

It was not long before Grandfather discovered that his wife was a woman of great talent. She was unusual in that she was remarkably

375

erudite, having studied under her own father. At thirteen she could compose poems, at fifteen she could write essays and, by the time she was eighteen, she was learned in history and the classics. She was known for her ability to write both good poetry and good prose. Her literary ability far exceeded Grandfather's, and she composed poems on his behalf, which he dedicated to his friends, as was the custom of the time. Yet she was skilled also in the martial arts, and taught her sons how to wield the broadsword and to bend the bow.

Exactly what Grandfather did in the decade after his marriage is unclear. A volume of poetry written by Grandmother indicates that he was away much of the time, traveling in the northeast and the northwest. It is possible that he rejoined General Zuo Zongtang, who was responsible for putting down an uprising in Xinjiang in the 1870s. In any event, despite their prolonged separations, their children continued to arrive, at two- or three-year intervals.

By 1880, when he was twenty-eight years old, he was an expectant assistant district magistrate. In that capacity, he was involved in the gathering of tribute grain from Zhejiang and its transportation to the capital by sea.[2] Such shipments were important because they included not only husked grain for consumption by the residents of Peking and its environs but also extra-fine polished rice for the use of the court. For having discharged his duties well, Grandfather was rewarded in mid-1882 by preemptive promotion: He was promised that, as soon as he obtained the office of assistant magistrate, he would be treated as a full district magistrate. That was a common form of reward in the last years of the dynasty. It had the appearance of a promotion and yet, for the time being, cost the court nothing.

Though the sea trip was arduous, Grandfather evidently enjoyed travel. He tarried so long in the north that, by the end of the year, he was still in Shandong province. Grandmother, left with her children in Zhejiang, composed the following poem:

> The year is going to end with the winter drums;
> My tears are dry before I hear the farewell song.
> Beware the winds and dew of strange lands;
> The pine and chrysanthemum at home await you.
> You will achieve your goal of self-fulfilment;
> Don't worry about our food, though life is difficult.
> You take care, no need to look back;
> Don't let your ambitious heart turn sour.

The following year, Grandfather moved on to Shaanxi province, perhaps to visit his mother's relatives, with whom he had grown up. He liked to play the flute and carried a metal one while riding, which he also used as a weapon to fend off wolves. In fact, he called himself "The Man With the Metal Flute," a sobriquet that Grandmother used in her poems about him.

Her husband's wanderlust thrust upon Grandmother the responsibility of caring for their children. The family had little money, and she had to supplement the family income by spinning at home, something that many women did. However, she was different from other women in that she became the modern-day equivalent of the free-lance writer. Using a pen name to disguise her sex, she contributed articles on current affairs to a journal published by the famous academy Kujing Jingshe in Hangzhou. In the evening, she taught her children Tang-dynasty poems and read to them from the classics. And often, she lay awake in bed at night, lonely and unhappy.

In the late 1880s, Grandfather became involved for several years in the delivery of large sums of silver to Peking, representing payment of taxes of one form or another. Extra taxes were often levied to fill special needs. In 1888, for example, the Ministry of Revenue ordered Zhejiang province to raise 400,000 taels of silver to pay for strengthening border defenses.

The province was unable to raise more than 50,000 taels at once, but pledged to do its best to raise the rest. In the meantime, Grandfather, then a thirty-seven-year-old probationary district magistrate, was ordered to transport the money to Shanghai and thence by ship to Tianjin before traveling overland to Peking.

In the company of an assistant magistrate, Grandfather carried not only the 50,000 taels for border defense but an additional 6,000 taels in other taxes. They started the trip on August 31 and on October 2 arrived in Peking, where they delivered the funds into the hands of officials of the Ministry of Revenue. Both men were rewarded by being advanced one grade and given two recordings of merit.

The wedding of the Guangxu Emperor in February 1889, at which time he ostensibly took over the reins of power from his aunt, the empress dowager, was the occasion for raising additional taxes to pay for the imperial celebrations. Zhejiang's share was 10,000 taels of silver.

That year, Grandfather journeyed to Peking to attend an imperial audience, a formality necessary to ratify his promotion. Only the year before he had finally mustered enough funds to pay the balance for the *jiansheng* degree he had purchased seventeen years earlier, an outstanding sum of more than 39 taels. Payment was probably necessary before he could be granted an imperial audience. He was received by the Guangxu Emperor on August 25, 1889. After the audience, the nineteen-year-old emperor issued an edict to the Ministry of Personnel that said: "The candidate seen by me today, Expectant District Magistrate Qin Guojun, will retain the rank of district magistrate and will be assigned for replacement of district magistrate in the original province," that is, he would continue to work in Zhejiang. However, he was only an "expectant," which meant he had to wait for an office to become available. This often meant years of waiting, since the expectants were many and the posts few. And when a post did come up, the candidate would first have to serve a period of probation.

For the next several years, Grandfather's primary responsibility, as a probationary district magistrate, continued to be to convey taxes from Zhejiang to Peking. The total amount that he carried in 1890 was 80,000 taels. The following year, he transported 50,000 taels and, in 1892, he was assigned to transport 60,000 taels of *likin* tax —20,000 for the capital's coffers and 40,000 taels for defense of the northeast.

All these funds were delivered into the hands of officials of the Ministry of Revenue. After this, according to regulations, Grandfather was entitled to request a promotion, supported by the recommendation of a metropolitan official. The time limit for transport from Zhejiang to Peking was seventy days, and all the deliveries had been made well within that limit. Successful transportation of each 50,000 taels of silver could be rewarded with advancement of one grade and two recordings of merit. As a result of his accomplishments in 1890, 1891 and 1892, Grandfather was rewarded in 1894 with three advancements in grade and six recordings of merit.

That year, China and Japan went to war over the former's most important tributary, Korea. Badly defeated, the Chinese entered into negotiations the following year and agreed not only to the independence of Korea (which would allow its dominance by Japan) but also the cession of the Liaodong Peninsula, Taiwan and the Pescadores to Japan. Grandmother, who was in poor health, wrote from her sickbed a poem deploring her impotence:

> For three years I learned to use the sword;
> I feel ashamed when I touch my dagger.
> Who will provide for the peace of the land?

China was in a state of national decline. Externally, it was suffering from the progressive encroachments of foreign powers. Internally, it was suffering from the lack of a firm hand at the nation's helm. Though Empress Dowager Cixi had ended her regency and moved into the Summer Palace, power remained in her hands, since she did not relinquish the reading of important state documents or the making of appointments to certain offices. Her nephew, the emperor, had been taught from infancy to fear and obey her, and found it almost impossible to go against her will. Moreover, the heavy indemnities China was obliged to pay to foreigners forced the government to impose more and more taxes, leading to widespread unrest. The young emperor was unable to institute reforms that were needed to restore the nation's health. Bureaucrats intent on protecting their sinecures dominated the government and blocked all attempts by reform-minded officials to make changes. Events finally came to a head in 1898.

That spring, serious food shortages were reported in a dozen provinces as a result of a poor rice harvest following a very wet year. Soaring grain prices led to riots as crowds stormed granaries and government offices. Those in Zhejiang were particularly serious. One eyewitness, a missionary named Edward Hunt, described it thus:

"On Thursday last there occurred a fierce and successful riot. The people rose, closed all the shops, and went in a body to the *yamens* [offices] of the three chief civil mandarins of the city and district. They beat several mandarins, cleared one *yamen* of everything portable, and smashed all the woodwork, etc. The new opium office [where opium could now be purchased] shared the same fate. The officials took refuge in the provincial military *yamen*, and thence issued successive proclamations to try and pacify the people. These were all torn down as they appeared, until one was put out promising the opening of granaries and the sale of rice at a fair price."[3]

Three days later, even more serious violence broke out and stores were looted. Troops were called out and two of the rioters were killed before order was restored.

Because of his incompetence, the incumbent district magistrate was dismissed. Guojun, my grandfather, was appointed acting district magistrate, with the specific task of searching out the leaders of the riot. In a telegram to the capital, the governor reported that after the arrival of the new magistrate, the price of rice had declined and investigations were being held into those responsible for the disturbances.

The situation was so serious that the British consul in Ningbo, G.M.H. Playfair, filed an urgent report to the embassy in Peking, which was forwarded to London. Although the outbreak was not directed at Europeans, Consul Playfair reported, it was "part and parcel of a movement which seems to be taking place in most parts of China.

"Two features have seemed to characterize the many disturbances recently reported, viz., scarcity of rice and the proposed imposition of fresh taxation," the consul wrote. Rice, he said, "has been selling at six dollars per picul instead of three dollars. Ningpo produces rice but not in sufficient quantity for home consumption; the supply has to be supplemented by imports from Wuhu and other river ports. When, therefore, in addition to this hardship, it was proposed to levy fresh taxes in field produce, the peasants rose. On the eighth [they] poured into the city from the country. The *yamen* of the district magistrate was sacked and he himself mistreated.

"That China is in straits for money to meet loans, indemnities, etc. is obvious, and her efforts to meet her pecuniary difficulties by drafts on the people's benevolence are one by one proving futile."[4]

Reports of food shortages in Zhejiang and elsewhere spurred the emperor on to action. On June 11, he issued his first reform decree, speaking in broad terms on the need for change to enable China to catch up with the West and Japan. In the next three months the emperor, assisted by a small group of young zealous reformers, issued a series of decrees to reform and streamline the government, including abolition of the traditional essay in the official examinations, removal of key conservative officials, setting up of a modern university in Peking and the adoption of Western military drill. All these reforms were opposed by conservative officials, who called upon the empress dowager for assistance. She, fearing that she, too, would be stripped of power, acted forcefully. On September 22, she summoned her nephew into her presence and had him placed in confinement, while she resumed her regency. For the remaining ten years of his life the emperor was, in effect, her prisoner, even though memorials were addressed to them jointly and edicts were issued in both their names. Between the outbreak of the food riots in Wenzhou and the imperial edict issued in response several months later, a coup had taken place in Peking.

The edict, issued on December 1, 1898, accused unnamed officials of lying about the existence of famine or drought in requesting tax exemptions. While paying lip service to the need to look after the welfare of the people, its conclusion was that taxes had to be collected in full and on time. Nothing was said about the need to take steps to see that sufficient food at reasonable prices was made available to the common people.

Because Western countries had generally been sympathetic to the cause of the reformers, the empress dowager's antiforeign bias was strengthened. This led two years later to her support for the xenophobic Boxers, who wanted to kill all foreigners and drive them from China.

Grandfather was successful in restoring order to Wenzhou and won the respect of his superiors and the admiration of the local people. But he did not have the seniority to enable him to obtain a permanent appointment, and so he had to give way to another man. Before long, though, trouble broke out again in Wenzhou, this time in connection with the Boxer Rebellion of 1900, and Grandfather's services were again required. In all, he spent almost six years in that city.

The Boxer disturbances began in the north and moved gradually toward Peking. Emboldened by the support given them by the empress dowager, the Boxers laid siege to the Legation Quarter. A Japanese diplomat and the German minister were killed. Troops from eight nations were sent to raise the siege and, on August 14, their expedition entered Peking. For the second time in four decades, the Chinese capital was occupied by foreign troops. The empress dowager, with the imprisoned emperor in tow, fled to Xi'an.

While these events were unfolding in Peking, the provinces in the southeast were, by and large, isolated from the conflict. After the Chinese court declared war on the foreigners on June 21, the governors-general in the south decided it was imperative that they not be dragged into a war with virtually all the powers simultaneously. These officials decided instead to protect foreigners and put down secret societies.

In spite of their efforts, the Boxer Rebellion did spill over into southern and eastern China, including Zhejiang province, causing considerable apprehension on the part of both Chinese officials and foreigners. An edict issued by the notoriously antiforeign Prince Tuan, which was suppressed in other southeastern provinces, was allowed to be published in Zhejiang by Governor Liu Shutang. This was seen by some as official sanctioning for the use of violence against foreigners, mostly missionaries, and their Chinese converts. In Wenzhou, the atmosphere was particularly tense.

On July 4, 1900, John Compton, constable of the British consulate in Wenzhou, sent an urgent letter to the British consulate in Ningbo, saying that members of the main missionary organization, the China Inland Mission, were "in great fear both for themselves and their converts, and asked me to write to you by overland courier, and ask you to try and get a gunboat sent here at once or it may be too late."[5]

A few days later, on July 9, the newly appointed British consul, Pierce Essex O'Brien-Butler, arrived to assume his duties. He found the British consulate, which was situated on Conquest Island in the middle of a river, crowded with refugee missionaries. These, together with customs officials and their families, accounted for almost the entire foreign community of Wenzhou, aside from two French priests and three Japanese merchants.

In a report to the Foreign Office, O'Brien-Butler reported that immediately after his arrival he sent a dispatch to the circuit intendant, or Taotai, "informing him that the high authorities of the centre and south of China had disassociated themselves from the north, and that, consequently, those parts of the empire were at peace with all foreign powers. I begged him to at once issue a proclamation to inform the people of this fact, so that their minds might be set at rest, and to threaten with dire penalties any person who should venture to molest foreigners or Christian converts or to injure their property."[6]

After meeting with the circuit intendant, the consul decided that, in view of the isolation of Wenzhou, which was visited only every ten days by a steamer from Shanghai called the *Poochi*, there should be an immediate evacuation of all foreigners. The decision was reinforced by the arrival of five Chinese Christians who reported that "the Boxers had a list with the names of twenty-eight Christians, and were openly declaring that they intended to have as many heads."

In his account to the Foreign Office, O'Brien-Butler concluded: "In the afternoon we heard that the Boxers were active in destroying at a distance of only 16 miles from Wenchow. It was evident that they were gradually approaching the city, and all doubts as to the advisability of leaving the port were set at rest. Finally, news came to us from three distinct sources that a party of Boxers about 3,000 strong was starting from a place only 10 miles distant with the intention of attacking the churches and foreigners in the city of Wenchow itself. The most circumstantial account was brought to the Roman Catholic priest by a native Christian who said that the rioters were advancing very slowly, as they were destroying the Christian property they found on the way, and, besides, had to offer certain sacrifices en route. It was expected that they would reach Wenchow at about dawn on Thursday. On receipt of this news I sent word to all the foreigners to come on board the 'Poochi' as soon as possible, and steam was at once got up."

The Italian-built *Poochi* left for Shanghai on July 12. On board were nineteen men, ten women and ten children, in addition to the crew.

Less than ten days after the evacuation of Wenzhou, a massacre of foreign missionaries occurred in a nearby prefecture, Chuzhou, where two men, six women and three children were killed, of whom nine were English and two Americans. This event aggravated tensions in Zhejiang, eventually leading to demands by foreign powers that provincial officials, including the governor, be executed.

Though the missionaries in Wenzhou were evacuated in time, their Chinese converts were less fortunate. Hundreds had to flee for their lives by going into hiding in the mountains. Some died from the hardship and others were killed. The prefect of Wenzhou, who was vehemently antiforeign, was widely seen as being responsible for fanning the flames.

In this highly charged atmosphere, marked by anti-Christian hysteria, Grandfather was again dispatched to Wenzhou. His job was to quell any unrest, look into complaints, determine the extent of damage and apprehend those responsible. And he was to participate in the negotiations over the amount of compensation to be paid by the Chinese authorities. He was dispatched to Wenzhou as a *weiyuan*, or commissioner for foreign affairs. His arrival was recorded in a dispatch dated August 12, 1900, in the English-language newspaper *Shanghai Mercury*:

"There also arrived by the Poochi this time a *weiyuan* specially deputed to inquire into the recent local troubles. The officials here don't in the least relish his coming, and when he calls on them offer the most paltry excuses for not seeing him."[7]

Grandfather's job, clearly, was not easy. But his handling of this task, combined with his pacification of Wenzhou two years previously, earned him a reputation as a capable administrator.

Few documents are extant setting out the details of what Grandfather did, but it is clear that he was applauded not only by his superiors but by foreigners as well. Two of the rioters' leaders were rapidly apprehended, and machinery was set in motion for the capture of others.

The Protestant claims were quickly settled. An indemnity of a little over 16,000 Mexican dollars was agreed to by both sides, Mexican dollars being the Western currency commonly accepted in China. However, the Roman Catholic claims were much more difficult. A report by the circuit intendant to the governor shows the delicate situation the Chinese officials found themselves in: "When we negotiated with the Protestants I was afraid that the Catholics might object to whatever decision was reached. So I asked Magistrate Qin to conduct discussions with their missionary at the same time. However Père Louat [the Catholic missionary in charge] told us that the case had been referred to their bishop in Ningbo and that negotiations should be conducted by the bishop. He refused to take part in meetings in Wenzhou."[8]

Père Louat sought substantial indemnities. He put losses of his mission at 20,000 Mexican dollars and of Chinese converts at another 20,000 dollars. The priest apparently had the backing of the French consul in Hangzhou, who threatened to send troops and warships to Wenzhou.

Grandfather again contacted Père Louat, hoping to resolve the issue as rapidly as possible, but the priest again declined. So Grandfather was instructed to go to Ningbo to negotiate directly with the bishop.

Grandfather went to Ningbo early in 1901, but the discussions with the bishop were inconclusive and, in the middle of March, the *North China Herald* reported that the Chinese and the Catholics "have been unable to come to terms—and those who know best seem not to wonder at this—for the Chinese say the claim is most exorbitant, and we incline to believe it. The claim has now been carried to the provincial capital, Hangchow."[9] Grandfather apparently also took part in the negotiations in Hangzhou, which were not concluded until late July.

An article in the *North China Herald* on April 24, 1901, paid tribute to Grandfather's efforts and those of his superior, the circuit intendant:

"Fortunately we have in our *taotai* a tolerant man who used his utmost efforts to undo the prefect's evil work. He was vigorously supported by the then *weiyuan* for foreign affairs, Ch'in [Qin], formerly and now again magistrate here. But for these two officials, the outbreak here would have been a terrible one. Through their influence the storm lasted but a few days, and many of the Christians were able to return to their homes within a month. Ch'in Ta-lao yeh [His Honor Qin] has worked splendidly in settling up the claims in his *hsien* [district], as well as rendering aid in others over which he has no direct control. He has personally visited the places which suffered most and supervised the return of goods removed from Christian homes. The Protestant claims are now all arranged and in process of payment."

The following year, Governor Ren Daoyong, in a special memorial to the emperor, highly commended Grandfather as one of three officials in the province deserving of promotion. The governor said: "When he was appointed, it was right after the incident involving missionaries in Wenzhou. He devoted himself to the task of resolving difficulties and he provided solutions for every problem he encountered. He adopted practical measures, instituting new policies where they were called for and discarding old ones. His decisions have been praised by gentry and commoners alike. This official has been courageous in the performance of his duties, he has displayed a firm resolve, is energetic and acts as the occasion requires. He possesses intelligence and determination. Truly, an outstanding man."[10]

Despite the glowing recommendation, Grandfather was not promoted. Instead, the emperor asked that the recommended officials be granted an imperial audience. But it took two years for Grandfather to be granted that privilege. One reason was that the number of expectant officials kept increasing while the number of government posts remained constant. Governor Ren, in a memorial, asked that no expectant officials be sent to his province. He pointed out that there already were 27 expectant circuit intendants, 74 expectant prefects, more than 150 expectant subprefects, and over 300 expectant magistrates—and openings for only 2 intendants, 5 prefects, 24 subprefects and 76 magistrates.[11] It is unlikely that his request was heeded; the selling of official posts was too important a source of revenue.

The Boxer-related incidents took up a large part of Grandfather's time in 1900 and 1901, but he still had to perform the other duties of a district magistrate. His two major ones were to maintain the peace and to collect taxes. The district magistrate was responsible for apprehending suspected lawbreakers, establishing their guilt or innocence and meting out appropriate punishment. China traditionally did not separate the executive and judicial arms of government. At the top, such powers were epitomized in the person of the emperor; at the bottom, where the ordinary citizen encountered officialdom, they resided in the office of the district magistrate.

As district magistrate, Grandfather was expected not only to investigate but to solve all cases by established deadlines, and since Wenzhou was a poor area, robberies frequently occurred. Grandfather's life was made even more difficult by clan feuds, often over ownership of farmland, which resulted in many deaths. Because the clans shielded their own, it was difficult for the magistrate to make arrests.

One case that he did succeed in solving occurred on the night of October 20, 1901, when Grandfather was in Hangzhou on official business. Robbers broke into the home of a Wenzhou resident named Wang Jiada. They used rocks to batter down his door and wounded two of the servants before fleeing with money, jewelry and clothes valued at 303 taels of silver.

Five months later, a band of robbers broke into the home of a family named Chen. Grandfather, upon receiving this report, accompanied the police and visited the scene of the crime. He found that the Chen home consisted of a complex of seven structures in a remote area several miles outside the city. Grandfather examined the back door, which had been smashed in, as well as boxes and cupboards that had been forcibly opened. A metal chopper was found in one room, and a stone pillar, presumably used to batter down the door, was discovered lying outside the back entrance. The loss was estimated at 639 taels of silver. On the basis of descriptions provided by the victims, pictures of the robbers were drawn and posted on walls.

Barely four days later, eight men were apprehended. Among the stolen goods recovered were items from both the Chen and the Wang households. After interrogation, it was discovered that the leader, a man named He Changlin, had been involved in both robberies. He was a thirty-five-year-old Hunanese who was basically a mercenary, having served in various irregular armies. Later, the force he had been serving with was disbanded and he became a drifter. He had gathered around himself a group of more than twenty robbers, most of whom were still at large. He admitted his involvement in both cases and described how they had been planned and carried out. He confessed that he had worn his military uniform and carried a pistol while committing the robberies. He also said that his share of the loot amounted to 40 Mexican dollars from the Wangs' home and 26 from the Chens'. As part of his confession, he said that he had taken part in only these two robberies, that none of his relatives had been involved and that he did not know the whereabouts of those of his confederates still at large.

The two other men involved in the Wang robbery were an umbrella repairer and another ex-militiaman who had been dismissed for dereliction of duty and then become a boatman. The boatman admitted that he had also been involved in a robbery in a different district. His share of the loot from the Wang household was 20 Mexican dollars, while the umbrella repairer, who kept watch and did not take part in the actual robbery, got 5.

Since capital punishment was called for by law for all robbers, whether gang leaders or followers, Grandfather meted out death sentences to the two former militiamen and ordered that their heads be put on display after their decapitation. The third man was sentenced to exile in Xinjiang, there to work as a slave for the rest of his life. His face was to be tattooed so that all would know what crime he had committed.

Turning his attention to the robbery of the Chen household, Grandfather sentenced two of the five other men to death. One was another former irregular soldier who had been fired for laziness and the other was a soldier who had served with the Qing army in Taiwan and been dismissed for repeated absences without leave. Each had received 26 dollars as his share of the loot from the Chen household. Both men had also been involved in another robbery. The three others were two demobilized soldiers and a former body-guard. Because they had acted as lookouts and did not take part in the actual robbery, they were given the lighter sentence of exile to Xinjiang, where they were to be given as slaves to soldiers serving in that border area.[12]

Most of the robbers in these two cases used to be soldiers. Soldiers came from the lowest levels of Chinese society and were usually poor and illiterate. As a Chinese saying has it, "Good iron is not made into nails, and good men do not become soldiers."

There were two types of death sentences: "immediate execution" and "execution after the assizes." The latter meant that final disposition of the case had to wait until the annual Autumn Assizes, presided over by the emperor, which often resulted in commutation of the sentence. But even those sentenced to immediate execution were not killed until after a long process of review.

First, the cases went up to the prefectural level for review. If no discrepancies were found between the magistrate's report and the testimony of the prisoners, the cases went to the circuit intendant for another review, and then to the judicial commissioner. If the original sentences were upheld at all these levels, reports were then sent to the Ministry of Punishments in Peking. Only after the ministry had confirmed the penalty of immediate execution were the condemned finally put to death.

These two cases handled by Grandfather were forwarded to the prefecture for review. There, the prisoners were examined by magistrates from other districts. In the Wang case, all the sentences were upheld and the case passed on to the circuit intendant. By the time it reached the Ministry of Punishments, two and a half years had elapsed. In the Chen case, while the death sentences were upheld, the remaining prisoners were ordered returned to the district level for reexamination because they had recanted their original confessions. By then, Grandfather was no longer in Wenzhou and they were questioned by a new magistrate who confirmed the original findings and the sentences. Despite the arrest and conviction of eight men, Grandfather was still liable to an official reprimand because the remaining members of the band had not been apprehended. A magistrate was supposed to arrest all lawbreakers, not just some of them. However, it was decided in this case not to reprimand him.

A district magistrate's responsibilities were manifold. In October

1902, seventeen Korean fishermen whose ship had broken down and drifted into the vicinity of Wenzhou were rescued. Three of them were injured and required medical attention. Grandfather arranged for all of them to be cared for before being returned to their own country. They were sent to Hangzhou, the provincial capital, where they joined another group of refugees and were escorted to Shanghai and put aboard a Japanese passenger liner.

The treatment of the Korean refugees reflected the changing triangular relationship among China, Japan and Korea. For centuries Korea, known to the West as the Hermit Kingdom, had been China's main tributary state. The Koreans openly acknowledged this status and adopted Chinese political and cultural institutions. However, China's decline and Japan's rapid rise as a modern power drastically changed the situation, and Korea came increasingly within Japan's orbit. After the opening of a Japanese consulate in Zhejiang, shipwrecked Korean fishermen were often simply handed over to the Japanese consulate, which arranged for them to be sent home by way of Japan. By such actions, the Chinese implicitly recognized Japanese authority in Korea.

Collection of taxes was an important part, possibly the most important part, of a district magistrate's job. Tax quotas were fixed and if taxpayers failed to pay on time, the district magistrate was held responsible. In prosperous areas, officials were able to impose surtaxes to cover their own expenses. In poorer areas, such as Wenzhou, it was often difficult to ensure the prompt delivery of all taxes. In 1903, because he had collected only 90 percent of the previous year's grain tax, Grandfather was demoted by one grade but retained at his post.

Failure to put adequate pressure on the people to pay their taxes on time ultimately led to the biggest setback of his career. On June 4, 1904, the governor asked for Grandfather's dismissal. In a memorial, the governor reported that Grandfather's collection of the poll tax for the previous year fell 147 taels short of the quota, while his collection of the grain tax was short by 7,000 strings of copper. In addition, he had fallen short by 129 Mexican dollars in the collection of a Wenzhou local tax. The governor said he had warned Grandfather twice, but he had still been unable to meet the deadlines. As a result, thirty-three years after he had bought his way into officialdom, Grandfather was removed from government service.[13]

Grandfather's reluctance to press for the prompt payment of taxes must have enhanced his popularity with the citizenry of Wenzhou. When he left, he was presented with a "10,000 citizens umbrella," on which were stuck pieces of paper with the names of numerous residents of Wenzhou. In addition, a plaque in his honor, known as a Remembrance Tablet, literally "Thinking of One Who Has Left," was erected on a hill. The esteem in which Grandfather was held was still evident in 1937, twenty-five years after his death, when several of his children and grandchildren passed through Wenzhou. A cousin who was present told me that one day while they were talking in a hotel an old chef came out and asked them where they had learned to speak the very difficult and distinctive Wenzhou dialect.

"When we were young, our father used to work in Wenzhou," one of my aunts told him.

The old man asked: "What work did your father do?"

"He was Magistrate of Yongjia District Qin Leping."

Upon hearing this, the old man held up both his thumbs and repeated, "An honorable man! An honorable man!"

From Wenzhou, Grandfather and his family returned to live in Hangzhou. Then as now, the most convenient way was to take a boat to Shanghai, then proceed to the provincial capital. While in Shanghai, Grandfather became enamored of a young girl who had been sold by her parents to work as a maid. Grandmother was aware of his feelings and, despite her education and her relatively modern outlook, the influence of traditional Chinese culture was such that she considered it her duty to buy the maid's freedom, then present her to Grandfather as a concubine. But the action broke her heart.

The month after Grandfather's dismissal, the governor informed the court that the tax deficiency had been made good and asked for Grandfather's reinstatement. It is not clear how Grandfather had been able to raise the funds. Perhaps he obtained a loan from one of the newly established native banks.

But while dismissal had been so swift, reinstatement was to take many months. Grandfather had first to be received in imperial audience to be formally reinstated as an expectant magistrate, and then to join the ranks of all the other expectant magistrates to await another opening.

Grandfather's reinstatement, approved in July 1904, was not formalized until November 9, when he was received in imperial audience again in Peking on the arrangement of the Ministry of Personnel.

After the audience, an imperial edict was issued approving the reinstatement of "the former Expectant Magistrate Qin Guojun," and sending him back to Zhejiang.[14]

The following month, on December 10, Grandfather was received in imperial audience yet again, and the recommendation made by Governor Ren two years before was finally acted on. He was elevated to magistrate of an independent department. Still, while promoted in theory, he was without a substantive post.

Exactly what Grandfather did during 1905 and 1906 is unclear. In all likelihood, he served in various districts in an acting capacity.

Depression and emotional strain took its toll on Grandmother and, in February 1905, she died at the age of fifty-six. My father told me that when his mother was on her deathbed, he tried to keep her mouth open in the hope that she would be able to continue breathing, and that she, in her death agony, almost bit his fingers off. In addition, he kept one hand over her head to prevent her soul from leaving her body.

This was a critical time for China. The occupation of Peking by foreign troops in 1900 had shocked the Qing court into action. Many Chinese were convinced that they faced national annihilation. The Qing dynasty finally recognized the need for reform and the empress dowager, while keeping the reins of power, began to implement the reform program her nephew had attempted to put in place in 1898. Even the age-old system of examinations was abolished in 1905. Students were sent abroad to study and a cabinet was formed.

But while the Qing dynasty was seeking to reform itself, increasingly large numbers of educated people became convinced that the dynasty itself was the problem, and that the Manchus would always be willing to sell out Chinese interests if it was to their benefit. Talk of revolution was in the air, one that would not only end the power of the Manchus but would result in a republican form of government, similar to that found in many Western countries.

As events were to prove, the Qing had waited too long to start their reforms. Moreover, the revolutionaries fed on the reforms, with each change being seen as not sufficiently far-reaching. Ironically, students sent abroad by the government returned with revolutionary ideas of democracy and republicanism and sought to overthrow the dynasty rather than to preserve it.

In Zhejiang province, illegal societies were formed in the early

391

1900s and became increasingly well organized. One of the most outstanding revolutionary leaders of the time was a Zhejiang woman named Qiu Jin, who had studied in Japan. After returning to China in 1906, she became an activist in an underground revolutionary society and founded a newspaper for women. Early in 1907, she returned to Shaoxing, her hometown, and made that her base. She became the head of the Datong Normal School, a center of revolutionary activities. She expanded the scope of the school by setting up a physical-education association in Zhuji District.

At about the same time, in late 1906 or early 1907, Grandfather was given the post of acting magistrate in Zhuji District. Just what role Grandfather played in the suppression of revolutionary activities there is unclear. He may have been totally unaware of the presence in his district of the woman revolutionary.

In any event, in the spring of 1907, he was temporarily transferred to other duties. At that time, several provinces were struck by natural disasters and Grandfather was assigned to work on famine relief. He traveled from city to city, primarily in Hubei province, seeing to the shipment of foodstuffs from other provinces, arranging for payment and transportation as well as inspecting the grain. On one occasion, he had to personally borrow 2,000 taels of silver from a native bank to meet expenses, and an urgent appeal was sent to Nanking for funds. On another occasion, he reported that six thousand bags of rice kept in storage awaiting transportation were rotting away as procedures were too rigid and rice scheduled to be placed on one ship could not be transferred onto another.[15]

For his contribution to the relief efforts, Grandfather earned another promotion, this time to subprefect, and was entitled to wear an azure-colored button in his headdress as a special honor.

From Hubei, Grandfather returned to Zhejiang. There, he was transferred to Jiaxing, where he was given his first permanent posting, that of district magistrate of Xiushui, where he arrived on July 17. He narrowly missed the July 13 arrest and execution of Qiu Jin, who had been plotting to stage an uprising in Shaoxing. She is today honored in both Taiwan and mainland China as a martyr to the revolutionary cause.

Grandfather spent three years in Jiaxing, officially described as an "important post" whose characteristics were "frequented, troublesome and difficult"; that is to say, it was an important transportation hub, presented many problems and was hard to administer.

One of the most serious problems in Jiaxing was banditry. The main trouble spot was a thriving town named Puyuan. At one time, a string of thirteen shops was held up. On another occasion, bandits spent hours carrying off load after load of merchandise from a shop on the main street. Even missionaries were not immune. Finally, Grandfather arranged to have gunboats and soldiers sent to Puyuan and put an end to the rash of robberies.

About the time of Grandfather's arrival in Jiaxing, the area suddenly suffered from an infestation of worms, which ruined what had been a promising rice crop. One September Sunday, a large crowd of farmers gathered outside the prefect's office demanding assistance. The prefect called in Grandfather and another district magistrate for help, and eventually the crowd dispersed. Such was the damage done by the worms that the government had to petition the court for a reduction in taxes.

In January 1908, rioting erupted in Tongxiang, another district in Jiaxing, as a result of a combination of high taxes and poor harvests. But a newspaper report said Xiushui was calm because Grandfather had handled matters well. Perhaps it was just because Grandfather desisted from heavy-handed methods of collecting taxes that he soon found himself in trouble. In March 1910, the Zhejiang governor submitted a memorial reporting delinquent officials who had fallen short by 10 percent or more of their tax obligations for 1909. Grandfather had fallen short by between 30 to 50 percent in the three categories of taxes for which he was responsible. For this, he was penalized, though not dismissed.[16]

The job of district magistrate included some pleasant activities. In the spring of 1909, Grandfather submitted a petition asking that "a woman of chastity, Madame Chi Shen," be honored. Her husband had died while a young man and the widowed Madame Chi had refrained from remarrying, taken in needlework to do at home and succeeded in raising her children single-handed. Moreover, she even managed to put some money aside from time to time and, after twenty years, had accumulated substantial savings.

While Grandfather was district magistrate, Madame Chi donated land valued at over a thousand taels of silver for the construction of a nursery. Grandfather felt that such an act of merit, coming from a virtuous widow, should not go unacknowledged. After her family background was investigated and a record prepared listing her ancestors for the last three generations, the provincial governor endorsed the proposal and submitted it to the imperial court in Peking, formally asking for approval for an arch to be built in her honor inscribed with the words "A Fondness For Charity." Three weeks later, permission from the court was granted.

A district magistrate had to resolve even such mundane matters as common brawling and fistfights. On one occasion, a fight broke out in a restaurant between some soldiers and the proprietor. "One onlooker was cut on the head and two soldiers were arrested," a newspaper account said. "The civil magistrate, who is a man of considerable ability and popular with all the people, settled the case without interference from the military authorities."[17]

Grandfather's tour in Jiaxing coincided with the implementation of the Qing dynasty's reform program. One important element was the control of opium. As part of a plan to gradually eradicate opium smoking, it had been decided that the drug could be sold only by licensed opium dealers, and the quantity that could be sold at any one time was controlled. A tax had been imposed on the prepared opium. The customers, too, were limited to people who were already habitual smokers. In this way, it was hoped, the number of addicts would decrease over time. In the effort to control the distribution of opium, Jiaxing was one of the most successful cities in the nation.

As China moved to enter the twentieth century, symbols of modernity began to appear. The railway connecting Hangzhou and Jiaxing began operating in March 1909. That year, the telegraph, too, finally reached Jiaxing. And as part of the natural development of Jiaxing, a chamber of commerce appeared, which worked closely with the government.

Another important development in the Qing court's attempts at reform was the formation of a National Assembly in the capital and of provincial and local assemblies elsewhere. Consisting primarily of people of some standing in the community, the assemblies were initially meant to be advisory bodies, but they became increasingly powerful. They regularly received copies of government documents and were consulted on policy or personnel changes and they even initiated proposals.

One of the most significant reforms was the recruitment of professional troops, a far cry from the untrained dregs of society that made up earlier Chinese armies. In the spring of 1907, a drill was held in Jiaxing by these new soldiers. Grandfather, who arrived at the parade ground borne on a sedan chair, was one of the civil officials present to view the exercise.

"Four hundred soldiers in dark uniforms with red shoulder straps, black caps and foreign leather shoes, the officers in navy blue uniforms with red stripes on pantaloons, red shoulder straps and gold-trimmed caps, presented quite a smart appearance," an eyewitness reported. "The battalion drill was on the whole creditable, though some of the soldiers were not quite up to a few of the movements." In conclusion, the report said: "No one viewing this drill could fail to see the advance that China is making along these lines. . . . We understand that the military authorities in the provincial capital are sending these troops to a number of places in the province to show the people what China is doing. It will serve to stir up patriotism and is an evidence of what the Chinese might do if they had proper leaders."[18]

Alas for the Manchus, this reform, like the sending of students overseas, ended up working against them. The professional armies became one of the main forces in the republican movement, especially in Zhejiang.

The goal of the administrative reforms was ultimately to set up a constitutional monarchy, with the provinces enjoying a high degree of autonomy. To pave the way for this, modern schools were established, including colleges of law and government, which were meant to turn out officials properly trained in law. In the past, magistrates had dispensed justice without benefit of any formal legal training. In Zhejiang, a College of Law and Government was set up in Hangzhou. Grandfather sent both his sons there, my father and his older brother. My uncle Lianyuan graduated in 1911 and my father in 1912, the year the Republic was proclaimed.

Grandfather, who had worked as commissioner for foreign affairs, continued to maintain good relations with missionaries, diplomats and others, though Jiaxing had a foreign community of only about twenty people. Grandfather was present at the wedding of a Scotswoman, a teacher at Miss Jewel's Music School in Shanghai, and an American missionary from the Presbyterian Mission Press. The ceremony, attended by Chinese officials as well as a considerable foreign contingent from Shanghai, including the American consul, was held in the compound of the Imperial Maritime Customs, since the bride's father was deputy commissioner of customs. (Foreigners were hired toward the end of the dynasty to run the customs service to see that foreigners obeyed trade regulations.) As the *North China Herald* observed, the Chinese officials "entered heartily into the spirit of the occasion though they could not understand English."[19]

In the fall of 1909, Governor Zeng Yun, who had been recently transferred to Zhejiang, recommended that Grandfather head the strategic district of Huangyan, a post that had been vacant for many months.

In asserting that Grandfather was the appropriate candidate, Governor Zeng said, "There are no unfinished court cases or any unarrested robbers in his jurisdiction." The case, as usual, was referred to the Board of Personnel for discussion, but there it ran into a hitch. The board said that Huangyan was an important post and regulations were that only someone with three years' experience could fill that vacancy. Since Grandfather did not have three years' experience as a full district magistrate and since he had not paid to have this requirement waived, the governor's request for him was turned down.

The following year, Governor Zeng filed a report on the officials within his jurisdiction. He divided all the provincial officials into three categories: Those who were guilty of serious wrongdoing and warranted permanent dismissal, those who ought to be dismissed but could be given another chance and a third group of outstanding officials who merited recommendation and promotion.

Topping the list of outstanding officials was Qin Guojun, whom the governor described as "kind and benevolent as a teacher, who sees the commoners as his own children, who manages all the new policies and succeeds in raising large amounts of funds, and imposes clear discipline."

In response, an imperial edict said that "good officials such as District Magistrate Qin Guojun who have performed well and properly administer their districts deserve rewards" while others should be dismissed.[20]

Three months later, Governor Zeng recommended that Grandfather be named to head the Dinghai Independent Subprefecture. Dinghai, an island that was part of an archipelago, was categorized as an "important" post. It was an antipirate stronghold, and foreign gunboats moving north toward the capital would have to pass it.

The governor pointed out that Grandfather had been an expectant subprefect for six years, so he would be filling a substantive position for which he was already qualified.[21]

This time, Governor Zeng's request was granted. However, Grand-father was not in his new post for long. In the autumn of the following year, he was asked to take over temporarily the position of subprefect of Haining, not far from Hangzhou.

But before he went, an uprising broke out in Wuhan, which signaled the outbreak of a nationwide revolution against the Qing dynasty. Gradually, political activists in province after province seized local power and declared their independence from Peking.

Governor Zeng was under pressure to declare Zhejiang's independence, but he refused. At two o'clock on the morning of November 5, the smartly trained new army in Zhejiang revolted, moving from its camps and marching into the city. The provincial capital was captured without bloodshed. Governor Zeng and his family were put under arrest and escorted from the province. A new provincial government was set up, which published a declaration of independence, denouncing Manchu rule and promising that officials could keep their posts if they gave allegiance to the new regime.

Grandfather had not arrived in Haining until some time in late October. He was in office for less than half a month before the revolutionaries descended on Haining on November 7. A family council was held and it was decided to surrender. A bedsheet was hung outside the government office. When the revolutionaries entered, Grandfather received them dressed in his official robes.

To his surprise, they showed him much courtesy. Then he noticed that his youngest son, Liankui, was waving to some of the revolutionary leaders. It turned out that Liankui, my father, was friendly with the leaders and had given some of the revolutionaries shelter in Grandfather's government office when troops were looking for them.

With the dynasty at an end, Grandfather went to live in Shanghai. But, sick and in his sixtieth year, he died of asthma on January 21, 1912. That same month, Liankui, my father, graduated from the Zhejiang College of Law and Government. And in Nanking, Dr. Sun Yatsen was sworn in as provisional president of the newly proclaimed Republic of China. A new era was dawning in China and, within my family, my father was establishing himself in the newly created profession of lawyer.

CHAPTER TWENTY-FIVE

Father: Legal Pioneer Qin Liankui

"Two years ago, one often saw an old man on the streets of Hong Kong and Kowloon. He was of a withered appearance, thin and emaciated. He wore a Chinese robe and a felt hat, and carried a rattan basket. He walked by himself, looking lonely and desolate. This was the famous Shanghai lawyer Qin Liankui."

The above account appeared in a Hong Kong magazine in 1960.[1] It was an accurate portrayal of the man I knew as Father, a man who was eccentric, unhappy, sick, querulous and, toward the end, paranoid. This was almost the only side of him I knew; certainly the side I remember most vividly. He was in his fifties when I was born and, though I am told that he doted on me when I was an infant, my only clear memories of him are of an old man who rarely spoke to his children, did not even know if they went to school and was obsessed with his own numerous physical ailments and the looming shadow of death.

But as the magazine article showed, there was much more to Father than the pale shadow that I had seen. The author said that when Father was a practicing lawyer, he "was extremely intelligent and was a man of honor and righteousness. Since China established the system of lawyers, his license was No. 7; he was one of the most senior of registered lawyers."

I started piecing together my father's life more than two decades after his death in January 1959. Much of my information came from my older brothers and sisters, as well as from my mother. But since Father was twenty-eight years older than she, there was much of his early life that even she did not know. Eventually, largely by reading old newspapers dating back to 1912, I was able to fill in the gaps.

Qin Liankui was born in 1888, probably in Hangzhou, the seventh and last child of my grandparents. Because Grandfather worked in different places in Zhejiang province, my father grew up speaking the Hangzhou and Wenzhou dialects fluently. Although Wuxi was his ancestral home, he never lived there and did not speak its local tongue.

My grandparents' first five children were girls, and so the two boys who followed were the recipients of special parental love. If the family was traveling, care was taken that the two sons were not on the same boat; if an accident occurred, one of them would thus remain to continue the family line. Grandmother used to dress her older son as a scholar and my father as a soldier. As a boy, Father was trained to climb hills with weights attached to his shoes so that, when the weights were removed, he would fly through the streets, easily outstripping other pedestrians. This was an ability that stayed with him almost to the end of his life, when he used to march determinedly along the sidewalks of Hong Kong, wielding a cane, seeking to assuage the abdominal pains that tortured him.

Father's early education was supervised by Grandmother, who taught him martial arts in addition to the classics and history. But when Father was eight years old, Grandmother died. From then on, his oldest sister, Peilan, seventeen years his senior, ran the household and became a substitute mother to him. But the sister to whom he was closest was Feiqing, the fifth daughter and, by all accounts, the most able.

When Father was a teen-ager, Grandfather began to pave the way for him to follow in his footsteps and become an official of the Qing dynasty. To this end, Grandfather purchased for him various official titles. And Grandfather sent him to the newly established College of Law and Government in Hangzhou, which had been set up to develop a corps of modern legal specialists to staff the new courts.

It was in school that Father met his political mentor, a man named Xu Dafu who was a member of an anti-Manchu secret society and the brother of one of Father's teachers. Through him Father became so involved with political activists in Zhejiang that he offered men wanted on sedition charges shelter in Grandfather's house, without the old man's knowledge. That is why, from very early times, Father had extremely good relations with revolutionaries under the leadership of Dr. Sun Yatsen, revered as the father of modern China.

At the three-year college, he studied ethics, Qing-dynasty law, the history of Chinese and foreign legislation, constitutional law, administrative law, civil law, criminal law, commercial law, legal procedure, international law and prison administration. In addition, he obtained a separate degree in jurisprudence. In January 1912 he graduated.

The same month, Dr. Sun Yatsen had been proclaimed provisional president of the Republic of China, with its capital in Nanking, while the Qing court in Peking was negotiating the terms for the abdication of the child emperor, Xuantong. Terms were finally reached the following month, and the six-year-old emperor, who in later life became known as Henry Puyi, formally abdicated, ending several thousand years of dynastic rule in China. As part of the agreement, Dr. Sun agreed to be replaced as provisional president by Yuan Shikai, a militarist and leading official of the Qing dynasty. Though there was widespread distrust of Yuan, Dr. Sun felt that since Yuan had pledged to abide by the republican constitution being drafted, his power would not be unfettered.

The fall of the Manchu dynasty coincided with attempts to modernize the Chinese legal system and bring it more into line with those of Western democracies. New courts, introduced in 1910, removed judicial functions from the district magistrate. But the abandonment of long-established practices inevitably brought new problems, and in 1912, when Father graduated from law school, the situation was quite confused.

Things were especially complicated in cosmopolitan Shanghai, where Father set up practice, because of the large foreign presence there. Of the roughly two million residents, only little more than half were governed by the Chinese authorities, the rest by foreigners. Foreigners had imposed the concept of extraterritoriality on China through a series of what the Chinese called "unequal treaties." The heart of the city was the International Settlement, formed in the 1860s when the British and American settlements merged. It was run by the consuls of major foreign powers, primarily Britain, the United States and Japan. In addition, the French had their own enclave, known as the French Concession. Chinese governmental control existed only in the Chinese section of Shanghai and neighboring counties. This offended Chinese sensitivities but because the foreign-administered areas of Shanghai were far better run than the rest of the city, many Chinese preferred to live there.

In the International Settlement, a unique legal institution had developed, known as the International Mixed Court, in which a deputy of the Shanghai magistrate shared the bench with foreign assessors. In theory it was a Chinese court administering Chinese law, but foreign consuls jointly adjudicated cases arising within the settlement or those involving foreign interests. This created an atmosphere in which lawyers from all over the world developed a thriving practice, even to the extent of establishing their own bar associations. The Americans, for instance, operated a Far East American Bar Association in Shanghai. But Chinese lawyers were not granted right of audience in the Mixed Court.[2]

In November 1911, Shanghai had been captured by revolutionaries under Chen Qimei, whom Father had known in Zhejiang. Chen Qimei led a successful attack on the Jiangnan Arsenal, a key installation, and became military governor of Shanghai. The Mixed Court was temporarily closed. The foreign consuls made use of this period of confusion to consolidate their control. From then on, Chinese magistrates were to act "under the guidance of and in concert with the assessors." And it was decided that even civil cases *not* involving foreigners would be tried in the presence of foreign assessors. There was no properly constituted Chinese authority to effectively oppose these measures, and so the International Mixed Court became, in effect, an appendage of the government of the International Settlement. This was known as the Shanghai Municipal Council and consisted *only* of foreigners. The Mixed Court, however, did not have the authority to enforce capital punishment. Capital cases were invariably transferred to Chinese courts.

Even in the Chinese Quarter, the judicial system was in a state of flux. The confusion stemming from the change-over from a monarchy to a republican system of government was compounded by the shifting fortunes of local warlords, who paid only lip service to the central authorities. The Ministry of Justice worked frantically to draft and promulgate new legislation, but it was often unclear what laws were in force in which locality at any particular time.

Many self-proclaimed lawyers had little or no legal training, having obtained their degrees from "diploma mills" that offered no courses. Others were ostensibly graduates of foreign institutions, though they had never been abroad; they had studied law through correspondence courses.

In this chaotic atmosphere Father set up practice. The arrival on the scene of Lawyer Qin Liankui, barely twenty-three years old, was disclosed in an announcement in the Shanghai newspaper *Shun Pao* on March 27, 1912. The advertisement, on an inside page, was repeated every other day for two weeks and was followed two months later by a bold announcement of a similar nature, this time on the front page, which appeared for seven days in a row.

In the announcement, Father declared that he was "qualified to practice law in Shanghai and the provinces of Jiangsu and Zhejiang, to act as either the defending or prosecuting attorney, to handle contracts, deal in purchase, sale or rental of property and to represent local or foreign clients, in the Settlements or the Chinese Quarter."

As a newcomer to Shanghai, Father found it useful to continue proclaiming his presence. In August, he launched a series of announcements to inform potential clients that his address remained unchanged. Then, in November, another barrage appeared, this time to proclaim that he had moved.

Meanwhile, in September, the Ministry of Justice had issued provisional regulations governing the registration of lawyers. The regulations were relatively general but provided that a major role be played by local bar associations. "The president of a bar association," one regulation said, "shall report at once to the District Court of the locality the name of the lawyer admitted to the association and the date of his admission." Shortly after, the ministry began to issue official certificates to qualified lawyers. Father's certificate was dated January 22, 1913.

These developments evidently galvanized Father and other lawyers in Shanghai into action. On February 27, 1913, an announcement of the formation of the Shanghai Bar Association appeared in *Shun Pao*.

On March 12, another notice appeared, which declared that the inaugural meeting of the Shanghai Bar Association had been held ten days previously. Only three names appeared in that announcement. One was that of the association's first president, Ding Rong, a vice-chairman of the National Association of Lawyers. Father and another man were designated as the people responsible for collecting fees from new members.

Exactly how many members the bar association started with is unknown. Father's bar-association membership card indicates he was the sixteenth member to be admitted. A membership list for 1918 carried the names of 256 men, of whom only 4 were founding members. The association was quasi-official in nature, since it in effect had the authority to decide who could or could not practice law within its jurisdiction, and a representative of the local prosecutor's office was entitled to be present at meetings.[3]

The atmosphere in Shanghai continued to be marked by turmoil. Ten days after the announcement of the setting up of the bar association, a leading political figure, Song Jiaoren, was assassinated in Shanghai. The thirty-year-old Song had drafted the Provisional Constitution under which President Yuan Shikai was ruling, and had been designated by Sun Yatsen as the leader of the Kuomintang, the newly formed revolutionary party. The youthful Song had been the most likely candidate to become premier in a new government, and so President Yuan had arranged for his assassination at the Shanghai Railway Station just as he was about to journey to Peking.

The murder of Song Jiaoren convinced Sun Yatsen and other revolutionaries that they had been betrayed by President Yuan, and so, in 1913, a Second Revolution was launched in Shanghai, with the aim of toppling the man Sun Yatsen had supported only a few months previously. An attack on the Jiangnan Arsenal in Shanghai was again led by Chen Qimei, who had been forced to resign as military governor by President Yuan. But the Chinese Navy sided with Yuan, and the attempt proved abortive.

Father gradually built up his legal practice. Still idealistic, he was willing to challenge the martial-law administrators of Shanghai, whose authority ultimately stemmed from President Yuan Shikai in Peking. In August 1913, he and the new president of the Shanghai Bar Association, Chen Zemin, accused Chief of Police Mu Xiangyao of having exceeded his authority in executing five robbers. Citing Article 9 of the Martial Law Code, the two lawyers argued that martial law applied only to military cases, and that the robbers should have been dealt with under civilian law. Police Chief Mu had wrongly exercised the martial-law powers of the commandant, they said.

The two lawyers lodged an action against the police chief with the Shanghai Prosecutor's Office, an action that was also a criticism of the military governor for having sanctioned the executions.

The following week, a newspaper report asserted that Police Chief Mu had lodged a countersuit, accusing the two lawyers of malicious prosecution, but in a letter to the editor, the two lawyers said they had checked with the Prosecutor's Office, and discovered that no such charge had been lodged. Contemporary newspaper accounts do not make clear how this sensitive political issue was eventually resolved. But the incident appears to depict Father as a man opposed not only to the arbitrary exercise of power by a police chief but also to the increasingly dictatorial rule of Yuan Shikai in Peking.

Father's actions may well have reflected the influence that his old mentor continued to exercise over him. With the overthrow of the Qing dynasty, Xu Dafu had joined the Kuomintang and was elected to China's first parliament as one of ten members of the Senate from Zhejiang province. The new parliament, which was dominated by the Kuomintang, convened in Peking in April 1913. After Sun Yat-sen launched the Second Revolution, many members of parliament dissociated themselves from this new civil war. A hundred and forty-eight members of the Senate, including Xu Dafu, withdrew from the Kuomintang in a tactical maneuver. Yuan Shikai, after success-fully pressuring parliament to confirm him in office as president, dissolved the body at the beginning of 1914. Impotent in the face of such unconstitutional behavior, Xu Dafu and other legislators dispersed.[4]

At this time, Father was in his mid-twenties and still officially unmarried, though he had fallen in love with a lovely young Suzhou woman named Cao Yueheng, whom he had met in a high-class pleasure house. The age-old custom of patronizing courtesans was still very popular, and Father formed a liaison with Miss Cao, whose face was the shape of a watermelon seed, like classical Chinese beau-ties. Father had known her mother, and had watched her grow up. At the time, he was just beginning his legal career and could not afford to monopolize her services. By the time he could, she had given birth to a daughter by another man. But so great was his love for her that he took her, her child and her mother into his household. He brought up the child as his own, and named her Jiaxiu. Even-tually, Miss Cao bore him six children, one of whom died in infancy.

Still, in accordance with prevailing practice, it was necessary for him to take a formal wife. It was suggested that Father marry Xu Dafu's younger sister, Xu Peihua, and Father, out of respect for his former teacher, agreed. They were married on April 20, 1914. Father had not seen his bride before the wedding night and, after the marriage, avoided seeing her too often. Not only was she pock-marked, but she also had extremely small eyes; her nickname within the family was "Tiny Eyes." Even after the formal marriage, he did not live with her, preferring to spend his nights with the lovely Cao Yueheng. Miss Cao was, in a real sense, his wife, though he could never acknowledge her as such.

To ease the loneliness of Tiny Eyes, Father gave her Cao Yue-heng's first son, a baby boy named Ah Xiang, to take care of. Unfortunately, Ah Xiang died at the age of four and Tiny Eyes was distraught. One day, she informed Father that she intended to commit suicide. He rushed to her home, where she told him that she had already taken poison. However, she said, she had an antidote. If he would agree to her terms she would take the antidote. If not, she would die before his eyes. Father gave in.

Her demand was simple: Father should stay with her until she became pregnant. He stayed and she conceived, and gave birth to a boy, whom she named Reborn, in memory of Ah Xiang. Tragically, Reborn, too, did not survive long, and Tiny Eyes resumed her lonely existence. She died in 1932, at the age of thirty-nine.

In 1914, Chinese lawyers were finally admitted to the Mixed Court. Father applied for, and was granted, right of audience. He could appear in the Mixed Court, the Shanghai District Court and the branch court at Zhabei as well as the High Court of Jiangsu province and the Supreme Court in Peking.

In 1916, Shanghai was shocked by another political assassination, this time of the revolutionary Chen Qimei. The former military governor had returned to Shanghai to organize activities against Yuan, who was becoming more and more unpopular, thanks in part to his attempt to revive the monarchy by proclaiming himself emperor in January: Yuan had been forced to reverse the decision in the face of overwhelming opposition. Chen Qimei had lived in the French Concession, beyond the reach of the Chinese police, and had been surrounded by bodyguards. But Yuan's agents, apparently with the assistance of someone within Chen's organization, obtained access to his house on the pretext of requiring his signature for a loan involving a mining corporation, the Hong Fong Company, and gunned him down. Six suspects were arrested by the Annamese police force and tried in the French Mixed Court. Two were convicted on the murder charge, one was found not guilty and the three others given minor sentences on lesser charges.

Because the punishment to be meted out was beyond the jurisdiction of the French court, the two convicted prisoners, Xu Guolin and Su Zhenfang, were handed over to the Chinese authorities "for punishment in accordance with the gravity of their crime." Thus, a new trial was scheduled in the Shanghai District Court.

The trial was almost a formality: It was generally assumed that the two men were guilty, since they had already been convicted. Nonetheless, they were assigned a defense attorney under the system of voluntary legal assistance in effect at the time. Ironically, of all the practicing lawyers in Shanghai, Father was selected to defend the two suspects accused of having murdered his friend.

However, Father put up the best defense possible. On behalf of Defendant Xu, Father said that although he was the owner of the Hong Fong Company, his purpose in setting up the company was purely commercial and he was not necessarily aware of the murder plot. Father conceded that his client had been present and, after the shooting, had jumped into his car and attempted to escape. But this action, he said, could be attributed to fear and panic, not guilt.

As to Defendant Su Zhenfang, the French court had convicted him in part on the strength of a confession he had signed. However, in the Shanghai District Court, Su repudiated this confession, and Father set about casting doubt on the remaining evidence, primarily the testimony of an eyewitness. He said that Su, who had visited the Hong Fong Company the day after the assassination, had been arrested because he was tall, and a witness had said that one of the killers was "a tall man." But, Father said, another witness had already identified the "tall man" as someone else.

In the midst of the murder trial, a lawyer representing Chen's widow rose to lodge a civil complaint. He demanded that Chen's killers be responsible for Chen's debts, which amounted to 350,000 dollars, adding that the creditors were pressing the widow for payment.

Father objected to the lawyer's demand, arguing that Chen's physical being had suffered but his estate was undamaged. Father and the other lawyer engaged in debate for over an hour before the court ordered an adjournment. The two suspects requested that the court assign Father to represent them also in the civil claims, but the judge said he lacked such authority. Father then volunteered his services.

As was expected, the court convicted both defendants, sentencing Xu to death and Su to fifteen years in prison. Both appealed and their sentences were subsequently reduced, with the former being given life imprisonment and the latter twelve years. Throughout the trial, there was no direct reference to the instigator of the political crime, President Yuan, who had died from natural causes the month after Chen's assassination.

The death of Yuan Shikai marked the beginning of the warlord period, when Peking was under the control of a succession of militarists who often received little more than lip service from local strongmen in the provinces. The man who assumed power in Peking was Premier Tuan Qirui. To legitimize his power, Premier Tuan recalled the parliament illegally abolished by President Yuan. This session of parliament fared no better than the first, for it was dissolved in June 1917, amid political upheavals that erupted when a conservative general attempted to restore the Manchu emperor. A rump parliament convened in Canton and established a military government headed by Sun Yatsen.

Meanwhile, in Shanghai, Father's practice had been steadily growing. But many legal battles were fought in the pages of newspapers as well as in the courtroom. In the autumn of 1922, for instance, a lawyer named Wang Huanqie announced that certain properties could not be disposed of without the consent of his client, Madame Xu Wang, a widow. Father put an announcement of his own in the papers disputing this claim, saying that he represented two brothers of the deceased, and that Lawyer Wang's original announcement appeared to infringe on the rights of the brothers and other relatives.

Gradually, both the government and the legal profession acquired greater sophistication. Lawyers were no longer authorized to appear in courts outside the jurisdiction of the bar association of which they were members. In addition, in 1919, the Ministry of Justice reviewed the qualifications of all the lawyers in Jiangsu province, of which Shanghai was a part, and asked all four to five hundred of them to be reexamined. The only exceptions were those who had had three years' experience as a judge. By the end of that year, a National Union of Bar Associations was inaugurated in Peking.

Father was active in the Shanghai Bar Association and was repeatedly elected to serve on its management committee. The association jealously guarded its prerogatives, objecting whenever someone who was not a member appeared in court in violation of Ministry of Justice regulations.

However, the bar association itself had problems. Not only was it riven by factions, such as foreign-educated versus Chinese-educated lawyers or those from one province vis-à-vis those from another province, but so many of its members did not bother to attend meetings that on many occasions, it could not hold valid meetings for lack of a quorum: The association's charter stipulated that at

407

least half the members had to be present to make up a quorum. On at least one occasion, outside help was sought. In March 1925, for example, a meeting for the election of officers was four short of a quorum. Four members arrived late, but by then four others had left. Father and three other leaders of the association decided to go ahead with the elections. Afterward the association wrote to the Supreme Court to ask if, under the circumstances, the results were valid. The answer was yes. In time, the association's bylaws were changed, reducing the necessary quorum from one half to one third of the membership. There was still much difficulty in mustering sufficient members to hold a valid meeting.

Despite the factionalism within the association, there was one issue on which almost all its members agreed: terminating the judicial powers enjoyed by foreigners in Shanghai. While the last decades of the Qing dynasty had witnessed the ever-increasing encroachment of foreign powers, the republican era was marked by incessant efforts to roll back the foreign tide. In 1918, Father was named to serve on a nine-member committee formed to look into the issue, which was inextricably linked with the politically sensitive question of extraterritoriality. The presence of foreign courts on Chinese soil was seen as a national insult, and rallied not only lawyers but also students, workers and businessmen. The successful conclusion of the First World War, which China had entered on the Allied side, fostered hope that the foreign powers would give up their extraterritorial rights. But this was not to be. Instead, the Paris Peace Conference decided to transfer Germany's rights in Shandong province to Japan, causing the eruption of nationwide student demonstrations known as the May Fourth Movement of 1919. The Shanghai Bar Association gave its support to the student protest.

At every opportunity, the bar association pressed for action on the Mixed Court. At a judicial conference in September 1922, the association introduced a resolution calling for the unconditional restoration to China of the administration of the Mixed Court. It pointed out that the administration of the Mixed Court by foreign consuls was not provided for in any treaty, and said that Chinese magistrates merely put their signatures to decisions arrived at by the assessors. It called for immediate action to be taken to "preserve the rights of the country."

While the bar association was seeking to purge Chinese courts of foreign domination, the country itself continued to be wracked by factional strife, as northern militarists attempted to gain control of the capital and forge alliances with local despots. In August 1922, the old parliament was once again called into session in Peking in a move to achieve peaceful unification of the country. Once again, a military strongman desired the legitimacy that parliament could confer on him. The strongman this time was Cao Kun, who wished parliament to elect him president. Xu Dafu, now Father's brother-in-law, again took part as a delegate. Pressure was brought to bear on the parliamentarians to vote for Cao Kun, but several hundred, unwilling to support his move, fled south. Their attempt to set up a rival parliament in Shanghai collapsed and, ultimately, some of them succumbed to Cao Kun's blandishments and returned to Peking to help vote him into office. Xu Dafu remained in the south, ending his days in political obscurity, living with his sister in Suzhou. It appears likely that Father joined him in Peking in 1923 and, when attempts to foil Cao Kun failed, fled with him to Shanghai. As a result of these early experiences, Father in later life took pains to stay away from politics and refused all offers of government posts. He warned his children, too, not to get involved in politics.

The campaign for the restoration of the Mixed Court went on desultorily for years without much progress. The foreign powers, while agreeing in principle to hold negotiations on the issue, countered by calling for talks on other problems, such as the enlargement and improvement of the port and the extension of the boundaries of the International Settlement. However, in 1925, an event occurred that provided the impetus necessary for the resolution of the issue. That year, Japanese-owned textile mills in Shanghai were hit by a wave of strikes, in one of which a Chinese worker was killed by a Japanese foreman. That triggered a demonstration by university students on May 30. Under orders from their foreign superiors, the police in the International Settlement, turbaned Sikhs and Chinese, opened fire on the students, killing eleven of them. This incident precipitated a series of protests by students, workers and merchants that paralyzed Shanghai for months and quickly spread to other cities. Known to history as the May Thirtieth Movement, it led to demands not only for the punishment of those responsible for the shooting but for the resolution of the underlying causes of discontent, in particular, foreign domination of the Mixed Court and foreign monopoly over the running of the International Settlement.

Inevitably, foreign lawyers resisted the restoration of the Mixed

Court's administration to China. A Committee of Foreign Lawyers was formed to safeguard their interests. The Far Eastern American Bar Association in Shanghai issued a strongly worded statement opposing the return of the Mixed Court to provincial authorities, asserting that the provincial government was no more than a military regime led by Marshal Sun Quanfang. "During the last two years," the statement said, "the so-called Kiangsu provincial authorities have changed four times with kaleidoscopic rapidity. Marshal Sun has only been in power for a short while, and, if newspaper reports are to be believed, it is probable that he will soon be succeeded by some other general who desires to control the wealthy Chinese territory surrounding the International Settlement of Shanghai." The American lawyers went on to say that the Chinese residents of Shanghai had greater confidence in the Mixed Court than in Chinese judicial institutions.

The statement by the American lawyers was extremely galling to Chinese sensitivities, because it contained a large kernel of truth. The local authorities were indeed not always responsive to central direction. Moreover, ever since 1921, two governments, each claiming exclusive legitimacy, functioned in China: the warlord government in Peking and the one formed by Sun Yatsen in Canton. Sun Yatsen was unsuccessful in winning the recognition of foreign powers, who continued to deal with whoever was in power in Peking. In 1921, another contender for political power had appeared in the form of the fledgling Chinese Communist party. And by 1924, the Communists and the Kuomintang had joined forces to topple the northern warlords.

On July 18, 1926, the day after the American lawyers' statement, Father and twelve other members of the Shanghai Bar Association met in urgent session. Afterward, a strong statement was issued in which the bar association not only called for the restoration of the Mixed Court to China but also declared that foreign lawyers should no longer be granted right of audience. "Foreigners are not allowed to practice in the Chinese court because they are ignorant of Chinese customs and the Chinese language," the statement said. "The use of interpreters involves the waste of too much valuable time on the part of magistrates and sometimes leads to misinterpretations." Moreover, it said that foreign lawyers who enjoyed extraterritorial rights should not be allowed to appear in court because if they misbehaved they could not be disciplined. "Are we going to conserve the interests of about a hundred foreign lawyers at the expense of justice and at the expense of the friendly relationship between Chinese and foreigners?" the Shanghai Bar Association asked.[5] Telegrams were sent to the American secretary of state, the American ambassador and the British ambassador in Peking. Meanwhile, the foreign lawyers sent a delegation to the capital to urge their ambassadors not to give in to the Chinese demands.

Spurred on by pressure from the Shanghai Bar Association and other groups, notably the Shanghai General Chamber of Commerce, the Foreign Ministry that summer successfully negotiated an agreement that provided for the replacement of the Mixed Court on January 1, 1927, by the Shanghai Provisional Court, marking one phase in the long process to bring an end to the era of foreign domination. The provisions of the agreement were meant to be temporary, as reflected in the name of the new court. Under the accord, all civil and criminal cases in the International Settlement were to be dealt with by the Shanghai Provisional Court, except for cases that involved the right of consular jurisdiction. Foreign assessors were abolished. In cases involving foreign interests, a foreign deputy could be appointed to sit with the judge, and though the deputy could record his objections, he would not be in a position to override the judge. Foreign lawyers could represent either side in cases involving foreigners. The agreement specified that the Provisional Court would function for three years and, if a final settlement was not reached by that time, its life could be extended. For the time being, at least, the issue was resolved.

The end of the Mixed Court moved China a step closer toward true independence. But it had other ramifications, including sartorial ones. Chinese judges and lawyers were required to wear special robes in court. The month after the Provisional Court was set up, a British attorney, a Mr. Covey, appeared in court before a Chinese judge, and this exchange took place:

Judge: Why are you not robed in the Chinese gown and silk?

Covey: Because I am not a Chinese lawyer.

Judge: Then I cannot hear you. . . .

Covey: Then I am to understand that because my standing as a British legal practitioner permits of my wearing the gown of a British solicitor in British courts and no other and provides that I shall not appear in any court outside my own in it or another gown, I am barred from practicing in this court. . . . I have no other alternative than to bow to Your Honor's ruling.

Covey's interpreter: May I speak to Mr. Covey's client?

Judge: No, you may not, as I cannot recognize you as an interpreter of a lawyer who is not dressed in Chinese robes.

Although Father had never lived in Wuxi and Grandfather had left it as a small boy, Father considered it his hometown. In fact, for a while, he used the Wuxi Clan School in Shanghai as his mailing address. Undoubtedly, his Wuxi connection helped to widen his circle of friends and acquaintances, from whom he obtained referrals and fresh clients. There were well over 100,000 people from Wuxi living in Shanghai, many of whom were prominent businessmen. There was in Shanghai a Wuxi Guild, whose members originated from that town. It served as a meeting place where fellow townsmen could socialize, hold meetings and exchange information. The guild served also as a hostel for visitors from Wuxi. Another service it offered was as a repository for coffins of Wuxi people, usually awaiting burial in Wuxi. After Grandfather's death in January 1912, Father had deposited his coffin with the Wuxi Guild. Although normally the guild asked its members to retrieve coffins within two years, Father did not do so for twenty-five years, while he looked for an auspicious burial site. Grandmother's body, too, lay in a coffin in a Hangzhou temple awaiting burial for thirty years.

Because of his Wuxi connection, it is not surprising that when a move began in late 1923 to establish a Wuxi Sojourners Association, Father was recruited as a founder member. The new association was different from the Wuxi Guild in that its primary purpose was not social but rather to provide assistance to Wuxi people in Shanghai and those still living in the old hometown. The association came into existence on March 16 at a meeting of the 150 promoters. The initial membership surpassed six thousand. Father acted as its legal adviser.[6]

The activities of the association included charitable works, legal aid, education and entertainment. Membership was open to all males from Wuxi over the age of twenty-one who were recommended by two members. The association set up a primary school for Wuxi children, established a shelter for the care of homeless women and children from Wuxi and published a journal.[7]

The new association's resources were sorely taxed early the next year after war broke out between the military governors of Jiangsu and Zhejiang provinces. Wuxi, in Jiangsu, was caught in the hostilities. When one of the warlord armies marched through Wuxi, leaving death and destruction in its wake, the association set up a special task force to deal with the emergency. Food and other supplies were sent to Wuxi. In addition, five to six thousand refugees were evacuated to Shanghai. In the process, one of the association's workers was shot and killed. An emotional mourning ceremony was held at which the bloody clothes of the dead man were put on display. Speeches were made by several officials of the association, including Father.

On August 27, the Wuxi Association held a general congress to mark the beginning of its second year. In a speech, Father said: "In the past, before we were organized, our fellow townsmen had nowhere to turn to when they were in trouble. Now, we can offer help whenever a situation arises. If both sides in a dispute are fellow Wuxi townsmen, the association can mediate and help resolve differences without the feelings of either side being hurt. As the legal adviser, I am willing to do whatever I can to help."

Father was active in the association for over a decade. In the summer of 1927, a banquet was held in honor of the newly appointed mayor of Wuxi, Yu Conghuan. At the time, district courts were being set up across the country and the functions of mayor and judge were being separated, but this had not yet happened in Wuxi. Father, in a speech, urged the mayor to support the principle of separation of executive and judicial powers. He said the local gentry often attempted to influence the outcome of cases, and the best way to avoid such problems was to have the judiciary truly independent.

Just about this time, the clan decided to publish the ninth edition of the family genealogy, first proposed in 1919 but repeatedly delayed for lack of funds. Announcements were placed in newspapers asking clan members to submit drafts of updated biographies, including such major changes as births, deaths and marriages. Father consented to serve as an appraiser of the information submitted and as legal consultant to the clan on the project. The clan sought to use his prestige to minimize any legal problems that might emerge as a result of the genealogy's being published. The genealogy was important because inclusion of a person's name implied his right to inheritance. Since there were Qin family members who had adopted

413

surnames of in-laws without male descendants, outsiders who had adopted Qin as their surname as the result of marriage, plus adoptions of cousins and other relatives, there were potential legal problems.

The chief editor was a scholar of distinction named Qin Dunshi, a *juren* who was the great-grandson of Qin Ying. His branch of the family had produced outstanding scholars for generations. Dunshi's son, Tongli, Father's eighth cousin, was assistant salt controller under Marshal Sun Quanfang. Father and Tongli had become very good friends. The two men were of the same age and shared similar interests, one of which was the Chinese theater. Both men were not only aficionados but were themselves trained singers. The highly stylized Peking Opera boasted beautiful costumes but was almost entirely bereft of props, often using only a table and two chairs to adorn the bare stage. There was a limited repertoire, and regular theatergoers knew all of the operas by heart. The initiated knew that a man brandishing a whip was on horseback, while one with banners sprouting from his back was a general with troops under his command. The pleasure lay not in watching the story unfold but rather in observing how an actor, through a flick of a sleeve or a shake of his head, was able to convey anger, fear or surprise. The roles included generals, scholars, clowns, women warriors and even animals, such as the popular Monkey King. Father's specialty was that of a *xiao-sheng*, or good-looking young man.

Tongli and Father shared another trait: Both were fond of beautiful women. Although Tongli had a wife and three children, he acquired and discarded concubines with considerable frequency. Several of his concubines were accomplished singers. When one of them referred to herself as "Mrs. Qin Tongli" in the newspapers, his wife was so angered that she placed an announcement in the papers declaring that "Mrs. Qin Tongli" was only a housewife and had no theatrical abilities. After that, the concubine referred to herself only as "Mrs. Qin," and Tongli's wife refrained from further public embarrassment of her husband.

Though Father did not take on additional wives or concubines, he is known to have had many mistresses, even after his formal marriage to Xu Peihua and his common-law marriage with Cao Yueheng. According to Chinese traditional values, there are four weaknesses common to men—womanizing, gambling, drinking and opium smoking. Father admitted to one of his friends that people accused him of being guilty of the first two. He drank only in moderation but was a heavy smoker, not of opium but of cigarettes, his favorite being the British-manufactured Garrick brand, of which he consumed a tin of fifty every day, so that his fingers were yellowed by nicotine. Another friend, writing about Father after his death, said that he had become sick in his later years because "he indulged too much in sensual pleasures when he was a young man."

Gambling, in all its forms, obsessed Father. He speculated in gold, currencies, stocks and bonds, went to the horse races, played Mah-Jongg, bought lottery tickets and bet on the popular jai-alai games, often until he had lost his last penny. Once, after receiving three thousand dollars in fees, he went to a casino and played roulette until he had lost all of it. So accustomed was he to a lucrative income from his law practice that he never thought it necessary to put money aside.

Actually, gambling was one way of meeting and cultivating clients, and many friendships were made at the mah-jongg table. It was at a casino that Father came to know one of the most important, and most feared, men in Shanghai, a complex man who was simultaneously head of the underworld, dealing in narcotics and prostitution among other things, and a businessman, banker and philanthropist: Du Yuesheng. It was to him that Chiang Kai-shek turned for assistance when he decided to crush the Communists in 1927, and Du Yuesheng helped him mightily, sending his men into the foreign settlements that Kuomintang troops could not enter openly. Du was a man of little formal education who, through force of personality, became the leader of the illegal secret society known as the Green Gang. Money derived from his criminal activities was channeled into legitimate businesses, and Du proved himself adept in that world as well, eventually controlling several banks and the stock exchange and serving on the boards of over a hundred companies. His friends ran the gamut of Shanghai society, and he was much sought after by politicians and business associates. One of his friends was a wealthy businessman named Zhu Rushan, who occasionally went to a casino operated by Du for a night of big-time gambling.

Zhu Rushan was also a friend of Father's. He, too, was a Peking Opera fan and amateur singer. And given Father's passion for gambling, it is not surprising that, one day, he asked to accompany Zhu Rushan to Du Yuesheng's mansion. That night, Father lost 4,000 silver dollars, a considerable sum. He paid for it with a check, then left.

According to one account of that evening's events, Du asked Zhu Rushan after Father's departure: "Who is your friend?" To which Zhu replied that he was the lawyer Qin Liankui. Du then took out the 4,000-dollar check and handed it to Zhu saying: "A lawyer makes painstaking efforts, wields the pen and has to talk endlessly. How much is he able to earn? I really do not want to win money from him. Please return the check to him on my behalf."

The next day, Zhu returned the check to Father, who at first refused to accept it. Zhu explained to him over and over: Du Yuesheng was sincere; he had nothing but respect for him. What is more, Du had an unwritten law: Money sent by him could not be refused. So Father took the check. From then on, the two men became close friends.[8] He became Du's voluntary legal adviser, devising strategies for Du for the next two decades. Of course, Du had other lawyers, but none of them were as close to him as Father. Often, Father would drop in unannounced at Du's house and stay for a meal. The two men addressed each other as "brother." Through Du's wide circle of friends, Father obtained many referrals, especially in his later years.

The death of Sun Yatsen in 1925 left the Kuomintang with no clear leader. By mid-1926, however, General Chiang Kai-shek had emerged as the military commander in chief, responsible for bringing to fruition the wishes of the deceased Sun Yatsen by unifying China through launching a Northern Expedition to quell the warlord armies.

So, while the Foreign Ministry in Peking was engaged in negotiations to abolish the Mixed Court, Chiang Kai-shek's armies were pushing northward toward Shanghai from Canton, quickly taking Changsha and, by October, capturing the central Chinese city of Wuhan. By March 1927, the Kuomintang forces were poised on the outskirts of Shanghai. The bar association had scheduled its annual spring meeting for March 20. That meeting was never held. Two days later, Kuomintang troops captured the city.

With the defeat of the old regime, which was allied with the northern warlords, the Kuomintang quickly moved to consolidate its position in the nation's largest and wealthiest city. It was welcomed by the Shanghai capitalists, who were fearful of the growing power of

416

the Communist party, which controlled the most powerful unions in the city. Chiang, too, had decided that the Communists posed an intolerable threat and, on April 12, he suddenly turned against his united front partners and launched a massacre, killing several thousand Communist party workers.

But the alliance between the business community and the Kuomintang did not last long. The Shanghai capitalists balked when Chiang's demands for large sums continued. Ultimately, though, the capitalists were cowed, for the Kuomintang, in alliance with the powerful underworld Green Gang, extorted money through kidnappings and other means. One foreign observer at the time reported that "wealthy Chinese would be arrested in their homes or mysteriously disappear from the streets. . . . Millionaires were arrested as 'Communists'!"[9]

As part of the attempt to control and milk the Shanghai capitalists to fund the Northern Expedition, the Kuomintang took over the Shanghai General Chamber of Commerce. The Shanghai branch of the Central Political Council, which exercised overall executive and legislative powers, set up a government-controlled supervisory committee to run the chamber. The Central Political Council was headed by Chiang Kai-shek himself.

The legal profession in Shanghai was another target in the campaign to bring influential bodies under the control of the Kuomintang. The first move in this direction was to set up a parallel body, known as the Shanghai Comrade Lawyers Association. Launched on March 25, days after the takeover of Shanghai, it was open only to members of the Kuomintang. The standing committee of its provisional executive committee consisted of Wen Chao, one of the founders of the Shanghai Bar Association who evidently commanded respect, and three other Kuomintang members. However, since the vast majority of the lawyers in Shanghai did not choose to join the new Kuomintang-controlled body, the party then sought to reconstitute the bar association itself.

On April 24, the association convened its delayed spring annual meeting. As was normal, a government representative was present, but this time he represented the Kuomintang. The lawyers were told that, until the association's constitution had been approved by the Nationalist government, that is, the government of the Kuomintang rather than that of Peking, the society was barred from holding regular meetings. The lawyers present decided to set up a Reorganization Committee, to which Father was elected with the most votes.

When other lawyers heard about the decision to reorganize, there was an uproar. Many called on Zhang Yipeng, who had been president of the bar association since 1917, not to yield control. Zhang wrote to the Political Council and the Prosecutor's Office for guidance. Meanwhile, a six-member Takeover Committee, including Father, was elected by the Reorganization Committee. This put Father in a delicate position. As a founder of the bar association, he undoubtedly wanted to preserve its independence. However, he was also a personal friend of many Kuomintang leaders and had a long history of supporting the Kuomintang against the northern warlords. Probably for this reason, Father declined to serve on the Takeover Committee. Then, more than a hundred and twenty members signed a letter repudiating the Reorganization Committee and asking President Zhang Yipeng to remain in charge until a formal election could be held. But when the Political Council decided that the proceedings were valid, Zhang Yipeng publicly announced his resignation as president.

The following week, the Reorganization Committee announced that a five-man standing committee had been set up to take over the bar association. Father was not part of the new leadership, which was Kuomintang-controlled.

But the Kuomintang itself was divided into left and right factions, and, in January 1927, a new government had been set up in Wuhan consisting of the Kuomintang and its Communist allies. In April, after his triumph in Shanghai, Chiang Kai-shek and other opponents of the Wuhan group proclaimed a rival government in Nanking. Counting the warlord regime in Peking, there were now three governments in China. In August, in the face of strong opposition, Chiang Kai-shek resigned. But he would reemerge the following year to continue the Northern Expedition.

His departure from the political scene was followed by the formation of a coalition Kuomintang government in Nanking. In this more relaxed atmosphere, both the General Chamber of Commerce and the bar association were able to regain some of their previous independence. At a meeting of the re-formed Shanghai Bar Association, the decision was made to abolish the posts of president and vice-president and to adopt a committee system of a fifteen-member executive committee, a three-man supervisory committee, and a three-member standing committee. In the elections, Father obtained the most votes, becoming the senior member of the executive committee as well as a standing committee member. By occupying those dual posts he became, in effect, head of the bar association. Not being a party member, he perhaps found it easier to bridge differences between the association and the party. In any event, he had apparently succeeded in easing the doubts about the Kuomintang harbored by many lawyers.

With the coming to power of the Kuomintang government, a reregistration of all lawyers was ordered, and new certificates were issued to those deemed qualified. The photograph on Father's certificate, issued on September 29, 1927, showed a thirty-nine-year-old man wearing a Chinese-style tunic over a high-collar robe buttoned on the side. His unparted hair was swept back, revealing a high forehead below which were a pair of piercing eyes, a straight nose and a firm mouth. His skin was like alabaster. There was about him a sense of purpose and determination. Father was then at the height of his career.

On the personal side, the death of his common-law wife Cao Yueheng had left six young children on his hands. Father put household matters in the hands of his mother-in-law, and several of the children were sent to Suzhou to be brought up by the old woman's other daughter, while Father continued to live the life of a carefree bachelor.

CHAPTER TWENTY-SIX

Mother: Zhaohua Enters the Picture

During the war of 1924–1925 between Jiangsu and Zhejiang, the fighting spilled over into Shanghai. The International Settlement and the French Concession were islands of tranquillity amid the general turmoil. Father's good friend Tongli wished to move his wife and children from the Chinese Quarter, but he could not very well put them together with his concubine in the French Concession. Since he and Father were so close, he did not think it an imposition to ask Father to shelter them temporarily, and Father agreed.

But Father could not take them into his own home. Because of the widespread unrest, many refugees were pouring into Shanghai, and Father had already offered his home to some other relatives. However, he arranged for them to stay for the time being in a hotel in the International Settlement.

Father had met Tongli's wife before, but this was the first time he had met their children. The oldest, Kaihua, was a boy of twelve while his sisters, Zhaohua and Wanhua, were aged eight and six. Since Father and Tongli were cousins, the children were told to call Father "Uncle."

This meeting, brief though it was, left its imprint on both Father and Zhaohua, a little girl in pigtails and bangs. To him, she was a comely young girl who was likely to grow up to be a beauty. To her, he was what a good-looking scholar should be—thin, with square shoulders, and wearing a traditional Chinese robe. But what struck her most were his personal quirks, the rapid blinking of his eyes whenever he was thinking, and his chain-smoking. He was extremely courteous, and bowed deeply to Tongli's wife, whom he called sister, upon both her arrival and her departure.

It would be years before Father and Zhaohua met again. In the meantime, he had his law practice to attend to while she still had to

420

go through school. After graduating from elementary school, she attended the British-run Besant Middle School for Girls. One of the students there was Jiaxiu, Father's oldest daughter. The two became friends and, years later, it would be Jiaxiu who would bring Father and Zhaohua together.

From Besant, Zhaohua moved to an American Baptist institution known as the Elizabeth School, after which Tongli had her transferred to the elite McTyeire School for Girls, where many of the daughters of the rich and the powerful were taught by American Methodist missionaries. Among its graduates were the famous Soong sisters: Ching-ling married Dr. Sun Yatsen, Mei-ling married Chiang Kai-shek and Ai-ling married H. H. Kung, banker, businessman and government official. It was Tongli's hope that, by attending McTyeire, his daughter would one day marry into a wealthy Shanghai family. He could not have guessed that, instead, she would become the wife of his good friend and distant cousin.

The success of the Northern Expedition in 1928 saw China unified under one government, officially proclaimed on October 10 in Nanking, and ushered in a period of impressive nation building, including the development of agriculture, industry, banking, education and railways.

Now that the country was unified, the Shanghai Bar Association was active in promoting the development of the legal system. In June 1928, it sent a proposal to the Ministry of Justice, the Supreme Court and other relevant bodies, for the setting up of the jury system. The association urged that the judiciary select the members of the jury, and that jury duty be obligatory. The smallest jury would consist of four persons, and a majority decision would be sufficient. All offenses that carried a penalty ranging from five years in prison up to capital punishment had to be tried before a jury. A special commercial-crimes court and a labor tribunal were proposed. And the bar association called for abolition of the old system in which the district magistrate served as both chief executive of a locality and judge.

Most of all, the bar association was in the forefront of the campaign to achieve a final solution to the question of foreign influence in Chinese courts. It also adopted a resolution that lawyers who were not members of the association not be allowed to practice in the Shanghai Provisional Court. This provoked a long article in the *North*

China Herald denouncing the bar association for attempting to impose a monopoly and described it as an organization controlled by "radicals." It charged that the fifteen men who made up the leadership at the time, including Father, were Kuomintang party members.

Nevertheless, the following January, the Jiangsu provincial government issued an order that any lawyer not a member of the bar association would not be allowed to practice in the Provisional Court. The order was put to the test almost immediately. On January 5, 1929, Tsah Lin-ching, a lawyer who was not an association member, appeared in the Provisional Court to represent a truck driver accused of negligent driving. The Chinese judge, citing the government order, denied him right of audience. This ruling was strongly opposed by the Dutch vice-consul, Mr. Van den Berg, who was sitting on the bench as the deputy. Van den Berg said that if Tsah withdrew from the case, so would he. Even the police prosecutor opposed the withdrawal of Tsah, and suggested that the government order was illegal. In the end, the case was indefinitely adjourned.[1]

The Mixed Court agreement of 1926 had provided that "in criminal cases which directly affect the peace and order of the International Settlement, the senior consul may appoint a deputy to sit with the judge to watch the proceedings." The difference in the authority of the judge and the deputy was defined: "The concurrence of the deputy shall not be necessary for the validity of the judgment, though he shall have the right to record his objections: He shall not, however, put any questions to the witnesses or prisoners without the consent of the judges."

On February 23, a Chinese judge was presiding over a case involving four coolies facing various charges, when a lawyer, Tsu Zuching, who had been sitting in the public gallery, suddenly injected himself into the discussions by saying that he represented the husband and father-in-law of a female complainant, both of whom wished to prosecute her for adultery. Judge Koh informed him that he had no standing, as no charge of adultery was before the court. Tsu, however, refused to be silent and argued with the judge. At that point the deputy, again the Dutch diplomat Van den Berg, intervened, but Tsu said the point at issue was of no concern to him. The judge ordered Tsu to withdraw and, when he did not comply, Deputy Van den Berg instructed the police to physically remove the lawyer from the courtroom. When the lawyer attempted to reenter the room, the police blocked him. At the conclusion of the hearing, Van den Berg endorsed the charge sheet thus:

"I suspend Mr. Tsu Zu-ching from practice before this court for a period of three months or till such time as he make a proper retraction and apology for his most improper and reprehensible conduct in court." Thus the deputy, who did not even have the authority to question witnesses without the consent of the judge, took it upon himself to suspend a lawyer from practicing. This incident shocked the Chinese legal community and added fuel to the debate on the future of the Provisional Court.

The president of the Provisional Court, Dr. He Shizhen, protested to the senior consul that his deputy had usurped the authority of the judge by suspending the lawyer. He said that until the matter was resolved, all the judges would refuse to serve with Van den Berg. He also wrote to the chief of police, Captain E.I.M. Barrett, telling him that the police officer who carried out the consular deputy's order without the consent of the judge was wrong in acting as he did. The senior consul, an American named Edwin S. Cunningham, defended the Dutch diplomat, saying that if the judge failed to discharge his duty, it was "incumbent upon the deputy" to take action. Moreover, he said that in the event of a boycott of Van den Berg, "your compatriots would be the first to suffer, as they would have to be detained in prison."

While events were unfolding in the Provisional Court, the Shanghai Bar Association added its voice to the dispute. In one strongly worded protest, it said:

"The consular deputy, Mr. Van den Berg, exceeded his rights, encroached on the judicial rights of China, and snapped his fingers in the face of the Chinese judges by doing this. This is a matter of the utmost importance." The bar association demanded the withdrawal of the Dutch diplomat and urged preparations for the appointment of Chinese judicial police.

To prevent matters from getting out of hand, arrangements were made for the lawyer, Tsu, to be present in court on March 14, when Van den Berg would lift the suspension order upon receiving an apology, thus saving face on all sides. After some preliminary discussion the Judge said: "The senior consul's deputy, Mr. Van den Berg, has been requested to cancel his order for your suspension. In future, no deputy may suspend any lawyer without the consent of the judge. I now ask for an apology because you were to blame."

423

The lawyer protested that the deputy did not have the authority to suspend anyone in the first place, but ultimately he did utter an apology. Van den Berg then withdrew the suspension order. The judge, turning to the lawyer, then said: "Everything is now settled. Your suspension is canceled. In future, you must obey the orders of the court. The police in future are not to carry out any orders in the court unless given by the judges."

But the judge was wrong. Everything was not settled. Van den Berg wanted to see the lawyer punished not only for his action in court but also for alleged threats he had made outside the courtroom to other individuals. Failing to persuade the president of the court to take action, he revived the suspension order that same afternoon.

The dispute was turning into a test between the Chinese judges, led by the president, and the foreign consuls and police. In response to Deputy Van den Berg's complaint, R. T. Bryan, the police advocate, brought three charges against Tsu. As soon as this action was taken, Van den Berg again rescinded his suspension order. But when the case came to court, the judge refused to hear it. Bryan then said: "If the learned judge refuses to hear these cases with the learned deputy, I, as a representative of the Shanghai Municipal Council, shall have no option but to request the senior consul to allow this deputy to try cases alone."

The judge responded: "If the police wish to protest they may do so, but all cases for this morning are hereby adjourned."

Van den Berg then wrote on the charge sheet: "I reserve my right to protest against the adjournment."[2]

In theory all authority was vested in the Chinese judge, but because the International Settlement was run like a foreign country, with its own government, its own police force and prison, it was difficult for the judge to prevail over a deputy. The Van den Berg saga underlined the need for the Provisional Court system to be revamped. In April 1929, the Nanking government informed foreign governments of its intention to abolish the Provisional Court at the end of the year when the three-year agreement expired.

A major weakness of the Provisional Court was its separation from the rest of the nation's judicial system. In district courts around the country, decisions could be appealed to the provincial high court and, if necessary, to the Supreme Court in the capital. The Shanghai Bar Association, in a submission in October 1929, argued forcefully that such a "three-tier" system of courts must apply to the International Settlement as well and called for this system to be instituted by the Provisional Court, even before its replacement by a wholly Chinese court.

Racing against the December 31 deadline, negotiators sought to reach an agreement, which was not signed until February 17. That agreement abolished the Shanghai Provisional Court and established a Special District Court as well as a branch of the Jiangsu Provincial High Court, from which cases could further be appealed to the Supreme Court in Nanking. The system of joint hearings, under which a foreigner shared the bench with a Chinese judge, was finally abolished. However, foreign cooperation in the administration of justice was still required, since the International Settlement still maintained its own police force. Moreover, those police were allowed to be present in court and to submit opinions to judges in cases related to police administration. The agreement provided for the right of foreign lawyers to appear in court, but only if they were certified by the Ministry of Justice.

The Provisional Court agreement marked another step forward in China's fight to rid itself of foreign dominance. But the path was tortuous. Of the major powers, only the Soviet Union voluntarily relinquished its rights in China. Negotiations with the Western countries were difficult and protracted. On April 27, 1929, the Chinese government sent identical notes to the American, British and French ministers in China expressing its desire to have restrictions on China's sovereignty removed as soon as possible. The response was unenthusiastic, but indicated a general willingness to enter into negotiations that would gradually lead to the end of extraterritoriality. The impatient Chinese made clear that, with or without agreement, they would unilaterally announce that, beginning January 1, 1930, all the old unequal treaties would be considered invalid. The foreigners attempted to minimize actual changes. The British, for instance, asserted that they were willing to agree that "January 1, 1930, should be treated as the date from which the process of gradual abolition of extraterritoriality should be regarded as having commenced in principle."

On December 28, China issued its long-expected declaration: "It is hereby decided and declared that on and after the first day of the first month of the nineteenth year of the Republic (January 1, 1930) all foreign nationals in the territory of China who are now enjoying extraterritorial privileges shall abide by the laws, ordinances and

425

regulations duly promulgated by the central and local governments of China."

But despite its ringing tones, the declaration had little impact. The Western powers chose to interpret it as an expression of intent. Indicative of the Western attitude was the American position, which was that change should be gradual, possibly involving a ten-year transition period, during which foreigners would continue to enjoy special rights in various treaty ports.

Ever since Sun Yatsen first became provisional president in 1912, he had wanted to hold a National People's Convention that would abolish all unequal treaties between China and other powers. Sun felt so strongly about this that he put it in his political will:

"For forty years, I have devoted myself to the cause of the National Revolution, the object of which is to raise China to a position of independence and equality. The experience of these forty years has convinced me that, to attain this goal, the people must be aroused and that we must associate ourselves in a common struggle with the peoples of the world who treat us as equals. The Revolution has not yet been successfully concluded. Let all our comrades follow my writings—the Plans of National Reconstruction, the Three Principles of the People, and the Manifesto of the First Congress of Representatives—and make every effort to carry them into effect. Above all, my recent declaration in favor of holding a National Convention of the People of China and abolishing the unequal treaties should be carried into effect as soon as possible. This is my last will and testament."

In December 1930, Chiang Kai-shek revived the idea of such a convention. Election procedures were announced on January 1, 1931. Both foreign and Chinese leaders knew that the National People's Convention would provide an avenue for the expression of the rising nationalistic feelings of the Chinese people. Yet the foreign powers continued to believe that nothing would change.

Delegates to the National People's Convention were chosen on the basis of their occupation. The legal profession was part of the educational constituency. Father decided to run and campaigned by giving speeches at law schools and universities around the province, including his ancestral hometown, Wuxi, where he obtained substantial support from both teachers and students. His campaign expenses were largely underwritten by his friend Zhang Danru, a banker and salt merchant. Of the six lawyers running, Father won by far the largest number of votes.

At 9:00 A.M. on Friday, May 5, the four hundred and seventy-five delegates, government officials and party leaders of the Kuomintang gathered in the auditorium of the Central University in Nanking. The opening of the National People's Convention was heralded by salvos fired by cannons mounted in forts and on warships in the harbor.

In his inaugural address, President Chiang said that the convention had two main purposes. First, to consolidate peace and national unification and to map out plans for national reconstruction. Second, to pave the way for an era of constitutional rule, when power would be returned to the people. According to Sun Yatsen's political philosophy, the era of constitutional rule was the culmination of a three-phase program, beginning with military campaigns to unite the country, followed by a period of political tutelage, during which the Kuomintang would exercise all power. This would eventually usher in the third and last stage, when a constitution would be promulgated and power placed in the hands of the people. The holding of the convention marked the end of phase one. Hence, a major task of the convention was to discuss and decide upon a provisional constitution, which would be in effect during the second phase, the period of political tutelage.

Before the meeting proper got under way, the several hundred delegates gathered before the tomb of Sun Yatsen for a solemn ceremony, during which they pledged to follow his teachings and carry out his will.

At an early session, one delegate moved an emergency resolution calling for the abolition of unequal treaties. He reflected the prevailing mood of the delegates, who keenly felt the disgrace of Chinese having foreign overlords in their own land. But President Chiang was not in full accord. He said: "We should exert ourselves in order that we might prove ourselves equal to the situation. It would require almost superhuman efforts to free ourselves from the various unequal treaties. In order to attain our object, we must first make our country powerful and independent. More shouting of cries of 'Down with the unequal treaties' would prove of little avail." He called for a concerted effort to reconstruct the nation, after which, he said, the unequal treaties could be easily abolished.

427

In between the plenary sessions, various committees met to scrutinize proposals and prepare drafts. Father took part in the discussion of the provisional constitution. As the chief representative of the country's lawyers, he had special interest in establishing a uniform judicial system within the country, including the foreign-administered enclaves, but he was unable to gain sufficient support for the measure. Another motion he raised dealt with human rights, and on this he received considerable backing. Thus, a clause was written into the new provisional constitution that individuals could not be detained for more than twenty-four hours. Another subject Father was particularly interested in was compensation for those wrongly detained or imprisoned. But on this measure, too, he was unable to muster enough interest.

By May 12, when the fourth plenary session was held, the provisional constitution was ready. The document, which consisted of eighty-nine articles, was adopted to the cheers of the joyful delegates.

The next day, the delegates resoundingly approved a document called "The Manifesto on the Abolition of All Unequal Treaties." It said in part: "The Chinese people have, as the result of their awakening to the sense of nationalism, come to feel the increasing irksomeness of these unequal treaties and dedicate themselves with added determination to the task of liberating China from her shackles. . . . In the opinion of the National People's Convention, the abrogation of the unequal treaties cannot be delayed any further." In conclusion, it declared:

> In view of the foregoing circumstances, the National People's Convention, being representative of the entire Chinese people, hereby solemnly declare the following to the entire world:
> 1. The Chinese people will not recognize all the past unequal treaties imposed by the Powers upon China.
> 2. The National Government shall, in conformity with the late Dr. Sun Yatsen's testamentary injunction, achieve with the least possible delay China's equality and independence in the family of nations.

Evidence of the high level of nationalistic sentiment at the convention was also reflected in a proposal calling on the government to begin "immediate negotiations with the various foreign countries relative to the amelioration of discriminatory legislation against overseas Chinese."[3] The delegates may well have had the United States in mind, where anti-Chinese practices were widespread, including discriminatory legislation against Chinese in immigration, employment, house ownership and even the courts, where Chinese were not allowed to testify.[4]

In the aftermath of the National People's Convention, talks with the Western powers, particularly the United States and Britain, over the abolition of extraterritoriality continued. The negotiations were still going on when, on September 18, 1931, the Japanese attacked Mukden, beginning their conquest of Manchuria. President Chiang Kai-shek called upon the toothless League of Nations to intervene.

The Japanese rapidly consolidated their hold on Manchuria and, to make it less obvious that they were embarked upon conquest, set up a puppet regime. For this purpose they turned to China's last Manchu emperor, Puyi, who had abdicated in 1912 at the age of six. Puyi, who had been living in Japan, agreed to head a new government in Manchuria, to be called Manchukuo. On March 9, 1932, he was formally installed, with his capital at Changchun.

In Shanghai, news of the Mukden Incident angered the populace, and an anti-Japanese movement developed. An umbrella group, known as the Anti-Japanese National Salvation Association, was formed. It included, along with the bar association, such diverse groups as fellow provincials associations, the Young Men's Christian Association, students' and women's groups, and even the Rickshaw Pullers' Association. The bar association held an emergency meeting on the night of September 30, 1931, which Father attended, and resolved to send a telegram to the government asking what steps, including military ones, were being taken to deal with the situation, and urging the government to stage an economic boycott of Japan. The bar association decided to stage its own economic boycott. Its members would no longer work with Japanese lawyers or accept cases from Japanese clients. Even economic relations such as those of landlord and tenant were to be terminated.

Despite national indignation over Japan's invasion of Manchuria, President Chiang Kai-shek's policy was one of nonresistance. Instead of fighting the Japanese, he was intent on waging war against the Communists. The mood of the people was reflected in a manifesto issued by the Shanghai Bar Association on December 18, 1931, which excoriated the Kuomintang government, blaming it for the proliferation of civil conflicts, restriction of human rights, loss of national territory and financial chaos. The bar association went so far as to say that the Kuomintang was little different from the warlords. It ended by saying that the most important thing was for China to return to the rule of law.

To raise funds for war victims in Manchuria, Father and a group of friends decided to put on a charity show. They were all good amateur performers, and it was fashionable at the time for men of good standing to hold such events. On three successive nights, they put on special performances of well-known operas. Many opera fans joined, including Tongli and his latest concubine, a Wuxi woman named Wang Jie, who had worked as a dancing girl in the Black Cat Ballroom. For this reason, she was sometimes called "Black Cat."

Tongli had gone into the Chilean saltpeter business and was doing fairly well. He had rented a two-story Spanish-style house in the French Concession for Black Cat and her mother, and had sent her to study singing, studying both Peking opera and its southern counterpart, Kunshan opera. She had turned out to be so gifted that, within two years, she became a celebrity and was considered as good as any professional. In the best courtesan tradition, she could not only sing and act but was also accomplished in languages, being able to speak French and Japanese.

One day, Tongli brought his daughter Zhaohua to meet his concubine, Wang Jie, and the two liked each other instantly. At first, Zhaohua stayed with them on rare occasions, then every other weekend, and eventually their home became her second home.

It was through Black Cat that Zhaohua learned to sing Kunshan opera. Though only in her mid-teens, she was especially adept at playing the role of a naughty maid in the opera *Cunxiang Teases the Moon*. She, Tongli and Black Cat all appeared in a peformance held at the Ningbo Fellow Provincials Association. Father was in the audience. It was the first time he had seen Zhaohua since that day many years before when Tongli's wife had brought her children to his house for asylum. Watching the performance, he was captivated by Zhaohua, who had blossomed into a beautiful young woman. From that time on, his interest in her rapidly increased. No longer did he see her as the daughter of Tongli; he saw her as a maiden in the full bloom of youth.

On January 28, 1932, Japanese troops launched an assault on Shanghai, throwing the people there into a panic. The Nineteenth Route Army gallantly defended the city. A campaign was launched by many of Shanghai's most prominent citizens to provide supplies and equipment for the army. The bar association set up a special fund-raising committee, on which Father served, to raise a hundred thousand dollars for the war effort. Zhaohua worked as a volunteer nurse, washing bandages and helping wounded soldiers write letters to their wives and children.

In mid-1932, Father announced that his oldest daughter, Jiaxiu, would be married to her first cousin, Wu Hanyuan, the son of Father's oldest sister. Since Jiaxiu was Father's adopted daughter, his common-law wife's first child, the two cousins were not related by blood. Father arranged for a huge wedding celebration in the beautiful resort city of Hangzhou. Friends and relatives from around the country were invited, and Father even provided them with train tickets. The wedding banquet was held in the best hotel in the city, known as the Xileng.

Taking advantage of the occasion to get to know Zhaohua better, Father asked Tongli if his daughter could be the maid of honor, and Tongli accepted on her behalf. The wedding was a major social event, complete with performances of Peking and Kunshan opera by well-known amateur singers and attended by many of the most influential men of the day. The performances went on for three days.

The night before the wedding, Father organized a boat tour of West Lake, followed by a banquet at the famous Louwailou Restaurant.

After the dinner, Father asked Zhaohua if she could help tutor his daughter Margaret in English. Zhaohua demurred at first, but then consented. From then on, she went often to Father's home, at first once or twice a week, later almost daily. Ostensibly, she was there to tutor Margaret, but since Father's office was in the same house, the two of them saw each other often.

Father at forty-four was in the prime of life. His formal wife had died in Suzhou and he was officially a widower. He was of an unconventional bent and thought nothing of showing interest in his friend's teen-aged daughter. Zhaohua, for her part, was unhappy at home, where her parents' affections centered on their son. Though only sixteen, she was very mature for her age, and was responding to the attention that many men were showering on her. At parties given by her McTyeire school friends, she met not only their brothers and cousins but much older men, men of the world, who were drawn

431

by her youth and her innocence. She enjoyed the attention she was getting, and responded to it.

It was Zhaohua's mother who, unintentionally, pushed her in the direction of one of these older men. One day, she confided to Zhaohua that for years she had speculated in gold. While she had done fairly well at first, recently she had lost not only all the money her husband had given her, but also money entrusted to her by other relatives. She desperately needed two thousand dollars, and did not know to whom to turn. Knowing that her daughter had been associating with influential men, she asked her for help. Quite naturally, Zhaohua's first thought was of "Uncle" Liankui. She asked him for the money, and he was more than happy to oblige, adding that he did not like to see her worried, and wanted to take care of her.

It was probably from this time on that the relationship between the middle-aged lawyer and the high-school student was transformed. No longer was he an uncle; he became a suitor. And she, for her part, could not continue as the light-hearted teen-ager. She began to consider assuming the responsibilities of adulthood. One day, Father took her aside and showed her a copy of an old thread-bound book, which turned out to be the genealogy of the Qin clan of Wuxi, containing the names of their common ancestors. He pointed out to her the names of her father and grandfather, and the people they were descended from, and also his own name and those of his forebears, showing her that their relationship was really very distant, and no impediment to marriage at all.

When Zhaohua's family found out that she was seriously considering marriage to a man who was so much older, and one to whom they were related as well, they were outraged. Her grandfather, the scholar Dunshi, exclaimed in the words of Confucius: "If even this can be tolerated, what is there that cannot be tolerated?" Her father, Tongli, asked her mother to quickly arrange a marriage for her with someone else.

Many of Father's friends tried to dissuade him from his course of action. Torn by indecision, he resorted to his knowledge of another ancient Chinese art: that of *ce-zi*, or the ability to tell fortunes by means of analyzing characters. A person in doubt about a certain question goes to a *ce-zi* expert, tells him what is troubling him, then picks a Chinese word at random. The *ce-zi* specialist analyzes the components of the word and interprets their meaning in the light of what is being asked. So good was Father at doing this that people used to say that he possessed "heaven-piercing eyes," that is, he could see things denied to ordinary mortals.

So Father turned to *ce-zi* for an answer. Of course, he himself could not both pick the word and analyze its meaning. He was invited to the home of the political leader Zhang Jingjiang for dinner. Upon entering the door, he encountered the Zhang family's accountant, a man named Li Lijing. Without telling Accountant Li what problem he wished to solve, Father asked him to pick a word. Since the accountant had just seen a friend named Gu, he suggested the word *gu*.

Father studied the word, which consists of twenty-one strokes, to see what it would disclose about his nuptial plans. Then he shouted in delight, "This is wonderful! This is wonderful!" He explained to Accountant Li that the left side of *gu* consisted of the word *hu*, meaning "house," over the word *jie*, or "virtuous." On the right, the two strokes on top resembled the word *ding*, which means "son," while the bottom is the word *bei*, which means "treasure." Right then and there, Father composed a couplet, based on his analysis of the word *gu*:

> A virtuous woman will enter the
>   household
> Sons will multiply and prosperity
>   increase.

The incident created such a deep impression on Accountant Li that half a century later, when I found him in Shanghai, he related it to me with relish.[5]

So, despite the whispers and the scandal, despite the strenuous objections of her family, Father and Zhaohua traveled to Hangzhou and were married there on May 22, 1933. In contrast to the festivities that had accompanied the wedding of his daughter a few months earlier, this marriage was subdued. No member of her family was there, while only a handful of his close relatives was present, together with two local lawyers who acted as witnesses. The ceremony was simple, with the bride and groom reciting the following:

"We, partners to the Marriage Contract, Qin Liankui and Qin Zhaohua, today join in wedlock at the wedding ceremony held in Hangzhou, home of the parents of the bridegroom, in accordance with the provisions of Section 2, Article 963 of the Civil Law."

433

After the wedding, the couple went to Peking on a honeymoon, and stayed in the Peking Hotel. As was the custom of the time, they had their pictures taken in a photographer's studio. Father's portrait showed a handsome man with jet-black hair, head slightly bent, dressed in a Chinese robe and cloth shoes. He had the look of a man who was ready to take on the whole world if necessary. Mother's photograph was of a thoughtful-looking young woman, with clear eyes, her hair parted in the center. She was in a high-collar Chinese dress with elaborate cloth buttons. From each ear dangled a white, spherical jade earring. She looked demure and slightly apprehensive, as if unsure of what fate had in store for her.

A shock awaited Mother when they returned to Shanghai after the honeymoon. She had been publicly disowned by her family for having married Father. Tongli had published an announcement in the newspaper in which he said that, at the behest of his father, he was severing all ties with his disobedient daughter Zhaohua.

Fortunately, her sister, Wanhua, and her mother did not repudiate her and came to see her from time to time. But her brother, Kaihua, would have nothing to do with her. Whenever she went to see her mother, Kaihua would leave the house.

Mother was deeply hurt. She had not thought her father would go so far. What hurt her even more was that while Tongli would not forgive her, he continued to be friends with Father, now his son-in-law. When she confronted Father over his continued relationship with Tongli, he said that he, as her husband, had to express his gratitude to her parents for bringing her up.

Father, too, was criticized for his marriage. A stormy meeting was held by the clan in Wuxi, during which he was denounced by conservative older members. Even in Shanghai, some of his friends distanced themselves from him. But eventually, they came to accept the situation. He was, after all, an excellent lawyer whose services were much sought after, and he could not be isolated. Gradually, Mother, too, was accepted by Father's circle of friends.

The following year, things started going badly for Zhang Danru, one of Father's closest friends. His bank, the Tungyi Commercial and Savings Bank, had serious problems.

In January 1934, the United States had devalued the dollar, causing silver prices to soar. This led to a rapid drain on China's silver reserves, a drain that amounted to several hundred million dollars during the year. Banks in Shanghai came under much pressure, because the country's currency was based on silver. The following year, the situation worsened. By November, China was forced to abandon the silver standard. The dwindling of silver stocks in Shanghai caused banks first to curtail and then to halt credit entirely. "Business came to a standstill and business failures became the order of the day," one economist wrote. "Land values in Shanghai receded much faster than general wholesale commodities. Due to the curtailment of credit the majority of mortgagors were unable to repay loans taken against land and buildings; many were even unable to meet interest charges."[6]

That year, twelve of the sixty-seven Chinese banks in Shanghai closed their doors, as did over a thousand factories. And one of the casualties was Zhang Danru's Tungyi Bank, which had much of its assets tied up in real estate. In January 1935, the bank suspended operations. Father attempted to get government support to stave off insolvency of the bank, of which he was a director, but to no avail.

For over a year, Father devoted himself to sorting out the legal problems of the Tungyi Bank, a task for which he sought no monetary compensation. He was incensed at the government's refusal to bail the bank out, and held strongly that the Zhang family's contribution to the Chinese revolution should be acknowledged.

In the spring of 1936, the Shanghai Bar Association launched a publicity drive for its proposal to compensate those wrongly imprisoned, a suggestion that had been turned down during the National People's Convention. Cinema owners were approached and asked to show slides on the subject; radio stations were urged to broadcast messages. Father and eight other members of the executive committee fanned out across Shanghai to broadcast radio speeches appealing for compensation for such innocent victims, and included those who were prosecuted and found not guilty, and those who on appeal had a guilty verdict reversed. Relatives of those wrongly executed would also be compensated, regardless of financial need. In addition, where a person's reputation was damaged, the government should formally publish an apology in the newspapers. As a result of their efforts, Article 26 was included in the Draft Constitution of the Republic of China. This said:

"Any public functionary who illegally infringes upon any private liberty or right shall, besides being subject to disciplinary punishment, be responsible under criminal and civil law. The injured per-

435

son may also, in accordance with law, claim indemnity from the State for damages sustained."

Meanwhile, plans for the convening of a constitution-making National Assembly on November 12, 1936, were announced. The legal profession was allocated ten seats. Father and the other candidates were nominated in August but, in mid-October, the ruling Kuomintang announced a one-year delay because of the unsettled conditions in the country.

The continuing Japanese encroachments on China at this time helped fan nationalist feelings—and growing opposition to President Chiang Kai-shek's policy of nonresistance. The president felt that the Communists posed a more serious long-term threat than the Japanese. Once they were vanquished, he thought, a united China could drive out the Japanese.

Many people differed vehemently with his assessment. They felt that the Chinese people were confronted with national extinction, and so Communists and Nationalists should close ranks in the face of the common enemy. In the forefront of the movement to press Chiang Kai-shek to fight the Japanese invaders were a group of prominent members of society, who in May 1936 formed the National Salvation Association. The leader was Father's longtime friend Shen Junru, now working as a lawyer. Their slogan was "Save the Nation." To this end, they urged cessation of the Kuomintang-Communist civil war. When Mao Zedong, then in Yanan, issued an open letter declaring willingness to cooperate against the Japanese, some Kuomintang officials suspected that the National Salvation Association was working with the Communists.

On November 23, 1936, Shen Junru was arrested on charges of associating with Communists and attempting to overthrow the government. Six other leaders of the National Salvation Association were also arrested, including three other lawyers—one of them a woman. Shen Junru, a standing-committee member of the bar association, submitted his resignation, but his fellow lawyers showed their solidarity with him by refusing to accept it. The subsequent trial became one of the most sensational political cases of the Republican period. The defendants were known collectively as the "Seven Gentlemen," even though one of them was a lady.

The arrest of these seven aroused the public and even divided the Kuomintang. Over twenty members of the party's Central Executive

Committee, including Sun Ke, son of Sun Yatsen, sent a telegram to Chiang Kai-shek calling for their release. Marshal Zhang Xueliang, commander in Xi'an, also urged their release, saying that their arrest created the impression that patriotism was a crime. Prominent Americans, including Albert Einstein and the philosopher John Dewey, sent telegrams to voice their concern.

On December 12, the attention of the country was riveted by another dramatic development. President Chiang Kai-shek, while in Xi'an, was kidnapped by Marshal Zhang. The nation waited in anguished suspense to see what would unfold next. Marshal Zhang, who had seen his Manchurian homeland come under the heel of the Japanese army, was unwilling to carry out Chiang Kai-shek's policy of nonresistance while continuing to fight the Communists. His soldiers had no heart in waging war against fellow Chinese. In Xi'an, Zhang—called the Young Marshal to distinguish him from his father, who was known as the Old Marshal—had made contact with Chinese Communist leaders and was convinced of their sincerity in wanting to unify China against the Japanese conquerors. His detention of the president had one main objective: to demand that Chiang Kai-shek join hands with the Communists in resisting Japan. And as a corollary, he wanted the Seven Gentlemen case dropped.

Three days after the detention of President Chiang, a Communist delegation headed by Zhou Enlai, Ye Jianying and Qin Bangxian[7] arrived in Xi'an to persuade Chiang that if he was willing to fight the Japanese, they would accept his leadership. After ten days of negotiations, agreement on a united front was reached. On Christmas Day, 1936, Chiang Kai-shek was released. As a sign of good faith, the Young Marshal accompanied him back to Nanking. But Chiang put him under arrest and had him tried by a military court which, on December 31, sentenced him to ten years in prison. Four days later he was granted an amnesty, but kept under house arrest, where he remained for the rest of Chiang Kai-shek's life, even being moved to Taiwan in late 1948, before Chiang himself fled there.

Chiang Kai-shek did end his policy of nonresistance to Japan, but the case of the Seven Gentlemen was not dropped. Instead, with the Xi'an Incident, it was given a more sinister dimension, as prosecutors suspected that the National Salvation Association leaders were in league with the Young Marshal in the kidnapping of the president.

In April 1937, when it became clear that the government was determined to proceed with the trial, Shen Junru and the other

437

defendants set about getting lawyers. By law, each of them was entitled to three lawyers. The seven decided that they would hire twenty-one of the best to work as a team. Two criteria were established: First, the lawyers had to be men of influence, and second, they could not be opposed to resistance against Japan.

As a result, the strongest team in Chinese legal history was put together. "These persons were highly distinguished members of society," one of the seven defendants wrote in his memoirs. "They were prepared to wage a fierce legal battle to expose the reactionary policy of the 'crime of national salvation.'" For his own defense, Shen Junru selected Father, who that month was reelected to the bar association's executive committee with the most votes, along with two other respected lawyers.

The trial, held in Suzhou by the High Court of Jiangsu Province, was scheduled for June 11. In the morning, the lawyers went to the prison to meet with their clients in the front yard. The court session was set for 2:00 P.M. The defendants were escorted from prison through the narrow, meandering streets and alleys of Suzhou to the High Court building. Guards were posted every five to ten paces, and soldiers with loaded rifles were positioned on the footboards on either side of each car. To an onlooker, it may well have appeared to be a parade of high-ranking officials.

Despite the fact that a large crowd had gathered outside the courtroom, it was announced that no observers would be allowed inside. The authorities were fearful of a demonstration in the courtroom, or even, in the feverish atmosphere, an attempt to forcibly gain the defendants' freedom. Eventually a compromise was reached and relatives of the accused as well as the press were admitted as observers.

The court consisted of a presiding judge, two assessors, a court clerk and the prosecutor. All were garbed in court attire. The defendants were led in first and told to stand facing the bench. The defending lawyers, in their robes, were seated on both sides of a long, rectangular table, with Father at the head. After that, each defendant was asked to state such particulars as his name, age, hometown, address and profession. Then the prosecution read out the charges. Shen Junru, the main defendant, was questioned first. With his beard, and in his long pale robe, he cut an impressive figure. For an hour and a half, he presented a forceful rebuttal to the bill of indictment that had been drawn up against him. His lawyers also spoke, asking in particular for an investigation into items in the indictment that pertained to the relationship between the accused and the Xi'an Incident. They also requested that Marshal Zhang be produced in court as a witness. But the presiding judge denied all of their requests, saying there was no need for any investigation.

Similarly, with the other defendants, the court denied all requests to investigate the evidence on which the charges were based and refused to summon relevant persons for questioning. Not only did the court deny requests for further investigation, it even rejected evidence presented by lawyers for the accused.

When the court adjourned at seven that evening after a five-hour session, the lawyers held a strategy session that lasted until past midnight. They feared that the very next day, all the accused would be convicted on the basis of the "Emergency Penal Code for Treason Against the Republic" and sentenced to prison terms. Something had to be done immediately.

According to one of the lawyers present, it was at this juncture that Father spoke up. He proposed that the defense file a motion of disqualification on the ground that the judges' impartiality was in question. China's criminal-procedure law was such that, when a defendant made such a request, the proceedings were halted awaiting a decision. A motion was immediately drawn up, worded thus: "Since the judges of the panel perform their duties en bloc, there obviously is great concern over their partiality. We petition that the judges of the panel disqualify themselves."

The stratagem worked. The following day, all legal proceedings were suspended pending the appointment of new judges, and precious time was won.

A second trial was set for June 25, with different judges. That day, Father and several other defending attorneys took the 8:00 A.M. express train from Shanghai to Suzhou, arriving in time for the morning court session. The hearing lasted a total of seven hours and centered around the charge that the defendants were connected with Marshal Zhang and the kidnapping of Chiang Kai-shek. The defense lawyers asked for the Young Marshal to be summoned so he could be questioned. Failing this, they argued, at least the court should send for the records of the military trial of the Young Marshal to see if there was any evidence of a link between him and the defendants. The presiding judge ignored these requests.

Finally, Father stood up. He said that, in his twenty-six years as a

439

lawyer, he had always tried to avoid unnecessary clashes with prosecutors. "Today," he said, "we have collectively requested that the records of Zhang Xueliang's case be summoned to use as collateral evidence. This request conforms to the law of the land and to human reason. The court must heed this point."

The presiding judge called a recess so he and the two assessors could discuss the situation. Upon their return, the judge announced that the court acceded to the request to ask for records of the trial of Marshal Zhang. Pending the receipt of such documents, he said, the trial stood adjourned. The defendants were returned to prison.

This won the seven one more breathing spell, during which events took another dramatic turn. Appeals to free the seven were transformed into a nationwide movement, led by Madame Soong Chingling, widow of Sun Yatsen, to join them in prison. Soon, several hundred celebrities, together with students and workers, were involved. If patriotism was to be considered a crime, they wanted to be locked up.

On July 7, the Japanese began their invasion of Peking, then known as Peiping, by attacking the Marco Polo Bridge. This incident so inflamed passions that it became politically impossible for the government to keep in prison seven people who had advocated resistance to the Japanese. On July 31, the seven were released "on bail." The trial was never resumed. But it was not until January 1939, when Suzhou, Shanghai and Nanking itself had fallen into Japanese hands, that all charges were formally dropped.

Shen Junru went on to become the first president of the Supreme People's Court after the People's Republic of China was proclaimed in 1949.

CHAPTER TWENTY-SEVEN

My Brother: Communist Martyr Qin Jiajun

With her marriage to Father, Mother at age seventeen found herself in the difficult position of being stepmother to six children —one of them married—only slightly younger than herself.

Those children had been separated at an early age, apparently to lighten the load on Father. The two daughters, Margaret and Alice, had been sent to live with their aunt in Suzhou. They remained with her until that lady died, and then returned home to live. The sons mainly grew up at home, except for the middle one, Jiajun.

Tongli's concubine, Yan Lizhen, who had been a close friend of Jiajun's mother, was very fond of Jiajun and adopted him. So Jiajun was sent to live with them while still an infant and stayed there until he was ten years old, at which time Miss Yan left Tongli to marry another man, and Jiajun returned home. But he continued to maintain a close relationship with Miss Yan to the end of his life. She was the only mother he ever really had, for his own mother died when he was an infant.

The death of his mother, combined with his being sent to live with foster parents for many years, undoubtedly had an effect on him. The marriage of his father to Tongli's daughter must have been especially unsettling; it must have seemed almost incestuous since now his foster sister was his stepmother.

His childhood experience appears to have turned him into someone deeply concerned with the ills of society. He was filled with the idealism of youth and became a vegetarian at an early age, when he considered himself a Buddhist. Once, after his friends had enjoyed a chicken meal, Jiajun composed a requiem in memory of the chicken.

By the time of my parents' wedding, all five of Father's unmarried children were living at home. Father set up two households, adjacent to each other, situated at Fuming Terrace at Avenue Foch in the

441

French Concession. He and Mother lived in one house, and the house next door was both his office and home for the five children. Father took great care that his seventeen-year-old bride was kept apart from his children. Jiaxiu, the just-married daughter, had been Mother's classmate and Margaret was only a year younger. But Father's concern lay not with his daughters but with his sons. The oldest, Jiaju, was fifteen, while Jiajun and Jiahua were fourteen and twelve respectively.

Mother tried to discharge her new duties as best she could, including seeing to the children's education. A few months after her marriage, she and Father arranged for Jiahua, the youngest son, to attend the Xuyi Elementary School. The two older boys were enrolled in the Zhengshi Middle School.[1] The school operated a dormitory, where the students lived. They went home only on holidays.

Its principal was Chen Qun, an early supporter of Sun Yatsen and an intimate associate of Chiang Kai-shek.

It is said that, in 1933, after citywide school graduation examinations were held at the elementary level, Chen went to the head of the education bureau and asked for the best graduates to be assigned to his school. That year, both Jiaju and Jiajun were admitted. Though Jiaju was a year older, the brothers were in the same grade.

Zhengshi Middle School was run like a military academy. The school attempted to cultivate a martial spirit in the students, who were forced to shave their heads. Military training was part of the school's curriculum. The students wore all-white military uniforms, complete with peaked caps. Discipline was extremely strict.

Because Principal Chen got the cream of the city's students, he was able to boast that none of his students failed the city-administered middle-school graduation examination. He even proclaimed in the newspapers that the top-ranking middle-school graduate each year came from his school.

Jiajun proved himself an intelligent and hardworking student. His favorite subjects were mathematics, physics and chemistry. In addition, he was fond of classical literature. He also studied two foreign languages, English and Japanese, and became passably fluent. He adopted an English name, Oliver, which he used on occasion.

Perhaps understandably, Jiajun was affected by the political atmosphere at Zhengshi. Since Principal Chen was a former associate of President Chiang Kai-shek, Jiajun at the time became an ardent admirer of Chiang.

His education was interrupted by the Japanese attack on Shanghai. The bombing of the Great World Amusement Park, in which more than a thousand people were killed and many more injured, made it clear that Shanghai was no longer safe. Even though the Japanese stayed out of the foreign concessions, Father made plans for the family to move to Hong Kong.

Before leaving, however, he had to attend to the burial of his parents. His mother had been dead for thirty years and his father for twenty-five, but he had put off the burial in the hope of finding an auspicious site that would bring good fortune to himself and his descendants.

Meanwhile, the mother of his first six children, his common-law wife, Cao Yueheng, had also lain unburied for over a decade, while his brother, Lianyuan,[2] had died in 1933. The beginning of the Sino-Japanese war imparted a sense of urgency, since the unburied coffins could well be lost or destroyed during the fighting, resulting in the desecration of the bodies. With the assistance of his fifth sister, who was closest to him in age, Father bought a piece of land outside Hangzhou. Three graves were dug. In one he buried his mother and father, in another his brother, and in the third he buried Cao Yueheng, the mother of Jiajun and his siblings. By burying her and not his formal wife with his parents, he was in effect publicly acknowledging her status as his wife. Even as the burials were proceeding, Japanese bombs were falling from the sky.

The Lloyd Triestino liner *Conte Verde* steamed out of Shanghai harbor on Saturday, August 28, 1937, carrying 1,042 passengers, including nine members of our family. By this time, Mother had given birth to two children, a daughter, Julia, and a son, Anthony. The 11,527-ton liner was scarcely out of the harbor when it witnessed one of the tragedies of the war: the bombing of the *President Hoover* by Chinese planes that mistook the American vessel for a Japanese transport. Passengers on the *Conte Verde* saw four Chinese planes appear in the sky above them. After circling over the *Conte Verde*, they flew off toward the *President Hoover* and began to drop bombs. The nervous passengers were fearful that they would be next. Apparently what saved the *Conte Verde* from a similar fate was its distinctive white and cream color.

After this narrow escape, the liner continued on its three-day voyage to Hong Kong, from which it was to continue on to Venice, Trieste and Brindisi by way of Singapore, Colombo, Bombay and Port Said. On September 1, the liner reached Hong Kong, and its passengers joined the hundreds of thousands of Chinese refugees pouring into the British colony. The very next day, Hong Kong was struck by the worst typhoon in the colony's history. Uncounted thousands of fishermen drowned. Twenty-seven steamers were sunk or blown ashore. Our family had just moved into a house in Kowloon, on Boundary Street. But the roof caved in because of the typhoon, and the family had to find new living quarters, this time on Arbuthnot Road. Eventually, more permanent accommodations were found in an apartment at 11A Robinson Road, halfway up Victoria Peak.

The three boys did not remain long in Hong Kong. Before the end of the year, they returned to Shanghai to continue their studies. Although much of Shanghai was in flames, the foreign settlements were still unaffected and classes continued in the Zhengshi Middle School. The school hired foreigners to serve on their board of directors as a shield against the Japanese. In this artificial atmosphere, the brothers continued their studies until graduation in mid-1938, but many students had dropped out. The class in which Jiaju and Jiajun had started out had about fifty students. When graduation time came, only eighteen remained.

Though the Kuomintang forces put up a valiant resistance in the defense of Shanghai, they were overwhelmed by Japanese troops, who inflicted a quarter of a million casualties.

Chiang Kai-shek traded space for time, repeatedly retreating before the well-trained, well-equipped Japanese soldiers. Jiajun, nineteen, watched helplessly from Shanghai as the Japanese seized Nanking. The Kuomintang then moved the capital to Hankow until that city, too, was lost. Finally, the Kuomintang government withdrew into Sichuan province, in the southwest, and established their wartime capital in Chungking.

Jiajun wanted to go to Chungking to join the government in resisting the Japanese, but Father would not hear of it and made him continue his studies.

A frustrated Jiajun enrolled in Datong University, where he pursued a curriculum in the sciences. Datong University was very different from the right-wing Zhengshi Middle School. Like much of

Shanghai at the time, it was a hotbed of intrigue. There were agents working for the Japanese, the Kuomintang and the Communists, all of them acting clandestinely, spying and reporting on one another. Most of the students were nationalistic, but many did not dare speak openly. Even in the foreign settlements, anti-Japanese activities were discouraged. There were no anti-Japanese public speeches and no public rallies. The united front between the Kuomintang and the Communists was holding, but neither side really trusted the other.

By the end of 1938, the Japanese controlled most of northern China and vast tracts of eastern and central China. So large was the territory that they set up several puppet administrations to help them govern. The puppet administration could control only key cities and communications lines, such as railroads. In the countryside, especially in border regions where provincial boundaries met, the Communists set up anti-Japanese bases.

When Jiajun entered Datong University, the Communist New Fourth Army had just been formed, with the sanction of the Kuomintang government, and was operating in central China, primarily in the southern part of Jiangsu province. Northern Jiangsu was dominated by Kuomintang troops. As long as these two forces, both ostensibly anti-Japanese, were on opposite sides of the Yangtze, there was no direct confrontation. But in the spring of 1940 the New Fourth Army moved into northern Jiangsu, and in July 1940, at a small town called Huangqiao, Communist forces wiped out a Nationalist unit. The Kuomintang brought in reinforcements and, at the beginning of September, another battle was fought at Huangqiao. Severe casualties were suffered by both sides, but ultimately the Communist troops succeeded in routing the Kuomintang army.[3] The Huangqiao battles brought into the open the deep rift between the Kuomintang and the Communists.

In January 1941, the Kuomintang government ordered the dissolution of the New Fourth Army, charging serious breach of military discipline. The Communists, instead of obeying the order, reorganized the army into seven divisions. From this time on, the Kuomintang-Communist alliance was, for all practical purposes, at an end. And the New Fourth Army, which was entrenching itself in northern Jiangsu, acted like a beacon for Shanghai's student intellectuals.

At Datong, Jiajun's interest in politics found expression in the Milky Way Drama Society, a students' organization. Jiajun probably did not know it at first, but the society was a Communist-front organization. It had only a small core of party members, and all public activities were done in the name of those who did not belong to the party. Gradually, Jiajun became one of the most active participants. He acted and directed, as well as wrote scripts. By the autumn of 1939, he was one of the three leaders of the group, only one of whom was an underground Communist-party member. Performances were held both on and off campus.

Underground party members at Datong had their eye on Jiajun. Though from a relatively well-off family, he was frugal, did not play cards or mah-jongg, and dressed simply. "He was very active and enthusiastic," one recalled. "He was engaged mostly in anti-Japanese propaganda. He was hardworking and patriotic; a very good comrade."

Jiajun was zealous in acting on his beliefs, easily attracted to new ideas. He had great sympathy for others and once, when he observed two policemen shoot and kill a robber, he voiced sympathy for the victim, saying that he had fallen like a "paper man" after being shot.

He thought all Chinese should speak Mandarin, the national language. Since he himself spoke only the Shanghai dialect, he devoted himself to the study of Mandarin, going to the park regularly to practice. After a month, he had made so much progress that he was able to speak Mandarin when he performed onstage.

Many of the underground Communists rose to positions of prominence at this time, but the person who undoubtedly exercised the greatest influence over Jiajun was a woman known as Qu Jin. She was the underground party secretary at Datong University.

Shanghai being the cosmopolitan city that it was, many of the students at Datong were very sophisticated and worldly, but Jiajun did not find them attractive. He found girls more appealing who were straightforward and warm. Qu Jin was such a person. Her father was a wealthy banker, but she wore no makeup and kept her hair short and straight. She was very lively and a good talker. She was also the editor of a school magazine.

The two of them often discussed politics, and she referred him to works on political philosophy. She told him that it was not necessary to go to Chungking to resist the Japanese, that revolutionary activities could be conducted anywhere. They often strolled through the streets of Shanghai until late at night, she propounding her political views and he listening silently while falling in love with her. Though she visited him at home several times, she never met other members of the family. Father, of course, was still in Hong Kong, and Margaret was married and not living at home.

Jiajun did not know at first of Qu Jin's Communist affiliation. To him, she was a like-minded thinker and the romance of his life.

There is no evidence that she led him on. In fact, it is likely that she let him know, gently but firmly, that he should put romance out of his mind. That is probably the reason he attempted suicide by taking poison. After he recovered, he decided to accept her on her terms. And with her introduction, he was inducted into the underground Communist party.[4]

In a simple ritual held in the home of a friend, attended by only two or three people, Jiajun officially became a Communist some time in August or September of 1940. In a plainly furnished room, bereft of flags or portraits, he swore that he was joining the party voluntarily and would strive all his life to fulfill the party's aims, preserve its secrets and never betray his comrades. In the interest of security, no membership card was issued.

Communist-party members were never publicly identified as such. In fact, party members might not know each other, as each cell of three was isolated from the others to minimize damage. Thus was forged a chain, each link of which could be exposed without the rest automatically suffering a similar fate. Of course, that also made it difficult for a Communist to know whom he could or could not trust. And when a link in the chain was severed, it was hard for those at lower levels to reestablish contact with party authorities. For this reason, during the Cultural Revolution, many party members were jailed for acts that they had carried out under party direction in the 1930s and 1940s, since they were unable to prove the facts. Their leaders had been arrested or killed and no records had been kept.

In March 1941, at the express instructions of the party, Jiajun went into hiding. To prevent capture, he had been advised not to live at home. He therefore went to stay with his foster mother, Yan Lizhen. Later, the party decided that he should leave for the Communist-held areas in northern Jiangsu, under the New Fourth Army.

In early 1942, Jiajun left Shanghai, having completed only the midterm of his third year at Datong. His foster mother gave him two hundred dollars. He and other students were led through enemy lines by guides who moved back and forth between the Japanese and the Communist areas. Strict secrecy was imposed, and even people within the same group did not know each other.

From Shanghai, he took a passenger ship up the Yangtze River to where the river divides into a number of narrow tributaries. There, the Japanese controlled the coast, but virtually all the inland counties were under the Communists. Trekking up to twenty miles a day, Jiajun made his way deep into the interior. There were stations set up along the way, where he was greeted warmly as a newly arrived comrade. He passed through Huangqiao, the scene of the two major battles between the Kuomintang and the Communists, and pressed on until he finally reached his destination, Dongtai, the stronghold of the New Fourth Army.

When Jiajun arrived in Dongtai, living conditions in the area were poor. There was enough to eat, but each person received only a dollar a month for such necessities as soap and toilet paper. The money given to him by his foster mother was gone, lost to robbers who accosted him on his journey. Jiajun wrote to his oldest brother in Shanghai, who managed to send him some money.

In the New Fourth Army, Jiajun adopted not only a new way of life but a new name, calling himself Wang Shengbai. It was the custom for party members to change their names once they were in the "liberated areas" controlled by the Communists. This was because, in those areas, they operated openly as Communists. If their real names were known, their friends might be endangered and their party connections exposed back home.

Jiajun donned the gray army uniform, complete with gray cap and cloth shoes. He was named political instructor. His duties included organization of cultural events, teaching and spreading anti-Japanese and pro-Communist propaganda.

But he was not satisfied with limiting himself to propaganda and educational work. He wanted to throw himself into the actual fighting. His high spirits were reflected in a rare letter he wrote to an old school friend in Shanghai: "I am very happy for today I exchanged my gold watch for a pistol."

His contacts with family and friends were by necessity sporadic. From time to time, he could arrange for letters to be sent indirectly to a family member or to one of his former colleagues at the Milky Way Drama Society. One day, a comrade of his arrived from Jiangsu and called on Father to seek financial assistance. Father, who at the time had been unemployed for years, took a ring off his finger and gave it to him.

Jiajun engaged in actual combat, going into the field armed with his pistol and with grenades strapped to his side. He fought several battles in northern Jiangsu.

In the autumn of 1942, his unit was in the vicinity of Dongtai, engaged in a major battle with the Japanese. The fighting was going well and the Communists clearly had the upper hand. Jiajun rose and called upon some enemy soldiers in a pillbox to surrender. He was struck by a bullet and killed. At the time of his death, Jiajun was only twenty-three years old.

It was a long time before our family knew about his death. Conditions at the time made it impossible for the New Fourth Army to notify bereaved family members of their loss. When the Communists took over Shanghai in May 1949, as they were sweeping to victory nationwide, Margaret hoped to see her brother return. When efforts to locate him failed, she placed a notice in the personal columns of the newspapers inquiring about his whereabouts. But there was no response.

Three years later, in 1952, Margaret received a letter from a former comrade of Jiajun's, informing her that "Comrade Jiajun joined the revolution in northern Jiangsu in the winter of 1940. He was a brave man. Unfortunately he was killed in the battle of Jiaoxie township in Dongtai during the autumn of 1942."

Jiajun had been buried where he fell, in an obscure, unmarked grave. But he was not forgotten. In 1953, the Shanghai municipal government issued a certificate to his surviving family members, hailing him as a martyr in the Communist cause. The certificate was delivered to Margaret's house with much clanging of gongs and clashing of cymbals to mark the joyous occasion.

The certificate turned out to be very useful in later years, as Margaret was able to overcome many problems by demonstrating that she was the sister of a Communist martyr. Unfortunately, it was lost during later political disturbances.

Although Margaret knew about Jiajun's death, the rest of the family in Hong Kong and the United States did not learn about it for many years. We were separated by great distances, and did not communicate often.

Father apparently did not find out until Margaret and her family moved to Hong Kong in 1957, and the news did not appear to affect him much. Of course, by that time he was already quite old, and had many serious problems of his own to contend with, including his deteriorating physical and mental health.

As for me, I was not quite two years old at the time of Jiajun's death and had never even seen him. After I grew up, the relatives I was with were unclear about what had happened to him. So it was not until my return to China to work as a correspondent for *The Wall Street Journal* that I was finally able to determine that I had had a brother who had been active as an underground Communist-party member and who had sacrificed his life fighting the Japanese.

CHAPTER TWENTY-EIGHT

Father: His Final Years

The year following our arrival in Hong Kong, Priscilla, Mother's youngest daughter, was born. And two years later, on December 13, 1940, I came into this world. Both Priscilla and I were born at the Hong Kong Sanatorium and Hospital in Happy Valley. My mother, an admirer of President Franklin D. Roosevelt, decided to name me Frank.

On December 7, 1941, when I was not quite a year old, the Japanese bombed Pearl Harbor. With that, World War II spread to the Pacific. The attack was synchronized with one on Hong Kong, which took place hours later. The airport was bombed, as was the center of the city. Simultaneously, Japanese troops already in Guangdong province swept across the border.

As soon as residents realized that Hong Kong was under attack for the first time in its history, the city was gripped by fear. Panic quickly cleared store shelves. Rice was no longer available. Fortunately, my sister Alice had a boyfriend who was able to buy some canned sardines and corned beef, as well as two bags of oats and two bags of what he thought was flour but turned out to be cornstarch. The food helped the family through the next eighteen days. At night, homemade black curtains were drawn across the windows to keep even the candlelight from showing.

My first birthday was spent with the family huddled together for safety while Japanese bombs fell from the sky. The building across from ours was bombed and burned to the ground. Father felt our home was too exposed and moved us to a friend's home in Happy Valley. Since there was no transportation available, the distance had to be covered on foot. The family made the move on the morning of December 16, with Alice carrying me on her back, while Mother carried Priscilla in her arms. Father held Julia by the hand, while a friend of his helped Anthony, who was asthmatic. When we arrived at the apartment, it was already full of other refugees. At night, all of us slept on the floor of one small room.

Hong Kong could not withstand the Japanese onslaught for long and, though the defenders put up a gallant stand, the colony surrendered on Christmas Day. The triumphant Japanese soldiers wandered the streets, helping themselves to food and women. Stories of plunder and killings swept the city.

Father decided it was better to return to our own home, and the family went back to Robinson Road, making the uphill climb on foot, with the grownups helping the children. At Alice's suggestion, the women and children in the family sought refuge in the Italian convent school she attended, which was a short walk from our home. (The Catholic Church ran some of the best schools in Hong Kong and students did not have to be believers.) Alice reasoned that the Japanese would not bother the nuns, especially Italian ones, because of the alliance between Japan and Italy. There, we found a temporary haven.

By early 1942, the situation had stabilized. Father resumed his custom of taking tea at the elegant Gloucester Hotel, located in the heart of Victoria City in Hong Kong. One day, he ran into an old friend who had just arrived from Shanghai, a tall, thin nervous-looking man named Xu Caicheng, who was related to Zhang Danru by marriage and, on the surface, was in the textiles business. He was, in reality, an undercover agent with Japanese connections. Less than a month after the fall of Hong Kong, he had flown in on a Japanese military plane to help family members of Chinese government officials go to Chungking, the temporary capital. At a time when ships were urgently needed by the Japanese army, the resourceful man had been able to find a freighter of slightly under ten thousand tons. On this vessel he accepted about two hundred passengers, mainly women and children, all of whom he carried free of charge to Shanghai. That city, too, was under Japanese occupation, but the food supply there was better than that in Hong Kong. So Father put the whole family aboard, staying behind himself in order to let a friend—a woman with two young children—go first. He joined us two months later.

The cargo ship flew a banner identifying her as being on a "refugee evacuation mission," so that it would not be bombed by Allied planes. The journey took a little over a week because of the stormy mid-February weather. The Chinese New Year was celebrated on board in a subdued atmosphere.

Once in Shanghai, the family moved in with my maternal grandmother, Tongli's wife, on Rue Retard, in what used to be the French Concession. Ironically, while China had been unable to abolish the foreign settlements in Shanghai, Japanese troops did this in one fell swoop after Pearl Harbor when their troops marched in.

With all the treaty ports occupied by the Japanese, the exercise of extraterritorial rights by Western powers became impractical. Besides, China was on the Allied side. Treaties to end such rights were signed between the Chinese government and those of the United States and Britain in January 1943. France was then under the Vichy regime, but that May, the Chinese government unilaterally declared that it considered itself no longer bound by agreements granting France extraterritorial rights.[1]

Grandmother's house was one of a cluster built by Tongli for his own retirement. The group consisted of a large house surrounded by a wrought-iron gate plus three semidetached Spanish-style townhouses. Tongli at the time was living in the coastal city of Tsingtao, where he had been named tax commissioner, and working for the northern Chinese puppet government headed by Wang Keming. In spite of the tragedies of war, the Japanese occupation did, in a way, bring about a reconciliation between him and his daughter. It began with a business transaction. At Grandmother's urging, Mother wrote to him asking if she could rent one of his houses. He could have leased it for a large sum, but he agreed instead to rent it to his daughter. Later, he invited her to visit him in Tsingtao, and suggested that the ocean air would be good for Anthony, who was suffering from an asthma attack.

Mother took Anthony and Priscilla with her, and a decade after he had disowned her, Tongli and his daughter were finally reconciled. They spent ten days together in Tsingtao, then went to Peking to see Tongli's father, the aged Dunshi. A reconciliation of sorts was also effected with Kaihua, Mother's brother. When she returned to Shanghai, he saw her off at the train station. It was to be their last meeting.

Though it was wartime, there was no actual fighting in Shanghai and life continued as usual. Alice was admitted to Aurora University and Julia to McTyeire Middle School. Father did not work. As a lawyer, he would have had to register with the Japanese-imposed puppet government, and he refused to accord it his recognition. Some other lawyers either did not have such scruples or could not afford to go for years without an income. For this, they would suffer in later years.

One day, Father received a call from one of his most respected colleagues, Zhang Yipeng, who for ten years had been president of the Shanghai Bar Association. He told Father that he had accepted the position of minister of justice under the pro-Japanese Wang Ching-wei administration, and asked Father to be his vice-minister. He declared that he wanted to ameliorate the horrendous conditions of Chinese prisons, and said that helping fellow Chinese could not be considered traitorous behavior. Father, always cautious, declined, saying he was in poor health.

Zhang Yipeng did try to ease the wretched conditions of the prisons, where disease was prevalent. Six months after he assumed office, he caught a disease from the prisoners and died. After the war, the Kuomintang labeled him a "traitor" and confiscated all his family properties.

Sometime in 1945, Tongli sold his Shanghai properties, and we had to look for a new home. Father decided that it would be safer for the family to move out of Shanghai, and so we went to Suzhou, which was less exposed. It was in Suzhou that Father first heard the news of the Japanese surrender. For eight years the Kuomintang had held out against the Japanese. Finally, victory was achieved in August 1945, in the aftermath of the American bombing of Hiroshima and Nagasaki. The entire Chinese nation celebrated the return of peace to their land. In Shanghai, people eagerly looked forward to the return of the "real" Chinese government, which had been based in Chungking.

But the return of the Kuomintang was not an unmixed blessing for people in Shanghai. While those who had gone to Chungking with the government were considered loyal citizens, all those who had remained behind were suspect, especially those who had prospered during the Japanese occupation. Many people were accused of being traitors, which almost inevitably meant the wholesale confiscation of their properties. It was, in a way, reminiscent of the situation in 1927, when the Kuomintang squeezed money from Shanghai capitalists by accusing them of being Communists.

On the whole, only people of substance faced such charges. Others who had worked for pro-Japanese puppet governments were not bothered. For the legal profession, the large-scale prosecution of "traitors" was a bonanza, as those so charged were invariably not only wealthy but willing to pay.

Father was approached by many people facing such charges. In spite of his poor financial situation, he steadfastly turned down all of them, including tearful appeals from wives of imprisoned husbands. At the time, payment was being made with gold bars or with American dollars, and many prominent lawyers gladly accepted these lucrative offers. But Father rejected all such clients, saying, "If I win this type of case, I will do my country a disservice; if I lose, I will do my client a disservice. I prefer to remain poor rather than suffer from a bad conscience."[2] Father's patriotism had been proved at the start of the war, when he was a leading member of the Anti-Japanese Support Association of All Circles of Shanghai, formed in July 1937 to organize civilian resistance to the Japanese invasion.[3]

Lawyers were not exempt from being branded as traitors. A recertification of all lawyers was required. All those who had practiced law during the Japanese occupation were permanently debarred. One of these was Mother's uncle, with whom she had stayed when she was young. Father was formally readmitted to practice before the Shanghai District Court in April 1946, and before the High Court the following month.

After eight years of enforced idleness, he was able to work again. He very quickly reestablished himself as one of the leading lawyers in Shanghai. One of those who required his services was his old friend Du Yuesheng, who was probably the most influential man in the city. Du had been chairman of the Shanghai Stock Exchange before the Sino-Japanese war. When the Japanese attacked on August 13, 1937, the exchange had suspended operations. But during the occupation the pro-Japanese Wang Ching-wei regime had set up its own stock exchange in the same building, on Hankow Road.

With the end of the war, the "traitorous" stock exchange was closed and many of those involved in it were prosecuted. However, the old one was not reopened. The shareholders of the old exchange were interested only in getting their money back by disposing of its assets. The Central Bank, the Bank of China and the Bank of Communications started a new stock exchange. Du found himself shut out.

Du asked Father for advice. He wanted to continue to play a key role in the postwar era. Father worked out a plan together with another lawyer and two accountants. Negotiations had to be held

455

with a number of parties, including the old shareholders and various government agencies. Permission was obtained from the Ministry of Economic Affairs to allow the old stock exchange to issue shares that left the names of the shareholders blank, so that they were easily transferable, like money.

The blank shares could be used as gifts to board members and government officials to obtain their support. A resolution was passed to turn the old stock exchange into a real-estate company.

The real-estate company then invested in the new stock exchange. As a result, Du was named to its board and actually became its chairman.[4]

As part of his compensation, Father was given a brokerage seat on the stock exchange, a highly-sought-after prize. Father gave it to his son-in-law Henry, who had married Margaret at the beginning of the war.

Another major case handled by Father at this time was the settlement of the estate of Silas A. Hardoon, an Iraqi Jew originally from Baghdad whose wealth was legendary. Educated in Bombay, he went to Hong Kong in 1873 and later settled down in Shanghai. There he married a Chinese woman, Liza Loo. Starting from lowly positions working for the well-known Sassoon family, he eventually struck off on his own as a trader. Through a combination of luck, industry and good judgment, he became a multimillionaire. He built a magnificent mansion, called Hardoon Gardens, for himself and his wife at the heart of the International Settlement, on a road named after him. At the time of his death in 1931, at the age of eighty-four, he owned most of the important pieces of land in both the International Settlement and the French Concession. He was reputed to be the wealthiest foreigner in the Far East. His estate was estimated at four million British pounds.

The Hardoons, who were childless, adopted many children. Silas and Liza Hardoon had drawn up identical wills, under which each named the other the sole beneficiary. If that beneficiary was not still alive, bequests would go to six adopted children. The residual property was to go to two other adopted sons, David George Hardoon, getting 70 percent, and Reuben Victor Hardoon, 30 percent. So, according to the terms of Hardoon's will, his entire fortune went to his wife. However, the will was contested by people from as far away as Iraq and India who claimed to be his relatives. One point at issue was whether British law, Chinese law or Iraqi law should prevail. Hardoon, while a British-protected person, was not a British subject.

A suit brought by a cousin, Ezra Hardoon, argued that Iraqi law should govern and that, by the laws of Iraq, a person's will can cover only one third of the property of the testator, and a will in favor of one heir is not valid without the consent of the other co-heirs, and a legatee of a different nationality from the testator cannot inherit. Lawyers for Hardoon's widow, who was of Chinese nationality, argued that Hardoon, as a British-protected person, was in effect a British subject, and that British law should prevail. This position was upheld by the British Supreme Court in Shanghai.

On September 30, 1937, Liza Hardoon drew up a drastically different new will. In it, she declared that David George Hardoon, the principal beneficiary under the old will, "has caused me many troubles and has actually threatened me with a revolver in order to get money from me" and that therefore "I no longer acknowledge him as my adopted son." However, she did not cut him out entirely. She put him on a par with nine other adopted children, each of whom was to inherit 140,000 dollars upon reaching the age of twenty-five. David George, the will said, could inherit "provided that my trustees shall then in their own absolute discretion be satisfied that he is leading a good and virtuous life."

The bulk of her estate was to go to Reuben Victor and to five of her nephews, all surnamed Loo, whom she had adopted as her sons.

On October 3, 1941, Liza Hardoon died. Immediately, David George Hardoon sought legal recognition of the original will in a civil action in the British Supreme Court in Shanghai. Chi Cho-mi, named an executor in both wills, testified that the second one was the last will and testament of Liza Hardoon. But before the case was finished, the Japanese army invaded the International Settlement, abruptly terminating court proceedings.

During the Japanese occupation, Hardoon and Company, the family business, was seized. David Hardoon cooperated with the Japanese. By offering money to the five Loo nephews, who had no source of income, he obtained from them in 1944 signed statements giving up their right of inheritance. With the end of the war, legal proceedings resumed. The Loo nephews took action against David and Reuben Hardoon in an attempt to have the terms of the new will implemented.

It was at this stage that Father was brought into the case, to act on behalf of the Loo nephews. By this time, the British no longer enjoyed extraterritorial rights and the British Supreme Court in Shanghai no longer existed.

In a petition to the Shanghai District Court in October 1945, Father set forth the history of this complex case. He argued forcefully that the agreements signed during the Japanese occupation waiving inheritance rights were not valid, having been obtained by duress. David Hardoon, Father declared, had been a collaborator and was trusted by the Japanese. The Loo nephews were in fear of him. Moreover, David Hardoon had clearly been disowned by his mother and the old will had been superseded by the new one. Father asked the court to declare that the old will was void, that David Hardoon had no right to inherit and that the agreements signed in 1944 were invalid.

The Loo nephews, however, were still in financial straits. As his legal fee, Father was to receive a proportion of whatever was realized from the sale of two designated pieces of property, at a price acceptable to him. The Loo brothers could not even afford court fees. Because of their failure to pay the required fees, the court refused to rule in their favor.

To avoid a protracted and expensive court battle, an attempt was made to settle the problem out of court. Du Yuesheng and another man, Gu Jiatang, who were acceptable to both sides, were invited to mediate. Father suggested that, in order to save face, the two sides drop any mention of either of the two wills and concentrate on the division of property. An agreement was finally reached in July 1946 that awarded David Hardoon the bulk of the estate, but that also gave substantial amounts to the Loo nephews.

In October 1948, Father received his first payment for work on the case, as one plot of land was sold. It is not clear if he ever received payment for the second plot, since he left Shanghai not long afterward.

Although Father was again doing well as a lawyer in Shanghai, he had doubts about the long-term outlook. The vast majority of the people had had high hopes for the future and had eagerly looked forward to the return of the Kuomintang government. They had welcomed the officials who flew from Chungking to Shanghai to take over the city from the Japanese.

But instead of treating the people of Shanghai like compatriots who had suffered under the Japanese, the Kuomintang officials behaved like conquerors, looking down on those who had lived under the Japanese as tainted. Students who had graduated during the Japanese occupation had to take special courses in Kuomintang ideology. Teachers had to be tested for their knowledge of the Kuomintang and their loyalty to it. A stigma was attached to everyone who had lived in Japanese-occupied territories.

The Kuomintang officials termed themselves patriots or righteous men, but their main aim seemed to be the acquisition of gold bars, cars, houses, women and face. By their behavior, they quickly lost the respect of people who formed their main base of support.

The Kuomintang also proved inadequate to the task of running the country. There appeared to be no clear economic policy, and the government resorted to the printing press to raise funds, resulting in perhaps the worst inflation the world has ever seen. Sackfuls of money had to be brought along for shopping, and a million dollars was insufficient to buy a meal. Then the government, in an attempt to stabilize the currency, introduced what was called the "gold dollar," which could be exchanged at the rate of one for three million old dollars. But this move, too, failed. A freeze on wages and prices had to be lifted, and another inflationary spiral set in.[5]

Father became disgusted quite early with the behavior of the Kuomintang. Privately, he told Mother that Kuomintang law was such that anyone who had so much as eaten a meal in occupied territory could be found guilty of treason.

In mid-1946, he told Mother that he had put aside some money and gave her a choice: Did she want him to buy a house in Shanghai or would she prefer to take the whole family to Hong Kong? Since Father was extremely possessive about Mother, the very suggestion that she consider moving to Hong Kong without him indicates how serious were his doubts about the future of China. He must have known that the tentative peace between the Kuomintang and the Communists would not last, and that the Kuomintang would be defeated. Mother, too, was appalled by the high-handed manner in which the Kuomintang officials were behaving, and decided that she did not wish to continue to live in Shanghai.

So, in the summer of 1946, our family was on the move again. Mother took her four children—Julia, Anthony, Priscilla and me— to Hong Kong. At Father's suggestion, Alice, then a senior at Aurora University, went also. He remained alone in Shanghai, to join us at some future date, which turned out to be two and a half years later. With the departure of his family, Father moved into his office, in the Chung Wai Bank Building, which was owned by Du Yuesheng.

Knowing that his new lease on life as a lawyer was limited must have had a sobering effect on him. It was natural that his thoughts should turn to death, and to permanent separation from his homeland. This helps to explain an incident that occurred the following year. At that time, a cousin of his, Qin Jinjian, who used to run the school operated by the Wuxi Sojourners Association, arrived in Shanghai on a visit with his son, Zhihao. Father took them out to coffee, and said, "I won't be able to return to Wuxi. As the saying goes, a falling leaf returns to the roots. Let me give you a tooth to take back and have buried in Wuxi. That will symbolize my return to my ancestral home." The cousin did as he was told, burying the tooth within the compound of the family's ancestral temple.

In Hong Kong, Mother and Alice were busy trying to get an apartment and to get the children enrolled in school. The war-ravaged colony was suffering from a housing shortage, and it was with some difficulty that Mother eventually found a place on Kennedy Road, a fairly good location. However, it was set against the mountain, and they had to ascend a hill and then climb long flights of steps before coming to the house. Even then, access to the building was difficult because of mounds of earth washed down by storms. Mother had to pay to have the earth removed by women laborers, who carried it away a basket at a time.

Alice did not stay long with us. Mother insisted that she return to Aurora University in Shanghai. Mother herself had not had an opportunity for advanced studies, and realized how important it was for Alice to get her degree.

We moved into the ground floor of a three-story building, sharing it with another family. In this house I was to spend the next fourteen years of my life. When I think of my childhood, it is this house that is conjured up in my memory, including the school next door for deaf-and-dumb children and the battles that were waged from time to time with our neighbors over the shared toilet or kitchen.

Meanwhile, in China, with the end of the war, preparations resumed for the holding of a National Assembly that would adopt a permanent constitution to end one-party rule. Delegates to it had been elected in 1936, but the congress had been postponed indefinitely because of the Japanese invasion.[6]

The eight years of war against Japan had been officially a period of cooperation between the Kuomintang and the Communists. Immediately after the end of the war, President Chiang Kai-shek invited Chairman Mao Zedong to Chungking for postwar talks. The two men agreed to appoint representatives, who met in October. These negotiations covered a wide range of subjects, which centered on the adoption of a national reconstruction program, political de- mocratization and the holding of a National Assembly.

The Communists felt that the original delegates, elected under Kuomintang-government auspices, were pro-Kuomintang. The gov- ernment representatives held that the elections already held should be deemed valid, but that the number of delegates could be in- creased. A compromise was reached, with the Communists agreeing to recognize the 1,200 who were elected in 1936 and the Kuomintang agreeing to the addition of 850 new ones, making up a National Assembly of 2,050 delegates.

As for the original draft constitution, it was decided that a com- mittee would be set up to examine that document and produce a revised draft constitution to be submitted to the National Assembly. All augured well for the future, as the Communists and the Kuo- mintang appeared finally to be working in harmony. Preparations went ahead for the constitution-making National Assembly to be held on May 5. Credentials of those elected previously were ex- amined and those found to have been properly elected were given official certifications. Father received his in March.

The Draft Constitution Examination Committee held its first meet- ing on February 14, 1946. While it was in session, however, the Central Executive Committee of the Kuomintang met and passed a number of resolutions that made it appear as though the party was reneging on major commitments made during the Political Con- sultative Conference. This precipitated a new debate between the Kuomintang and the Communists. As a result, on April 24, while many delegates to the National Assembly had already arrived in the capital, another delay was ordered.

The National Assembly finally did meet in Nanking on November 15, but it was boycotted by the Communists as well as one of the minor parties. Of the originally planned 2,050 delegates, about 1,400 attended.

The constitution-making National Assembly met for forty days. Lawyers, accountants, doctors and journalists all had their own rep- resentatives. The legal profession had ten delegates, led by Father.

On November 28, President Chiang presented the revised draft constitution to the delegates for deliberation. Each delegate had a chance to express his own views. Father's speech, delivered on December 4, showed that he was, as always, concerned with human rights:

"The property of citizens should be protected, and this is already set out in Article 91 and Article 16. However, it is necessary to further strengthen the rights of the individual, including the freedom to choose his own place of residence. We should therefore retain the guarantees of citizens' rights provided for in the [original] May 5 Draft."

This proposal of Father's was enshrined in Article 10 of the Constitution of the Republic of China, which states:

"The people shall have the freedom of domicile and of change of domicile."

This article may appear to be trivial on the surface, but in China, where traditionally each person had to register his place of abode with the government, it was not an insignificant right. Even today, in both Taiwan and on mainland China, each family has to register with the government the name of each member of the household. Any friend or relative staying overnight must be reported to the police.

President Chiang held a series of banquets, lasting three days, to which he invited all the delegates in turn to dine or lunch with him. According to Father, at one of the banquets, Chiang Kai-shek walked by when Father was eating. He paused and said, "Why, Lawyer Qin, you're in very good spirits. You're even gnawing on the chicken bones." Father, fearful that he would be asked to take on an official post, immediately reached inside his mouth and pulled out his dentures. "See, I don't have any teeth left. They are all false."

The constitution was unanimously approved on December 25, 1946, and was to come into force on December 25, 1947. Thirty-five years after the overthrow of the Qing dynasty, it appeared, China was finally about to enter into the era of constitutional rule.

However, even as the National Assembly was in session, scattered fighting had resumed between Communist and Kuomintang forces, with each side probing the other's strengths and weaknesses. With the Kuomintang refusal to dissolve the National Assembly and the Communists' refusal to return to the military status quo of January 1946, open war became inevitable. Even so, few among the delegates suspected that in less than three years, the Kuomintang government would be swept off the China mainland by Communist forces and the constitution on which they had labored would have little meaning outside of Taiwan. Even there, key provisions would be suspended as long as the mainland was in a state of "Communist rebellion."

Father remained working in Shanghai as long as possible. As a result of the reregistration of all lawyers, he was issued a new membership card by the bar association in February 1948. Twenty-one years had elapsed since the reregistration in the wake of the Northern Expedition, and, judging from the photograph, time had taken its toll. The face that peered out from the membership card was that of an old man with sunken cheeks. His gray hair was cut short, almost into a crew cut, and the hairline was noticeably receding. The eyes, still piercing, were somewhat cloudy. The mouth showed a hint of a droop.

By the summer of 1948, the Communists were surging south toward Shanghai. In early 1949, Father decided that it was time to go to Hong Kong. There he joined Mother and their children, as well as Alice.

Alice had left Shanghai in 1947, after her graduation. In Hong Kong, she had been working as a ground stewardess for an airline, the China National Aviation Corporation, one of two Chinese airlines. She left Hong Kong for the United States in 1949, the first member of our family to do so. Her departure left a vacuum in my life. She, as the big sister, used to take all of us out on Sundays, first to church and then to lunch. Often, even when she was on a date, she would let us tag along. I was only eight years old when she left and, for months afterward, I used to dream about her return.

At the time of Alice's departure, the Nationalist forces were in full retreat, with the Communists pressing inexorably southward. On October 1, 1949, Mao Zedong proclaimed in Peking, "The Chinese people have stood up!" and established a new government, that of the People's Republic of China. The political division of China into the Communist-ruled mainland and Nationalist-ruled Taiwan had begun. For decades, the division separated husbands and wives, parents and children, as well as brothers and sisters.

In Hong Kong, the airline for which Alice had worked, China National Aviation Corporation, divided into pro-Communist and pro-Nationalist factions. On November 9, nine CNAC commercial aircraft and two owned by its sister company, Civil Aviation Transportation Corporation, defected by flying unannounced to Communist-controlled sites in China. Senior officials of the airlines went with the pilots.

The defections created legal problems in Hong Kong. Britain still recognized the Kuomintang government, but the Communists immediately laid claim to the airline's assets in the British colony. With the airline inoperational, its employees, who were no longer receiving salaries, submitted a winding-up petition. The situation was later complicated by Britain's announcement that it was switching diplomatic recognition from the Kuomintang to the Communists. The legal wrangle was ultimately settled with the new Communist government assuming responsibility for the airline. The company was not wound up, but remained inactive for the next two decades. It has now been revived, not as an airline but as the agent of China's national airline, CAAC (or the Civil Aviation Administration of China).

Before Alice left for the United States, she helped Mother place all four children in Catholic missionary schools. I was taught first by Italian nuns, then by Irish Christian brothers. Father took almost no interest in us, and had only a vague awareness that we were in school.

At that time, of Father's earlier children, Jiaxiu, his eldest daughter, had died of illness in 1949. Margaret remained in Shanghai with her husband, Henry, and their children. Our eldest brother, Jiaju, was working for a bank in Shanghai, Jiajun had been killed and Jiahua, the third son, was doing odd jobs in various places between periods of unemployment. In any event, they were all adults and no longer his responsibility.

Though his second set of children was much younger, Father made no provision for them. He had brought substantial sums out from China, amounting to a modest fortune, but he no longer had a regular income. Nevertheless, instead of making prudent investments, he continued to persue an uninhibited life-style, squandering his funds on speculation and gambling. He made periodic visits to the casinos of Macao, invariably returning with empty pockets. Perhaps he thought that this was but another interlude in his life, and that he would be able to resume his career later on.

When he was young, Father gave himself another name that he used throughout the rest of his life except on formal occasions. The name he chose was Daishi, or "Waiting for the Time." Father always felt that, one day, his time would come and so he waited. He had

464

been attracted to Mother when she was a young girl, and he waited for her to grow up. During the Japanese occupation, he waited for eight years, and finally came victory. Now, with the Communists entrenched on the mainland, Father had to bide his time again. But at some point, he must have realized that his time was running out.

Still, he never lacked for friends, even in Hong Kong. He had always been generous, both with his money and his time, and his friends responded in kind. When he was in need, he often received gifts of money from one old friend or another. Two million people flooded into the British colony to flee from the Communists. Among them were some of his closest friends, including Du Yuesheng and Zhang Danru. Like Father, they preferred to live in the British colony rather than under the Communists on the mainland or under the Kuomintang in Taiwan.

Mao Zedong sent an emissary to Hong Kong to persuade well-known personages like Du Yuesheng to return to the mainland. The emissary was Zhang Shizhao, an eminent legal scholar and a good friend of Father's. According to those present at the encounter between Du and Zhang, the conversation went like this:

Du: Is it true, Mr. Zhang, that you have decided to live in Peiping [Peking]?

Zhang: Yes.

Du: Are you going to continue to practice law?

Zhang: Er, well, under Communist rule there won't be any need for lawyers. I won't be able to practice but . . .

Du: Well, since you can't be a lawyer, are you planning to go into business?

Zhang: The Communist system may not permit private enterprise. But Chairman Mao has told me personally that he will be responsible for my welfare. With such a promise from Chairman Mao, why should I still have any worries about my livelihood?

Du: Ah, so you don't have to worry about making a living.[7]

Du Yuesheng decided not to return to the mainland. Father, too, was invited to return to China, but declined even though his old friend Shen Junru had been appointed president of the Supreme People's Court. Another friend of Father's, the match and wool entrepreneur O. S. Lieu, did decide to return. By 1951, he was under attack as a capitalist as the Communists began to nationalize industry and commerce.

Zhang Shizhao returned to live in Peking but, in 1970, he was back in Hong Kong to be with his fourth wife, who was thirty years his junior. Actually, Mrs. Zhang was undecided about the wisdom of marrying him, and Father was the one who had talked her into it. He told her that a thirty-year age difference was not an obstacle. She did not know, until I happened to tell her many years later, that Father himself had married a woman twenty-eight years younger than he.

In the early years of the People's Republic, it was still relatively easy to leave the country. In 1951, our oldest brother, Jiaju, suddenly appeared in Hong Kong with his common-law wife. Father told him that he should not have left Shanghai, where he had a job, for the uncertainty of Hong Kong. Moreover, Father himself was without an income at the time. My oldest brother had always been Father's favorite, and it must have pained the old man to tell him to go back to China.

In the early 1950s, both Julia and Anthony left Hong Kong, she for the United States and he for France. As far as I could see, Father took little interest in these events. Before Anthony left for France, he gave Father a character to analyze, the word *fa*, which means both "law" and "France." Father took one look at it and said, "Oh, you're going abroad." He explained that the word *fa* was made up of the water radical on the left and the word *chu*, which means travel, on the right. So, taken in combination, it meant that Anthony was about to cross the ocean. It was uncanny, or so I thought. Before my brother left, Father told him that he would not mind if Anthony married a non-Chinese. Ultimately, that was exactly what my brother did.

Mother had to work to support the family and take care of all domestic problems. Once, frustrated because I was falling behind in school, she dragged me to Father and complained that I was lazy. He was so angered that he immediately took off his shoe and started to smack me on the face with it. Mother quickly stopped him. She never asked him to take an interest in the children's education again.

That is not to say that he was not concerned about us. When he saw Priscilla and me roller-skating outside the house one day, he told us that it was dangerous and asked us to stop. On another occasion, on my birthday, he invited some friends to dinner in a restaurant and, even though he was paying, told them I was the host. He was so pleased at the thought that his youngest son was now old enough to invite him to dinner.

Father's health, which had never been good, deteriorated as his spirits declined. His eyesight became poor and his hearing, too, was impaired. But his worst problem was his abdominal pains. Being superstitious, he refused to see a doctor, convinced that a doctor would diagnose cancer. To dull the pain, for years he kept a hot-water bottle constantly pressed against his side. Eventually, the skin in that area turned black.

As he got older, he was constantly constipated, and found it necessary to go for long walks to help his digestion. He also became highly photosensitive. At his request, I painted all the windowpanes in his room green, but he still complained about the light. Ultimately, I had to board up all the windows so that, even during the day, his room would be pitch dark. He had only one tiny desk lamp, with a five-watt bulb covered by a dark green shade. He used to pile towel upon towel over the shade, so that there was only a tiny pinprick of light.

His room, which was always dark and dirty, became a haven for rats and mice, especially because he often kept food lying around. Because Father was born in the Year of the Rat, he would not harm them. Once, when he was out, I went into his room to investigate. I moved the furniture around but could find no sign of the rodents. I sat on the bed to think, and immediately heard loud squeaking. The mice, it turned out, had turned Father's bed into their home, nesting beneath the mattress, in the boxspring. Ultimately, Father said that he had to fight back. It was either he or the rats, he said. I set a trap and at night heard fearful screams. Our cat was caught in it.

But worse than his physical decline was his mental deterioration. Father became paranoid, suspecting that people, especially Mother, were trying to kill him. He even suspected me. One night, I was playing with a flashlight with another boy who lived upstairs. Father said I was signaling someone to set off poison gas. He survived, he said, only because he sat up all night with an orange peel against his nose to act as a gas mask.

Married as he was to a much younger woman, Father had always been prone to jealousy. Now that he felt old and helpless, he accused Mother of wanting to kill him so that she could marry again. Finally, Mother said that if he suspected that, then it would be better for them to get a divorce, so she would have no reason to kill him. He objected strenuously but, in the end, consented. He insisted on drawing up the divorce papers, taking two years to do so. After the papers were drawn, my parents considered themselves divorced, though there had been no legal formality.

The "divorce" actually made very little difference. Father always

467

had his own room, even before the divorce, and continued to live in it afterward. He would sleep till noon, ask Priscilla to read him the weather forecast, and then go on his constitutional walk, often not returning until ten or eleven at night. Even on these nocturnal walks, he carried an umbrella to shield him from streetlamps. For a long time, Jiaxiu's husband accompanied him on these walks, helping him up the slope and the steps. Later, Jiaxiu's daughter assumed the task as her father, too, was getting old and weak.

On one occasion I was asked to accompany him for the day. We spent hours walking, then he stopped in a restaurant for lunch, a place that he apparently frequented. It was then that I had my one and only conversation with Father about my future career. Since he was a lawyer, I mustered my courage and asked, "Father, do you think I should be a lawyer?" Immediately, he responded, "No, no, you have to be very smart to be a lawyer."

Because our house was on a hill, and access to it could only be gained by a long series of stone steps, Father found the ascent difficult. Sometimes, when he felt particularly weak, he would not come home at all, staying in a hotel for days. His favorite hotel was a place called Winner House. Priscilla and I would visit him while he lay in his hotel bed.

In 1957, Margaret and Henry came from Shanghai with their children, Edward, Michael and Rita. Though they are my nephews and niece, they are my age; Edward, in fact, is five days older than I. Their arrival made life much more interesting for me.

The day Margaret arrived, she came to see Father. Although Margaret was devoted to him, Father's superstition caused him to keep her at a distance, because she was born in the year of the snake, and snakes eat rats.

Father's stays in hotels became more and more frequent as he got weaker. Often, Priscilla would spend the night with him, sleeping on the floor next to his bed. Every time he coughed, she would jump up and hand him a Garrick cigarette tin lined with newspaper, which he used as a cuspidor. He commended her for her filial piety, but she says she responded so quickly because she dreaded a lump of spittle landing on her as she lay on the floor.

Even toward the end, Father was concerned about his appearance. He dyed his hair, but not with enough regularity to prevent the gray from showing. His face was completely smooth, not because he shaved but because he plucked out all the hairs. He had an aversion to baths. Occasionally, he would wipe himself clean with a wet towel. Perhaps once a year, he took a steam bath. He would order pots of boiling water poured into the bathtub, after which he would sit on the edge and let the steam envelop his body, emerging clean and refreshed.

His paranoia never left him. He used to say that he had left a letter in his safety-deposit box accusing my mother of murdering him, a letter to be opened in the event of his death. He accused the children of taking sides, once telling me that half of me belonged to him, and only half to my mother. He dreaded the thought of death, and told Priscilla that it was a pity that she could not give him some years of her life, since she had so many years left.

On January 27, 1959, at the age of seventy, Father was found dead in bed, his upper body slumped over a chair. He had evidently attempted to get up but could not.

We were all worried about the letter that Father had said accused Mother of murder. By law, his bank-deposit box was automatically sealed upon his death. Finally, through the good offices of a sympathetic bank official, we got the safety-deposit box opened. It yielded only a stack of old letters and some bottles of medicine.

When I first discovered that Father was dead, my immediate feeling was one of relief. I felt that he had made life difficult for all of us, Mother as well as the children. When I returned home with the death certificate, I saw Margaret at a distance, her face contorted. I thought she, too, was showing relief at his death. But as I got closer, I realized that she was torn by grief. It came as a surprise to me that Margaret could have loved Father so much, when I thought of him only as a self-centered old man who was nothing but trouble. But then, of course, Margaret had known him when he was at the height of his career, and all I saw was his shell.

Looking back on these events, I see Father in a very different light. He was, I think, a man of many contradictions; a man who was loyal to his friends, yet neglected his closest family members; a man who cared deeply about principles, yet was practical enough to stay out of political entanglements; a romantic willing to defy convention, yet cruel to the women in his life. He was a brilliant lawyer who had achieved great success in his career in a turbulent period of Chinese history. But flaws in his personality, evidenced by his addiction to speculation and gambling, caused him to be controlled by events rather than to be master of his own destiny. In the final analysis, he was a tragic figure. His motto in life, which he imparted to his wife and his earlier children, was this:

Harbor no desire to injure anyone
But always be on guard against everyone.

News of Father's death did not reach his sons in China for some time. It is doubtful if he had much knowledge about their whereabouts. If he did it would not have made his last days any easier, for both of them were in political trouble. In the autumn of 1957, Jiahua, who was working at the Xinhua Bookstore, was labeled a "rightist." He was sent to be "reeducated through labor" by working in the countryside outside Shanghai. A few months later, Jiaju, too, was sentenced to reeducation through labor and sent to Anhui province, under the supervision of the Public Security Ministry, where he worked first as a cook, then cultivated vegetables and finally made wooden boxes.

Both brothers were victims of the same political climate. In the spring of 1957, Chairman Mao had raised the slogan "Let a hundred flowers bloom, let a hundred schools of thought contend," urging anyone with criticisms to step forward. The massive discontent with Communist rule that this disclosed caused Mao to clamp down hard, and hundreds of thousands of people were labeled as rightists.

At the time of Father's death, few outside China suspected that there were serious rifts within the highest leadership of the Communist party. Certainly, China's political campaigns were not foremost in our minds in the months following his death. There were more pressing matters at hand. Our family was getting ready to leave Hong Kong. Within months of Father's death, both Priscilla and Mother left, Priscilla for the United States and Mother for the British colony of Borneo, where she would work for the government and, we hoped, start a new life. The following year, I, too, left for the United States. Returning to China in quest of my origins could not have been further from my mind.

Paradoxically, it was Henry Kissinger's secret trip to China in 1971, followed by President Richard Nixon's official visit a few months later, that turned my attention back to my old homeland. The thaw in U.S.-China relations made it possible for Chinese-Americans to visit long-separated relatives, and awakened in me a yearning to learn more about my own origins. The call of my ancestors was one I did not hear for years but, when I finally did, responding to it became a consuming passion.

NOTES

Prologue

1. Interview in Peking on June 30, 1984, with Lu Dingyi of Wuxi, a former alternate Politburo member and propaganda chief of the Chinese Communist Party.

2. Subsequently, I discovered that both volumes are available in many libraries, including those in Peking and Hangzhou. The two volumes are called *Ming Qiu Guan Wenji* (*Essays from the Clear Autumn Study*) and *Ming Qiu Guan Shiji* (*Poems from the Clear Autumn Study*). These volumes yielded details of my grandparents' personal lives, including the only picture of my grandmother, who died thirty-four years before I was born.

3. *Wen Hui Bao*, July 26, 1982, p. 2.

4. *The Wall Street Journal*, February 2, 1983.

5. For lack of funds, the Wuxi authorities were unable to construct a road to the gravesite, so it is still quite difficult to find. But in 1987 a tramline was built from the foot of Mount Hui to the peak.

Chapter One

1. This incident is described in the chronological biography of Qin Guan prepared by Qin Ying, his twenty-eighth-generation descendant. It is also recorded in *Qin Shaoyou Yanjiu* (*A Study of Qin Shaoyou [Qin Guan]*) by the scholar Wang Pao-chen (Taiwan: Hsueh Hai Publishing House, 1981), p. 7, citing *Leng Zai Ye Hua* (*Night Chats in the Cold Studio*). Many details of Qin Guan's life in this and the following chapter are taken

from these two sources. Because the Wang volume is more easily accessible, it is the source more frequently cited here. I am grateful to Madame Wang for providing me with a copy of her work.

2. Edwin O. Reischauer, *Ennin's Travels in T'ang China* (New York: Ronald Press Co., 1955, p. 163).

3. *The Travels of Marco Polo* (The Broadway Travellers' Series), (London: Routledge & Kegan Paul, 1950), pp. 224–225. Translated into English from the text of L. F. Benedetto by Professor Aldo Ricci. Cited by Reischauer, *Ennin's Travels,* p. 2.

4. Wang Pao-chen, op. cit., p. 1. Also in the narrative biography prepared by Hilary Kromelow Josephs in "The *tz'u* of Ch'in Kuan" (1049–1100), Dissertation, Harvard University 1973, and Julia Ching's essay on "Ch'in Kuan" in *Sung Biographies,* edited by Herbert Franke (Wiesbaden: Steiner, 1976), pp. 235–241.

5. For details on the education of Song dynasty children, see "Life in the Schools of Sung China," by Thomas H. C. Lee, *Journal of Asian Studies,* November 1977.

6. This is different from the *San Zi Jing,* or *Three Character Classic,* which became popular in later centuries.

7. John William Chaffee, "Education and Examinations in Sung Society," Ph. D. dissertation, University of Chicago, 1979, p. 82.

8. Wang Pao-chen, op. cit., p. 3.

9. Adapted from Joseph Needham, *Science and Civilization in China,* (New York: Cambridge University Press, 1954), Vol. 1, p. 103.

10. Edwin O. Reischauer, *East Asia: The Great Tradition,* (Boston: Houghton Mifflin, 1960), p. 166.

11. Prescribed mourning ceremonies are to be found in *Da-Dai li-ji* (*The Book of Rites According to the Elder Dai*).

12. Personal data on Qin Guan's in-laws have been presented by Peter Bol in "Culture and the Way in the Northern Sung," doctoral dissertation, University of Chicago, 1981. The information was drawn from Qin's Guan's writings, especially the funerary biographies of his in-laws. Qin

Guan's works have been published in Chinese as *Huai Hai Ji* (*Collected Works of Huai Hai*). Huai Hai was another name by which Qin Guan was known.

13. Marriage customs during the Song dynasty are described in detail in *Songdai Zheng Jiao Shi* (*History of Political and Cultural Customs in the Song Dynasty*) and in *Dongjing Meng Hua Lu* (*A Record of Dreaming of Hua in Dongjing*), the richest source for urban life in the Northern Song. For information on this important book, see Stephen H. West, "The Source, Evaluation and Influence of the Dongjing Meng Hua Lu," in *T'oung Pao*, Vol. LXXI (1985), pp. 63–105.

14. The word for "chopsticks," *kuaizi*, is a homonym for "quick—a son." The word for fish, *yu*, bears the same sound as a word that means "to have more than enough," that is, "prosperity." Another marriage custom, which survives to this day, is the eating of lotus seeds (*lian-zi*) because the sound of the term is the same as that for "one son after another."

15. See *History of Chinese Society, 907–1125*, by Karl A. Wittfogel and Feng Chia-hsiang (New York: The MacMillan Co., 1949), for a detailed account of Liao society.

16. Needham, op. cit., Vol. I, p. 132, with minor modifications.

17. Bol, op. cit., p. 279.

18. I am indebted to Peter Bol for the explanation of the name "Great Void." See his dissertation, pp. 278–282.

19. Wang Anshi's culinary peculiarities are presented in Lin Yutang, *The Gay Genius: The Life and Times of Su Tungpo*, (New York: John Day Co., 1947), pp.76–77. I am grateful to Professor James T. C. Liu of Princeton University for pointing out that Lin's stereotypical account of Wang Anshi using evil characters to implement badly conceived policies is not generally accepted today.

20. For a fuller account of Wang Anshi, see James T. C. Liu's *Reform in Sung China: Wang An-shih (1021–1086)* (Cambridge, Mass.: Harvard University Press, 1959). Also see *Wang An-shih: Practical Reformer?*, ed. John Meskill (Boston: D.C. Heath and Co., 1963).

21. E. A. Kracke, Jr., *Civil Service in Early Sung China, 960–1067* (Cambridge, Mass.: Harvard University Press, 1953), pp. 33–37.

22. Cited by James T. C. Liu in *Reform in Sung China,* p. 66.

23. For the biography of Sun Jue, see the official history of the dynasty, *Song Shi* (*Song History*), Vol. 103.

24. During the Song, unlike in later dynasties, the conferring of the *juren* degree was not permanent. If a candidate failed to pass the metropolitan examinations, he had to take the qualifying examinations at the prefectural level again before he could take part in the next metropolitan examinations. Furthermore, unlike later *juren*, who were graduates of provincial-level examinations, the Song dynasty *juren* could not hold office. I am indebted to Professor Deng Guangming of Peking University for this information.

25. *China's Examination Hell: The Civil Service Examinations of Imperial China,* by Ichisada Miyazaki, translated by Conrad Schirokauer, (New Haven: Yale University Press, 1981), p. 92.

26. Much of the description of the examination system is drawn from Miyazaki.

27. A detailed account of the arrest and trial of Su Dongbo is found in Lin, op. cit., pp. 187–204.

28. The compactness of the Chinese language, the frequent usage of classical references and literary allusions, together with a grammar that permits lines with verbs without subjects or objects, render the task of translating poems from Chinese into English extraordinarily difficult. In this poem, the word translated as "Fairyland" is *Penglai,* the name of a Daoist paradise that also happened to be the name of the pavilion in which Qin Guan stayed. Qin Guan is said to have fallen in love during his sojourn in Yuezhou, and the poem suggests that he was recalling a personal experience. The first line of the poem, "Mountains rubbed by light clouds," is *Shan mo wei yun* in Chinese or, literally, "mountain rub slight cloud." Su Dongbo liked this poem so much that he copied it down on his fan, and took to calling Qin Guan "Mr. Mountain Rub Slight Cloud." The piece became one of the most popular tunes sung by courtesans in Kaifeng and other major cities. Both the translation and the explanation are derived from James J. Y. Liu's

Major Lyricists of the Northern Sung (Princeton, N.J.: Princeton University Press, 1971). Reprinted by permission of Princeton University Press.

29. Translated by Burton Watson in *Su Tung-p'o: Selections from a Sung Dynasty Poet* (New York: Columbia University Press, 1965), pp. 78–79.

30. Miyazaki, op. cit., p. 74.

31. Bol, op. cit., pp. 316–321, explains significance of new name.

Chapter Two

1. "Let us take a look at Buddhism from its practice," Cheng Yi wrote. "In deserting his father and leaving his family, the Buddha severed all human relationships. It was merely for himself that he lived alone in the forest. Such a person should not be allowed in any community. Generally speaking, he did to others what he himself despised. Such is not the mind of the sage, nor is it the mind of a gentleman." Quoted from *Sources of Chinese Tradition,* ed. William Theodore de Bary, (New York: Columbia University Press, 1960), Vol. 1, p. 478.

2. Lin, op. cit., pp. 154–155.

3. Translation by Josephs, op. cit., pp. 81–82. Reprinted with permission. Josephs cites "Kao-chai shih-hua" to the effect that this woman was an army courtesan.

4. Translation by James J. Y. Liu, op. cit., p. 113, who cites this as example of Qin Guan's "daring eroticism and no less daring use of colloquial language." Reprinted by permission of Princeton University Press.

5. James J. Y. Liu, op. cit., pp. 110–111. Reprinted by permission of Princeton University Press.

6. Titled "New Year's Day," written in January 1930, in *Mao Tsetung Poems,* (Peking: Foreign Languages Press, 1976), p. 7.

7. Alan Ayling and Duncan Mackintosh, *A Collection of Chinese Lyrics* (London: Routledge and Kegan Paul, 1965), p. 131.

8. The criticism of "maiden's poetry" was made by Yuan Haowen, who, upon reading Qin's poem "Spring," which he felt contained an excess

475

of sentimentality, said he "finally realized yours was maiden's poetry." This was cited in Kojiro Yoshikawa, *An Introduction to Sung Poetry*, translated by Burton Watson, Harvard-Yenching Monograph Series, XVII (Cambridge, Mass.: Harvard University Press, 1967), p. 133.

9. Wang Pao-chen, op. cit., p. 27.

10. Bol says, (op. cit., p. 317), "Attacks on his conduct plagued [Qin] even after he received an appointment. Appointments were withdrawn and promotions were deferred repeatedly. Was it moral turpitude? Were his romantic lyric songs too suggestive of (illicit) pleasures? His accusers are not specific in our present records, and an accusation alone may well have been sufficiently damning at the time."

11. The description of Kaifeng is drawn from *A Record of Dreaming of Hua in Dongjing*. An English-language account is E. A. Kracke, Jr.'s "Sung Kaifeng: Pragmatic Metropolis and Formalistic Capital" in *Crisis and Prosperity in Sung China,* edited by John Winthrop Haeger (Tucson: University of Arizona Press, 1975). A remarkable scroll depicting scenes from everyday life in the Northern Song is the "Qing Ming Shang He Tu," and this has been transformed into an illustrated book, *A City of Cathay* (Taipei: National Palace Museum, 1980), with textual matter provided by Lin Yutang.

12. The courtesans in those days were themselves accomplished poets who could improvise when necessary. The late Professor Fang Chaoying, in a private communication dated Nov. 5, 1984, written in Englewood, N.J., recalled something that had happened in his undergraduate days sixty years previously: "I still remember a story my professor told the class. At a banquet the government geisha was asked to sing this song. After the first line the audience shouted 'Wrong!' for she ended the first line with *xieyang* instead of *chaomen*. The prefect was about to punish her when the honored guest intervened by suggesting to have her finish the song with the *yang* rhyme. After a moment she started singing. When she finished even the prefect applauded." By merely substituting a few words, she had been able to compose an excellent poem.

13. Biography of Qin Guan by Julia Ching in *Sung Biographies*, p. 237.

14. Volume 463 of *Xu Zi Zhi Tong Jian Chang Pian (Long Draft of the Comprehensive Mirror for Aid in Government Continued)*, an account of the Northern Sung dynasty that continues the work of Sima Guang (*Com-*

prehensive Mirror for Aid in Government), which ended with the beginning of the Song dynasty.

15. Ibid., Vol. 484.

16. The story of Qin Guan and Zhaohua is found in *Mo Zhuang Man Lu* (*Scattered Records of Mo Zhuang*), Vol. 3.

17. *Long Draft of the Comprehensive Mirror . . .* Vol. 83, where an official, Liu Cheng, accused Qin Guan of having relied on the prestige of Su in order to distort the Veritable Records.

18. *Night Chats in the Cold Studio.*

19. Translated by James J. Y. Liu, op. cit., p. 116. Reprinted by permission of Princeton University Press.

20. Translated by Josephs, op. cit., p. 22.

21. Accounts of Qin Guan's death are found in *Dong Du Shi Lue* (*Events in the Eastern Capital*), the biography of Qin Guan, and *Night Chats in the Cold Studio*, Chapter 7.

22. *Song History*, Vol. 19, and Kojiro Yoshikawa, op. cit., pp. 134–135, which said: "A list of the names of one hundred twenty men of the conservative party who were to be purged was drawn up and distributed to the provinces, together with orders that the list be carved in stone and set up in public places. . . . Orders were also given that the publication of literary works by the men whose names appeared on the list was to be halted."

23. Changzhou Fuzhi (*Changzhou Gazetteer*), Chapter 13.

24. *Song History*, Vol. 19.

25. *Hui Chen Lu* (*Removal of Obstructions*), Vol. 3, p. 14.

26. *Wuxi Xianzhi* (*Wuxi Gazetteer*), 1881 edition, Chapter 35, pp. 27–18. There have been many editions of the *Wuxi Gazetteer*, some of which will be referred to later in this book, but all citations will be from this, the most recent, edition, edited by Qin Xiangye. This was reprinted in Taipei in 1968 by the Wuxi Fellow Townsmen's Association under the supervision of the eminent historian Ch'ien Mu.

Chapter Three

1. "Peking Gains Favor with Chinese in U.S.," *The New York Times*, February 22, 1971. p. 1.

2. *Xishan Qin Shi Zongpu* (*Ancestral Genealogy of the Qin Clan of Wuxi*), Preface. Since nine editions of the family genealogy were published, references throughout will be to the last one, the editing of which, under the supervision of my maternal great-grandfather, Qin Dunshi, was completed in 1928, and probably appeared in 1929.

3. *Wuxi Gazetteer*, Chapter 35, pp. 27–28.

4. *Yongzheng Zhupi Yuzhi* (*Vermilion Edicts of the Yongzheng Emperor*), written on the sixth day of the sixth month of the fifth year of the Yongzheng reign era, or July 24, 1727.

5. For loss of northern China to the Jurchens, see *Sung Biographies,* pp. 1092–1095.

6. Text of 1123 treaty documents can be found in Herbert Franke's "Treaties Between Sung and Chin," in *Sung Studies, Series 1,* ed. Françoise Aubin (Paris: Mouton & Co., 1970), pp. 60–64.

7. Ibid., pp. 68–73, for the 1126 treaty documents.

8. Ibid., pp. 77–78, for the 1141 treaty documents.

9. The official biography of Qin Kui in *Song History* is categorized under "Evil Officials," Chapter 473, p. 13747 (Peking: Zhenghua Publishing House, 1977). A more objective one, written in German, can be found in *Sung Biographies,* pp. 241–247.

10. James T. C. Liu, "Yueh Fei (1130–41) and China's Heritage of Loyalty," *Journal of Asian Studies,* Vol. XXXI, No. 2, February 1972, p. 295.

Chapter Four

1. The interview with the Shanghai Museum curator provided my introduction to the City God. Much of the information he supplied, it turned out, is also available in *Shanghai Xianzhi* (*Shanghai Gazetteer*).

2. The life story of Qin Yubo as well as his later exploits as the City God of Shanghai was compiled into one volume, *Qin Jingrong Xiansheng Shiji Kao* (*An Examination of the Historical Record of Mr. Qin Jingrong*) in 1933 by Qin Xitian, a member of the Shanghai branch of the Qin clan. "Jingrong" was another name for Yubo.

3. Reischauer, *East Asia: The Great Tradition,* p. 272.

4. The Mongols divided the population into four categories—Mongols; "people with colored eyes," such as people of Turkish or other Central Asian or Western origin; northern Chinese; and southern Chinese, with the southerners at the bottom of the scale. One indication of the contempt in which Chinese were held was the suggestion by a chief councillor that killing off all people with the five commonest surnames—Zhang, Wang, Liu, Li and Zhao—about half the population, would minimize trouble. See Charles O. Hucker's *The Ming Dynasty: Its Origins and Evolving Institutions,* Michigan Papers in Chinese Studies (Ann Arbor: University of Michigan, Center for Chinese Studies, 1978). No. 34.

5. Biography of Qin Zhirou is in *Shanghai Gazetteer.*

6. Biography of Qin Lianghao is in *Shanghai Gazetteer.*

7. The last Mongol to ascend the throne was a teen-ager, who had so little concern for his subjects that he forbade all women in the empire to marry until after he had finished selecting his harem. See Hucker, op. cit., p.7.

8. For more information on Zhang Shicheng, see entry under his name, Chang Shih-cheng, in *Dictionary of Ming Biography, 1368–1644,* edited by L. Carrington Goodrich and Fang Chaoying (New York: Columbia University Press, 1976), pp. 99–102.

9. See *Ming Shi* (*Ming History*) for biography on Qin Yubo. Taipei: Kaiming Shudian, p. 705.

10. See *Songjiang Gazetteer.*

11. For details of Zhu's rise to power and his defeat of Zhang see Goodrich and Fang, op. cit., pp. 381–385, biography of Chu Yuan-chang.

12. Texts of all letters from Zhu Yuanzhang to Qin Yubo and Qin's re-

sponses are found in *An Examination of the Historical Record of Mr. Qin Jingrong*, which cites the Qin ancestral genealogy as the source.

13. Arguments based on loyalty and filial piety were the most persuasive that could be used in traditional China. This portion of Qin Yubo's response is cited in most biographies of him, including that in the *Ming History*.

14. The significance of the saying is that "barbarian horses" from the north are moved by breezes blowing in from their homeland while birds from the south build their nests on the southern branches of trees. Since even horses and birds instinctively know where they belong, Zhu Yuanzhang argued, then a man such as Qin Yubo should know that his real loyalties should lie with his fellow Chinese and not with the Mongols.

15. Edward L. Dreyer, in *Early Ming China* (Stanford, Calif.: Stanford University Press, 1982, p. 105), says that the emperor abolished all posts above that of minister and ordered those officials "to report to him personally." However, as Dreyer points out on p. 213, grand secretaries, who were originally used to help the emperor draft documents, eventually "rose from clerks to great ministers of state."

16. Charles O. Hucker, in *The Traditional Chinese State in Ming Times* (Tucson: University of Arizona Press, 1961, pp. 9–10), declares: "Every male descendant of every Ming emperor in the male line, all bearing the surname Chu, theoretically received some title of royalty and a corresponding emolument from state funds. . . . It has been estimated that by the end of the Ming period the number of living clansmen had swelled to one hundred thousand."

17. Cao Yishi, "Shanghai-xian Cheng-huang Shen-ling Yi-ji" ("Record of Strange Occurrences Regarding the City God of Shanghai") in *An Examination of the Historical Record of Mr. Qin Jingrong*, pp. 24–31.

18. *North China Herald*, August 21, 1935.

19. Details of what occurred to the City God and his temple during the Cultural Revolution were provided by a spokesman for the Daoist Association of China in an interview on May 28, 1986.

Chapter Five

1. In 1819, an attempt was made to uncover portraits of all major ancestors. Portraits of Qin Guan and Qin Weizheng, done by contempor-

aries, were found. In addition, the portrait of Qin Guan's son, Qin Zhan, was found in the *Ancestral Genealogy of the Qin Clan of Piling*. However, those of eight figures could not be uncovered. Ultimately, a painter was commissioned to prepare fourteen portraits, some based on old ones, but the majority based on little more than descriptions found in writings about the men. At least six of the portraits remain.

2. The odds against success at the examinations were almost astronomical, as quotas were set for successful candidates at all levels. In addition, the cost of hiring teachers, travel to and from examination centers in various cities, and lost earning power was such that families became impoverished by sending their sons to the examinations time after time.

3. *Xiancheng Jipu (Additional Information on Ancestral Tombs)*, a book compiled in 1795 with information primarily on the graves of prominent clan members, together with some personal information, p. 18.

4. Research done in the nineteenth century revealed that Weizheng had a younger brother, known as Ruiba, who was not mentioned in the Wuxi genealogy. This discovery was made by Qin Zhenjun, who, while in Majishan to locate the tomb of Weizheng's grandfather, encountered the descendants of Ruiba.

5. The legend of Wang Yazhou's dream was carried on as an oral tradition within the family. A number of sources refer to the dream, including articles written by Gu Guangxu, Liu Yong and Zhou Xiying, all of which can be found in *Zu De Lu (Record of the Virtues of the Ancestors)*, a four-volume handwritten work compiled in 1852, only two volumes of which remain. The most detailed account is by Qin Yuzhang, an eighteenth-generation descendant of Weizheng, prepared in the nineteenth century, which can be found in *Xishan Qinshi Wenchao (Prose Writings by Members of the Qin Family of Wuxi)*, Chapter 8, p. 17.

6. Wang's proposal to marry a daughter to Qin Weizheng is in Gu Guangxu's article.

7. *Additional Information on Ancestral Tombs* carries a description of Mr. Wang's grave, which was to the right of that of Qin Weizheng.

8. The poem is part of an anthology, *Xishan Qin Shi Shi Chao (Poetic Writings by Members of the Qin Family of Wuxi)*, published circa 1839. The painting itself is no longer extant.

9. The account by Yin Bangzhan is still extant and is included in *Records of the Virtues of the Ancestors*.

10. Text of Liu Yong's tombstone inscription is found in *Record of the Virtues of the Ancestors*.

11. Article by Zhou Xiying, which is also in Volume 1 of *Record of the Virtues of the Ancestors*.

12. The stories on Gou-jian and Fan Li are drawn, with minor alterations, from *Selections from Records of the Historian*, translated by Yang Hsien-yi and Gladys Yang (Peking: Foreign Languages Press, 1979).

13. When Lu Yu visited Wuxi in 1170, he recorded that Tin Mountain was still tin-bearing. However, he went on to cite a Han dynasty prophecy to the effect that "when there is no tin, the empire is stable; when there is tin, there is strife." His diary, published in English translation by the Chinese University Press, Hong Kong, under the title *South China in the Twelfth Century*, says on p. 46, "Even now, whenever tin is discovered, it is hastily covered up. No one dares obtain it."

Chapter Six

1. The legend regarding the birth of Qin Xu is to be found in *Xijin Shi Xiaolu* (*Tales of Wuxi*), Chapter five, p. 79. Xijin is another name for Wuxi.

2. Qin Xu was considered one of the most important scholars of the Qin family. Aside from Qin Guan, he is one of three men for whom a chronological biography, listing his activities on a year-by-year basis, was prepared. This is part of the seventeen-volume *Ancestral Genealogy of the Qin Clan of Wuxi*.

3. *A Persian Embassy to China: Being an Extract from Zubdatu't Tawarikh of Hafiz Abru*, translated by K. M. Maitra (New York: Paragon Book Reprint Corp., 1970), pp. 83–85.

4. Information on Qin Xu's life is drawn from his chronological biography, from his various epitaphs and his own writings, which have been gathered and published as part of *Qin Shi San Fu Jun Ji* (*Writings of the Three Gentlemen of the Qin Family*), published in 1929. The three

ancestors so honored are Qin Xu (1410–1494), Qin Jin (1467–1544) and Qin Han (1493–1566).

5. Official court dress for civilian and military officials was prescribed from the beginning of the Ming dynasty. Details, in English, are provided in *The Emperor's Procession: Two Scrolls of the Ming Dynasty* (Taipei: National Palace Museum, 1970), pp. 156–160.

6. Qin Kuai's writings were collected after his death and put together in a four-volume work entitled *Wu Feng Yi Gao (Fifth Peak Manuscript Left by Deceased* (because his home had been on the fifth peak). This work, which was never printed, is still available in hand-copied form.

7. Essays and poems about the bamboo stove have been collected and published in a small book entitled *Annals of the Bamboo Stove of the Ting Song Temple on Mount Hui,* to which my mother's grandfather, Qin Dunshi, contributed a preface.

Chapter Seven

1. See *The Book of Filial Duty*, translated by Ivan Chen (London: John Murray, 1908), for stories of Wu Meng and other filial sons.

2. Quoted from *A History of Chinese Philosophy*, by Fung Yu-lan, translated by Derk Bodde (Peiping: Henri Vetch, 1937).

3. Sometimes, the virtue of filial piety came into conflict with other Confucian virtues, such as loyalty to the state. For example, Derk Bodde, in his *Essays on Chinese Civilization* (Princeton, N.J.: Princeton University Press, 1981), quotes Confucius that father and son have the duty to hide each other from the authorities if one has committed a crime. A son who informs against his father or a wife against her in-laws would be guilty of a crime. As Bodde says: "Probably China is the world's only country where the true reporting of a crime could entail legal punishment for the reporter." According to Confucius, if a son finds his parents are guilty of wrongdoing, all he can do is "gently remonstrate with them. If he sees that they are not inclined to follow his suggestion, he should resume his reverential attitude but not abandon his purpose. If he is belabored, he will not complain" (Analects IV:18, cited in *Sources of Chinese Tradition*, Vol. 1, pp. 27–28).

NOTES

4. Article by Qin Yo, Yongfu's grandnephew, in the handwritten book *Records of the Virtues of the Ancestors,* Vol. 2.

5. Both the use of blood for medicinal purposes and treatment of the infected knee are recounted in the *Wuxi Gazetteer,* Chapter 24, biographies of filial sons, p. 5.

6. Long Jin proposal is in *Record of the Virtues of the Ancestors,* Vol. 2.

7. The names of these two filial sons are recorded in *Ming History,* Vol. 296, p. 4.

8. The Wen Zhengming text can be found in *Record of the Virtues of the Ancestors,* Vol. 2.

9. Quoted from the request to honor Tang as a filial son. Text found in *Record of the Virtues of the Ancestors,* Vol. 2.

10. Notation appended to Zhang Dalun request.

11. Quoted from biography of Qin Tang by Xu Wen, *Record of the Virtues of the Ancestors,* Vol. 2.

12. The Ministry of Personnel's copy of the request by Huai's son is in *Record of the Virtues of the Ancestors,* Vol. 2.

13. *Wuxi Gazetteer,* Chapter 24, pp. 6–7.

14. Xu Wen biography in *Record of the Virtues of the Ancestors,* Vol. 2.

15. Text of Qin Tang's letter declining nomination as a filial son is in *Records of the Virtues of the Ancestors,* Vol. 2.

16. Article on how Qin Tang was honored in the Temple of Worthies is in *Record of the Virtues of the Ancestors,* Vol. 2.

17. The story of two filial brothers in the nineteenth century was compiled into a book, *Xishan Qin-shi hou shuang-xiao wei-wen hui-lu (A Collection of Essays About the Later Filial Pair of the Qin Family of Wuxi).* A copy of this is in the Peking Library.

18. For Sung-yun, see *Eminent Chinese of the Ch'ing Period,* ed. Arthur W.

Hummel (Washington, D.C.: U.S. Government Printing Office, 1943), pp. 691–692.

19. Details of dream and filial activities, including the dialogue and the process of honoring the two brothers are from *A Collection of Essays About the Later Filial Pair* . . .

Chapter Eight

1. For the official biography of Qin Jin, see *Ming History*, Chapter 294, pp. 12–15. Also, *Ming Ming-chen yan-xing lu (Words and Acts of Famous Officials of the Ming Dynasty)*, Chapter 47, and *Ben Chao Jing-sheng Ren-wu kao (A Study of Capital Personages in the Current Dynasty)*, Chapter 28. In addition, there is a chronological biography of Qin Jin in the family genealogy.

2. The *Xiancheng Jipu*, compiled by Qin Jin's great-great-great-great-great-great-grandson, Qin Yunjin.

3. Story of the household god is in *Tales of Wuxi*, Chapter 11, p. 14.

4. Almost three hundred years later, Linqing would be the site of the defeat of the White Lotus uprising of 1774, when one of the descendants of the Qin family of Wuxi would play a central role.

5. An extremely detailed account of the battle is the article by Liu Wuchen in *Fengqiu Xianzhi (Fengqiu Gazetteer)*, Chapter 7, pp. 21–24.

6. Several accounts of the building and later reconstruction of the "life temple" in honor of Qin Jin are included in the *Fengqiu Gazetteer*, Chapter 7, pp. 21–30.

7. *Selected Works of Mao Tse-tung* (Peking: Foreign Languages Press, 1965), Vol. 2, p. 308.

8. *Veritable Records of the Zhengde Emperor*, Chapter 91, p. 1.

9. Ibid., Chapter 119, p. 3.

10. Ibid., Chapter 126, p. 10.

11. Ibid., Chapter 152, p. 2.

12. *Hong Yu-lu (Records of Great Bandits)* by Gao Dai, published in 1557, Chapter 14, pp. 168–170. This forms part of the collectanea *Ji-lu hui-pian (An Edited Classification of Records)* by Shen Jiefu, printed in 1617. *Records of Great Bandits* begins with Chapter 80. For life of Gao Dai, see Goodrich and Fang, op. cit., biography of Kao Tai, pp. 710–711.

13. Since Qin Jin and Qin Rui were fifth cousins, they were no longer close relatives and were not even obliged to mourn each other's death. The fact that they cooperated in the construction of the ancestral temple shows that both men meant this not for their own families but for the clan as a whole. It also shows the cohesiveness of the clan at that point, six generations after having moved to Wuxi.

Chapter Nine

1. Text of the memorial can be found in *Huang Ming jing-shi wen-pian,* a collection of essays and memorials of the Ming dynasty concerning political and economic problems, compiled in 1638. Taipei edition, 1964, Chapter 174, p. 1775.

2. Ibid., pp. 1774–1775. The Tai-ah Sword is the name of a fabled sword in ancient times.

3. For the text of the memorial see *Qin-ting si-ku quan-shu (Imperially Sanctioned Complete Library in Four Branches of Literature,* section on Ho Meng-cun memorials, Chapter 10, pp. 61–62.

4. *Veritable Records of the Jiajing Emperor,* Chapter 55, pp. 4–5.

5. Ibid., Chapter 56, pp. 1–2.

6. Ray Huang, in his book *Taxation and Governmental Finance in Sixteenth-Century Ming China* (New York: Cambridge University Press, 1974), says unequivocally on page 12 that Qin Jin, "after fighting losing battles with the eunuchs, retired in 1527."

7. *Veritable Records of the Jiajing Emperor,* Chapter 74, p. 7.

8. Ibid., Chapter 133, pp. 8–9.

9. Ibid., Chapter 191, p. 12.

10. Ibid., Chapter 282, p. 5.

11. The funeral service for Qin Jin and the description of his tomb are found in *Xiancheng Jipu* and the "Rites" section of *Siku Imperial Library*, Chapter 31, compiled by Yu Rujic.

12. This story is from *Tales of Wuxi*, Chapter 9.

Chapter Ten

1. *Tales of Wuxi*, Chapter 9, p. 34. This prophecy, however, is included in the section "Of Doubt," meaning that this is a story that should be treated with some skepticism.

2. "Account of Conduct," written after the death of Qin Liang by his cousin Chen Yizhong, published in *Liang Qi Wen-chao* (*Essays of Wuxi*), Chapter 11, pp. 10–17. "Liang Qi" was another name for Wuxi. Much of the information on Liang's life is drawn from this document.

3. Qin Han is one of the three prominent members of the Wuxi Qin clan for whom a year-by-year chronological biography was prepared. The story of Han's aunt's adopting him is from this account, which is part of ancestral genealogical records.

4. The two-volume *Xijin you xiang lu* (*Record of Those Who Attended the Confucian Academy in Wuxi*), published in 1878, provides a detailed listing of all students from the Wanli period of the Ming dynasty on for 254 years. Qin Liang's attendance predates this period. However, a preface written by Qin Gengtong, the uncle of my maternal great-grandfather, cites a stone plaque engraved in 1602, which gives the names of such famous officials as Shao Pao, Qin Jin, Qin Liang, Qin Yao, Qin Huai, Gu Xiancheng and Gao Panlong as having been educated there.

5. This is quoted in the epitaph of Qin Han, composed by Grand Secretary Li Shifang. This attitude is in line with the belief that it is the duty of an official to remonstrate with the emperor when he departs from the path of righteousness, even at the cost of his life.

6. *Guo-chao lieh-qing-ji* (*List of Officials of the Present Dynasty*), covering the period 1368 to 1566, compiled by Lei Li in the Ming dynasty and reprinted in Taiwan, 1970, in twenty-four volumes. See p. 5175.

7. The revival of the Blue Mountain Poetry Society was marked by an outpouring of essays by prominent scholars, including the future Grand Secretary Xu Jie. These have been collected and published in the book *Writings of the Three Gentlemen of the Qin Family*, which refers to Qin Xu, Qin Jin and Qin Han. Available in Peking Library.

8. From the epitaph of Qin Han.

9. Preface in *Wuxi Gazetteer*.

10. This essay is in "Writings of the Three Gentlemen of the Qin Family," appended to the section on Qin Han, and in *Essays of Wuxi*, Chapter 10, pp. 12–18.

11. Liang's last words are quoted by Chen Yizhong in his epitaph.

Chapter Eleven

1. For background on the pirate situation in the 1550s, see "Hu Tsung-hsien's Campaign Against Hsu Hai, 1556," in *Two Studies on Ming History*, by Charles O. Hucker, Michigan Papers in Chinese Studies, No. 12 (Ann Arbor: University of Michigan, Center for Chinese Studies, 1971).

2. *Jinhua Fuzhi* (*Jinhua Prefectural Gazetteer*), Chapter 2, p. 707. The gazetteer added that he "loved the people, admired literature, observed the rites and exhibited the style of a Confucian scholar."

3. Details of Yao's career can be found in his epitaph, written by Shi Ce, the text of which is in *Essays of Wuxi*, Chapter 11, pp. 5–9.

4. *Ming History*, Chapter 224, p. 2587, says that the Minister of Personnel had no choice but to go along with Grand Secretary Zhang. It adds that Qin Yao and Zhang's other protégés plotted against critics of the Grand Secretary.

5. The defeat of Li Yuanlang by Qin Yao, together with a biography of the bandit chieftain, is recorded in *Wanli Wu-gong lu* (*Military Exploits of the Wanli Era*), pp. 203–207.

6. *Essays of Wuxi*, pp. 32–33. Qin Yao's memorials from Huguang were compiled into a book and published as *Quan Qu Zou Shu* (*Complete*

Memorials from Huguang). A microfilm copy of this is kept in the National Central Library, Taipei.

7. *Tales of Wuxi*, Chapter 9.

8. See Ray Huang's excellent account in the book *1587: A Year of No Significance* (New Haven: Yale University Press, 1981).

9. *Prose Writings by Members of the Qin Family of Wuxi*, Chapter 2, p. 33.

10. Ibid., Chapter 7, pp. 27–28.

Chapter Twelve

1. Liao Mosha, director of the United Front Department of the Peking Municipal Committee, collaborated with Deng Tuo and Wu Han in a series of articles criticizing the party leadership through historical analogies or satire, published in the Peking party's theoretical journal *Frontline* between October 1961 and July 1964.

2. Defense Minister Peng Dehuai was likened to Hai Rui, the upright Ming dynasty official.

3. A graphic description of persecution of Donglin partisans is provided in Charles O. Hucker's "Su-chou and the Agents of Wei Chung-hsien, 1626," in *Two Studies in Ming History*.

4. Cited by Heinrich Busch, "The Tung-lin Academy and Its Political and Philosophical Significance," MS, XIV (1949–55), p. 123.

5. Ibid., p. 129.

6. The conversation between Qin Ercai and his teacher was recorded by Gao Panlong in an epitaph he wrote for his student. See *Donglin shuyuan zhi* (*Annals of the Donglin Academy*), pp. 34–36.

7. From Preface to *Qingjiang Gazetteer*.

8. Yong's activities in Qingjiang are detailed in his epitaph, which was prepared by his brother and was published in *Essays of Wuxi*, Chapter 39, pp. 25–35.

9. The "Four Prohibitions" appear in an anthology of Qing-dynasty poems known as *Qing shi duo,* Chapter 19, pp. 630–631.

10. For a graphic account of the final days of the last Ming emperor, see Frederic Wakeman, Jr.'s "The Shun Interregnum of 1644" in *From Ming to Ching,* edited by Jonathan D. Spence and John E. Wills, Jr. (New Haven and London: Yale University Press, 1979.)

11. Ibid., p. 59.

12. *Jiashen chuanxin lu (A Record of the Messages of 1644),* p. 96.

13. Wakeman, loc. cit., p. 59.

14. *A Record of the Messages of 1644,* p. 97.

15. Zhang Youyu, a *jinshi* of 1622, served the Ming and the Southern Ming and was named grand guardian of the heir apparent. He spent his last years as a Daoist philosopher.

Chapter Thirteen

1. For Schall's relationship with Shunzhi, see *Jesuits at the Court of Peking,* by C. W. Allan (Shanghai: Kelly and Walsh, reprinted in 1975 by University Publications of America, Inc., Arlington, Va.), especially pp. 143–147. The Shunzhi Emperor honored the Jesuit in the Chinese style, granting honorary titles first to his parents, then extending them to his great-grandparents.

2. On the legend of the Shunzhi emperor entering a monastery, see his biography in *Eminent Chinese of the Ch'ing Period,* edited by Arthur W. Hummel, pp. 255–259.

3. One Catholic missionary, Andreas Xavier Koffler, writing back to Europe at the time, commented: "The sign of defeat or submission for the Chinese was the cutting of their hair which they wore very long and well arranged. They esteem it so highly that many preferred to have their throats under the knife than their hair under the scissors." I am indebted to Albert Chan, S.J., for providing me with his translation of this document, which deals with the fall of the Ming dynasty and which was uncovered by him in the National Library of Madrid.

4. Lawrence D. Kessler, in *K'ang-hsi and the Consolidation of Ch'ing Rule, 1661–1684* (Chicago: University of Chicago Press, 1976, p. 170) has this to say: "The Southern Tours gave K'ang-hsi ample opportunity to self-consciously display these complementary virtues of Confucian sagacity and Manchu vitality: he was the 'serious-minded scholar' on the first tour in 1684 and the 'sensitive aesthete' in 1689, but by the third tour in 1699 he had become the hard-riding Manchu."

5. Much of the general information on the Kangxi Emperor's southern tours is drawn from Jonathan D. Spence, *Ts'ao Yin and the K'ang-hsi Emperor* (New Haven: Yale University Press, 1966).The information on Wuxi is culled from the *Veritable Records* of that emperor.

6. This first meeting with the emperor is described in the biography of Qin Dezao that appears in the book *Guochao qixian leicheng chupian (First Edition of the Various Categories of Venerable Personalities of the Present Dynasty)*. Compiled by Li Huan, it covers the period 1616 to 1850. The biography of Qin Dezao appears in the section on "Filial Piety and Brotherly Harmony," Chapter 383, pp. 1–3. The biography itself was composed by Zhang Yushu, an official and scholar who rose to become grand secretary.

7. The imperial conversation with Songqi is recorded in the chronological biography of Qin Dezao.

8. In *Qiu Shui Wenji (Collected Essays of Autumn Waters)*, pp. 5–7, appears a funerary biography of Qin Dezao written by the Wuxi scholar Yan Shengsun.

Chapter Fourteen

1. The appointment of Qin Songling to the Hanlin Academy is in *Veritable Records of the Shunzhi Emperor,* Chapter 111, p. 19. He was one of three men during the Qing dynasty to gain the *jinshi* degree before he was married.

2. *Veritable Records*, Chapter 117, pp. 8–10, dated June 12, 1658, only a week after the honor accorded the late consort of Prince Haoge.

3. Qin Dezao's advice to Songling against defending himself is reported in the funerary biography of the older man written by Yan Shengsun.

4. For reversal of Shunzhi's policies toward the Chinese by the regents, see Robert B. Oxnam, "Policies and Institutions of the Oboi Regency, 1661–1669," *Journal of Asian Studies,* February 1973. Oxnam says that Shunzhi's will was intercepted and replaced by another forged by his mother and the regents.

5. Meng Sen, "Zou Xiao An" ("Taxation Case"), in *Ming-Qing shi lun-zhu ji-kan* (Taipei: 1961), pp. 434–452. The case of Qin Songling is specifically dealt with on p. 451, where the author points out that the official history deliberately omitted all reference to the taxation case in reporting the dismissal of Songling.

6. *Tales of Wuxi,* Chapter 11, p. 20.

7. Yu Huai, "Ji Chang Yuan wen-ke-ji" ("Enjoyment of Songs in Ji Chang Garden"), in *Yu chu xin-zhi,* Chapter 4, pp. 3–4.

8. For more information on the significance of these special examinations, see Helmut Wilhelm "The Po-hsueh Hung-ju Examination of 1679," *Journal of the American Oriental Society,* LXXI (1951), pp. 60–66. Wilhelm describes the holding of these examinations as appeasement of defiant Chinese scholars to invite them back into the official fold.

9. *Veritable Records of the Kangxi Emperor,* February 14, 1678, translation by Wilhelm, slightly abridged.

10. A comprehensive account of these examinations, with biographies of each of the successful candidates, was compiled by Qin Ying, great-great-grandson of Qin Songling.

11. *Qing-dai wen-xian man-gu-lu (Ancient Facts on Qing Dynasty Literature),* Chapter 7, p. 203, lists Qin Songling as the first of eleven men during the dynasty to gain admission twice to the Hanlin Academy.

12. See Adam Y. C. Lui, *Chinese Censors and the Alien Emperor, 1644–1660,* (University of Hong Kong, 1978), Appendix II, Case No. 1, on impeachment of the examiners.

13. *Kangxi qi-ju-zhu (Diary of Kangxi),* First Historical Archives of China (Zhonghua Publishing House, 1984), Vol. 2, pp. 871–872.

14. Ibid., pp. 897–898.

15. Ibid., pp. 937–938.

16. Ibid., pp. 949–950. Kangxi's mistrust of the imperial diarists extends at least as far back as 1679. That year, for example, "his mistrust was revealed by his inquiry whether any personal inventions had been added to the records." See Adam Yuen-chung Lui, *The Hanlin Academy* (New York: Archon Books, 1981), p. 31.

17. *Diary of Kangxi*, pp. 984–985.

18. Ibid., p. 1009.

19. Ibid., pp. 1056–1057.

Chapter Fifteen

1. Hummel, op. cit., p. 899, adds that Yao's death "occurred early in the following year—hastened, it is said, by disappointment and chagrin."

2. *Diary of Kangxi*, Vol. 2, pp. 1066–1067.

3. Much of the description of the assizes procedure is drawn from M. J. Meijer, "The Autumn Assizes in Ch'ing Law," *T'oung Pao*, LXX (1984), pp. 1–17.

4. *Diary of Kangxi*, Vol. 2, pp. 1079–1082.

5. Ibid., pp. 1100–1101.

6. Ibid., pp. 1148–1149.

7. *Veritable Records of the Kangxi Emperor*, Chapter 116, p. 11.

8. Ibid., p. 25.

9. *Qing Shi Gao (Draft History of the Qing Dynasty)*, Chapter 271, biography on Xu Qianxue. The Xǔ family produced many outstanding scholars. Xu Qianxue himself came third in the *jinshi* examinations the year he graduated while one brother came first and another also came third.

10. *Ming-Qing shi lun-zhu ji-kan*, pp. 510–511, citing Qin Ying's book *Jiwei Ci Ke Lu*.

11. This conversation is recounted by Zhang Ying, who accompanied the emperor on this trip, in his book account of his southern journey included in the *Imperially Sanctioned Complete Library in Four Branches of Literature*. The relevant account appears on pages six and seven of Zhang Ying. According to legend, the camphor tree in which Kangxi showed so much interest withered and died at the emperor's demise. This is recorded, among other places, on page 20 of *Qing Gong Yi Wen* (*Strange Stories of the Qing Court*).

12. Account by Yan Shengsun in *Wuxi Gazetteer*, Chapter 38, pp. 1–3.

13. *Memoirs of Father Ripa*, selected and translated from the Italian by Fortunato Prandi (New York: Wiley & Putnam, 1846), Chapter 16, pp. 99–100.

14. *Wanshou Shengdian Chuji*, a book recording the celebration of the Kangxi Emperor's sixtieth birthday on April 12, 1713, was not completed until 1716. Songling's participation appears in Chapter ten of the 120-chapter work.

Chapter Sixteen

1. The most complete biography on Qin Daoran is his epitaph, composed by Qian Weicheng, noted official and artist, and can be found in the collection of Qian's writings known as *Chashan wenji*, Chapter 12, pp. 12–15.

2. *Liang Qi Shi Chao* (*Poetry of Wuxi*), Chapter 27, pp. 1–2. "Liang Qi" was another name for Wuxi.

3. Biographical notes on Daoran in *Prose Writings by Members of the Qin Family of Wuxi*, Chapter 5, p. 14.

4. Qin Daoran is listed among outstanding calligraphers of the Qing dynasty in the work *Qing Ming shu-hua-jia pi-lu* (*Record of calligraphers and painters of the Qing and Ming Dynasties*), Chapter one, p. 10.

5. *Poetry of Wuxi*, republished in 1912, Chapter 27, p. 2.

6. An excellent study of the Kangxi Emperor's relationship with his sons is *Passage to Power*, by Silas H. L. Wu, Harvard East Asian Series, no.91 (Cambridge, Mass.: Harvard University Press, 1979). The recruiting

of He Chao (or Ho Ch'o) as tutor of the Eighth Prince is recounted by Wu on p. 75.

7. "Qing-dai Huangzi jiaoyu" ("Education of Princes in the Qing Dynasty"), in *Jindai shi yu renwu (Modern History and Personalities)*.

8. Wu, op. cit., p. 47.

9. Wu, op. cit., p. 127, where Qin Daoran is quoted as saying, "They made every effort to please old Prince Yu and asked him to recommend Yin-ssu [the Eighth Prince] to the Emperor. Therefore, even while seriously ill, Prince Yu strongly recommended Yin-ssu to the Emperor for his talent and virtue."

10. Wu, op. cit., pp. 118–120.

11. Wu, op. cit., p. 164.

12. Wu, op. cit., pp. 138–140.

13. *Memoirs of Father Ripa*, p. 96.

14. Quotation from Kangxi's valedictory is condensed from *Emperor of China*, by Jonathan D. Spence (New York: Vintage Books, 1975), pp. 143–151.

15. *Diary of Kangxi*, Vol. 3, pp. 2466–2467.

16. Ibid., p. 2467.

17. Ibid., pp. 2467–2468.

18. Ibid., pp. 2468–2469.

19. Ibid., pp. 2469–2470.

20. Ibid., p. 2472.

21. Ibid., pp. 2472–2473.

22. Adam Yuen-chung Lui, "The Hanlin Academy," p. 31. More specifically, the article "Qing-dai qi-ju-zhu" ("Qing Imperial Diarists"), by Dan Shiyuan, says that Kangxi suspected that imperial diarists might

be agents for his sons and pass on information to them regarding his feelings on an heir apparent. "He Chao and Qin Daoran were later found guilty of involvement," Dan says.

23. Wu, op. cit., p. 128, says that Yin-tang made Qin Daoran his household and financial manager in violation of an imperial order that such a position could be held only by a household bond servant, not by a government official.

Chapter Seventeen

1. Whether the Yongzheng Emperor was a usurper remains a question debated by historians today. For example, Robert C. I. King, in his article "Emperor Yung-cheng's Usurpation: The Question of Yin-t'i," published in *Ch'ing-shi Wen-t'i*, Volume 3, November 1978, pp. 112–121, argues persuasively that the intended heir was the fourteenth son.

2. Hummel, on p. 917 of his biography of the Yongzheng Emperor, says: "Knowing that some official records of the latter part of his father's reign were unfavorable to himself and that some were favorable to his opponents, he decided to suppress or alter any records which he disliked. One of the revealing facts about the shih-lu, or veritable records, of his father's eventful reign is that they occupy a smaller compass per year than the shih-lu of any other Emperor of the Ch'ing period." The article also says that Yongzheng "suppressed so many documents concerning his brother, Yin-t'i, that little is now known about the latter's expedition to Lhasa." In light of this, the King article cited above is particularly intriguing.

3. This incident is recounted in *Wenxian Congpian* (*Miscellaneous Qing Historical Documents*) (Taipei reprint, 1964), which contains the text of depositions by Qin Daoran in a section titled "The Case of Yin-ssu and Yin-tang." On p. 26, Qin Daoran confirmed that he had been warned by an emissary from Yin-tang.

4. *Veritable Records of the Yongzheng Emperor*, Chapter 4, pp. 8–10.

5. Ibid., Chapter 12.

6. *Memoirs of Father Ripa*, p. 137.

7. Shao Yuanlong, who was also assigned to tutor Yin-tang, was shunted aside to teach that prince's son instead. In his testimony, he declared that Qin Daoran used to visit the prince every day by a private door, not leaving until late at night. He also said that Qin Daoran's gaining of the *jinshi* degree was due to Yin-tang's influence and that Daoran and the eunuch He Yuzhu were sworn brothers. Both these allegations were denied by Daoran. See "Case of Yin-ssu and Yin-tang," pp. 34–35.

8. See *Veritable Records*, Chapter 41, March 10, 1726 (2d month, 7th day, 4th yr.).

9. The text of Daoran's "confession," on which this section is based, can be found in "The Case of Yin-ssu and Yin-tang," pp. 26–33.

10. This second deposition can be found in "The Case of Yin-ssu and Yin-tang," pp. 4–10.

11. Ibid., p. 17.

12. *Yongzheng Zhu-pi Yu-zhi* (*Vermilion Edicts of the Yongzheng Emperor*), written on the sixth day of the sixth month of the fifth year of the Yongzheng reign era, or July 24, 1727.

13. *Prose Writings by Members of the Qin Clan of Wuxi*, Chapter 5, p. 14.

Chapter Eighteen

1. See Harold L. Kahn *Monarchy in the Emperor's Eyes*, (Cambridge, Mass.: Harvard University Press, 1971, p. 11), where it is also said that Qianlong was the putative author of "some 1,260 prose pieces—study notes, discourses, opinions, records, prefaces, colophons, inscriptions, prose poems, epitaphs and eulogies." Many of these may well have been written with the help of courtiers.

2. Epitaph of Qin Huitian, written by the scholar Qian Daxin, which can be found, among other places, in *Guochao Qixian Leicheng Chubian* (*First Edition of the Various Categories of Venerable Personalities in the Present Dynasty*). This funerary biography was classified in the section "Ministers," Chapter 81, pp. 20–24.

3. Examination topics for that year are found in *Qing Bi Shu Wen* (*Secret*

Information on the Qing Dynasty), Chapter 5, p. 154, compiled in 1798
by the Mongol scholar Fa-shih-shan, which lists examiners in the provincial and metropolitan examinations, topics and the top successful
candidates.

4. Qin Huitian's examination paper is reprinted in *Prose Writings by Members of the Qin Clan of Wuxi,* Chapter 6, pp. 9–12.

5. Description of Qianlong's ranking of the 1736 palace examination candidates is found in *Veritable Records of the Qianlong Emperor,* Chapter
16, pp. 7–8.

6. Ibid., p. 10. The ceremony of announcing the names of the top graduates is described in Miyazaki, op. cit., pp. 83–85.

7. *Veritable Records,* Chapter 17, p. 18.

8. Ibid., Chapter 18, p. 22.

9. Huitian actually never saw his adoptive father, Yiran, since that man
had died two days before Huitian's birth. This fact probably played a
part in assigning the baby as his posthumously adopted son, since it
was considered possible that Huitian was his reincarnation.

10. Actually, it was something of a miracle that Daoran, who had been
imprisoned in his late sixties, should have survived thirteen years of
incarceration. Though his book describing prison life is no longer
extant, it is known that prison conditions were in general horrendous.
A description of the prison administered by the Ministry of Punishments, where Daoran was held part of the time, is the article "Prison
Life in Eighteenth Century Peking," in *Essays on Chinese Civilization,* by
Derk Bodde. An eyewitness is quoted there as saying: "Every evening,
when the locks are closed, all the urine and excrement are left inside
to mix their vapors with the food and drink. And with destitute prisoners sleeping on the floor during the height of winter, there are few
who don't fall ill when the spring vapors begin to stir. . . . Throughout the night living persons and those who have died sleep next to
each other head to head and foot to foot, without any means of
turning away."

11. The text of this memorial is in the family genealogy. The original is
still in the Ming-Qing Archives in Peking, and I am grateful to Mr.
Liu Kui for locating it.

12. The other filial son of this era was Fang Guancheng, whose father and grandfather were banished to Tsitsihar. Fang, who lived in Nanking as a youth, used to visit them and eventually ended up living in Tsitsihar himself for years. He was favored by the Qianlong Emperor and rose to the rank of governor general.

13. This edict, too, was found in the Ming-Qing Archives. Its wording shows that, at least at this point, Qianlong did not fully trust Daoran and was not prepared to repudiate some of his father's actions.

14. The practice continues to this day. In fact, the word *fu*, or "good fortune," is often pasted upside down on the door, because the term "upside down" is a homonym for the word meaning "arrived." Thus, *fu dao le* can mean either that the word *fu* is upside down or, more propitiously, "good fortune has arrived."

15. Qin Huitian's diaries, actually titled *Random Jottings*, are primarily recordings of edicts concerning himself, imperial gifts and some essays, apparently not in any particular order, at least in the form they exist today. It is unclear how many volumes originally existed, but in the aftermath of the Cultural Revolution, only two volumes remain. Some appears to be in Huitian's own hand, while other parts were apparently copied down by later generations. The most recent date on them is 1878, when my mother's great-granduncle, Qin Gengtong, affixed his seal after having read the contents "with reverence."

16. The description of the ceremony of imperial plowing is drawn from three essays, which are in the Ming-Qing Archives, written by Huitian and two other officials. The *Veritable Records*, Chapter 63, p. 7, gives it only passing mention.

17. *Veritable Records*, Chapter 90, p. 8.

18. *Qing-dai Dingjia Lu* (*Records of the Three Top Graduates in the Qing Dynasty*), Chapter 1, p. 10.

19. *Veritable Records*, Chapter 159, p. 8.

20. Ibid., Chapter 200, pp. 7–13, and Chapter 201, pp. 1–11.

21. Ibid., Chapter 205, p. 4.

22. Text of this memorial can be found in *Huang Qing Zou Yi (Memorials to the Throne in the Qing Dynasty)*, Chapter 41, pp. 13–16.

23. Ibid., Chapter 42, pp. 1–8.

24. Qianlong's response to Huitian's memorial can be found in Vol. 7, Chapter 81, pp. 1–2, of the book *Qinding Nanxun Shengdian, (Imperially Approved Record of Southern Tours)*, the official record of the emperor's first four southern journeys, compiled in 1771.

25. Details on Wuxi's preparations for the imperial visit are culled from *Zhuo Quan Lu (Record of the Pouring Forth of the Spring)*, a book about Wuxi.

26. *Veritable Records*, Chapter 383, pp. 4–5. *Record of the Pouring Forth of the Spring*, in its section on "Southern Tours," provides more details.

27. Qianlong's meeting with the Nine Old Men of the Qin family is described in *Wuxi Gazetteer*, Chapter 38, pp. 25–26.

28. Qianlong's poem can be found, among other places, in the *Wuxi Gazetteer*, p. 6 (section on imperial writings).

29. Quoted in "Ji Chang Yuan: An Enchanting Garden," by You Qi, *PRC Quarterly*, Premier Issue, p. 216.

Chapter Nineteen

1. *Prose Writings of the Members of the Qin Clan of Wuxi*, Chapter 6, pp. 21–22. To a large extent, the development of the system of justice in China was a mingling of Confucian principles with the harsh punishments advocated by the Legalist school of philosophy. See *Law in Imperial China*, by Derk Bodde and Clarence Morris (Philadelphia: University of Pennsylvania Press, 1967), especially section entitled "Legalist Triumph but Confucianization of Law," and following sections.

2. File in Ming-Qing Archives, under category "Officials," subcategory "Punishments." Unfortunately, it is not possible to identify more precisely individual documents in the archives, since they are not numbered. Often, it is necessary to go through many bundles of files, wrapped in paper and tied with string, before a specific document can be located.

3. The information on official income is drawn from the excellent study by Chung-li Chang, *The Income of the Chinese Gentry* (Seattle: University of Washington Press, 1962), in particular from Chapter 1: "Office as a Source of Income."

4. *Literary Records of the Qing Dynasty*, Chapter 9, p. 231. In addition, three other families produced Hanlin academicians for four generations in a row. The importance of the examination system throughout the dynastic period is reflected in the fact that such statistics were deemed of interest.

5. *Veritable Records of the Qianlong Emperor*, Chapter 500, p. 17. The ancient practice of the emperor's meeting with eminent officials to read and discuss texts from the classics and histories was institutionalized in the Ming dynasty, when sessions were held twice a year. See Charles O. Hucker *A Dictionary of Official Titles in Imperial China* (Stanford, Calif.: Stanford University Press, 1985), p 173.

6. *Veritable Records*, Chapter 580, pp. 14–17.

7. For Huitian's first lecture, see *Prose Writings*, Chapter 6, pp. 14–17.

8. *Veritable Records*, Chapter 630, pp. 4–6.

9. For Huitian's second lecture, see *Prose Writings*, Chapter 6, pp. 15–17.

10. *Veritable Records*, Chapter 530, p, 23.

11. Ibid., Chapter 543, pp. 36–37. Because Huitian was head of the Ministry of Works for a relatively brief time, this is the only proposal he made in that capacity that I was able to uncover. It shows the systematic way in which Huitian's mind worked to manage and to solve problems.

12. Ibid., Chapter 546, pp. 11–17. "Nominal dismissals" were perhaps a uniquely Chinese form of punishment, under which an official guilty of a relatively minor offense could technically lose his title but keep his job. See *Ch'ing Administrative Terms*, translated and edited by E-tu Zen Sun, (Cambridge, Mass.: Harvard University Press, 1961), p. 18.

13. *Veritable Records*, Chapter 555, p. 21. Although the heads of the six ministries all carried the same grade, the minister of works was considered the lowest ranking, while the minister of personnel was the

highest. Thus, Huitian's transfer to minister of punishments can be seen as a promotion.

14. See *Prose Writings,* Chapter 6, pp. 20–21 for text of memorial. The *Veritable Records,* Chapter 558, pp. 12–13, attributes the proposal to the Manchu minister of punishments "and others." This is in conformity with protocol, since the Manchu minister outranked the Chinese minister, and his name always appeared first on memorials from the ministry. But the presence of the memorial in Huitian's collected works indicates that this was his proposal.

15. Ming-Qing Archives. While searching through the Ming-Qing Archives for cases where Huitian was held culpable, I was told by Mr. Chu Deyuan that he had once come across a document indicating that Huitian had been punished by Qianlong because he had become friends with one of the emperor's sons, a grievous offense since social intercourse between high officials and the imperial family was banned. However, we were unable to uncover the document, despite examination of many files.

16. *Veritable Records,* Chapter 560, pp. 21–22. The *bao-jia* was a system that began in the Song dynasty in which every household was part of a security network. Ten *jia,* or households, made up a *bao.* The entire *bao* was held responsible for the behavior of a household, and the entire household was responsible for the behavior of each of its members. For history and development of the system, see Philip A. Kuhn *Rebellion and Its Enemies in Late Imperial China* (Cambridge, Mass.: Harvard University Press, 1970.)

17. See *Veritable Records,* Chapter 601, pp. 24–26, and Chapter 606, pp. 5–8, for information on this episode. Relevant edicts can be found in *Gaozong Shun Huangdi Shengxun,* a collection of Qianlong's decrees and writings printed in 1799.

18. *Veritable Records,* Chapter 608, p. 9. This was another instance when Huitian, despite his personal involvement, attempted to devise a system for preventing such problems from arising in future.

19. By contrast, when Ho-shen was chief examiner in 1795, he was so sure of himself that he submitted only eight papers to Qianlong.

20. Daoran was posthumously granted a series of increasingly exalted titles as his son rose in the hierarchy, beginning with vice-minister of pun-

ishments and culminating with the exalted title of Guanglu great officer and lecturer of the classics colloquium, titles that Huitian had earned.

21. *Veritable Records,* Chapter 657, p. 22. Internal exile was a frequently imposed punishment, but it had many gradations, such as "very near," "nearby frontier," "distant frontier," "farthest frontier" and "in a malarial region." If a criminal was already living in a frontier region, he would not be kept there but sent to another frontier region. See Bodde and Morris, op. cit., pp. 87–91.

22. See *Veritable Records,* Chapter 687, pp. 5–22 and Chapter 688 pp. 10–14. Some memorials on the Qin Rong case are available in the compilation put out by the Palace Museum in Taiwan covering the Qianlong period. Qianlong's edicts are in the "Cha Li" ("Investigation of Officials") section of *Gaozong Shun Huangdi Shengxun.* Qin Rong came from a very distinguished branch of the family. His brother and two of his sons were all members of the Hanlin Academy.

23. *Veritable Records,* Chapter 717, p. 1.

24. Ibid., Chapter 717, pp. 4–5.

25. Ibid., Chapter 719, p. 2.

Chapter Twenty

1. This information is in a biography of Zhenjun written by his nephew Qin Ying and can be found in *Prose Writings by Members of the Qin Family of Wuxi,* Chapter 7, pp. 51–53.

2. This quotation is from an essay in a handwritten booklet titled *Qin-shi Wenxian (Qin Family Literature)* found in Wuxi. A number of handwritten articles by Qin Zhenjun are also there.

3. Much of the information in this chapter is drawn from Susan Naquin, *Shantung Rebellion: The Wang Lun Uprising of 1774* (New Haven and London: Yale University Press, 1981).

4. *Shouzhang Gazetteer,* Chapter 10, p. 7.

5. Zhenjun's role in the siege of Linqing is largely culled from his diary, as well as from the *Veritable Records of the Qianlong Emperor.*

6. *Veritable Records*, Chapter 966, pp. 14–16.

7. Translation by Naquin, pp. 89–90.

8. Shu-ho-te was Huitian's colleague when he served as the Manchu minister of punishments.

9. Translation by Naquin, pp. 90–91.

10. Some of the lurid details of this attack were provided by Yu Qiao, who was visiting Linqing at the time and who later wrote *Linqing kou-lue* (*Brief Account of the Attack on Linqing*).

11. *Veritable Records*, Chapter 966, p. 53.

12. Ibid., Chapter 967, pp. 10–11.

13. Text of Qianlong edict is in *Veritable Records*, Chapter 968, p. 26.

14. *Jiao-pu Linqing ni-fei ji-lue*, a collection of documents relating to the Wang Lun uprising published in 1781, Vol. 2, Chapter 16, pp. 40–41.

15. *Veritable Records*, Chapter 1006, pp. 9–11.

16. Biography by Qin Ying.

17. Ibid.

18. Article titled "The Rebuilding of Liuhu Academy" in *Tan-jing-zhai quan-ji*, by Kong Jinghan.

19. Article on "The 60th Birthday of Mr. Qin Rongzhuang [Zhenjun]" in Kong Jinghan's book.

Chapter Twenty-one

1. *Veritable Records of the Qianlong Emperor*, Chapter 1005, p. 1.

2. *Banli Siku Quanshu Dongan* (*Files on the Handling of the Complete Library in Four Branches of Literature*), by Chen Heng.

3. Ying wrote funerary biographies of his parents and his brother, which can be found in an anthology of his essays, *Xiaoxian Shanren Wenji.*

4. Poems by Ying to his sons can be found in the section on his works in *Poetry by Members of the Qin Family of Wuxi,* Chapter 8, p. 6.

5. Qianlong's edict to King George III is quoted from *China's Response to the West,* by Ssu-yu Teng and John K. Fairbank (Cambridge, Mass., and London: Harvard University Press, 1979), p. 19.

6. Ying's account of this incident can be found in *Xiaoxian Shanren Wenji,* Vol. one, p. 20.

7. Role of his wife is recounted by Ying in his funerary biography of her.

8. The memorials in this section were discovered in the Institute of History and Philology of the Academia Sinica in Taiwan.

9. Letter to Ruan Yuan is in Volume 2 of *Xiaoxian Shanren Wenji,* pp. 9–12.

10. I am indebted to Dr. Wei Peh T'i, author of the doctoral dissertation on Ruan Yuan called "Juan Yuan: A Biographical Study with Special Reference to Mid-Ch'ing Security and Control in Southern China, 1799–1835," for many helpful comments and suggestions.

11. Ying's second letter to Ruan Yuan is in Vol. 2 of *Xiaoxian Shanren Wenji,* pp. 10–12.

12. *Veritable Records of the Jiaqing Emperor,* Chapter 66 p. 11.

13. Ibid., Chapter 75, p. 29.

14. *Draft History of the Qing Dynasty,* Chapter 357, p. 11292, biography of Qin Ying.

15. *Veritable Records,* Chapter 130, p. 40.

16. This incident is in the biography of Qin Ying engraved on the *shendaobei* over his grave. It was written by Tao Shu, a well-known official and man of letters.

Chapter Twenty-two

1. *Na Wen-yi gong Liang Guang Zongdu zou-yi* (*Memorials of Governor-General of Liang Guang Na-yen-cheng*), Chapter 12, pp. 1614–1630.

2. Some of the background material on piracy in Guangdong and the role of Na-yen-cheng was drawn from a doctoral dissertation by Dian Hechtner Murray, "Sea Bandits: A Study of Piracy in Early Nineteenth Century China," Cornell University, 1979.

3. *Xinhui Gazetteer*, Chapter 14, p. 4.

4. Na-yen-cheng memorial in collection cited above, Chapter 12, pp. 1511–1517.

5. Ibid., pp. 1547–1556.

6. Ibid., pp. 1932–1958.

7. *Veritable Records of the Jiaqing Emperor*, Chapter 151, pp. 7–9.

8. Ibid., Chapter 154, p. 10.

9. *Essays of Wuxi*, Premier Volume, pp. 21–30.

10. *Veritable Records*, Chapter 154, p. 10.

11. Ibid., Chapter 179, pp. 6–8.

12. Ibid., Chapter 187, pp. 18–21.

13. Ibid., Chapter 195, p. 19.

14. Ibid., Chapter 194, pp. 4–5.

15. Ibid., Chapter 215, pp. 28–29.

16. *Qing Shi Lie Zhuan* (*Biographies of the Qing Dynasty*), biography of Qin Ying under section on "Great Officials," Chapter 32, pp. 42–44.

17. *Veritable Records*, Chapter 208, p. 5.

18. Ibid., Chapter 208, pp. 9–10.

19. Ibid., Chapter 210, p. 15.

20. Ibid., Chapter 214, pp. 8–11.

21. Ibid., Chapter 212, pp. 12–15.

22. Obituary of Qin Ying by Chen Yongguang in *Xiaoxian Shanren Wenji,* pp. 4–8.

23. *Veritable Records,* Chapter 224, p. 22.

Chapter Twenty-three

1. Xiangye's mother's words are cited by him in his biography of her, which can be found in an anthology of his writings, *Hongqiao Laowu Yigao.*

2. A draft of Qin Xiangwu's official biography can be found in the Palace Museum Archives in Taipei. An anthology of his poems, titled *Cheng Xi Caotang Shiji (Poems of the Western City Cottage),* can be found in the Library of Congress.

3. The loss and recovery of Wuxi during the Taiping Rebellion is described in *Xu Xijin Xiao Lu (Tales of Wuxi Continued)* and in Chapter 5 of *Zhongguo Jindai Shiliao Congkan (A Collection of Modern Chinese Historical Materials).*

4. Xiangye's letter to the magistrate, whom he addresses as "Wen Mei," is in the Shanghai Library.

5. Xiangye's obituary of his mother and the biography of his son are in his anthology.

6. Cited and translated by Chung-li Chang in his book *The Income of the Chinese Gentry,* p. 135.

7. Epitaph by Sun Yiyan can be found in *Beizhuang Jibu,* published in 1932 by Yanjing University.

Chapter Twenty-four

1. The original document attesting to the payment, dated December 11, 1889, is from the Ministry of Revenue to the Ministry of Personnel, and can be found in the Ming-Qing Archives in Peking.

2. Grandfather's official career in this period was largely reconstructed from memorials of various governors of Zhejiang province held by the Palace Museum Archives in Taipei.

3. Edward Hunt, *China's Millions*, 1898, p. 136.

4. Great Britain, Foreign Office Records, preserved on microfilm in general correspondence files, FO 17 series. Unfortunately, records for Wenzhou, like those for consular posts elsewhere, were often not very well kept and have suffered from neglect.

5. Foreign Office Records, FO 17 series.

6. O'Brien Butler's report is included in *Correspondence Respecting the Disturbances in China*, published by the British Foreign Office (London: Harrison & Sons, 1901), No. 1, pp. 119–121.

7. Dispatch in *Shanghai Mercury* dated August 12, 1900, reprinted in *The Boxer Rising* (New York: Paragon Book Reprint Corp., 1967).

8. Document from Ming-Qing Archives. I am indebted to Wang Daorui, a researcher at the archives, for locating this document.

9. *North China Herald*, March 13, 1901.

10. Memorial enclosure by Governor Ren Daoyong, which can be found in *Yu Zhe Hui Cun (Classified Preservation of Imperial Documents)* (Wenhai Publishing House), Vol. 41, pp. 3462–3463.

11. Memorial in Palace Museum Archives.

12. Records of these and other cases can be found in the Ministry of Punishments files in the Ming-Qing Archives.

13. The memorial by Governor Nie Jigui of Zhejiang is in the Palace Museum Archives in Taipei.

14. Documents relating to Grandfather's reinstatement are in the Qing-Ming Archives, categorized under "Officials."

15. Grandfather's role in Hubei disaster relief work can be sifted from the files of Tuan-fang, the Manchu official in charge, in the Qing-Ming Archives.

16. Documents relating to Grandfather toward the end of the dynasty can be found in the "Huiyi Zhengwuchu" files of the Ming-Qing Archives.

17. *North China Herald,* February 14, 1908.

18. *The Missionary,* April 1907, pp. 154–155.

19. *North China Herald,* January 23, 1909.

20. Governor Zeng's memorial and the imperial edict are in the Qing-Ming Archives.

21. *Zhengzhi Guanbao* (*Government Gazette*), the third year of the Xuantong reign era (1911), No. 1049, pp. 17–18.

Chapter Twenty-five

1. The article, "Du Yuesheng Wai Zhuan," appeared in *Chun Qiu* (*The Observation Post*), a semimonthly magazine, 1961, Issue 88, p. 9. It was a serialization of the book *Du Yuesheng Wai Zhuan,* by Wei Yang.

2. For further information on the Mixed Court, see A. M. Kotenev, *Shanghai: Its Mixed Court and Council* (Shanghai: North China Daily News and Herald, Ltd., 1925).

3. Information on the Shanghai Bar Association was culled from *Shun Pao* as well as the association's *Journal,* some issues of which are preserved in the Shanghai Library and the Shanghai Municipal Archives. The archives also hold the association's files.

4. The travails of early Chinese parliaments are discussed in the book *Zhongguo Huiyi Shi* (*A History of Chinese Parliaments*). Xu Dafu is identified there by his formal name, Xu Shen. A good English-language source is Andrew Nathan's *Peking Politics, 1918–1923* (Berkeley, Calif.: University of California Press, 1976).

5. *North China Herald,* July 24, 1925.

6. The activities of the association's first decade were recorded in the book *Wuxi Lu-Hu Tongxianghui Shizhounian Jiance* (*The Tenth Anniversary Commemoration of the Wuxi Association in Shanghai*), which is held by the library of the History Institute of the Shanghai Academy of Social Sciences.

7. Some issues of the journal, *Wuxi Lukan,* are available in the Shanghai Library.

8. Father's meeting with Du Yuesheng is recounted in *Du Yuesheng Zhuan* (*Biography of Du Yuesheng*), by Zhang Jungu (Taipei: 1978), pp. 241–242. According to *The Observation Post* magazine, 1961, Issue 88, p. 9, the incident occurred in 1929 or 1930.

9. Parks M. Coble, Jr., *The Shanghai Capitalists,* Harvard East Asian Monographs (Cambridge, Mass.: Harvard University Press, 1986), p. 35. Coble also discusses the takeover of the Chamber of Commerce by the Kuomintang.

Chapter Twenty-six

1. *North China Herald,* January 12, 1929.

2. *North China Herald,* March 2 to March 23, 1929.

3. The proceedings of the convention are recounted in *China Year Book 1931,* Chapter XIX: "Unequal Treaties—Provisional Constitution."

4. For information on anti-Chinese measures, see *Chink!,* edited by Cheng-Tsu Wu (New York: World Publishing Company, 1972).

5. The interview with Accountant Li Lijing took place in his home in Shanghai on February 23, 1982.

6. E. Kann, in *China Year Book 1935,* Chapter XIV: "Currency and Banking."

7. Qin Bangxian, better known by his pseudonym, Bo Gu, was a member of the Qin clan of Wuxi. He was general secretary of the Communist Party from 1931 to 1935 and was killed in a plane crash in 1946.

Chapter Twenty-seven

1. Du Yuesheng was the chairman of the board of the school.

2. In a death notice, Father described Lianyuan as the center of the family around whom his siblings revolved after their parents' death. "How can I take over and continue the family traditions?" he lamented. "My brother's death may signal the fall of our family."

3. The Huangqiao battles and the New Fourth Army's role in northern Jiangsu are described by Chalmers A. Johnson in his book *Peasant Nationalism and Communist Power* (Stanford, Calif.: Stanford University Press, 1962).

4. Qu Jin, now known as Zhang Hong, provided some of these details during an interview in her home in Peking on August 8, 1983.

Chapter Twenty-eight

1. For a more detailed treatment on the subject, see *The End of Extraterritoriality in China,* by Wesley R. Fishel (Berkeley, Calif.: University of California Press, 1952).

2. Father's refusal to handle "traitor" cases earned him much respect and was mentioned in an article in *The Observation Post* magazine, 1966, Issue 25, p. 10.

3. *Shun Pao,* July 23, 1937, reported Father was on the standing committee and, the following day, that he had been elected to the Secretariat.

4. Father's strategy for Du Yuesheng to gain control of the new stock exchange was explained to me by Li Wenjie, a lawyer and accountant who had worked with him on the project.

5. The hyperinflation of the last years of Kuomintang rule on the mainland is treated in depth by Shun-hsin Chou in his book *The Chinese Inflation, 1937–1949* (New York: Columbia University Press, 1963).

6. The drafting of the Chinese constitution up to the eve of the National Assembly meeting is described by Pan Wei-tung in his book *The Chinese Constitution: A Study of Forty Years of Constitution-Making in China,* sponsored by the Institute of Chinese Culture, Washington, D.C., in 1945.

7. "Biography of Du Yuesheng", Vol. 4, pp. 201–203.